Chapter 11: Performance Appraisal

Measuring performance
Performance criteria
Graphic rating scales
Rating errors
Behaviorally anchored rating
　　scales
Behavioral observation scales
Management by objectives
Conducting appraisals
Appraisal interviews

Chapter 12: Reward Systems

Common types of rewards
Rewards and membership
Rewards and attendance
Pay for performance
Pay incentive plans
Scanlon plans
Comparable worth
Cafeteria-style benefits
Lump sum increases

Chapter 13: The Design of Work

Scientific management
Job enlargement
Job enrichment
Herzberg's approach
Job characteristics model
Autonomous work groups
Diagnosing problems
Implementing solutions
Individual vs. group approaches

Chapter 14: Managerial Decision Making

The decision-making process
Classical theory
Behavioral theory
Bounded rationality
Satisficing
Stress and decisions
Procedural rationality
Group decision making
Groupthink

Chapter 15: Organizational Entry

Career choice
Job choice
Realistic job previews
Interviews
Ability tests
Personality tests
Assessment centers
Legal environment
Improving predictive validity

Chapter 16: Managing Job Stress

General Adaptation Syndrome
Role ambiguity and conflict
Organizational climate
Holmes and Rahe scale
Physical health
Psychological well-being
Type A personality
Tolerance for ambiguity
Coping strategies

Chapter 17: Innovative Approaches to Organizing

Need for innovation
Quality of work life (QWL)
QWL programs
Japanese management
Applicability of Japanese
　　techniques
Search for excellence
Excellent American companies
Sources of excellence
Applying innovative techniques

Chapter 18: Organization Development

Nature of organization
　　development (OD)
OD and change
Resistance to change
Steps in OD
Data collection techniques
Feedback and action planning
OD consulting
Implementing change
OD interventions

Chapter 19: Careers in Organizations

Career and life stages
Entry shock
Organizational socialization
Training and orientation
Transfers and promotions
Geographical moves
Mid-career crisis
Plateaud performance
Career development programs

Organizational
Behavior

McGraw-Hill Series in Management

FRED LUTHANS AND KEITH DAVIS, Consulting Editors

ALLEN   The Management Profession
ARNOLD AND FELDMAN   Organizational Behavior
BUCHELE   The Management of Business and Public Organizations
CASCIO   Managing Human Resources: Productivity, Quality of Work Life, Profits
CLELAND AND KING   Management: A Systems Approach
CLELAND AND KING   Systems Analysis and Project Management
DALE   Management: Theory and Practice
DAVIS AND FREDERICK   Business and Society: Management, Public Policy, Ethics
DAVIS AND NEWSTROM   Human Behavior at Work: Organizational Behavior
DAVIS AND NEWSTROM   Organizational Behavior: Readings and Exercises
DEL MAR   Operations and Industrial Management: Designing and Managing for Productivity
DOBLER, LEE, AND BURT   Purchasing and Materials Management: Text and Cases
DUNN AND RACHEL   Wage and Salary Administration: Total Compensation Systems
FELDMAN AND ARNOLD   Managing Individual and Group Behavior in Organizations
FINCH, JONES, AND LITTERER   Managing for Organizational Effectiveness: An Experiential Approach
FLIPPO   Personnel Management
GERLOFF   Organizational Theory and Design: A Strategic Approach for Management
GLUECK AND JAUCH   Business Policy and Strategic Management
GLUECK AND JAUCH   Strategic Management and Business Policy
GLUECK AND SNYDER   Readings in Business Policy and Strategy from *Business Week*
HAMPTON   Contemporary Management
HICKS AND GULLETT   Management
HICKS AND GULLETT   Modern Business Management: A Systems and Environmental Approach
HICKS AND GULLETT   Organizations: Theory and Behavior
JAUCH AND TOWNSEND   Cases in Strategic Management and Business Policy
JOHNSON, KAST, AND ROSENZWEIG   The Theory and Management of Systems
KARLINS   The Human Use of Human Resources
KAST AND ROSENZWEIG   Experiential Exercises and Cases in Management
KAST AND ROSENZWEIG   Organization and Management: A Systems and Contingency Approach
KNUDSON, WOODWORTH, AND BELL   Management: An Experiential Approach

KOONTZ, O'DONNELL, AND WEIHRICH   Essentials of Management
KOONTZ, O'DONNELL, AND WEIHRICH   Management
KOONTZ, O'DONNELL, AND WEIHRICH   Management: A Book of Readings
KOPELMAN   Managing Productivity in Organizations: A Practical, People-Oriented
    Perspective
LEVIN, McLAUGHLIN, LAMONE, AND KOTTAS   Production/Operations
    Management: Contemporary Policy for Managing Operating Systems
LUTHANS   Introduction to Management: A Contingency Approach
LUTHANS   Organizational Behavior
LUTHANS AND THOMPSON   Contemporary Readings in Organizational
    Behavior
McNICHOLS   Executive Policy and Strategic Planning
McNICHOLS   Policymaking and Executive Action
MARGULIES AND RAIA   Conceptual Foundations of Organizational Development
MAYER   Production and Operations Management
MILES   Theories of Management: Implications for Organizational Behavior and
    Development
MILES AND SNOW   Organizational Strategy, Structure, and Process
MILLS   Labor-Management Relations
MITCHELL   People in Organizations: An Introduction to Organizational Behavior
MOLANDER   Responsive Capitalism: Case Studies in Corporate Social Conduct
MONKS   Operations Management: Theory and Problems
NEWSTROM, REIF, AND MONCZKA   A Contingency Approach to Management:
    Readings
PORTER, LAWLER, AND HACKMAN   Behavior in Organizations
PRASOW AND PETERS   Arbitration and Collective Bargaining: Conflict
    Resolution in Labor Relations
QUICK AND QUICK   Organizational Stress and Preventive Management
REDDIN   Effective Management by Objectives: The 3-D Method of MBO
RUE AND HOLLAND   Strategic Management: Concepts and Experiences
RUGMAN, LECRAW, AND BOOTH   International Business: Firm and
    Environment
SARTAIN AND BAKER   The Supervisor and the Job
SAYLES   Leadership: What Effective Managers Really Do . . . and How
    They Do It
SCHLESINGER, ECCLES, AND GABARRO   Managing Behavior in Organizations:
    Text, Cases, Readings
SCHROEDER   Operations Management: Decision Making in the Operations
    Function
SHORE   Operations Management
STEERS AND PORTER   Motivation and Work Behavior
STEINHOFF AND BURGESS   Small Business Management Fundamentals
SUTERMEISTER   People and Productivity
VANCE   Corporate Leadership: Boards, Directors, and Strategy
WALKER   Human Resource Planning

WEIHRICH Management Excellence: Productivity through MBO
WERTHER AND DAVIS Personnel Management and Human Resources
WOFFORD, GERLOFF, AND CUMMINS Organizational Communications: The
  Keystone to Managerial Effectiveness

Organizational Behavior

Hugh J. Arnold
University of Toronto

Daniel C. Feldman
University of Florida

McGraw-Hill Book Company

New York   St. Louis   San Francisco   Auckland   Bogotá   Hamburg
Johannesburg   London   Madrid   Mexico   Montreal   New Delhi
Panama   Paris   São Paulo   Singapore   Sydney   Tokyo   Toronto

Library of Congress Cataloging-in-Publication Data

Arnold, Hugh J.
   Organizational behavior.

   (McGraw-Hill series in management)
   Bibliography: p. 579
   1. Organizational behavior.   I. Feldman, Daniel C.
II. Title. III. Series.
HD78.7.A76 1986   658   85-18139
ISBN 0-07-002300-X

ORGANIZATIONAL BEHAVIOR

1 2 3 4 5 6 7 8 9 0 HALHAL 8 9 8 7 6

ISBN 0-07-002300-X

This book was set in Times Roman by University Graphics, Inc. (ECU).
The editors were John R. Meyer, Elisa Adams, and Peggy Rehberger;
the design was done by INK, Graphic Design;
the production supervisor was Charles Hess.
The drawings were done by Fine Line Illustrations, Inc.
Halliday Lithograph Corporation was printer and binder.

About the Authors

Hugh J. Arnold is a professor of organizational behavior at the University of Toronto. He received his B.A. in psychology from the University of Alberta, his M.A. in psychology and philosophy from Oxford University, his M.A. in administrative sciences from Yale University, and his Ph.D. in organizational behavior from Yale. Coauthor of *Managing Individual and Group Behavior in Organizations,* Dr. Arnold has also published extensively in the areas of motivation, job design, and decision making. He has served on the editorial board of the *Academy of Management Journal,* and has conducted executive development programs with a wide variety of private and public sector organizations.

Daniel C. Feldman is a professor of management at the University of Florida Graduate School of Business. He received his B.A. in sociology from the University of Pennsylvania, his M.A. in administrative sciences from Yale University, and his Ph.D. in organizational behavior from Yale University. Coauthor of *Managing Individual and Group Behavior in Organizations,* Dr. Feldman has also published extensively in the areas of career development and group dynamics. He serves on the editorial boards of the *Academy of Management Journal* and *The Industrial Psychologist.* Before joining the faculty at the University of Florida, Dr. Feldman was on the faculty at the University of Minnesota Industrial Relations Center and the J. L. Kellogg Graduate School of Management at Northwestern University.

For C. A.
J. A.
S. F.

Contents

Preface   xix

Part One *The Nature of Organizational Behavior*   1

Chapter 1   **Introduction to Organizational Behavior**   3

The Nature of Organizations   4
Systems View of Organizations   5
Levels of Analysis   7
The Individual ● The Group ● The Organization
Organizational Effectiveness   9
Components of Organizational Effectiveness ● Assessing Organizational
Effectiveness ● Determinants of Organizational Effectiveness
The Manager's Job   13
Characteristics of the Manager's Job
Plan of This Book   15
Notes   18

Part Two *Individuals in Organizations*   21

Chapter 2   **Determinants of Individual Performance**   23

A Model of Individual Behavior and Performance   23
Motivation   26
Attitudes ● Beliefs ● Values ● Needs ● Goals

Ability   30
Aptitudes ● Learning Opportunities

Perception   34
*Characteristics of the Entity ● Characteristics of the Person ● Characteristics of
the Situation*

Personality   37
*Personality Traits and Characteristics ● Determinants of Personality ●
Personality and Behavior*

Organizational Systems and Resources   41
Facilities ● Organization Structure and Design ● Leadership ● Reward Systems

Keys to Effective Management   43
Review Questions   44
Case for Chapter 2: Robert Morton   45
Notes   47

Chapter 3   Motivation   **51**

Need Theories   52
Maslow's Need Hierarchy Theory ● Other Need Theories

Expectancy Theory   57
*Expectancy That Effort Leads to Performance (E→P) ● Expectancy That
Performance Leads to Outcomes (P→O) ● Valence of Outcomes (V) ●
Combining the Factors ● Expectancy Theory in Practice*

Equity Theory   61
*Determinants of Feelings of Equity ● Consequences of Perceived Inequity ●
Equity Theory in Practice*

Goal Setting Theory   64
Goal Setting in Practice

Reinforcement Theory   68
*Reinforcement ● Schedules of Reinforcement ● Organizational Behavior
Modification (OB Mod) ● Ethical Issues in OB Mod*

Keys to Effective Management   74
Review Questions   75
Case for Chapter 3: Lincoln Electric   77
Notes   79

Chapter 4   Job Satisfaction   **85**

Sources of Job Satisfaction   86
*Pay ● The Work Itself ● Promotions ● Supervision ● Work Group ● Working
Conditions ● A Model of Job Satisfaction*

Consequences of Job Satisfaction   92
*Performance ● Withdrawal Behavior: Turnover and Absenteeism ● Union
Activity*

Trends in Job Satisfaction Levels   95
How Satisfied Are Workers Today?   Recent Changes in Job Satisfaction Levels

Job Satisfaction Surveys   99
*Measuring Job Satisfaction ● Uses of Job Satisfaction Surveys ● Survey
Administration*

Keys to Effective Management   107
Review Questions   108
Case for Chapter 4: Perfect Pizzeria   110
Notes   113

Part Three Interpersonal and Group Behavior   117

Chapter 5   **Leadership**   119

The Nature of Leadership   120
    Sources of Leader Influence on Followers
Trait Theories of Leadership   122
Behavioral Theories of Leadership   124
    The Ohio State Studies
Fiedler's Contingency Theory   127
    The Leader ● The Situation ● The Model
Path-Goal Theory   130
    Styles of Leader Behavior ● Contingency Factors
The Vroom and Yetton Model   133
    Alternative Decision Styles ● Decision Effectiveness ● Choosing a Decision Style
Current Issues in Leadership   138
    Leadership as Mutual Influence ● Constraints on Leadership Behavior ●
    Attribution Theory of Leadership
Keys to Effective Management   142
Review Questions   144
Case for Chapter 5: Which Style Is Best?   146
Notes   148

Chapter 6   **Communication**   154

Attention   155
    Amount of Information ● Formal Communication Channels ● Informal
    Communication Networks ● The Message Itself
Comprehension   159
    Semantics of the Message ● Perceptions ● Opportunity for Feedback
Acceptance of the Information as True   165
    Characteristics of the Communicator ● Defensive Communication
Retention of Information   169
    Explicit versus Implicit Conclusions ● One-Sided versus Two-Sided Arguments ●
    Oral versus Written Communication ● Single Presentation versus Repetition
Keys to Effective Management   171
Review Questions   173
Case for Chapter 6: Dashman Company   175
Notes   177

Chapter 7   **Groups in Organizations**   180

The Nature of Work Groups   181
Work Groups Defined ● Types of Work Groups

Group Cohesiveness   182
Cohesiveness Defined ● Sources of Group Cohesiveness ● Consequences of Group Cohesiveness ● Factors Influencing the Productivity of Cohesive Groups

Group Performance   187
Potential Assets of Groups ● Potential Liabilities of Groups

Group Norms   192
Norms Defined ● Types of Group Norms ● Why Norms Are Strongly Enforced ● How Group Norms Develop

Deviance   195
Deviance Defined ● Functions of Deviance ● Rejection of the Deviant ● Deviance and Group Effectiveness

Keys to Effective Management   200
Review Questions   201
Case for Chapter 7: Phantoms Fill Boy Scout Rolls   203
Notes   206

Chapter 8   **Intergroup Conflict**   209

Changing Views of Intergroup Conflict   210
Traditional View of Conflict ● Contemporary View of Conflict ● Can There Ever Be too Little Conflict?

Causes of Intergroup Conflict   212
Coordination of Work ● Organizational Reward Systems

The Dynamics of Intergroup Conflict   217
Changes within Each Group ● Changes in Relations between Groups ● Strategies Groups Use to Gain Power ● Consequences of Winning or Losing a Conflict

Managing Intergroup Conflict   223
Conflict Avoidance Strategies ● Conflict Defusion Strategies ● Conflict Containment Strategies ● Conflict Confrontation Strategies

Keys to Effective Management   230
Review Questions   232
Case for Chapter 8: The Open Budget   234
Notes   236

Part Four   Organizational Structure and Design

   239

Chapter 9   **The Structure of Organizations**   241

Functional Organizations   242
Advantages of the Functional Structure ● Disadvantages of the Functional Structure ● Overall Assessment

Divisional Organizations 245
Advantages of the Divisional Structure ● Disadvantages of the Divisional Structure ● Overall Assessment

Lateral Relations 252
Dotted-Line Supervision ● Liaison Roles ● Temporary Task Forces ● Permanent Teams ● Integrating Managers ● Overall Assessment

Matrix Structures 256
Project Management Matrix ● Geography-by-Product Matrix ● Advantages of the Matrix Structure ● Disadvantages of the Matrix Structure ● Overall Assessment: Making the Matrix Work

Keys to Effective Management 262
Review Questions 264
Case for Chapter 9: Organization Structure in Practice 266
Notes 269

Chapter 10 **Designing Effective Organizations** 271

Classical Theories of Organization Design 272
Principles of Classical Management ● Assessment of Classical Management Principles

Technology and Structure 278
Types and Examples of Technology ● Contingency Theories of Technology ● Overall Impact of Technology on Structure

Environment and Structure 284
Dimensions of Organizational Environments ● Contingency Theories of Organizational Environments ● Coping with Environments ● Overall Impact of Environment on Structure

Keys to Effective Management 294
Review Questions 295
Case for Chapter 10: Avondale Shipyards, Inc. 297
Notes 299

Part Five *Improving Employee Performance*

303

Chapter 11 **Performance Appraisal** 305

Functions of Performance Appraisal 306
Individual Evaluation and Reward ● Individual Motivation and Development ● Organizational Planning and Decision Making

What Should Performance Appraisals Measure? 307
Activities versus Results

Graphic Rating Scales 309
Problems with Graphic Rating Scales ● Common Rating Errors ● Reducing Rating Errors

Behaviorally Anchored Rating Scales (BARS) 317
Advantages of BARS ● Disadvantages of BARS ● Evaluation of BARS

Behavioral Observation Scales (BOS) — 320
Advantages and Disadvantages of BOS

Management by Objectives (MBO) — 322
Advantages of MBO ● Disadvantages of MBO

Comparison of Appraisal Techniques — 325

Managing the Appraisal Process — 326
Who Evaluates ● When to Evaluate ● The Appraisal Interview

Keys to Effective Management — 329
Review Questions — 331
Case for Chapter 11: Problems in Performance Evaluation — 332
Notes — 334

Chapter 12 **Reward Systems** — 340

Types and Characteristics of Rewards — 341
Characteristics of Rewards ● Comparison of Rewards

Functions of Reward Systems — 344
Encouraging Membership ● Rewarding Attendance ● Improving Performance

Pay and Performance — 346
Methods of Pay Administration ● Pay for Performance ● Evaluating Pay-for-Performance Plans

Comparable Worth — 352

Innovative Reward Systems — 354
Cafeteria-Style Benefits ● Lump-Sum Salary Increases ● Open Salary Information

Keys to Effective Management — 359
Review Questions — 360
Case for Chapter 12: Recognition Won't Buy Bread — 362
Notes — 364

Chapter 13 **The Design of Work** — 367

Historical Development of Work Design — 368
Scientific Management ● Job Enlargement ● Job Enrichment

Individual Job Design — 374
Critical Psychological States ● Core Job Characteristics ● Differences among People ● Outcomes of Enriched Work ● Job Design in Practice

Work Design for Groups — 381
Factors Influencing Effort of Group Members ● Design Factors Influencing Group Knowledge and Skill

Work Design for Groups: An Example — 384
Work Design ● Status Differentials ● Authority and Decision Making ● Reward System ● Results

Individual versus Group Work Design — 387
Keys to Effective Management — 388
Review Questions — 389
Case for Chapter 13: Job Enrichment in Data Processing — 391
Notes — 393

Chapter 14   **Managerial Decision Making**   395

Classical Decision Theory   396
*Steps in the Decision-Making Process ● Assumptions of Classical Theory ●
Assessment of Classical Theory*

Behavioral Theory of Decision Making   403
*Bounded Rationality ● Satisficing ● Stress and Decision Making ● Procedural
Rationality*

Group Decision Making   406
*Quality of Decisions ● Creativity of Decisions ● Acceptance of Decisions ●
Groupthink: Group Decision Making Gone Awry ● Alternative Group
Techniques*

Keys to Effective Management   415
Review Questions   416
Case for Chapter 14: The Structure of a Business Decision   418
Notes   420

Part Six *Improving Organizational Effectiveness*   425

Chapter 15   **Organizational Entry**   427

Job Choice: The Individual's Perspective   428
*Developing a Career Identity ● Making a Job Choice ● Improving Job Choice
Decision Making*

Selection: The Organization's Perspective   434
*Assessing Job Applicants ● Criteria for Selection Devices ● Making Selection
Decisions*

Job Interviews   437
The Negative Side ● The Positive Side ● Improving the Interview

Tests   442
Ability Tests ● Personality Tests

Assessment Centers   445
*Structure of Assessment Centers ● Content of Assessment Centers ● Success of
Assessment Centers ● Potential Problems and Solutions*

Keys to Effective Management   449
Review Questions   450
Case for Chapter 15: Gigantic Aircraft Company   452
Notes   454

Chapter 16   **Managing Job Stress**   458

The Nature of Job Stress   459
*The Dual Nature of Stress ● Inevitability of Stress ● Personal Reactions to Stress ●
Importance for Organizational Effectiveness*

Sources of Job Stress   461
Job Characteristics ● Interpersonal Relationships ● Personal Factors

Consequences of Job Stress 468
Physical Health •*Psychological Well-Being* •*Performance* •*Individual Decision Making*
Individual Differences and Stress 472
Self-Esteem •*Tolerance for Ambiguity* •*Type A Personality*
Coping with Job Stress 474
Work-Focused Coping Strategies •*Emotion-Focused Coping Strategies* •
Organizational Programs to Manage Stress
Keys to Effective Management 478
Review Questions 480
Case for Chapter 16: The Company Man 481
Notes 483

Chapter 17 Innovative Approaches to Organizing 487

Factors Generating the Need for Innovation 488
Lagging Productivity Growth •*Increasing Foreign Competition* •*The Revolution in Microelectronics* •*A Changing Work Force*
Quality of Work Life (QWL) 491
Examples of QWL Programs •*Future Prospects for QWL*
Japanese Management 496
The Nature of Japanese Management •*Japanese Techniques Applicable in North America*
Excellent Companies Research 503
The Nature of the Research •*Problems with American Management* •
Characteristics of Excellent Companies •*Implications of the Excellent Companies Research*
Keys to Effective Management 510
Review Questions 511
Case for Chapter 17: Nissan: Robotics Comes to Tennessee 513
Notes 515

Chapter 18 Organization Development 518

The Nature of Organization Development 519
Examples of Organizational Problems Calling for Change •*Distinguishing Features of Organization Development*
The Organization Development Process 522
Unfreezing •*Movement* •*Refreezing*
Phases in Organization Development 523
Problem Recognition •*Entry* •*Diagnosis* •*Feedback* •*Action Planning* •
Intervention/Implementation •*Evaluation*
Organization Development Interventions 534
Individual Interventions •*Process Interventions*
Keys to Effective Management 540
Review Questions 541
Case for Chapter 18: Resolving Intergroup Conflict 542
Notes 544

Chapter 19   **Careers in Organizations**   **545**

The Nature of Careers   546
Career and Life Stages

Early Career Issues   550
Entry Shock ●Organizational Socialization ●Stages of Organizational Socialization ●Managing Organizational Socialization

Transfers and Promotions   557
Benefits of Transfers and Promotions ●Special Problems of Transferred and Promoted Employees ●Managing the Transfer and Promotion Process

Middle- and Later-Career Issues   560
Professional Concerns of Mid- and Late-Career Managers ●Personal Concerns of Mid- and Late-Career Managers ●The Mid-Life Crisis

Career Development   564
Career Management: The Organization's Perspective ●Career Development: The Individual's Perspective

Keys to Effective Management   569
Review Questions   571
Case for Chapter 19: Gordon Company   572
Notes   575

Bibliography   579
Indexes   609
  Name Index   611
  Subject Index   617

Preface

Overview

This book is about organizations, and the people who work in them. Each of us will spend about 10,000 days working in organizations over the course of our careers. Even in the time we are not at work, organizations like government agencies, churches, schools, and hospitals have a strong impact on the quality of our day-to-day lives. Therefore, it is important to understand how organizations influence the feelings and behaviors of their employees and clients—and how the feelings and behaviors of employees and clients influence the effectiveness of organizations.

The effective management of organizations has always been important. Today, increased competition from abroad and rising expectations of employees entering the work force have made good management of organizations even more critical. In this book we will describe the day-to-day problems managers face at work, present theories and research on why organizations operate the way they do, and suggest guidelines on how to manage organizations more effectively.

While the book is designed to acquaint students with theories and concepts of organizational behavior, theories are not presented merely for their own sake. Good theories help managers analyze and understand problems they may face in their careers, today and in the future. Throughout the book we make a point of discussing how theories and concepts can be applied to actual managerial situations. The Keys to Effective Management at the conclusion of each chapter summarize the implications of what we know about each chapter topic for effective managerial action in organizations.

Structure of the Book

This text consists of nineteen chapters, divided into six sections.

Part One, *The Nature of Organizational Behavior,* introduces the field of organizational behavior, the nature of organizations, and an overview of the manager's job.

Part Two, *Individuals in Organizations,* examines the feelings, behaviors, and performance of individual employees. It consists of three chapters: Chapter 2 (Determinants of Individual Performance), Chapter 3 (Motivation), and Chapter 4 (Job Satisfaction).

Part Three, *Interpersonal and Group Behavior,* looks at the relationships among employees and work groups in organizations. Part Three has four chapters: Chapter 5 (Leadership), Chapter 6 (Communication), Chapter 7 (Groups in Organizations), and Chapter 8 (Intergroup Conflict).

Part Four, *Organizational Structure and Design,* focuses on the strategies organizations as a whole use to coordinate and control the activities of their employees. This section of the book also focuses on the strategies organizations as a whole use to deal with external clients, customers, and competing firms. It consists of two chapters: Chapter 9 (Structure of Organizations) and Chapter 10 (Designing Effective Organizations).

Part Five, *Improving Employee Performance,* examines a variety of management techniques that can facilitate employee performance. Part Five has four chapters: Chapter 11 (Performance Appraisal), Chapter 12 (Reward Systems), Chapter 13 (Design of Work), and Chapter 14 (Managerial Decision Making).

Part Six, *Improving Organizational Effectiveness,* examines a series of practices that managers can use to improve the effectiveness of the organization as a whole. Part Six consists of five chapters: Chapter 15 (Organizational Entry), Chapter 16 (Managing Job Stress), Chapter 17 (Innovative Approaches to Organizing), Chapter 18 (Organization Development), and Chapter 19 (Careers in Organizations).

In general, we cover topics relevant to individual performance first (e.g., job satisfaction and motivation), topics relevant to interpersonal and group behavior second (e.g., leadership and communication), and topics relevant to organizations as a whole third (e.g., organization structure and design). Also, we cover the basic theoretical material about behavior in organizations (e.g., Parts One, Two, Three, and Four) before the more applied material on how to improve the effectiveness of employees and organizations (e.g., Parts Five and Six).

Content

The book is comprehensive in its coverage of the field of organizational behavior. Professors and students in a variety of courses—organizational behavior, personnel, human resource management, public, educational, and hospital administration, and executive development—will find the book appropriate for their uses. The chapters integrate the perspectives and findings of a wide range of social science disciplines, including social psychology, sociology, industrial psychology, and management.

The text is also up-to-date and innovative in its coverage of traditional organizational behavior topics. For instance, the chapter on determinants of individual behavior covers the topics of perception, personality, and learning in an integrated fashion that demonstrates the relevance and implications of this material to understanding behavior in organizations. The chapter on leadership includes material on power and authority, attribution theory, and substitutes for leadership. The chapter on organizational entry integrates the literature on selection with material on occupational and job choice. The chapter on decision making examines both the information-processing aspects of decision making and the non-rational, stressful elements of that activity. The chapter on communication synthesizes what we know about perception, cognitive dissonance, communication networks, information channels, and cognitive complexity. The chapter on careers includes recent research on socialization, the transfer and promotion process, and career development programs in industry.

Another important feature is the book's extensive coverage of material often not found in traditional organizational behavior textbooks. Frequently ignored topics in the groups area—such as norms, conformity, deviance, cohesiveness, group performance, group decision making, and autonomous work groups—are all covered here, and in substantial detail. We devote whole chapters to topics such as careers in organizations, managing job stress, designing reward systems, job satisfaction, organizational entry and organization development. Chapter 17, Innovative Approaches to Organizing, covers in great depth three areas of recent interest to managers: quality of working life programs, Japanese management, and the search for excellence among major U.S. and Canadian corporations.

Pedagogy

There are several features designed to facilitate student learning. Each chapter concludes with a section entitled *Keys to Effective Management,* which help students make clear connections between theory and practice. These sections answer the oft-heard question: *How can I use this material to become a better manager?*

Two other devices aid students to master the material more effectively. Each chapter concludes with a series of review questions about the major topics covered in the text. These clarify the main points of the chapter and assist students in remembering the important issues. Each chapter also is followed by a short (two- or three-page) case. These cases have been carefully chosen to help students relate the textbook material to actual situations in real organizations. Each case illustrates several different topics in the chapter and highlights the relationships among these topics.

Within each chapter we have used figures and tables extensively to help students organize and remember the material more easily. Also within each chapter, we have included excerpts from recent business journals and magazines. These inserts demonstrate the chapter's concepts and principles applied in real-world organizations.

Accompanying the text is an instructor's manual to help professors utilize the book more effectively. The manual provides answers to review questions, detailed suggestions about teaching the cases, exam questions for each chapter, transparency masters, and information about supplemental teaching devices like exercises and films.

Textbook authors are often influenced by what they liked (and disliked) about the textbooks they used as students themselves. We have been no exception. We remember all too vividly reading books overloaded with jargon, mind-numbing descriptions of research methodology, and uninterpretable results.

Consequently, we have dealt with relatively sophisticated concepts in an understandable and accessible writing style, rather than simplifying ideas to trivialities and dressing them up with jargon. We present a coherent point of view about what we know about behavior in organizations, rather than letting students flounder in a catalogue of briefly described theories. We have devoted as much effort to describing organizations as they are, as we have to describing how we would like them to be. Finally, we have tried to make explicit the implications of organizational behavior theory for the practice of management. We want students to be as enthusiastic about their study of the theory as they are about the prospects of managing.

Acknowledgments

We were fortunate to have had such excellent assistance from our editors. Our developmental editor, Elisa Adams, provided consistently constructive and creative suggestions for improving the manuscript; her help at every stage in the project was invaluable. Peggy Rehberger, our editing supervisor, managed the logistics of production with an organizational ability and an eye to detail that made our lives in the last few months of this project much easier. John Meyer, our acquisitions editor, and Fred Luthans, our consulting editor, helped us structure the manuscript and provided useful feedback on the overall direction and content of the book.

We also received many thoughtful comments from outside reviewers: John Daley, City University (Bellevue, Washington); Bruce Eberhardt, University of North Dakota; Mark Fichman, Carnegie-Mellon University; Robert Fischer, University of Central Arkansas; Stephen Green, University of Cincinnati; Nell Hartley, Robert Morris College; David Herold, Georgia Institute of Technology; Robert Hollmann, University of Montana; Fred Luthans, University of Nebraska; James McElroy, Iowa State University; Jim McFillen, Bowling Green University; Martin Markowitz, Rutgers Univesity; Mabry Miller, Drake University; Paula Morrow, Iowa State University; Joe Pecenka, Northern Illinois University; Tim Peterson, Texas A & M University; Sam Rabinowitz, Rutgers University; Michael Rush, University of Tennessee; Brad Shrader, Iowa State Universtiy; Pamela Specht, University of Nebraska; Susan Taylor, University of Maryland; and Mary Ann Von Glinow, University of Southern California. Their comments substantially helped us to refine the manuscript.

Our secretaries typed the manuscript with much care and attention. We appreciate their efforts all the more, knowing how illegible our handwriting can be and how many deadlines they had to meet. In particular, we want to thank Edith Kosow, Mary Lynch, Kathy Levy, Marlene Baccala, Barbara Washington, and Maria Balanos for the long hours they put in at the word processor, and for the good cheer they showed in making last-minute revisions and corrections.

A number of people in our own organizations provided a supportive environment for the writing of this book. We especially want to thank our deans (Douglas Tigert and Robert Lanzillotti), our department chairmen (Martin Evans and Tony Majthay), and our colleagues, (Robert House, Jitendra Singh, Joe Reitz, Jerry Young, and Carrie Leana) for their encouragement, ideas, and technical assistance. From them we have learned more than they know about being good managers and coworkers. We also want to thank the students in our classes, whose reactions and feedback on drafts of the manuscript helped us improve the book in countless ways.

Finally, we want to express our gratitude and appreciation to our families and friends. Their patience and forebearance during the past three years have not gone unnoticed. Most importantly, they helped us keep our sense of humor and our sense of perspective when it looked like the book would become the master of us rather than vice versa.

Hugh J. Arnold
Daniel C. Feldman

Organizational
Behavior

Part 1

The Nature of Organizational Behavior

Chapter 1 *Introduction to Organizational Behavior*

Introduction to Organizational Behavior

CHAPTER OUTLINE

The Nature of Organizations

Systems View of Organizations

Levels of Analysis

Organizational Effectiveness

The Manager's Job

Plan of This Book

*O*rganizations have a pervasive influence on our lives. Most of us will spend the majority of our working lives as members of organizations. The way these organizations are set up and managed influences the work we do, how effectively we perform our jobs, and how we feel about ourselves.

The work organizations that we belong to are not the only organizations that influence our lives. Each of us also deals with many other types of organizations on a daily basis. Supermarkets, department stores, specialty shops, government agencies, churches, schools, and hospitals are all organizations that we frequently come into contact with. These organizations have a strong collective influence on the nature of our day-to-day experiences and the quality of our lives.

This book is about the field of *organizational behavior.* Organizational behavior is concerned with two basic issues. The first issue is the way organizations influence the thoughts, feelings, and actions of their members. The organizations of which we are members influence the way we see the world, the way we feel about our jobs and ourselves as people, and the way we behave in the course of performing our duties and obligations as organization members. Organizational behavior is concerned with trying to understand the var-

3

Figure 1-1   Two basic issues of organizational behavior.

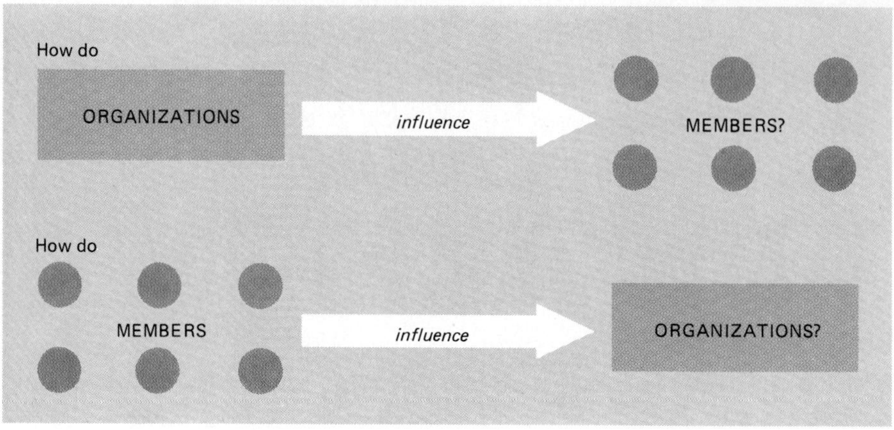

ious ways in which organizations influence their members in order to create healthier and more productive organizations.

Organizational behavior is also concerned with understanding the ways in which behavior and performance of individual organization members influence the performance and effectiveness of the organization as a whole. The way in which organizations coordinate and integrate the activities of their members determines whether the organization will succeed in accomplishing its goals and objectives.

Because of the significant role that organizations play in our lives, we all share a common stake in understanding organizational behavior. By understanding how organizations influence us and how we in turn can influence organizations, we gain a valuable perspective on events that shape our experiences on a daily basis.

The Nature of Organizations

Organizational behavior explores the nature and functioning of all types of organizations, not just private-sector, profit-oriented organizations. The field is equally concerned with understanding educational organizations, hospitals, government agencies, voluntary organizations, and so on. Organizational behavior seeks to develop general principles and concepts that are relevant to understanding the operation and performance of all types of organizations.

What are the common defining characteristics of an organization? Many attempts have been made to define just what an organization is.[1] While each definition differs somewhat from the other, they do share some common themes that permit us to identify the following three factors that characterize all types of organizations.[2]

1   *Organizations are composed of individuals and groups.*   While at first glance it may seem obvious that all organizations are made up of people, the key point is that people *are* the organization. We may have a tendency to identify an organization with the building it occupies, the technology it employs, or the products and services it creates. But buildings are simply places for people to work, technology is something that the people make use of, and products and services are created by people. It is the people who are the organization, and without them there is no organization.

2   *Organizations are oriented toward the achievement of goals.*   Organizations are created and continue to exist only because some group of people share a common goal that they cannot accomplish alone. Private sector organizations exist for the purpose of creating products or providing services to clients or customers. Educational institutions have the goal of providing an education to certain groups of people. Hospitals exist in order to meet the goal of providing health services to people who are sick. Every organization is goal-oriented.

3   *Organizations employ specialization and coordination in order to accomplish their goals.*   Organizations exist because a single individual is unable to perform all the functions and activities necessary to create a product or provide a service to a group of customers or clients. The members of an organization do not each attempt to do all the jobs and perform all the functions that need to be carried out for the organization to accomplish its goals. Instead, the organization divides up the work to be performed and each person or group of people takes responsibility for performing some set of specialized functions. However, once the work has been divided up and people have become specialized, the organization requires some means for coordinating their activities. Without such coordination we would not have an organization working toward common goals. Instead we would have various individuals and groups each performing their own specialized function in an uncoordinated and potentially chaotic manner.

Systems View of Organizations

It can also be very helpful to think of an organization as a system of interdependent parts that interact with one another and that also must interact with the broader world within which the organization exists. Figure 1-2 summarizes what is known as the *systems view* of organizations.

Within the organization we see that **people** employ **technology** in perform-

Figure 1-2   Systems view of organizations.

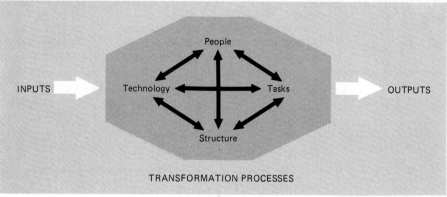

ing the **tasks** that they are responsible for, while the **structure** of the organization serves as a basis for coordinating all their different activities. The systems view emphasizes the interdependence of each of these elements within the organization, as indicated by the arrows among them in the figure. Each element within the organization depends upon all the other elements, if the organization as a whole is to function effectively.

The other key aspect of the systems view of organizations is its emphasis on the interaction between the organization and its broader environment. Organizations do not exist in a vacuum but instead are influenced by the social, economic, political, and cultural environments within which they operate. As indicated in Figure 1-2, organizations are dependent upon their environments in two key ways.

First, the organization requires **inputs** from the environment if it is to operate. These inputs can take the form of people, raw materials, money, ideas, and so on. If an organization cannot attract the inputs it requires from the environment in order to function, it will rapidly decline and go out of existence. The organization itself can be thought of as performing certain **transformation processes** on its inputs in order to create outputs in the form of products or services. For example, an automobile manufacturer takes inputs in the form of labor, ideas, production techniques, steel, rubber, and the like, and transforms these into finished cars.

This brings us to the second key way in which the organization is dependent upon its environment. If people outside the organization do not want the products or services provided by the organization (i.e., the **outputs** of the organization), it will very quickly go out of existence. Schools and hospitals exist because people want the educational and health services that these organizations provide (such services are the outputs of these organizations). Similarly, an automobile manufacturer can continue to exist only as long as people want and are willing to buy the cars that the company makes. For example, Chrysler nearly went out ot existence in the early 1980s because people no longer wanted the types of cars that the company was making. The company had not been paying sufficient attention to its external environment (i.e., its customers) to know what types of outputs (i.e., cars) they would be willing to buy.

The systems view of organizations thus emphasizes the key interdependencies that organizations must manage. Within themselves organizations must trade off the interdependencies among people, tasks, technology, and structure in order to perform their transformation processes effectively and efficiently. Organizations must also recognize their interdependence with the broader environments within which they exist. Failure to recognize and manage these key interdependencies can lead to rapid decline and ultimately to the demise of the entire organization.

Levels of Analysis

Organizational behavior can be viewed from a number of different perspectives or levels of analysis. At one level we can view organizations as consisting of individuals working on tasks in the pursuit of the organization's goals. A second level of analysis focuses upon the interaction among organization members as they work in teams, groups, and departments. Finally, we can attempt to analyze organizational behavior from the perspective of the organization as a whole. Each of these levels of analysis, outlined in Figure 1-3, contributes a unique perspective and generates its own insights into the nature and functioning of organizations.

The Individual

Our definition of organizations emphasized the fact that they consist of people. From this it would seem to follow that a sensible way to approach the study of organizational behavior would be from the perspective of individual organization members. This approach to organizational behavior draws heavily on the discipline of psychology in developing theories and explanations regarding why individuals behave and react as they do in response to different organizational policies, practices, and procedures. Within this perspective, **psychologically based** theories of learning, motivation, satisfaction, leadership, and so on are brought to bear upon the behavior and performance of individual organization members. Factors such as attitudes, beliefs, perceptions, and personalities are taken into account and their impact upon individuals' behavior and performance on the job is studied.

The Group

People rarely work completely alone in organizations. Organization members must work cooperatively and coordinate their actions if the organization's goals are to be met. This frequently results in people working together in teams,

Figure 1-3   Three levels of analysis of organizational behavior.

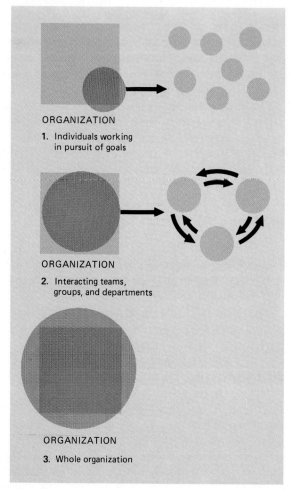

ORGANIZATION

1. Individuals working
   in pursuit of goals

ORGANIZATION

2. Interacting teams,
   groups, and departments

ORGANIZATION

3. Whole organization

committees, task forces, and the like. Thus, an alternative and fruitful perspective on organizational behavior analyzes the functioning of these work groups. How do people work together in groups? What factors determine whether a group will be cohesive and productive as opposed to fragmented and unproductive? What kinds of tasks and assignments are groups particularly good at performing? How does leadership influence group members and their ability to work together cooperatively and productively? These are only some of the questions that can be asked about the effective functioning of groups in organizations. An important component of organizational behavior involves the application of knowledge and theories from **_social psychology_** to the study of groups in organizations. The insights and understanding generated by this level of analysis are unique from those generated by the study of individuals working alone.

The Organization

Rather than focusing more narrowly upon individuals and groups within organizations, some organizational behavior researchers take the organization as a whole as their object of study. This *macro* perspective on organizational behavior draws heavily on theories and concepts from the discipline of *sociology*. Researchers seek to understand the implications of the relationship between the organization and its environment for the effectiveness of the organization. Emphasis is placed upon understanding how organizational structure and design influence the effectiveness of the organization (for example, how different ways of assigning duties and responsibilities to departments may influence the ability of these departments and the whole organization to do their work effectively). Other factors, such as the technology employed by the organization, the size of the organization, and the organization's age, are also examined, and their implications for effective organizational functioning are explored.

These different perspectives on the study of organizational behavior are not in conflict with one another. Instead, they are complementary. A full and complete understanding of the nature of organizations and the determinants of their effectiveness requires a blending together of knowledge derived from each perspective.

Organizational Effectiveness

The study of organizational behavior is ultimately concerned with understanding the nature and determinants of *organizational effectiveness.* What is it that causes certain organizations to perform effectively and grow rapidly while other organizations remain stagnant, perform poorly, and may ultimately go out of existence? Organizational effectiveness is an important but complex issue. Understanding the factors related to the measurement and determination of organizational effectiveness is a key to the field of organizational behavior.

Components of Organizational Effectiveness

How can we tell just how effective an organization really is? If we want to measure organizational effectiveness, what should we measure? Many suggestions have been made regarding different criteria that can be employed in the assessment of organizational effectiveness.[3] Table 1-1 summarizes a variety of the different components of organizational effectiveness that have been suggested. This list is not exhaustive, but instead focuses on those factors that have been most commonly employed and that appear to be most useful as indicators of effectiveness.

TABLE 1-1

Components of Organizational Effectiveness

Profitability	Can be measured in a variety of ways, such as total gross profits, profits as a percentage of total sales, and amount of money paid to each shareholder in the company
Growth	Can also be measured many different ways, such as growth in profits, growth in revenues, growth in number of products or services offered, and growth into new locations
Resource acquisition	The organization's ability to acquire the resources (i.e., inputs) it requires to perform its functions. Resources can be in the form of capital, raw materials, people, or new ideas
Adaptability	The organization's capacity to adapt to changing conditions in terms of its suppliers, its customers, its competitors, and its employees
Innovation	The organization's ability to innovate in terms of new products, new services, new technology, and new managerial systems
Productivity	The efficiency of the organization in creating products and services of maximum value at minimum cost or expense
Customer/client satisfaction	The level of satisfaction of customers or clients with the products or services provided by the organization
Employee satisfaction/ commitment	The level of satisfaction and commitment to the organization among its members

An interesting and important point to note about the components of organizational effectiveness contained in the table is that it may not be possible for any organization to be judged effective according to all the components simultaneously. Achieving effectiveness according to one of the components may make it difficult or impossible to be effective in terms of one or more of the other components. For example, actions such as closing down a plant or laying off employees, though required of an organization to increase profitability and productivity, may generate dissatisfaction among remaining employees. Alternatively, an organization that is investing heavily in order to grow rapidly and develop innovative products or services may not be as profitable (at least in the short run) as an organization not taking such actions.

Assessing Organizational Effectiveness

Thus, it is impossible to say that any organization must be performing effectively in terms of *all* the components of organizational effectiveness in order to be judged effective. In fact, the assessment of an organization's effectiveness is very much dependent upon whose perspective is used in assessing effectiveness, the time frame employed for the assessment, and the standard of comparison being applied.[4]

Perspective

Different individuals and groups, both inside and outside the organization, may focus upon different components of the organization's performance and as a result develop different assessments of the organization's effectiveness. For example, shareholders and investors may evaluate an organization's effectiveness solely in terms of its profitability, growth, and productivity. Managers within the same organization tend to focus more upon the adaptability and innovativeness of the organization, as well as on the satisfaction of customers or clients with the products or services offered by the organization. Lower-level employees may judge the organization's effectiveness primarily in terms of how they are treated by the organization and their resulting levels of commitment to the organization. It would be incorrect to assume that the assessments of organizational effectiveness from one perspective are right while the others are wrong. The key point is that whether an organization is judged to be effective or not depends largely on who is asked for an assessment and what their particular perspective is.

Time Frame

Assessments of organizational effectiveness are very much dependent upon the time period during which effectiveness is measured. For example, an organization may be able to increase its profitability in the short-to-medium term by cutting expenditures on maintenance, research and development, and the like. These same actions, however, may inhibit the organization's capacity to innovate and adapt effectively to changing conditions in the longer term. Thus, an assessment of the same organization over a longer time period might lead to the conclusion that the organization was very ineffective in terms of innovation, adaptability, and ultimately profitability. Any discussion of organizational effectiveness must clearly specify the time frame employed in the assessment.

Standard of Comparison

Whether an organization is judged to be effective according to any of the components depends upon the standard against which the organization is being assessed. There are three standards of comparison commonly used in assessing organization effectiveness. The first standard is the performance of other, similar organizations making the same types of products or offering the same types of services. For example, if compared to organizations in general, Apple Computer might be judged to be very effective in terms of innovation. But the key to assessing Apple's effectiveness on this dimension might well be in determining whether Apple's computers are *more* innovative than those of IBM, Hewlett-Packard, and its other top competitors.

The second common basis for assessment of effectiveness is the past level of performance of the organization itself. In the rapidly growing personal computer industry a company that grew by 20 percent in one year might be judged ineffective if it had been growing in size by 50 percent each year for the previous five years. In a declining industry such as steel manufacturing, a company that had been shrinking for several years might be judged extremely effective if its sales grew by 5 percent in a subsequent year.

Finally, organizational effectiveness may be judged in terms of the levels of performance that the organization had hoped or planned to attain, i.e., the organization's own performance goals. An organization that had set a target of a 5 percent increase in profits might feel it had performed very effectively if a 7 percent increase in profits were achieved. Another organization that had projected a 15 percent profit improvement might be judged ineffective if the same 7 percent growth in profits were attained.

Determinants of Organizational Effectiveness

The levels of effectiveness achieved by an organization are influenced by a multitude of factors. Figure 1-4 summarizes some of these factors in terms of four major categories: environmental characteristics, organizational characteristics, employee characteristics, and managerial policies and practices.[5]

Organizational effectiveness is influenced by the nature of the external environment within which the organization operates. The external environments faced by organizations can vary in terms of how predictable they are (e.g., how certain the organization can be of a supply of raw materials), how complex they are (e.g., how many different groups, suppliers, and government agencies must be dealt with), and how hostile they are (e.g., whether people tend to view the organization's existence as desirable—a hospital—or undesirable—a company making nerve gas).

Organizational effectiveness is also influenced by certain key characteristics of the organization as a whole. Is the organization properly structured into different departments, and are the activities of these departments adequately coordinated? Is the organization making effective use of technology, and does its structure reflect the demands inherent in the technology employed? Is the design of the organization appropriate for the organization's size, and has this design evolved appropriately as the organization has grown over time?

Characteristics of the members of the organization also influence the effectiveness of the organization. Do employees possess the skills and abilities necessary for effective performance? Are the personal goals of employees consistent with the goals of the organization? Are employees motivated to perform effectively and committed to the organization? Do employees' attitudes and values foster or hinder the achievement of effectiveness?

Finally, the managerial policies and practices employed within the organization have a key impact upon its effectiveness. The way in which managers develop strategy and design techniques to reward and control employees influences the effectiveness of the organization. Similarly, the communication and leadership skills of managers, combined with the methods they employ for making decisions, determine in large measure how effective the organization will be. Each of these sets of factors influencing organizational effectiveness will be examined in detail throughout the book.

Figure 1-4   Factors influencing organizational effectiveness.

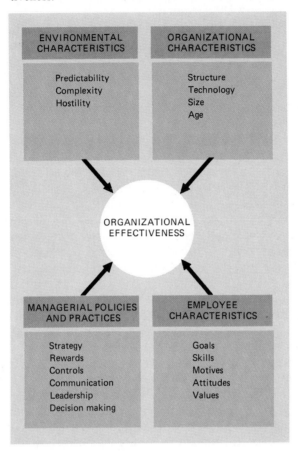

The Manager's Job

You may be thinking about pursuing a career in management. Perhaps full-time work experience in organizations has already given you an opportunity to observe something of what being a manager is all about. Or you may not yet have had such experience and may only have a fairly vague idea about what managers actually do in their jobs. Many common stereotypes exist regarding managerial work. It is often assumed that managers spend their time giving orders, making decisions, analyzing technical reports, developing strategic plans, and the like. The picture that emerges from this stereotype of a manager is of a systematic planner who engages in a good deal of contemplation and reflection, makes decisions on the basis of technical analyses, and focuses attention on key problems and issues rather than on routine duties and responsibilities.[6]

It turns out that what managers actually do in their jobs is rather dramatically different from the common stereotype held by many of us.

Characteristics of the Manager's Job

Over the past few years numerous studies have been conducted to ascertain the real nature of managerial work and how managers actually spend their time.[7] These studies have focused upon managers from the bottom (first-line supervisors) to the top (chief executive officers, or CEOs) of many different organizations. From this research the following more accurate and realistic picture emerges of the manager's job.

High Quantity of Work

Managers typically perform a great quantity of work, have little free time for breaks, and put in additional time after regular working hours. Three different studies of CEOs found these senior managers engaging in anywhere from twenty-two to seventy-seven different activities in an average working day. It is clear that managers work hard and put in long hours, and that they must be capable of performing many different types of tasks.

Brief and Varied Activities

The notion that managers spend long periods of time engaged in careful reflection on problems and decisions appears to be a myth. In fact, managers' jobs are characterized by brevity, variety, and fragmentation. Half or more of the activities engaged in by CEOs last for less than ten minutes. The average CEO gets the opportunity to work uninterruptedly for a half hour or more about once every two days. At lower levels in the organization the pace and variety of activities is even more hectic. A study of first-level supervisors found these managers averaging 583 different activities in an eight-hour shift—with a separate activity to be performed every forty-eight seconds. Clearly, managers must be able to work quickly and must be capable of shifting gears rapidly from one issue or problem to another many times during their working day.

Highly Structured Work Days

It is often assumed that senior managers are masters of their own fate who are free to set their own schedules and allocate their time as they see fit. The studies of CEOs clearly indicate that this is not the case. Scheduled meetings consume more of senior managers' time than any other activity. The average CEO has four scheduled meetings every day. When we add to these scheduled meetings the other daily routines CEOs must engage in, only about 15 percent of the senior managers' time is left available for unscheduled activities. Senior managers turn out to have much less discretion over how they spend their time than is commonly assumed.

Much Verbal Contact

The picture of the manager studying lengthy written reports and analyzing technical data also turns out to be more myth than reality. Managers frequently express a strong dislike for written material and reports. In fact, they show a significant preference for verbal contacts with others, either in meetings or over the telephone. Studies of CEOs indicate that these senior managers spend almost 75 percent of their time on the phone or in meetings. The importance of verbal communication skills for effective performance in senior management roles is obvious.

Considerable Time with Subordinates

Managers are often thought of as people who make decisions and then give orders to their subordinates regarding what they want them to do. If this were true, managers would not have to spend much time with their subordinates, other than on those occasions when orders were being given. Such appears not to be the case. Of the time they spend in contacts with other people, senior managers spend anywhere from one-third to three-quarters of it dealing with their subordinates. The ability to work effectively and productively with subordinates appears to be a key element in the manager's job.

The manager's job is thus quite different in nature from the stereotype commonly held by people unfamiliar with managerial work. Technical knowledge and skill may be essential prerequisites for successful performance in relatively specialized and often lower-level analytic jobs in organizations. However, once a person moves out of such a job and into a position that entails responsibility for managing other people, the nature of the job begins to change dramatically. The manager must be capable of working hard, performing many different activities quickly and efficiently, communicating effectively with others, and dealing with subordinates productively and positively. The manager's job essentially involves getting the organization's work done *through* the people that he or she is responsible for managing.[8] The knowledge of organizational behavior that you will acquire throughout this book will provide you with a sound basis for performing the job of manager effectively and productively.

Plan of This Book

The material contained in *Organizational Behavior* is designed to accomplish two objectives. The first objective is to provide you with a better understanding of the nature of organizations and organizational behavior, and the factors that influence the effective performance of organizations and their members. The second objective is to spell out the implications of our knowledge of organizational behavior for more effective management. This latter objective is achieved in three ways. First, each subsequent chapter contains short descriptions of actual organizational situations demonstrating the concepts and principles being discussed. Second, each subsequent chapter concludes with a listing of keys to effective management, which summarize clearly what managers should and should not do in order to apply what we know about organizational behavior to their own managerial situations. Finally, each subsequent chapter concludes with a case that permits you to apply what you have learned to the analysis of a concrete organizational problem or issue. All these elements will help you in making the transition from the general concepts and principles of organizational behavior to the concrete situations that you will have to deal with as a manager.

This first chapter has provided you with an overview of what the field of organizational behavior is all about. We have had an opportunity to discuss the nature and determinants of organizational effectiveness in addition to examining what managers' jobs are really like. This introduction to organizational behavior provides the basis for the more in-depth examination of topics and issues in the chapters to follow.

Part Two, *Individuals in Organizations,* focuses upon how individuals and organizations influence one another. Chapter 2 provides an overview of the factors that influence individual performance in organizations. A comprehensive model is presented of the ways individual abilities, expectations, attitudes, and motives influence how people perform on the job. Chapter 3 addresses the topic of motivation. The chapter examines in depth the factors that account for differences in motivation among employees, as well as techniques managers can use to influence the motivation of the people they manage. Job satisfaction is the focus of Chapter 4. It is important for managers to understand the factors that influence the job satisfaction of their subordinates, as well as the implications of levels of job satisfaction for employee behavior and job performance.

In Part Three, *Interpersonal and Group Behavior,* we broaden our focus from the individual to the group level of analysis. Chapter 5 begins the section with a discussion of leadership in organizations. Different styles of managerial leadership are described, and the implications of these leadership styles for subordinates' motivation, performance, and satisfaction are discussed. Chapter 6 deals with the critical topic of communication in organizations. The key role of effective communication in organizational life is examined. Various common barriers and strategies for improving organizational communication are suggested. In Chapter 7 the nature and functioning of groups in organizations are considered. A good deal of work gets done by groups in organizations. The chapter describes the nature of groups and the factors that influence work group effectiveness. Part Three concludes with Chapter 8 on intergroup conflict. It is very common for different groups in an organization to become enmeshed in conflict with one another. These intergroup conflicts can seriously hinder the effective functioning of the organization as a whole. The chapter discusses how these conflicts get started, what their implications are, and how they can be resolved.

Part Four, *Organization Structure and Design,* broadens our perspective still further to that of the total organization. Chapter 9 presents an overview of alternative approaches to organizational structure. Different methods of setting up departments and coordinating their activities are discussed, and the advantages and disadvantages of the different approaches are analyzed. Chapter 10 explores how factors such as an organization's size, its technology, and the type of environment within which it operates influence the appropriateness of different types of organizational designs. The emphasis is upon understanding how organizational structure and other organizational characteristics interact with one another to determine the effectiveness of the organization as a whole.

The chapters in Part Five, *Improving Employee Performance,* focus upon a variety of managerial techniques and processes that influence the effectiveness of individual employee performance. Chapter 11 deals with the problem of measuring and evaluating employee performance. Different techniques of performance appraisal are presented, and their strengths and weaknesses are analyzed. Chapter 12 takes up the topic of how organizations can design reward systems that will motivate and sustain effective performance among their members. This chapter demonstrates how a number of the concepts of motivation presented in Chapter 3 can be concretely applied to encourage this type of behavior. In Chapter 13 we explore how the type of work that employees are required to perform can influence their motivation, satisfaction, and performance. In turns out that managers can have a significant impact on the performance of their employees by carefully attending to how jobs are designed for people. Chapter 14 completes this section of the book with a detailed look at the decision-making process. Much of what managers do involves making decisions, and this chapter explores ways in which the decision-making process can be handled more effectively both by individuals and by groups.

Finally, in Part Six, *Improving Organizational Effectiveness,* we deal with a variety of topics relevant to improving the effectiveness of the organization as a whole. Chapter 15 discusses the issue of organizational entry. The methods that organizations employ for selecting, training, and socializing new employees into the organization have important and far-reaching implications for the organization and its long-run effectiveness. In Chapter 16 we take up the topic of job stress. Stress can be both functional and dysfunctional. We will examine the factors that generate job stress, what the implications of different stress levels are for organization members, and how organizations and their members can attempt to manage stress effectively. Chapter 17 describes a number of the innovative approaches to organization design and management that have emerged recently. The quality of work life (QWL) movement, Japanese management techniques, and the research on excellent companies are presented, and their implications for effective management are explored. Chapter 18 deals with the difficult problem of managing change in organizations. All organizations exhibit some degree of resistance to change. The chapter describes the techniques of organization development that can help an organization overcome resistance and manage the change process effectively and productively. Finally, in Chapter 19 we conclude with a discussion of career development. You are already involved in the process of developing and implementing a plan for your own career. This chapter will provide you with ideas on how to manage your own career development creatively and effectively in the future.

Notes

1   Etzioni, A. (1964). *Modern organizations.* Englewood Cliffs, NJ: Prentice-Hall.

March, J. G., & Simon, H. A. (1958). *Organizations.* New York: Wiley.

Parsons, T. (1956). Suggestions for a sociological approach to the theory of organizations: I and II. *Administrative Science Quarterly, 1,* 63–85, 225–239.

Schein, E. (1970). *Organizational psychology* (2nd ed.). Englewood Cliffs, NJ: Prentice-Hall.

Simon, H. A. (1952). Comments on the theory of organization. *American Political Science Review, 46,* 1130–1139.

2   Porter, L. W., Lawler, E. E., III, & Hackman, J. R. (1975). *Behavior in organizations.* New York: McGraw-Hill.

3   Cameron, K. S., & Whetten, D. A. (Eds.). (1983). *Organizational effectiveness: A comparison of multiple models.* New York: Academic Press.

Gaertner, G. H., & Ramnarayan, S. (1983). Organizational effectiveness: An alternative perspective. *Academy of Management Review, 8,* 97–107.

Goodman, P. S., & Pennings, J. M. (1977). *New perspectives on organizational effectiveness.* San Francisco: Jossey-Bass.

Spray, S. L. (1976). *Organizational effectiveness: Theory, research and application.* Kent, OH: Kent State University Press.

Steers, R. M. (1977). *Organizational effectiveness: A behavioral view.* Santa Monica, CA: Goodyear.

Zammuto, R. F. (1982). *Assessing organizational effectiveness.* Albany, NY: State University of New York Press.

Zammuto, R. F. (1984). A comparison of multiple models of organizational effectiveness. *Academy of Management Review, 9,* 606–616.

4   Ford, J. D., & Schellenberg, D. A. (1982). Conceptual issues in the assessment of organizational performance. *Academy of Management Review, 7,* 49–58.

Kelley, M. (1982, August). Participant based theories of organizational effectiveness. Paper presented at the 42nd Annual Meeting of the Academy of Management, New York.

Salancik, G. R. (1984). A single value function for evaluating organizations with multiple constituencies. *Academy of Management Review, 9,* 617–625.

5   Steers, *loc. cit.*

6   Mintzberg, H. (1975, July–August). The manager's job: Folklore and fact. *Harvard Business Review,* 49–61.

7   Choran, I. (1969). The managers of a small company. Unpublished MBA thesis, McGill University, Montreal.

Kurke, L. B., & Aldrich, H. E. (1983). Mintzberg was right!: A replication and extension of the nature of managerial work. *Management Science, 29,* 975–984.

McCall, M. W., Jr., Morrison, A. M., & Hannan, R. L. (1979). *Studies of managerial work: Results and methods* (Tech. Rep. No. 9). Greensboro, North Carolina: Center for Creative Leadership.

Mintzberg, H. (1973). *The nature of managerial work.* New York: Harper & Row.

Stewart, R. (1967). *Managers and their jobs.* London: Macmillan.

Stewart, R. (1982). A model for understanding management jobs and behavior. *Academy of Management Review, 7,* 7–13.

8   London, M. (1985). *Developing managers.* San Francisco: Jossey-Bass.

Part 2

Individuals in Organizations

Chapter 2 *Determinants of Individual Performance*

Chapter 3 *Motivation*

Chapter 4 *Job Satisfaction*

Determinants of Individual Performance

CHAPTER OUTLINE

A Model of Individual Behavior and Performance

Motivation

Ability

Perception

Personality

Organizational Systems and Resources

Keys to Effective Management

Review Questions

*P*eople are the basic building blocks of organizations. Therefore, to understand the determinants of effective organizational performance, we must first discover what determines the effectiveness of the performance of individual organization members. This chapter presents a comprehensive model of the determinants of individual performance in organizations and examines the key factors influencing individual performance effectiveness.

A Model of Individual Behavior and Performance

Figure 2-1 contains a model of the determinants of individual behavior, performance, and effectiveness within organizations. The distinctions drawn between the behavior, the performance, and the effectiveness of individuals in organizations are important ones. Individual *behavior* refers to the concrete

Figure 2-1   A model of the determinants of individual behavior, performance, and effectiveness in organizations.

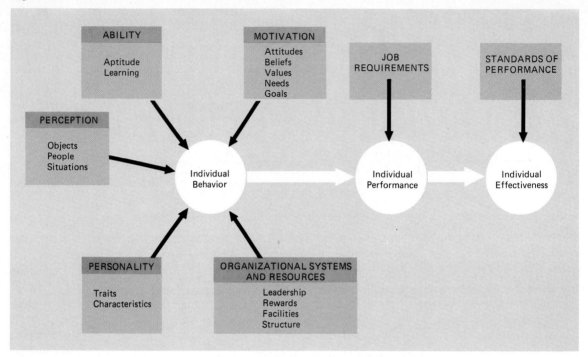

actions engaged in by a person. However, whether any particular set of behaviors or actions constitutes **performance** depends upon what the organization expects or demands of the person. Two members of an organization might behave in an almost identical manner, but if their jobs require or demand different types of behaviors, one person might be performing effectively and the other person not. Notice also that the notion of **effective** performance requires some standard of comparison for the performance of the individual. Only when we have well-defined standards and a knowledge of the organization's expectations and demands can we assess whether a person's behavior constitutes effective individual performance.[1]

The goal of the organization and its managers is to encourage individual organization members to engage in the kinds of behavior that will constitute effective performance for the organization. Thus, the behavior of individual organization members is the primary concern of management, and it is essential that managers have an understanding of the factors influencing the behavior of the individuals they manage. Figure 2-1 identifies five sets of factors that have an impact upon individual behavior in organizations.

1   *Motivation.*   A person's motivation is a key determinant of his or her behavior on the job. Motivation refers to all of the forces operating within a person to cause him or her to want to engage in certain kinds of behavior rather than others. Even if all the other factors are in place to facilitate effective individual behavior on the job, these factors will amount to nothing unless the person is motivated to perform well. A person's motivation is influenced by his or her attitudes, beliefs, values, needs, and goals.

2   *Ability.*   All the motivation in the world won't help a person perform effectively if the necessary ability just isn't there. Ability refers to the actual skills and capacities that a person possesses and that are required for the effective performance of his or her job. Organizations have to ensure that people possess the necessary abilities to engage in the behaviors required for effective performance. This can be accomplished either by careful selection of people or by a combination of selection and training.

3   *Perception.*   Perception has to do with the way in which we receive messages and interpret information. Organization members are constantly being bombarded with information, requests, demands, suggestions, and so on. What people do depends to a large extent upon which of these many perceptual inputs they pay attention to, as well as how the inputs and messages are interpreted and understood. Of particular relevance to understanding individual behavior are the messages the organization sends to its members regarding the kinds of behaviors and activities expected of them. These expectations are communicated in a variety of ways (job descriptions, policies and procedures manuals, informal norms, discussions with supervisors, etc.). A key factor is that an individual's behavior is influenced *not* by the organization's *actual* expectations of him or her, but rather by how these expectations are *perceived* by the person. Thus, we need to take into account the process of perception and understand how perceptual processes operate in organizations.

4   *Personality.*   Personality refers to the personal traits or characteristics—sociability, dominance, aggressiveness, persistence, and so on—that a person possesses. An individual's personality influences the types of activities that she or he is suited for and the likelihood that the person will be able to perform effectively in a particular job or situation. As a result, personality factors must be taken into account in assessing the suitability of an individual for a position in an organization.

5   *Organizational systems and resources.*   Individual behavior is influenced by a wide variety of organizational systems and resources. Systems such as the organizational structure and hierarchy strongly influence and constrain both *what* individuals do and *how* they do it. In addition, individual behavior is influenced by various types of resources provided by the organization, such as advice and direction from leaders and physical support in terms of facilities and technology.

In the remainder of the chapter we will explore each of these sets of factors and their influence on individual behavior in organizations in more depth. This discussion will provide a sound basis for understanding the nature of individuals and why they behave as they do in organizations.

Motivation

In studying motivation we are interested in understanding why people choose to do certain things rather than others, and also why different people put different amounts of effort or intensity into the activities they engage in. The nature of individual motivation in organizations is a broad and complex topic that we will explore in considerable depth in the next chapter. At this point we will outline some of the basic components or building blocks of motivation in organization members.[2] These components are summarized in Figure 2-2 and discussed in turn below.

Attitudes

An ***attitude*** refers to the way a person feels about and is disposed towards some "object."[3] The term *object* is used here very generally. The object of a person's attitude could be a physical object or a set of objects (e.g., What's your attitude toward foreign cars?), a specific person (e.g., What's your attitude toward your boss?), a group of people (e.g., What's your attitude toward professors?), or a more abstract entity (e.g., What's your attitude toward business?). Each of us obviously has many different attitudes. When we ask someone what his or her attitude is toward some object, we are asking the person: (1) how he or she feels about the object; and (b) how he or she is disposed to act toward the object (supportively or critically).

Attitudes are relevant to our understanding of individual motivation and behavior because of the links that exist between attitudes and behavior. A person who has a negative attitude toward another department in the organization may be unlikely to behave in a friendly and cooperative manner with members of that department. A person with a very positive attitude toward his or her company will be more likely to come to work regularly and to remain with the company even if offered a job with another organization. However, a person's attitude is not the only factor influencing the way he or she will behave toward a given object. People do sometimes act in ways that are inconsistent with their attitudes (e.g., the person says one thing and does another). A full understanding of why people actually behave the way they do requires us to take into account the many additional factors that influence individual motivation and behavior.

Beliefs

A person's ***beliefs*** have a critical impact upon motivation in two ways. First of all, people must believe that they are capable of performing the behaviors that

Figure 2-2   Factors influencing individual motivation in organizations.

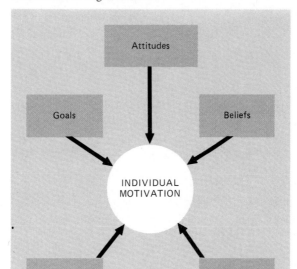

the organization expects of them. If people do not believe that effective performance is even possible, then motivation is bound to be very weak. Second, people must believe that engaging in the behaviors desired by the organization will have positive consequences for them personally. Unless people believe that some personal benefits will follow from performing effectively, they are unlikely to be highly motivated.[4]

A person's beliefs regarding his or her ability to perform effectively and the rewards likely to follow from effective performance are influenced by a wide variety of factors, some of which are summarized in Figure 2-3. Perhaps the key point to keep in mind is that people's motivation is influenced by their beliefs, and that these beliefs may not be based upon accurate perceptions of the world. For example, a person may mistakenly believe that he or she is incapable of performing a certain job effectively, and as a result lack the motivation to try. Even if the belief is incorrect, the person's motivation will still be very low because it is the belief that serves as the basis for the person's actions. Similarly, if a person believes that performing well is more likely to lead to unpleasant results (e.g., more work assignments) than to pleasant ones (e.g., a pay bonus), the person will not be motivated to perform well, even if those beliefs are invalid. Each of us takes action based upon our beliefs about ourselves and the world around us. When our beliefs are incorrect or inaccurate we may end up being motivated to engage in inappropriate or ineffective patterns of behavior. An important implication is that organizations and their

Figure 2-3 Factors influencing individual beliefs
about effective performance.

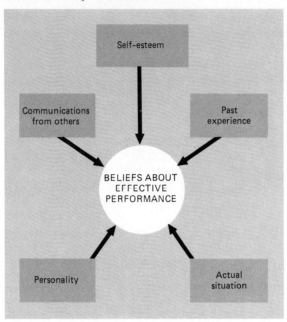

(*Source:* Adapted from Lawler, E. E., III. (1973).
Motivation in work organizations. Monterey, CA:
Brooks/Cole, pp. 55,58. Used by permission.)

managers must try to ensure that organization members hold accurate and
realistic beliefs about their capacities to perform effectively and the likely consequences of such effective performance.

Values

The *values* that a person holds can influence his or her motivation and subsequent behavior in two ways. First, they influence the general types of activities
that the person will find appealing. Second, they influence a person's motivation to obtain specific outcomes, such as money, promotion, and prestige.[5]

There is some evidence that people with different general patterns of values gravitate toward different types of occupational groups and organizations.[6]
For example, we would expect to observe different patterns of values among
members of the banking industry than among voluntary workers in social service organizations. Even within a single organization the patterns of values
among individuals may be quite different across different departments (e.g.,
sales vs. manufacturing vs. research), as well as across different hierarchical
levels (e.g., senior management vs. blue-collar workers).[7]

On a more specific level, the values that people attach to various types of
organizational outcomes can exert a strong impact on their motivation.[8] For
example, the person who places a high value on monetary rewards and promotional opportunities may be highly motivated in a situation in which he or

she believes that effective performance will lead to these outcomes. On the other hand, exactly the same situation might elicit very little motivation from a person who values money and promotion very little, but who places high value on opportunities for friendship and pleasant working conditions. Obviously, poeple differ in what they value, and organizations must take these value differences into account in attempting to motivate their members.

Needs

People can be thought of as having a variety of different **needs** that influence their motivation. These can vary from very basic needs for items such as food and shelter to the more complex needs for friendship, a sense of self-esteem, and personal achievement. To the extent that a person is experiencing a particular need, we might expect that person to be motivated to engage in behavior that would lead to the satisfaction or gratification of the need. The prescription for organizations would then be to set up situations in which people are able to satisfy their most important needs by engaging in the types of behavior most desired by the organization for effective performance.[9]

A number of specific motivation theories based on the analysis of human needs have been developed. Perhaps the best-known is the need hierarchy theory developed by Abraham Maslow.[10] This theory suggests that people have a set of five different types of needs that vary from the most basic physiological needs to the most advanced needs for personal growth, development, and accomplishment (known as *self-actualization needs*). This theory and several other motivation theories based upon an analysis of human needs are discussed in detail in Chapter 3. Table 2-1 provides an idea of the variety of different types of needs that can have an influence on motivation.[11] This list represents a sampling of only about half of the needs that have been analyzed and studied.

Goals

Goals influence motivation in two ways. First, a goal provides a person with a target to shoot for, something to aspire toward. The existence of the goal then generates motivation within the person to work toward the attainment of the goal. Second, goals influence motivation by providing a basis for assessing how well a person is doing in terms of how close he or she has come to reaching the goal. People can't really tell how well they're doing without some standard of comparison, and goals provide that standard.

The importance of goals and their impact upon motivation has been recognized in the management literature since the early part of this century.[12] More recently, a considerable amount of research has focused explicitly on understanding how and why goals have the influence they do on motivation.[13] This research has led to the conclusion that in order for goals to influence motivation, they must be *specific* and they must be sufficiently *difficult* to be challenging to the person. Of additional importance is the fact that goals only influence motivation to the extent that they are *accepted* by the person. In other

TABLE   2-1

A Sample of Some of the Needs Whose Influence on Motivation Has Been Studied

Need	Characteristics
Achievement	Aspires to accomplish difficult tasks; maintains high standards and is willing to work toward distant goals; responds positively to competition; is willing to put forth effort to attain excellence
Affiliation	Enjoys being with friends and people in general; accepts people readily; makes efforts to win friendships and maintain associations with people
Aggression	Enjoys combat and argument; is easily annoyed; is sometimes willing to hurt people to get his or her way; may seek to "get even" with people perceived as having harmed him or her
Autonomy	Tries to break away from restraints, confinement, or restrictions of any kind; enjoys being unattached, free, not tied to people, places, or obligations; may be rebellious when faced with restraints
Endurance	Is willing to work long hours; doesn't give up quickly on a problem; is persevering, even in the face of great difficulty; is patient and unrelenting in work habits
Exhibition	Wants to be the center of attention; enjoys having an audience; engages in behavior that wins the notice of others; may enjoy being dramatic or witty
Harm avoidance	Does not enjoy exciting activities, especially if danger is involved; avoids risk of bodily harm; seeks to maximize personal safety

words, a goal has to be *my* personal goal if it is to motivate me. If my boss tells me that my goal is to achieve a certain standard of performance, that goal won't motivate me unless I accept it as my own.

Ability

A person's ability is obviously a crucial factor influencing his or her behavior and performance as an organization member.[14] Regardless of how motivated a person is to perform effectively, if the necessary ability is lacking it is impossible for the person to achieve an adequate level of performance. Below a certain level, a person cannot make up for lack of ability simply by trying harder.

TABLE   2-1 (*Continued*)

A Sample of Some of the Needs Whose Influence on Motivation Has Been Studied

Need	*Characteristics*
Impulsivity	Tends to act on the "spur of the moment" and without deliberation; gives vent readily to feelings and wishes; speaks freely; may be volatile in emotional expression
Nurturance	Gives sympathy and comfort; assists others whenever possible, is interested in caring for children, the disabled, or the infirm; offers a "helping hand" to those in need; readily performs favors for others
Order	Is concerned with keeping personal effects and surroundings neat and organized; dislikes clutter, confusion, lack of organization; is interested in developing methods for keeping materials methodically organized
Power	Attempts to control the environment and to influence or direct other people; expresses opinions forcefully; enjoys the role of leader and may assume it spontaneously
Succorance	Frequently seeks the sympathy, protection, love, advice, and reassurance of other people; may feel insecure or helpless without such support; confides difficulties readily to a receptive person
Understanding	Wants to understand many areas of knowledge; values synthesis of ideas, verifiable generalizations, logical thought, particularly when directed at satisfying intellectual curiosity.

Source: Adapted from Jackson, D. N. (1974). *The Personality Research Form Manual.* Port Huron, MI: Research Psychologists Press. Copyright © 1967, 1974 by Douglas N. Jackson. Used by permission.

A person's ***ability*** to perform an activity can be thought of as having two components.[15] The first component is the person's aptitude for the activity. Second are the learning opportunities that permit the person to develop his or her abilities.

Aptitude refers to the person's basic, built-in capacity for performing some activity effectively.[16] For example, people differ considerably in their aptitudes for athletics, music, and mathematics. A person with a high level of athletic aptitude may be able to develop considerable ability in a wide variety of sports very quickly after taking up each sport. The same person may be tone-deaf (lacking any musical aptitude) and utterly baffled by mathematics no matter how hard he or she studies the subject (low mathematical aptitude).

At the same time, however, a person's aptitudes are not translated into actual abilities until the person is provided with ***learning opportunities*** to develop those aptitudes. For example, a person possessing considerable musical aptitude still requires music lessons in order to develop the acutal ability to play the piano well. The development of aptitudes into abilities can occur via two methods. The first, more structured method is formal *training,* while the second is the provision of opportunities to obtain *experience* in the activity. Both training and experience create the conditions for learning to occur. It is this general process of learning that transforms an inherent aptitude into an actual ability to perform effectively. This model of ability as a combination of aptitude and learning opportunities is summarized in Figure 2-4.

Aptitudes

Many attempts have been made to describe and classify the various aptitudes that people may possess.[17] One fundamental distinction that we can draw is between *mental* and *physical* aptitudes. For certain types of jobs (e.g., research scientist), particular mental aptitudes may be crucial while physical aptitudes may be quite irrelevant to effective performance. For other types of jobs (e.g., manual laborer), physical aptitudes may be important and mental aptitudes relatively unimportant. Finally, another class of jobs (e.g., brain surgeon, football quarterback) may require a combination of key mental and physical aptitudes.

Mental Aptitudes

The classification and measurement of mental aptitudes began with the first intelligence tests, developed in the early part of this century. Since then a tremendous number of different mental aptitudes have been suggested, measured, and analyzed.[18] Table 2-2 provides examples of several relatively independent sets of mental aptitudes.[19] The extent to which a person possesses each of these aptitudes can be measured. Each aptitude can then be related to the person's ability to engage in different types of behavior and hence to perform successfully in different types of jobs.[20]

Figure 2-4   Ability results from the combination of aptitudes and development opportunities.

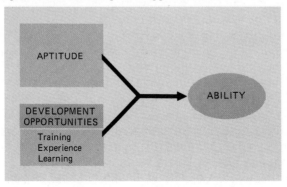

TABLE   2-2

Examples of Some Different Types of Mental and Physical Aptitudes

Mental aptitudes	Verbal comprehension	Understanding of the meaning of words and their relationship to each other; ready comprehension of what is read
	Number	Speed and accuracy in making simple arithmetic computations such as adding, subtracting, multiplying, and dividing
	Space	Accuracy of perception of fixed geometric or spatial relations among figures and ability to visualize how they might look if transformed or changed in position
	Memory	Accuracy of rote memory for words, symbols, and lists of numbers
Physical aptitudes	Control precision	Ability to perform tasks requiring finely controlled muscular adjustment
	Multilimb coordination	Ability to coordinate the movements of a number of limbs simultaneously
	Reaction time	Speed of a person's response when a stimulus appears
	Manual dexterity	Skill of arm and hand movements in handling rather large objects under speeded conditions

---

Physical Aptitudes

A variety of distinct physical skill aptitudes have been identified. These types of physical aptitudes are obviously highly relevant to the effective performance of jobs whose content is physical or manual in character. Table 2-2 also summarizes some groups of physical aptitudes[21] that, interestingly, appear to be highly specific and quite independent of one another. Thus, a person with quick reaction times may be quite lacking in manual dexterity, and vice versa. This suggests the importance of careful testing of physical aptitudes prior to selection of a person for a job requiring certain specific physical skills.

Learning Opportunities

The ability to perform an activity effectively requires not only that the person possess the necessary aptitude for the activity, but also that he or she have had the opportunity to develop that aptitude in real work settings. This development can occur either in a relatively formal and structured manner, via ***training,*** or more informally, via **experience.** The reinforcement mechanisms that underlie these learning processes will be explored in detail in the next chapter.

Training   Organizations generally spend large amounts of money each year to provide job-related training to their members. This training can take a wide variety of forms, from formal classroom instruction to simulated work situations to actual on-the-job training. The appropriateness and effectiveness of different training techniques is very much dependent upon the particular skills that are the focus of the training. The effective use of training requires that the organization clearly identify the needs that training is to fulfill, and specifically state the skills to be developed. The organization then must choose the training methods and techniques that are most likely to facilitate the acquisition and development of the target abilities. The training must be designed with principles of learning and motivation in mind, to ensure that the appropriate abilities will be developed at a rapid pace and subsequently retained and used by the trainees.[22]

Experience   Work experience can be used either as a substitute for, or as a supplement to, formal training. The complete development and perfection of complex work-related abilities almost always requires extensive practice and experience. If organizations expect their members to develop certain abilities, then they must ensure that individuals are provided with adequate opportunities to obtain experience in using those abilities. This may require the organization to tolerate some less-than-optimal performance from members as they are progressing through the skill acquisition process. On-the-job training is, in fact, a technique for combining some of the structured elements of formal training programs with the opportunity for the individual to obtain actual work-related experience.

Perception

Perception plays a key role in determining individual behavior in organizations. In a variety of forms, organizations send their members messages regarding what they are expected to do and not do. No matter how hard an organization may try to send clear messages to its members regarding what is expected of them, those messages are still subject to distortion in the process of being *perceived* by organization members.[23] Our perceptions of the world serve as the basis for our actions. If our perceptions of what is expected of us are consistent with the actual expectations of the organization, then the result can be effective performance. If, on the other hand, our perceptions are a distorted or inaccurate picture of reality, then the outcome will be inappropriate behavior and ineffective performance.[24]

To understand how perceptions may become distorted, let us look at the different factors that influence our perceptions. Figure 2-5 outlines three sets of factors that influence how a person perceives something (whether that something is a physical entity, such as a car or an office, another person, such as

Figure 2-5   Factors influencing a person's perceptions.

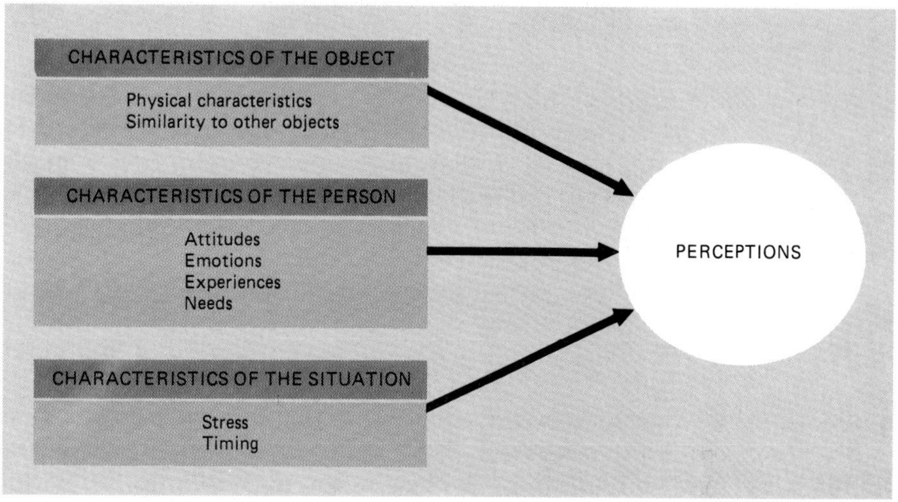

one's boss, or a more abstract entity, such as one's job or role in the organization).

Characteristics of the Entity

Naturally we would hope and expect that the primary determinants of a person's perception of any entity would be the actual characteristics of the entity itself. This should apply not only to physical objects but also to our perceptions of people and more abstract entities like jobs and organizations. Notice, however, that as the object of perception becomes more abstract, there are fewer actual physical characteristics to influence our perceptions of the object. Thus, as objects of our perception become more ambiguous, our perceptions of those objects become more subject to influence by the other personal and situational factors outlined in Figure 2-5. For example, different people's perceptions of a physical object such as an office building will be much more similar than will the same people's perceptions of a more abstract entity such as the strategy of their organization.

Stereotyping is a common form of perceptual distortion that arises as a result of the similarity of an object to other objects previously perceived by the person. Stereotyping occurs when a person decides (usually unconsciously) that all objects of a certain type share certain characteristics.[25] Stereotyping can occur regarding physical objects, people, or abstractions. For example, a person may develop a stereotype regarding all cars made by a certain manufacturer as a result of his or her experiences with only one car made by that manufacturer (e.g., "All Fords are poorly made."). Stereotyping is unfortunately common with respect to different groups of people based upon certain observable characteristics, such as race and sex. Finally, stereotyping can occur in perceptions of more abstract entities like jobs and organizations (e.g., "All unions are undesirable.").

Stereotyping is dangerous because it results in perceptions being influenced not by the actual characteristics of a particular object, but rather by the apparent similarity of that object to some previously perceived object or group of objects. It is almost certainly true that there are some poorly made Fords on the road and some undesirable unions in existence. However, it is equally certain that there are many well-made Fords and many desirable unions in existence. Each member of a class or grouping must be perceived and evaluated on its own, not in terms of an inaccurate stereotype of *all* members of that class or group.

Characteristics of the Person

A variety of personal characteristics influence our perceptions. The more ambiguous the objects of our perception are, the greater is the influence of these personal factors on our perceptions.

Attitudes

Our attitudes have a powerful influence upon what we pay attention to, what we remember, and how we interpret information.[26] For example, people's perceptions of political parties are strongly influenced by their attitudes toward the parties. A person with a positive attitude toward the party in power will tend to perceive and remember the positive accomplishments of the party (e.g., reduced inflation and increased economic growth). A person with a negative attitude toward the party will be much more likely to perceive and remember the negative events that have occurred (e.g., increased unemployment and higher deficits).

Emotions

A person's emotional state strongly influences the perceptual process. When people are highly agitated, frustrated, or angry, their perceptual processes become impaired. People actually don't hear or see things at times because their emotional state may be causing them to ignore any inputs that they are receiving.

Experience

A person's previous experiences with objects of a similar type or under similar circumstances can influence perception. For example, if a person has had many unhappy experiences in performance appraisal meetings with his or her previous bosses, those experiences will influence how that person will perceive his or her first appraisal interview with a new boss.

Needs

People's needs influence their perceptions. For example, people who are hungry tend to see images of food in even the most ambiguous stimuli. A person with a strong need for security will focus his or her perceptions more strongly on the stability of the organization when offered a new job than will a person whose strongest need is for variety and challenge.

Characteristics of the Situation

Various situational factors can influence the nature and accuracy of a person's perceptions.

Stress

Information is often either distorted or ignored when a person is under a high level of stress. The existence of stress impedes the person's capacity to process and perceive information that he or she may be receiving. Sufficient stress to impede accurate perception may result from deadlines, time pressures, crises, and the like.

Timing

A person may have become accustomed to receiving certain kinds of information at certain times or under certain circumstances. If the information is then received at another time or under other circumstances, it may be ignored, for example, if a regular report arrives at a time other than when it was expected.

Our perceptions are obviously influenced by many factors. When perceptions are distorted or inaccurate, people may end up engaging in behavior that is inappropriate or undesirable from the organization's standpoint. It is thus critical that organizations work hard at ensuring that their members accurately perceive what is expected of them if they are to perform effectively.

Personality

Personality is another key factor influencing individual behavior in organizations.[27] The term *personality* is one that we all tend to use quite frequently and that most people feel they have an intuitive understanding of. We talk quite freely of our own personality, of the personalities of other people, and even of disagreements among people being due to personality conflicts. However, coming up with an accurate and comprehensive definition of personality is not an easy task. We will define ***personality*** as a stable set of personal characteristics and tendencies that determine the commonalities and differences in people's thoughts, feelings, and actions. These characteristics of personality exhibit continuity over time and are not solely the result of the pressures of the moment.[28]

There are several aspects of this definition that we need to look at closely. First, personality refers to a relatively *stable* set of characteristics and tendencies of a person. When we want to understand someone's personality we need to look for characteristics of the person that are relatively unchangeable or that change only very slowly. Thus we would not characterize someone as having a very outgoing personality if that person tended to be very outgoing and friendly only some of the time and on other occasions behaved in a very shy and retiring manner.

In studying personality we are interested in factors that explain both *commonalities* and *differences* in the behavior of people. Thus, a knowledge of personality should help us to explain commonalities in a person's behavior in a variety of different types of situations (e.g., why does the person tend to behave very similarly with friends, family, coworkers, and superiors?). At the same time, knowledge of individual personalities should help us to understand differences in the behavior of different people in the same situation (e.g., why is one person quiet and obedient with the boss while someone else is forceful and opinionated?).

Finally, our definition of personality draws attention to the fact that in studying personality we are interested in factors *within people* that cause them to behave as they do. Behavior that is clearly caused by social factors (e.g., doing a job a certain way because the boss told you to do it that way) or biological pressures (e.g., stopping work to have lunch because you're hungry) doesn't require any explanation in terms of personality factors. Behavior that can't be explained in terms of clear social or biological causes requires us to look to the personality of the individual for its causes.

Personality Traits and Characteristics

In order to understand how personality influences individual behavior in organizations, we require a method of describing the nature of an individual's personality. One method is to identify various **traits** or **characteristics** of personality and attempt to measure them. Measures of personality traits can then be related to observations of individual behavior to see what influence, if any, the personality factors have on behavior. We will examine a number of personality traits which have been frequently studied and that have some direct relevance to individual behavior in organizations.

Authoritarianism

The **authoritarian** personality is characterized by a strong belief in the legitimacy of established mechanisms of formal authority, such as the government, the legal system, and the organizational hierarchy.[29] A person who is highly authoritarian tends to hold conventional values, believe in the moral correctness of his or her position, and view obedience to authority as essential. The authoritarian tends to be quite rigid in his or her beliefs and strongly oriented toward conformity with rules and regulations. Not surprisingly, authoritarian people tend to prefer to work in organizational situations that are highly structured and unambiguous. In addition, they are likely to respond positively to a relatively autocratic and directive leadership style, since they view it as the legitimate right of people in positions of authority to give orders and directions to others. Box 2-1 provides a description of the management style of Harold Geneen, former president of ITT, who exhibited many of the characteristics of authoritarianism.

BOX 2-1

An Authoritarian Manager

Harold S. Geneen built International Telephone and Telephone (ITT) Corporation into the biggest conglomerate in the world in the 1970s. Then he saw its assets gradually sold off and himself squeezed out of the company. Geneen showed the classic characteristics of the authoritarian manager.

Geneen was considered a superstar at acquiring companies but opinions about his abilities as an operating manager of an organization were mixed. He was "an absolute disaster" in the words of a business analyst quoted by *Fortune* magazine (January 11, 1982), although others claim his colleagues considered him an excellent manager. All of them agree he was not well liked. He formed no close alliances, made few friends, and was feared by his managers. He was demanding, impatient, antagonistic, and blunt. Subordinates were scared to death of his sudden flailing criticisms of them at meetings where other colleagues were present. He was relentless in his pursuit of short-term goals and pressured his managers without mercy to meet quarterly budgets. "If you make your quarters, you'll make your year" was his watchword. He insisted on regular reporting and tight cost control.

He was brutal in his punishment of any manager who didn't measure up and maintained teams of corporate "overseers" at headquarters whose job was to find problems in other people's operations and report them to Geneen. Meetings with Geneen were an ordeal, and they were meant to be. They were held regularly, monthly in some cases. At them, managers reported on their operations, shared information, discussed ideas, and took their turns submitting to Geneen's grillings. These were so brutal it is said some managers were brought to tears. The meetings tested not only the performance of a subordinate, but his attachment to the Geneen organization.

But many people couldn't take it. Geneen attracted some of the brightest business executives to ITT, but he lost many of them. As one disgruntled manager said: "The pressures here have made many say 'the hell with it.' Nothing matters to him but the job—not the clock, not your personal life, nothing."

Geneen had the reputation as a master manager and a financial wizard when he went to ITT, and his secret wish seems to have been to operate the company all by himself, relying on no one else. "If I had more arms, legs, and time, I could run the entire corporation," he is supposed to have said. When he relinquished his post as chief executive officer at ITT, he made no secret of his hope to become chairman of the board so that he could continue to exercise some control. Geneen was temperamentally incapable of refraining from playing a role at ITT and, in the nature of his record and personality, it would be a powerful one. In fact, Geneen engineered the ousting of his successor within 18 months.

Source: Adapted from House, R. J. (1986). *Power,* forthcoming. Used by permission.

Locus of Control

People have different perceptions about the factors responsible for what happens to them. These perceptions are referred to as perceived *locus of control.* Some people tend to see the things that happen to them as primarily under their own control. In other words their perceived locus of control is internal or within themselves. Such people are referred to as *internals.* Other people may tend to see what happens to them as largely outside their own control. They believe that events are controlled by other people, other things, or simply luck or chance. Such people have an external locus of control and are referred to as *externals.* A personality inventory has been developed that can be used to classify people according to where they fall on the continuum of internal-external locus of control. A good deal of research has been carried out exploring the implications of locus of control for behavior in organizations.[30]

Internals are more likely than externals to be in managerial positions and tend to be more satisfied with their jobs. Internals respond more positively to a participative style of management than do externals.[31] Internals are also more likely to try to influence others as to the way they would like them to behave and, conversely, are less prone to accept the influence attempts of others. In addition, internals appear to be more capable than externals of coping effectively with stressful and ambiguous situations.[32]

Introversion/ Extroversion

Introversion and *extroversion* are two ends of a different personality continuum.[33] A person who is highly introverted tends to be quiet, shy, and retiring. The introvert is characterized by a sensitivity and concern for feelings and is comfortable dealing with abstract notions and concepts. The extrovert, on the other hand, is highly social and outgoing and wants to be constantly interacting with people and involved in events.

Introverts and extroverts will naturally be differentially suited to different types of positions in organizations. The extrovert will want to be dealing with other people and to be involved in a constant stream of activities. For example, extroverts would be well suited to sales positions in an organization. The introvert, on the other hand, will function more effectively in positions that permit him or her to work independently on tasks that require some reflection and thought regarding abstract ideas and concepts. We might expect to find introverts in technical staff groups and research departments of organizations.

Dominance

As the term implies, individuals whose major personality trait is *dominance* like to be in positions in which they can exert influence and control over others.[34] Highly dominant people like to be at the center of attention and activity and to feel that they are in control of situations. There is some evidence to indicate that dominance is related to success in sales jobs, and that leaders tend to be somewhat higher on dominance than followers.[35]

Determinants of Personality

A number of different factors determine the nature of an individual's personality. Obviously a key factor in the determination of personality is heredity.

While the genetic background inherited from our parents does not absolutely determine the precise type of personality we will have, it does profoundly influence and constrain the type of personality each of us develops.

Cultural factors play a broad and general role in the development of individual personality. Different cultures encourage and prohibit different types of behaviors and attitudes, and these broad social and cultural norms influence the nature and development of the personalities of the members of the cultural group.

Social factors have a direct and pervasive impact on the nature of personality. We are each profoundly influenced by our interactions with other people. Parents construct the world for their children when they are very young. Throughout our lives friends and peers influence what we do and how we develop. The people with whom we interact provide us with models of behavior and also reinforce and punish us for different types of behavior.

Finally, our environment and the situations within which we find ourselves also influence our personalities. The types of experiences that we have and the contexts within which we have them can strongly influence the development of personality. For example, personality developement is influenced by where we live, what schools we attended, and what kinds of organizations we have worked in.

Personality and Behavior

A considerable amount of research has been carried out exploring the relationship between personality and individual behavior in organizations. The results of much of this research have been rather disappointing. It is difficult to predict accurately how a person will perform in an organization simply from a knowledge of his or her personality. However, if we look back at Figure 2-1, we should not find this result surprising. Personality is but one of many factors influencing the behavior of individuals in organizations. Effective understanding and prediction of such behavior cannot be based upon an analysis of only one of the multiple factors operating. More recent research has begun to attempt to take into account these multiple influences in the models and theories being tested.[36]

Organizational Systems and Resources

The behavior and performance of individual organization members is also influenced by a variety of organizational systems and resources.

Facilities

The *physical facilities* and accompanying support systems provided by the organization obviously influence the behavior and performance of individual organization members. People must be provided with the space and equipment they require if they are to perform well. In addition, adequate provision of such things as secretarial support and adequate staffing can often free more senior managers to focus their attention on the issues most critical to the effective performance of the organization. The importance of the nature and design of the organization's physical facilities has been underlined by recent research demonstrating the impact that such facilities can have upon the attitudes, motivation, and performance of individual members.[37]

Organization Structure and Design

Organization structure and design have to do with the way in which the different groups and departments in the organization are set up and the way in which the reporting relationships and lines of communication are established among different positions in the organization. The behavior and performance of an individual is influenced by where that person fits into the overall structure and design of the organization.[38] The basis upon which the organization structures itself into departments, divisions, and so on has an indirect but pervasive impact on the organization's members. For example, the structural design of the organization influences people's ability to coordinate their activities with one another in an informal fashion. When different people are put into the same department, they become subject to common supervision and may have common measures of performance applied to their output. These factors can influence the ability and willingness of people to work together cooperatively to solve problems and achieve common goals.[39] The ways in which organizational structure and design influence the behavior of organization members are explored in detail in Chapters 9 and 10.

Leadership

The organization establishes a system of *leadership* and supervision to provide direction, assistance, advice, and coaching to individual organization members. The leadership behavior of individuals occupying positions of authority is thus a potential source of influence on the behavior and performance of organization members.[40] The ways in which different styles of leadership can influence the effectiveness of individuals in organizations are explored in depth in Chapter 5.

Reward Systems

Organizations set up a variety of systems to provide their members with *rewards* such as money, time off, recognition, and awards. Most organizations believe that their reward systems help them to obtain the types of behavior that they desire from their members. Whether reward systems are in fact effective in accomplishing this objective is not always clear.[41] In Chapter 12 we discuss organizational reward systems in detail and examine how they can be designed in order to have maximum positive benefit in terms of encouraging and reinforcing effective individual performance.

Keys to Effective Management

Our analysis of the determinants of individual behavior in organizations has a variety of implications for effective management.

1 *Managers must recognize that the behavior of individuals in organizations is determined by multiple factors.*   The way organization members behave and perform is influenced by characteristics of the organization as well as by characteristics of the individual. From the organizational perspective, the expectations that are set up and communicated, as well as the systems and resources that are provided for members, all have a direct impact on individual behavior. From the individual's viewpoint, motivation, ability, and personality all jointly interact in determining how the person will behave.

2 *Managers must recognize the key role of motivation and the multiple factors that influence individual motivation.*   Motivation is an essential prerequisite to effective behavior and performance. It, in turn, is influenced by the person's attitudes, beliefs, values, needs, and goals. A thorough understanding of the nature and determinants of individual motivation is indispensable for the effective manager.

3 *Managers must ensure that a good fit exists between the abilities of the individual and the demands of the job.*   If a person does not possess the ability to perform effectively, all the motivation in the world cannot help. Managers must ensure that people are placed into positions suited to their aptitudes, and must provide adequate learning opportunities to permit individuals to develop the required levels of proficiency.

4 *Managers must ensure that individuals clearly perceive what the organization expects of them.*   It is extremely difficult for people to do a good job if they don't understand what is expected of them. Managers must work hard to ensure that jobs and roles are defined clearly and unambiguously for people. Managers must also recognize that it is the job as *perceived* by the individual that influences the person's behavior. Efforts must be made to overcome barriers and ensure accurate and clear perceptions of duties and responsibilities on the part of organization members.

5 *Managers must take into account the influence of personality on the behavior and performance of organization members.*   Individuals differ widely in the nature of their personalities. Managers must recognize the need for a good fit between the personality of the individual and the requirements and demands of the person's job.

6 *Managers must design and deliver the systems and resources that individuals require in order to do their jobs well.*   Even if a person understands clearly what needs to be done, if he or she lacks the necessary resources and support, the person will not be able to perform effectively. Such support can take the form of physical resources, such as facilities and equipment, or of organizational support, such as effective leadership, planning, and reward systems.

Review Questions

1 Discuss the differences between the behavior, the performance, and the effectiveness of individuals in organizations. Why is it important to keep these distinctions in mind?

2 Outline a model of the determinants of individual behavior in organizations. Briefly describe and justify your model.

3 What role does motivation play in determining how individuals behave in organizations?

4 Discuss some of the factors that influence the motivation of individuals in organizations.

5 What factors influence the current levels of ability of organization members? Discuss how these factors interact with one another.

6 Describe the joint influence of motivation and ability on the behavior of individuals in organizations.

7 What are some of the factors influencing a person's perceptions of what the organization expects of him or her?

8 Describe several personality characteristics and discuss their relevance to individual behavior in organizations.

9 Discuss ways in which an individual's personality may interact with other factors in determining his or her behavior and performance in the organization.

10 Outline and discuss some of the organizational systems and resources that have a direct impact on the behavior and performance of organization members. Which factor or factors do you believe have the strongest influence on individuals?

Robert Morton

Robert Morton was an intelligent 29-year-old high school graduate. He was married, but separated from his wife, and he had no children. Morton had been hired by the Crystal City subsidiary of a major corporation in the defense industry. His guard job required using an automobile to get from place to place to check locks on a specified schedule. The considerable time between checking locks was to be spent cruising around the plant looking for unauthorized persons and, as the chief of the plant protection department said, "to provide a tight security image to both insiders and outsiders." It was generally agreed by many plant employees that a lapse in security could have international implications for military defense.

During his first six months on the job Morton carried out his duties without any problems. However, during the next six months he began to report late for work, to fail to report to work at all, to use his sick leave, and to leave work without permission. Frequently he was found sleeping in his guard car. Consequently the night shift captain of the guard force gave Morton a verbal warning about his attendance and about his failure to report that he was not coming to

work or that he was leaving early. Morton said he understood the seriousness of the problem, especially the need for tight plant security, and indicated he would try to improve. Soon he was failing to report for work, was late for work, and was leaving early. Again the night shift captain gave him verbal warnings, the last of which was written and placed in the files of the plant protection department. Morton was then found sleeping in his guard car, which was reported to the chief of plant protection, who placed a reprimand in Morton's file with the personnel department. Morton was informed of this action by a copy of the reprimand placed in his mailbox. Morton's continued attendance problems became serious enough that the captain of the night shift decided that after the next incident Morton would be laid off for three days without pay. One morning the captain went looking for Morton when he failed to respond to calls over the radio. The captain found Morton's guard car parked in the lot provided for the force. Morton had apparently left work forty-five minutes early. Morton was informed of his layoff by a note in his box when he next reported for work; he said nothing, left, and reported to work three days later. A few weeks later the night captain again could not find Morton, but eventually located him sleeping in his guard car. The incident was reported to the chief of plant protection, who initiated discharge procedures that gave Morton two weeks to find another job at the plant before he was terminated from the company.

The chief of plant protection then called the plant services manager and asked him to interview Morton, who the chief said should make a good employee because of his intelligence and ability and his twelve months of experience with the company. Morton was interviewed and given a job in janitorial services where he would take a 5 percent pay cut and lose all of his union seniority (in guard services) and the prestige of working in plant protection.

When Morton first reported to plant services he was assigned to the crew in the administration building. After the probationary period of ninety days it was decided that Morton should be moved to the production crew. This switch was decided upon by the two crew supervisors when the administration building supervisor reported that Morton was again reporting late for work (40 percent of the time), having unexcused absences, taking his sick leave as soon as it was earned, sitting in the back of the building where he could not be found, sleeping on the job, having a "bad attitude" toward his supervisor and other members of the crew, and being a "poor influence" on others in the administration crew. During the ninety-day period he missed twenty-four days of work. He was evaluated every thirty days as is required when an employee is on probation in a new job. These evaluations went into Morton's permanent personnel file and were never discussed with him because, as his supervisor said, "he knows what he is doing." Despite this poor performance Morton was not given the "extremely unsatisfactory" necessary to be terminated at the end of the probationary period.

When he reported to the production crew, his behavior changed very little other than that he began to take college courses away from the plant, which his new supervisor said provided him with some excuses for his lateness. In response to the new supervisor Morton's attitude did not change. He still was frequently found "hiding out" and sleeping on the job. Several members of his crew described Morton as "arrogant" and they felt he defied them to make comments implying that he was inferior to or different from other members of the crew.

Morton has now been in plant services for a year and a half, and the complaints about his lateness, work habits, and attitude persist. He does have two brothers who are successfully employed in the same plant. One was formerly in plant services and had good work habits; he got along well with his coworkers and was promoted to a production job. Morton's financial needs are apparently being met as he has never borrowed money from the credit union or coworkers despite his being frequently docked for lateness or for not reporting to work at all. Another of his coworkers mentioned that all Robert really needed was some personal attention and counseling and for someone to explain what the company expects, what he can get in return, and what supportive services are available to him.

Questions for Discussion

1   If you were the plant services manager in this organization, how would you handle Robert Morton's case?

2   Generate a list of possible reasons for Robert Morton's behavior in terms of factors such as motivation, ability, personality, perception, and organizational systems.

3   Based on your list of reasons for Morton's behavior, suggest ways to try to change his behavior on the job.

Source: Adapted from a case written by Richard W. Beatty. Used by permission of the author.

Notes

1   Campbell, J. P., Dunnette, M. D., Lawler, E. E., III, & Weick, K. E. (1970). *Managerial behavior, performance, and effectiveness.* New York: McGraw-Hill.

2   Pinder, C. (1984). *Work motivation.* Glenview, IL: Scott Foresman.

3   Rosenberg, M. J. (1960). A structural theory of attitudes. *Public Opinion Quarterly,* 319–340.

4   Lawler, E. E., III. (1973). *Motivation in work organizations.* Monterey, CA: Brooks/Cole.
Vroom, V. H. (1964). *Work and motivation.* New York: Wiley.

5   Elizur, D. (1980). Facets of work values: A structural analysis of work outcomes. *Journal of Applied Psychology, 69,* 379–389.

6   Costa, P. T., Jr., McCrae, R. R., & Holland, J. L. (1984). Personality and vocational interests in an adult sample. *Journal of Applied Psychology, 69,* 390–400.
Flowers, V. S., et al. (1975). *Managerial values for working.* New York: American Management Association.

7   Tagiuri, R. (1965). Value orientations and relationships of managers and scientists. *Administrative Science Quarterly, 10,* 39–51.

8   Vroom, *loc. cit.*

9   Alderfer, C. P. (1972). *Existence, relatedness, and growth: Human needs in organizational settings.* New York: Free Press.

10   Maslow, A. H. (1954). *Motivation and personality.* New York: Harper.

11   Dreher, G. F., & Mai-Dalton, R. R. (1983). A note on the internal consistency of the Manifest Needs Questionnaire. *Journal of Applied Psychology, 68,* 194–196.
Murray, H. A. (1938). *Explorations in personality.* New York: Oxford University Press.
Stahl, M. J., & Harrell, A. M. (1982). Evolution and validation of a behavioral decision theory measurement approach to achievement, power, and affiliation. *Journal of Applied Psychology, 67,* 744–751.

12   Taylor, F. W. (1911). *The principles of scientific management.* New York: Harper.

13   Garland, H. (1982). Goal levels and task performance: A compelling replication of some compelling results. *Journal of Applied Psychology, 67,* 245–248.

Kim, J. S. (1984). Effect of behavior plus outcome goal setting and feedback on employee satisfaction and performance. *Academy of Management Journal, 27,* 139–149.

Locke, E. A. (1968). Toward a theory of task performance and incentives. *Organizational Behavior and Human Performance, 3,* 157–189.

Locke, E. A., Frederick, E., Bobko, P., & Lee, C. (1984). Effect of self-efficacy, goals, and task strategies on task performance. *Journal of Applied Psychology, 69,* 241–251.

Locke, E. A. et al. (1981). Goal setting and task performance: 1969–1980. *Psychological Bulletin, 90,* 125–152.

14 Hunter, J. E., & Hunter, R. F. (1984). Validity and utility of alternative predictors of job performance. *Psychological Bulletin, 96,* 72–98.

15 Dunnette, M. D. (1976). Aptitudes, abilities, and skills. In M. D. Dunnette (Ed.), *Handbook of industrial and organizational psychology.* New York: Wiley.

16 Schneider, B., Reichers, A. E., & Mitchell, T. M. (1982). A note on some relationships between the aptitude requirements and reward attributes of tasks. *Academy of Management Journal, 25,* 567–574.

17 Fleishman, E. A. (1962). The description and prediction of perceptual-motor skill learning. In R. Glaser (Ed.), *Training in research and education.* Pittsburgh: University of Pittsburgh Press.

Guilford, J. P. (1959). Three faces of intellect. *American Psychologist, 14,* 469–479.

Guilford, J. P. (1967). *The nature of human intelligence.* New York: McGraw-Hill.

18 Dunnette, *loc. cit.*

19 Thurstone, L. C. (1938). Primary mental abilities. *Psychometric Monographs* (No. 4).

20 Ghiselli, E. E. (1973). The validity of aptitude tests in personnel selection. *Personnel Psychology, 26,* 461–477.

21 Fleishman, *loc. cit.*

22 Dossett, D. L., & Hulvershorn, P. (1983). Increasing technical training efficiency: Peer training via computer-assisted instruction. *Journal of Applied Psychology, 68,* 552–558.

23 Bartley, S. H. (1980). *Introduction to perception.* New York: Harper & Row.

24 Nord, W. R. (Ed.). (1976). *Concepts and controversy in organizational behavior.* Santa Monica, CA: Goodyear.

25 Secord, P., & Backman, C. (1964). *Social psychology.* New York: McGraw-Hill.

26 Maier, N. R. F. (1973). *Psychology in industrial organizations* (4th ed.) Boston: Houghton-Mifflin.

27 Gough, H. G. (1984). A managerial potential scale for the California Psychological Inventory. *Journal of Applied Psychology, 69,* 233–240.

28 Maddi, S. R. (1980). *Personality theories: A comparative analysis* (4th ed.). Homewood, IL: Dorsey, 10.

29 Adorno, T., et al. (1950). *The authoritarian personality.* New York: Harper & Brothers.

30 Miller, D., Kets de Vries, M. F. R., & Toulouse, J–M. (1982). Top executive locus of control and its relationship to strategy-making, structure, and environment. *Academy of Management Journal, 25,* 237–253.
Rotter, J. B. (1966). Generalized expectancies for internal versus external control of reinforcement. *Psychological Monographs, 80,* (No. 609).
Spector, P. E. (1982). Behavior in organizations as a function of employee's locus of control. *Psychological Bulletin, 91,* 482–497.

31 Mitchell, T. R., Smyser, C. M., & Weed, S. E. (1975). Locus of control: Supervision and work satisfaction. *Academy of Management Journal, 18,* 623–631.

32 Anderson, C. R. (1977). Locus of control, coping behaviors, and performance in a stress setting: A longitudinal study. *Journal of Applied Psychology, 62,* 446–451.

33 Jackson, D. N., & Paumonen, S. V. (1980). Personality structure and assessment. *Annual Review of Psychology, 31,* 503–551.

34 Byrne, D., & Kelley, K. (1981). *An introduction to personality* (3rd ed.). Englewood Cliffs, NJ: Prentice-Hall.

35 Ghiselli, *loc. cit.*

36 Schneider, B. (1978). Person-situation interaction: A review of some ability-situation interaction research. *Personnel Psychology, 31,* 281–295.
Terborg, J. R. (1981). Interactional psychology and research on human behavior in organizations. *Academy of Management Review, 6,* 569–576.
Terborg, J. R., Richardson, P., & Pritchard, R. D. (1980). Person-situation effects in the prediction of performance: An investigation of ability, self-esteem, and reward contingencies. *Journal of Applied Psychology, 65,* 574–583.

37 Davis, T. R. (1984). The influence of the physical environment in offices. *Academy of Management Review, 9,* 271–283.
Steele, F. (1973). *Physical settings and organization development.* Reading, MA: Addison-Wesley.
Oldham, G. R., & Brass, D. J. (1979). Employee reactions to an open-

plan office: A naturally occurring quasi-experiment. *Administrative Science Quarterly, 24,* 267–284.

38 Green, S. G., Blank, W., & Liden, R. C. (1983). Market and organizational influences on bank employees' work attitudes and behaviors. *Journal of Applied Psychology, 68,* 298–306.

39 Mintzberg, H. (1979). *The structuring of organizations.* Englewood Cliffs, NJ: Prentice-Hall.

40 House, R. J., & Baetz, M. (1979). Leadership: Some generalizations and new research directions. In B. M. Staw (Ed.) *Research in organizational behavior.* Greenwich, CT: JAI Press.

41 Lawler, E. E., III. (1981). *Pay and organization development.* Reading, MA: Addison-Wesley.

Chapter 3

Motivation

CHAPTER OUTLINE

Need Theories

Expectancy Theory

Equity Theory

Goal Setting Theory

Reinforcement Theory

Keys to Effective Management

Review Questions

*M*anagers frequently talk about motivation problems among their employees. These problems can take many different forms, such as lack of effort, frequent tardiness and absenteeism, and unwillingness to finish projects or meet deadlines. What distinguishes motivation problems from other types of employee performance problems is the manager's assumption that poor performance is *not* being caused by lack of ability or competence on the part of the employee. Instead, when an employee is referred to as having a "motivation problem," the manager is assuming that the employee *does* possess the skills and abilities necessary for good performance, but lacks the *desire* or *willingness* to use those skills and abilities to perform the job effectively.

Theories of motivation deal with two interrelated issues regarding individual behavior in organizations. The first issue has to do with the *choices* that people make regarding the things that they will and will not do. For example, why do some people choose to come to work regularly and promptly while others often choose to be absent or late for work? The second issue concerns the *effort* or *intensity* that people put into the activities they choose to perform. Why is it that some people constantly put a great deal of effort into performing effectively while others only put enough effort into their jobs to avoid being fired? The theories discussed in this chapter help us develop answers to these types of questions regarding individual motivation in organizations.[1]

The chapter begins with a discussion of need theories of motivation, often referred to as **content** theories of motivation, since they focus on the content of an individual's personal needs and motives. We then turn to a number of

51

process theories of motivation. Process theories, such as expectancy theory, equity theory, and goal-setting theory, help us to understand some of the underlying psychological processes that generate motivation within individuals. The chapter concludes with a discussion of reinforcement theory and organizational behavior modification. Reinforcement theory highlights the ways in which various types of rewards and punishment influence how people behave and perform in organizations.

In reviewing each theory we will analyze how the theory can be used to diagnose and understand motivation problems. In addition, we will explore what each theory tells us about what managers can do to increase the levels of motivation in their subordinates.

Need Theories

A number of theorists have attempted to explain the nature of motivation in terms of the types of needs that people experience. The basic idea of such theories is that people have certain fundamental needs and that people are motivated to engage in behavior that will lead to the satisfaction of these needs. The implication for managers is that situations must be created at work that will result in the satisfaction of employees' most important needs when employees are performing effectively. We will briefly examine several of the most influential need theories and also discuss the theories' implications for diagnosing motivational problems and taking corrective managerial action.

Maslow's Need Hierarchy Theory

The *need hierarchy theory* developed by Abraham Maslow has been one of the most popular and widely known theories of motivation among practicing managers.[2] The theory hypothesizes that all people possess a set of five needs and that these needs are arranged in a hierarchy from the most fundamental or basic survival needs up to the most advanced needs for personal growth and development. According to the theory, people are motivated to engage in behavior that will result in the satisfaction of the lowest level of needs currently not fulfilled. It is hypothesized that once a need has been satisfied the next need upward in the hierarchy then becomes dominant. The five levels of needs, arranged in hierarchical order, are outlined in Figure 3-1 and are briefly summarized below.

1   *Physiological needs.*   These comprise our most basic survival needs for food, water, and adequate shelter from the environment to permit our continued existence.

2   *Safety needs.*   The second set of needs has to do with physical and psychological safety from external threats to our well-being. These needs become salient when the basic physiological needs have been met.

Figure 3-1 The five needs hypothesized as sources of motivation by Maslow's need hierarchy theory.

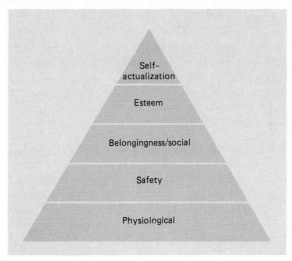

3 *Belongingness/social needs.* The third level comprises our needs for the company and companionship of other people and our need for a sense of personal belongingness. These needs for contact and interaction with other people are triggered once physiological and safety needs have been met.

4 *Esteem needs.* The fourth level (the first of the so-called growth needs) has to do with our need for a sense of self-esteem and a feeling of self-worth. Such needs for personal recognition become salient only when all the lower-order needs have been satisfied.

5 *Self-actualization needs.* The final and highest level in the hierarchy comprises needs for personal growth, for the development of one's full potential, and for the fulfillment associated with the realization of all of one's capabilities. Self-actualization needs are unique in that once activated, they can never be fully satisfied or fulfilled. The more self-actualization needs are fulfilled, the stronger they become, according to the theory.

Need Hierarchy Theory in Practice

The need hierarchy theory implies that motivational problems will occur when people find themselves in a situation at work in which it is not possible to satisfy the needs that are dominant for them. For example, Box 3-1 describes a group of workers whose physiological and safety needs were being met by the basic salary they received. In the old work situation, the workers were able to satisfy their belongingness needs (by interacting with one another in small groups), as well as their esteem needs (by using their personal judgment regarding how the work should be done). Now, in the new plant, these workers are unable to satisfy their belongingness and esteem needs since they work alone

BOX 3-1

New Technology Reduces Need Satisfaction

The manufacturing process employed by Home Electric, a manufacturer of household appliances, had relied upon small groups of workers operating as a team. Each team was responsible for the complete assembly of a particular line of small appliances and had a good deal of freedom in deciding what each team member would do at any particular time. The team as a whole was responsible for manufacturing a certain number of appliances each day and also for testing and insuring the quality of the appliances that they produced. Team members were all experienced in performing all the various activities associated with the manufacture of the appliances and would rotate from one work position to another as required. The production of each work group was stacked next to the group's work station so that at the end of the day the members of each group could observe their own productivity and compare their output to that of other work groups.

As a result of increasing foreign competition and the development of new production methodologies, management had decided that it was essential to develop new production techniques. It was felt that a new plant should be built, embodying the latest in sophisticated technology and machinery. When the ideas for the new plant were initially presented to the workers, they were reasonably enthusiastic, believing that the new methods and techniques would in fact increase their productivity and performance.

When the new plant was built and the machinery installed, the nature of the work to be performed was changed quite radically. Rather than working in small groups of four, each person now worked at a single work station along an assembly line. The work was much more highly automated and required fewer skills and abilities on the part of each worker. In addition, each worker was expected to specialize in a particular work station and was not permitted to rotate or move from that position during the day. Workers were no longer responsible for checking or correcting any defects in the appliances they were working on. In addition, workers were unable to gauge how productive they had been on any given day since the finished appliances simply carried on down the production line and were then handled by the packing and shipping department.

After a few months in the new plant, productivity and quality began to decline. Management was extremely concerned because of the large investment they had made in the new machinery and technology. Rather than reaping the benefits in terms of productivity, management was instead subjected to increasing levels of complaint and absenteeism on the part of the workers. In order to deal with this problem, management decided to increase the wage rates paid to employees in the hope that this would motivate them to perform more effectively. When the new wage rates were implemented there was no noticeable change in either productivity or the satisfaction expressed by the workers with their jobs.

Source: Unexpected outcomes of new plant design. *Interfaces,* May–June 1982, *12,* 31–41.

and have lost the autonomy and freedom they previously enjoyed. However, their basic salaries continue to provide the means to meet their physiological and safety needs. The management's offer of a pay increase in response to the motivation problem is unlikely to increase motivation since the increase does nothing to help satisfy the workers' belongingness or esteem needs, and their more basic needs are already met.

In general, need hierarchy theory implies that when a manager is faced with a motivation problem, he or she must attempt to discover what needs are most salient or important to the "problem" employees. The manager then must attempt to create an on-the-job situation that permits the employees to satisfy their dominant needs whenever they engage in the types of performance desired by the manager.

Status of the Theory

While the need hierarchy theory has enjoyed popular appeal among practitioners, it has not been faring so well among systematic scientific researchers. Because of its popularity, a great deal of research has been carried out aimed at assessing the theory's validity. Unfortunately, the results of the research are not particularly encouraging.[3] There appears to be little evidence in favor of the notion that there are five distinct categories of human needs. In addition, there is little support for Maslow's argument that needs are structured into a hierarchy. What supporting evidence there is points in the direction of a very broad classification of needs into "deficiency" needs (physiological, safety, and belongingness) and "growth" needs (esteem and self-actualization). Finally, it does not appear that the lowest set of unfulfilled needs exclusively dominates the attention and behavior of the individual. It appears quite feasible that an individual might orient his or her behavior toward the satisfaction of more than a single set of needs simultaneously.

Given this rather discouraging summary of the scientific status of need hierarchy theory, what is it sensible for the manager to conclude from the theory? On the one hand, it seems clear that need hierarchy theory cannot provide the practicing manager with a complete or adequate basis for understanding and dealing with motivational problems. On the other hand, however, the need categories suggested by the theory may be helpful to the manager as he or she attempts to understand the factors most important to a particular employee who may not be performing up to expectations. A manager does not have to "buy" need hierarchy theory as a whole in order to use some of its concepts in understanding and diagnosing sources of motivational problems among individual employees.

Other Need Theories

Several other theories of motivation based upon human needs have been developed. We will briefly examine two of these alternative need theories.

ERG Theory

ERG theory hypothesizes that individual motivation in organizations can be understood in terms of ***existence (E), relatedness (R),*** and ***growth (G)*** needs.[4] These three needs and their correspondence to the five needs hypothesized by

Figure 3-2   A comparison of need hierarchy theory and ERG theory.

NEED HIERARCHY THEORY	ERG THEORY
Physiological needs Safety needs	Existence needs
Belongingness/social needs	Relatedness needs
Esteem needs Self–actualization needs	Growth needs

Maslow are outlined in Figure 3-2. Existence needs are roughly comparable to the physiological and safety needs of the Maslow theory and refer to people's needs for sustenance, shelter, and physical and psychological safety from threats to their well-being. Relatedness needs correspond approximately to the belongingness/social needs hypothesized by the need hierarchy theory and have to do with needs for personal relationships and interaction with other people. Growth needs are the ERG-theory counterpart to the esteem needs and self-actualization needs contained in the Maslow theory. Growth needs refer to the human needs to grow, to develop, and to fulfill one's potential by seeking new opportunities and overcoming new challenges.

ERG theory does not propose that people move up or down a hierarchy of needs in a fashion similar to that suggested by Maslow's need hierarchy theory. Instead, ERG theory argues that it is possible for more than one set of needs to be activated at the same time. The theory also suggests that people may move down, as well as up, the three-step hierarchy of needs. Satisfaction of needs at one level leads to progression to the next higher level of needs. However, when people become frustrated in their attempts to fulfill needs at one level, this frustration can also lead to increased importance for lower-level needs. For example, a manager whose attempts to satisfy her growth needs by obtaining greater job responsibilities are frustrated may respond by demanding more pay in order to satisfy her existence needs.

Although the greater flexibility of ERG theory is probably an accurate reflection of the complexity of human needs, this flexibility also means that the implications of ERG theory for management practice are less clear-cut than those of need hierarchy theory. ERG theory implies that individuals will be motivated to engage in behavior that will satisfy one of the three sets of needs hypothesized by the theory. To predict what behavior any given person will be motivated to engage in would require an assessment of that person to determine which of the three needs are most salient and most important to him or her. The individual would then be expected to engage in behavior that would lead to the fulfillment of these salient needs.

Learned Needs

While Maslow's theory and ERG theory argue that people have certain inherent, or "built-in" needs, others have argued that many needs take on importance to people as a result of learning processes experienced by the person. Many different needs of this type have been suggested,[5] but the three that have received greatest attention have been the need for achievement, the need for affiliation, and the need for power.

People with a strong need for achievement tend to set moderately difficult goals for themselves, to engage in activities in which there is a moderate degree of risk that they may not succeed, to seek out feedback on the quality and quantity of their performance, to wish to be personally responsible for their actions, and to generally be preoccupied with accomplishment and achievement. Such individuals will find many of the preceding types of experiences to be motivating. Highly challenging jobs such as investment banking or new product marketing frequently provide opportunities for these kinds of experiences and hence may be highly motivating to individuals who have a strong need for achievement.

Individuals with a high need for affiliation, on the other hand, tend to place greatest value upon human companionship and opportunities for obtaining personal reassurance from others. People with a high need for affiliation thus tend to be motivated to seek out personal approval, to conform to the wishes and expectations of those they admire, and to demonstrate a strong and sincere interest in the feelings of others. As a result such individuals find opportunities for meaningful relationships with others to be highly motivating and may tend to gravitate to jobs in professions such as social work and counseling.

Finally, the need for power refers to a desire to influence others and to exert a high degree of control over one's physical and social environment. People who are dominated by the need for power tend to try to influence other people directly via personal appeals or arguments and also frequently seek out positions of leadership in groups to which they belong. Such people find it motivating to be in situations that permit them to exert influence and control over others and may be attracted to a career in a military or quasimilitary organization.

Research indicates that assessing the strength of these learned needs can be helpful in identifying individuals who will respond positively to different types of work environments.[6] People differ in the extent to which they experience needs for achievement, for affiliation, and for power. This suggests that it may be important for managers to think about the extent to which their employees possess these needs and to design motivational strategies that permit employees to satisfy those needs that are strongest for each individual.

Expectancy Theory

Expectancy theory explains motivation in terms of the expectations (or **expectancies**) that people have about their ability to perform effectively on the job and about the kinds of rewards they expect to obtain if they do perform effectively.[7] According to this theory, there are three separate factors that influence a person's motivation to perform effectively. We will examine each component in turn and will then discuss how the components combine to determine a person's overall level of motivation.

Expectancy that Effort Leads to Performance (E → P)

The first component of motivation according to expectancy theory is a person's belief or expectation regarding the link between putting effort into a job (E) and performing effectively on the job (P). If a person believes that no matter how much effort he or she puts into a job it will still be almost impossible to perform well, then that person has a very low or weak *effort → performance (E → P) expectancy*. The more strongly a person believes that he or she can perform effectively if effort is put into the job, the stronger is the E → P expectancy. According to the theory, a strong E → P expectancy is a necessary condition for the existence of high levels of work motivation. Unless a person believes that putting in effort on the job is likely to lead to effective performance, there is little reason for even trying to perform well.[8] For example, a person who is placed in a job for which he or she feels underqualified and lacking in necessary skills may feel that there is little point in putting much effort into the job since the chances of successful performance are almost nil.

Expectancy that Performance Leads to Outcomes (P → O)

People also hold beliefs regarding the likelihood that they will obtain or experience various types of outcomes (O) as a result of performing effectively on the job (P). For example, a person might feel that if she meets certain standards of performance on her job, it is very likely that she will receive a salary bonus, but very unlikely that she will be promoted. In this case we would say that the person has a very high performance → outcome (P → O) expectancy associated with the salary bonus, but a weak P → O expectancy for promotion. A person's beliefs regarding what desirable (and undesirable) outcomes may occur as a result of performing effectively have an important influence upon his or her motivation. The more strongly a person believes that positive outcomes will follow from effective performance, the more motivated he or she will be to perform effectively.[9] For example, a person who believes that positive outcomes such as pay increases and promotions will follow as a result of effective performance will be highly motivated to perform well. Another person, who may believe that only negative outcomes such as frustration and fatigue will result from performing at a high level, will not be motivated to perform well.

There is no limit to the type and number of outcomes that an individual may perceive as being linked in some fashion to effective performance on the job. A person's motivation is influenced by the links (P → O expectancies) that he or she perceives to exist between performing effectively and attaining desirable outcomes.

Valence of Outcomes (V)

Naturally, the degree of impact that any outcome may have on a person's motivation will depend on how much the person values that outcome. People differ in the extent to which they value outcomes. One person may place a very high value on money, while someone else will feel that recognition and praise from others are much more valuable than money. The extent to which any outcome is capable of influencing a person's motivation is very much dependent upon the value that the person places upon the outcome. The more positively that a person values an outcome, the greater potential power that outcome has to influence the person's motivation.[10]

Expectancy theory takes into account the fact that people value outcomes differently. However, expectancy theory employs the concept of **valence (V)** of outcomes rather than the concept of actual value of outcomes to the person. The term *valence* refers to the degree of satisfaction that a person *anticipates* that he or she will experience when an outcome is attained at some point in the future, while *value* refers to the amount of satisfaction a person actually receives from an outcome.[11]

The reason for using the concept of valence rather than that of value is as follows. A person's motivation to perform effectively *now* is based upon what the person expects or anticipates will happen *in the future* as a result of current effective performance. The ability of any outcome to influence current motivation is thus dependent upon the extent to which the person *expects* or *anticipates* that he or she will positively value the outcome when it is in fact obtained. Thus it is the valence (i.e., the anticipated value and satisfaction) rather than the actual value of an outcome that determines its impact upon a person's motivation. For example, a person may attach a very high positive valence to the outcome of being promoted. Because of this, the individual is motivated to work hard and perform effectively in order to obtain the promotion. If the person is successful and eventually is promoted, he or she may find that the actual experienced value of the promotion is much lower than was anticipated. Regardless, it is the valence (i.e., the anticipated value) of the promotion that motivated the person to work hard in order to obtain the promotion.

Combining the Factors

Figure 3-3 summarizes the way in which the three components of expectancy theory combine in determining a person's motivation.[12] The figure makes it clear that a high effort → performance expectancy is essential to high levels of work motivation. Unless a person actually believes that he or she is capable of performing effectively as a result of putting effort into the job, none of the other factors come into play at all. If, however, the E → P expectancy is reasonably high, then it is the outcomes associated with effective performance that determine a person's motivation. In order for an outcome to influence a person's motivation, two things are necessary. First, the person must perceive obtaining the outcome as being contingent upon performing effectively; in other words, the performance → outcome expectancy must he high. Second, the outcome must have a strong positive valence; that is, the person must anticipate that receiving the outcome will be very satisfying. The outcomes that influence

Figure 3-3 Summary of the major components in expectancy theory.

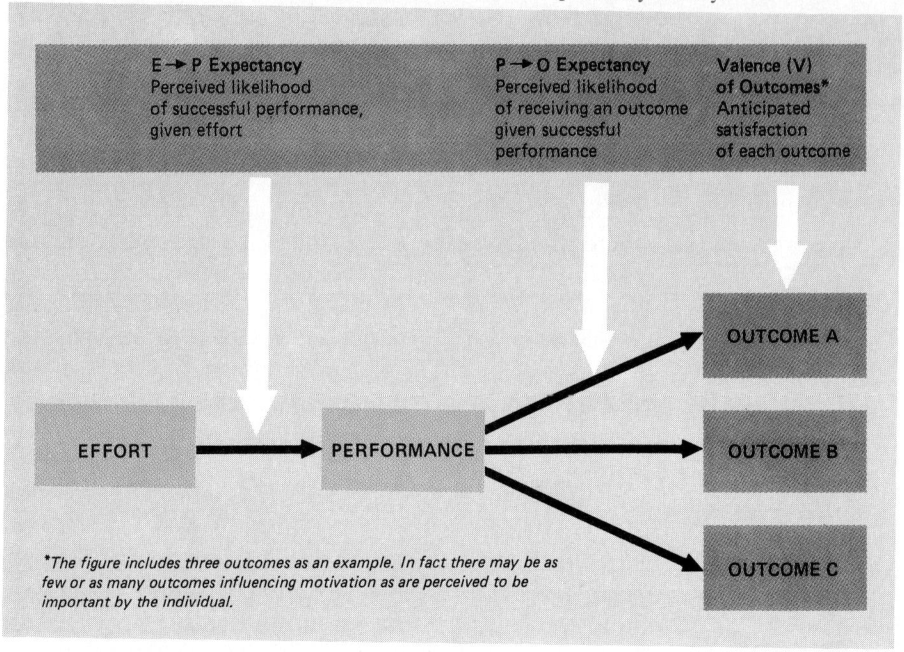

E → P Expectancy
Perceived likelihood
of successful performance,
given effort

P → O Expectancy
Perceived likelihood
of receiving an outcome
given successful
performance

Valence (V)
of Outcomes*
Anticipated
satisfaction
of each outcome

EFFORT → PERFORMANCE

OUTCOME A

OUTCOME B

OUTCOME C

*The figure includes three outcomes as an example. In fact there may be as
few or as many outcomes influencing motivation as are perceived to be
important by the individual.

[*Source:* Adapted from Nadler, D. A., & Lawler, E. E., III (1983). "Motivation: A
diagnostic approach," in J. R. Hackman, E. E. Lawler, III, & L. W. Porter (Eds.),
Perspectives on behavior in organizations, (2nd Ed.) (pp. 67–78). New York: McGraw-
Hill. Used by permission.]

motivation most strongly are those that simultaneously have strong P → O
expectancies and strong positive valence.

Table 3-1 outlines how different combinations of high and low expectancies and valences combine to influence motivation. A high level of motivation
requires that all three components of the expectancy model be high. Moderate
levels of motivation result when the effort → performance expectancy is high
and either the performance → outcome expectancies or the valences are high.
Even when the E → P expectancy is high, motivation is low when both the P
→ O expectancies and the valences are low. A low E → P expectancy creates
low motivation regardless of the strength of the P → O expectancies or the
valences. When all three components are low, motivation is virtually
nonexistent.

Expectancy Theory in Practice

The fundamental implication of expectancy theory is that the manager should
attempt to ensure that all three components of motivation are present and
strong for each of his or her subordinates. This can be done in a number of
ways.

First, high effort → performance expectancies are dependent upon two factors: ability and self-confidence. The manager must first ensure a good match

TABLE 3-1

How the Components of Expectancy Theory Combine to Influence Overall Motivation

$E \rightarrow P$ Expectancy	$P \rightarrow O$ Expectancies	Valences	Motivation
High	High	High	High
High	High	Low	Moderate
High	Low	High	Moderate
High	Low	Low	Low
Low	High	High	Low
Low	High	Low	Low
Low	Low	High	Low
Low	Low	Low	Very low

between a subordinate's skills and abilities and the requirements of the subordinate's job. If a person perceives that he or she lacks the ability to perform effectively, then the person's $E \rightarrow P$ expectancy will naturally be weak and motivation will be correspondingly low. However, a person may possess all the skill necessary to perform effectively but still have a low $E \rightarrow P$ expectancy due to lack of self-confidence. This type of situation requires a supportive approach from the manager to help the subordinate bring his or her $E \rightarrow P$ expectancy up to a realistic level in light of his or her ability and competence.

A manager can also influence the motivation of subordinates by altering the rewards available to them. Expectancy theory implies that the manager must first discover which outcomes have highest valence for subordinates and then attempt to make the attainment of these outcomes contingent upon effective performance. Notice also how important it is for the manager to clearly communicate to subordinates just what the relationships are between performance and rewards. It is the performance $\rightarrow$ outcome expectancies of subordinates that influence their motivation. If outcomes of high valence *are* contingent on performance, but these contingencies are not clearly communicated to the subordinates themselves, then performance $\rightarrow$ outcome expectancies may be low. Thus the manager must make outcomes of high valence contingent on performance and ensure that subordinates understand that the outcomes they desire can be obtained if they perform their jobs effectively.

Equity Theory

The motivation of organization members is influenced by the extent to which they feel that they are being treated fairly and equitably by the organization.

When a person feels that he or she is being treated unfairly by the organization, these feelings can have a variety of adverse effects on the person's motivation and performance on the job. The ***equity theory*** of motivation helps us understand both the causes and the likely consequences of feelings of inequitable treatment among organization members.[13] In what follows we will first examine the factors that lead to feelings of inequity among organization members. Then we will look at the kinds of things that people often do (and don't do) when they are feeling unfairly treated.

Determinants of Feelings of Equity

What is it that causes people to feel that they are being treated fairly by their organizations? What sorts of things do people take into account when they assess how they feel about how equitably their organization treats its employees? Equity theory suggests that each of us measures ourselves against a "comparison person," someone in a comparable sort of organizational situation.[14] If we see ourselves and our comparison person being treated approximately the same, we then feel that we are being treated fairly or equitably. If, however, we perceive that our comparison person is being treated quite differently we feel that the situation is inequitable and we will be motivated to do something to try to establish or restore a more equitable situation.

The next question then becomes, What is it that people take into account when they are measuring themselves against a comparison person? Do they compare themselves on the basis of the time and effort put into the job, or their years of experience, or the amounts they are paid, or some other factor or factors? According to equity theory the comparison process takes into account both the ***inputs,*** or contributions that each person makes to the organization, and the ***outcomes,*** or rewards that each person receives from the organization. Some examples of inputs and outcomes are summarized in Table 3-2.

According to equity theory people compare themselves to one another in terms of their ***ratios*** of inputs to outcomes. In other words, the person thinks first about him or herself and evaluates the level of inputs he or she is providing to the organization in return for the level of outcomes that he or she is receiving. The person then compares this ratio of inputs to outcomes to what he or she perceives the ratio to be for some other comparison person in the organization. If the person perceives these ratios to be approximately equal, he or she feels that the situation is equitable. However, if the ratios are not in balance, a situation of inequity exists, and the person will be motivated to take some action to resolve the inequity.

The key notion to keep in mind is that people compare themselves to one another in terms of their ratios of inputs to outcomes. This is a very sensible notion. For example, it helps us explain why we might feel that it is quite fair for someone else to be paid a great deal more than we are paid. Such a situation would be the case if we felt that the greater outcomes (i.e., pay) received by the other person were balanced off by the higher inputs (e.g., time, effort, experience) to the organization provided by that person. Alternatively, the notion of

TABLE   3-2

Examples of Job Inputs and Outcomes

Inputs	*Outcomes*
Time	Pay
Effort	Promotion
Education	Recognition
Experience	Security
Training	Personal development
Ideas	Benefits
Ability	Friendship opportunity

comparison of ratios of inputs to outcomes can also explain why we might feel that it is inequitable for someone at our own level in the organization to receive the same pay. Such a situation could arise if we felt that we were providing a higher level of inputs to the organization than our comparison person in return for the same level of outcomes.

Consequences of Perceived Inequity

According to equity theory, feelings of inequity are uncomfortable and create a sense of tension within the individual. A situation of perceived equity can be reestablished via any one of six different mechanisms.[15]

1   *Changing inputs.*   The person may choose to increase or decrease his or her inputs to the organization, for example, by working harder or, alternatively, working less hard.

2   *Changing outcomes.*   A person may attempt to change his or her outcomes by requesting a salary increase or asking for a bigger office or a personal secretary. Anything perceived to be an outcome important to the individual can shift his or her ratio of inputs to outcomes.

3   *Changing perceptions of inputs and outcomes.*   Rather than actually changing inputs or outcomes, a person may change his or her perceptions of these factors. For example, a person who at first was feeling overpaid in return for his inputs to the company could reestablish equity by distorting upward his perception of his own inputs (e.g., "I now realize that I really do work a lot harder than anyone else does").

4   *Changing the inputs or outcomes of others.*   A person could try to restore equity by attempting to convince a comparison person to reduce his or her inputs, for example by not working as hard in the future. Equity can also be restored by changing one's perceptions of the inputs and outcomes of

other people. For example, a person could distort downward her perception of the inputs provided by someone else to the organization (e.g., "I used to think that Jim was really talented, but now I realize he's only very average").

5 *Changing the comparison person.* If comparing yourself to one person creates feelings of inequity, choosing someone else for comparison purposes may result in less uncomfortable feelings.

6 *Leaving the situation.* If a given situation seems to invariably leave a person feeling inequitably treated, the most drastic solution is to leave that situation. This could take the form of requesting a transfer to another department or location or, in the most extreme case, leaving the organization altogether.

Equity Theory in Practice

Equity theory has a number of important implications for managerial practice. First, and perhaps most obviously, equity theory underlines the importance to organizations of establishing and maintaining fair and equitable methods of treating their employees. In addition, equity theory draws attention to the fact that organizations must not only treat their members fairly and equitably; they must be *seen* to do so in the eyes of the members themselves. Equity is in the mind of the beholder.

The fact that perceptions of equity and inequity arise from a process of social comparison (people comparing themselves to one another) helps underline the interconnectedness and interdependence that exists within organizations. Organization members are not totally isolated and independent of one another. As a result, the way that management treats one employee influences not only that particular employee, but all the other employees in the organization who come in contact with that person. For example, an organization may be overpaying one person in comparison with others in the hope that this will generate positive motivation and commitment from the overpaid person. What such a policy fails to address is the spin-off costs associated with the inequity perceived by others in the organization who compare themselves to the overpaid person. An example of the types of problems that can be generated by such a situation is presented in Box 3-2. Equity theory can help draw the attention of managers to the factors generating feelings of unfair treatment and hence help them to avoid situations that may be costly to the organization.

Goal Setting Theory

The importance of goals as a determinant of the motivation and performance of organization members has been formally acknowledged in the management literature for many years. Frederick Taylor, in his book *The Principles of Sci-*

BOX 3-2

Salary Compression in the Business Schools

During the past twenty years there has been a dramatic growth in student enrollment in business programs. One outcome of this growth has been a tremendous surge in the demand for professors to teach in such programs. In certain areas, such as accounting and management information systems, the supply of well-trained new faculty members with doctorates has been far lower than the demand.

Because of the low supply, new graduates with PhDs in certain functional areas of business have been in great demand. This has sometimes led to a type of "bidding war" in which various universities have raised their salary offers in an attempt to attract competent and bright new faculty members. This has sometimes resulted in salary offers being made to new PhD graduates that are significantly higher than the salaries being earned by individuals already teaching in the business schools and performing well in their jobs.

This type of situation can easily lead to strong feelings of inequitable treatment on the part of the individuals receiving the lower salaries. Such individuals may feel that they are providing the organization with higher levels of inputs in terms of their experience and past performance. However, they see themselves receiving a lower level of outcomes from the organization in terms of salary. These feelings of inequity can manifest themselves in complaints to university administrators and requests for some redress in regard to the inequitable salary situation. Moreover, budget constraints at universities do not always make it possible to alleviate some of these inequities. The result has been in some cases that very competent and productive faculty members have chosen to leave their university in order to become part of the competitive market for jobs at other universities. This is obviously a potentially serious loss to each institution, since it is the most talented and productive faculty members that will be most easily able to leave for other universities.

Source: Report of the annual salary survey. *AACSB Newsline,* February 1985, 3–6.

---

entific Management,[16] published in 1911, emphasized how giving workers clear and specific goals or standards to attain generated higher levels of performance.

The average workman will work with the greatest satisfaction, both to himself and to his employer, when he is given each day a definite task which he is to perform in a given time, and which constitutes a proper day's work for a good workman. This furnishes the workman with a clearcut standard, by which he can throughout the day measure his own progress, and the accomplishment of which affords him the greatest satisfaction (pp. 120-121).

A considerable body of systematic scientific research over the past fifteen years has addressed the subject of why goals influence motivation and performance as they do.[17] This research is extremely consistent and persuasive in demonstrating that goals can and do have a positive impact on the motivation and performance of organization members.[18] However, it is also clear that goals must meet certain conditions if they are to have this influence. The mere act of setting a goal does not ensure higher levels of motivation among employees. In fact, there appear to be three important criteria that goals must meet if they are to influence the behavior of organization members. The three characteristics are summarized at the top of Figure 3-4 and discussed in turn below.

Specificity

Goals must be stated in very specific terms if they are to motivate effective performance.[19] Vague and general goals, such as to "do your best," have little or no impact on motivation. In order to influence motivation a goal must provide a specific, concrete target against which the person can measure and evaluate how well he or she is doing. Knowing that a specific goal has been met provides a sense of personal satisfaction and accomplishment. Goals must be set in terms of measurable criteria of work performance (e.g., number of units produced, defect rate, new sales, or number of customer complaints) and must specify a time period within which the goal is to be attained (e.g., one month, six months, one year).

Difficulty

The relationship between goal difficulty and work motivation is clear and unambiguous. The more difficult the goal, the higher the level of motivation and performance.[20] Setting goals that can be attained easily simply encourages people to work only at the pace required to achieve the easy goals. High levels of motivation and performance are observed when goals are set at levels sufficiently difficult to be challenging to the individual. Naturally, even though more difficult goals lead to higher levels of performance, it is essential that goals be set at levels that are realistic to the person. Goals that are so difficult to achieve that they are viewed as impossible lose their capacity to motivate;

Figure 3-4 Examples of goals that do and do not meet the three key criteria of effective goals.

KEY CHARACTERISTICS OF GOALS			
	Specificity	Difficulty	Acceptance
Effective Example	"Increase sales by 20% over the next six months."	"Achieve a 10% increase in market share over the next year."	"This is my goal and I personally care about achieving it."
Ineffective Example	"Do your best to increase sales over the next little while."	"Achieve a 1% increase in market share over the next year."	"This goal is impossible to reach and besides, who's concerned about meeting it? Not me."

they are simply ignored by the person as being beyond his or her capacity and hence irrelevant.

Acceptance

In order to influence motivation and performance, a goal must be internalized by the individual. In other words, the person has to feel some personal investment in and ownership of the goal and must care personally about achieving it.[21] This implies that goals are unlikely to accomplish their potential to motivate if managers simply *tell* their subordinates what their goals are. When this occurs the goals are likely to be the manager's rather than the subordinate's. The manager's job is instead to encourage subordinates to set their own goals, so that they can experience a sense of personal ownership and responsibility for achieving them.

Goal Setting in Practice

The most obvious implication of goal-setting theory is that managers should be helping subordinates to set goals that are specific and reasonably difficult, and that subordinates accept and internalize as their own. Beyond this relatively straightforward advice, however, there are a number of issues that arise in implementing goal setting in practice.

Setting goals in specific terms is essential, and it is always worthwhile to invest effort in trying to identify meaningful and valid objective measures that can serve as indicators of goal attainment. However, a danger that sometimes arises in the goal-setting process is the tendency to set goals in terms of the *measurable* criteria of performance rather than the most *important* criteria (which may not be so easily measurable). While specificity is essential and measurability is desirable, these criteria should not result in goals that focus the attention and activity of the individual away from the key areas of responsibility associated with his or her job.

A second common issue related to implementing goal setting has to do with how the manager can go about generating high levels of goal acceptance among subordinates.[22] The manager can stimulate goal acceptance in at least three ways. The first is to involve subordinates participatively in the goal-setting process. By listening to subordinates' points of view and permitting them to have direct input into the goal-setting process, the manager is much more likely to generate feelings of personal ownership of goals and hence internalization and acceptance of goals. Second, the manager can stimulate goal acceptance by demonstrating a supportive attitude and approach toward his or her subordinates. By indicating that he or she is there to help subordinates when help is needed and by expressing confidence in subordinates' abilities, the manager generates acceptance of and commitment to the attainment of goals. Finally, goal acceptance and motivation to attain goals can be increased by tying various rewards to the achievement of goals. Such rewards can vary from personal recognition and praise from the manager to more concrete rewards such as salary increases and monetary bonuses.[23]

Management by objectives (MBO) is a managerial technique for improving motivation and performance using goal-setting principles.[24] Under MBO a manager meets regularly with each of his or her subordinates to review progress toward previously set goals and to set goals for the next performance period. In addition to stimulating employee motivation, MBO also provides a basis for the appraisal of employee performance. The use of MBO for performance appraisal is discussed in detail in Chapter 11.

Reinforcement Theory

Reinforcement theory applies principles from the psychology of learning and conditioning to the process of influencing the motivation and performance of people on the job. ***Reinforcement theory,*** also sometimes known as ***operant conditioning theory,*** was developed initially by the well-known psychologist B. F. Skinner.[25] Basically, reinforcement theory argues that the behavior of people is largely determined by its consequences. In other words, those actions that tend to have positive or pleasant consequences tend to be repeated more often in the future, while those actions that tend to have negative or unpleasant consequences will be less likely to be repeated again. The obvious implication is that managers should try to structure the contingencies of rewards and punishments on the job in such a way that the consequences of effective job behavior are positive while the consequences of ineffective work behavior are negative or unpleasant. Since the focus of this approach is upon changing or modifying the actual behavior of people on the job, applications of these concepts in organizations have been labeled *organizational behavior modification (OB Mod).*

Reinforcement

The key notion underlying reinforcement theory is the concept of reinforcement itself. An event is said to be ***reinforcing*** if the occurrence of the event following some behavior makes the behavior more likely to occur again in the future. For example, a manager may observe an employee performing a task effectively and congratulate the employee on his or her good work. If, after being congratulated, that employee performs the task effectively more frequently than he or she did in the past, then the congratulations from the supervisor has served as a reinforcer of effective performance. Notice that the definition of a reinforcer is such that we can't tell whether any event is actually a reinforcer until we see whether the behavior that preceded the event occurs more often in the future. We can only discover whether events are reinforcing by trying them out and then observing their consequences.

The example above is an instance of *positive reinforcement.* In fact, there are a total of four different types of reward and punishment contingencies that can be employed. The different types of situations arise as a result of either the application or the withdrawal of either pleasant or unpleasant events. The four different situations are summarized in Figure 3-5.

Figure 3-5   Classification of different types of reinforcement situations.

	Pleasant or Desirable Events	Unpleasant or Undesirable Events
Event is Applied	POSITIVE REINFORCEMENT Behavior becomes more likely to occur again	PUNISHMENT Behavior becomes less likely to occur again
Event is Withdrawn	EXTINCTION Behavior becomes less likely to occur again	NEGATIVE REINFORCEMENT Behavior becomes more likely to occur again

Positive Reinforcement

Positive reinforcement occurs when a pleasant or desirable event is supplied to a person following some behavior. The pleasant event (e.g., praise, contingent pay, time off) is said to be a positive reinforcer if the behavior that preceded it recurs more frequently again in the future.

Negative Reinforcement

Negative reinforcement, much less common than positive reinforcement, occurs when an unpleasant or undesirable situation is removed or withdrawn following some behavior. The event is said to be a negative reinforcer if the behavior that preceded its removal occurs more frequently in the future. For example, a supervisor may continually harass and badger an employee until the employee begins performing a job correctly, at which point the harassment stops. If the employee continues to perform the job correctly in the future, then the *removal* of the unpleasant situation (the harassment) is said to have negatively reinforced effective job performance.

Punishment

Punishment occurs when an unpleasant or undesirable event occurs following some behavior and makes the behavior less likely to occur in the future. For example, a supervisor might harass or berate an employee each time the employee performs a task incorrectly. The supervisor's hope is that the harassment will act as punishment for the ineffective performance and hence result in fewer instances of ineffective performance in the future.

Extinction

Extinction occurs when the withdrawal of a pleasant or desirable event results in behavior becoming less likely to occur in the future. For example, a supervisor may have been giving recognition and support to an employee each time the employee performed a job in a particular fashion. If the supervisor stops giving recognition and support and the employee stops performing the job in that fashion, the employee's previous approach to job performance is said to have been extinguished.

An important question to address at this point is which type of reinforcement is most effective in influencing employees in organizations to perform their jobs effectively. There is a good deal of evidence available on this matter, and the evidence is extremely consistent in pointing to positive reinforcement as by far the most powerful and effective tool for influencing behavior.[26] Positive reinforcement is most appropriate because it *increases* the occurrence of effective job behavior on the part of employees. In contrast, punishment and extinction can only be used to *decrease* the frequency of ineffective performance by organization members.[27] While the employee may learn what he or she is *not* supposed to do, neither punishment nor extinction indicates to the person what he or she *should* be doing instead. Finally, negative reinforcement is frequently cumbersome, even impossible, to implement since it requires establishing an unpleasant situation for the employee that continues unabated until the desired behavior occurs. In addition, the unpleasant events employed in negative reinforcement and punishment generate undesirable side effects in terms of employee anger and frustration as a result of being subjected to such unpleasant situations.

Schedules of Reinforcement

Schedules of reinforcement are methods of categorizing the frequency and timing of reinforcement. A **continuous** schedule of reinforcement involves administering the reinforcer each and every time the desired behavior occurs. While this schedule can be very effective in the early stages of learning new types of behavior, it becomes difficult to employ in practice over extended periods of time.

Figure 3-6   Types of partial reinforcement schedules.

| | | BASIS FOR DETERMINING FREQUENCY OF REINFORCEMENT | |
		Passage of Time	Number of Times Behavior Occurs
SPACING OR TIMING OF REINFORCERS	**Fixed**	FIXED INTERVAL Reinforcement administered every *x* minutes.	FIXED RATIO Reinforcement administered every *x*th occurrence of the behavior.
	Variable	VARIABLE INTERVAL Timing of reinforcers varies randomly around some average time period.	VARIABLE RATIO Number of occurrences of the behavior required to receive reinforcer varies randomly around some average number.

Partial reinforcement involves administering the reinforcer only after some occurrences of the desired behavior. There are four different types of partial reinforcement schedules diagrammed in Figure 3-6. These schedules differ in terms of whether reinforcement is administered on the basis of the passage of time or on the basis of the frequency of the occurrence of the desired behavior. They also differ in terms of whether the spacing, or timing, of reinforcers is fixed or variable.

Under a *fixed interval* reinforcement schedule a reinforcer is administered after some fixed passage of time, as long as the person continues to engage in the desired behavior during that time. Most pay systems in which people receive a salary check once every two weeks or once a month can be thought of as fixed interval reinforcement schedules. Under the *variable interval* schedule the time between reinforcers is not fixed but varies around some average. A supervisor who makes a point of seeing each of his employees once a day in order to offer them encouragement and praise, but who varies the time of day of his visits, is employing a variable interval reinforcement schedule. A *fixed ratio* reinforcement schedule requires administration of reinforcement following some fixed number of occurrences of the behavior. Piece-rate pay systems, under which individuals are paid a certain amount for each unit produced, are examples of fixed ratio schedules. Under the *variable ratio* schedule the administration of reinforcement is still based upon the number of occurrences of the desired behavior, but the precise number varies each time the reinforcer is administered. Slot machines are one of the best examples of variable ratio reinforcement. People know that the machines pay jackpots after a certain number of plays of the machine. However, the precise number of plays of the machine required to win the next jackpot is unknown.

While continuous reinforcement is very effective in the early stages of learning new forms of behavior, the partial reinforcement schedules are more effective for maintaining effective behavior at high levels over extended periods of time.[28] The variable ratio schedule is most powerful in this regard and can establish very strong patterns of behavior that are extremely resistant to extinction.[29] The feverish behavior of slot machine players in Las Vegas is testimony to the power of the variable ratio reinforcement schedule.

Organizational Behavior Modification (OB Mod)

Organizational Behavior Modification (OB Mod) is the label used to refer to techniques designed to change employee behavior on the job using reinforcement theory. OB Mod employs the series of steps summarized in Table 3-3 for the analysis of employee behavior and the development of effective strategies for changing it.[30]

Step 1   *Identification of critical behaviors.*   The starting point of the process of OB Mod must be to identify which behaviors should be reinforced. This requires a determination of exactly which behaviors are the critical determinants of success on any given job.

TABLE   3-3

Steps in Implementing OB Mod

1   Identification of critical behaviors
2   Measurement of the behaviors
3   Causal analysis of the behaviors
4   Development of a change strategy
5   Evaluation to assure performance improvement

Step 2   *Measurement of the behaviors.*   Before implementing a positive reinforcement program managers must determine whether it is realistic to expect improvement in the quality or quantity of the critical behaviors identified. If the critical behaviors are already being performed very effectively, there is no need for a new program of positive reinforcement. Measuring behavior prior to implementing OB Mod also provides a baseline measure to which performance can be compared after positive reinforcement is introduced.

Step 3   *Causal analysis of the behaviors.*   Once the behaviors that are critical to successful job performance have been identified and measured, it is then necessary to determine what the causes and consequences of these behaviors are. This involves analyzing: (1) the factors that seem to instigate the behavior, or get it started; and (2) the consequences, or the results which follow as a result of engaging in the behavior.

Step 4   *Development of a change strategy.*   In choosing a strategy to change employee behavior in OB Mod, the emphasis is upon identifying rewards that can serve as positive reinforcers and then establishing methods of providing these reinforcers contingent upon subordinates engaging in the desired behaviors. Positive reinforcement is employed to increase the likelihood of desirable behavior. Extinction may also be used to attempt to decrease the frequency of undesirable behavior. Punishment and negative reinforcement are used as little as possible.

Step 5   *Evaluation to assure performance improvement.*   The results of a systematic evaluation of an OB Mod program can be used both to determine whether the program should be continued and also to "fine-tune" the program to increase its value and its ability to increase effective performance.

OB Mod programs have now been implemented by a variety of organizations. The positive experiences of two organizations with such programs are summarized in Box 3-3. However, it is important to keep in mind that while there are a number of success stories regarding the effects of OB Mod,[31] there has been relatively little careful scientific research on the impact of such programs.[32] This situation is improving as more research is carried out, and the

---

BOX 3-3

OB Mod Successes

At Michigan Bell-Operator Services a program was established that involved setting productivity goals for a group of operators, providing the operators with feedback on how they were performing, and positively reinforcing performance improvements. The program resulted in service promptness (time to answer a call) improving from 94 to 99 percent of standard, average work time per call (time taken to give information) decreasing from 60 to 43 units of work time, the percentage of work time completed within ideal limits increasing from 50 to 93 percent of ideal time, and the percentage of times in which operators made proper use of references going from 80 to 94 percent. The overall outcome was a significant improvement in the productivity of the operators.

In another example, the B. F. Goodrich chemical plant in Avon Lake, Ohio, introduced an OB Mod program at a time when the plant was in serious danger of failing. The program involved setting goals and providing feedback and positive reinforcement regarding scheduling, targets, costs, and problem areas. Supervisors received feedback once a week on sales, costs, and productivity. The plant production manager credits the program with turning the plant around, resulting in significant cost savings and a 300 percent productivity improvement over 5 years.

Source: Hamner, W. C., and Hamner, E. P. (1976, Spring). Behavior modification on the bottom line. *Organizational Dynamics,* 12–24.

---

results that are available from well-designed studies are quite encouraging regarding the positive outcomes associated with OB Mod programs.[33]

Ethical Issues in OB Mod

Objections have sometimes been raised to OB Mod on ethical grounds. The basic thrust of most of the criticism seems to be that OB Mod is a technique for controlling and manipulating the behavior of organization members. It is argued to be ethically undesirable since its application deprives organization members of their freedom and may result in their engaging in behavior which they would not otherwise engage in.

The basic issues of control, manipulation, and freedom are obviously extremely important, and those who raise these issues do so with considerable justification. It is extremely important to think through very carefully the ethical issues involved in the treatment of people in work organizations and to analyze the potential for misuse or misapplication of any techniques that may be developed for application to people in organizations.

Clearly, the goal of OB Mod is to increase a manager's ability to control and direct the behavior of other members of the organization. But it is equally clear that the fundamental nature of a manager's job is to control and direct the behavior of the people under his or her supervision. Surely the organization is controlling the behavior of its members by insisting that in order to remain a member of the organization, people must be physically present on the job from 9 a.m. to 5 p.m., or some variant of such hours. And just as surely a manager is attempting to control and direct the behavior of members of the organization when he or she exhorts them on to higher levels of productivity or greater levels of accomplishment. OB Mod, properly directed and applied, simply attempts to make the process of control and direction more systematic, more effective, and more clearly based upon positive rewards rather than negative punishment.

Ethical issues regarding manipulation and freedom are by no means irrelevant to considering the application of OB Mod. Indeed they are very important. However, they are important issues to address in analyzing any technique of management, indeed any approach designed to influence the behavior of people in organizations. People who study organizations and people who work in them must all remain conscious of these ethical issues in order to ensure that available techniques are not misused or placed in the service of unethical goals. Such ethical issues are pervasive and are relevant not only to OB Mod but to management techniques in general.

Keys to Effective Management

1 *Managers must be sensitive to the differences in needs and values among the people they supervise.* Every individual is unique and will respond differently to attempts to motivate him or her. Above all, managers must avoid assuming that subordinates need and value exactly the same things the manager does. In order to discover the key needs and values of subordinates the manager must work hard at listening to and understanding those he or she is managing.

2 *Managers must try to increase subordinates' expectations that their effort can result in effective performance (i.e., increase E → P expectancies).* Low effort → performance expectancies guarantee low levels of motivation. In order to ensure that these expectancies are high, the manager must ascertain that subordinates possess the necessary *ability* to perform effectively and that they possess sufficient self-confidence to *believe* that their effort will result in effective performance. Key elements in this process must be careful hiring and placement of employees based upon their ability, as well as the effective use of training to overcome any ability deficiencies.

3 *Managers must take whatever steps are available to them to make the attainment of rewards by their subordinates dependent upon effective performance.* They must also ensure that subordinates correctly *under-*

stand the basis upon which rewards are administered and that they *believe* that promised rewards will be provided if stated standards of performance are attained.

4 *Managers must ensure that subordinates feel they are being equitably treated by the organization.* This places three sets of demands on management. First, management must treat members of the organization fairly and equitably in comparison to one another. Second, the policies and practices in place in the organization must compare favorably to those in other organizations of a similar type. Finally, members of the organization must be provided with accurate and complete information regarding the organization's policies and practices in order to ensure that they accurately perceive and understand them.

5 *Managers should encourage their subordinates to set performance goals that are specific, challenging, and realistic.* The manager also must ensure that goals are not simply dictated to subordinates, but rather are generated in a fashion that creates a sense of personal ownership and acceptance of those goals by the subordinate responsible for their implementation.

6 *Managers should be making use of positive reinforcement whenever and wherever possible.* This requires some analysis of the types of behavior desired from subordinates plus some effort from the manager to ensure that those desired behaviors are reinforced. At the same time managers should make a point of avoiding the use of punishment and negative reinforcement as far as possible.

Review Questions

1 Describe a theory of motivation based on the needs of organization members. What are the strengths and weaknesses of the theory? What does it imply for managerial practice?

2 Discuss the two different types of expectancies referred to in the expectancy theory of motivation. What can a manager do to influence these expectancies?

3 What types of outcomes do you feel have the highest positive valences for young people starting their careers in organizations today? Do you think these have changed much over the past five to ten years?

4 Think of a job that you have had at some point in your life. Think of another person who was doing a similar job in the same organization. Conduct an equity theory comparison of yourself to the other person. To what extent were your feelings and actions in the situation similar to what equity theory would have predicted they would be?

5   What types of factors do you think generate such strong feelings of inequity that a person becomes likely to take drastic action such as quitting the organization?

6   What kinds of goals are most likely to generate high levels of motivation among subordinates? What can a manager do to try to ensure that subordinates set such goals for themselves?

7   What are the advantages and disadvantages associated with the uses of positive reinforcement, negative reinforcement, extinction, and punishment? Which approach would you recommend to a manager?

8   Under what circumstances is it desirable to employ continuous as opposed to partial schedules of reinforcement? When partial reinforcement schedules are used, which specific type would you recommend? Why?

9   Is it ethical for managers to attempt to influence the motivation and behavior of their subordinates? Defend your position.

Lincoln Electric

The productivity incentive program at Lincoln Electric is based on maximizing output, minimizing inputs, and increasing efficiency. The savings generated by the program are passed on to the customer, while additional earnings generated are apportioned between the customer in terms of lower prices and employees in terms of an annual bonus. Both the customer and the employee share in the gains from increased efficiency. Thus, the partnership between employees and customers is emphasized since both are essential for the success of the enterprise and both share the gains from increased productivity.

In James Lincoln's philosophy, "the incentives that are most potent when properly offered and believed in by the worker" are the following: (1) money in proportion to production; (2) status as a reward for achievement; and (3) publicity of the worker's contribution and skill and imagination and the reward that is given for it. This results in added status.

Each employee is evaluated regularly by his or her immediate superior. Managers make annotations on their employees' performance at least monthly and often more frequently when a particular event justifies it. The importance of the evaluation of workers by their superiors, and the direct connection between this evaluation and the dollar bonus paid at the end of the year, emphasizes the relationship between the employee, his or her superior, and the overall performance of the company. The better the performance of the company in economic terms, the larger the dollar pool from which bonuses will be paid; and the higher the employee is rated by the supervisor, the greater his or her share of the pool will be. The combination of these two factors results in the annual bonus the employee receives. Thus, the relationships among the employee, the supervisor, and the company as a whole are directly tied together; and this relationship is demonstrated in very tangible terms:

a check at the end of the year. Year-end bonuses for employees normally range from 60 to 150 percent of their regular salary. In a recent year the company's 2,369 workers received a total of $27.5 million in bonuses, an average of $11,608 an employee. The recognition is further emphasized by in-house publications and also in newspaper and magazine articles released by the company's public relations department.

All employees are included in this program: production employees, support employees (like floor sweepers), and management. The fact that all employees are included in the program and treated in a similar manner adds an element that is absent in most so-called incentive programs. It tends to emphasize the unity of purpose and the common objectives of all employees, regardless of status or function, as they work toward the success of the common enterprise.

An outstanding performance citation is given each year to ten people who are recommended by department heads to the president. Anyone is eligible for this award, including a floor sweeper. The winners of these citations get an additional bonus, which is determined by the president. Another incentive is appointment of promising employees to the company's junior board of directors. This is an advisory group of ten people selected from among employees who are identified as exhibiting executive potential. This group meets once a month and can make recommendations on any subject to the company's board of directors. This junior board of directors is given a high degree of visibility within the company.

Questions for Discussion

1 What assumptions docs the Lincoln Electric plan make about human needs and motives?

2 How can expectancy theory concepts be used to understand the effectiveness of the productivity incentive program?

3 How does the plan deal with issues of perceived equity of treatment among employees?

Source: Adapted from a case written by DeWayne Piehl. Used by permission of the author.

Notes

1   Mitchell, T. R. (1982). Motivation: New directions for theory, research, and practice. *Academy of Management Review, 7,* 80–88.

2   Maslow, A. H. (1954). *Motivation and personality.* New York: Harper.

3   Miner, J. (1980). *Theories of organizational behavior.* Hinsdale, IL: Dryden Press, 18–45.

Naylor, J., Pritchard, R., & Ilgen, D. (1980). *A theory of behavior in organizations.* New York: Academic Press, 159–223.

Wahba, M. A., & Bridwell, L. G. (1976). Maslow reconsidered: A review of research on the need hierarchy theory. *Organizational Behavior and Human Performance, 15,* 212–240.

4   Alderfer, C. P. (1972). *Existence, relatedness, and growth.* New York: Free Press.

5   Murray, H. A. (1938). *Explorations in personality.* New York: Oxford University Press.

6   Atkinson, J. W., & Raynor, J. O. (1974). *Motivation and achievement.* Washington, D. C.: R. H. Winston & Sons.

Harrel, A. M., & Stahl, M. J. (1981). A behavioral decision theory approach for measuring McClelland's trichotomy of needs. *Journal of Applied Psychology, 66,* 242–247.

Litwin, G. H., & Stringer, R. A., Jr. (1968). *Motivation and organizational climate.* Boston: Division of Research, Graduate School of Business Administration, Harvard University.

Steers, R. M., & Braunstein, D. N. (1976). A behaviorally based measure of manifest needs in work settings. *Journal of Vocational Behavior, 9,* 251–266.

7   Lawler, E. E., III. (1973). *Motivation in work organizations.* Monterey, CA: Brooks/Cole.

Vroom, V. H. (1964). *Work and motivation.* New York: Wiley.

8   Eden, D., & Ravid, G. (1982). Pygmalion versus self-expectancy: Effects of instructor- and self-expectancy on trainee performance. *Organizational Behavior and Human Performance, 30,* 351–364.

Garland, H. (1984). Relation of effort-performance expectancy to performance in goal-setting experiments. *Journal of Applied Psychology, 69,* 79–84.

Janz, T. (1982). Manipulating subjective expectancy through feedback: A laboratory study of the expectancy-performance relationship. *Journal of Applied Psychology, 67,* 480–485.

Matsui, T., Okada, A., & Mizuguchi, R. (1981). Expectancy theory prediction of the goal theory postulate, "The harder the goals, the higher the performance." *Journal of Applied Psychology, 66,* 54–58.

9   Mowen, J. C., Middlemist, R. D., & Luther, D. (1981). Joint effects of assigned goal level and incentive structure on task performance: A laboratory study. *Journal of Applied Psychology, 66,* 598–603.

Pinder, C. C. (1984). *Work motivation.* Glenview, IL: Scott, Foresman.

10   León, F. R. (1981). The role of positive and negative outcomes in the causation of motivational forces. *Journal of Applied Psychology, 66,* 45–53.

Schmitt, N., & Son, L. (1981). An evaluation of valence models of motivation to pursue various post high school alternatives. *Organizational Behavior and Human Performance, 27,* 135–150.

11   Pecotich, A., & Churchill, G. A., Jr. (1981). An examination of the anticipated satisfaction importance valence controversy. *Organizational Behavior and Human Performance, 27,* 213–226.

12   Arnold, H. J. (1981). A test of the multiplicative hypothesis of expectancy-valence theories of work motivation. *Academy of Management Journal 24,* 128–141.

Fusilier, M. R., Ganster, D. C., & Middlemist, R. D. (1984). A within-person test of the form of the expectancy theory model in a choice context. *Organizational Behavior and Human Performance, 34,* 323–342.

Ilgen, D. R., Nebeker, D. M., & Pritchard, R. D. (1981). Expectancy theory measures: An empirical comparison in an experimental situation. *Organizational Behavior and Human Performance, 28,* 189–223.

Stahl, M., & Harrell, A. M. (1981). Modeling effort decisions with behavioral decision theory: Toward an individual differences model of expectancy theory. *Organizational Behavior and Human Performance, 27,* 303–325.

13   Adams, J. S. (1965). Injustice in social exchange. In L. Berkowitz (Ed.), *Advances in Experimental Social Psychology* (Vol. 2). New York: Academic Press.

Goodman, P. S., & Friedman, A. (1971). An examination of Adams' theory of inequity. *Administrative Science Quarterly, 16,* 271–288.

14   Birnbaum, M. H. (1983). Perceived equity of salary policies. *Journal of Applied Psychology, 68,* 49–59.

Greenberg, J. S., & Ornstein, S. (1983). High status job title as compensation for underpayment: A test of equity theory. *Journal of Applied Psychology, 68,* 285–297.

Vecchio, R. P. (1984). Models of psychological inequity. *Organizational Behavior and Human Performance, 34,* 266–282.

15   Cosier, R. A., & Dalton, D. R. (1983). Equity theory and time: A reformulation. *Academy of Management Review, 8,* 311–319.

Duchon, D., & Jago, A. G. (1981). Equity and the performance of major league baseball players: An extension of Lord and Hohenfeld. *Journal of Applied Psychology, 66,* 728–732.

Eden, D., & Ravid, G. *loc. cit..*

Mowday, R. (1983). Equity theory predictions of behavior in organizations. In R. M. Steers & L. W. Porter (Eds.), *Motivation and Work Behavior* (3rd ed.). New York: McGraw-Hill.

Vecchio, R. P. (1982). Predicting worker performance in inequitable settings. *Academy of Management Review, 7,* 103–110.

16   Taylor, F. W. (1911). *The principles of scientific management.* New York: Harper.

17   Latham, G. P., & Yukl, G. A. (1975). A review of the research on the application of goal setting in organizations. *Academy of Management Journal, 18,* 824–845.

Locke, E. A. (1968). Toward a theory of task performance and incentives. *Organizational Behavior and Human Performance, 3,* 157–189.

Locke, E. A. (1978). The ubiquity of the technique of goal setting in theories of and approaches to employee motivation. *Academy of Management Review, 3,* 594–601.

Locke, E. A., Shaw, K. N., Saari, L. M., & Latham, G. P. (1981). Goal setting and task performance: 1969–1980. *Psychological Bulletin, 90,* 125–152.

18   Chacko, T. I., & McElroy, J. C. (1983). The cognitive component in Locke's theory of goal setting: Suggestive evidence for a causal attribution interpretation. *Academy of Management Journal, 26,* 104–118.

Ivancevich, J. M., & McMahon, J. T. (1982). The effects of goal setting, external feedback, and self-generated feedback on outcome variables: A field experiment. *Academy of Management Journal, 25,* 359–372.

Kim, J. S. (1984). Effect of behavior plus outcome goal setting and feedback on employee satisfaction and performance. *Academy of Management Journal, 27,* 139–149.

Locke, E. A., Frederick, E., Bobko, P., & Lee, C. (1984). Effect of self-efficacy, goals and task strategies on task performance. *Journal of Applied Psychology, 69,* 241–251.

19   Jackson, S. E., & Zedeck, S. (1982). Explaining performance variability: Contributions of goal setting, task characteristics, and evaluative contexts. *Journal of Applied Psychology, 67,* 759–768.

Latham, G. P., & Steele, T. P. (1983). The motivational effects of participation versus goal setting on performance. *Academy of Management Journal, 26,* 406–417.

McCaul, K. D., & Kopp, J. T. (1982). Effects of goal setting and commitment on increasing metal recycling. *Journal of Applied Psychology, 67,* 377–379.

   Mowen, J. C., Middlemist, R. D., & Luther, D., *loc. cit..*

   Reber, R. A., & Wallin, J. A. (1984). The effects of training, goal setting, and knowledge of results on safe behavior: A component analysis. *Academy of Management Journal, 27,* 544–560.

20   Garland, H. (1982). Goal levels and task performance: A compelling replication of some compelling results. *Journal of Applied Psychology, 67,* 245–248.

   Locke, E. A. (1982). Relation of goal level to performance with a short work period and multiple goal levels. *Journal of Applied Psychology, 67,* 512–514.

21   Erez, M., & Kanfer, F. H. (1983). The role of goal acceptance in goal setting and task performance. *Academy of Management Review, 8,* 454–463.

   Erez, M., & Zidon, I. (1984). Effect of goal acceptance on the relationship of goal difficulty to task performance. *Journal of Applied Psychology, 69,* 69–78.

   Garland, H. (1983). Influence of ability, assigned goals, and normative information on personal goals and performance: A challenge to the goal attainability assumption. *Journal of Applied Psychology, 68,* 20–30.

   Locke, E. A., Frederick, E., Bobko, P., & Buckner, E. (1984). Effect of previously assigned goals on self-set goals and performance. *Journal of Applied Psychology, 69,* 694–699.

22   Ivancevich, J. M., & Smith, S. V. (1981). Goal-setting interview skills training: Simulated and on-the-job analysis. *Journal of Applied Psychology, 66,* 697–705.

   Latham, G. P., & Saari, L. M. (1979). Importance of supportive relationships in goal setting. *Journal of Applied Psychology, 64,* 151–156.

23   Locke, et al. (1981), *loc. cit.*

24   Carroll, S. J., Jr., & Tosi, H. L., Jr. (1973). *Management by objectives.* New York: Macmillan.

   Pringle, C. D., & Longenecker, J. G. (1982). The ethics of MBO. *Academy of Management Review, 7,* 305–312.

   Tosi, H. L., Jr., Rizzo, J. R., & Carroll, S. J., Jr. (1970). Setting goals in management by objectives. *California Management Review, 12*(4), 70–78.

25   Skinner, B. F. (1953). *Science and human behavior.* New York: Macmillan.

26   Dowrick, P. W., & Hood, M. (1981). Comparison of self-modeling and small cash incentives in a sheltered workshop. *Journal of Applied Psychology, 66,* 394–397.

Komaki, J. Barwick, K. D., & Scott, L. R. (1978). A behavioral approach to occupational safety: Pinpointing and reinforcing safe performance in a food manufacturing plant. *Journal of Applied Psychology, 63,* 434–445.

Komaki, J., Heinzmann, A. T., & Lawson, L. (1980). Effect of training and feedback: Component analysis of a behavioral safety program. *Journal of Applied Psychology, 65,* 261–270.

Scott, W. E., Jr., & Erskine, J. A. (1980). The effects of variation in task design and monetary reinforcers on safe behavior. *Organizational Behavior and Human Performance. 25,* 311–335.

27 Luthans, F., Paul, R., & Baker, D. (1981). An experimental analysis of the impact of a contingent reinforcement intervention on salespersons' performance behaviors. *Journal of Applied Psychology, 66,* 314–323.

28 Pritchard, R. D., Hollenback, J., & DeLeo, P. J. (1980). The effects of continuous and partial schedules of reinforcement on effort, performance, and satisfaction. *Organizational Behavior and Human Performance, 25,* 336–353.

29 Saari, L. M., & Latham, G. P. (1982). Employee reactions to continuous and variable ratio reinforcement schedules involving a monetary incentive. *Journal of Applied Psychology, 67,* 506–508.

30 Luthans, F., & Kreitner, R. (1974, July-August). The management of behavioral contingencies. *Personnel,* 7–16.

Luthans, F., & Kreitner, R. (1975). *Organizational behavior modification.* Glenview, IL: Scott Foresman.

31 Hamner, W. C., & Hamner, E. P. (1976, Spring). Behavior modification on the bottom line. *Organizational Dynamics,* 12–24.

32 McGehee, W., & Tullar, W. L. (1978). A note on evaluating behavior modification and behavior modeling as industrial training techniques. *Personnel Psychology, 31,* 477–484.

33 Haynes, R. S., Pine, R. C., & Fitch, H. G. (1982). Reducing accident rates with organizational behavior modification. *Academy of Management Journal, 25,* 407–416.

Komaki, et al. (1978), *loc. cit.*

Luthans, et al. (1981), *loc. cit.*

Luthans, F., & Schweizer, J. (1979, September). How behavior modification techniques can improve total organizational performance. *Management Review,* 43–50.

Snyder, C. A., & Luthans, F. (1982, August). Using O.B. Mod to increase hospital productivity. *Personnel Administrator,* 67–73.

Chapter 4

Job Satisfaction

CHAPTER OUTLINE

Sources of Job Satisfaction

Consequences of Job Satisfaction

Trends in Job Satisfaction Levels

Job Satisfaction Surveys

Keys to Effective Management

Review Questions

*T*he recessions in the 1970s and 1980s brought to focus an issue that better economic times had masked: that many workers, at all levels of organizations, were not particularly satisfied with their jobs. Blue-collar workers were frustrated with the tedium of factory work; secretarial workers were being replaced by, or made servants to, video display terminals; white-collar workers were confronted with layoffs and salary cuts. At the same time, the popular press brought to focus another related issue: that workers overseas, in countries like Japan and Sweden, were much more satisfied with their jobs and organizations than American workers were. Indeed, in the case of Japan, they were also more productive.

Thus, managers today are concerned about job satisfaction for two reasons. First, many feel morally responsible for maintaining a high level of job satisfaction in their organizations. Whether people find their work satisfying or frustrating, challenging or boring, meaningful or pointless, is a strong personal concern for managers.[1] Second, managers are concerned about the impact that job satisfaction has on performance. Most managers believe that job dissatisfaction leads to low productivity, high absenteeism and turnover, and increased unionization.

In this chapter, we'll be exploring more fully the nature of job satisfaction and its impact on employee behavior. The first section of the chapter defines job satisfaction and identifies its major sources. We also examine here a model of job satisfaction; this model helps us determine whether, overall, employees will feel satisfied or dissatisfied with their jobs. In the second section of the chapter, we consider the consequences of job satisfaction with respect to a variety of job behaviors—performance, absenteeism, turnover, and unionization. In the third section of the chapter, we turn to some of the broader issues of job satisfaction. At the societal level, what changes have occurred in the levels of job satisfaction and dissatisfaction? Why have these changes occurred? What are the results of these changes? Finally, the chapter concludes with a section on job satisfaction surveys and some guidelines on how to design and administer these surveys more effectively.

Sources of Job Satisfaction

For our purposes, ***job satisfaction*** will be defined as the *amount of overall positive affect (or feelings) that individuals have toward their jobs.* When we say that an individual has high job satisfaction, we mean that the individual generally likes and values his job highly and feels positively toward it.

As Box 4-1 suggests, there are a variety of factors that lead people to feel positively or negatively about their jobs. Below, we look at the six most frequently studied causes of job satisfaction: (1) pay; (2) the work itself; (3) promotions; (4) supervision; (5) the work group; and (6) working conditions. We will see that, in general, pay and the work itself are the most important sources of job satisfaction, that promotional opportunities and supervision are moderately important sources of job satisfaction, and that the work group and working conditions are relatively minor sources of job satisfaction.[2]

Pay

Wages do play a significant role in determining job satisfaction, and are as significant to white-collar workers as to blue-collar workers.[3] ***Pay*** is such an important determinant of job satisfaction because it is instrumental in fulfilling so many of the needs we talked about in the last chapter. Money facilitates the obtaining of food, shelter, and clothing and provides the means to enjoy valued leisure interests outside of work. Moreover, pay can serve as a symbol of achievement and a source of recognition. Employees often see pay as a reflection of management's esteem for their contribution to the organization.

However, fringe benefits have not been found to have as strong an influence on job satisfaction as direct wages. Employees tend to underestimate how much they actually receive in indirect benefits. Often, employees underestimate by 33 percent how much they are receiving in "real dollars" in fringe benefits. Employees also tend to undervalue receiving some of these benefits. For instance, young workers tend to undervalue receiving life and disability insurance.[4]

BOX 4-1

Working: How People Feel About Their Jobs

Studs Terkel has interviewed over 100 workers from all walks of life about their experiences on their jobs. Below are some excerpts from these interviews. As you will see, even jobs of high status and income are not necessarily highly satisfying.

Ernest Bradshaw (bank auditor):   "The job is boring. It's a real repetitious thing. I don't notice the time. I could care less about the time. I don't really know if it's 5:00 until I see somebody clean up their desk. . . ."

"It's just this constant supervision of people. It's more or less like you have a factory full of robots working the machinery. You're there checking and making sure the machinery is constantly working. If it breaks down or something goes wrong, you're there to straighten it out. You're like a foreman on the assembly line; if they break down, replace them. You're just like a man who sits and watches computers all day. Same thing."

John Fortune (media supervisor in an advertising agency):   "There's a kind of cool paradox in advertising. There's a pressure toward the safe, tried, and true that has worked in the past. . . . But there's a tremendous need in the agency business for the fresh and the new, to differentiate this one agency from another. Writers are constantly torn between these two goals: selling the product and selling themselves. If you do what they tell you, you're screwed. If you don't do what they tell you, you're fired. . . ."

"There are five (career) stages. 'Who is this guy, John Fortune?' The second stage: 'Gee, it would be great if we could get that guy, what's his name? John Fortune.' The third stage: 'If we could only get John Fortune.' The fourth stage: 'I'd like to get a young John Fortune.' The fifth stage: 'Who's John Fortune?' There are no old writers."

Nancy Rogers (bank teller):   "We work right now with the IBM. . . . There are two tellers to a cage, and the machine is in between our windows. I don't like the way the bank is set up. It separates people. People are already separated enough. . . . It's not quite like being in prison, but I still feel very locked in."

"I like the person who shares my cage very much. I have fun with her. She's originally from the South. She's a very relaxed type of person. I can be open and not worry I might offend her. . . . It's nice and relaxed—we sit around and gossip about our boyfriends, which is fun."

Source: Reprinted from Terkel, S. (1974). *Working.* New York: Pantheon Books, pp. 398–401, 73–78, 257–262. Used by permission of Random House.

The Work Itself

Along with pay, the content of **the work itself** plays a very major role in determining how satisfied employees are with their jobs. By and large, workers want jobs that are challenging: they do not want to be doing mindless jobs day after day.[5] The two most important aspects of the work itself that influence job satisfaction are *variety* and *control over work methods and work pace.*

In general, jobs with a moderate amount of variety produce the most job satisfaction. Jobs with too little variety cause workers to feel bored and fatigued. Jobs with too much variety and stimulation cause workers to feel psychologically stressed and "burned out."[6]

Jobs that give workers some autonomy in how they do their work also provide the greatest job satisfaction. In contrast, management control over work methods and work pace consistently leads to high levels of job dissatisfaction. It is dehumanizing for employees to have their every action determined by their supervisors, down to when they can have a rest break. Moreover, many workers report their own productivity varies widely over the course of a day. Often, employees are least efficient the first and last half hours of the day and just before and after lunch. They are most efficient in the middle of the morning and the middle of the afternoon. Mechanical pacing does not allow employees to pace their work according to their energy levels.[7]

Ironically, in the 1970s and 1980s, the problems of unchallenging work seem to be moving out of the blue-collar factory and into the white-collar office. As Box 4-2 suggests, computers can create the same mind-numbing effects on workers today as assembly lines created for their counterparts in the past.

Promotions

Promotional opportunities have a moderate impact on job satisfaction. A **promotion** to a higher level in an organization typically involves positive changes in supervision, job content, and pay. Jobs that are at the higher levels of an organization usually provide workers with more freedom, more challenging work assignments, and higher salary.[8]

However, the rewards associated with a particular promotion differ greatly from one situation to another. One person may be promoted to a company presidency with a salary increase of $100,000 a year, whereas another person who is promoted from senior secretary to administrative assistant may receive only a $1,000 salary increase. For this reason, promotions are a much greater source of job satisfaction to business executives than to blue-collar and white-collar clerical workers.[9] Executives gain comparatively greater rewards from their promotions.

Supervision

Like promotions, **supervision** is a moderately important source of job satisfaction. Two dimensions of supervisor style, in particular, seem to have some impact on employee job satisfaction. The first dimension is **employee-centeredness** or **consideration.** Supervisors who establish a supportive personal rela-

BOX 4-2

Terminal Tedium

As automation has come to more and more white-collar offices, people are beginning to question whether the new technology is improving the lot of office workers. Could computers be producing, instead, new forms of old factory-life abuses—namely tedium, piecework rates, and exploitation of labor?

At Blue Shield of Massachusetts, data processors sit for six hours a day before their video display terminals, transferring data from claims forms to a company computer system. The computer keeps track of how much work is done by each employee and prints out a production report for each employee each week. The company has also developed time standards for each of the jobs performed by processors. The computer compares individual productivity with company standards, and wages are adjusted accordingly, up or down, every two months.

At Equitable Life Assurance, claims processors used to need a variety of skills when claims were being processed manually. Workers had to do math calculations, check the wording, and verify the format of the claim. Now all the claims processors do is punch numbers into the video display terminal. Workers who once performed a variety of tasks now do just one task; computer systems have rendered many of their other job duties superfluous.

On the positive side, automation has increased the productivity of several companies, including American Express. For instance, Blue Shield of Massachusetts reports productivity has tripled in some areas since the company automated. Blue Shield also feels it provides job opportunities to housewives who don't want to work full-time; the automated processing jobs are much more amenable to part-time workers than are regular secretarial jobs.

However, workers report increased physical problems since the introduction of video display terminals, especially headaches and backaches. These ailments seem to be caused by a combination of improper lighting, uncomfortable seating arrangements, and insufficient rest periods. At least two states, Maine and Massachusetts, are currently considering legislation addressing some of the health concerns about video display terminals. The proposals would require, among other things, regular inspection of terminals, free eye examinations for frequent users, and more frequent rest breaks during the working day. A recent study by the U.S. Public Health Service offers some support for the new concern about automated office workers. Clerical workers using the video display terminals report, by far, the most symptoms of physical and mental stress.

Source: Andrews, J. (1983, May 6). Terminal tedium. *Wall Street Journal,* pp. 1, 15. Used by permission of Dow Jones.

tionship with subordinates and take a personal interest in them contribute to their employees' satisfaction.[10] The other dimension of supervisory style that seems to contribute to employees' satisfaction is ***influence,*** or ***participation,*** in decision making. Employees who participate in decisions that affect their jobs display a much higher level of satisfaction with their supervisors and with their overall work situation.[11]

While employee-centeredness and influence in decision making are positively correlated with employee satisfaction, the participative leadership style does not always improve workers' attitudes toward their jobs. For instance, while employees in small, close-knit work groups prefer democratic leaders, employees in large, impersonal work groups actually prefer autocratic leaders.[12] Thus, while there is generally a positive relationship between an employee-centered supervisory style and employee satisfaction, there are several circumstances in which the relationship does not hold up.

Work Group

Having friendly and cooperative coworkers is a modest source of job satisfaction to individual employees. People like the opportunity to have conversation with each other as they work, and especially dislike jobs in which they are physically separated from each other.[13] The ***work group*** also serves as a social support system for employees. People often use their coworkers as a sounding board for their problems or as a source of comfort.

Ironically, however, while most people are very satisfied with their relationships with coworkers, having good relationships with coworkers is not as important to employees as most other factors are. In a study called "What You Really Want from Your Job," researchers found that while employees said they were very satisfied with the friendliness of their coworkers, they rated the work group only fourteenth in importance out of eighteen factors.[14] Employees seem to expect to like their coworkers, and only when they have to continuously deal with people whom they dislike does the work group become an important factor in their thinking.

Working Conditions

Working conditions, too, contribute in a modest way to job satisfaction. Features such as temperature, humidity, ventilation, lighting and noise, work schedules, cleanliness of the workplace, and adequate tools and equipment can all affect job satisfaction.[15]

The reasons for this are fairly straightforward. First, employees desire good working conditions because they lead to greater physical comfort. For instance, too much heat or too little light can cause physical discomfort; unclean air or poor ventilation can be physically dangerous. Second, working conditions are important to employees because they can influence life outside of work. If people are required to work long hours and/or overtime, they will have very little time left for their families, friends, and recreation outside of work. On the other hand, if workers have relatively short workweeks and/or some flexibility in the hours they have to work, it will be much easier for them to improve the quality of their lives outside of their jobs.[16]

Generally, however, unless working conditions are either extremely good or extremely bad, they are taken for granted by most employees. Moreover, quite often complaints about working conditions are manifestations of deeper frustrations. Complaints about the size of offices, for instance, often reflect individuals' anger toward management and feelings of lack of appreciation, rather than true problems in actual working conditions.[17]

A Model of Job Satisfaction

What determines whether employees feel generally satisfied or dissatisfied with their jobs? How do the specific satisfactions with pay, promotions, and the other job factors combine to produce an overall attitude of liking or disliking of the job? The model of job satisfaction presented in Figure 4-1 summarizes what we know about what determines whether employees will be generally satisfied.

Basically, job satisfaction is determined by the *discrepancy* between what individuals expect to get out of their jobs and what the job actually offers. A person will be dissatisfied if there is *less* than the desired amount of a job characteristic in the job. For instance, if a person expects to be promoted in six months and then is not, the person will be dissatisfied. A person will be satisfied if there is *no* discrepancy between desired and actual conditions (e.g., I expected a 10 percent raise and I received it). If there is *more* than the

Figure 4-1   A model of job satisfaction.

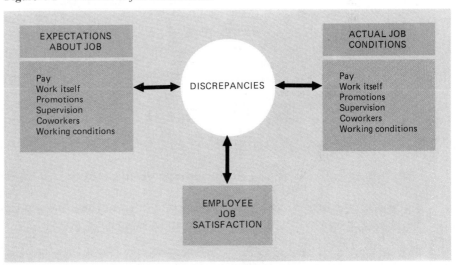

(*Source:* Adapted from Lawler, E. E., III (1973). *Motivation in work organizations.* Monterey, CA: Brooks/Cole, figure 3-4, p. 75. Used by permission.)

employee expected of some job factor and the excess is beneficial (e.g., a larger bonus, a faster promotion), then the person will be very highly satisfied.[18]

Now, let's examine cases of both job satisfaction and job dissatisfaction, using the model in Figure 4-1. A newly graduating MBA is hired to be an assistant brand manager at a major corporation at $30,000. Although she has no previous work experience, she expects, on the basis of job interviews, to be given significant job challenges right away. Not long after she starts working, she realizes that: (1) this entry-level position does not require MBA skills; (2) friends from graduate school working for other marketing corporations are doing significantly more challenging work; and (3) the salary does not cover as many expenses as expected, due to the high cost of living in a large city. In short, there are major discrepancies between job expectations and actual working conditions, and the new graduate is dissatisfied.

Next, let's examine a case of job satisfaction. A newly graduating MBA is hired to be an assistant brand manager at a major corporation for $30,000. Although the student has no previous work experience, he expects, on the basis of job interviews, to be given significant job challenges right away. Not long after he starts working, he realizes that: (1) he is doing the type of work promised in the interview; (2) he is doing the same level of work as friends from graduate school in comparable firms are doing; and (3) since he has lived in other major metropolitan areas, his personal estimates about how far $30,000 would go were accurate. There is no discrepancy between job expectations and actual job conditions, and the graduate is satisfied.

There is also a third case, in which there is a discrepancy between actual job conditions and job expectations, but the job is better than expected. For instance, the new MBA assistant brand manager discovers that the brand manager is being transferred to another position, and so the assistant takes on additional, challenging responsibilities and gets a corresponding pay raise. Not only are the coworkers enjoyable, but there is also an active social life with them after work. The new assistant does extremely well in the first job assignment and is promoted six months ahead of schedule. Since the actual job conditions exceed job expectations, job satisfaction is especially high.

Consequences of Job Satisfaction

While job satisfaction is obviously of great personal concern, managers are also concerned about the consequences of job satisfaction for employee behavior. In this section, we examine the ways in which job satisfaction affects employee behavior.

Performance

Of all the behaviors that job satisfaction or dissatisfaction could affect, there is none so important to managers as **performance**. Are satisfied workers more productive workers? It seems somehow natural that more positive feelings about work would lead to greater output and higher-quality work.[19] Unfortunately, four decades of research into this issue does not lend support to this belief.

First, *the relationship between job satisfaction and job performance is weak.* Empirical research studies suggest that these two variables are not closely related to each other in any simple fashion. Other factors besides job satisfaction—for instance, the condition of the work equipment or the worker's own abilities—have a much greater impact on how much a person can produce than his or her job satisfaction does.[20]

Second, *there is substantial evidence to suggest that job performance leads to job satisfaction, rather than vice versa.* As the model in Figure 4-2 indicates, performance leads to satisfaction, and rewards play a major role in the relationship.

Employees who perform well should receive both more ***intrinsic*** rewards and more ***extrinsic*** rewards. Workers who have successfully completed their jobs will receive more intrinsic rewards (e.g., feelings of accomplishment) as a result of their efforts. Moreover, employees who perform well should also receive more extrinsic rewards (e.g., pay and promotions) in recognition of their superior work. As a result of all these rewards, the best performers will also be the most satisfied workers.[21]

In contrast, employees who perform poorly will probably feel worse about their competence and will probably also receive less pay and fewer promotions.

Figure 4-2 The relationship between satisfaction and performance.

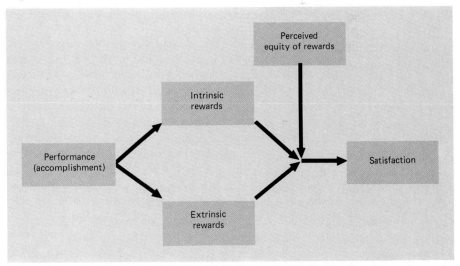

(*Source:* Adapted from Lawler, E. E., III, & Porter, L. W. (1967). The effect of performance on job satisfaction. *Industrial Relations, 7,* p. 23. Used by permission of authors and publisher. Copyright 1967, *Industrial Relations.*)

Consequently, the model would predict that these poor performers will be *less* satisfied with their jobs.[22]

Withdrawal Behavior: Turnover and Absenteeism

Dissatisfied employees are the most likely to quit their jobs altogether (turnover) and to be absent frequently from work. Withdrawing from the workplace allows employees to avoid the unpleasant or punishing aspects of their work environments.

Turnover

Turnover is of considerable concern to managers because it disrupts normal operations and necessitates the costly selection and training of replacements. Workers who have relatively low levels of job satisfaction are indeed the most likely to quit their jobs. In addition, organizational units with the lowest average satisfaction levels tend to have the highest turnover rates.[23]

However, while the relationship between job satisfaction and turnover is strong, it is important to note that the *availability of other places of employment* also influences turnover. If employees do not have a variety of alternative places of employment—due to geographical constraints, family responsibilities, bad economic times, or very specialized skills—they will be unlikely to leave their jobs even if they are highly dissatisfied.

Absenteeism

Job satisfaction is also highly related to **absenteeism.** Workers who are dissatisfied are more likely to take "mental health" days (i.e., days off not due to illness or personal business).[24] In an interesting experiment, researchers at Sears, Roebuck examined what would happen if salaried employees could choose to attend work or to be absent without financial penalty. On April 2, 1975, an unexpected blizzard hit Chicago, greatly hampering the city's transportation system. Attendance to work on April 3 would require considerable personal effort, but workers would not be penalized financially for absence. In work units where job satisfaction was high, attendance was high; in work units where job satisfaction was low, attendance was much lower. Those groups of workers with the highest levels of job satisfaction were more likely to exert the high level of effort necessary to get to work.[25]

Because absenteeism, like turnover, disrupts normal operations and necessitates the employment of costly substitute personnel, this form of withdrawal behavior, too, seriously concerns management. Relatively low-paid workers are especially likely to take days off when they are frustrated with work. This is because low-paid workers will incur relatively little loss of income if they are absent. In fact, one company—Parsons Pine Products of Ashland, Oregon—started giving "well pay" bonuses to workers who are neither absent nor late for a full month. By using "well pay" bonuses, Parsons Pine Products increased the financial incentives for workers to come to work even if they were not feeling positively toward their jobs on a given day.[26]

Union Activity

Why do employees want unions? This question concerns many diverse groups in the business community: the National Labor Relations Board, which regulates union organizing in the private sector; employers and managers who wish to avoid unionization; labor lawyers and management consultants who make a business of it. The evidence is strong that job dissatisfaction is a major cause of unionization.[27]

In an important study of union organizing, researchers found that employees' interest in unionization is based on dissatisfaction with working conditions and a perceived lack of influence to change those conditions. Employees become frustrated by low wages, by arbitrary and capricious discipline, and by uncorrected safety hazards. When employers fail to respond to employee complaints, employees realize that their power is not sufficient to deal with their employers. Collective action—*unionization*—may be their best solution. Satisfied employees are seldom interested in unions; they don't perceive that they need them.[28]

It is also not surprising that job dissatisfaction has an impact on other union activities, such as calling strikes or filing union grievances. Work units with low levels of job satisfaction do have more strikes and file more grievances than units with high levels of job satisfaction.[29]

Trends in Job Satisfaction Levels

In the first two sections of this chapter, we looked at job satisfaction from the individual's point of view. In this section, we consider some of the larger aspects of job satisfaction. Just how satisfied are workers in general today? What have been the trends in the levels of job satisfaction and why? We turn, next, to answer some of these questions.

How Satisfied Are Workers Today?

Despite some particularly gloomy predictions, major surveys of the American work force reveal that workers are generally satisfied with their jobs. Probably the most highly publicized of these surveys are those carried out by the University of Michigan's Survey Research Center and the National Opinion Research Center. In both these surveys, between 80 and 90 percent of employees working on a wide range of jobs across a diverse set of organizations consistently report that they are satisfied with their jobs.[30]

Does this mean that most workers are really happy with their jobs? The survey results are not so positive on this point. When employees were asked the question "What type of work would you try to get into if you could start all over again?" only 43 percent of the white-collar workers and 24 percent of the blue-collar workers said they would choose the same kind of work if given another chance. Employees were also asked the question "What would you do with the extra two hours if you had a twenty-six-hour day?" Two out of three college professors and one in four lawyers said they would use the extra time in a work-related activity. Strikingly, only one out of twenty nonprofessional workers would make use of the extra time in work activity.

A survey respondent summed up his feelings in the following way: "Don't get me wrong. I didn't say it is a *good* job. It's an okay job—about as good a job as a guy like me might expect. The foreman leaves me alone and it pays well. But I would never call it a good job. It doesn't amount to much, but it's not bad."[31]

Thus, while there are very few employees who have classically alienating jobs, there are also very few employees who are really happy with their work. Most people have jobs that are satisfactory, but not truly satisfying.

Recent Changes in Job Satisfaction Levels

There has probably been a *very slight trend downward* in the overall level of job satisfaction over the past 15 years—probably no more than 5 percent.[32] While more than 80 percent of the work force still report that they are either somewhat or very satisfied with their jobs, that percentage seems to have been inching downward since the early 1970s. Why is this the case? Let's look at the changes in attitudes among three large groups of workers: the young (under 30); middle managers; and blue-collar workers (see Table 4-1).

Young Workers

Demographic changes in the work force are contributing to the downward trend in job satisfaction. Probably the most significant of these changes is the growing number of young employees. In the United States, out of a work force of more than 85 million, 22.5 million are now under age 30. The baby-boom generation of the 1950s is entering the labor market in full force, and younger employees are consistently more dissatisfied than other employees.[33]

TABLE 4-1

Three Dissatisfied Work Groups

Young workers
1 Unrealistic job expectations
2 Overqualification for jobs
3 Unresponsiveness to authoritarian management

Middle managers
1 Lack of influence in decision making
2 Frequent layoffs during recessions
3 Declining earning power

Blue-collar workers
1 Lack of mobility out of blue-collar jobs
2 Lack of respect given by media
3 Low pay, uninteresting work

Part of the reason young employees are dissatisfied with their jobs is the nature of their job expectations. Many young employees begin their jobs with unrealistic expectations about how fulfilling and challenging their jobs will be. Finding that reality falls short of expectations, they are very disillusioned in their first decade of work. For instance, when workers under 30 are asked "How often do you leave work feeling you have done something particularly well?" only 23 percent answer "very often." In contrast, half the workers over age 50 respond "very often" to the same question.[34] After age 30, expectations are modified and the job is seen in a more positive light.

Another reason young employees are dissatisfied is that many of them are overqualified for their jobs. The Bureau of Labor Statistics, for instance, estimates that by the beginning of 1986, the number of college degrees will exceed job openings that require college degrees by *one million*.[35] Thus, college graduates are moving down to lower-income and lower-status jobs, generating even further frustration. Recent interviews with new college graduates illustrate this frustration with work:

"I didn't go to school for four years to type. I'm bored; continuously humiliated. They sent me to Xerox school for three hours. . . . I realize that I sound cocky, but after you've been in the academic world, after you've had your own class (as a student teacher) and made your own plans, and someone tries to teach you to push a button—you get pretty mad. They even gave me a gold plated plaque to show I've learned how to use the machine."

"You can't wait to get out and get a job that will let you do something that's really important. . . . You think you're one of the elite. Then you go to a place like the Chicago Loop and there are all these lawyers, accountants, etc., and you realize that you're just a lawyer. No, not even a lawyer—an employee: you have to check in at nine and leave at five. I had lots of those jobs—summers—where you punch in and punch out. You think it's going to be different, but it isn't. You're in the rut like everybody else."[36]

Yet a third reason young employees seem to be more dissatisfied is their response to authority. In the 1960s and 1970s, students received a greater voice in setting the goals of the university and in determining what was taught in the classroom; as new entrants into the work force, they are disappointed that they have less influence as adults than they did as students.

Middle Managers   A disturbing trend in the job satisfaction figures is the growing disenchantment of such traditionally privileged groups as the nation's five million middle managers. Whereas in 1957 William H. Whyte almost parodied the subservience of these managers in his *Organization Man,* today one out of three middle managers indicates some willingness to join a union. What thirty years ago was seen as dedication—late nights of work, working vacations—is seen today as compulsive behavior and evidence of workaholism. Many middle managers feel that their company would not act to do something about their individual problems; loyalty to the employer, once high among this group of workers, is now much lower.

Middle managers today feel they lack influence in organization decision making. They often have to implement company policies that they don't understand and don't agree with. Moreover, because middle managers' productivity is often hard to measure and their functions often seem nonessential, middle management is the easiest place to cut during recessions. Even the relative earning power of the middle manager has declined substantially. Very few middle managers can afford to support their families on their own salaries. Today, only 14 percent of these workers come from the "traditional family"— a one-earner household in which the husband is employed and the wife and children are not. In 1950, that figure was 70 percent.[37] Middle managers continue to share the goals of top management, but are more nervous than ever about their own personal careers.[38]

Blue-Collar Workers

Many blue-collar workers do not believe that there is a great deal of opportunity for them or their children to move up the ladder of success. First of all, employers have raised education requirements for most blue-collar jobs. Now it takes more education just to keep the same blue-collar jobs and much more education to move up to higher-status jobs. Today, almost half of all blue-collar workers have high school diplomas: in 1960, the figure was 25 percent. For the first time, the children of blue-collar workers are predominantly becoming blue-collar workers as well.

Second, many blue-collar workers are frustrated by the lack of respect with which they are portrayed by the media. Television shows often present blue-collar workers as racist or authoritarian hard hats. Newspaper coverage of unions has focused on the "fat cats" among laborers, such as the plumbers who work only twenty-hour weeks and earn $500. The portrait of blue-collar workers that emerges from the mass media implies that they *are* the problem, not that they *have* problems.

Third, there is an increasing feeling among blue-collar workers that there are not enough of the good things in life to go around—and that they have received the short end of the stick. Despite the rich union contracts available to some workers in the United States today, two-thirds of the blue-collar workers have no paid vacations and no private pension plans. Most blue-collar workers are barely keeping up with inflation; many of their jobs are being automated or eliminated; many of their jobs are still characterized by low skill variety and little real autonomy.[39]

Whether the improved economic conditions of the mid-1980s will turn around these job satisfaction trends, it is too soon to tell. The most recent data available from the National Opinion Research Center suggest that the decline in job satisfaction may be leveling off, with about 81 percent of the work force being at least "moderately satisfied" and with white-collar workers in general being more satisfied than blue-collar workers.

Job Satisfaction Surveys

In this final section we address the use of job satisfaction surveys in organizations. More specifically, we are concerned with three issues: (1) What are the most reliable and valid methods of measuring job satisfaction?; (2) When should job satisfaction surveys be utilized?; and (3) How should job satisfaction surveys be administered?

Measuring Job Satisfaction

While a wide variety of instruments are available for use in surveying job-related attitudes, a few stand out as especially useful: the Job Descriptive Index (JDI), the Minnesota Satisfaction Questionnaire (MSQ), and the Porter Need Satisfaction Questionnaire (NSQ). Sample items from these questionnaires are presented in Figures 4-3, 4-4, and 4-5.

Job Descriptive Index

Probably the most well known job satisfaction survey is the ***Job Descriptive Index (JDI).***[40] The JDI has separate satisfaction scales for pay, promotion, supervision, work, and coworkers (see Figure 4-3). It has been used in a large variety of organizations, with employees from all different levels of education and income. It requires only ten to fifteen minutes to administer and is also available in a Spanish-language version.[41]

Minnesota Satisfaction Questionnaire

The ***Minnesota Satisfaction Questionnaire (MSQ)*** has 100 items, 5 items for each of the following 20 factors:[42]

1	Ability utilization	11	Moral values
2	Achievement	12	Recognition
3	Activity	13	Responsibility
4	Advancement	14	Security
5	Authority	15	Social service
6	Company policies and practices	16	Social status
7	Compensation	17	Supervision—human relations
8	Coworkers	18	Supervision—technical
9	Creativity	19	Variety
10	Independence	20	Working conditions

A short form of the MSQ, shown in Figure 4-4, has twenty items: general satisfaction can be measured by summing the scores for all twenty items. The regular form takes about a half hour to administer; the short form, only ten minutes. While the JDI gives a broad picture of employees' attitudes toward five major components of their jobs, the Minnesota Satisfaction Questionnaire gives a more detailed picture of employees' specific satisfactions and dissatisfactions.

Figure 4-3 The Job Descriptive Index.

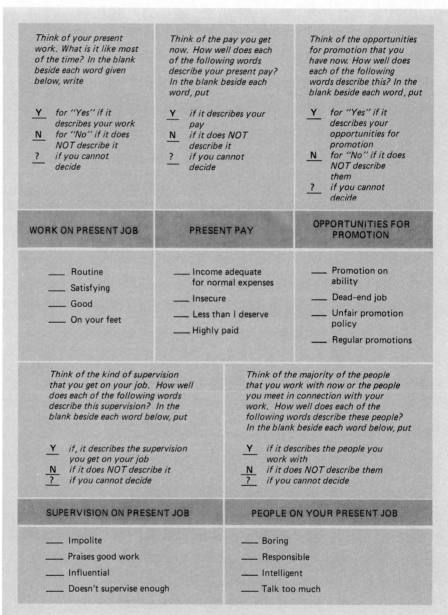

(*Source:* Reprinted by permission of Dr. P. C. Smith. Copyright 1975, Bowling Green University, Department of Psychology, Bowling Green, Ohio 43403.)

Figure 4-4   Minnesota Satisfaction Questionnaire.

Ask Yourself: *How satisfied am I with this aspect of my job?*

> **Very Sat.** *means I am very satisfied with this aspect of my job.*
> **Sat.** *means I am satisfied with this aspect of my job.*
> **N** *means I can't decide whether I am satisfied or not with this aspect of my job.*
> **Dissat.** *means I am dissatisfied with this aspect of my job.*
> **Very Dissat.** *means I am very dissatisfied with this aspect of my job.*

On my present job, this is how I feel about . . .	Very Dissat.	Dissat.	N	Sat.	Very Sat.
1. Being able to keep busy all the time	☐	☐	☐	☐	☐
2. The chance to work alone on the job	☐	☐	☐	☐	☐
3. The chance to do different things from time to time	☐	☐	☐	☐	☐
4. The chance to be "somebody" in the community	☐	☐	☐	☐	☐
5. The way my boss handles the staff	☐	☐	☐	☐	☐
6. The competence of my supervisor in making decisions	☐	☐	☐	☐	☐
7. Being able to do things that don't go against my conscience	☐	☐	☐	☐	☐
8. The way my job provides for steady employment	☐	☐	☐	☐	☐
9. The chance to do things for other people	☐	☐	☐	☐	☐
10. The chance to tell people what to do	☐	☐	☐	☐	☐
11. The chance to do something that makes use of my abilities	☐	☐	☐	☐	☐
12. The way company policies are put into practice	☐	☐	☐	☐	☐
13. My pay and the amount work I do	☐	☐	☐	☐	☐
14. The chances for advancement on this job	☐	☐	☐	☐	☐
15. The freedom to use my own judgment	☐	☐	☐	☐	☐
16. The chance to try my own methods of doing the job	☐	☐	☐	☐	☐
17. The working conditions	☐	☐	☐	☐	☐
18. The way my coworkers get along with each other	☐	☐	☐	☐	☐
19. The praise I get for doing a good job	☐	☐	☐	☐	☐
20. The feeling of accomplishment I get from the job	☐	☐	☐	☐	☐
	Very Dissat.	Dissat.	N	Sat.	Very Sat.

(*Source:* Weiss, D. J., Dawis, R. V., England, G. W., & Lofquist, L. H. (1967). *Manual for the Minnesota Satisfaction Questionnaire.* (Minnesota studies in vocational rehabilitation, Vol. 22). Minneapolis: University of Minnesota Industrial Relations Center. Reprinted by permission.)

Porter Need Satisfaction Questionnaire

The *Porter Need Satisfaction Questionnaire (NSQ)* is typically used for management workers only. Its questions focus mostly on the particular problems and challenges of managerial jobs. Sample items appear in Figure 4-5.

The NSQ is based on the discrepancy model of job satisfaction discussed earlier (see Figure 4-1). Each item has two questions, one for "should be" and one for "is now" (e.g., "How much feeling of security should there be in this job?" and "How much is there now?"). An item in this scale is scored by subtracting the numerical value of the choice on the "is now" part from the numerical value of the choice on the "should be" part. The greater this difference, the more dissatisfied the employee is with this aspect of the job. Overall job dissatisfaction can be measured by summing the scores on all the items.[43]

Figure 4-5 Sample items from the Porter Need Satisfaction Questionnaire.

Instructions: Circle the number on the scale that represents the amount of the characteristic being rated. Low numbers represent low or minimum amounts, and high numbers represent high or maximum amounts.

1. The opportunity for personal growth and development in my management position.
   a. HOW MUCH IS THERE NOW?
   (Minimum)   1   2   3   4   5   6   7   (Maximum)
   b. HOW MUCH SHOULD THERE BE?
   (Minimum)   1   2   3   4   5   6   7   (Maximum)

2. The feeling of security in my management position.
   a. HOW MUCH IS THERE NOW?
   (Minimum)   1   2   3   4   5   6   7   (Maximum)
   b. HOW MUCH SHOULD THERE BE?
   (Minimum)   1   2   3   4   5   6   7   (Maximum)

(*Source:* Porter, L. W. (1961). A study of perceived need satisfaction in bottom and middle management jobs. *Journal of Applied Psychology, 45,* p. 3. Copyright 1961 by The American Psychological Association. Reprinted by permission of the publisher and author.)

Attributes of Good Surveys

There are several characteristics that make these three instruments so well respected:[44]

1 *Validity.* These instruments measure what they are intended to measure. Their items are highly related to other, previously validated measures of job satisfaction.

2 *Reliability.* These instruments have been demonstrated to produce stable, consistent results. They include several items to measure each particular facet of job satisfaction, and provide clear instructions to respondents.

3 *Content.* These survey instruments identify the wide range of factors that affect work life and organizational effectiveness. They provide data on the factors most managers are interested in.

4 *Language level.* Writing good items is not as easy as it appears. Items have to be written so that they are understandable to the respondents and can be used across a wide variety of organizations. The items in these scales are clearly and unambiguously worded and can be used in many different firms.

Since most of the better survey instruments are copyrighted, there is a modest charge to companies that want to purchase these surveys and have them scored and interpreted. To avoid paying these fees for services, many managers are tempted to write their own questionnaires. However, as mentioned earlier, it is very difficult to develop a reliable and valid instrument.

Thus, while ultimately a manager will want to establish the validity of a survey instrument for his or her own organization, developing a reliable survey from scratch is a tall order and demands quite a good deal of knowledge about measurement theory and statistics. Beginners, especially, would be well advised to use previously validated instruments.

Uses of Job Satisfaction Surveys

Job satisfaction surveys can help employers manage their workers more effectively. Surveys are generally used to accomplish five goals:

1 *To diagnose potential problems in organizations.*   Many companies find that job satisfaction surveys serve as a barometer of employee satisfaction with respect to a variety of organizational issues. If management sees a downward trend in satisfaction with pay, for instance, it will be alerted to potential future complaints about pay and can reexamine its policies to discover why pay dissatisfaction is increasing.[45]

For example, at Texas Instruments (TI), attitude surveys picked up two potential problems: (1) employees complained that people from outside the organization were being hired for desirable jobs that insiders were qualified to fill; and (2) sometimes employees were not told until Friday night that they were expected to work on Saturday. As a result of these two complaints, Texas Instruments decided to post job openings on bulletin boards and to improve the procedures for bidding on these jobs. TI also implemented a policy whereby all employees had to be given two days' notice if they were required to work on weekends.[46]

2 *To discover the causes of absenteeism and turnover.*   If an organization is disturbed by high rates of turnover and absenteeism it might appropriately turn to job satisfaction surveys to discover what it is about the job situation that is leading to withdrawal behavior. Perhaps it is low pay; perhaps it is lack of promotional opportunities; perhaps it is unchallenging jobs. Without satisfaction surveys, there would be random guessing on the part of management.

For instance, at Geosource, Inc. (Houston), attitude surveys showed that one group of employees—its welders—were very dissatisfied with their pay. Management was concerned about this problem, especially since they perceived that they were paying industry standards and did not want further turnover among the welders. In discussing the problem with the welders, management discovered that welders were reading want ads offering "up to $7.84 per hour." When management could produce evidence that no welders were in fact being hired at that wage, the welders' job dissatisfaction decreased substantially.[47]

Similarly, at American Can, a survey showed that employees were concerned about a lack of career opportunities. Not wanting to lose its best employees, the corporation initiated a job information center. Staff were made available to counsel employees on career planning and training opportunities. Also, senior executives gave a series of talks on career opportunities in their respective areas to interested employees.[48]

3 *To assess the impact of organizational changes on employee attitudes.* Satisfaction surveys can be used fruitfully to help evaluate various changes in organizational policies and programs. By comparing prechange attitudes with postchange attitudes, management can determine what impact changes in organizational policies and programs are having on worker satisfaction.

In a survey of over 20,000 employees, General Electric (GE) found that a majority of its workers were very unhappy with the amount of information they received from top management about developments in the corporation. As a result, GE's management instituted monthly meetings with its employees, brought in experts to answer questions, and initiated a newsletter. One year later, General Electric used a follow-up attitude survey to discover whether its changes had the desired impact on worker satisfaction. Results showed, in fact, that the percentage of employees dissatisfied with the amount of information they received dropped from fifty percent to zero.[49]

4 *To stimulate better communication between management and workers.* Since surveys typically guarantee anonymity to respondents, workers should feel free to communicate information that would not normally be expressed directly to management. Thus, the survey can sometimes function as a catalyst and a safe channel for upward communication. Surveys can stimulate downward communication, too. Feedback sessions can provide opportunities for management to discuss important issues with workers and put to rest unfounded worker concerns.[50]

Sears, Roebuck has been especially active in running feedback meetings from top to bottom of the organization to discuss attitude survey results. One of the main discussion topics that emerged among middle managers was the company's relocation policies. The executives noted that: (1) often they could get as challenging a work assignment in the current geographical location as in the proposed new job location; (2) moving children of high school age was especially problematic; and (3) often the financial costs that the transferred family had to bear (e.g., loss of spouse's earnings) were substantial. In view of these findings, Sears's moving policy was changed to increase financial compensation to relocated employees. Moreover, wherever possible, employees were given career-path alternatives to geographical relocation, such as rotation across jobs within the same store or within the same metropolitan area.[51]

5 *To provide accurate information about the degree to which employees may be willing to vote for a union if given the chance.* Since we have already noted the strong link between job satisfaction and the likelihood of voting

for union representation, it makes sense for the employer who wishes to remain nonunion to systematically evaluate employee attitudes. If employees are honest in filling out the survey, management should be able to identify what working conditions are unsatisfactory and make the necessary changes before union-organizing efforts begin. In fact, when companies are faced with the threat of a union, they often hire consulting firms to come in and conduct such systematic surveys for them.

It is important to note here that it is far preferable to survey employee satisfaction *before* a union-organizing campaign begins. If a survey is conducted during a campaign, the National Labor Relations Board might infer that the employer is engaging in an unfair labor practice—implying a promise to alleviate unsatisfactory conditions.[52]

In short, attitude surveys can act as both a sensor of important organizational problems and a catalyst to widespread corporate policy changes. In Box 4-3, we briefly describe the recent impact attitude surveys have had on PepsiCo, Inc.[53]

Survey Administration

The way in which the satisfaction survey is administered can also influence how honestly people will respond to it and how useful the results will be. Some important factors that managers might want to consider in conducting job satisfaction surveys include the following:[54]

1 *Timing.* Satisfaction surveys are most effective if they are set up as part of a regularly scheduled, long-term program. First, this resolves the problems of scheduling. Managers can anticipate and plan for employees being away from their work station to participate. Moreover, scheduling eliminates the need for "crisis" surveying, unscheduled surveying carried out in response to an acute problem.

2 *Sampling.* Obviously it is much less expensive to sample (i.e., survey a representative subgroup of the population) than to canvas (survey the entire population). Before managers become overly influenced by this cost factor, however, they should consider the potential reactions of respondents to sampling. Imagine being bombarded with a chorus of "Why am I being singled out to participate?" and "Why am I being left out?" The hesitancy of those singled out to answer honestly can damage the usefulness of the results. In this situation, the added expense of a canvas might well be justified.

3 *Explaining the purposes of the survey.* One of the most damaging things a manager can do in surveying employees is to create false expectations. Particularly when an organization is just starting to use attitude surveys, employees may interpret the survey as a precursor to change. Management

BOX 4-3

Attitude Surveys at Pepsi Cola

Last spring, two attitude surveys of PepsiCo's 470 executives turned up some troubling job alienation. Many managers complained that they didn't feel cared about as people, that they didn't know enough about what was happening in the company as a whole, and that they weren't told how they were doing in their jobs. Although PepsiCo prizes the fast pace and demanding standards that make it so successful, it now worries more about the battle fatigue in its ranks. Some changes PepsiCo is in the process of implementing, as a result of these surveys, include:

More feedback   At annual merit-increase reviews, the company will be more specific in showing what kinds of behavior are rewarded. The forms for such reviews have been rewritten. Instead of dwelling on generalities, they now ask how a manager is doing daily, how effectively he or she is planning for the long term, and how personal development is progressing. Each year, the supervisor must explain to each subordinate precisely what determined the size of his or her bonus.

More personal concern   PepsiCo has a good deal of turnover at the top of its ranks. Each year, 4 percent of its top executives leave voluntarily, and an additional 4 percent or 5 percent are fired. Of the twenty-six officers listed in the 1982 annual report, ten were gone by the time the 1983 report was issued. In large part, this has been due to an implicit "up or out" policy: make the big play, or move on. PepsiCo will try to convince its solid achievers that it cares about them as well as its fast-track stars.

Reducing stress   As the company's president notes, "We probably attract people who give ulcers rather than those who get them." PepsiCo is a results-oriented company, and its promise of quick promotions attracts ambitious, aggressive people from other companies and top business schools. While PepsiCo does not want its standards to slip, its recent financial gains have given the company some time and resources to put into the human side of the enterprise. The organization is beginning to consider ways to develop its people and its business more thoughtfully and more fully. In particular, the company now wants to emphasize the value of coaching and training, management traits that are not currently rewarded. In fact, promotions and pay raises will now be based partly on how well an executive furthers the development of his or her subordinates.

Source: Hall, T. (1984, October 23). Demanding PepsiCo is attempting to make work nicer for managers. *Wall Street Journal*, p. 31. Used by permission of Dow Jones.

has to be honest with employees about the purposes of the survey and what will be done with the results. If there is going to be feedback, explain when the feedback will come and in what form (e.g., aggregated by department, by division, by job categories). If changes are going to be based on survey results, explain what role employees will have in planning or discussing those changes.

4 *Standardizing the conditions of survey administration.* It takes a lot of lead time to administer a survey in a professional manner. Times for employees to complete the survey have to be arranged; rooms for taking the survey have to be provided. It is important, too, that survey administrators be trained in how to answer frequent or typical questions, such as "Why are we doing a survey now?" Research suggests that deviations from standard practice in administering the questionnaire—including jokes and asides—can seriously lower the reliability of the results.

5 *Feedback meetings.* It is generally a good idea to hold discussions between managers and workers after the results of the satisfaction survey have been tabulated. These forums, run in an open and constructive climate, can elicit comments from employees that might explain survey results that are surprising from management's point of view.

Moreover, problem-solving committees can be set up to work on specific problems identified by the attitude survey. Good managers use job satisfaction surveys to measure the level of well-being among their employees; even better managers use surveys to encourage their employees' participation in improving upon that well-being.

Keys to Effective Management

A better understanding of the causes and consequences of job satisfaction can help managers diagnose and solve employee problems. Below we consider some practical issues related to job satisfaction that should be of particular concern to managers.

1 *Managers should be especially concerned with employee complaints about low pay and unchallenging work.* Too often managers delude themselves into thinking that employee dissatisfaction can be lessened by painting the work area, piping in music, giving out a few more words of praise, or giving people longer work breaks. While these issues sometimes are very important to workers, it is much more likely that the tougher issues of low pay and tedious work need to be addressed.

2 *Managers need to be aware that increasing job satisfaction is not a likely solution to increasing productivity.* Satisfaction and performance are not closely related to each other. Moreover, there is more evidence to suggest that job performance leads to job satisfaction than that job satisfaction leads to job performance. Job satisfaction is more likely to tell managers how reasonably employees feel they have been rewarded in the past rather than how well employees are likely to perform in the future.

3 *Managers should be more concerned about the impact of job satisfaction on employee turnover, absenteeism, and unionization.* The research evidence is consistent that dissatisfied employees are more likely to leave their jobs permanently and to be frequently absent from work. The costs of employee withdrawal behavior to organizations are high because turnover and absenteeism disrupt normal operations and necessitate the hiring and training of replacement personnel. Employers who wish to avoid unionization or to avoid strikes and grievances from current unions would likewise do well to attend to employee dissatisfaction. Employees who are dissatisfied are much more likely to join unions and, once unionized, to file grievances and call strikes.

4 *In assessing the levels of job satisfaction, it is important for managers to look not only at overall job satisfaction, but also at who is satisfied.* If the poor performers or those in less skilled job categories are less satisfied with pay, then that is in fact a sign of organizational effectiveness; the employees who are valued the most are receiving the greatest rewards. However, if the most talented employees are leaving because of factors that are within the organization's control, then that is a legitimate—perhaps pressing—area of concern.

5 *If designed and administered effectively, job satisfaction surveys can provide managers with a wealth of data about their work units.* In addition to diagnosing sources of problems in the organization, job satisfaction surveys can be used to assess the impact of organizational changes on employee attitudes and to stimulate better communication between management and workers. Feedback meetings held to discuss survey results can be used to elaborate the problems identified by the survey and to generate solutions to those problems.

Review Questions

1 What is job satisfaction?

2 What are the major sources of job satisfaction? Which two factors are particularly important?

3 What two aspects of the work itself especially influence employees' satisfaction?

4 Comment on the following statement: "The happy worker is the productive worker."

5 What impact does job satisfaction have on turnover and absenteeism?

6 In what ways does job satisfaction influence union activity?

7 How satisfied are workers in general today? What have been the trends in the level of job satisfaction?

8 Comment on the changes in job satisfaction among the following groups of workers: (a) workers under 30; (b) middle-managers; and (c) blue-collar workers.

9 What are the five purposes of job satisfaction surveys?

10 What three job satisfaction surveys are most well known?

11 What are the key attributes of a good job satisfaction survey?

12 Identify five important guidelines in administering an attitude survey.

Perfect Pizzeria

Perfect Pizzeria in Southville, in deep southern Illinois, is the second largest franchise of the chain in the United States. The headquarters is located in Phoenix, Arizona. Although the business is prospering, it has employee and managerial problems.

Each operation has one manager, an assistant manager, and from two to five night managers. The managers of each pizzeria work under an area supervisor. There are no systematic criteria for being a manager or becoming a manager trainee. The franchise has no formalized training period for the manager. No college education is required. The managers for whom the case observer worked during a 4-year period were relatively young (ages 24 to 27) and only one had completed college. They came from the ranks of night managers or assistant managers, or both. The night managers were chosen for their ability to perform the duties of the regular employees. The assistant managers worked a two-hour shift during the luncheon period five days a week to gain knowledge about bookkeeping and management. Those becoming managers remained at that level unless they expressed interest in investing in the business.

The employees were mostly college students, with a few high school students performing the less challenging jobs. Since Perfect Pizzeria was located in an area with few job opportunities, it had a relatively easy task of filling its employee quotas. All the employees, with the exception of the manager, were employed part-time. Consequently, they worked for less than the minimum wage.

The Perfect Pizzeria system is devised so that food and beverage costs and profits are set up according to a percentage. If the percentage of food unsold or damaged in any way is very low, the manager gets a bonus. If the percentage is high, the manager does not receive a bonus; rather, he or she receives only his or her normal salary.

There are many ways in which the percentage can fluctuate. Since the manager cannot be in the store twenty-four hours a day, some employees make up for their paychecks by helping themselves to the food. When a friend comes in to order a pizza, extra ingredients are put on the friend's pizza. Occasional nibbles by eighteen to twenty employees throughout the day at the meal table also raise the percentage figure. An occasional bucket of sauce may be spilled or a pizza accidentally burned. Sometimes the wrong size of pizza may be made.

In the event of an employee mistake or a burned pizza by the oven man, the expense is supposed to come from the individual. Because of peer pressure, the night manager seldom writes up a bill for the erring employee. Instead, the establishment takes the loss and the error goes unnoticed until the end of the month when the inventory is taken. That's when the manager finds out that the percentage is high and that there will be no bonus.

In the present instance, the manager took retaliatory measures. Previously, each employee was entitled to a free pizza, a salad, and all the soft drinks he or she could drink for every 6 hours of work. The manager raised this figure from 6 to 12 hours of work. However, the employees had received these 6-hour benefits for a long time. Therefore, they simply took advantage of the situation whenever the manager or the assistant was not in the building. Though the night manager theoretically had complete control of the operation in the evenings, he did not command the respect that the manager or assistant manager did. That was because he received the same pay as the regular employees; he could not reprimand other employees; and he was basically the same age or sometimes even younger than the other employees.

Thus, apathy grew within the pizzeria. There seemed to be a further separation between the manager and his workers, who had started out as a closely knit group. The manager made no attempt to alleviate the problem, because he felt it would iron itself out. Either the employees who were dissatisfied would quit or they would be content to put up with the new regulations. As it turned out, there was a rash of employee dismissals. The manager had no problem in filling the vacancies with new workers, but the loss of key personnel was costly to the business.

With the large turnover, the manager found he had to spend more time in the building, supervising and sometimes taking the place of inexperienced workers. This was in direct violation of the franchise regulation, which stated that a manager would act as a supervisor and at no time take part in the actual food preparation. Employees were not placed under strict supervision with the manager working alongside them. The operation no longer worked smoothly because of differences between the remaining experienced workers and the manager concerning the way in which a particular function should be performed.

Within a two-month period, the manager was again free to go back to his office and leave his subordinates in charge of the entire operation. During this two-month period, in spite of the differences between experienced workers and the managers, the percentage had returned to the previous low level and the manager received a bonus each month. The manager felt that his problems had been resolved and that conditions would remain the same, since the new personnel had been properly trained.

It didn't take long for the new employees to become influenced by the other employees. Immediately after the manager had returned to his supervisory role, the percentage began to rise. This time the manager took a bolder step. He cut out any benefits that the employees had—no free pizzas, salads, or drinks. With the job market at an even lower ebb than usual, most employees were forced to stay. The appointment of a new area supervisor made it impossible for the manager to "work behind the counter," since the supervisor was centrally located in Southville.

The manager tried still another approach to alleviate the rising percentage problem and maintain his bonus. He placed a notice on the bulletin board stating that if the percentage remained at a high level, a lie detector test would be given to all employees. All those found guilty of taking or purposefully wasting food or drinks would be immediately terminated. This did not have the desired effect on the employees, because they knew if they were all subjected to the test, all would be found guilty and the manager would have to dismiss all of them. This would leave him in a worse situation than ever.

Even before the following month's percentage was calculated, the manager knew it would be high. He had evidently received information from one of the night managers about the employees' feelings toward the notice. What he did not expect was that the percentage would reach an all-time high. That is the state of affairs at the present time.

Questions for Discussion

1   What are the major sources of dissatisfaction to the college student employees in Perfect Pizzeria?

2   What are the consequences of employees' dissatisfaction for the manager of the franchise?

3   Why isn't turnover even higher at Perfect Pizzeria?

4   What could the manager of the pizzeria do to increase job satisfaction?

Source: Adapted from a course assignment prepared by L. Neely for J. G. Hunt. In Dittrich, J. E., and Zawacki, R. A. (1981). *People and organizations.* Plano, TX: Business Publications, pp. 126–128. Used by permission of the authors and publishers.

Notes

1   Reitz, H. J. (1981). *Behavior in organizations* (2nd ed.). Homewood, IL: Irwin, 202.

2   Locke, E. A. (1976). The nature and causes of job satisfaction. In M. D. Dunnette (Ed.), *Handbook of industrial and organizational psychology.* Chicago: Rand McNally, 1297–1349.
   Terkel, Studs (1974). *Working.* New York: Pantheon Books.

3   Locke, E. A., *op. cit.,* 1321–1323.

4   Lawler, E. E., III, (1971). *Pay and organizational effectiveness.* New York: McGraw-Hill.
   Goodman, P. S. (1974). An examination of referents used in the evaluation of pay. *Organizational Behavior and Human Performance, 12,* 170–195.

5   Barnowe, J. T., Mangione, T. W., & Quinn, R. P. (1972). The relative importance of job facets, as indicated by an empirically derived model of job satisfaction. Unpublished report, University of Michigan Survey Research Center, Ann Arbor.
   Gilbreth, F. B., & Gilbreth, L. M. (1979). *Fatigue study.* New York: Macmillan.

6   Scott, W. E., Jr. (1966). Activation theory and task design. *Organizational Behavior and Human Performance, 1,* 3–30.

7   Mann, F. C., & Hoffman, L. R. (1960). *Automation and the worker.* New York: Holt.
   Walker, C. R., & Guest, R. H. (1952). *The man on the assembly line.* Cambridge: Harvard University Press.
   Walker, J., & Marriott, R. (1951). A study of some attitudes to factory work. *Occupational Psychology, 25,* 181–191.
   Andrews, J. (1983, May 6). Terminal tedium. *Wall Street Journal, 1,* 15.

8   Sirota, D. (1959). Some effects of promotional frustration on employees' understanding of, and attitudes toward, management. *Sociometry, 22,* 273–278.

9   Vroom, V. H. (1964). *Work and motivation.* New York: Wiley.

10   Fleishman, E. A., Harris, E. F., & Burtt, H. E. (1955). *Leadership and supervision in industry.* Columbus: Ohio State University, Bureau of Educational Research.

11   Coch, L., & French, J. R. P., Jr. (1948). Overcoming resistance to change. *Human Relations, 1,* 512–532.

12 Vroom, V. H., & Mann, F. C. (1960). Leader authoritarianism and employee attitudes. *Personnel Psychology, 13,* 125–140.

13 Walker, J., & Marriott, R., *op. cit.,* 181–191.

14 Renwick, P. A., Lawler, E. E., III, & the *Psychology Today* staff (1979). What you really want from your job. *Psychology Today, 11,* 53–64, 118.

15 Barnowe, J. T., Mangione, T. W., & Quinn, R. P., *loc. cit.*

16 Locke, E. A., *op. cit.,* 1324–1325.

17 Chadwick-Jones, J. K. (1969). *Automation and behavior.* New York: Wiley.

18 Lawler, E. E., III (1973). *Motivation in work organizations.* Monterey, CA: Brooks/Cole.

19 Gannon, M. J., & Noon, J. P. (1971). Management's critical deficiency. *Business Horizons, 14,* 49–56.

20 Herman, J. B. (1973). Are situational contingencies limiting job attitude-job performance relationships? *Organizational Behavior and Human Performance, 10,* 208–224.

21 Lawler, E. E., III, & Porter, L. W. (1967). The effect of performance on job satisfaction. *Industrial Relations, 7,* 20–28.

22 Cherrington, D. J., Reitz, H. J., & Scott, W. E., Jr. (1971). Effects of contingent and non-contingent rewards on the relationship between satisfaction and task performance. *Journal of Applied Psychology, 55,* 531–536.

23 Arnold, H. J., & Feldman, D. C. (1982). A multivariate model of job turnover. *Journal of Applied Psychology, 67,* 350–360.

24 Breaugh, J. A. (1981). Predicting absenteeism from prior absenteeism and work attitudes. *Journal of Applied Psychology, 66,* 555–560.

25 Smith, F. J. (1977). Work attitudes as predictors of attendance on a specific day. *Journal of Applied Psychology, 62,* 16–19.

26 *Business Week,* June 12, 1978, 143–146.

27 Brett, J. B. (1980, Spring). Why employees want unions. *Organizational Dynamics.* 47–59.
Schriesheim, C. A. (1978). Job satisfaction, attitudes toward unions, and voting in a union representation election. *Journal of Applied Psychology, 6,* 548–552.

28 Getman, J. G., Goldberg, S. B., & Herman, J. B. (1976). *Union representation elections: Law and reality.* New York: Russell Sage Foundation.

29 Hamner, W. C., & Smith, F. J. (1978). Work attitudes as predictors of unionization activity. *Journal of Applied Psychology, 63,* 415–421.

30   Weaver, C. N. (1980). Job satisfaction in the United States in the 1970's. *Journal of Applied Psychology, 65,* 364–367.

31   *Work in America* (1973). (Report of the Secretary of Health, Education and Welfare). Boston: MIT Press, 14–16.

32   Weaver, *op. cit.,* 364–367.

33   Weaver, *op. cit.,* 364–367.

34   *Work in America, op. cit.,* 14–16.

35   *Business Week,* February 20, 1978, 78.

36   *Work in America, op. cit.,* 44–45.

37   Longworth, R. C., & Neikirk, B. (1977, September 15). The changing American worker. *Chicago Tribune,* 1, 16.

38   *Business Week*/Harris Poll: Middle managers still think positively. (1983, April 25). *Business Week,* 64.

39   *Work in America, op. cit.,* 1–28.

40   Smith, P. C., Kendall, L. M., & Hulin, C. L. (1969). *The measurement of satisfaction in work and retirement.* Chicago: Rand McNally.

41   Katterberg, R., Smith, F. J., & Hoy, S. (1977). Language, time, and person effects on attitude scale translations. *Journal of Applied Psychology, 62,* 385–391.

42   Weiss, D. J., Dawis, R. V., England, G. W., & Lofquist, L. H. (1967). *Manual for the Minnesota Satisfaction Questionnaire* (Minnesota studies in vocational rehabilitation, Vol. 22). Minneapolis: University of Minnesota Industrial Relations Center.

43   Porter, L. W. (1961). A study of perceived need satisfaction in bottom and middle management jobs. *Journal of Applied Psychology, 45,* 1–10.

44   Dunham, R. B., & Smith, F. J. (1979). *Organizational surveys.* Glenview, IL: Scott, Foresman.

45   Roberts, K. H., & Savage, F. (1973). Twenty questions: Utilizing job satisfaction measures. *California Management Review, 15,* 21–28.

46   Myers, M. S. (1967). How attitude surveys can help you manage. *Training and Development Journal, 21,* 34–41.

47   *Business Week,* October 16, 1978, 168–171.

48   Ibid.

49   Ibid.

50   Dunham & Smith, *loc. cit.*

51   Smith, F. J., & Porter, L. W. (1977). What do executives really think about their organizations? *Organizational Dynamics, 6,* 68–80.

52   Brett, *op. cit.,* 57.

53   Hall, Trish (1984, October 23). Demanding PepsiCo is attempting to make work nicer for managers. *Wall Street Journal,* 31.

54   Dunham & Smith, *loc. cit.*

Part 3

Interpersonal and Group Behavior

■	Chapter 5	Leadership
■	Chapter 6	Communication
■	Chapter 7	Groups in Organizations
■	Chapter 8	Intergroup Conflict

Leadership

CHAPTER OUTLINE

The Nature of Leadership

Trait Theories of Leadership

Behavioral Theories of Leadership

Fiedler's Contingency Theory

Path-Goal Theory

The Vroom and Yetton Model

Current Issues in Leadership

Keys to Effective Management

Review Questions

*T*he term *leadership* tends to conjure up in our minds pictures of great military commanders such as General Patton, stirring politicians and statesmen such as Winston Churchill, or charismatic leaders of national movements such as Gandhi. But while people such as these were undoubtedly great leaders, they are only the most visible and obvious examples of leadership in action. In fact, every time a person attempts to get other people to do something that the person wants them to do, he or she is functioning as a leader. Seen in this light, leadership is exercised in organizations from the chief executive officer right down to the first-level supervisor on the shop floor. Because leadership is so pervasive and important to the effective functioning of organizations, it is obviously essential to understand what factors determine the effectiveness of leadership in organizations.[1]

We begin our discussion in this chapter by looking briefly at the nature of leadership in organizations. What exactly do we mean by the term *leadership* and what does it imply? We then turn to what are known as **trait theories** of leadership, theories that have sought to identify traits, or personality characteristics, that distinguish leaders from followers and good leaders from poor leaders. Next, we discuss several attempts to describe the **behavioral styles** of effective leaders. These approaches have sought to identify the activities that effective leaders engage in and that ineffective leaders do not. We then deal with the most recent approaches to understanding leadership in organizations, the ***contingency theories*** of leadership. These theories seek to understand what kinds of leaders and what kinds of leadership behavior are most likely to be effective in different kinds of situations. The basic assumption of contingency theories of leadership is that what constitutes effective leadership depends upon (or, in other words, is *contingent* upon) the nature of the situation. By combining the insights offered by each of the different theories and approaches to leadership, we arrive at a variety of important implications for more effective organizational leadership.

The Nature of Leadership

Many attempts have been made to come up with a definition of ***leadership.*** In fact, there are almost as many definitions of leadership as there are researchers who have studied the topic (over 3,000 empirical studies of leadership have been carried out).[2] For our purposes, we will define leadership as an ***influence process;*** leadership involves the exercise of influence on the part of the leader over the behavior of one or more other people. In other words, leadership essentially involves one person (the leader) consciously trying to get other people (the followers) to do something that he or she wants them to do. The study of leadership then becomes an attempt to understand how a leader comes to have influence over the thoughts, feelings, and actions of followers. What is it about the nature of the leader, the nature of followers, the organizational situation, or the leader's behavior that results in the leader's capacity to influence followers? And what is it that ultimately results in some leaders being labeled as effective and others as ineffective?

Sources of Leader Influence on Followers

What provides a leader with the capacity to influence followers? Why will subordinates respond to the influence attempts of a leader by doing what the leader intends or wishes them to do? In other words, what is the source of the leader's power over subordinates? Five distinct sources of leader power or influence have been identified.[3] Any particular leader may have at his or her disposal any combination of these different sources of power.

1   ***Reward power*** refers to the leader's capacity to reward followers. To the extent that a leader possesses and controls rewards that are valued by subordinates, the leader's power increases. Rewards at a leader's disposal fall into two categories. Rewards such as praise, recognition, and attention are sources of *personal power* possessed by the leader as an individual. In addition, a leader also usually controls certain organizational rewards, such as

pay raises, promotions, and other perquisites. These are sources of power that depend upon the leader's *position* in the organization.

2   *Coercive power* is the flip side of reward power and refers to the leader's capacity to coerce or punish followers. Sources of coercive power also break down into personal and positional components. Leaders personally possess coercive power to the extent that followers experience criticism or lack of recognition from their leader as unpleasant or punishing. In addition, leaders possess coercive power to the extent that their position permits them to administer organizational sources of punishment (such as demotion, withholding of pay increases, or firing) to followers.

3   *Legitimate power* refers to the power a leader possesses as a result of occupying a particular position or role in the organization. In every organization, certain types of requests and directions issued by leaders to subordinates are viewed to be legitimate and valid. Subordinates are obligated to comply with such requests because of the norms, policies, and procedures accepted as legitimate by all members of the organization. Legitimate power is clearly a function of the leader's position in the organization and is completely independent of any of the leader's personal characteristics.

4   *Expert power* refers to power that a leader possesses as a result of his or her knowledge and expertise regarding the tasks to be performed by subordinates. Subordinates are more likely to respond positively to a leader's attempts to influence their behavior if they view the leader as competent and in possession of knowledge and information regarding effective task performance that they themselves lack. The possession of expert power by a leader obviously depends upon the personal characteristics of the leader (i.e., his or her personal expertise) and is not determined by the formal position that the leader occupies in the organization.

5   *Referent power* is dependent upon the extent to which subordinates identify with, look up to, and wish to emulate the leader. The more that subordinates admire and identify with the leader, the greater the leader's referent power over subordinates. Referent power, like expert power, is totally dependent upon the personal characteristics of the leader and does not depend directly upon the leader's formal organizational position.

These five distinct sources of a leader's power to influence subordinates are summarized in Figure 5-1. Two of the sources (reward power and coercive power) have both personal and positional components. Legitimate power depends solely on the leader's position, while expert and referent power are determined solely by the leader's personal characteristics. Since legitimate power and the components of reward and coercive power involving organizational outcomes such as raises and firing are dependent upon the leader's position in the organization, these are sometimes referred to as sources of a leader's *position power* or *organizational power.* On the other hand, expert power, refer-

Figure 5-1 Total power available to a leader is determined by both personal and organizational factors.

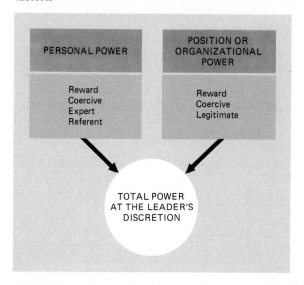

ent power, and the components of reward and coercive power involving personal outcomes such as praise and criticism are dependent upon the leader's personal characteristics and hence are often referred to as sources of a leader's *personal power.*

Naturally, the more sources of power leaders have at their disposal, the more likely that they will be successful in influencing subordinates to do those things they would like them to do. However, possessing a high degree of power in no way assures that a leader will be effective. Leadership effectiveness will depend not only upon the leader's power, but also upon what the leader uses his or her influence to encourage subordinates to do.[4] It is also important to note that a significant proportion of the leader's potential power derives from his or her own personal characteristics and style. Thus, it would be a mistake to assume that anyone can become an influential leader purely on the basis of the power inherent in the position he or she occupies in the organization. Such a viewpoint ignores a large segment of the potential sources of power and influence available to a leader.

Trait Theories of Leadership

The prevailing assumption among early researchers interested in leadership was that leaders are born, not made. This approach has also been characterized as the "great person" theory of leadership. It was assumed that some people are set apart from others by virtue of their possession of some quality or qualities of "greatness" and that it is such great persons who become leaders.

This approach to leadership implies that understanding leadership requires the identification and measurement of those personal characteristics, or ***traits,*** that differentiate leaders (the "great") from followers (the "not so great"). A considerable amount of research has been conducted in an effort to identify these traits. The research has focused on a wide variety of leader traits, including personality characteristics (e.g., adaptability, dominance, self-confidence), physical characteristics (e.g., height, weight, appearance), and ability (e.g., intelligence, task expertise, sensitivity in dealing with others).

A comprehensive review of the results of 124 studies of leadership traits published around 1950 indicated that leaders could be differentiated from nonleaders on the basis of traits such as intelligence, alertness to the needs of others, understanding of the task, initiative and persistence in dealing with problems, self-confidence, and the desire to accept responsibility and occupy a position of dominance and control.[5] While these results are consistent with the notion that leaders differ from nonleaders in their personal traits in ways that we might expect, the results were not especially strong. In particular, the results tended to vary from situation to situation, leading to the conclusion that a person does not become a leader only by virtue of the possession of some combination of traits. Rather, the pattern of personal characteristics of the leader must also fit effectively with the characteristics, activities, and goals of the followers.

Later research on trait theories of leadership focused more specifically on predicting leadership effectiveness in *managerial* settings, and the results were much more encouraging. The results of this more recent research are contained in Table 5-1. The table summarizes the personality traits, abilities, and social skills found most frequently to be characteristic of effective and successful leaders. The findings suggest that leaders are characterized by a strong desire for responsibility and task completion, vigorous persistence in the pursuit of goals, and originality in solving problems. Leaders also tend to take the initiative in social situations; they are highly self-confident and are able to influence the behavior of other people. Finally, leaders are willing to accept the consequences of their own decisions and actions, are capable of tolerating frustration and delay, and are able to absorb considerable levels of stress.[6]

While it is clear, then, that leader traits alone cannot completely explain leadership effectiveness, it is equally clear that such traits are not irrelevant to effective leadership. Since all leadership situations share certain common characteristics, research should continue to attempt to identify the specific traits required for effectiveness in all leadership situations.[7] While a focus on leadership traits alone cannot explain all we need to know regarding effective leadership in organizations, leadership traits are also far from irrelevant to such an understanding.[8] A balanced and complete approach to leadership effectiveness in organizations must take into account the personal traits and skills of the leader.

TABLE 5-1		

Personality Traits, Abilities, and Social Skills Most Frequently Associated with Effective Leadership

Personality traits	*Abilities*	*Social skills*
Adaptability	Intelligence	Ability to enlist cooperation
Adjustment (normality)	Judgment and decisiveness	Administrative ability
Aggressiveness and assertiveness	Knowledge	Cooperativeness
Dominance	Fluency of speech	Popularity and prestige
Emotional balance and control		Sociability (interpersonal skills)
Independence (nonconformity)		Social participation
Originality and creativity		Tact and diplomacy
Personal integrity (ethical conduct)		
Self-confidence		

Source: Reprinted with permission of Macmillan Publishing Co., Inc., from Stogdill, R. M. (1974). *Handbook of leadership: A survey of theory and research.* Copyright © 1974 by The Free Press, a division of Macmillan Publishing Co., Inc.

Behavioral Theories of Leadership

Trait theories of leadership focus upon personal characteristics of the leader and try to explain leadership effectiveness on the basis of what type of person the leader is. An alternative approach is to focus instead on what the leader actually *does* when he or she is dealing with subordinates. What are known as behavioral theories of leadership effectiveness focus upon leader *behavior* and seek to understand the relationship between what the leader does and how subordinates react emotionally (their levels of satisfaction with work) and behaviorally (their job performance).

The task facing researchers adopting this perspective was twofold. First, they had to develop some method of characterizing or describing *patterns* of leader behavior. It is obviously impossible to study links between every particular thing that a leader does and the way subordinates respond to each aspect of a leader's behavior. Consequently, general patterns had to be sought that could be used to characterize and describe leadership behavior, and methods had to be developed for classifying leaders on the basis of the patterns identified. The second part of the task was to study the relationship between the various patterns of leader behavior and the performance and satisfaction of subordinates. While several different behavioral theories of leadership have been developed, we will focus our attention most closely upon the theory developed at the Ohio State University since it is most representative of this approach to leadership and has generated the largest body of empirical research.

The Ohio State Studies

Researchers at Ohio State University identified two distinct, relatively broad categories of leader behavior. The two categories were labeled *consideration* and *initiating structure.*

Consideration

Consideration refers to the extent to which a leader is considerate of subordinates and concerned about the quality of his or her relationship with subordinates. Among the specific examples of leader behavior included in the consideration dimension are friendliness, consultation with subordinates, recognition of subordinates, open communication with subordinates, supportiveness, and representation of subordinate interests.

Initiating Structure

Initiating structure refers to the extent to which a leader is task-oriented and concerned with utilizing resources and personnel effectively in order to accomplish group goals. Specific types of leader behavior included in the initiating structure dimension include planning, coordinating, directing, problem solving, clarifying subordinate roles, criticizing poor work, and pressuring subordinates to perform more effectively. The nature of these two dimensions of leader behavior is summarized in Table 5-2.

Relationship to Effectiveness

Consideration and initiating structure are thought of as two relatively independent dimensions of a leader's behavior.[9] In other words, a leader with a high degree of consideration need not necessarily be low on initiating structure. Similarly a leader who is characterized by a high level of initiating structure may be high or low on consideration. Figure 5-2 plots these two dimen-

---

TABLE 5-2

Examples of Behaviors Associated with Leader Consideration and Initiating Structure

Leader consideration	*Leader initiating structure*
Friendliness	Planning
Consultation with subordinates	Coordinating
Recognition of subordinates	Directing
Open communication with subordinates	Problem solving
Supportiveness	Clarifying subordinates' roles
Representation of subordinates' interests	Criticizing poor work
	Pressuring subordinates

Figure 5-2 The Ohio State dimensions of consideration and initiating structure.

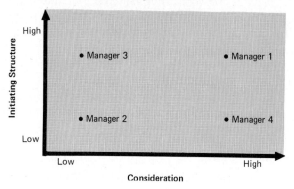

sions of leadership behavior in the form of a grid wherein the positions of four hypothetical managers are plotted. Manager 1, who rates high on both dimensions, has a leadership style characterized by a high degree of directing and controlling subordinates *and* a high level of concern and warmth toward employees. Manager 2 shows neither of these characteristics in his leadership style and would probably be characterized as a "laissez-faire" or a "do nothing" manager. Manager 3 does a lot of planning, directing, and so on, but does little to show his concern or interest in subordinates. Manager 4 is just the opposite of manager 3. He is very friendly and supportive toward his subordinates, but does little to control, direct, or plan their work.

The key question that must be addressed is: Which style of leadership is most effective? As we would expect, leaders who rate high on consideration tend to have subordinates who are more satisfied, who express fewer grievances, and who stay with the organization longer.[10] However, when we turn to the issue of subordinate *performance,* the pattern of results is much less clear-cut. It does not appear that being either high or low on consideration or initiating structure alone has a straightforward impact on the performance of subordinates.[11] There is some evidence, however, to indicate that leaders exhibiting high levels of *both* consideration and initiating structure generate higher levels of subordinate performance.[12] Thus, the main conclusion that can be drawn from the behavioral theories of leadership is that a more considerate leadership style will cause subordinates to be more satisfied. The conclusions that can be drawn regarding which style of leadership will result in the highest levels of performance by subordinates are much more tentative, with some indication of the desirability of a style characterized by high levels of both leadership dimensions.

One reason for the lack of a clear-cut relationship between leadership style and subordinate performance may be that leaders do not consistently employ a single leadership style. Evidence is accumulating that a leader may adjust his or her leadership style to the demands of the particular situation being faced[13]

Figure 5-3   Leadership effectiveness depends on a fit between the leader's behavior and the demands of the situation.

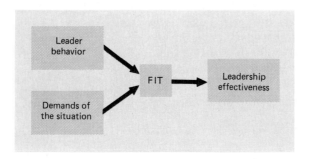

and may behave differently toward different subordinates.[14] A second reason for the lack of conclusive results is that it is highly unlikely that there exists *any* leadership style that will be universally effective. Rather than trying to identify *the* effective leadership style, perhaps we should instead be trying to understand which *different* leadership styles are most appropriate to different types of organizations, different types of tasks, different types of subordinates, and so on. In other words, we need to understand the complexities involved in achieving a "fit" between the leader's behavior and the leadership demands of the situation. This approach leads us to what are labeled ***contingency theories of leadership.***

The basic idea behind contingency theories of leadership is that leadership effectiveness depends upon the existence of a "fit" between the leader's behavior and the demands of the situation. This basic notion is diagramed in Figure 5-3. The contingency theories that we will be discussing draw attention to some specific dimensions of leader behavior and some specific characteristics of leadership situations in order to make predictions regarding the conditions under which a good fit will occur.

Fiedler's Contingency Theory

The first contingency theory we'll discuss was developed by Fred Fiedler.[15] Fiedler's theory consists of (1) a method of classifying leaders; (2) a framework for classifying leadership situations; and (3) a model specifying which types of leaders are best suited to which types of situations.

The Leader

According to Fiedler's contingency theory, leaders can be classified in terms of the extent to which they are either relationship-oriented or task-oriented. A ***relationship-oriented*** leader is primarily motivated to establish close interpersonal relationships with subordinates; he or she emphasizes socializing with subordinates and behaves toward them in a considerate and supportive manner. Achievement of task objectives is only a secondary motive and only takes on importance when the primary affiliation motive is satisfied. A **task-oriented** leader, on the other hand, is primarily motivated by task accomplishment. Such a leader's main concern is with doing a good job; establishing good interpersonal relationships with subordinates will only receive attention if the work is going well and no serious problems exist. A questionnaire known as the Least Preferred Coworker (LPC) Scale is used to classify leaders in terms of their relationship-orientation versus their task-orientation.[16]

The Situation

According to Fiedler, managerial situations can be classified on a continuum ranging from situations that are very favorable to the leader to situations very unfavorable for the leader. A situation is classified as favorable for the leader to the extent that the situation gives the leader influence and control over subordinate performance. Three factors determine how favorable any managerial situation is for the leader.

1 *Leader-member relations.* When the relationship between the leader and followers is good and the leader can count on the loyalty and support of followers, the leader's influence and control are high. Poor leader-member relations, on the other hand, impair the leader's control and contribute to a more unfavorable situation for the leader.

2 *Task structure.* A high degree of task structure contributes to a favorable situation for the leader, since the leader can more easily monitor and influ-

Figure 5-4 Fiedler's classification of managerial situations in terms of how favorable they are for the leader.

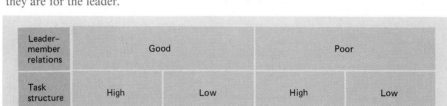

Leader–member relations	Good				Poor			
Task structure	High		Low		High		Low	
Position power	Strong	Weak	Strong	Weak	Strong	Weak	Strong	Weak
Situations	I	II	III	IV	V	VI	VII	VIII

Very favorable ⬅━━━━━━━━➡ Very unfavorable

[*Source:* Fiedler, F. E. (1967). *A theory of leadership effectiveness.* New York: McGraw-Hill. Used by permission of McGraw-Hill Book Company.]

ence subordinates' behavior on a highly structured task. When a task is unstructured, the leader is less likely to be sure of the best way of performing the task, and disagreements with subordinates regarding how to accomplish the task are likely. As a result, the leader's ability to control and direct subordinates is reduced.

3 *Position power.*   The greater the legitimate authority associated with the leader's position, and the greater the range of rewards and punishments at the leader's disposal as a result of his or her position, the greater the leader's control over subordinates and the more favorable the situation is to the leader.

These three factors can be used to construct a continuum of situational favorability. This continuum is constructed by determining whether leader-member relations are good or poor, task structure is high or low, and position power is strong or weak. The result is the classification of eight distinct types of leadership situations, varying from very favorable to very unfavorable, diagramed in Figure 5-4.

The Model

When Fiedler examined the relationships among type of leader, situational favorability, and task performance, the pattern diagramed in Figure 5-5 emerged. Task-oriented leaders turned out to be most effective in highly favorable and highly unfavorable situations. When the favorability of the situation is only moderate (the central segment of Figure 5-5), task-oriented leaders are not as effective. Relationship-oriented leaders, on the other hand, exhibit the opposite pattern of results. They are effective in situations of moderate favorability, but less effective in both highly favorable and highly unfavorable situations.

The explanation for this pattern is as follows. First, the effectiveness of task-oriented leaders in highly unfavorable situations is easily explained, since

Figure 5-5   Relationships among leadership style, situational favorability, and performance effectiveness according to Fiedler's contingency theory.

		SITUATIONAL FAVORABILITY		
		Very Favorable	Moderately Favorable	Very Unfavorable
PERFORMANCE EFFECTIVENESS	High	Task-oriented leader	Relationship-oriented leader	Task-oriented leader
	Low	Relationship-oriented leader	Task-oriented leader	Relationship-oriented leader

such situations would clearly require the directive, task-oriented leadership approach. Task-oriented leaders can also be seen to be suitable to highly favorable situations, since they would respond very positively to a situation that facilitated the accomplishment of performance goals by the work group. The effectiveness of relationship-oriented leaders in moderately favorable situations is less easy to explain. The most plausible explanation is probably that the relationship orientation of leaders may help overcome poor leader-member relations and may facilitate a participative approach to the clarification of ambiguous task demands.[17]

A great deal of research has been carried out on the validity of Fiedler's contingency theory. The majority of findings have been supportive of the theory.[18] While not every prediction of Fiedler's theory has been supported,[19] the theory represents an important contribution to our understanding of leadership effectiveness. For the first time we have a theory that: (1) explicitly recognizes that leadership effectiveness is jointly determined by the fit between the leader and the nature of the situation; and (2) makes some specific predictions regarding precisely what characteristics of leaders and what characteristics of the situation are the critical factors determining this fit, and hence the effectiveness of the leader.

Path-Goal Theory

The path-goal theory of leadership is based upon research by Martin Evans[20] and by Robert House and his colleagues.[21] The basic idea behind the theory is that a leader can influence the satisfaction, motivation, and performance of subordinates primarily by (1) providing subordinates with rewards; (2) making the attainment of those rewards contingent upon the accomplishment of performance goals; and (3) helping subordinates obtain rewards by clarifying the paths to the goals (i.e., helping subordinates understand exactly what they must do to obtain rewards) and making these paths easier to travel (i.e., providing subordinates with coaching, direction, and assistance when needed).[22] The theory argues that in order to accomplish the foregoing, a leader will have to engage in different types of leadership behavior, depending upon the nature and demands of the particular situation.

Styles of Leader Behavior

Path-goal theory identifies four distinct styles of leader behavior.

1   *Directive leadership* characterizes a leader who lets subordinates know what is expected of them, gives specific guidance regarding what is to be done and how it should be done, and ensures that his or her role as leader of the group is clearly understood. Such a leader also schedules work to be done, maintains definite standards of performance, and encourages group members to follow standard rules and regulations.

2 *Supportive leadership* characterizes a friendly and approachable leader who shows concern for the needs and well-being of subordinates. A supportive leader treats subordinates as equals and frequently does little things to make the work more pleasant and enjoyable.

3 *Participative leadership* characterizes a leader who, when faced with a decision, consults with subordinates, solicits their suggestions, and takes ideas seriously in arriving at a decision.

4 *Achievement-oriented leadership* constantly emphasizes excellence in performance and simultaneously displays confidence that subordinates can and will achieve the high standards that are set. Such a leader sets challenging performance goals and encourages subordinates to take personal responsibility for the accomplishment of those goals.

Contingency Factors

Path-goal theory argues that no single style of leader behavior will universally result in high levels of subordinate motivation and satisfaction. Instead, the theory suggests that different types of situations require different styles of leader behavior. Two sets of situational factors are addressed by the theory: (1) the personal characteristics of subordinates; and (2) the characteristics of the work environment facing subordinates.

Personal Characteristics

A number of personal characteristics of subordinates are thought to influence the extent to which subordinates will experience a leader's behavior as acceptable and satisfying.

1 *Ability.*   When subordinates perceive their ability to be low, they are likely to find directive leadership acceptable and to see it as helping them to perform more effectively in the future. However, when subordinates perceive their ability to be high, directive leadership is likely to be perceived as unacceptable and is unlikely to have any positive effects upon satisfaction or motivation.

2 *Locus of control.*   As discussed in Chapter 2, people who view what happens to them as being under their own direct control and influence are referred to as having an *internal* locus of control; those who view what happens to them as determined by circumstances and events outside themselves and beyond their own control are referred to as having an *external* locus of control. Research indicates that internals find a participative leadership style to be both acceptable and satisfying, while externals tend to respond more positively to directive leadership.[23]

3 *Needs and motives.*   The particular needs, motives, and personality characteristics of subordinates may influence their acceptance of and satisfaction with different leadership styles. For example, subordinates with a strong need for achievement may react positively to achievement-oriented

leadership, while those with a strong need for affiliation might respond more positively to a supportive or participative leadership style.

Characteristics of the Work Environment

Certain characteristics of the work environment influence the extent to which the various leadership styles will have a positive impact upon subordinate motivation and performance. Three important contingency factors in the work environment are:

1 Subordinates' tasks

2 The formal authority system of the organization

3 The primary work group

An effective leadership style (in terms of motivating subordinates) is one that complements the subordinates' environment by providing direction, assistance, and support that would otherwise be missing. Thus, if subordinates are working on a highly ambiguous task in an organization with few set policies and procedures, the theory predicts that a directive leadership style will increase motivation and performance by helping subordinates understand what they need to do in order to perform effectively. On the other hand, the theory predicts that if subordinates are working on a highly routine and structured task in an organization with elaborate rules and regulations, directive leadership will not facilitate performance but will simply create frustration and

---

TABLE 5-3

Summary of Path-Goal Relationships

Leader behavior	*and*	*Contingency factors*	*cause*	*Subordinate attitudes and behavior*
Directive		Subordinate characteristics:		Job satisfaction:
Supportive		Ability		Job rewards
Achievement-oriented		Locus of control		Acceptance of leader:
Participative		Needs and motives		Leader rewards
		Environmental factors:		Motivational behavior:
		The task		Effort–performance
		Formal authority system		Performance–rewards
		Primary work group		

Source: Adapted from House, R. J., & Mitchell, T. R. (1974). Path-goal theory of leadership. *Journal of Contemporary Business,* 3. Used by permission.

resentment among subordinates. According to path-goal theory, the leader must analyze the nature of the situation being faced by subordinates and then choose a leadership style that, in light of this situational analysis, provides the direction and support to subordinates that would otherwise be missing.

The basic tenets of path-goal theory—that leader behavior and contingency factors combine to cause subordinate attitudes and behavior—are summarized in Table 5-3. The theory provides a useful framework for thinking about leadership in organizations by drawing attention not only to the existence of alternative leadership styles, but also to a variety of characteristics of subordinates and of leadership situations that will influence the effectiveness of any given style of leadership.[24]

The Vroom and Yetton Model

Decision making constitutes a central component of any manager's job. A critical determinant of leadership effectiveness therefore will be the extent to which the leader is an effective decision maker. Vroom and his colleagues have developed a theory that focuses explicitly upon the decision-making component of the leader's role.[25] Consistent with the contingency viewpoint, the theory tries to identify those circumstances in which different styles of decision making are most effective.

Alternative Decision Styles

Vroom and Yetton identify five alternative decision styles that may be adopted by a leader. These five decision styles are summarized in Table 5-4. Two of the alternatives (AI and AII) involve an *autocratic* decision style, since the leader does not tell subordinates about the problem that he or she is dealing with. In the AI style the leader makes the decision without any inputs whatsoever from subordinates, while in AII the leader may ask subordinates for specific pieces of information prior to making the decision. In the two *consultative* styles (CI and CII) the leader consults with subordinates by sharing the problem with them and asking for their inputs. In the CI style the leader consults with subordinates individually, while in CII the leader consults with subordinates in a group meeting. However, in all the autocratic and the consultative styles it is important to note that the leader makes the final decision alone. In the fifth style (GII), the leader employs a *group consensus* approach to decision making and shares both responsibility and authority for arriving at a decision with his or her subordinates.

Decision Effectiveness

According to the Vroom and Yetton contingency theory there are three critical components that influence the overall effectiveness of a decision: quality, acceptance, and time.

TABLE 5-4

The Five Alternative Decision Styles of the Vroom-Yetton Model

AI   You solve the problem or make the decision yourself using the information available to you at the present time.

AII   You obtain any necessary information from subordinates, then decide on a solution to the problem yourself. You may or may not tell subordinates the purpose of your questions or give information about the problem or decision you are working on. The input provided by them is clearly in response to your request for specific information. They do not play a role in the definition of the problem or in generating or evaluating alternative solutions.

CI   You share the problem with the relevant subordinates individually, getting their ideas and suggestions without bringing them together as a group. Then you make the decision. This decision may or may not reflect your subordinates' influence.

CII   You share the problem with your subordinates in a group meeting. In this meeting you obtain their ideas and suggestions. Then, you make the decision, which may or may not reflect your subordinates' influence.

GII   You share the problem with your subordinates as a group. Together you generate and evaluate alternatives and attempt to reach agreement (consensus) on a solution. Your role is much like that of chairman, coordinating the discussion, keeping it focused on the problem, and making sure that the critical issues are discussed. You can provide the group with information or ideas that you have but you do not try to "press" them to adopt "your" solution and are willing to accept and implement any solution that has the support of the entire group.

Source: Vroom, V. H., & Jago, A. G. (1978). On the validity of the Vroom-Yetton model. *Journal of Applied Psychology, 63,* 151–162. Copyright © 1978 by the American Psychological Association. Reprinted by permission of the publisher and authors.

Decision Quality   Problem situations differ in the extent to which they possess a *quality* requirement. A situation is said to possess a quality requirement if it is clear that the problem is important and that alternative decisions or solutions to the problem will differ from one another in the extent to which they achieve the goals of the decision maker. Typical situations that possess a quality requirement are decisions regarding strategic planning, setting of goals and priorities, determination of work procedures, solution of technical problems, and assignment of tasks to subordinates of differing ability. Decision situations that do not possess a quality requirement are those in which the decision concerns a trivial matter (e.g., which brand of paper clips to purchase) and those in which all of the alternatives are approximately equally desirable (e.g., which subordinate to assign to a project when all subordinates are equally competent).

Decision Acceptance   Problem situations also differ in regard to the importance of decision acceptance. *Decision acceptance* refers to the extent to which subordinates will understand, accept, and commit themselves to implementing a particular decision. Decision acceptance is especially critical in those situations in which the leader is dependent upon subordinates for implementation. Even if a decision is the best possible in terms of its objective decision quality, the decision will not be effective if it is not implemented. For example, a manager in the head office of a company may make certain decisions regarding various policies and procedures to be followed by managers working in branch offices. However, if the branch office managers do not accept these decisions they may simply ignore the new policies and procedures and continue to operate as they had in the past.

Timeliness

Finally, problem situations vary in terms of the time available for decision making. ***Timeliness*** refers to the extent to which decisions need to be made quickly or according to a fixed schedule. It is neither efficient nor effective for leaders and subordinates to invest more time than is necessary in arriving at acceptable decisions of high quality. This implies the desirability of choosing a decision-making style that minimizes the time required to arrive at a decision. For example, if a bid on a project must be submitted by a certain deadline, any decision on what the bid should be that is arrived at after the deadline is of no value whatsoever.

Choosing a Decision Style

According to the Vroom and Yetton theory, the likelihood that an effective decision will be made is heavily determined by the decision style adopted by the leader. However, the theory does not see the leader as having only a single approach to making decisions or dealing with subordinates. Instead, the Vroom and Yetton theory views the leader as highly flexible and as capable of adjusting his or her decision style to the demands of the *situation*. Thus, different types of problem situations require different types of decision styles, and the effective leader must be capable of diagnosing a problem situation in order to choose the decision style that is most likely to result in an effective decision.

The model specifies a set of seven diagnostic questions that a manager can employ in determining which decision style to adopt in any given situation. These diagnostic questions are contained in Figure 5-6, along with the decision tree developed by Vroom and Yetton that guides the manager to a "feasible set" of decision-making styles. The feasible set of decision styles for a problem situation consists of all those decision styles that do not violate any of the rules that are designed to protect decision quality and decision acceptance in the model. When the feasible set contains more than one alternative, the leader must choose one style on the basis of some additional criterion. For example, the leader may choose the least time-consuming decision style. The time required to implement each decision style increases from AI (the least time-consuming) to GII (the most time-consuming). On the other hand, a leader interested in developing his or her subordinates' decision-making skills might choose always to employ the most participative feasible decision style.

The Vroom and Yetton decision-tree flowchart begins by asking managers the first of the seven diagnostic questions (labeled question A). Managers then follow the lines on the flowchart according to their answers ("yes" and "no") to each of the diagnostic questions. Each time a square is encountered on the chart, managers refer to the question corresponding to the letter above the

Figure 5-6 Vroom and Yetton decision process flowchart.

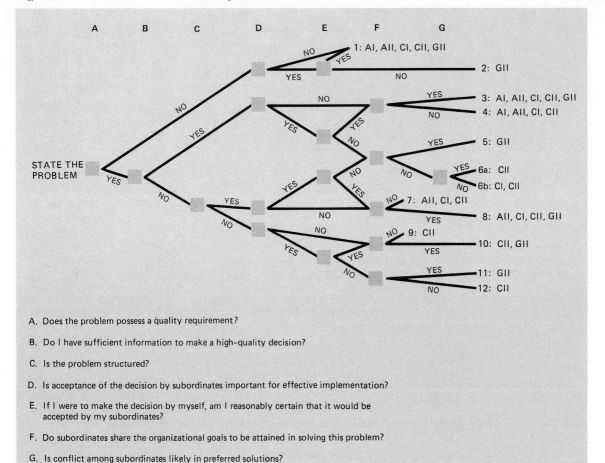

A. Does the problem possess a quality requirement?

B. Do I have sufficient information to make a high-quality decision?

C. Is the problem structured?

D. Is acceptance of the decision by subordinates important for effective implementation?

E. If I were to make the decision by myself, am I reasonably certain that it would be accepted by my subordinates?

F. Do subordinates share the organizational goals to be attained in solving this problem?

G. Is conflict among subordinates likely in preferred solutions?

square and continue on, based upon their answers, until an endpoint is reached that specifies the feasible set of alternative decision styles for the problem situation. Box 5-1 contains an example of how the decision flowchart would be applied to a managerial problem.

Overall, the Vroom and Yetton model is a promising development.[26] It provides a model of leadership and decision making that is based upon sound theory and research and that also has the advantage of being presented in a form that permits relatively easy and direct application by the practicing manager.

BOX 5-1

An Example of the Application of the Vroom-Yetton Model to a Managerial Problem Requiring a Decision

You are manufacturing manager in a large electronics plant. The company's management has always been searching for ways of increasing efficiency. They have recently installed new machines and put in a new, simplified work system, but to the surprise of everyone, including yourself, the expected increase in productivity has not been realized. In fact, production has begun to drop, quality has fallen off, and the number of employee separations has risen.

You do not believe that there is anything wrong with the machines. You have had reports from other companies who are using them and they confirm this opinion. You have also had representatives from the firm that built the machines go over them, and they report that they are operating at peak efficiency.

You suspect that some parts of the new work system may be responsible for the change, but this view is not widely shared by your immediate subordinates, who are four first-line supervisors, each in charge of a section, and your supply manager. The drop in production has been variously attributed to poor training of the operators, lack of an adequate system of financial incentives, and poor morale. Clearly, this is an issue about which there is considerable depth of feeling within individuals and potential disagreement among your subordinates.

This morning you received a phone call from your division manager. He had just received your production figures for the last six months and was calling to express his concern. He indicated that the problem is yours to solve in any way that you think best, but that he would like to know within a week what steps you plan to take.

You share your division manager's concern with the falling productivity and know that your men are also concerned. The problem is to decide what steps to take to rectify the situation.

The Vroom and Yetton decision tree contained in Figure 5-6 can be used to analyze this problem situation and to choose a decision style as follows:

Question A	(Quality requirement?)	:	Yes
Question B	(Do I have sufficient information?)	:	No
Question C	(Problem structured?)	:	No
Question D	(Acceptance important for implementation?)	:	Yes
Question E	(Would subordinates accept my decision?)	:	No
Question F	(Do subordinates share organization goals?)	:	Yes

Feasible set of decision styles: GII

Source: Vroom, V. H. (1973, Spring). "A New Look at Managerial Decision Making," *Organization Dynamics.* New York: AMACOM, a division of American Management Associations, p. 72.

Current Issues in Leadership

In addition to focusing on the validity of the various contingency theories discussed above, leadership researchers have also recently identified a number of new and important issues that deserve our attention.

Leadership as Mutual Influence

The very term *leadership* naturally serves to draw our attention to leaders themselves and focuses our interest on the ways in which leaders influence their followers. As a result, research on leadership has tried to understand how different types of leaders and different types of leader behaviors cause followers to react in different ways.

An important contribution of recent research on leadership has been to point out the shortsightedness of this view of leader-follower relations. While it is no doubt true that leaders can and do influence their followers, it is also true that leaders and followers engage in *interaction* with one another, which necessarily implies the existence of **mutual influence.** In other words, not only is it true that leaders influence followers, but it is equally true that followers influence leaders.

The validity of this claim has been demonstrated in a variety of recent research studies.[27] Researchers have found that the performance of subordinates can have a strong causal impact upon the behavior of their leaders. Leaders whose subordinates have performed incompetently tend to begin supervising their subordinates much more closely, to remind subordinates of their mistakes, to criticize unauthorized breaks, and to spend more time checking on the subordinates' whereabouts and activities.[28] In addition, incompetent performance by followers tends to result in leaders becoming more directive and insistent about how work should be carried out and more likely to refuse a subordinate's request to switch from one task to another. Leaders of incompetent subordinates also tend to become less considerate and less friendly toward their subordinates. Subordinates who perform effectively, on the other hand, tend to elicit behavior from their leaders that is less directive, more personally supportive, and more oriented towards delegating authority to their followers.[29]

Thus, it is clear that when we are studying leadership we are studying a mutual influence process wherein leaders influence followers and followers also influence leaders.[30] Any approach that views leadership as a one-way influence process whereby what the leader does causes subordinates to react in certain ways is of necessity incomplete and oversimplified.

Constraints on Leadership Behavior

In thinking about leadership as a mutual influence process we are taking into account the fact that the behavior of subordinates has a causal influence upon the behavior of the leader. In other words, leaders do not decide how they are going to behave in total isolation from their subordinates. Leaders must select and adjust their leadership style in light of how their subordinates are performing and responding. But acknowledging that the behavior of subordinates can influence how leaders behave raises the question of what other factors may be influencing and constraining what leaders do.[31] In fact, it turns out that leaders are far from totally free and unencumbered in choosing their leadership style.[32] A variety of factors summarized in Table 5-5 all have an impact upon a leader's behavior.

Subordinate Behavior

As was pointed out in our discussion of leadership as a mutual influence process, the evidence is quite clear that the performance of subordinates has a critical causal impact upon what a leader does and how he or she behaves toward followers.

Characteristics of Subordinates

In addition to what subordinates do and how they perform, other identifiable traits, or characteristics, of subordinates may influence the leader's behavior as well as the behavior of the subordinates themselves. For example, a leader may behave differently toward males and females, older and younger people, and those with similar as opposed to different personal backgrounds from his or her own.

Characteristics of the Leader

The leader's abilities and personal characteristics obviously influence and constrain what the leader does and how he or she behaves toward subordinates. On the ability side, task-relevant knowledge and skill, as well as supervisory skills and sensitivities, will have an important impact. In terms of traits, personality characteristics such as assertiveness, dominance, and self-confidence all have an influence on leadership behavior.

Leaders' Superiors

How leaders treat their subordinates is strongly influenced by how the leaders themselves are treated by their own immediate superiors. Superiors serve both as role models for the leadership behavior of individuals toward their own sub-

---

TABLE 5-5

Factors that Influence and Constrain Leadership Behavior

Subordinate behavior
Characteristics of subordinates
Characteristics of the leader
Leader's superiors
Leader's peers
Organizational policies, norms, and climate
Nature of subordinates' tasks

ordinates and as sources of rewards and punishments. Leaders with immediate superiors who preach, practice, and reward a participative management style, for example, are unlikely to treat their subordinates in a directive and authoritarian fashion.

Leaders' Peers

As in almost all things, peers have an important influence upon how leaders behave. Peer pressure has a potent homogenizing impact upon leadership behavior in an organization. Other managers in an organization are likely to exert both direct and indirect pressure on individual leaders to behave toward their subordinates in a fashion that is consistent with that practiced by other managers at that level in the organization.

Organizational Policies, Norms, and Climate

Some organizations are characterized by a very open, democratic, and participative management style. Such an organizational climate and policy will obviously influence a leader to behave as a participative manager. Very different leadership behaviors would be expected in an organization characterized by a very closed and authoritarian policy of management.

Nature of Subordinates' Tasks

The nature of the tasks that subordinates are performing also influences the behavior of leaders toward subordinates. A very vague and ambiguous task such as developing the design of a new product from scratch is bound to elicit different types of leadership behavior than is a highly structured and routine task such as producing a particular number of units on an assembly line.

Attribution Theory of Leadership

Researchers have recently begun to focus on the important role that attributional processes may play in leadership.[33] The term **attributions** refers to the assumptions that people make about the reasons why other people behave the way that they do. For example, when a leader observes one of her subordinates performing poorly she may *attribute* this poor performance to any of a number of factors such as poor training, lack of motivation, too heavy a workload, or inadequate facilities or equipment. The important point that researchers have been making is that what the leader decides to do in response to poor subordinate performance will depend in large part on what cause the leader *attributes* that performance to. If poor performance is attributed to poor training, the leader may try to offer improved training and coaching. If the attribution is to lack of motivation, on the other hand, the leader may decide to issue a reprimand or a warning, or even to fire the person. If poor performance is attributed to a heavy workload or inadequate facilities, the leader may attempt to lighten the load or provide improved facilities. The key point to note is that we cannot predict what the leader will do in response to any particular type of behavior by his or her subordinates without knowing what attributions the leader is making about the causes of subordinate behavior.

Figure 5-7 summarizes the attribution model of leadership. As the figure indicates, the process begins with the leader observing both the performance

Figure 5-7 A model of the attribution approach to understanding leadership.

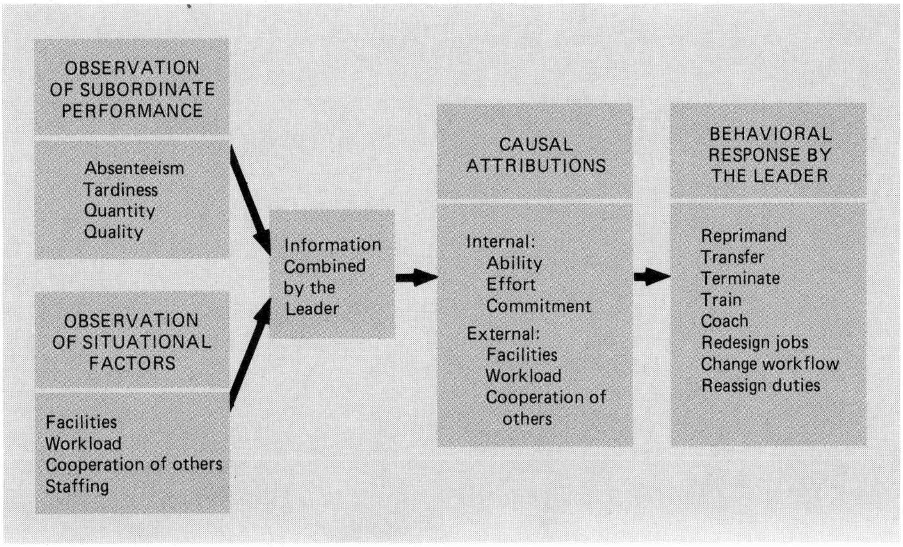

OBSERVATION
OF SUBORDINATE
PERFORMANCE

Absenteeism
Tardiness
Quantity
Quality

Information
Combined
by the
Leader

OBSERVATION
OF SITUATIONAL
FACTORS

Facilities
Workload
Cooperation of others
Staffing

CAUSAL
ATTRIBUTIONS

Internal:
  Ability
  Effort
  Commitment
External:
  Facilities
  Workload
  Cooperation of
    others

BEHAVIORAL
RESPONSE BY
THE LEADER

Reprimand
Transfer
Terminate
Train
Coach
Redesign jobs
Change workflow
Reassign duties

[*Source:* Adapted from Mitchell, T. R., & Wood, R. E. (1979). "An empirical test of an attributional model of leaders' responses to poor performance." *Academy of Management Proceedings,* 94–98.]

of the employee and the key characteristics of the situation within which the employee is working. This information about the employee's performance and the nature of the employee's situation is then combined by the leader and results in an attribution in the leader's mind regarding what has caused the employee to behave as he or she has. These attributions fall into two broad categories. Attributions to *internal* causes of performance, such as ability, effort, and commitment, indicate that the leader is assuming that the cause of the behavior is within the subordinate. Attributions to *external* causes of performance, such as poor equipment, excessive workload, and lack of cooperation from others, indicate an assumption on the part of the leader that the causes of the employee's behavior lie outside the person.

In addition to the obvious implications of the different types of attributions in terms of the corrective action to be taken by the leader, the leader's attributions also influence how he or she *feels* about subordinates.[34] Leaders feel most positively toward subordinates who perform effectively and whose effective performance is attributed to internal causes (e.g., effort and perseverance). On the other hand, subordinates whose poor performance is attributed to internal factors (e.g., laziness, carelessness) are viewed most negatively by their leaders.

The attribution approach to leadership is quite new and has not yet been subjected to in-depth research investigation. However, the attributions that leaders make about the causes of their subordinates' performance would appear to be an important factor to include in any comprehensive understanding of leadership in organizations.

Keys to Effective Management

In this chapter we have reviewed a wide variety of approaches and theories regarding leadership in organizations. While our discussion has made it clear that there is no single theory of leadership that we can endorse as the "correct" or "valid" theory, an overall look at what we know about leadership does permit us to develop some relatively clear implications for managers regarding leadership in organizations.

1   *In making appointments to leadership positions, managers must recognize that while the personal traits of the leader are not the sole determinant of leadership effectiveness, these traits do matter and do make a difference.* Managers making appointments to leadership positions must take into account individuals' personal traits and characteristics in assessing their suitability. Individuals differ in their appropriateness and capacity for handling different types of leadership situations effectively.

2   *To the extent that managers are concerned about employee satisfaction, they should adopt a considerate, employee-oriented leadership style.*   The evidence is quite consistent that employees are more satisfied with leaders who are considerate and oriented toward employee needs. Levels of satisfaction are in turn related inversely to employee absenteeism and turnover. To the extent that absenteeism and turnover are problematic or especially disruptive to the organization, the desirability of a considerate, employee-oriented leadership style is implied.

3   *Managers should adopt a contingency approach to leadership.*   The nature of effective leadership is not universal but is in fact contingent upon the nature of the leadership situation. It is clear that factors such as the nature of subordinates (e.g., their skills, background, training, orientation, and values), the nature of the task (e.g., whether it is routine and unambiguous or ill-defined and challenging), the nature of the work group (e.g., whether it is highly cohesive or fragmented), the nature of the organization (e.g., the extent to which it is rigid, formalized, and inflexible versus adaptive, informal, and flexible), the nature of the leader (e.g., the extent to which the leader is highly skilled and experienced), and so on, will all have an impact upon what is required of a leader in order to operate successfully. While no single theory adequately captures and explains the interdependent influence of all these situational and personal factors, there is a clear implication for managers that these factors must be carefully attended to in either selecting a leader for a particular position or in personally choosing a leadership style. Effective leadership requires a match or fit between the demands of the situation and the capabilities of the leader. Managers must attend carefully and systematically to the nature of those situational demands.

4   *Managers need to recognize that leadership is a mutual influence process.*
While it was once assumed that leadership was a one-way influence process, with leaders influencing their subordinates' feelings and behaviors, it is now recognized that subordinates' behavior and performance also have a strong influence on what leaders do. Thus, leadership is a process of mutual influence between leader and subordinates. This implies that managers need to recognize the ways in which their subordinates' behavior is influencing and affecting their own leadership style. In addition, it implies that in judging and evaluating the performance of other managers, senior managers must recognize that each manager's leadership style is in part determined by the nature of the subordinates he or she is currently supervising.

5   *Managers need to recognize that the impact of leadership is limited.*   It has not been uncommon in recent years for leadership researchers to express disappointment at the weakness of their findings. Instead of causing disappointment, such findings should serve as a reminder that the behavior of the leader is but one of many factors influencing the feelings, motivation, and performance of organization members. Many other factors besides leadership influence individuals in organizations, factors such as the characteristics of the individuals themselves (e.g., their needs, motives, and skills), the nature of their jobs, the nature of their peers and their work group, and the nature of the organization's policies, rules, and procedures. The important implication for the manager is that the manager or leader is only one of many factors influencing subordinates, and a change in leadership style or behavior cannot be expected to yield clear, unequivocal, and immediate changes in subordinates feelings and performance.

6   *Managers need to take advantage of the fact that the impact of leadership can be expanded.*   Our previous point drew attention to the fact that the impact of leadership is limited, since the behavior of the leader is but one of many factors influencing subordinates. At the same time, however, this awareness of the existence of additional factors and substitutes for leadership can help leaders recognize alternative avenues and approaches to influencing their subordinates. Leaders who assume that their ability to influence subordinates is limited only to face-to-face interactions with them are doomed to have relatively little influence and impact. In addition to interacting directly with subordinates, the leader is generally in a position to influence many of the additional factors that have a significant impact upon subordinates. For example, a leader may influence subordinates by offering coaching and direction to increase levels of ability; by influencing task characteristics through job redesign to increase the jobs' motivating potential; or by attempting to change the degree of organizational formalization and

flexibility by lobbying with more senior managers for changes in policies and procedures affecting subordinates. The clear implication is that managers do not influence their subordinates' satisfaction, motivation, and performance solely on the basis of direct, face-to-face interactions. To be effective, leaders must recognize and influence the many areas of leverage at their disposal that have an impact upon the total work experience of subordinates.

Review Questions

1   Discuss some of the sources of power that may be at a leader's disposal in his or her attempts to influence subordinates. What sorts of things should a leader do to attempt to increase his or her level of personal power to influence subordinates?

2   What personal characteristics, or traits, would you look for in an individual to be appointed to a leadership position in an organization? How would the nature of the leadership position influence the traits you would be looking for?

3   What do we know about the relationship between leader consideration and initiating structure on the one hand and subordinates' satisfaction and performance on the other?

4   What do you feel is the primary contribution of the behavioral theories of leadership to our understanding of leadership effectiveness in organizations?

5   What makes a theory of leadership a contingency theory? Discuss the advantages and disadvantages of adopting a contingency approach to understanding leadership.

6   Describe Fiedler's contingency theory and discuss what you feel are its primary strengths and weaknesses.

7   Describe some of the alternative decision styles outlined in the Vroom and Yetton model. How should a manager go about choosing which style to employ?

8   Discuss the predictions of path-goal theory regarding the impact of subordinate characteristics and the nature of the work environment on the effectiveness of alternative styles of leadership.

9   Do you believe leadership makes much of a difference in the satisfaction, motivation, and performance of organization members? What other factors need to be taken into account?

10 Do you feel that a manager's leadership style is relatively fixed and unchangeable or flexible and adaptable? What are the implications of your position for organizations seeking to improve leadership effectiveness?

11 What personal traits, or characteristics, do you feel have the greatest impact upon a leader's capacity to adopt alternative leadership styles?

12 What do we mean when we say that leadership is a mutual influence process?

13 Outline some of the factors that have an important influence upon a leader's behavior. Which factors do you feel are most potent in determining what a leader does?

14 Discuss some of the ways in which leaders can broaden their influence upon subordinates beyond their face-to-face interactions. Which techniques or approaches do you feel have the greatest potential to influence subordinates' work effectiveness?

Which Style Is Best?

The ABC Company is a medium-sized corporation that manufactures automotive parts. Recently, a survey was done of the leadership styles of three key managers in one of the company's divisions.

Ancil Able

Ancil is very proud of the output of his section. He has always stressed the necessity for good control procedures and efficiency, and is very insistent that project instructions be fully understood by his subordinates and that follow-up communications be rapid, complete, and accurate. Ancil serves as the clearinghouse for all incoming and outgoing work. He gives small problems to one individual to complete, but if the problem is large he calls in several key people. Usually, his employees are briefed on what the policy is to be, what part of the report each subordinate is to complete, and the completion date. Ancil considers this to be the only way to get full coordination without lost motion or an overlap of work.

Ancil considers it best for a boss to remain aloof from his subordinates and believes that being "buddy-buddy" tends to hamper discipline. He does his "chewing out" in private, and his praising, too. He believes that people in his section really know where they stand.

According to Ancil, the biggest problem in business today is that subordinates just will not accept responsibility. He states that his people have lots of opportunities to show what they can do but not many really try too hard.

One comment Ancil made was that he does not understand how his subordinates got along with the previous section head, who ran a very "loose shop." Ancil stated that his boss is quite happy with the way things go in his section.

Bob Black

Bob believes that every employee has a right to be treated as an individual and espouses the theory that it is a boss's responsibility and duty to cater to the employee's needs. He noted that he is constantly doing little things for his subordinates and gave as an example his gift to an employee of two tickets to an art show to be held at the City Gallery next month. He stated that the tickets cost $15 each but that it will be both educational and enjoyable for the employee and his wife. This was done to express his appreciation for a good job the man had done a few months back.

Bob says he always makes a point of walking through his section area at least once each day, stopping to speak to at least 25 percent of the employees on each trip.

Bob does not like to "knock" anyone, but he noted that Ancil Able runs one of those "taut ships" you hear about. He stated that Ancil's employees are probably not too happy but there isn't much they can do but wait for Ancil to move.

Bob said he had noticed a little bit of bypassing going on in the company but that most of it is just due to the press of business. His idea is to run a friendly, low-keyed operation with a happy group of subordinates. Although he confesses that they might not be as efficient as other units in terms of speedy outputs, he believes that his subordinates have far greater loyalty and higher morale and that they work well as an expression of their appreciation of his (Bob's) enlightened leadership.

Charles Carr

Charlie says his principal problem is the shifting of responsibility between his section and others in the division. He considers his section the "fire drill" area that gets all of the rush, hot items, whether or not they belong in his section. He seems to think this is caused by his immediate superior not being too sure who should handle what jobs in the division.

Charlie admits he hasn't tried to stop this practice. He stated (with a grin) that it makes the other section heads jealous but they are afraid to complain. They seem to think Charlie is a personal friend of the division manager, but Charlie says this is not true.

Charlie said he used to be embarrassed in meetings when it was obvious he was doing jobs out of his area, but he has gotten used to it by now, and apparently the other section heads have also.

Charlie's approach to discipline is just to keep everybody busy and "you won't have those kinds of problems." He stated that a good boss doesn't have time to hold anybody's hand, like Bob Black does, and tell the guy what a great job he's doing. Charlie believes that if you promise people that you will keep an eye on their work for raises and promotion purposes, most of the problems take care of themselves.

Charlie stated that he believes in giving a guy a job to do and then letting him do it without too much checking on his work. He believes most of his subordinates know the score and do their jobs reasonably well without too much griping.

If he has a problem, it is probably the fact that the role and scope of his section has become a little blurred by current practices. Charlie did state that he thinks he should resist a recent tendency for "company people above my division manager's level" to call him up to their offices to hear his ideas on certain programs. However, Charlie is not too sure that this can be stopped without creating a ruckus of some kind. He says he is studying the problem.

Questions for Discussion

1 How would you describe the leadership styles of each of the three managers presented in the case?

2 What predictions would you make regarding the satisfaction and performance of the subordinates of each of the three managers?

3 Is it possible that each manager's style is appropriate to the particular situation he is working within? Why or why not?

Source: Adapted from a case prepared by W. D. Heirer and used by permission.

Notes

1   Eden, D., & Shani, A. B. (1982). Pygmalion goes to boot camp: Expectancy, leadership, and trainee performance. *Journal of Applied Psychology, 67,* 194–199.

Smith, J. E., Carson, K. P., & Alexander, R. A. (1984). Leadership: It can make a difference. *Academy of Management Journal, 27,* 765–776.

Graen, G. B., Liden, R. C., & Hoel, W. (1982). Role of leadership in the employee withdrawal process. *Journal of Applied Psychology, 67,* 868–872.

2   House, R. J., & Baetz, M. L. (1979). Leadership: Some generalizations and new research directions. In B. M. Staw (Ed.), *Research in organizational behavior.* Greenwich, CT: JAI Press.

Stogdill, R. M. (1974). *Handbook of leadership: A survey of theory and research.* New York: Free Press.

Yukl, G. A. (1981). *Leadership in organizations.* Englewood Cliffs, NJ: Prentice-Hall.

3   French, J. R. P., & Raven, B. (1959). The bases of social power. In D. Cartwright (Ed.). *Studies in social power.* Ann Arbor, MI: Institute for Social Research.

4   Ashour, A. S. (1982). A framework of a cognitive-behavioral theory of leader influence and effectiveness. *Organizational Behavior and Human Performance, 30,* 407–430.

5   Stogdill, R. M. (1948). Personal factors associated with leadership: A survey of the literature. *Journal of Psychology, 25,* 35–71.

6   Bass, B. M. (1982). *Stogdill's handbook of leadership.* New York: Free Press.

Stogdill, R. M. (1974), *loc. cit.*

7   House & Baetz (1979), *loc. cit.*

8   Drory, A., & Gluskinos, U. M. (1980). Machiavellianism and leadership. *Journal of Applied Psychology, 65,* 81–86.

Kenny, D. A., & Zaccaro, S. J. (1983). An estimate of variance due to traits in leadership. *Journal of Applied Psychology, 68,* 678–685.

McClelland, D. C., & Boyatzis, R. E. (1982). Leadership motive pattern and long-term success in management. *Journal of Applied Psychology, 67,* 737–743.

9   Weissenberg, D., & Kavanaugh, M. H. (1972). The independence of initiating structure and consideration: A review of the evidence. *Personnel Psychology, 25,* 119–130.

10   Fleishman, E. A., & Harris, E. F. (1962). Patterns of leadership behavior related to employee grievances and turnover. *Personnel Psychology, 15,* 43–56.

Yukl, G. A. (1971). Toward a behavioral theory of leadership. *Organizational Behavior and Human Performance, 6,* 414–440.

11   Kerr, S., & Schriesheim, C. A. (1974). Consideration, initiating structure, and organizational criteria—An update of Korman's 1966 review. *Personnel Psychology, 27,* 555–568.

Schriesheim, J. F. (1980). The social context of leader-subordinate relations: An investigation of the effects of group cohesiveness. *Journal of Applied Psychology, 65,* 183–194.

Stogdill, R. M. (1974), *loc. cit.*

Yukl, G. A. (1971), *loc. cit.*

12   Tjosvold, D. (1984). Effects of leader warmth, and directiveness on subordinate performance on a subsequent task. *Journal of Applied Psychology, 69,* 422–427.

13   Hill, W. (1973). Leadership style: Rigid or flexible? *Organizational Behavior and Human Performance, 9,* 35–47.

Vroom, V. H., & Yetton, P. W. (1973). *Leadership and decision making.* Pittsburgh, PA: University of Pittsburgh Press.

14   Dansereau, F., Jr., Graen, G. B., & Haga, W. J. (1975). A vertical dyad linkage approach to leadership within formal organizations: A longitudinal investigation of the role-making process. *Organizational Behavior and Human Performance, 13,* 46–78.

Liden, R. C., & Graen, G. B. (1980). Generalizability of the vertical dyad linkage model of leadership. *Academy of Management Journal, 23,* 451–465.

Scandura, T. A., & Graen, G. B. (1984). Moderating effects of initial leader-member exchange status on the effects of a leadership intervention. *Journal of Applied Psychology, 69,* 428–436.

Vecchio, R. P. (1982). A further test of leadership effects due to between-group variation and within-group variation. *Journal of Applied Psychology, 67,* 200–208.

Vecchio, R. P., & Gobdel, B. C. (1984). The vertical dyad linkage model of leadership: Problems and prospects. *Organizational Behavior and Human Performance, 34,* 5–20.

15   Fiedler, F. E. (1964). A contingency model of leadership effectiveness. In L. Berkowitz (Ed.), *Advances in experimental social psychology.* New York: Academic Press.

Fiedler, F. E. (1967). *A theory of leadership effectiveness.* New York: McGraw-Hill.

16   Fiedler, F. E. (1971). Validation and extension of the contingency model of leadership effectiveness: A review of empirical findings. *Psychological Bulletin, 76,* 128–148.

Fiedler, F. E. (1972). Personality, motivational systems, and the behavior of high and low LPC persons. *Human Relations, 25,* 391–412.

Rice, R. W. (1981). Leader LPC and follower satisfaction: A review. *Organizational Behavior and Human Performance, 28,* 1–25.

Singh, R. (1983). Leadership style and reward allocation: Does least preferred coworker scale measure task and relation orientation? *Organizational Behavior and Human Performance, 32,* 178–197.

17   House and Baetz (1979), *loc. cit.*

18   Chemers, M. M., & Skrzypek, G. J. (1972). An experimental test of the contingency model of leadership effectiveness. *Journal of Personality and Social Psychology, 24,* 172–177.

Fiedler, F. E. (1978). The contingency model and the dynamics of leadership. In L. Berkowitz (Ed.), *Advances in experimental social psychology.* New York: Academic Press.

Rice, R. W. (1981), *loc. cit.*

Strube, M. J., & Garcia, J. E. (1981). A meta-analytic investigation of Fiedler's contingency model of leadership effectiveness. *Psychological Bulletin, 90,* 307–321.

19   Graen, G., Alvares, K. M., Orris, J. B., & Martella, J. A. (1970). Contingency model of leadership effectiveness: Antecedent and evidential results. *Psychological Bulletin, 74,* 285–296.

Vecchio, R. P. (1977). An empirical examination of the validity of Fiedler's model of leadership effectiveness. *Organizational Behavior and Human Performance, 19,* 180–206.

20   Evans, M. G. (1970). The effects of supervisory behavior on the path-goal relationship. *Organizational Behavior and Human Performance, 5,* 277–298.

Evans, M. G. (1974). Extensions of a path-goal theory of motivation. *Journal of Applied Psychology, 59,* 172–178.

21   House, R. J. (1971). A path-goal theory of leader effectiveness. *Administrative Science Quarterly, 16,* 321–339.

House, R. J., & Dessler, G. (1974). The path-goal theory of leadership: Some post hoc and a priori tests. In J. G. Hunt & L. L. Larson (Eds.), *Contingency approaches to leadership.* Carbondale, IL: Southern Illinois University Press.

House, R. J., & Mitchell, T. R. (1974, Autumn). Path-goal theory of leadership. *Journal of Contemporary Business. 3,* 81–98.

22   Podsakoff, P. M. (1982). Determinants of a supervisor's use of rewards and punishments: A literature review and suggestions for future research. *Organizational Behavior and Human Performance, 29,* 58–83.

Podsakoff, P. M., Todor, W. D., & Skov, R. (1982). Effects of leader contingent and noncontingent reward and punishment behaviors on subordinate performance and satisfaction. *Academy of Management Journal, 25,* 810–821.

Podsakoff, P. M., Todor, W. D., Grover, R. A., & Huber, V. L. (1984). Situational moderators of leader reward and punishment behaviors: Fact or fiction? *Organizational Behavior and Human Performance, 34,* 21–63.

23 Mitchell, T. R., Smyser, C. M., & Weed, S. E. (1975). Locus of control: Supervision and work satisfaction. *Academy of Management Journal, 18,* 623–631.

Runyon, K. E. (1981). Some interactions between personality variables and management styles. *Journal of Applied Psychology, 66,* 589–597.

24 Schriesheim, C. A., & DeNisi, A. S. (1981). Task dimensions as moderators of the effects of instrumental leadership: A two-sample replicated test of path-goal leadership theory. *Journal of Applied Psychology, 66,* 589–597.

Schriesheim, C. A., & Von Glinow, M. A. (1977). The path-goal theory of leadership: A theoretical and empirical analysis. *Academy of Management Journal, 20,* 398–405.

Yukl, G. A. (1981), *loc. cit.*

25 Jago, A. G., & Vroom, V. H. (1978). Predicting leader behavior from a measure of behavioral intent. *Academy of Management Journal, 21,* 715–721.

Vroom, V. H., & Jago, A. G. (1978). On the validity of the Vroom-Yetton model. *Journal of Applied Psychology, 63,* 151–162.

Vroom, V. H., & Yetton, P. W. (1973). *Leadership and decision making.* Pittsburgh, PA: University of Pittsburgh Press.

26 Field, R. H. G. (1982). A test of the Vroom-Yetton normative model of leadership. *Journal of Applied Psychology, 67,* 523–532.

Heilman, M. E., Hornstein, H. A., Cage, J. H., & Herschlag, J. K. (1984). Reactions to prescribed leader behavior as a function of role perspective: The case of the Vroom-Yetton model. *Journal of Applied Psychology, 69,* 50–60.

Jago, A. G., & Vroom, V. H. (1980). An evaluation of two alternatives to the Vroom-Yetton normative model. *Academy of Management Journal, 23,* 347–355.

27 Farris, G. F., & Lim, F. G., Jr. (1969). Effects of performance on leadership, cohesiveness, satisfaction, and subsequent performance. *Journal of Applied Psychology, 53,* 490–497.

28 Lowin, A., & Craig, J. R. (1968). The influence of level of performance on managerial style: An experimental object lesson in the ambiguity of correlational data. *Organizational Behavior and Human Performance, 3,* 440–458.

29 Greene, C. N. (1979). *A longitudinal investigation of modification to a situational model of leadership effectiveness.* Paper presented at the National Meeting of the Academy of Management, Atlanta, GA.

30 Ilgen, D. R., Mitchell, T. R., & Frederickson, J. W. Poor performers: Supervisors' and subordinates' responses. *Organizational Behavior and Human Performance, 27,* 386–410.

Sims, H. P., Jr., & Manz, C. C. (1984). Observing leader verbal behavior: Toward reciprocal determinism in leadership theory. *Journal of Applied Psychology, 69,* 222–232.

Watson, K. M. (1982). An analysis of communication patterns: A method for discriminating leader and subordinate roles. *Academy of Management Journal, 25,* 107–120.

Zahn, G. L., & Wolf, G. (1981). Leadership and the art of cycle maintenance: A simulation model of superior-subordinate interaction. *Organizational Behavior and Human Performance, 28,* 26–49.

31 Reitz, H. J. (1981). *Behavior in organizations* (rev. ed.). Homewood, IL: Irwin.

32 Ford, J. D. (1981). Departmental context and formal structure as constraints on leader behavior. *Academy of Management Journal, 24,* 274–288.

33 Calder, B. J. (1977). An attribution theory of leadership. In B. M. Staw & G. R. Salancik (Eds.), *New directions in organizational behavior.* Chicago: St. Clair Press.

Green, S. G., & Mitchell, T. R. (1979). Attributional processes of leaders in leader-member interactions. *Organizational Behavior and Human Performance, 23,* 429–458.

Mitchell, T. R., & Kalb, L. S. (1982). Effects of job experience on supervisor attributions for a subordinate's poor performance. *Journal of Applied Psychology, 67,* 181–188.

Mitchell, T. R., Larson, J. R., Jr., & Green, S. G. (1977). Leader behavior, situational moderators, and group performance: An attributional analysis. *Organizational Behavior and Human Performance, 18,* 254–268.

34 Knowlton, W. A., Jr., & Mitchell, T. R. (1980). Effects of causal attributions on a supervisor's evaluation of subordinate performance. *Journal of Applied Psychology, 65,* 459–466.

Mitchell, T. R., & Wood, R. E. (1980). Supervisors' responses to subordinate poor performance: A test of an attributional model. *Organizational Behavior and Human Performance, 25,* 123–138.

Chapter 6

Communication

CHAPTER OUTLINE

Attention

Comprehension

Acceptance of the Information as True

Retention of Information

Keys to Effective Management

Review Questions

*H*ow often do we hear managers explain an organizational problem by saying, "It's a communication problem"? Managers are constantly frustrated by projects that fail because the right hand doesn't know what the left hand is doing, and by quarrels among employees who misunderstand or misinterpret each other's actions.

The ability to communicate effectively is critical to a manager's success. All important management functions depend upon effective communication among managers and subordinates. To motivate employees, managers need to set goals with employees and instruct them how to perform their jobs correctly. To conduct effective performance appraisals, managers need to give employees feedback on their performance and justify their assessments to those evaluated. In making important business decisions, managers need to elicit information from a variety of different people in the organization, and then clearly convey the nature of the ultimate decisions back to their subordinates.[1]

In this chapter we will be examining communication in organizations. By the term **communication,** we simply mean the *exchange of information between people in organizations.* It is useful, however, to think about communication as an activity that actually takes place in four stages:

1 First, we need to attract people's *attention* to our communication.

2 Second, we want to make sure that people *understand* our message in the way we mean them to understand it.

3   Third, we want to influence others to *accept as true* the information we are giving them.

4   Finally, we want to make sure that people *remember* the information we have given them.

We'll explore each of these four stages in the communication process in some depth, and provide some guidelines for improving communication at each stage as well. We begin by considering what aspects of communication attract people's attention.

Attention

Every day, managers are inundated with memos, letters, phone calls, newspapers, television and radio programs, and conversations. Much of that communication simply goes in one ear and out the other.

Four key factors influence which communications catch people's attention: (1) the amount of communication they are receiving; (2) their position in formal communication channels; (3) their position in informal communication networks; and (4) the nature of the information itself. A brief summary of these factors appears in Figure 6-1.

Figure 6-1   Attention to communication

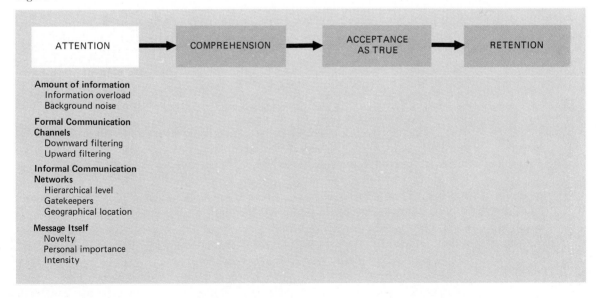

Amount of Information

People in organizations do not pay attention to a lot of the information given them because they are receiving so much information they cannot possibly process all of it carefully. When there is too much information coming in for a person to handle adequately, that situation is called *information overload.* Ample evidence suggests that managers are often greatly overloaded with both written and oral communication.

For instance, most organizations doing business with the federal government are faced with hundreds of government forms to complete. In fact, the U.S. Government prints well over 15 billion forms a year. The problem became so bad that the White House set up a fourteen-member panel to probe all facets of the growing paperwork burden—but the President's personnel staff itself became so engulfed in paperwork (security forms, political clearances, and interagency memoranda) that it took two years just to produce a slate of commissioners for the President's review and approval.[2]

A second aspect of the information overload problem is that there is often quite a bit of *background noise* during communication. Not only the *total* amount of information coming in but also the amount of *simultaneous* information coming in influences whether a manager will pay attention to a specific communication. The sender's communication must compete with a number of (frequently) irrelevant stimuli: the manager is on a phone call; the receptionist buzzes that another call is waiting; the secretary brings in some letters for the manager to sign; a subordinate is waiting in the office to continue the conversation the phone call interrupted. The person on the other end of the phone line is competing with the background noise of at least three other stimuli to get his or her message across.

Formal Communication Channels

Organizations realize that managers would be terribly overloaded with information if employees were free to communicate with all their superiors in the organization about any issue. For this reason, organizations set up *formal communication channels.* These communication channels indicate to whom employees should bring their concerns, problems, and questions.[3]

As a result, subordinates are often hesitant about communicating upward to their bosses. In a study of supervisors, engineers, white-collar workers, and blue-collar workers in eight companies, a large majority of employees believed that their boss was not interested in their problems and that they would get into "a lot of trouble" if they were completely open with their boss.[4] Subordinates are likely to cover up mistakes and difficulties, so that only information that reflects positively about themselves and their units is likely to be passed upward.[5] This *filtering* of upward communication is particularly strong when subordinates are ambitious for advancement and are very competitive with each other for the boss's approval.[6] As a result, managers often don't receive either sufficient information to help subordinates deal with their problems or accurate enough information to make high-quality decisions.

Formal communication channels are also supposed to protect employees from being inundated with irrelevant information from their managers. However, managers often filter out information that might be helpful to subordinates. In a study conducted in a public utility, 92 percent of the supervisors said that they always or nearly always told workers in advance about changes which would affect them or their work, but only 47 percent of the workers said they were always or nearly always informed about changes which would affect them.[7]

Moreover, at each successively lower level of the organization, less information gets passed down. In another study conducted in a manufacturing plant, top management held a meeting with middle managers and told them about tentative plans for a layoff. The layoff information was passed on to 94 percent of the foremen, but the foremen only passed that information on to 70 percent of the assistant foremen.[8] Managers make decisions about what employees need to know to do their jobs, and filter out all the other information. Unfortunately, sometimes the manager guesses wrong, and work effectiveness of subordinates can suffer substantially as a result.

Informal Communication Networks

In every organization there are informal communication networks as well as formal communication channels. Often called the **grapevine,** an informal communication network is used by employees to bypass the normal chain of command or to pass along personal information, gossip, or rumors. It is often used by top management to make unofficial announcements, "off-the-record" statements, and intentional leaks of upcoming announcements. Grapevine information almost always travels quickly because most of it is carried over the phone or in face-to-face conversation. As a result, when a key employee is fired or promoted, the grapevine often carries that information throughout the organization well before the official announcement is posted.[9]

What determines whether somebody receives and sends on grapevine information? People at *higher levels* in the formal communication network receive and send more information through the grapevine than do people at lower levels. *Gatekeepers*—employees who have a lot of contact with colleagues outside the organization—also tend to initiate a lot of informal communication. Gatekeepers are most likely to pass on information about developments in their own technical specialty, job changes of other people in their areas, and social news about colleagues. People who are *geographically central* are much more likely to receive grapevine information. For instance, people at headquarters will probably hear much more grapevine information than employees in geographically isolated field locations.[10]

Every manager, then, has to find the delicate balance between being inundated with information and being shut out from it. The manager also has to find the fine line between hearing too many trivial complaints from too many subordinates and being ill informed about major (or potentially major) problems.[11] Box 6-1 illustrates what some chief executives are doing to stay in touch with their subordinates.

BOX 6-1

How the Boss Stays in Touch with the Troops

Chief executives have developed some effective techniques for staying in touch with lower-level employees. These techniques enable executives to acquire information they might not otherwise get.

Dining out on the road   W. Michael Blumenthal, former president of Bendix and former Secretary of the U.S. Treasury, used to schedule lunches and dinners with divisional executives at all levels whenever he was traveling on business. "The conversations jump all over the place," he says. "One minute we're talking business, the next minute we're talking politics. Everybody learns." Robert Quittmeyer, president of Amstar, regularly goes to the company cafeteria and sits down with any group of employees, executive or clerical, whose table has an empty chair.

Looking over the office   Blumenthal also used the technique of occasionally hand-delivering memos himself to subordinates in the same building. Often the employee would take advantage of his few minutes with the chairman to tip him off to some potential problem or opportunity for the company. While this information was rarely earth-shattering, Blumenthal reports it often gave him a good feel for what was happening on a day-to-day basis. Fletcher Byrom, the chairman of Koppers, makes it a practice to take the local elevator rather than the express "on the chance that someone will want to say something to me when he sees me."

No-agenda meeting   Richard B. Loynd, president of Eltra Corporation, holds open, no-agenda meetings. Participants include a wide range of employees, from secretaries to vice presidents. They are encouraged to say whatever is on their minds about the business in general, the company, or the work they are doing. Some CEOs have "unprotected" office hours a couple of times a month; employees can call the CEO directly without having to fight through a phalanx of secretaries and receptionists.

Visits to the production area   Anthony Bryan, president of Ameron Iron Works, makes forays down to the production areas, even during the late night shifts. Sometimes an employee has a problem that isn't being satisfactorily handled via the usual channels; sometimes the employee has a suggestion to offer and doesn't quite know whom he should be telling about it. Bryan reports, "Our employees get to feel that their ideas, their own contributions to the company's productivity, matter to management." Bryan also cautions, "You must discipline yourself to do these things. If not, your isolation increases. You may think you know what you're doing, but you don't test yourself sufficiently. That's dangerous."

Source: Adapted from: Meyer, Herbert E. How the boss stays in touch with the troops. *Fortune.* (1975, June), 152–155. Used by permission.

**The Message
Itself**

The *characteristics of the message itself* play an equally strong role in whether people hear the information being sent them. What is it about the message itself that makes people take notice?

First of all, the *novelty,* or *newness,* of the information draws employees' attention. If information about potential labor problems, new business ventures, or recent job postings comes across their desks, and all the information is new and unfamiliar to them, they will pay more attention to it. Advertisers have long known the importance of novelty, and they effectively reach consumers with messages featuring a variety of exotic animals and catchy jingles that extol the virtues of their products.

Second, people pay the most attention to messages that are *important* to them, that affect them *directly.* Employees pay a lot more attention to information about pay raises than they do to the details of a charity drive; they pay more attention to how their bonus is calculated than to how replacement-cost accounting procedures are implemented.

Third, the *intensity* of the message affects how closely employees attend to it. If their manager strongly demands immediate action, they take heed. If the same request is more mildly stated in a list of ten other requests, it draws less attention.

Thus, if we look at the characteristics of messages that attract our attention—novelty, importance, and intensity—we can discover why so much communication in organizations is ignored. Much of the information that managers receive is irrelevant to their jobs (e.g., retirement notices of people they have never met), routine and uninteresting (e.g., menus for the company cafeteria), and of no immediate importance (e.g., the schedule of legal holidays for the next three years). Managers frequently find they are missing the information they currently need but are inundated with information that they won't ever use.

Comprehension

Attracting people's attention is only the first step in the communication process. The next step is communicating the information in such a way that people understand the information in the way it was meant to be understood. Three factors determine how completely employees understand the messages they are sent: (1) the semantics of the message; (2) the perceptions of the people receiving the information; and (3) the opportunity for feedback between the sender and receiver of the communication. A brief summary of these factors appears in Figure 6-2.

**Semantics
of the Message**

People communicate with each other through symbols—words, facial expressions, body language. They try to transmit information through symbols that they think others will clearly understand—vocabulary they think others will

Figure 6-2   Comprehension of information

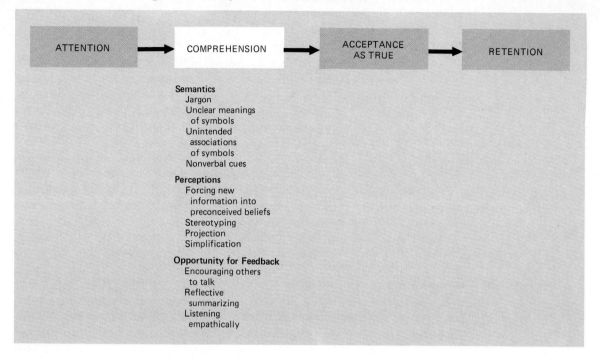

know, facial expressions and body gestures they think are easily interpreted. However, sometimes people do not comprehend the information the way others mean it because of *semantic* problems—people do not understand the symbols others are using or do not interpret them in the same way. Semantic problems arise from several sources.

Jargon

Every occupational and professional group has its own jargon, or specialized language. While jargon certainly helps professionals communicate with each other more quickly and more precisely, it is easy to forget that members of other groups in the organization and clients outside the organization may not understand some of the words that are used.

Consider this anecdote about a plumber who discovered that hydrochloric acid opened clogged drains, and who wrote to a government bureau to ask if it was a good substance to use. The reply was as follows: "The efficacy of hydrochloric acid is indisputable, but the corrosive residue is incompatible with metallic permanence." The plumber was not very well educated and interpreted the message to mean that it was all right to use the acid. After he thanked the bureau for their assistance, the bureau sent him another message with simpler language: "Don't use hydrochloric acid, it eats the hell out of pipes."[12]

Unclear Meanings of Symbols

Some words, like "tardy," "absent," and "superstar," have very clear meanings. Other words, like "aggressive," have much broader meanings. When a prospective employee is called "aggressive," is the term conveying praise (energy, initiative, perseverance) or criticism (pushiness, belligerence, authoritarianism)? Some symbols leave a lot more room for nuance and interpretation than others.

Unintended Associations of Symbols

Sometimes a message contains words that evoke emotions in the recipient that the sender did not mean to elicit. These associations can bias the recipient's interpretation of the message. For instance, in the early years of commercial aviation, a flight attendant would tell the passengers: "We're flying through a *storm.* You had better fasten your *safety* belts; it will be less *dangerous.*" These instructions caused some passengers to fear that the plane was likely to crash. So the language of the instructions was eventually changed to elicit more pleasant and secure associations. Today the flight attendant says: "We're flying through some *turbulence* now. Please fasten you *seat* belts; you will be more *comfortable.*"[13]

Nonverbal Cues

Much communication is carried on nonverbally. People convey their feelings and emotions through their facial expressions, their tone of voice, their posture, their eye contact, and where they position themselves in a room.[14] For instance, people are frequently suspicious of those who don't look them squarely in the eye. They often interpret fidgeting with hands as nervousness. When others "keep their distance," people take that as a sign of negativism or hostility. Semantic problems arise in three ways in regard to nonverbal cues.

First, nonverbal cues are generally even more *ambiguous* than verbal cues. Was Sue's smile a friendly smile? a nervous smile? a smirk? Did Bob not sit near me because he feels hostile? came in late? needed to speak to somebody else? A lot of nonverbal cues are very difficult to interpret.

Second, while people typically try to use nonverbal cues to help them interpret verbal communication, they sometimes find the nonverbal message is *inconsistent* with the verbal message. The tone of voice, facial expressions, and body gestures contradict what is being said orally. For example, someone may say "That's great with me," while the surly tone of voice, down-turned mouth, and slouch indicate substantial disapproval. The *overt* message (positive feelings) is very different from the *latent* message (negative feelings).[15]

Third, there are *cultural differences* in the ways different groups interpret nonverbal behavior. In Japan, for instance, it is customary to bow upon being introduced to someone new. In America, the same behavior would be seen as terribly affected.[16] If people are not aware of what nonverbal behaviors mean to different cultural groups, substantial misunderstandings might result.

Perceptions

Semantics is the first part of the comprehension problem. The second part is perception. Listeners often hear what they expect to hear rather than what is actually being said. For instance, pronounce the following four words slowly:

M-A-C-T-A-V-I-S-H

M-A-C-D-O-N-A-L-D

M-A-C-B-E-T-H

M-A-C-H-I-N-E-R-Y

If you pronounced the last word *Mac-Hinery* instead of *machinery* you—like most other people—were caught in a perceptual trap. Having read three other *Mac* words, you expected to hear yet a fourth. That "expecting-to-hear" phenomenon remains true in organizations as well.[17] People expect to hear certain messages in a communication and sometimes do not hear what is actually being communicated. When we use the term **perception,** we are talking about the ways in which people organize and interpret the information they receive (see Chapter 2). The way people perceive information influences how well they comprehend it. Several ways we perceive information inhibit complete and accurate comprehension of a communication.

Forcing Information to Fit Preconceived Beliefs

We frequently try to force new information into previously formed ideas. We often try to fit later impressions of people or events into our initial impressions—even if the circumstances have changed dramatically. But if we force new information to fit with our preconceived beliefs, we may not understand the communication the way the sender meant it.[18]

Consider, for instance, the following examples of how subordinates who perceive their bosses as hostile "hear" something very different from what was "said" to them:[19]

Example 1

The manager said: Your performance was below par last quarter. I really expected more out of you.

The subordinate heard: If you screw up one more time, you're out.

Example 2

The manager said: I'd like that report as soon as you can get to it.

The subordinate heard: Drop that rush order you're working on and fill out that report today.

Stereotyping

Stereotyping refers to the tendency to categorize people into a single class on the basis of some trait.[20] For instance, people often stereotype others on the basis of sex ("That's just like a man" or "That's just like a woman") or their functional department ("a hard-nosed engineer" or "an aggressive salesperson"). Young MBAs are often stereotyped as being too theoretical, while older managers are often stereotyped as resistant to change (see Chapter 2).

Stereotypes interfere with accurate perception.[21] If employees stereotype, they are unable to see the individual differences and variability among members of other groups. For instance, if employees use age stereotypes, they are less likely to see the theoretical aspects of an older manager's position, and less likely to see any practical considerations in the young MBA's position. Moreover, if employees stereotype, they are more likely to discount what others say ("Isn't it just like a new MBA to come up with an idea like that?") without seriously considering the merits of the specific case at hand.[22]

Projection

Projection is the perceptual process by which people attribute *their own* thoughts and feelings to others. People often project onto others the negative characteristics or feelings they have about themselves.

For instance, a manager may call in her subordinate to ask him to redo some financial analyses. There are some careless calculation errors that need to be fixed. The manager displays no real emotion, but the subordinate later describes her as angry and hostile. In truth, the subordinate was angry *at himself.* As a consequence, he *projects* anger onto his manager where there was none at all. Projection interferes with accurate comprehension of communication because people only perceive mirror images of their own thoughts, *not* the actual images trying to be conveyed by others.[23]

Simplification

Another perceptual problem that people often have is the need to *simplify* information. As information gets passed along in organizations, it tends to get simplified in two ways. First, the details of the message get dropped; the context of the message and the qualifications to the message get simplified. Second, the message is retold more vividly and dramatically as time goes on. As a result, messages get conveyed with a force and an unequivocality that the sender never meant.[24]

For instance, a division manager may ask her assistant to arrange a meeting for her with her subordinates to facilitate cooperation in problem solving. The assistant relays the following message: "Ms. Jones will meet with you on April 10 to discuss problems you are having." First of all, the context of the message has been completely deleted: the meeting is to help subordinates, not to punish them. Second, the message has been relayed more vividly than was intended: *problem solving* has become *problems;* problems *in general* have become the subordinates' *own* problems. Such simplification—in which important qualifications are dropped and the amount of emotion or force behind the communication gets exaggerated—clouds comprehension of the message.

Opportunity for Feedback

A third factor influencing the accuracy of communication is *opportunity for feedback.* Sometimes people are so busy talking *at* somebody that they don't stop and check to see whether their listeners are understanding the message as they mean it—or understanding it at all.

BOX 6-2

Strategies for Effective Active Listening

1   *Encouraging others to talk.*   Friendly facial expressions and an attentive but relaxed attitude encourage others to talk. Comments like "Could you tell me more?" or "I'd be interested in your point of view" also prompt others to open up with their feelings. When the other person pauses during the conversation, sometimes it is a good idea to refrain from talking yourself to signal the other person to keep on talking.

2   *Reflective summarizing.*   Occasionally during a conversation, it is important to try to summarize and restate what you believe the other person is trying to tell you. This shows that you are giving the other person's ideas careful consideration and allows the person a chance to restate or clarify his or her position.

3   *Listening empathically.*   Active listening requires that you put yourself in the other person's shoes. It is important to try to hear how the person is feeling as well as what he or she is saying. Often it is a good idea to tell listeners how you think they are feeling, (for example, "You sound pretty disappointed right now.") Sometimes people are surprised to learn what their words and emotions mean to you, and that sparks additional useful feedback.

4   *Avoiding arguments.*   It is important not to correct the other person when he or she is saying something you believe is wrong, especially at the beginning of the conversation. It conveys to others that you want to persuade them of the rightness of your position rather than listening to the validity of theirs.

5   *Avoiding premature judgment.*   Making moral judgments or personality assessments of others puts them on the defensive. Even if the people do not argue back, they will begin to edit what they say in order to win your approval.

6   *Avoiding armchair analysis.*   Subordinates often resent managers' attempts to analyze them in psychological terms. It is one thing to say to an employee, "You seem really upset these days"; it is quite another to say, "You seem clinically depressed."

Source: Adapted from: Sayles, L. R., and Strauss, G. (1981). *Managing human resources (2nd ed.).* Englewood Cliffs, NJ: Prentice-Hall, 117–124. Used with permission.

Perhaps the most effective way to obtain feedback from others is ***active listening***—listening for both the facts *and the feelings* of the audience.[25] In Box 6-2, we provide six guidelines for active listening. These guidelines should help you obtain more useful feedback from your listeners, and in so doing, ensure that your audience is understanding your message the way you mean it.

Acceptance of the Information as True

When managers use the expression "communicate effectively," what they frequently mean is *persuade.* They don't want to settle for others merely understanding what they mean; they also want others to agree with their position.

Two sets of factors most strongly influence whether the information communicated to others is accepted as true (see Figure 6-3). The first set of factors has to do with the characteristics of the communicator that increase his or her credibility. The second has to do with defensive communication—whether the communication poses some threat to the individual who is receiving it.

Characteristics of the Communicator

What makes a communicator particularly believable? Characteristics such as technical expertise, trustworthiness, and physical attractiveness are all characteristics that increase a person's credibility.[26]

Expertise

People are more likely to be persuaded by someone with special competence in the subject they are concerned about. They more readily accept the engineer's advice on what type of concrete to use, the personnel department's advice on affirmative action guidelines, and the legal department's advice on tax law questions. However, it is important to note that people also put *bounds* on the expertise of those they listen to. When the engineer offers suggestions on personnel matters, when the personnel manager dispenses financial advice, and when the corporate lawyer favors a particular engineering design, their comments are on subjects *outside* their realm of expertise and are thus taken with much more skepticism.

Figure 6-3   Acceptance of information as true

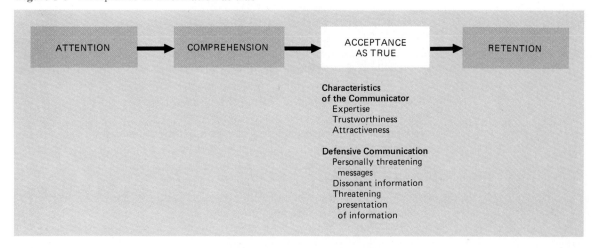

Trustworthiness

"Would you buy a used car from this man?" expresses in everyday terms the question of trustworthiness. Is the communicator telling a straight story? Two factors, in particular, influence a communicator's trustworthiness.

The first is the *past behavior of the communicator.* People tend to believe individuals who have followed through on their promises in the past, and tend to discount those who have not delivered.

The second factor that can enhance a communicator's credibility is *formal status.* Most people expect their leaders to be honest in their dealings with others. The example of Richard Nixon during the Watergate scandal illustrates this point. Many people simply refused to believe that the President of the United States would lie or knowingly deceive the public. Only after months of intensive news reporting, with a steady stream of incriminating evidence, did a majority of the public finally come to believe in Nixon's guilt.[27]

Attractiveness

If we look at people on television who are promoting products, we certainly couldn't conclude that they are particularly expert about the products they were selling or that they were motivated to communicate with us without bias.

It seems inconsistent, at first, that movie stars or sports figures could influence our beliefs about the products they are selling when they are not particularly expert or trustworthy. However, physically attractive people—simply because of their attractiveness—*can* have a major impact on our opinions. Fortunately, the answer to this paradox lies in the nature of the issue being discussed. On important issues, expertise and trustworthiness still matter; we wouldn't take somebody's advice on key issues just because they were attractive to us. However, we are influenced by people we are attracted to on *trivial* issues. We might not be influenced by their opinions about whether to build a new headquarters facility, but we might be influenced by their opinion about how to decorate the office. Expertise and trustworthiness are still the key dimensions of communicator effectiveness in organizational life.[28]

Defensive Communication

Defensive communication also influences whether people accept the information given them as true.[29] When employees perceive or anticipate some sort of threat in a communication, they react negatively, or defensively. They are unable to concentrate upon what is being said to them. They are less likely to see the motives of the people who are talking to them as positive or honorable. They are so concerned with escaping some punishment or trying to dominate the conversation that they don't accept what they are hearing as true.

Three factors produce defensive communication: (1) a message that is personally threatening to the receiver; (2) a dissonant message, that is, a message that is inconsistent with the beliefs of the receiver; and (3) a message presented in a threatening or hostile manner.

Personally Threatening Messages

People may build defenses against hearing information or messages that are personally threatening.[30] Consider, for instance, an individual who interviews for several advertising jobs and gets turned down repeatedly. It is very upsetting and threatening to hear the message of rejection over and over again. The individual starts to build defenses against the bad news, perhaps by distorting the message. For instance, the individual in our example might say, "I still haven't heard from a lot of places," or "The letter said that they didn't need me at this time . . . maybe I'll hear from them later." Part of the communication has been received, but the disturbing information has been distorted and is not perceived accurately.

Dissonant Information

In recent years, a great deal of psychological research has been conducted on how people cope with information that runs counter to other information they already possess—information that is *dissonant* with other beliefs. This research on **cognitive dissonance** suggests that there are very strong differences between reactions to information that is consistent with what the receiver already believes and reactions to information that is inconsistent with those beliefs. In general, people respond to dissonant information in one of four ways:[31]

1   *Avoid exposure to it.*   When new information is dissonant with existing beliefs, the receiver is likely to avoid exposure to the message (e.g., stop reading a newspaper article or turn off the television program presenting the information).

2   *Reject its validity.*   When new information runs counter to existing beliefs, the receiver is likely to reject that information as invalid (e.g., question the credibility of the source of the information or the research methodology and statistics used to generate it).

3   *Forget it quickly.*   When a communication is dissonant, receivers more easily and quickly forget the message (i.e., have trouble recalling important parts of the information soon after hearing or reading it).

4   *Distort the information in memory.*   When a communication is dissonant, people's memories tend to distort the information over time (e.g., recall the information inaccurately at a later time).

Cognitive dissonance helps explain why it is so difficult to get employees to accept as true the negative feedback given them by their managers. Employees try to block out the bad news, question the motives of their supervisors, and repress the criticisms in their memory after the conversation is over. Consequently, most negative feedback is presumed by employees to be inaccurate.

BOX 6-3

Guidelines for Nondefensive Communication

1 *Discipline your subordinates in private.*   It is difficult enough for people to deal with negative feedback without receiving it in front of others.

2 *Don't attack the employee personally.*   Focus on the specific behaviors you want the individual to change, not on his or her personality. People become very defensive when they feel you are making global personality assessments about them on the basis of a very small sample of their behavior.

3 *Get the facts first.*   Before confronting a subordinate, it is important to know as many specifics of the situation as possible. It is unwise to base your communication on hearsay evidence or "general impressions."

4 *Don't act while angry.*   Very few people can act sensibly and objectively when they are angry. Therefore, it is a good idea to calm down before confronting your subordinate. It is also a good idea not to initiate a serious negative conversation with a subordinate while he or she is very angry.

5 *Get the other side of the story.*   It is always a good idea to let your subordinate fully explain what happened and why it happened. You may find there were mitigating circumstances, or that he or she wasn't aware of the problem.

Source: Adapted from: Bittel, L. R. (1985). *What every supervisor should know.* New York: McGraw-Hill, pp. 295–299. Reprinted with permission.

Threatening Manner of Presentation

The third aspect of a communication which makes people defensive is a *threatening manner of presentation.* When people are being scolded, publicly ridiculed, or presented with sarcastic memoranda, they become defensive. Their attention focuses on the way they are being treated rather than on the content of the information. They are so sure they are being treated unfairly that they believe the content of the information is also unfair. Therefore, to the extent that managers can avoid making subordinates feel defensive, they increase the chances of subordinates accepting new or dissonant information as true.

Unfortunately, sometimes managers have to give employees personally threatening information. For instance, a manager may have to discipline the subordinate for violating some important rules. While it is probably impossible to communicate negative feedback to subordinates without making them defensive at all, there are some strategies managers can use to lessen the threat in the manner of presentation.[32] Some of these are reviewed in Box 6-3.

Retention of Information

The final step in the communication process is getting the people we are communicating with to *remember* the information presented (see Figure 6-4). Indeed, we often judge the effectiveness of our communication by looking at whether the people we communicate with remember what we said a while after we have said it. Four aspects of *message presentation* influence whether people will remember our communication over time.

Explicit versus Implicit Conclusions

Should managers explicitly draw conclusions from the facts that they present, or should they let the audience draw its own conclusions?

In general, it is more effective to draw conclusions *explicitly.* No matter how cogently the facts are marshaled, the audience may still not interpret the message the way the sender meant it—there could be either semantic misunderstandings or perceptual distortion of the information. For instance, a manager may be extolling the excitement and opportunities a city like New York offers, in order to convince a subordinate to accept a transfer to New York City. However, the subordinate may be opposed to big-city living, and he or she may be hearing the manager's arguments as good reasons for *not* moving. Drawing explicit conclusions allows the manager a second chance to reduce ambiguity in the message and ensure that people remember the argument correctly.[33]

Figure 6-4   Retention of information

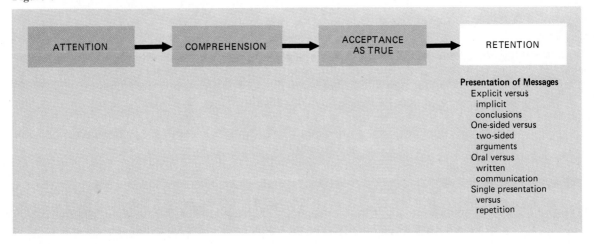

ATTENTION → COMPREHENSION → ACCEPTANCE AS TRUE → RETENTION

Presentation of Messages
Explicit versus
  implicit
  conclusions
One-sided versus
  two-sided
  arguments
Oral versus
  written
  communication
Single presentation
  versus
  repetition

One-Sided versus Two-Sided Arguments

Consider the case in which management is trying to convince workers to vote against the union. Is it more effective to present only the arguments against the union (a one-sided argument), or is it more effective to address both sides of the unionization argument and attempt to refute the union's position? Will presenting two sides of the argument confuse the workers even further, or will it make management seem more fair-minded?

By and large, it is more effective to present *both sides of the argument* in organizational settings. Most of the people a manager will be communicating with are fairly well informed. When the communicator avoids mentioning the counterarguments, the listeners are likely to conclude that the speaker is either unfair or is unable to refute the opponent's arguments.[34]

If employees are *predisposed to disagree* with the manager, then it is even more important for the manager to present both sides of the argument. In the union campaign example, if the manager knows employees are favorably inclined toward unions, it is in the manager's best interest to acknowledge the prounion position before attempting to discredit it. Otherwise, employees will be even more hostile, since the union position is being dismissed out of hand as completely worthless.

Finally, by presenting both sides of the argument, a manager can *forewarn* the employees of how the other side will try to manipulate them: "The union will try to persuade you we are insensitive to your needs and care only about the almighty dollar. Let me address those issues head-on." Forewarning substantially decreases the effectiveness of the other side's position. In fact, this phenomenon is so strong it is called the **inoculation effect.** By presenting a small dose of negative information about their own position and refuting it, speakers inhibit listeners from seriously believing and remembering those negative pieces of information later.[35]

Oral versus Written Communication

Oral communication is more effective than written communication in increasing employees' retention of information over time.[36]

First, face-to-face communication allows the sender to obtain some feedback from the receiver. The speaker can explicitly ask the listeners if they understand the communication, or, at the least, can get a feel from nonverbal behavior how the listeners are reacting. People remember two-way conversations longer than one-way conversation.

Second, when a manager is trying to communicate negative information, written criticism tends to provoke stronger emotional reactions than do oral warnings. Face-to-face exchanges can soften the blow of bad news. Moreover, the impact of praise is stronger when given in person than when relayed in memo.[37]

To get employees to remember particularly important messages, both oral and written communication should be used. New policies or procedures could first be outlined orally, and the manager could make clarifications and answer questions. Then, the information could be put in writing to reinforce the message and to serve as a future reference.[38]

Single Presentation versus Repetition

Finally, is it more effective in getting people to remember a message to present the message *once* or to repeat the same information *several times?* On one hand, people feel demeaned if they have to repeat themselves. What's wrong with them that other people aren't paying attention? Moreover, a person doesn't want to feel like a broken record, going over and over the same material. On the other hand, as discussed earlier, there is so much information overload and background noise that any one message—if only delivered once—may not be heard at all.

In general, it is better to err on the side of *repeating* the message. First of all, repetition of a message is attention-getting; it increases employees' sensitivity and alertness to the information.[39] If employees are reminded every day about a report that is due, they take more notice of it. Moreover, repeating a communication *prolongs* its influence. Employees tend to remember things they hear over and over again.[40] Most commercials, for instance, repeat the name of the product or a jingle over and over again, both to attract people's attention and to implant the product name in their memories. Sometimes people do find the repetition annoying ("Call GR5-5600 right now, that is GR5-5600, call GR5-5600 before midnight tonight . . ."), but in fact they remember those messages longer.

Keys to Effective Management

Common themes running throughout this chapter give us clues on how to improve communication in organizations. Before concluding, let's examine some strategies for making communication more effective.

1   *Managers need to more effectively control the flow of information.*   Regulating the flow of information can substantially increase the efficiency of communication and can be accomplished in several ways.

a   *Exception principle.*   Only communications regarding deviations from orders, plans, and policies should be communicated on a routine basis.

b   *Queuing.*   Managers should postpone handling low-priority messages until a slack period. Unimportant mail, phone calls, and reports can be put on hold, and low-priority meetings and appointments can be rescheduled.

c   *Critical timing.*   Managers need to become more sensitive to sending employees information at the time that they need it—not three months early so that it is discarded as irrelevant and not three months late when it is no longer of any use.

d *Lessening isolation from subordinates.* In order to lessen isolation from subordinates, managers need to get out of their offices occasionally and visit with a broad spectrum of employees at their jobs.

2 *Managers can increase the effectiveness of their communication by increasing redundancy and repetition.* A major principle of communication is to provide *multiple* channels of communication that reinforce each other. For example, a verbal request may be followed up with a memo, or a written report might be followed up by a phone call. Even *within* a message, it is probably good to have some redundancy. When addressing a group, managers might want to make their main arguments early in the speech, give several examples that illustrate their main points, and then reiterate the key points in conclusion.

3 *Managers should try to reduce ambiguity in their communication.* Independent of all the other sources of confusion in communication, a major cause of misunderstanding can reside in the message itself. People do not understand what is being communicated when the information given them is vague.

Managers can use simpler, more direct language. The level of language and the vocabulary should be that of the receiver, not the sender. A series of short messages with a few ideas in each is easier to understand than a long message with many different ideas.

4 *Managers should utilize face-to-face communication wherever possible.* On almost every dimension of communication effectiveness, face-to-face oral communication rates higher than written. People enjoy it more. It enhances the impact of praise and softens the impact of criticism. In addition, people believe information more when they get it "straight from the horse's mouth" and remember it longer. Face-to-face communication is also more effective since it gives people an opportunity to get feedback from their listeners.

5 *Managers should avoid putting listeners on the defensive.* People do not clearly hear information that they find personally threatening or that is inconsistent with what they already believe. They block it out, they distort it, they forget it. As a result, managers need to take care not to put their subordinates on the defensive. They should go easy on argument and criticism, for instance, and try to put their listeners at ease.

6 *Managers should address objections and arguments to their communications head-on.* Managers frequently have to communicate information that they think their listeners may disagree with. In such situations, they need to acknowledge that counterarguments to their position do indeed exist. To be effective in these situations a manager should: (1) present both sides of the argument; (2) forewarn the audience about the objections to the position being presented and systematically refute those objections; (3) draw explicit conclusions; and (4) make explicit their recommendations for action. Obviously, someone who is dead set against a communication can find every way to avoid hearing it or believing it, but the strategies above can be effective in dealing with the true undecideds and even the undecideds leaning in the opposite direction.

Review Questions

1 What is meant by the term *communication?* What are the four stages of the communication process?

2 How do information overload and background noise reduce the amount of attention people pay to a communication?

3 Why do people listen more carefully to communication coming down the chain of command than to communication being passed upward?

4 What characteristics of the informal communication network influence how much grapevine information employees send and receive?

5 What are some strategies managers can use to make sure they keep in touch with their subordinates?

6 Identify the three characteristics of the message itself that attract people's attention.

7 Name two semantic problems that frequently arise in communication. How does each of these interfere with accurate comprehension of the message?

8 Why is nonverbal communication so difficult to interpret correctly?

9 Briefly define the four perceptual biases that distort accurate comprehension of information.

10 Why is two-way feedback so important in communication?

11 What is meant by the term *active listening?* What are some strategies managers can use to improve their active listening?

12 What three factors make people defensive during a conversation?

13 How do people typically respond when they receive dissonant information?

14 Briefly describe four guidelines for nondefensive communication.

15 Which is more effective in getting people to remember communication longer?

   a Explicit or implicit conclusions?

   b One-sided or two-sided arguments?

   c Oral or written communication?

   d Single presentation or repetition?

16 What is the inoculation effect?

Dashman Company

The Dashman Company was a large concern making many types of equipment for the armed forces of the United States. It had over twenty plants, located in the central part of the country, whose purchasing procedures had never been completely coordinated. In fact, the head office of the company had encouraged each of the plant managers to operate with their staffs as separate, independent units in most matters. Late in 1940, when it began to appear that the company would face increasing difficulty in securing certain essential raw materials, Mr. Manson, the company's president, appointed an experienced purchasing executive, Mr. Post, as vice president in charge of purchasing, a position especially created for him. Mr. Manson gave Mr. Post wide latitude in organizing his job, and he assigned Mr. Larson as Mr. Post's assistant. Mr. Larson had served the company in a variety of capacities for many years, and knew most of the plant executives personally. Mr. Post's appointment was announced through the formal channels usual in the company, including a notice in the house organ published by the company.

One of Mr. Post's first decisions was to begin immediately to centralize the company's purchasing procedures. As a first step he decided that he would require each of the executives who handled purchasing in the individual plants to clear with the head office all purchase contracts which they made in excess of $10,000. He felt that if the head office was to do any coordinating in a way that would be helpful to each plant and to the company as a whole, he must be notified that the contracts were being prepared at least a week before they were to be signed. He talked his proposal over with Mr. Manson, who presented it to his board of directors. They approved the plan.

Although the company made purchases throughout the year, the beginning of its peak buying season was only three weeks away at the time this new plan was adopted. Mr. Post prepared a letter to be sent to the twenty purchasing executives of the company. The letter follows:

Dear _____ :

The board of directors of our company has recently authorized a change in our purchasing procedures. Hereafter, each of the purchasing executives in the several plants of the company will notify the vice president in charge of purchasing of all contracts in excess of $10,000 which they are negotiating at least a week in advance of the date on which they are to be signed.

I am sure you will understand that this step is necessary to coordinate the purchasing requirements of the company in these times when we are facing increasing difficulty in securing essential supplies. This procedure should give us in the central office the information we need to see that each plant secures the optimum supply of materials. In this way the interests of each plant and of the company as a whole will best be served.

Yours very truly,

Mr. Post showed the letter to Mr. Larson and invited his comments. Mr. Larson thought the letter an excellent one, but suggested that, since Mr. Post had not met more than a few of the purchasing executives, he might like to visit all of them and take the matter up with each of them personally. Mr. Post dismissed the idea at once because, as he said, he had so many things to do at the head office that he could not get away for a trip. Consequently he had the letters sent out over his signature.

During the two following weeks replies came in from all except a few plants. Although a few executives wrote at greater length, the following reply was typical:

Dear Mr. Post:

Your recent communication in regard to notifying the head office a week in advance of our intention to sign contracts has been received. This suggestion seems a most practical one. We want to assure you that you can count on our cooperation.

Yours very truly,

During the next six weeks the head office received no notices from any plant that contracts were being negotiated. Executives in other departments who made frequent trips to the plants reported that the plants were busy, and the usual routines for that time of year were being followed.

Questions for Discussion

1 What errors did Mr. Post make in composing his memorandum to the twenty purchasing executives?

2 Would oral communication have been more effective here? Why?

3 Why did the purchasing agents not comply with Mr. Post's requests?

4 What should Mr. Post have done differently to effectively communicate with the purchasing agents?

Source: Copyright 1947 by the President and Fellows of Harvard College. Case prepared by G. F. F. Lombard, R. S. Meriam, F. E. Folts, and E. P. Learned as the basis for class discussion rather than to illustrate either effective or ineffective handling of an administrative situation. Reprinted by permission of Harvard Business School.

Notes

1   Mintzberg, H. (1973). *The nature of managerial work.* New York: Harper and Row.

2   Glass, A. (1975, May 31). Paperwork bogs down paperwork probe. *The Miami News,* 1.

3   Likert, R. (1961). *New patterns of management.* New York: McGraw-Hill, 91.

4   Lawler, E. E., Porter, L. W., & Tennenbaum, A. (1968). Managers' attitudes toward interaction episodes. *Journal of Applied Psychology, 52,* 432–439.

5   Vogel, A. (1967). Why don't employees speak up? *Personnel Administration, 30* (May–June), 20–22.

6   Athanassiades, J. (1973). The distortion of upward communication in hierarchical organizations. *Academy of Management Journal, 16,* 207–226.

7   Davis, K. (1968). Success of chain-of-command oral communication in a manufacturing group. *Academy of Management Journal, 11,* 379–387.

8   Ibid.

9   Davis, K. (1978). *Human relations at work* (5th ed.). New York: McGraw-Hill, 267.

10   Sutton, H., & Porter, L. W. (1968). A study of the grapevine in a governmental organization. *Personnel Psychology, 21,* 223–230.
Davis, K. (1953). Management communication and the grapevine. *Harvard Business Review, 31,* 43–49.

11   Meyer, H. E. (1975, June). How the boss stays in touch with the troops. *Fortune,* 152–155.

12   Wexley, K. N., & Yukl, G. A. (1977). *Organizational behavior and personnel psychology.* Homewood, IL: Irwin, 55.

13   Haney, W. V. (1973). *Communication and organizational behavior.* Homewood, IL: Irwin, 443.

14   Hall, E. T. (1959). *The silent language.* New York: Doubleday.

15   Wexley & Yukl, *op. cit.,* 57.

16   Hall, *loc. cit.*

17   Luthans, F. (1981). *Organizational behavior* (3rd ed.). New York: McGraw-Hill, 90.

18   Bruner, J. S., & Tagiuri, R. (1954). The perception of people. In G. Lindzey (Ed.), *Handbook of social psychology* (Vol. 2), 601–633. Reading, MA: Addison-Wesley.

19   Hodgetts, R. M., & Altman, S. (1979). *Organizational behavior.* Philadelphia: W. B. Saunders.

20   Secord, P. F., & Backman, C. W. (1964). *Social psychology.* New York: McGraw-Hill.

21   Haire, M. (1955). Role perception in labor-management relations: An experimental approach. *Industrial and Labor Relations Review, 8,* 204–216.

22   Triandis, H. C. (1971). *Attitudes and attitude change.* New York: Wiley.

23   Sayles, L. R., & Strauss, G. (1981). *Managing human resources* (2nd ed.). Englewood Cliffs, NJ: Prentice-Hall, 117–124.

24   Lewis, P. V. (1980). *Organizational communication: The essence of effective management* (2nd ed.). Columbus, OH: Grid.

25   Rogers, C., & Farson, R. E. (1977). Active listening. In C. Anderson & M. J. Gannon (Ed.), *Readings in management.* Boston: Little, Brown, 284–303.

26   Aronson, E. (1976). *The social animal* (2nd ed.). San Francisco: W. H. Freeman, 55–62.

27   Secord, P. F., Backman, C. W., & Slavitt, D. R. (1977). Impression formation and interaction. In B. M. Staw (Ed.), *Psychological foundations of organizational behavior,* 147–157. Santa Monica, CA: Goodyear, 154.

28   Mills, J., & Aronson, E. (1965). Opinion change as a function of communicator's attractiveness and desire to influence. *Journal of Personality and Social Psychology, 1,* 173–177.
Aronson, *op. cit.,* 61–62.

29   Gibbs, J. (1961). Defensive communication. *Journal of Communication, 3,* 141–148.

30   Aronson, *op. cit.,* 85–139.
Luthans, *op. cit.,* 81–106.

31   Haire, M., & Grunes, W. F. (1950). Perceptual defenses: Processes protecting an organized perception of another personality. *Human Relations, 3,* 403–412.

32   Bittel, L. R. (1985). *What every supervisor should know.* New York: McGraw-Hill, 295–299.

33   Zimbardo, P. G., Ebbesen, E. B., & Maslach, C. (1977). *Influencing* *attitudes and changing behavior* (2nd ed.). Reading, MA: Addison-Wesley, 98–100.

34   Ibid.
Aronson, *op. cit.,* 67–68.

35   Zimbardo, et al., *loc. cit.*

36   O'Reilly, C. A., & Pondy, L. R. (1979). Organizational communication. In S. Kerr (Ed.), *Organizational behavior,* 119–150. Columbus, OH: Grid.

37   Strauss, G., & Sayles, L. R. (1980). *Behavioral strategies for managers.* Englewood Cliffs, NJ: Prentice-Hall, 143.

38   Rue, L. W., & Byars, L. (1980). Communication in organizations. In L. L. Cummings & R. B. Dunham (Eds.), *Introduction to organizational behavior: Text and readings,* 556–572. Homewood, IL: Irwin.

39   Morgan, C. T., & King, R. A. (1966). *Introduction to psychology* (3rd ed.). New York: McGraw-Hill.

40   Zimbardo, et al., *op. cit.,* 100.

Chapter 7

Groups in Organizations

CHAPTER OUTLINE

The Nature of Work Groups

Group Cohesiveness

Group Performance

Group Norms

Deviance

Keys to Effective Management

Review Questions

*T*here is probably no facet of organizational life about which we are more ambivalent than working in groups. On one hand, most of us believe that working together in groups can sometimes result in synergy; that is, that the product of the group will be better than what any one individual group member could have produced alone. On the other hand, most of us can readily recall the antics of some of the groups of which we have been members. The often-told joke "A camel is a horse designed by a committee" reveals that we do not always believe groups are effective in accomplishing their assignments. We can all think of groups in which we enjoyed the companionship of our coworkers and made strong friendships, but we can also think of groups that we disliked and couldn't wait to leave.

In this chapter, we will be examining the most important issues involved in managing groups in organizations today. First, we will look more closely at the nature of work groups, and the types of work groups to which employees belong. Next, we will examine group cohesiveness. What causes some groups to have very strong bonds among group members, and other groups to be marked by indifference or animosity? Do cohesive groups produce more than noncohesive groups? Third, we will look at the factors that influence the productivity of work groups. What are the assets and liabilities of work groups? What factors influence whether groups do achieve some synergy?

In the second half of the chapter, we will be focusing on the interpersonal relationships among members of work groups. We'll examine group norms, the informal rules of a group, and how they influence group dynamics. Finally, we'll explore why some individuals conform to group pressure and others do not. Throughout the chapter, we hope to help the reader understand why groups operate the way they do, and develop some strategies for designing and leading work groups more effectively.

The Nature of Work Groups

Work Groups Defined

By the term **work group,** we mean a collection of two or more people who (1) interact with each other; (2) share similar interests; and (3) come together to accomplish some work activity.

Interaction

In studying groups in organizations, we are interested in how groups influence the feelings and actions of their members. Obviously, for this to occur, there must be opportunity for interaction. If individuals do not interact with each other at work, they won't be aware of each other. They will not be affected by the feelings and actions of others, and thus we really can't consider them a group at all.

Similar Interests

The second element of the definition of work groups refers to similar interests or goals among members. Ten people who happen to be eating in the company cafeteria at the same time would not necessarily be considered a work group. They do not have any interests or goals in common. However, ten stockbrokers who lunch together regularly to discuss the latest Wall Street trends would be considered a work group. They share a common interest in improving their knowledge of the stock market, and a common goal of improving the quality of their recommendations to clients.

Work Orientation

In this chapter, we will further restrict our discussion to groups who come together to accomplish some work activity.

There are many types of *social groups* to which people might belong, such as friendship groups (e.g., college fraternities or alumni associations), special interest groups (e.g., clubs for stamp collectors, science fiction buffs, or astronomers), or sports groups (e.g., bowling teams, softball leagues, bicycling clubs). While all of these collections of people are indeed groups, for our purposes we will be examining only groups that are work-related or that accomplish a work-related project. An audit team in an accounting firm that works together to prepare a client's tax return is a good example of such a work group.

Types of Work Groups

There are three types of work groups to which employees are likely to belong.[1]

Command Groups	A ***command group*** consists of a supervisor and his or her subordinates. A university president and respective college deans, a head nurse and respective floor nurses, and a first-line supervisor and respective assembly line workers are all command groups. These command groups are a permanent part of the organization structure. Even if a particular supervisor or subordinate leaves the group, the group itself remains intact.
Task Groups	A ***task group*** consists of employees who work together to complete a particular task or project, but who do not necessarily report to the same supervisor. For example, in many organizations there is a Safety and Accident Committee. This committee consists of individuals from different departments and divisions who coordinate the development of safety rules and monitor compliance with those rules. Being a member of a task group is not a full-time assignment; it is a work assignment that temporarily takes individuals away from their command groups to work on a common problem.
Informal Groups	***Informal groups*** are those in which membership is voluntary; they evolve gradually among employees with common interests. For instance, in many companies the female executives get together once or twice a month to discuss the particular challenges or problems they are facing in their jobs. A group of junior commercial loan officers in a bank might also constitute an informal work group. They might meet for lunch regularly to discuss common problems or to share work-related information. Employees may be members of several informal groups.

Group Cohesiveness

Not all groups influence their members equally. In some groups there is a genuine liking and mutual respect among members, an almost intangible sense of group spirit. In these groups the bonds among members are strong, and people are strongly influenced by the statements and actions of their fellow workers. In other groups there is only minimal attraction among group members, and being a member of the group is only a tangential part of a member's life. Group membership has much less impact on the feelings and behaviors of these group members.

Cohesiveness Defined	The term ***cohesiveness*** means the extent to which members of a group like each other and want to remain members of the group.[2] In this section, we examine what makes some groups more cohesive than others, and why cohesive groups have such a strong influence on the feelings and behaviors of their members.

■

**Sources
of Group
Cohesiveness**

Group Size

Three factors influence how cohesive a group becomes: (1) group size; (2) shared success in meeting goals; and (3) similarity of attitudes and values.

All things being equal, small groups are more likely to be cohesive than large groups. The reason for this is simple: smaller groups allow for much more interaction among group members than larger groups. When a group gets too large, it is hard to sustain a lot of contact among all the group members. The group tends to split into smaller cliques that are cohesive within themselves, but may be isolated from the others.[3]

**Shared Success in
Meeting Goals**

Shared success in meeting goals also increases group cohesiveness. When the group meets its goals, it reaffirms its self-image as an effective group and solidarity is sustained. Group failure, on the other hand, makes the group much less attractive to its members; people begin to question the abilities and motives of their coworkers.[4]

In the television industry, for example, the success and group cohesiveness of the cast is easily detected at the "wrap party," the party given after the last taping of the season. When a show's ratings have been high, the party is lavish, the stars remain at the party well into the night, and spirits run high. When the show has done poorly, the food is meager, most of the big stars do not show up or only make a brief appearance, and people leave as soon as they can politely do so. People want to revel in success with those who helped make success possible; they want to avoid being reminded of failure by avoiding those with whom they failed.

**Similarity
of Attitudes
and Values**

One of the strongest sources of group cohesiveness is shared attitudes and values among group members. We enjoy spending time with others who hold the same opinions we do because they provide us with a feeling that our opinions are right. In contrast, people whose views differ greatly from our own evoke some fear in us that we are wrong-headed.

Box 7-1 illustrates how the management of a computer firm, Data General, went about attracting young engineers to work for Eclipse Group, a particularly intense computer design project.[5] Management wanted to make sure that group members would form a cohesive unit and would be excited about working the long, hard hours the project demanded. As the excerpt illustrates, Data General tried to ensure that recruits shared similar attitudes and values about their jobs.

There is no question that groups seek out new recruits who are like themselves, and that groups consisting of individuals with similar attitudes and values are more cohesive. Whether such cohesiveness is good for the organization is another question altogether, and one we consider next.

BOX 7-1

Building a Team at Data General

There was a mysterious rite of initiation through which, in one way or another, almost every member of the Eclipse Group computer design team passed. The term that the old hands used for this rite was "signing up." By signing up for the project an engineer agreed to forsake, if necessary, family, hobbies, and friends— if he had any of these left. From a manager's point of view, the practical virtues of the ritual were manifold. Employees were no longer coerced; they volunteered. When an engineer signed up, he in effect declared, "I want to do this job and I'll give it my heart and soul."

What enticements could the Eclipse Group at Data General offer to young computer engineers that companies such as IBM could not? Clearly, Data General's strongest pitch would be the project itself. As one manager reasoned, "Engineering school prepares you for big projects and a lot of guys wind up as transformer designers. It's a terrible letdown, I think. . . . By contrast, it was thought to be a fine thing in the fraternity of hardware engineers—in the local idiom, it was 'the sexy job'—to be a builder of new computers. . . . You can sign a guy up to that any day of the year. And we got the best there was. . . ."

The ideal interview of a potential group member would proceed in this fashion:

Interviewer: "It's going to be tough. If we hired you, you'd be working with a bunch of cynics and egotists and it'd be hard to keep up with them."

Recruit: "That doesn't scare me."

Interviewer: "There's a lot of fast people in this group. It's gonna be a real hard job with a lot of long hours. And I mean *long* hours."

Recruit: "No, that's what I want to do, get in on the ground floor of a new architecture. I want to do a big machine. I want to be where the action is."

Interviewer: "Well, we can only let in the best of this year's graduates. We've already let in some awfully fast people. We'll have to let you know."

After it was all done, the project manager remarked: "It was kind of like recruiting for a suicide mission. You're gonna die, but you're gonna die in glory."

Source: Adapted from: Kidder, John Tracy. (1981). *The soul of a new machine.* New York: Avon, pp. 63–66. Used by permission of Little, Brown and Company, in association with the Atlantic Monthly Press.

Consequences of Group Cohesiveness

Morale

On almost every index of satisfaction and morale, cohesive groups rank higher than noncohesive groups. Members of cohesive groups evaluate other members in their group more positively, and have a more favorable opinion of the group as a whole. There tends to be little conflict in cohesive groups, for members of cohesive groups tend to feel less tense and anxious with each other.

Communication	Members of cohesive groups communicate with each other more frequently. Members of cohesive groups tend to have more in common with each other, and therefore find conversation with each other to be more pleasurable. Research suggests that members of cohesive groups also show greater sensitivity to each other; they are more accurate in perceiving the feelings of fellow group members.[6]
Hostility and Aggression toward Non-group Members	Unfortunately, members of cohesive groups tend to have an overly negative view of individuals outside their own group. Because individuals in cohesive groups are so positive about their own groups, they tend to downplay the competence and effectiveness of other groups. As a result, members of cohesive groups tend to express increased hostility and aggression toward non-group members.[7]
Productivity	The strongest influence group cohesiveness has on productivity is that it *decreases productivity differences among members of a work group.* Members of a cohesive group value the group's good opinion and are unlikely to risk losing the group's esteem by producing much more or less than the group expects.[8]

However, group cohesiveness *does not necessarily lead to higher overall productivity.* In the largest-scale study of the impact of group cohesiveness on productivity, researchers found that high cohesiveness is as frequently associated with low productivity as with high productivity.[9]

Let's consider our Eclipse Group computer design team (see Box 7-1) again. This computer team was highly cohesive, and in addition it felt that management was highly supportive of its mission to develop the state-of-the-art computer. Team members felt a sense of pride in their work, and felt appreciated by Data General's management. As a result, members of the team worked incredibly hard to finish their design on time, often working late into the evening and through the weekends. Here, cohesiveness worked to enhance productivity.

In contrast, Box 7-2 provides a vivid example of how high cohesiveness can lead to lower productivity. Many factory workers are paid on what is called **the piece-rate system:** they are paid so many cents for each unit they produce. Often workers feel that if they produce too many units in an hour, management will lower the amount paid for each unit produced. Workers would have to produce more units just to get the same amount of pay. In these threatening situations, cohesive groups will strongly ostracize any "ratebusters" who refuse to abide by the informally established ceiling on output.[10] Cohesiveness here works against productivity.

Thus, cohesiveness will decrease the amount of variability in performance among members of a work group, but will not necessarily increase the productivity of the group as a whole. In the next section, we'll look more closely at the factors that influence whether group cohesiveness will have a positive or a negative impact on group performance.

BOX 7-2

Piece-Rate Jobs at a Furniture Factory

One day while picking up sawdust, I began to find pieces (of furniture dowling) in the sawdust or behind a woodpile or under a machine. The first few times, with great delight, I would announce to the operator, "Hey, look what I found!" I should have figured something was wrong by the lack of any similar enthusiasm from the operator. Sam was a generally quiet Midwesterner who never seemed to raise his voice much, but now when I showed him my finished work discovery behind his milling machine he shouted, "Who the hell asked you to be a detective? Keep out from behind my machine. I'll tell you what to pick up. . . ."

Confused, troubled, almost in tears, not knowing what to do or where to go, I lit a cigarette and began pacing up and down, puffing at my Camel. While I'm pacing and puffing, Sam comes in, saying, "Lissen, kid, don't get sore. I was trying to set you straight. Let me tell you what it's all about. The guys around, that is the machine operators, agree on how much we are gonna turn out, and that's what the boss gets, no more, no less. Now sometimes any one of us might just fall behind a little, so we always keep some finished stuff hidden away just in case." The more he talked, the more I really began to feel like the enemy. I tried to apologize, but he just went on. "Look, kid, the boss always wants more and he doesn't give a damn if we die giving it to him, so we agree on how much we're going to give him—no more, no less. You see, kid, if you keep running around, moving the stuff too fast, the boss will get wise to what's going on."

Sam put his arm on my shoulder. "So look," he says, "your job is to figure out how to move and work no faster than we turn the stuff out. Get it? O.K.? You'll get it." I said, "Yes, of course, I understand everything."

I was beginning to learn a lesson that would be taught me many times over in a variety of different jobs. Don't do more work than is absolutely necessary.

Source: Reprinted from: Schrank, R. (1978). *Ten thousand working days.* Cambridge, MA: MIT Press, pp. 7–8. Used by permission.

Factors Influencing the Productivity of Cohesive Groups

Antagonism/ Friendliness between Workers and Management

If we look carefully at the two cohesive groups we described in the boxed inserts—the Eclipse computer design team at Data General and the furniture dowling pieceworkers at the furniture factory—we see two factors that lead some cohesive groups to be more productive and other cohesive groups to be less productive.[11]

In the furniture factory, workers believed management was trying to work them too hard. In fact, they felt that even if they worked harder to produce more furniture dowlings, they would be punished by having the piecerate lowered. As a result, the group became cohesive around the goal of beating management at its own game.

In contrast, the computer designers at Data General had very positive feelings toward their managers. Management gave them the best equipment and resources they could afford, and gave them positive feedback for the extra effort they were exerting. Consequently, members of the Eclipse team became cohesive around helping management meet its production goals on time.

Dull Jobs/ Interesting Jobs

When jobs themselves are not interesting, group members are likely to become cohesive around avoiding hard work. The jobs are boring and tedious, so group members want to make sure that they don't have to work any harder on the jobs than is absolutely necessary. That is one reason why the ratebuster in the furniture factory was ostracized. If management discovered that the workers could produce even more, then the workers would have to exert more effort on jobs that they disliked.

In contrast, the computer designers at Data General were very enthusiastic about designing a state-of-the-art computer. By working hard for Data General, they were not only meeting the firm's goals, but they were also growing professionally as well. The harder they worked, the more glory they would receive, too. Consequently, the interesting nature of the jobs motivated the cohesive Eclipse team to work even harder.

In this section, we have discussed the impact of group cohesiveness on group productivity. In the next section, we will discuss group productivity in much more detail, and discover other factors besides cohesiveness that influence whether groups perform effectively at work.

Group Performance

If a group could take advantage of all the efforts and abilities of its members, then the larger the group, the greater its potential productivity. Potential productivity should increase directly with group size. However, when we look at what actually happens as groups get larger, we see that groups do not perform up to their ideal potential. There is some loss of productivity when individual contributions are combined. ***Actual productivity*** is lower than ***potential productivity.***[12]

The relationship between potential productivity and actual productivity is diagrammed in Figure 7-1. On the horizontal axis is the size of the group; on the vertical axis is group output. The potential productivity curve is a straight line; the greater the size of the group, the greater the potential output of the group. In contrast, the actual productivity curve plateaus out; the larger the actual size of the group, the less additional output each successive group member contributes.

By looking at the ***assets*** of groups we can discover why both potential and actual group productivity increase as the group gets larger. Conversely, by looking at the ***liabilities*** of groups, we can discover why there is some loss of effectiveness as groups grow larger.[13]

Figure 7-1   Model of group performance

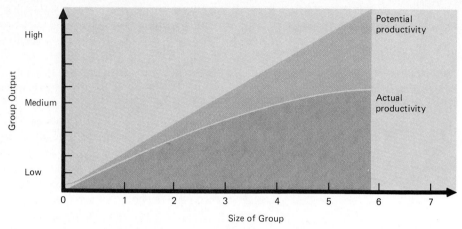

[*Source:* Adapted from I. D. Steiner (1966). Models for inferring relationships between group size and potential group productivity. *Behavioral Science, 11,* 273–283. Reprinted by permission.]

Potential Assets of Groups

Groups can potentially enhance the productivity of individual members in three ways: (1) by increasing their job-relevant knowledge and skills; (2) by increasing their level of job satisfaction; and (3) by increasing the level of effort they exert.

Job-Relevant Knowledge and Skills

Groups increase individual productivity by increasing individual members' job-relevant knowledge and skills. Group members can give direct instruction to coworkers on how to do their jobs more effectively. They can show them shortcuts, teach them how to work more efficiently, and help them to better organize their work. For example, senior accountants can give useful knowledge to junior accountants as they work together on internal audit teams.[14]

Also, individuals can learn the correct behavior to engage in at work by observing the behavior of other group members. By observing how other members of the group act, an individual can learn what behaviors are desired in the group. For example, most people pick up cues on how formal or informal to be in interactions with employees at different levels of the organization by observing how their coworkers behave.[15]

Satisfaction of Group Members

As we discussed in Chapter 4, the relationship between job satisfaction and job performance is relatively weak and the direct impact of job satisfaction on individual productivity is relatively small. However, the *social* rewards of working with other individuals can increase productivity *indirectly*.

Particularly when the jobs are uninteresting and routine, having congenial coworkers can make the workday more enjoyable. Sometimes the stimulation of friends at work can compensate for the lack of stimulation from the job.

Even if the work is highly challenging, having friendly coworkers can facilitate performance. People under stress actively seek out others with whom to share their anxieties.[16] By relieving some of the stress through talking, coworkers can help each other sustain their performance until the high-stress period passes.[17]

Moreover, satisfied workers have lower absenteeism, lower turnover, and less industrial conflict. All of these can also get translated into higher productivity.[18]

Level of Effort

Groups have the potential to increase the level of effort and intensity individual members put into their jobs. Working in the presence of other people does have an energizing effect on individuals, causing them to work with greater intensity. This phenomenon is called ***social facilitation.***[19] Moreover, when workers are being observed by people who might be evaluating their performance (such as their supervisors), their level of effort and work intensity increases even more substantially.[20]

However, it is important to note the one major exception to the above findings. If individuals are working on jobs that involve a lot of thinking or creativity (for instance, designing circuits or coming up with ideas for a commercial), working in the presence of others interferes with performance. In these situations, people get overly nervous and lose their concentration. Their anxiety gets in the way of better performance.

Potential Liabilities of Groups

Just as it is possible for individuals working together to produce some overall group benefits, the opposite is also true. Sometimes the group is less than the sum of its parts. Somewhere along the line, the group doesn't marshal its resources effectively and a lot of individual talent is untapped or wasted.

There are at least three ways groups can potentially decrease the productivity of individual members: (1) by decreasing their motivation to perform well; (2) by creating problems of coordination among group members; and (3) by decreasing individual feelings of responsibility.

Motivation Losses

As we discussed in Chapter 3, employee motivation to perform well is strongly influenced by the perception that good performance will lead to rewards; that is, that rewards are *contingent* upon performance. If an individual's reward is contingent upon his or her own *individual* performance, he or she will be motivated to perform at a high level.

The group setting complicates this scenario. If individuals are being rewarded contingent upon the *group's* performance, the performance-reward link is much less clear.[21] For instance, an individual could work very hard on a group project, but the incompetence of a coworker could prevent the group from turning out a good project. The individual performed well, but didn't get the reward. Conversely, an individual could do very sloppy work on a project, but could have colleagues who take up the slack by redoing that portion. In this case, the individual is likely to be rewarded despite the poor performance. Motivation often drops in group settings because there is less connection between individual performance and group rewards.

Coordination Losses

Actual productivity of groups also falls short of potential productivity because groups can lose a lot of productive time in trying to coordinate individual members' activities.[22]

Working on group projects requires some setup time: the group must be brought together, a suitable meeting time determined, and an agenda established. Moreover, it takes time to divide up all the work and then put the different parts of the project back together again after they have been completed. While an individual working alone might need seventy hours to do a job, it might take 10 people ten hours apiece, or one hundred employee-hours, to complete the project together.

Diffusion of Responsibility

In group situations individuals are more likely to shirk responsibilities that are not *theirs alone*. Consequently, some shared responsibilities fall through the cracks and remain undone.[23]

A good example of this phenomenon can be seen in retail department stores. It used to be the common practice in department stores for salespersons in each department to be responsible for taking back returns and exchanges. However, because no new sales commission would result, no one wanted to perform these tasks, and customers making returns and exchanges were shunted from one salesperson to another like hot potatoes. Each salesperson would claim that he or she had just handled a return, so it was somebody else's turn to deal with the customer. Now, many department stores have separate return and exchange departments. Even those that don't have separate departments make special arrangements for the Christmas season, when both the volume of returns and the volume of shoppers is high. In most group settings, diffusion of responsibility presents a real liability unless specific individual members can be given personal responsibility for completing specific tasks.

The consequences of diffusion of responsibility can also be seen in the development of the M-16 rifle for use in the Vietnam War. As Box 7-3 suggests, the lack of coordination among the different branches of the U.S. armed forces, the Pentagon, and weapons manufacturers yielded tragic results for the soldiers that had to use the rifle in combat.[24]

Box 7-3 also illustrates that the performance of a group is not entirely dependent on the skills and abilities of group members. The interpersonal dynamics among the members of a group come into play as well. In the last two sections of the chapter, we'll look more closely at these group dynamics and the role they play in group effectiveness.

BOX 7-3

The Development of the M-16 Rifle:
The Liabilities of Groups in Practice

In 1957, a new rifle called the AR-15 was developed by Eugene Stoner. It had several advantages over the previously used M-14. The rifle itself was lighter than the M-15, so that a soldier using the AR-15 could carry almost 3 times as many rounds of ammunition as a man with the M-14. This promised to eliminate one of the soldier's fundamental problems in combat: running out of ammunition during a fire fight. The AR-15 was also highly reliable. It could feed, fire, extract, and eject 600 or 700 cartridges a minute and practically never jam. In a 1962 test of 1,000 AR-15s shipped to Vietnam in actual combat, there were no broken parts reported in the firing of 80,000 rounds, and only two replacement parts were issued for all 1,000 rifles.

However, the Army Ordnance Corps (the unit in charge of purchasing rifles) had every reason to dislike the AR-15. It came from an outside inventor (Stoner) and threatened to replace a product of their own arsenal system, the M-14. The Army Ordnance Corps got hold of the AR-15, declared it to be "inadequately developed," and "militarized" it into the M-16 by making three modifications.

First, it added a manual bolt, a handle that would permit the soldier to load the gun manually. The Air Force and Marine Corps objected vehemently, complaining the device would add cost, weight, and complexity to the weapon, thereby reducing the reliability that had been its greatest asset. Second, the Ordnance Corps modified the rifle's barrel to make the bullet spin faster, but in so doing greatly reduced the damage a bullet would inflict on the enemy. Third, the Ordnance Corps insisted on changing the type of gunpowder in the M-16, to a powder manufactured by a long-time supplier to the Ordnance Corps.

The consequences of these changes were immediate and grave. What had been a supremely reliable rifle was now given to chronic breakdowns and jams. One Marine was killed as he ran up and down the line in his squad, unjamming rifles, because he had the only cleaning rod in the squad. Officials from the Pentagon would go on inspection tours to Vietnam and scold the soldiers for not keeping the rifles clean enough, but there never seemed to be enough cleaning supplies for the M-16.

In Congressional hearings, when representatives of the Ordnance Corps were pressed to explain their decisions, they fell back on citations from the rule books. They seemed to have a hard time remembering who was responsible for crucial decisions; they tended to explain things by saying, "The feeling was," or "The practice has been. . . ." They seemed not to see a connection between these choices and the soldiers who were dying with jammed rifles in their arms.

Source: Reprinted from: Fallows, J. (1981). *The national defense.* New York: Vintage, pp. 76–95. Used by permission of Random House.

Group Norms

Norms Defined

Group norms are the informal rules of behavior that provide some order to group activities.[25] While rarely written down and mostly unspoken, these norms can regulate group behavior with a consistency and a power that even formal organizational rules fail to engender. The set of norms with which a group operates also strongly influences how effectively the group can perform its job. Let's look now at some examples of group norms that are frequently found in work settings.

Types of Group Norms

Groups typically develop two types of norms: behavior norms and performance norms. *Behavior norms* are rules that standardize how people act at work on a day-to-day basis. *Performance norms* are rules that standardize employee output and number of hours worked.[26]

Behavior Norms

One behavior a group might want to regulate is the amount of participation in group meetings. Group members who sit back and say nothing are not appreciated, but people who monopolize the conversation also receive disapproval. Behavior norms will exert pressure on more silent members to carry their weight in group meetings and on overly talkative members to tone down their participation.

Another behavior that groups may regulate is the use of humor. The person who is completely humorless receives disapproval, for he or she makes other members feel uncomfortable and awkward. The person who is completely flip also receives disapproval because he or she is acting like the group fool or clown. Group norms will often exert pressure on dour group members to be a little more relaxed and easygoing, and on overly comical members to tone down their remarks.

Performance Norms

Production groups use performance norms to regulate the output of individual workers. The person producing too many pieces of work may be ostracized for encouraging management to reset the piece rate. On the other hand, the person producing too little puts a burden on coworkers to produce more to compensate. Thus, groups will often develop performance norms to regulate how much workers produce on the job.

Groups also frequently develop performance norms about the amount of time worked. For instance, in many offices secretaries are given a fifteen-minute coffee break in the morning. If a secretary doesn't take the break, he or she will receive some disapproval from coworkers because of increased pressure on them to skip their breaks too. On the other hand, secretaries who disappear for thirty or forty-five minutes per break will also receive disapproval. They will be shirking their responsibilities and displacing them onto coworkers.

Thus, groups will often want to regulate not only how much workers produce, but also how many hours they put in on the job.

While group norms indicate what the most desired behaviors on the part of group members are, there is also a *range of acceptable behavior.* For instance, being on time for work may be a group norm, but there will be no crisis if someone is occasionally five or ten minutes late. Producing 50 widgets an hour might be a group norm, but producing between 45 and 55 widgets an hour is likely to be acceptable to the group as well. Most group norms leave some latitude for individual discretion.

Why Norms Are Strongly Enforced

Groups don't have the time or energy to regulate each and every action of group members. Only those behaviors that are viewed as most important by group members will be brought under control.

Groups, like individuals, try to operate in such a way that they maximize their chances of task success and minimize their chances of task failure. Groups want to facilitate their performance and overcome barriers to reaching their goals. Moreover, groups want to increase morale and prevent any embarrassment or interpersonal discomfort to their members. Norms that will help groups meet these twin aims of performing successfully and keeping morale high are likely to be strongly enforced.[27] Below we consider four conditions where group norms will be especially enforced.

1 *Norms are likely to be strongly enforced if they facilitate group success or ensure group survival.*   For example, a group will strongly enforce norms that protect it from interference or harassment by members of other groups. Group members might develop a norm prohibiting discussion of salaries with members of other groups in the organization for this reason; they do not want attention brought to pay inequities in their favor. Some groups might also strongly enforce norms about not drinking at lunch and not being late for work. Individual group members who do not drink at lunch and who are on time for work are able to help the group accomplish its work goals more readily.

2 *Norms are likely to be strongly enforced if they simplify, or make predictable, what behavior is expected of group members.*   Group members may be uncertain about how to behave in certain types of situations. For instance, when attending meetings where proposals are presented and suggestions are requested, do the presenters really want feedback or are they simply going through the motions? Groups may develop norms that reduce this uncertainty and provide a clearer course of action (e.g., make suggestions in small, informal meetings but not in large, formal meetings). Norms about how to dress and where to sit in group meetings are also enforced to simplify, or make predictable, member behavior.

3 *Norms are likely to be strongly enforced if they reinforce specific members' roles within a group.* A number of different **roles** emerge within a group. These roles are simply expectations that are shared by group members about who is to perform specific duties in the group.[28] For instance, a group might have one person whom others expect to break the tension when tempers become too hot. Another group member might be expected to keep track of political developments in other parts of the organization. A third member might be expected to take care of the creature comforts of the group—making the coffee or making the dinner reservations, for example. A fourth member might be expected by others to take notes, keep minutes, or maintain files.

None of these roles are formal duties, but they are activities that the group needs accomplished and has somehow parceled out among members. Therefore, norms that reaffirm such roles are likely to be strongly enforced. If the role expectations are not met, some important jobs might not get done or other group members might have to take on additional responsibilities.

4 *Norms are likely to be strongly enforced if they help the group avoid embarrassing interpersonal problems.* Groups enforce norms that discourage certain topics of conversation which might prove awkward to group members. For instance, groups often have norms prohibiting discussion of religion or politics, topics that could cause tension and friction among group members. A group might also have a norm ensuring that social gatherings take place only in restaurants or public places and not in people's homes, so that differences in taste or income do not become salient. Groups will do what they can so that their members will not be embarrassed or made to feel awkward in public.[29]

How Group Norms Develop

Norms usually develop gradually and informally as group members learn what behaviors are necessary for the group to function effectively. Below we look at the four most common ways in which group norms develop.[30]

Carryover from Past Situations

Particularly among professional workers, there are existing norms about the appropriate ways to behave. For instance, accountants typically expect their colleagues to be formally dressed when going out on an audit; design engineers typically expect to have to work some overtime. Individual group members often bring expectations about appropriate behaviors with them from organization to organization.

Primacy

The first behavior pattern that emerges in a group often sets the group norm. If the first group meeting is marked by very formal interaction between supervisors and subordinates, then the group often expects future meetings to be conducted in the same way. Where people sit in meetings or rooms is also frequently a matter of primacy. People generally continue to sit in the same seats they sat in at their first meeting, even though those original seats are not assigned and people could change where they sit at every meeting.

Critical Incidents   Sometimes there is an important incident in the group's history that establishes a precedent. In one organization, the head of a department invited the entire staff to his house for dinner. The next day, people discovered that not one person on the staff had attended. The unpleasantness of this incident caused a norm to be established that prohibited outside entertaining for several years.

Conscious Decision of the Group   While norms generally develop gradually, it is also possible for the norm development process to be shortcut by some conscious decision of the group leader or of the group members themselves. For example, group members might note that they typically accomplish too little in a meeting and then consciously set norms (e.g., circulating agendas ahead of time, not interrupting others while they are talking, not starting meetings after 4:30 p.m.) to regulate the ineffective behavior.

Deviance

Most group members comply with the group's norms. The phrase "Get along by going along" captures much of what we have been taught over the years about how to succeed in groups and organizations. In school, the troublemakers are punished by the teachers and thought of as different by their classmates. When we start looking for jobs, we get further reinforcement for following standard practices. How a résumé should look, how we should dress, and how we should behave in our job interviews are all prescribed by norms. Of course, we don't have to conform, but we notice that people who don't conform have a much more difficult time getting good jobs, or any jobs at all.

In the previous section, we examined why groups develop norms and try hard to enforce them. In this section, we'll be looking more closely at how individuals respond to these group pressures. In particular, we'll be exploring what happens to group *deviants*—those who systematically refuse to conform to the group norms—and how they affect the performance of the group as a whole.

Deviance Defined   The term *deviance* refers to behaviors that other members of the group consider so threatening, embarrassing, or irritating that they bring special sanctions to bear against the persons who exhibit them.[31] Ratebusting is threatening to the survival of production groups, and is labeled deviant; unattractive, unstylish clothing is embarrassing and irritating to executives and is labeled deviant.

Each group develops its own set of norms to facilitate the group's particular task goals and prevent uncomfortable interpersonal situations for its particular members. What is deviant in a group is likewise unique to that group. Different groups will label different behaviors as deviant. For instance, ratebusting is threatening in production groups but individual competitive behavior is positively rewarded among executives. In contrast, unattractive and unstylish clothing is irritating and embarrassing to executives, but is the norm on production lines. What a group labels deviant reflects its own internal standards.

Functions of Deviance

Labeling certain behaviors as deviant serves three major functions for the group.[32]

First, labeling behavior as deviant *gives expression to the group's central values.* It clarifies what is distinctive about the group and central to its identity. When the production group labels ratebusting as deviant, it says, "We care more about maximizing group security than about individual profits." When an advertising agency labels wearing unstylish clothes deviant, it says, "We think of ourselves, personally and professionally, as trendsetters, and being fashionable conveys that to our clients and our public."

Second, labeling behavior as deviant *makes salient the power and authority of the group.* Each time a group punishes a deviant member, it reinforces in the minds of all members the power and authority of the group. Punishment of group deviants—in the form of ostracism or ridicule—reminds other group members what will happen to them if they do not conform.

Third, labeling behavior as deviant *makes explicit the range of acceptable behavior for each group norm.* By observing a series of incidents (a person produces 50 widgets and is praised; a person produces 60 widgets and is sharply teased; a person produces 70 widgets and is ostracized), group members learn the *limits* of the group's patience: this far, and no further.

Rejection of the Deviant

Deviants tend to irritate and embarrass their colleagues and make them feel uncomfortable. Consequently, coworkers and supervisors will pressure dissenters to get back into line. Box 7-4 provides an interesting example of how middle managers try to punish "reformers," subordinates who agitate to change significant organization practices.[33] The intimidation tactics become increasingly severe as the employee becomes increasingly recalcitrant.

Box 7-4 nicely illustrates the paradox of group deviance. While deviant members obviously make their colleagues feel uncomfortable, the group is very reluctant to do anything to directly exclude the offenders. Supervisors are reluctant to directly exclude the deviant because they want to preserve their carefully managed image of reasonableness.

BOX 7-4

Intimidation Rituals: Middle Managers Dealing with Deviants

Intimidation rituals are ways middle managers deal with "reformers," people who emerge from the lower levels of the organization and demand significant changes in the organization. In order to protect their interests, middle-level managers use four types of intimidation against reform-minded subordinates.

1 *Nullification.*   When a reformer first approaches his immediate supervisors, they will assure him that his accusation or suggestions are invalid—the result of misunderstandings on his part. His superiors, in this phase, hope that the reformer will be so awed by authority that he will simply take their word that his initiative is based on error. If, however, the reformer insists, his superiors will often agree to conduct an investigation. The explicit message is: "You don't know what you're talking about, but thank you anyway for telling us. We'll certainly look into the matter for you." Members of the middle hierarchy then proceed to cover up whatever (for them) embarrassing truth exists in the reformer's arguments.

2 *Isolation.*   If the reformer persists in his efforts, middle management will separate him from his peers, subordinates, and superiors, thereby softening his impact on the organization and making it extremely difficult for him to mobilize any support for his position. Most forms of isolation are designed to persuade the reformer of the futility of trying to initiate change.

3 *Defamation.*   If the reformer refuses to remain silent, and instead mobilizes support for his position, middle management will begin to impugn his character and his motives. Middle managers will often distort events or even fabricate instances of misconduct in order to intimidate not only the reformer but also those who would listen to or believe him. Supervisors will use their offices and positions of trust and responsibility to create the impression in the minds of others in the organization that their accusations of incompetence, self-interest, or psychopathology are true.

4 *Expulsion.*   When nullification, isolation, and defamation fail to silence the reformer or force his withdrawal from the organization, the middle hierarchy seeks an official decision for his dismissal. An official dismissal serves as a warning to other budding reformers that middle management has the necessary power and authority to expel troublemakers. The act of expulsion supports the contention that the reformer is an immoral or irrational man.

Source: Adapted from: O'Day, R. (1974). Intimidation rituals: Reactions to reform. *Journal of Applied Behavioral Science, 10* (No. 3), 373–386. Used by permission.

In the eyes of *their* managers, they do not want to appear unable to control their subordinates, and punishing deviance might bring negative attention to themselves. Coworkers are also reluctant to directly reject the deviant. While supervisory attention is focused on one deviant, their own flaws and failings are more likely to go unnoticed. Thus, expulsion of the deviant is a last-ditch strategy of groups; groups will do everything they can to bring the deviant back into line before taking that step.

However, there are three circumstances in which groups do seem willing to exclude the group deviant.

1 *The group is more likely to reject the deviant when the deviant has not been a good group citizen over a long period of time.* Group members can build up goodwill with their coworkers by being good group citizens—that is, by contributing effectively to the attainment of group goals and by generally conforming to the norms of the group. However, individuals expend this goodwill when they deviate—either by performing poorly at work or by failing to comply with group norms. In essence, it has been said that individuals earn ***idiosyncrasy credits*** by conforming to group norms and lose them for deviating from group norms. When a group member no longer has a positive balance of credits to draw upon, he or she is much more likely to be rejected for deviance.[34]

For instance, consider a veteran production worker whose output has climbed too sharply over the past couple of months. The group will be hesitant to ostracize the worker, since he or she has been such a good group member over the past years, producing acceptable amounts and being a congenial coworker. However, if a new worker produces too much in his or her first two months on the job, that deviance will be punished. The new worker hasn't earned any credits upon which to draw.

2 *The group is more likely to reject the deviant when the group is failing to meet its goals.* When the group is successful, it is somewhat tolerant of deviant behavior. The group may disapprove of deviant behavior, but it has some margin for error. When the group is faced with failure, then deviance is much more sharply punished. Any behavior that negatively influences the success of the group becomes much more salient and threatening to group members.

For instance, if the overall organization is making sufficient profits, ratebusting, or deviance from the piece-rate norm—while undesirable—is less threatening. The work group figures the one high producer will be a barely noticed blip in the otherwise routine production figures. However, when the organization is making concerted efforts to cut all costs, such deviance is much more threatening. Even one case of ratebusting could draw attention to the group's restrained pace, and all deviance must be viewed as the potential "straw that could break the camel's back."[35]

3 *The group is more likely to reject the deviant when the deviant is seen as completely incorrigible or uninfluenceable.* Groups will try to change a deviant member whenever they can, and will revert to rejection of the deviant *when change seems hopeless.*[36]

For instance, consider a student who consistently disagrees with the solutions to cases the class is discussing. In the beginning both the professor and other classmates will volunteer to address the student's objections. A lot of communication will be addressed to the deviant to get him or her to understand the class's point of view. However, if the student repeatedly states that there is no utility in doing cases, or that he or she hates the subject matter and finds it irrelevant, then others will tune out the deviant. Psychologically the deviant student will be rejected. Neither the professor nor fellow classmates will seriously address the student's continued objections to case solutions since they know that no answer would ever be satisfactory.

Deviance and Group Effectiveness

Caught between the desire to keep the deviant and the desire to reject him or her, the group all too often resolves the dilemma by *institutionalizing the role of the deviant* within the group. The person is labeled an oddball, and few pay much attention to his or her opinions or behaviors. "Don't mind Bob, he's always like that" or "Carol's at it again" are the kind of phrases used to brush aside the offending statement or behavior. People recognize the deviance but ignore it.

Group members simply find themselves unable and unwilling to handle the sensitive interpersonal issues that would be involved in rejecting a fellow worker. By gradually imposing the role of deviant on the offending member, the group solves the problem of the deviant's behavior in the short run without any emotional upheaval. However, such treatment of deviants can lower the group's effectiveness in two ways.[37]

First, by not tolerating deviance, the group loses the fresh perspectives of new members and diminishes their enthusiasm for improving the group. New members of a group are most likely to be punished for any deviance because they have the fewest idiosyncrasy credits. However, stifling the dissent or the questioning attitude of new recruits too seriously diminishes their enthusiasm. Their ideas for innovation, however fanciful, are too sharply curtailed. Two of the greatest assets new recruits bring to an organization are a fresh perspective and a desire to improve the group, and overbearing punishment for deviance deadens both of these quite quickly.

Second, by extinguishing all deviance, the group loses the opportunity to test the usefulness and ultimate validity of the very norms it is enforcing.[38] Ignoring the issues raised by deviants may prevent the group from discovering whether a norm is still helpful to the achievement of group goals and maintenance of group morale. Perhaps a norm in favor of long work hours, developed when the organization was short of staff, is no longer appropriate with added personnel. Perhaps some work procedures were efficient before the advent of personal computers, but are now inappropriate with the new technology. Perhaps norms prohibiting the hiring of husbands and wives by the same organization are no longer appropriate with so many two-career couples in the work force. More open and conscious decisions about what norms to enforce and what deviance to curtail would greatly enhance the long-term effectiveness of groups.

Keys to Effective Management

In closing, let's examine some of the managerial implications of this material more closely.

1   *In order to build group cohesiveness, managers should try to increase the amount of contact among group members, keep group size rather small, and develop common goals and interests among coworkers.*   The more employees interact with each other, the more likely they will be to develop close bonds of friendship. It is hard to develop a cohesive group if members don't spend much time with each other. This is also why smaller groups tend to be more cohesive; smaller groups allow much more interaction among group members than large groups. Shared goals and interests among coworkers also increase the attractiveness of the group to its members, and reduce potential sources of friction and conflict.

2   *In order to enhance group effectiveness, group leaders need to assign specific duties to individual group members, and reward them for their efforts.*   The three greatest liabilities of groups are decreased motivation, increased coordination problems, and diffusion of responsibility. Assigning specific duties to individual group members and rewarding them for their efforts will increase individual motivation. Members will know exactly what is expected of them, and will be certain of getting rewarded for their output. There will also be less diffusion of responsibility, since group members will each know for which tasks they are being held accountable. Moreover, clear division of labor helps the leader coordinate group members' individual efforts more effectively.

3   *The manager should diagnose which group norms are obsolete or dysfunctional to the work unit, and try to eliminate those soon after assuming his or her position.*   The group's norms can either enhance or detract from the group's effectiveness. Therefore, it is important to eliminate those norms that are unproductive for the group and set new norms for the group that are more functional. Because group norms often stay in place long after the initial circumstances that gave rise to them have passed, it is critical that the manager continually reassess the group's norms.

Moreover, it is much easier and more effective to change group norms at the outset of a relationship than to change the group norms later. If a new manager allows the old norms to carry over without questioning them, his or her attempts to change group norms months later will be seen as betrayal of some implicit understanding with subordinates.

4 *In trying to change the group's norms, the manager should draw the group's attention explicitly to the problem areas and suggest specific alternative ways of behaving.*   Groups resist examining their own interpersonal relationships; indeed, one of the biggest obstacles to the changing of group norms is a lack of recognition that the norms even exist. Therefore, the manager cannot rely on subtle social cues in changing the group's norms. He or she must draw the group's attention explicitly to the problem areas, suggest specific alternative ways of behaving, and reinforce the new behaviors as needed.

5 *Managers of groups should tolerate deviance without ignoring the offenders completely.*   If a group is too punitive toward its deviants, especially those who are newer group members, it is likely to deaden members' enthusiasm and desires to improve the group. Moreover, by extinguishing any signs of deviance, the group loses the opportunity to test the usefulness and validity of its norms. Discussion of the issues raised by deviants can, in fact, increase group effectiveness in the long run.

Review Questions

1   Define the term *work group*.

2   What is the difference between a command group and a task group? Give an example of each.

3   Define the term *group cohesiveness*.

4   Identify the major sources of group cohesiveness.

5   Consider a group of which you are currently a member (e.g., a class or a work crew). Is the group cohesive or not? Why?

6   Critically evaluate the following statement: Cohesive groups produce more than noncohesive groups.

7   What are the two factors that influence whether highly cohesive groups will be productive?

8   What are the potential assets of groups? the potential liabilities?

9   When will the presence of other people increase an individual's level of effort and work intensity? When will it decrease it? Why?

10   Define the term *group norm.*

11   What is a behavior norm? a performance norm? Give one example of each.

12   When will groups strongly enforce group norms?

13   Identify four ways in which group norms develop.

14   Define the term *deviance.*

15   Why do groups label behaviors as deviant?

16   Give an example of deviant behavior in a group of which you are now a member. Why is the behavior considered deviant?

17   Under what three circumstances is the group deviant most likely to be rejected? Why does ignoring the issues raised by the deviant hurt the long-run effectiveness of the group?

Phantoms Fill Boy Scout Rolls

The Boy Scouts have been a tradition in America for most of this century. To the public, scouting conjures up images of camping in the woods, hikes, and troop meetings. But there is another side of scouting that is not seen, a Tribune reporter discovered during a 4-month investigation. It includes massive cheating on the part of paid professional staff members to make their quotas.

The Boy Scouts of America—that venerable institution devoted to keeping boys physically strong, mentally aware, and morally straight—is in trouble.

A $65 million national campaign to expand scouting by more than 2 million boys in 1976 is nearly 2 years behind schedule.

And professionals within the Scout organization claim the problem has been aggravated by extensive cheating which has inflated membership figures. Scouting officials claim to have 4.8 million boys enrolled nationwide.

Like most charitable organizations, scouting also has been plagued with the problem of finding enough adult volunteers to run programs and raising enough money to keep up with inflation, Scout officials concede.

Many officials blame scouting's problems on the inability to recruit and keep volunteers, especially in the inner cities.

But the root of the problem is scouting's Boypower 76 program—a national effort to increase the membership rolls to include one-third of all eligible boys in America—an estimated 6 million youngsters.

Dissidents within scouting's 4,600-member professional staff, which raises funds and recruits boys and volunteers, also claim that efforts to streamline the organization and use improved business techniques have encouraged cheating.

What has happened, past and present Scout professionals claim, is that many professionals under pressure continually to make increasing membership quotas have been meeting those quotas with nonexistent boys belonging to nonexistent units. The boys exist only on rosters filed away in Scout offices throughout the country.

Actually, the cheating is confined largely to the professional organization and has had little or no effect on existing Scout programs operated by adult volunteers. Once started, the troops, packs, and posts operate almost independently of the professional organization.

Thus, the 15 Cub Scouts who meet each week in a Detroit ghetto church aren't aware that their unit has 65 members on official Scout reports. And the PTA of a west side Chicago school is not aware it is sponsoring a nonexistent, 44-member Boy Scout troop.

Scout professionals interviewed during the Tribune's 4-month investigation revealed that sometimes they cheat with federal money. The nonexistent boys and units were paid for with poverty funds from Washington.

"This thing is national in scope," claimed one Scout executive from the national organization. He asked that his name be withheld.

"They don't know themselves how many boys they have," he said.

"As far as they are concerned, the name on a roster is a Scout until someone proves it different."

An independent report on scouting in the New York area in 1971 by the Institute of Public Affairs said that many Scout professionals believe that the pressure to meet membership goals there resulted in a "numbers game and a possible cause of paper troops." The report never was publicly released.

But nowhere is the problem more critical than in Chicago—the place where scouting started in America in 1910 and the city that gave America the Boypower 76 program.

Some Scout professionals here estimate that anywhere from 25 to 50 percent of the 87,000 Cub Scouts, Boy Scouts, and Explorers registered in the Chicago Area Council are inactive or exist only on paper.

A suppressed 1968 audit of Scout operations in Chicago shows that of the council's 2,555 units, 1,694 were substandard and 623 were phony. Though Scout officials in Chicago claimed at the time to have 75,000 boys enrolled, the actual number of Scouts was less than

40,000, the audit showed. The Scout official who ordered the audit was quietly reassigned elsewhere.

Joseph Klein, the head of scouting in Chicago, claims to have 87,000 members—making Chicago the largest council in the nation.

However, confidential membership reports obtained by the Tribune show that on April 12 the actual membership was about 52,000 boys— nearly 40 percent less than quoted.

Though cheating also exists in the suburbs, it is worse in the inner city, Scout professionals said. They claim that it is extremely difficult to determine the exact extent of the cheating, but said that Scout districts with widely fluctuating membership totals and few promotions indicate large numbers of phony boys and units. Nonexistent boys can't be promoted.

Though 2,321 Boy Scouts were registered in the Midwest District on the West Side last December, only 117 boys received promotions to the six ranks of scouting. Only 32 boys were promoted to Tenderfoot—an almost automatic jump.

The adjacent Fort Dearborn District listed no promotions for its 1,511 Boy Scouts, although the predominantly white Timber Trails district on the southwest side had 245 promotions for its 850 registered boys for the same period.

Membership in the Midwest District has fluctuated widely since 1966, confidential Scout records show. On December 31, 1972, the district reported having 4,577 Scouts, but 2,797 of them—more than half—had evaporated in just 2 months. The district claimed to have recruited 3,270 new boys during its membership drive last fall, making it the largest district in the city, with 5,050 boys. But by the beginning of April, 2,981 boys—nearly 60 percent of the district—had somehow disappeared.

The seven Scout districts on the West Side claim to have recruited 8,630 new Scouts during last fall's membership drive, but lost 9,000 in the following three months. The six South Side districts in the Chicago Council lost more than 8,000 scouts during the same period—nearly half of the total membership.

The worst cheating actually occurs in the federally funded programs administered through the Chicago Model Cities program, the professionals claim. The programs, collectively known as Project 13, pay the Scout dues and fees for inner-city blacks and Hispanics, many of whom live in housing projects.

The Chicago Council has received $341,000 in federal funds for the program during the last 4 years, reportedly to provide a scouting program for more than 40,000 poor youngsters, federal records show.

"It's not hard to paper your project boys," bragged one Scout professional who asked to remain anonymous. "You register all the boys in December. You can put an extra 1000 boys in a unit because they drop out in 2 months and there's no record of them," he said.

An official of the Lawndale Urban Progress Center, which sponsors one federally funded program on the West Side, said that not more than 500 of the 2000 boys on the books are actually Scouts.

Scout professionals, past and present, admitted to a Tribune interviewer that they registered thousands of non-existent boys to meet their quotas.

One of the most common ploys the professionals claim they used was to reregister units year after year without bothering to check to see whether the units actually exist.

"You simply change a few names so the charter looks different, then reregister it," said one former professional. "Who's going to walk through those housing projects to check you out?"

"We've got to clean the cheating up," he said. "The minute we find it (cheating) we terminate the professional."

Klein said he constantly lectures his staff on maintaining a quality scouting program, "but maybe they're not hearing me."

"I firmly believe there's a hell of a lot more good in this program than there is bad," he said.

Questions for Discussion

1   How did the norm of cheating develop among Boy Scout professionals?

2   Is cheating deviant in this setting? Why?

3   Why do the individual Boy Scout professionals lack commitment to the national organization's recruiting goals?

4   What should the national organization do to change the norms of cheating among its staff?

Source: Copyright 1974, *Chicago Tribune.* Appeared under byline of David Young. Used by permission.

Notes

1   Dalton, M. (1959). *Men who manage.* New York: Wiley.

2   Shaw, M. E. (1981). *Group dynamics* (3rd ed.). New York: McGraw-Hill, 213–215.

3   Festinger, L., Schachter, S., & Back, K. (1950). *Social pressures in informal groups.* Stanford, CA: Stanford University Press.

4   Aronson, E. (1976). *The social animal* (2nd ed.). San Francisco: W. H. Freeman, 213–246.

5   Kidder, J. T. (1981). *The soul of a new machine.* New York: Avon, 63–66.

6   Lott, A. J., & Lott, B. E. (1965). Group cohesiveness as interpersonal attraction: A review of relationships with antecedent and consequent variables. *Psychological Bulletin, 64,* 259–309.

7   Dion, K. L. (1973). Cohesiveness as a determinant of ingroup-outgroup bias. *Journal of Personality and Social Psychology, 28,* 163–171.

8   Schachter, S., Ellertson, N., McBride, D., & Gregory, D. (1951). An experimental study of cohesiveness and productivity. *Human Relations, 4,* 229–238.
    Golembiewski, R. T. (1962). *The small group.* Chicago: University of Chicago Press, 223–224.

9   Seashore, S. (1954). *Group cohesiveness in the industrial work group.* Ann Arbor: Institute for Social Research, University of Michigan.

10   Whyte, W. F. (1955). *Money and motivation.* New York: Harper.
    Schrank, R. (1978). *Ten thousand working days.* Cambridge, MA: MIT Press, 7–8.

11   Back, K. W. (1951). Influence through social communication. *Journal of Abnormal and Social Psychology, 46,* 190–207.

12   Steiner, I. D. (1966). Models for inferring relationships between group size and potential group productivity. *Behavioral Science, 11,* 273–283.

13   Ibid.

14   Hackman, J. R. (1976). Group influences on individuals in organizations. In M. D. Dunnette (Ed.), *Handbook of industrial and organizational psychology,* 1455–1526. Chicago: Rand McNally.

15   Sarbin, T. R., & Allen, V. L. (1968). Increasing participation in a natural group setting: A preliminary report. *The Psychological Record, 18,* 1–7.

16 Rabbie, J. M. (1963). Differential preferences for companionship under threat. *Journal of Abnormal and Social Psychology, 67,* 643–648.

17 Feldman, D. C., & Brett, J. M. (1983). Coping with new jobs: A comparative study of new hires and job changers. *Academy of Management Journal, 26,* 258–272.

18 Roethlisberger, F. J., & Dickson, W. J. (1939). *Management and the worker.* Cambridge, MA: Harvard University Press.

19 Zajonc, R. B. (1969). Social facilitation. *Science, 149,* 269–274.

20 Henchy, T., & Glass, D. C. (1968). Evaluation apprehension and the social facilitation of dominant and subordinate responses. *Journal of Personality and Social Psychology, 10,* 446–454.

21 Steiner, *loc. cit.*

22 Ibid.

23 Shaw, *op. cit.,* 172.

24 Fallows, J. (1981). *The national defense.* New York: Vintage, 76–95.

25 Jackson, J. (1966). A conceptual and measurement model for norms and roles. *Pacific Sociological Review, 9,* 35–45.

26 Wallace, M. J., & Szilagyi, A. D. (1982). *Managing behavior in organizations.* Glenview, IL: Scott, Foresman, 110–111.

27 Much of this discussion is based on Feldman, D. C. (1984). The development and enforcement of group norms. *Academy of Management Review, 9,* 47–50.

28 Bales, R. F., & Slater, P. E. (1955). Role differentiation in small groups. In T. Parsons, R. F. Bales, et al., (Eds.), *Family, socialization, and interaction process.* Glencoe, IL: Free Press.

29 Goffman, E. (1955). On face-work: An analysis of ritual elements in social interaction. *Psychiatry, 18,* 213–231.

30 Much of this discussion is based upon Feldman, D. C. (1984). The development and enforcement of group norms. *Academy of Management Review, 9,* 50–53.

31 Erikson, K. T. (1966). *Wayward Puritans.* New York: Wiley, 1–31.

32 Dentler, R. A., & Erikson, K. T. (1959). The functions of deviance in groups. *Social Problems, 7,* 98–107.

33 O'Day, R. (1974). Intimidation rituals: Reactions to reform. *Journal of Applied Behavior Science,* 1974, *10* (No. 3), 373–386.

34   Hollander, E. P. (1958). Conformity, status, and idiosyncrasy credit. *Psychological Review, 65,* 117–127.

35   Wiggins, J. A., Dill, F., & Schwartz, R. D. (1965). On status-liability. *Sociometry, 28,* 197–209.

Alvarez, R. (1968). Informal reactions to deviance in simulated work organizations: A laboratory experiment. *American Sociological Review, 33,* 895–912.

36   Sampson, E. E., & Brandon, A. C. (1964). The effects of role and opinion deviation on small group behavior. *Sociometry, 27,* 261–281.

37   Dentler & Erikson, *loc. cit.*

38   Hackman, *loc. cit.*

Chapter 8

Intergroup Conflict

CHAPTER OUTLINE

Changing Views of Intergroup Conflict

Causes of Intergroup Conflict

Dynamics of Intergroup Conflict

Managing Intergroup Conflict

Keys to Effective Management

Review Questions

*S*o far we have focused on the manager's responsibilities toward individual employees and the work group as a whole. In this chapter, we look at another level of behavior in organizations—the relations *between* groups in organizations. We will be especially concerned here with ***intergroup conflict***—overt expressions of hostility between groups and intentional interference with each other's activities.[1]

We'll be examining a broad range of issues dealing with intergroup relations and managing conflict. In the first section of the chapter, we'll explore the nature of intergroup relations in organizations, and how managers' attitudes towards conflict have been changing. In the second section, we'll look more closely at the causes of intergroup conflict. In the third section, we'll examine the dynamics of intergroup conflict: the changes that occur between groups engaged in conflict; the changes that occur within the conflicting groups; and the strategies groups use to advance their causes and to gain power. Finally, we'll explore the wide range of conflict resolution strategies available to managers, and discuss the circumstances under which each strategy is most effective.

Throughout the chapter, we will see that intergroup conflict is not necessarily destructive in and of itself. Conflict, if kept to a reasonable level of intensity and a limited number of important issues, can actually help the organization operate more effectively.

Changing Views of Intergroup Conflict

**Traditional
View of
Conflict**

Traditionally, intergroup conflict in organizations has been viewed very negatively. It has been considered dysfunctional primarily because of the adverse effects it could have on organizational productivity. Conflict could cause losses in productivity because groups wouldn't cooperate in getting projects finished and wouldn't share important information. Too much conflict could also distract managers from their work and reduce their concentration on the job.

Moreover, conflict was felt to affect the morale of employees. Over a prolonged period of time, it could cause stress, frustration, and anxiety, which were detrimental to employees' well-being.

Because of this view, managers have traditionally been negatively evaluated for allowing conflict to surface in their units. Senior managers in most organizations have praised and rewarded middle managers who maintain peace and harmony in their units, while punishing those whose units are marked by confrontation. Since absence of conflict has frequently been used at evaluation time as a sign of managerial effectiveness, historically most managers have been concerned with eliminating or suppressing *all* conflicts. In an ideal world, conflict would be avoided altogether; when it appeared, it would be stopped as quickly as possible by managerial fiat.[2]

**Contemporary
View of
Conflict**

More recently, however, a broader view of conflict has been emerging, a view that sees the functional aspects of conflict as well as the dysfunctional.

First, while the potential negative consequences of conflict are certainly costly, there are some benefits to be derived from conflict as well. Conflict can be a catalyst for change. It can force organizations to re-examine corporate goals or reset priorities. It can force managers to face important issues they have been ignoring and make higher-quality decisions on those issues. Intergroup conflict can jolt organizations out of the status quo and lead them toward more innovation.

Second, sometimes suppressing all conflict leads to further negative consequences. People begin to sabotage each other covertly rather than confronting each other directly. Groups waste energy trying to undercut their opponents rather than directing their efforts to solving problems with their adversaries. Confrontation can sometimes be more effective than suppression as a strategy for resolving conflict.

Third, conflict is seen as inevitable rather than avoidable. The products and services most organizations provide today are very complex and require many different groups to work closely together. It is virtually impossible that there will be no conflict when so many groups are working together on so many projects. In addition, the financial fortunes of the firm and the strength of the economy as a whole may shift several times during a year. These shifts often set in motion some conflicts about budgets and resources, conflicts which cannot be easily foreseen or always averted.

Therefore, according to this view, the manager's job is not to suppress all conflict at all costs. It is to allow some optimal level of conflict to surface, and to resolve conflicts in a way that enhances organizational effectiveness without creating further hostility or destructive behavior. It is conflict diagnosis and management skills on the part of managers that should be recognized and rewarded.[3]

Can There Ever Be Too Little Conflict?

Taking the contemporary view of conflict to its logical conclusion, in fact, we can see that there *are* situations where there is too little conflict for the organization's own good. While there is no definitive method for assessing the need for more conflict, managers might ask themselves the following questions:[4]

1   Are managers surrounded by "yes men"?

2   Are subordinates afraid to admit ignorance and uncertainties to their bosses?

3   Do decision makers concentrate so much on reaching a compromise that they lose sight of long-term objectives and company welfare?

4   Do managers believe that it is in their best interest to maintain the impression of peace and cooperation in their units, regardless of the price?

5   Do decision makers show an excessive concern for not hurting the feelings of others?

6   Do managers believe that popularity is more important than competence and high performance for the obtaining of organizational rewards?

7   Are managers unduly enamored of obtaining consensus for their decisions?

8   Do employees show unusually high resistance to change?

9   Is there a lack of new ideas forthcoming?

10   Is there an unusually low level of employee turnover?

Affirmative answers to these questions suggest that managers do, indeed, need to allow more conflict into the open.

In the next section of the chapter, we turn our attention away from *how much* intergroup conflict an organization experiences to consider *why* intergroup conflicts occur.

Causes of Intergroup Conflict

Intergroup conflicts generally do not emerge out of irrationality or petty griev-ances. Instead, they result from the ways in which organizations coordinate the work of different groups and distribute rewards among those groups. A brief summary of the causes of intergroup conflict appears in Figure 8-1.

Coordination of Work

Probably the most common source of intergroup conflict is the coordination of work among several different departments. Organizations need coordination among several departments' activities to manufacture products or to provide a service, and friction often arises in the process.

Sequential Task Interdependence

By the term *task interdependence,* we mean the amount of reliance a work group has to put on other organizational units to complete its projects. In *sequential* task interdependence, the product (output) of one group becomes the raw material (input) of another group. For example, the consumer surveys of a market research function become the raw data for the design of promo-tional activities in advertising; the specifications of an architect's construction plans provide the starting point for the engineering function's activities. The more the activities of one group affect the performance of another group, the greater the intergroup conflict is likely to be.[5]

Line and staff groups often have conflicts resulting from sequential task interdependence. Staff groups generally perform a monitoring function, report-

Figure 8-1   Causes of intergroup conflict.

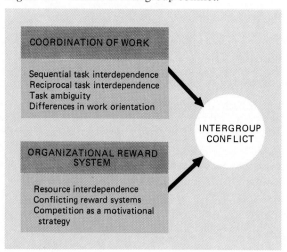

ing to top managers problems they see in line operations. Needless to say, line employees often view staff's work as "ratting" rather than as constructive guidance. Moreover, line employees often reject the suggestions of staff to improve productivity. Line managers typically complain that while staff employees have a good deal of technical expertise, they do not have good political instincts for implementing their ideas effectively.[6]

Reciprocal Task Interdependence

In *reciprocal task interdependence,* some outputs of each group become inputs of the other group. Reciprocal task interdependence is probably best exemplified by the relationship between production and quality assurance: production produces goods for quality assurance to test for safety and other standards, and quality assurance sends back to production products that are substandard and in need of alteration. Reciprocal task interdependence also occurs between production and sales. Production provides the goods for the sales force to sell, and orders and estimates provided by the sales force help determine the volume to be produced. Intergroup conflict arises from reciprocal task interdependence over differences in performance expectations. Each group is dissatisfied with the quality or quantity of work received from the other group.

Purchasing agents and engineers typically experience intergroup conflict as a result of reciprocal task interdependence. Purchasing agents are charged with securing raw materials for an organization at the lowest cost, consistent with quality constraints. Purchasing agents strongly prefer that engineers avoid telling them what specific brands to purchase; they only want the functional specifications of the needed product so that they can bargain more effectively with several suppliers. However, this request from the purchasing agent causes more work for the engineers, who must then provide greater detail in materials orders and must also test several brands to see which meet all the specifications. Engineers and purchasing agents both feel that the other group intrudes into areas which are none of its business.[7]

Task Ambiguity

Intergroup conflict is also likely to arise when it is unclear which group is responsible for certain activities. This lack of clarity over job responsibilities is called *task ambiguity,* and it frequently leads to hostility between work units. Important job duties fall between the cracks, and each group is upset with the other for what it perceives to be the other's shortcomings.

A good example of task ambiguity leading to intergroup conflict occurs in the recruitment of new employees. Both the personnel department and the specific functional areas (e.g., marketing, operations, finance) of a firm have responsibilities in recruiting: identifying candidates, interviewing candidates, making selection decisions, and negotiating salaries. Sometimes there is conflict over who has the final authority to make and execute selection decisions. Final offers are held up as personnel and the functional areas each assert what they perceive to be their prerogatives.

Task ambiguity often arises when the organization is growing quickly or the organization's environment is changing rapidly. As Box 8-1 illustrates, sev-

BOX 8-1

AT&T's Split Leads to Frustration

Dozens of interviews by *Wall Street Journal* reporters throughout the United States showed that the breakup at AT&T has caused maddening experiences for both residential customers and businesses. Many problems in phone service and repairs are the result of competition—and occasionally downright enmity—between AT&T and the regional companies. AT&T and the regionals are actively competing to sell equipment to businesses and are quick to disparage each other's products. Moreover, employees of AT&T and the seven regional companies often don't seem to know which company does what. The companies continually blame each other for causing problems, forcing customers to spend days just trying to find someone to take responsibility for getting a job done. Some of the more frustrating problems which emerged:

- Eagle Expediting, Inc., a trucking company in Flint, Michigan, waited five days for repairs while the phone companies bickered over whether the problem was in the equipment, which would be AT&T's responsibility, or on the line, which is the local company's concern.

- Reis Neckwear (New Haven, Connecticut) ordered a newly introduced Merlin Telephone System for its New York showroom. Within a ten-day period, the company was told: (a) the promised date of delivery could not be met; (b) no firm commitment could be made on future delivery dates; (c) the equipment would be delivered that day; (d) if the equipment did end up being delivered, no commitments could be made on installment dates; and (e) there was a new, unexpected $140 installation charge.

- Fidelity Group, the Boston money-management house, got caught in the middle of a dispute over whether its problem was equipment or line, so the repairs weren't done for three days. Now Fidelity is spending $25,000 on diagnostic systems for its headquarters so that it can figure out quickly if it has an equipment problem or a line problem, and therefore know immediately whether AT&T or the local company should respond.

- In Maple Heights, Ohio, there is no listing for AT&T phone stores in the regular phone book. There is a number listed in the yellow pages, but a recording says the number has changed and reads out a new number. That number has changed, too, so another recording gives another new number. But that's not much help either, because there's no answer at that number. An employee at the phone store sheepishly explains: "Our phone doesn't work."

- Probably the most fitting story about the AT&T breakup comes from Peggy Stevens of Los Angeles, who was angry she could not rent a pink telephone. Ms. Stevens was informed she could buy such a phone, but she was concerned about who would fix it if it broke. When asked by the customer service representative how often her phone broke, she replied: "Every time I throw it against the wall."

Source: Adapted from: AT&T's split proves frustrating to homes, businesses, across U.S. (1984, January 13). *The Wall Street Journal,* pp. 25, 37. Used by permission.

eral intergroup problems due to task ambiguity emerged in the Bell System after its massive breakup in 1984.[8]

Differences in Work Orientation

The ways in which employees go about their work and deal with others vary widely across functional areas of an organization. First, functional groups differ in their *time perspectives.* For example, research and development (R&D) scientists have much longer-range goals than do manufacturing groups. Manufacturing is evaluated on how quickly it can turn out high-quality products, while R&D scientists can only be evaluated after a long period of product development and testing. Second, the *goals* of different functional groups vary greatly. The goals of a manufacturing unit are more specific and clear-cut than the goals of an R&D unit: manufacturing has precise targets for volume, cost savings, and percentage of rejects, while R&D has much broader and less easily measurable goals such as developing basic science knowledge and suggesting potential market applications. Third, the *interpersonal orientations* of people in different departments vary. R&D labs need and encourage a level of informality, a looseness of structure, and a collegiality that would be dysfunctional in a manufacturing group.

Lawrence & Lorsch contingency theory

The greater the differences in goal, time, and interpersonal orientation between two work units, the more likely it is that conflict will arise between the groups when they have to coordinate their work efforts. These differences in work orientation lead groups to be frustrated with, and to misinterpret, the behavior of other groups.[9]

For instance, when manufacturing and R&D have to work together to implement a product idea, there is often conflict between the two groups. Manufacturing may feel it is being too closely monitored while the people in R&D are getting away with murder. People in manufacturing may interpret the casual atmosphere of R&D people as lack of seriousness, while people in R&D may view manufacturing's concern with volume and cost indices as narrow and shortsighted.

These differences in work orientation also help to explain why marketing and manufacturing units often do not work together effectively. As Table 8-1 illustrates, many of the day-to-day goals of the two groups are in conflict. Marketing groups try to increase the variety of products offered, and the speed with which they can be produced and delivered; manufacturing groups try to decrease the variety of products offered, and to keep costs down by limiting inventory and the number of design changes.[10] Inevitably, the two groups come into conflict as they each try to achieve their goals.

Organizational Reward Systems

The way in which an organization monitors group performance and distributes resources (e.g., money, personnel, equipment) is the second major source of intergroup conflict. Groups come into conflict as they compete for scarce resources.

TABLE 8-1

Differences in Goal Orientations Between Marketing and Manufacturing

Goal area	Typical marketing comment	Typical manufacturing comment
1 Breadth of product line	"Our customers demand variety."	"The product line is too broad— all we get are short, uneconomical runs."
2 Capacity planning and long-range sales forecasting	"Why don't we have enough capacity?"	"Why didn't we have accurate sales forecasts?"
3 Production scheduling and short-range sales forecasts	"We need faster response. Our lead times are ridiculous."	"We need realistic customer commitments and sales forecasts that don't change like wind direction."
4 Delivery and physical distribution	"Why don't we ever have the right merchandise in inventory?"	"We can't keep everything in inventory."
5 Quality assurance	"Why can't we have reasonable quality at reasonable cost?"	"Why must we always offer options that are too hard to manufacture and that offer little customer utility?"
6 Cost control	"Our costs are so high that we are not competitive in the market-place."	"We can't provide fast delivery, broad variety, rapid response to change, and high quality at low cost."
7 New product introduction	"New products are our life blood."	"Unnecessary design changes are prohibitively expensive."
8 Adjunct services such as spare parts inventory support, installation, and repair	"Field service costs are too high."	"Products are being used in ways for which they weren't designed."

Source: Reprinted from Shapiro, B. S. (1977). Can marketing and manufacturing coexist? *Harvard Business Review, 55* (September–October), 104–114. Used by permission.

Resource Interdependence

ej budgets corporate support

Frequently, groups are relatively independent of each other in getting their work done but compete with each other for resources. Two separate manufacturing plants making the same product may compete for additional budget allocations or additional personnel from corporate headquarters. Two departments or project groups may compete for the limited services of a support group; for example, different product groups may compete for the time of the marketing research department. When organizations are experiencing slow growth or no growth, the inevitable conflict over resources becomes even more intense.[11]

Conflicting Reward Systems

Sometimes the ways in which reward systems in organizations are designed create a situation in which one group can only accomplish its goal at the expense of other groups. For example, staff departments may be rewarded for cutting costs and personnel, while line departments are rewarded for increasing the amount of products sold or services provided. To increase the amount of products sold, the line group may have to lean even more heavily on staff groups such as advertising. However, the staff groups are being rewarded for cutting costs and personnel, and providing the types of services asked for by line groups can prevent them from meeting their own goals. Conflicting reward systems inevitably result in poor intergroup relations.[12]

Competition as a Motivational Strategy

Managers sometimes use competition between groups as a way of motivating workers. The rationale behind this strategy is that people will produce more under pressure, and that competition between groups is healthy for the organization.

Unfortunately, as seductive as this theory may seem, competition between groups frequently *increases conflict* between groups *without* increasing productivity.[13] When examined systematically, the research on this issue reveals that noncompetition results in higher productivity for groups. Groups that cooperate with each other can coordinate their activities better and have a fuller exchange of information and ideas. As a result, cooperative groups generally produce more and higher-quality products.[14]

Moreover, if the groups that are competing are highly task interdependent, competition lowers productivity even further. If groups are not task interdependent, the only way they can gain an advantage is to produce more. However, if the groups are task interdependent, they may spend time and energy *blocking* the activities of other groups. Such blocking simultaneously lowers the productivity of other groups and takes productive time and energy away from the blocking group.[15]

A good example of the effects of cooperation and competition on productivity is seen in sales groups. Frequently, sales groups are pitted against one another in a competitive fashion so that the group that sells the most receives some special bonus. However, organizational productivity might be even higher if the sales groups cooperated, shared expenses for clerical and support groups, and tried to sell several product lines to the same customer.

The Dynamics of Intergroup Conflict

When there is intergroup conflict in an organization, systematic changes occur in the perceptions, attitudes, and behaviors of the participants. In this section, we'll be looking more closely at the dynamics of intergroup conflict as it unfolds. First, we will look at the systematic changes in interpersonal relationships and work orientation that take place within each group and between the conflicting groups. Next, we will examine the strategies groups use to gain power in intergroup conflict situations. Finally, we will focus on the effects that winning and losing the conflict have on subsequent group dynamics.

Changes within Each Group

Five changes in the perceptions, attitudes, and behaviors of a group are particularly noticeable at the onset of intergroup conflict.[16] They are outlined in Table 8-2, and discussed in more detail below.

1 *Loyalty to the group becomes more important.*   In the face of an external threat, the group demands more loyalty from individual members. Not only is social interaction with people outside the group not encouraged; it is expressly discouraged. Such interaction could lead to inadvertent betrayal of group strategy and secrets. Deviance is more closely monitored and punished.

Loyalty

2 *There is increased concern for task accomplishment.*   There is additional pressure for the group to perform at its best. Therefore, the concern for group members' personal needs declines and the concern for task accomplishment increases. The climate of the group becomes much less informal.

accomplishment

3 *Leadership in the group becomes more autocratic.*   When intergroup conflict is present it is especially important for a group to be able to respond

autocratic

TABLE 8-2

Dynamics of intergroup conflict

Changes within Each Group

1   Loyalty to the group becomes more important.
2   There is increased concern for task accomplishment.
3   Leadership in the group becomes autocratic.
4   The organization and structure of the work group become more rigid.
5   Group cohesiveness increases.

Changes In Relations between Groups

1   There are distortions of perception, both about one's own group and about the other group.
2   Interaction and communication between groups decrease.
3   There is a shift from a problem-solving orientation toward other groups to a win-lose orientation.
4   There is increased hostility toward the rival group.

quickly and in a unified manner to the activities of other groups. A democratic work style can reduce the group's capacity to respond quickly. Moreover, democratic leadership allows the expression of differing opinions. A more autocratic leadership style, in contrast, strengthens the group's ability to respond quickly to external threats and to present a unified front.

rigid

4 *The organization and structure of the work group become more rigid.*   Consistent with both the increased concern for task accomplishment and a more autocratic leadership style, the organization and structure of the work group become more rigid. Coordination of activities is increased, additional rules and procedures are outlined and enforced, and specific responsibilities are allocated to different group members.

cohesiveness

5 *Group cohesiveness increases.*   In the face of an external threat, past differences and difficulties between group members are forgotten. The group closes ranks to meet the challenge. Individual group members find both the group as a whole and other group members more attractive.

A good illustration of these intergroup dynamics appears at the peak of the annual planning cycle in most organizations. Once a year, each subunit in the organization prepares to meet with top management to set group performance objectives for the upcoming year and to obtain as many resources as possible to meet those objectives. Groups are competing with each other for scarce resources, and the dynamics discussed above are often observed. For instance, the groups become more task-oriented: there is both an increased work load (preparing the next year's plans) and an increased need for the group to perform well. Lunchtime tennis games become business lunches. People are expected to work longer hours and weekends, even at the expense of their personal lives. The leader becomes more directive, assigning the additional responsibilities of the planning review to specific group members and coordinating their activities. Differences of opinion between group members are deemphasized and feelings about the group become more positive.

Changes in Relations between Groups

The nature of the relationships between groups also changes markedly during intergroup conflicts. Four changes in particular occur at this time.[17]

distortions

1 *There are distortions of perception, both about one's own group and about the other group.*   First, perception of one's own group is highly selective: people see only the best aspects of their own group and deny any weaknesses in their own group's performance. Second, and more importantly, perception of the other groups is systematically distorted: groups see only the worst parts of other groups and deny other groups' positive accomplishments. Thus, intergroup conflict leads to increased use of stereotypes. Each group develops a more positive stereotype of itself and a more negative stereotype of others.

2   *Interaction and communication between groups decrease.*   Because group members feel hostile toward members of rival groups, there is less desire for interaction with them. Moreover, decreased interaction makes it easier for each group to maintain its negative stereotype of the other.

Even when groups are forced to interact with each other, those interactions become fairly rigid and formal. Whatever information is passed between groups is very carefully rationed and sometimes deliberately distorted. Groups tend to ignore the similarities between their positions and exaggerate the differences.[18]

3   *There is a shift from a problem-solving orientation toward other groups to a win-lose orientation.*   There are several facets to this shift in orientation. First, there is a much clearer distinction drawn between the groups, resulting in a "we-they" rather than a "we-versus-the-problem" orientation. Second, all exchanges with the other groups are evaluated in terms of victory or defeat. Third, the groups tend to see the problem only from their own point of view, rather than in terms of the needs of both groups. Fourth, the parties emphasize the benefits of winning the conflict in the short run and tend to ignore the long-term consequences of the conflict for the relationship between the groups.[19]

4   *There is increased hostility toward the rival group.*   As a result of negative stereotyping, decreased communication between groups, and a win-lose orientation, increased hostility inevitably occurs between rival groups. Members of the other group are seen as the enemy, and deserving of hostile attacks.[20]

Union-management relationships during contract negotiations illustrate some of these dynamics. At these times it becomes difficult for each side to see anything positive about the other side; each party emphasizes the good it is doing for its side and undervalues the interests of the other side. The relationship is adversarial, not problem-solving, in tone. During bargaining, each side tries to engineer a solution that it can label as a victory for itself. The relationship is viewed as a win-lose proposition. Short-run outcomes loom much more important than long-run union-management relations. When the two sides are forced to interact with each other, these interactions are very formalized. Each side tries to withhold as much information from the other as is legally allowed. Each side overstates its position and adds demands simply so that they can be bargained away. There is marked hostility and mistrust between the two parties.

Strategies Groups Use to Gain Power

There are several strategies groups can use to gain power in an intergroup conflict situation. Some of these strategies allow cooperation and sharing between groups; other strategies are more competitive and increase the power of one group at the expense of others.

Contracting

Contracting refers to the negotiation of a *quid pro quo* (this for that) agreement between two groups. Each group makes some concessions to the other so that there can be some predictability and stability in their relationship. As a result of contracting, groups know in advance how they will split the profits from the joint ventures.

A common example of contracting occurs between labor and management. Collective bargaining agreements are the results of such contracting. The union guarantees to management that its workers will work so many hours for so many weeks under specified work conditions. Management guarantees to the union some due process in the hiring, disciplining, and termination of employees and in regard to changes in the design of the work. Union and management agree on how to divide the economic gains of the enterprise; the union knows precisely what the wage rates, benefits, and profit-sharing formula will be.

Co-opting

A second power acquisition strategy is **co-opting.** Co-optation occurs when a group gives some of its leadership positions to members of other groups or includes them in its policy-making committees. Hence, the criticism and threat from these out-groups is blunted. How can they attach or criticize a group of which they themselves are a part?

A co-optation strategy frequently employed in industry involves the use of boards of directors. In order to maintain stable relationships with financial lending institutions and to blunt any criticism from them, corporations may add to their boards of directors representatives of the banks on whom they are most dependent for financial support.

Forming Coalitions

A third form of power acquisition is **coalition formation.** In forming a coalition, two or more groups cooperate or combine their resources in order to increase their power over groups not in their coalition. It is an interesting mix of cooperation and competition: member groups cooperate with each other in order to compete more effectively with nonmembers.

In recent years, the managements of major airlines have developed cooperative arrangements with each other so that if one airline is having a strike, it will receive 25 percent of the revenues it would have received had it been operating under normal business conditions. Although the managements of competing airlines obviously stand to gain by the loss of one competitor during a strike, there are greater benefits to be gained by exerting general management's power against the union.

Influencing Decision Criteria

Top management often cannot make decisions about resource allocation among groups using strictly rational criteria. Purely rational decision making is very difficult (perhaps impossible) to achieve because organization members disagree about what the goals of the organization should be and what criteria should be used in measuring contributions to organizational effectiveness.

Groups can exert power by influencing which criteria are selected as the basis for resource distribution. Groups can look at the *relative* position of their subunit in light of several criteria, and then argue that those criteria on which their subunit is relatively high be adopted as the basis for distributing resources.

For instance, in university budget allocations, a department like geology, which typically has few majors, will try to obtain funds on the basis of national research reputation. A department like economics, which typically teaches large survey classes to nonmajors, will try to obtain funds on the basis of total students taught. A department like psychology, which typically has a lot of majors, will try to obtain funds on the basis of number of undergraduate majors produced.[21]

Controlling Information

Another very competitive strategy groups can use to exert power in intergroup conflict situations is to control important information. Gaining access to sensitive information and then limiting other groups' access to it increases the power of the information-rich group vis-à-vis other subunits.[22]

For example, management information systems (MIS) departments frequently exert power in this way. The MIS department has almost exclusive control over the collection, analysis, and interpretation of sensitive organizational data for many important functions. As a result, MIS groups can use withdrawal or slowdown of their services to influence other groups in the organization.[23]

Forcing and Pressure Tactics

Pressure tactics to force others to give in represent the most competitive, or hostile, strategy a group can use to gain power. For instance, a union might threaten a strike or slowdown if management does not grant significant wage increases. In a similar vein, management might make nonnegotiable, final offers to the union. Both sides will aggressively try to demonstrate that they can back up their threats. Unions will publicize the size of their strike funds and management will publicize its plans for shutting down a facility if a contract is not signed. However, while such pressure tactics are highly competitive, they are rarely highly effective. The use of threats usually provokes counterthreats rather than concessions.[24] In general, cooperative strategies among groups in organizations yield more positive results for all concerned than competitive strategies do.

Consequences of Winning or Losing a Conflict

As we would expect, the "winners" and "losers" react in substantially different ways to the end of an intergroup conflict.[25]

Effects of Success

The most systematic change in the perceptions of the winning group is a stronger belief in the negative stereotype of the losing group. Winning the conflict reaffirms both the group's positive self-image and its negative evaluation of the other group.

In regard to group climate, the winning group becomes much more concerned again with the satisfaction and needs of individual members. The work atmosphere becomes more casual, more complacent. Group cohesiveness and group cooperation are likely to increase as well.

At least in the short run, the concern for work and task accomplishment decreases. The winning group has little reason to reexamine its operations and little incentive to think about ways of improving. The winning group loses some of its fighting spirit.

Effects of Failure   The losing group responds to failure by attempting to deny or distort the reality of losing. A lot of energy is put into finding excuses for the loss (e.g., "The deck was stacked"). It is unlikely that the losing group will simply admit that other groups were better and more deserving, and that nothing would have changed the results of the conflict.

The losing group also experiences a noticeable decline in the quality of interpersonal relationships. Unresolved conflicts come to the surface as different factions of the group blame each other for the loss. The group becomes more tense. There is lower group cohesiveness, less cooperation, and less concern for individual members' needs.

However, if the group gets over its initial disappointment and anger and accepts its loss realistically, there can be some positive changes in the way it operates. The group can learn a lot about itself because its stereotypes have been upset; it is forced to reevaluate its own strengths and weaknesses. The group is also likely to reorganize to become more effective, and commit itself to working even harder in the future.

Thus, neither winning nor losing a conflict has unambiguous results for the participants in intergroup conflict. Winning increases self-satisfaction, but the price is complacency; losing decreases group morale but provides an impetus for improving group performance.

Managing Intergroup Conflict

There is perhaps no topic on which managers receive more contradictory advice than conflict management. Just consider the following three proverbs that we all, at one time or another, take to be sound advice: "Come, let us reason together"; "Put your foot down where you mean to stand"; "Turn the other cheek."[26] In this final section of the chapter, we will try to make some sense out of all the conventional wisdom about how to effectively manage intergroup relations.

Intergroup conflict resolution strategies vary widely in how openly they address the conflict. Some of the strategies used to resolve intergroup conflict depend quite heavily on conflict *avoidance*—keeping the conflict from coming into the open at all. A second group of strategies depends instead on conflict *defusion*—keeping the conflict in abeyance and "cooling" the emotions of the parties involved. A third group of strategies depends upon conflict *containment*—allowing some conflict to surface but tightly controlling which issues are discussed and the manner in which they are discussed. A fourth set of strategies depends on conflict *confrontation*—openly airing all the issues of the conflict and trying to find a mutually satisfactory solution.[27]

In general, which strategy is most appropriate depends on how *critical* the conflict is to task accomplishment and how *quickly* the conflict needs to be resolved. When the conflict is over a trivial issue or needs to be resolved quickly, avoidance and defusion are more likely to be employed; when the conflict is over an important work issue and does not have to be resolved quickly, then containment and confrontation are more likely to be used.

Below we examine eight different strategies managers can use to deal with intergroup conflict. For each strategy, we also discuss the situations where the strategy is most appropriate and effective. A brief summary of these strategies appears in Table 8-3.

Conflict Avoidance Strategies

Ignoring the Conflict

Ignoring the conflict is characterized by the absence of behavior: the executive avoids dealing with the dysfunctional aspects of the conflict. He or she might fire or transfer one of the managers of the conflicting groups, for instance, or simply refuse to listen to attacks of one group on the other. Quite often, executives who utilize this strategy disregard the causes of the conflict, and, as a result, the conflict situation frequently continues or gets worse over time.

While ignoring the conflict is generally ineffective for resolving important policy issues, in some circumstances it is at least a reasonable way of dealing with problems. One such circumstance occurs when the conflict issue is trivial. For instance, there may be differences in opinion over the wisdom of giving employees release time to go to a one-shot company training program. This is such a short-run, temporary issue that it does not warrant much attention.

Another circumstance in which ignoring the conflict is a reasonable strategy is when the issue seems symptomatic of other, more basic conflicts. For example, two groups may experience conflict over amount and quality of office space. While office space is not in and of itself a trivial issue, conflicts over space reflect more important battles about relative power and status. Simply resolving the office space problem does not address the key issues, and attention would be more fruitfully directed to the basic concerns.

Imposing a Solution

Imposing a solution means forcing the conflicting parties to accept a solution devised by a higher-level manager. In effect, this strategy does not allow much conflict to surface or offer much room for the participants to air their griev-

TABLE   8-3

Conflict Management Strategies

Conflict resolution strategy	Type of strategy	Appropriate situations
Ignoring the conflict	Avoidance	When the issue is trivial When the issue is symptomatic of more basic, pressing problems
Imposing a solution	Avoidance	When quick, decisive action is needed When unpopular decisions need to be made and consensus among the groups appears very unlikely
Smoothing	Defusion	As a stop-gap measure to let people cool down and regain perspective When the conflict is over nonwork issues
Appealing to superordinate goals	Defusion	When there is a mutually important goal that neither group can achieve without the cooperation of the other When the survival or success of the overall organization is in jeopardy
Bargaining	Containment	When the two parties are of relatively equal power When there are several acceptable, alternative solutions that both parties would be willing to consider
Structuring the interaction	Containment	When previous attempts to openly discuss conflict issues led to conflict escalation rather than to problem solution When a respected third party is available to provide some structure and could serve as a mediator
Integrative problem solving	Confrontation	When there is a minimum level of trust between groups and there is no time pressure for a quick solution When the organization can benefit from merging the differing perspectives and insights of the groups in making key decisions
Redesigning the organization	Confrontation	When the sources of conflict come from the coordination of work When the work can be easily divided into clear project responsibilities (self-contained work groups), or when activities require a lot of interdepartmental coordination over time (lateral relations)

ances. Like ignoring the conflict, imposing a solution is generally an ineffective conflict resolution strategy. The peace it achieves is frequently short-lived. The real issues do not get addressed, and conflict reappears under other guises and in other situations.

However, imposing a solution can be appropriate at times. It is useful when quick, decisive action is needed. For instance, when there is high conflict over some investment decisions, where delays can be very costly, forcing a solution may be the only strategy available to top management. Another situation in which forcing the solution may be necessary occurs when unpopular decisions need to be made and there is very little chance that the participants involved could ever come to an agreement.[28] When companies have to cut back on the funding of different manufacturing plants, it is unreasonable to expect that any plant would agree to substantially cut its staff (or close down altogether) for the greater good, yet ultimately some hard, unpleasant decisions have to be made.

Conflict Defusion Strategies

Smoothing

A manager may choose to *smooth* over the conflict, playing down its importance and magnitude. He or she might try to persuade the groups that they are not as far apart in their viewpoints as they think they are, point out to the groups their similarities rather than their differences, try to appease group members whose feelings have been hurt, or downplay to the groups the importance of the issue. By smoothing the conflict, the manager hopes to decrease the intensity of the conflict and avoid an escalation of open hostility. Like forcing a solution, smoothing is generally ineffective because it does not address the key points of conflict, which are likely to keep resurfacing.

However, smoothing can sometimes be effective as a stop-gap measure to let people cool down and regain perspective. In the heat of battle, people are likely to make statements that escalate, rather than de-escalate, the conflict, and smoothing can bring the disagreement back to a manageable level. For instance, when unpopular actions or decisions are discussed in meetings, tempers often run high and hostile behavior increases dramatically. Smoothing helps get the groups back to a point where they can deal with each other with less friction.

Smoothing may also be appropriate when the conflict is over nonwork issues. For instance, intergroup conflict frequently occurs between older and younger employees because of their different political beliefs and moral values. Smoothing can help defuse the tension so that the conflict does not spill over into more central work issues.[29]

**Appealing to
Superordinate
Goals**

Another way managers can defuse conflict is by ***appealing to superordinate goals.*** The manager diverts attention from the current conflict to the overarching aims that both groups share. The current problem is made to seem insignificant beside these more important common goals.

Finding such superordinate goals is not easy. The goal must be important to both groups. Attaining the goal must require cooperation between groups. The rewards from obtaining the common goal must be high.[30]

Perhaps the most frequently used superordinate goal is organizational *survival:* if the subunits do not cooperate sufficiently, the continued existence of the larger organization is severely jeopardized.[31] This strategy was recently employed by the Chrysler Corporation. Ordinarily, contract negotiations between union and management would have entailed a great deal of conflict and bargaining over wages, working conditions, and benefits. However, given Chrysler's economic troubles in the early 1980s, a large wage increase for the workers would have seriously hurt the corporation's chances of economic survival. Such a wage increase would have depleted Chrysler's already low resources and reduced the corporation's chances of obtaining more federal loan guarantees. The superordinate goal of sustaining Chrysler as an ongoing enterprise—and as an employer—defused the potential for conflict in what would have been, under other circumstances, a very heated contract negotiation.

**Conflict
Containment
Strategies**

Bargaining

Bargaining is probably the most common intergroup conflict resolution strategy. In essence, bargaining is a form of compromise: two groups exchange concessions until a compromise solution is reached. This strategy does allow some conflict to surface, but usually without much openness on the part of the groups involved and without much real problem solving.

Typically what happens in bargaining is that each side begins by demanding more than it really expects to get. Both sides realize that some concessions will be necessary in order to reach a solution, but neither side wants to make the first concession because it will be seen as a sign of weakness. A lot of what happens in bargaining is ***tacit communication:*** each party signals a willingness to be flexible in exchanging concessions, without actually making an explicit offer or promise. There is thus little danger of appearing weak, since a tacit proposal can later be denied if it fails to elicit a positive response from the other party.[32] Bargaining continues until some sort of mutually satisfactory agreement is reached.

It is also important to note that bargaining often results in a compromise agreement that fails to deal with the underlying problem in a rational manner and that is not in the long-term interests of the parties. In one manufacturing company, for instance, two departments were competing for control over a new production process. The conflict was resolved by an agreement to divide the new machines and personnel equally between the two departments. The cost of running duplicate operations became so excessive that departments continually had to compete for available work. Ultimately, the compromise turned out to be not only unprofitable for the company, but unsatisfactory to both departments as well.[33]

For bargaining to be feasible at all as a conflict resolution strategy, both parties should be of relatively equal power. Otherwise, one group could simply impose its will upon the other and the solution would not be mutually acceptable; the weaker group would have no recourse in obtaining its concessions from the more powerful group. In addition, bargaining is more likely to work if there are several acceptable alternatives that both parties would be willing to consider. If each party has only one acceptable settlement, bargaining will likely end in deadlock.

The trading of players among professional sports teams probably illustrates bargaining at its best. Each sports team generally has several players it wants and several players it would like to trade, and there are often several potential trade deals between the teams—particularly when future draft choices and money are also considered as items to be traded. Moreover, because the sports teams are members of larger professional associations (like the National Football League), there are rules and procedures that guide how bargaining is to occur and how contracts and agreements are to be enforced.

Structuring the Interaction between Groups

Providing constraints on the number of issues and the manner in which they will be discussed can facilitate conflict resolution. While there are many ways to *structure the interaction between groups* to deal with conflict, some of the most frequently used and effective strategies include: (1) decreasing the amount of direct interaction between the groups in the early stages of conflict resolution; (2) decreasing the amount of time between problem-solving meetings; (3) decreasing the formality of the presentation of issues; (4) limiting the application of historical precedents; and (5) using third-party mediators.

All these strategies allow some conflict to surface and be addressed but prevent the conflict from getting out of hand and the parties from hardening their positions. For instance, decreasing the amount of direct interaction between groups early in the conflict helps to prevent the conflict from escalating; as mentioned earlier, when the groups are hostile, they use additional interaction simply to confirm their negative stereotypes of each other. Decreasing the amount of time between problem-solving meetings decreases the amount of time groups will have in which to backslide from tentative agreements and harden their original positions. Decreasing the formality of the presentation of issues helps induce a problem-solving, rather than a win-lose, orientation to the conflict. Limiting the application of historical precedents helps the parties focus on finding a solution to the current conflict; if past conflicts and solutions are extensively discussed, hostility will again increase, reducing the likelihood of finding a solution consistent with all the precedents cited. Finally, a mediator can act as a go-between who transmits offers and messages, helps the groups clarify their positions, presents each group's position more clearly to the other, and suggests possible solutions not obvious to the opposing parties.[34]

Structuring the interaction between groups as a means of intergroup conflict resolution is seen most frequently in governmental relations (such as diplomatic talks) and in union-management relations. While structuring the interaction can frequently be used to help resolve conflict, it is especially useful in two situations: (1) when previous attempts to openly discuss conflict issues led to conflict escalation rather than to problem solution; and (2) when a respected third party is available to provide (and maintain) some structure to the interactions between the groups and to serve as mediator.

Conflict Confrontation Strategies

Integrative Problem Solving

Integrative problem solving is a conflict resolution strategy that attempts to find a solution that reconciles, or integrates, the needs of both parties. The two groups work together to define the problem and to identify mutually satisfactory solutions. Moreover, there is open expression of feelings as well as exchange of task-related information.[35]

In order to implement integrative problem solving, organizations generally bring in an outside consultant. The consultant tries to establish some initial trust between the conflicting groups, and to set up ground rules for further discussions.[36] The consultant also helps the groups identify their most important problems working with each other and assists them in designing solutions (see Chapter 18 for more details).

There are two preconditions for integrative problem solving to work. The first is a minimal level of trust between the groups. Without this minimal trust, each group will be unlikely to reveal its true preferences and will expect the other group to give it inaccurate information in return. Second, integrative problem solving takes a lot of time and can only really succeed in the absence of excessive pressure for a quick settlement. However, the gains from integrative problem solving can be high. When the organization could benefit from merging the different perspectives and insights of the two groups in making key organizational decisions, integrative problem solving is especially needed.

It is also important to note here that integrative problem solving can be used to manage intergroup conflict even within a unionized company. For example, at the McCormick Works of International Harvester, the following issue arose. As soon as the company announced the shutdown of the plant, the union wanted employees released so they could apply for work at other International Harvester plants. For its part, the company desired to keep many of these employees since they were necessary to the phasing-out operation. The solution reached established a "pegged" seniority date at other plants: employees continued on in the plant being terminated, while acquiring seniority at the plant to which they would eventually be transferred. Union and management got together to discuss what they *really* wanted from each other, rather than making overstated, impossible demands which could never be met by the other side.[37]

Redesigning the Organization

Organization redesign can be an effective intergroup conflict resolution strategy, especially when the sources of conflict come from the coordination of work among different departments or divisions.

Probably the most frequently used method of reducing conflict through organization redesign is to create **self-contained work groups** that have enough resources to accomplish their goals. One illustration of the use of self-contained work groups to reduce organizational conflicts comes from a manufacturing plant in which all the mechanics belonged to a separate maintenance department with its own supervisor. Conflict developed between the mechanics and the production supervisors—and among the production supervisors—because of competition over whose machines should be repaired first by the mechanics. Attempts to establish standard criteria for processing requests for service failed, and higher-level managers were being inundated with requests for help. Finally, the organization was redesigned so that the mechanics reported to the head of production. In some cases, mechanics were also assigned to individual production supervisors. No additional mechanics were needed for this reorganization, and the result was an end to the conflict and reduction in workflow delays.[38]

There can also be projects that do not fall clearly within any one department's responsibilities but require the contributions and expertise of several departments. Developing new products is one such activity. If the organization arbitrarily assigned new product development to one department, it would decrease potential conflict but at a high cost to the quality of the product. Instead, the organization might try to incorporate **lateral relations** mechanisms to better manage the conflict.[39]

For instance, when coordination among members of several different departments is needed for short periods of time, organizations can use **task forces,** made up of representatives from each of the affected departments. Some organizations create new **integrator roles,** such as product or program managers, to coordinate the activities of several departments working on the same project over time. These structural changes, as well as others, are discussed in more detail in the following two chapters.

Keys to Effective Management

We have outlined some of the most frequently used strategies of intergroup conflict resolution and the circumstances under which each strategy is most appropriate. Next, let's look more carefully at the implications of this material for managing conflict in organizations more effectively.

1 *The assignment and coordination of work activities among groups should be clarified so that daily frictions over minor issues can be avoided.* For many projects, the coordination of different groups' contributions is essential to achieve a high-quality product. The coordination of work activities should be modified, not so that there will be no conflict among groups, but so that conflict will arise over important, policy-related issues rather than over petty day-to-day irritations.

2 *Managers should monitor reward systems to eliminate any win-lose conflicts they might be inducing inadvertently among groups.* Often organizational reward systems induce conflict among groups in organizations. Intergroup competition for rewards, often encouraged to increase group productivity, actually acts to reduce it. Changes in dysfunctional reward systems can help eliminate unproductive conflict and enhance organizational effectiveness.

3 *The use of cooperative strategies among groups in organizations often leads to more positive results than does the use of competitive strategies.* When groups try to achieve some mutually satisfactory solution to a conflict through contracting or integrative problem solving, both sides are more likely to achieve several of their important goals. However, when groups try to bully or harass other groups into accepting their position, the outcome is much less satisfactory. Threats and attacks are more likely to lead to counterthreats and counterattacks than to capitulation. Even if one group can outpressure other groups in the short run, the losing groups will use covert tactics to get even in the long run.

4 *The use of avoidance and defusion as conflict resolution strategies is generally ineffective because neither strategy addresses the key sources of the conflict.* Moreover, conflict which is suppressed in one arena frequently reappears in others. Conflict avoidance and defusion are most appropriate as stop-gap measures or when the conflicts are over relatively unimportant issues.

5 *Managers can establish rules and standard procedures to regulate conflict in more constructive ways.* These rules and procedures allow some conflict to be expressed but carefully check the conflict from escalating or spreading. Some of the most frequently used and effective guidelines include: (a) decreasing the amount of direct interaction between the groups in the early stages of conflict resolution; (b) decreasing the amount of time between problem-solving meetings; (c) decreasing the formality of the presentation of issues; (d) limiting the application of historical precedents; and (e) using third-party mediators.

6 *When high-quality decisions and solutions are needed, top managers should sustain constructive confrontation between the groups.* Under these circumstances, intergroup conflicts can force managers to face important issues they have been ignoring and lead them toward more innovation. Integrating managers or task forces can be used structurally to coordinate the contributions of different groups to a project. Integrative problem-solving sessions can be used among managers to improve their joint decision-making processes. Conflict here can actually help the organization operate more effectively.

Review Questions

1 What is meant by the term *intergroup conflict?*

2 Compare and contrast the traditional view of conflict with the contemporary view of conflict.

3 What are some signs that suggest that not enough conflict is being allowed to surface in an organization?

4 Define sequential and reciprocal task interdependence. Give an example of how each leads to intergroup conflict.

5 What is task ambiguity? Why does task ambiguity contribute to intergroup conflict?

6 What are the differences in goal, time, and interpersonal orientation between marketing and production that might cause intergroup conflict?

7 How effective is competition between groups as a motivational strategy? Why?

8 What systematic changes occur in the perceptions, attitudes, and behaviors of group members during intergroup conflict? What changes occur in relations between groups?

9 What strategies can groups use to gain power in intergroup conflict? Which strategies are most cooperative? Which are most competitive?

10 What are the effects of winning a conflict on group dynamics? What are the effects of losing a conflict?

11 Identify and define the four types of intergroup conflict resolution strategies.

12 When are avoidance strategies most appropriately used?

13 How effective is appealing to superordinate goals in resolving intergroup conflict?

14 How can interactions between groups be structured to facilitate conflict resolution?

15 What are the key elements of integrative problem solving?

16 When should organization redesign be used to reduce conflict?

The Open Budget

Command Press, Incorporated, manufactures and sells a complete line of greeting cards, invitations, party favors, etc. In 1981, total sales exceeded $100 million and the company employed 360 people.

Preparation of the annual budget for marketing is the combined responsibility of the budget officer, the division sales managers, and the vice president. The budgeting process revolves around a fiscal year which runs from July 1 through June 30 of the following year. Around April 1 of each year, each sales division manager is requested to submit his or her budget proposal for the next fiscal year. After each division manager submits the personnel and financial needs, the budget officer and vice president meet, analyze the requests, and propose a budget.

After the budget is prepared, the president briefs the board of directors. If they approve the budget, the document becomes the new budget for the fiscal year beginning July 1. While the budget is reviewed at midyear (six-month point)

and adjusted internally, the general tendency is to leave the budget "as is" once approved.

Linda Seigmiller, sales manager of Division A, prepared her budget proposal on April 6 and submitted it to the vice president. In her budget proposal, she requested one new salesperson because the sales of Division A had increased 7.5 percent during the past year. The unwritten guideline in the company was that a division received an additional person for every 7.5 percent increase in sales. She also requested a proportional increase in supplies, travel expenses, and telephone expenses for Sales Division A. She knew that her division had, by far, the largest sales increase for the year and she felt confident that her requests would be honored.

After preparing and sending her budget proposal to the vice president, Linda received the third-quarter sales figures and observed the following sales increases for each division: A (30%); B (6.3%); C (4.3%); D (8.8%). After seeing these figures, she called a staff meeting on May 1. In this meeting, her section managers indicated that they believed the increase in sales would continue for Division A through the next fiscal year. Linda did not inform the vice president of this new projection.

At a staff meeting on June 1, the vice president told the division sales managers that the president had approved the new budget and that it would be distributed within the week. The sales manager of Division C asked a question about new people needed because of increased sales. The vice president responded that Division A would receive 1 additional salesperson, Division B would receive 2.5, Division C would receive 7, and Division D would receive 1. Linda was shocked by the response and immediately requested a reevaluation of the budget because her division had the largest increase in sales and the smallest increase in new personnel.

After leaving the meeting, Linda telephoned the budget officer and asked if he could explain to her the logic for the allocation of new personnel. He replied that she had requested one new position and she received one new position. She countered by informing him of the third-quarter sales figures and said she now needed three new people to meet anticipated sales. She also asked, "Why did Division C receive 7 new authorizations with only a 4.3 percent increase in sales?" The budget officer responded that he didn't exactly know the reasoning behind the allocation

of new people; however, he did know that Division A received 100 percent of its requested budget while the other divisions received less than they requested.

After the telephone conversation, Linda felt disgusted because she had been honest during the budgeting process and had requested only those increases that could be documented by increases in productivity, whereas it appeared that other departments had "padded" their budget requests.

Discussion Questions

1 What are the major sources of conflict among the divisions?

2 What strategy did Linda Seigmiller use to deal with other divisions? What strategies did other divisions use to accumulate resources?

3 How has competition among divisions hurt the overall effectiveness of Command Press?

4 Do you think that Linda Seigmiller will act differently the next time budgets are reviewed? Why?

Source: Case written by Robert A. Zawacki. Reprinted with permission from Dittrich, J. E., and Zawacki, R. A. (1985). *People in organizations* (2nd ed.). Plano, TX: Business Publications, pp. 261–262.

Notes

1   Wexley, K. N., & Yukl, G. A. (1977). *Organizational behavior and personnel psychology.* Homewood, IL: Irwin, 172–173.

2   Robbins, S. P. (1978). Conflict management and conflict resolution are not synonymous terms. *California Management Review, 21* (Winter), 67–69.

3   Ibid., 69–70.

4   Ibid., 70–71.

5   Alderfer, C. P. (1977). Group and intergroup relations. In J. R. Hackman & J. L. Suttle (Eds.), *Improving life at work.* Santa Monica, CA: Goodyear, 248–253.

6   Dalton, M. (1959). *Men who manage.* New York: Wiley, 75–76.

7   Strauss, G. (1964). Work flow frictions, interfunctional rivalry, and professionalism: A case study of purchasing agents. *Human Organization, 23,* 137–149.

8   AT&T's split proves frustrating to homes, businesses, across U.S. (1984, January 13). *The Wall Street Journal, 25,* 37.

9   Lawrence, P. R., & Lorsch, J. W. (1969). *Organization and environment: Managing differentiation and integration.* Homewood, IL: Irwin.

10   Shapiro, B. S. (1977). Can marketing and manufacturing coexist? *Harvard Business Review, 55* (September–October), 104–114.

11   Jewell, L. N., & Reitz, H. J. (1981). *Group effectiveness in organizations.* Glenview, IL: Scott, Foresman.

12   Merton, R. K. (1940). Bureaucratic structure and personality. *Social Forces, 18,* 560–568.

13   Deutsch, M. (1949). An experimental study of the effects of cooperation and competition upon group process. *Human Relations, 2,* 199–232.

14   Hammond, L. K., & Goldman, M. (1961). Competition and noncompetition and its relationship to individual and group productivity. *Sociometry, 24,* 46–60.

15   Miller, L. K., & Hamblin, R. L. (1963). Interdependence, differential rewarding, and productivity. *American Sociological Review, 28,* 768–777.

16   Much of this discussion is taken from Sherif, M., & Sherif, C. W. (1953). *Groups in harmony and tension.* New York: Harper.

17   Ibid.

18   Blake, R. R., & Mouton, J. S. (1961). Loyalty of representatives to ingroup positions during intergroup competition. *Journal of Conflict Resolution, 5,* 304–310.

19   Filley, A. C. (1977). Conflict resolution: The ethic of the good loser. In R. C. Huseman, C. M. Logue, & D. L. Freshley (Eds.), *Readings in interpersonal and organizational behavior.* Boston: Holbrook Press, 234–252.

20   LeVine, R. A., & Campbell, D. T. (1972). *Ethnocentrism: Theories of conflict, ethnic attitudes, and group behavior.* New York: Wiley.

Thomas, K. W. (1977). Toward multi-dimensional values in teaching: The example of conflict behaviors. *Academy of Management Review, 2,* 484–490.

21   Pfeffer, J. (1977). Power and resource allocation in organizations. In B. Staw & G. Salancik (Eds.), *New directions in organizational behavior.* Chicago: St. Clair.

22   Salancik, G., & Pfeffer, J. (1974). The bases and uses of power in organizational decision making. *Administrative Science Quarterly, 19,* 453–473.

23   Crozier, M. (1964). *The bureaucratic phenomenon.* Chicago: University of Chicago Press.

24   Wexley & Yukl, *op. cit.,* 180–181.

25   Sherif & Sherif, *loc. cit.*

26   Lawrence, P. R., & Lorsch, J. W. (1967). *Organization and environment.* Boston: Harvard University Graduate School of Business Administration.

27   Feldman, D. C. (1985). A taxonomy of intergroup conflict resolution strategies. In L. Goodstein (Ed.), *Developing human resources.* La Jolla, CA: University Associates, 169–176.

28   Ibid.

29   Thomas, *loc. cit.*

30   Alderfer, *loc. cit.*

31   Sherif & Sherif, *loc. cit.*

32   Pruitt, D. G. (1971). Indirect communication and the search for agreement in negotiations. *Journal of Applied Social Psychology, 1,* 205–239.

33   Blake, R. R., & Mouton, J. S. (1961). Comprehension of own and of outgroup positions under intergroup competition. *Journal of Conflict Resolution, 5,* 304–310.

34   Wexley & Yukl, *op. cit.,* 181–182.

35   Ibid. 183.

36   Blake, R. R., Shepard, H. A., & Mouton, J. S. (1964). *Managing intergroup conflict in industry.* Houston: Gulf.

Burke, W. W. (1972). Managing conflicts between groups. In J. D. Adams (Ed.), *Theory and method in organizational development: An evolutionary process.* Arlington, VA: National Training Laboratories Institute, 255–268.

37   Walton, R. E., & McKersie, R. B. (1965). *A behavioral theory of labor negotiations: An analysis of a social interaction system.* New York: McGraw-Hill, 130.

38   Chapple, E., & Sayles, L. R. (1961). *The measure of management.* New York: Macmillan.

Duncan, R. B. (1979). What is the right organization structure? *Organizational Dynamics, 7,* 59–80.

39   Galbraith, J. R. (1974). Organization design: An information processing view. *Interfaces, 4,* 28–36.

Lawrence, P. R., & Lorsch, J. W. (1967). New management job: The integrator. *Harvard Business Review, 45,* 142–151.

Part 4

Organizational Structure and Design

Chapter 9   The Structure of Organizations

Chapter 10   Designing Effective Organizations

The Structure of Organizations

CHAPTER OUTLINE

Functional Organizations

Divisional Organizations

Lateral Relations

Matrix Structures

Keys to Effective Management

Review Questions

I n this chapter, we will be examining the ways in which organizations are structured. By the term *organization structure,* we mean the formal arrangement of operations and activities within an organization.

Organization structures allow companies to achieve three interrelated goals.[1] First, organization structures define lines of responsibility and authority within corporations. They indicate to managers which employees they are responsible for supervising, and they indicate to employees which managers they are to take orders and instructions from.

Second, organization structures help channel the flow of information in companies. There would be chaos in an organization if all employees were free to communicate directly with top management on all business matters. Organization structures indicate the supervisors to whom employees may legitimately bring their problems. In so doing, organization structures also help control the amount of information flowing directly to top management.

Third, organization structures help achieve coordination of the work activities of different individual employees. Organization structures make it possible for employees who are working on the same products or services to be grouped together in the same work group, and to report to the same supervisor.

In this chapter we will be examining four types of organizational structure: (1) functional organizations; (2) divisional organizations; (3) lateral relations; and (4) matrix structures. For each type of structure, we will first give some examples of current business organizations that use that particular structural form. Next we will discuss the advantages and disadvantages of that type of organizational structure. Finally, we'll examine the conditions under which each organizational structure works best, and when organizations should consider changing their structural form.

Functional Organizations

A *functional organization* is one in which employees are grouped together on the basis of the primary skill (or business *function*) they need to do their jobs. For instance, all accountants are grouped together in the same department, all marketing specialists are grouped together in the same department, and so on. Most of the authority and power in these organizations is held by the *functional department heads* (e.g., the department manager of accounting and the department manager of marketing). Coordination of projects and activities that involve several functional areas is done by *top general managers* (the president and his or her chief assistants).

Figure 9-1 contains the organizational charts of two functional organizations, a city government and a manufacturing company. (In these organizational charts, vertical lines denote a superior-subordinate relationship; horizontal lines link people at the same hierarchical level.)

In the city government example, municipal employees are grouped together on the basis of their major business function. Employees are grouped by technical specialty: police officers are situated in the police department, sanitation engineers in the public works department, and so on. Employees in each functional department report to their respective department head: fire officers report to the fire chief and school principals report to the superintendent of schools. These department heads have most of the authority and power over day-to-day work activities and projects in their departments. When there is a project that involves the coordination of several departments (e.g., public relations and civil defense), the mayor's office has the major responsibility.

In the manufacturing company, we see another example of a functional structure. First, all employees are grouped by technical specialty: the sales force is in the sales department; engineers are in the engineering department, and so on. Notice, though, that within the manufacturing department yet another level of functional departmentalization has been instituted. Painters are in the painting department; packagers are in the packaging department, and so on. The department heads have the major responsibilities for the day-to-day work activities within their departments. Vice presidents have the major responsi-

Figure 9-1   Functional Organizations.

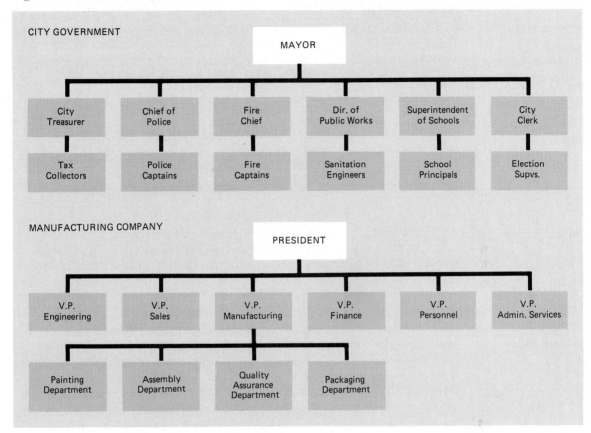

bilities for coordinating the different departments within their areas. For example, the vice president of manufacturing is responsible for coordinating the activities of the painting, assembly, quality assurance, and packaging departments. When there is a project that involves the coordination of several business areas (e.g., budgeting and legal affairs), the president's office has the major responsibility.

Advantages of the Functional Structure

The functional structure offers the organization two key advantages: It encourages technical expertise, and it reduces duplication of activities.[2]

Encourages Technical Expertise

One of the greatest advantages of the functional structure is that it supports and reinforces technical expertise. For instance, in the manufacturing company example, a functional structure facilitates sharing of technical knowledge and

TABLE 9-1

Advantages and Disadvantages of Functional Organizations

Advantages

1 Encourages technical expertise
2 Reduces duplication of activities

Disadvantages

1 Fosters narrow perspectives in the functional departments
2 Makes it difficult to coordinate interdepartmental activities

work experience by locating all the engineers in the same department. Moreover, since the vice president of engineering will have the most influence on the allocation of pay raises and promotion decisions, he or she can reward the engineers doing the highest quality work.

Reduces Duplication of Activities

Another big advantage of the functional structure is that it achieves some economies of scale. For instance, in the manufacturing company example, there is one vice president of personnel. This vice president and his or her staff are responsible for screening all company job applicants, keeping all payroll records, filing all affirmative action information to the government, and so on. If there were not one business unit whose job was to perform these personnel activities, each separate business unit would have to hire people to perform these functions. The engineering department, the sales department, and the finance department would each have to do its own screening of job applicants, keep payroll records, and file affirmative action plans. It is much more efficient—in terms of time, money, and human resources—for one department to carry out all the personnel activities for the corporation as a whole.

Disadvantages of the Functional Structure

While the functional structure has its strong points, it has two major disadvantages as well: It fosters narrow perspectives in functional groups and it makes it difficult to coordinate interdepartmental activities.[3]

Fosters Narrow Perspectives in Functional Groups

When each functional group is doing what is best for itself, an organization may not achieve its overall corporate objectives. For instance, in the city government example, each department will try to obtain as much money for itself as it can. Each department is only secondarily concerned with the overall financial situation of the city as a whole, and whether taxes will need to be raised or higher deficits endured. We see this same phenomenon at the national level.

In 1985, while President Reagan was trying to lower the overall national debt, cabinet secretaries like Caspar Weinberger of Defense were doing everything they could to prevent their units' budgets from being cut.

Makes It Difficult to Coordinate Interdepartmental Activities

When many different departments have to be coordinated for a special project, top managers of functional organizations often find that they are facing a very difficult task. For example, in the city government structure, the mayor's office is responsible for coordinating all the parties involved in a major parade or concert—police officers, fire officers, public works directors, and so on. In situations such as these, there can be serious lapses in communication between the units involved and long delays as each department waits for final instructions from the mayor's office. We also see this disadvantage of the functional structure operating in city governments when they try to coordinate emergency responses to major fires, floods, snowstorms, and accidents.

Overall Assessment

Three situational factors seem to be particularly favorable to the functional structure: (1) relatively small organization size; (2) geographical centralization, i.e., all operations are in the same geographical location; and (3) specialization of the organization on three or four products or services.

Under these circumstances, the disadvantages of the functional structure are quite modest. Because the organization is small and geographically centralized, there can be relatively simple communication and decision making among departments, and overall corporate goals can be kept in sight. Because the organization only provides a few products or services, there is not substantial difficulty coordinating interdepartmental activities. At the same time, the functional organization is able to develop technical expertise among its employees and achieve some economies of scale.

However, as the organization grows, spreads out geographically, and provides many more products and services, the functional design weakens. There is simply too much difficulty in coordinating interdepartmental activities, and too many bottlenecks occur in decision making at the top manager's level. At this point, many organizations turn to the divisional structure, and we turn next to analyze that structural form.

Divisional Organizations

In *divisional structures,* employees are grouped together in one of three ways: (1) by the products on which they work; (2) by the geographical locations in which they work; or (3) by the sets of customers they serve.[4]

1   *Product divisions.* This type of divisionalization groups together all the people needed to produce a product or provide a service. For instance, at

General Motors there is a Chevrolet division, a Pontiac division, and so on. Each division contains most of the people, raw materials, and technology needed to produce its goods.

2 *Geographical divisions.* This type of divisionalization groups together in a geographical unit most of the people, raw materials, and technology needed to produce the unit's goods and provide its services. For instance, retail stores like Walmart are largely divisionalized geographically. All the employees in the same geographical area report to the same general managers.

3 *Customer divisions.* This type of divisionalization groups together all the people needed to produce a product or provide a service to a specific set of customers. For instance, AT&T has separate divisions for residential customers and commercial customers. Universities often have separate divisions for undergraduate students, graduate students, and continuing education students.

In divisional organizations, most of the power and responsibility for the day-to-day running of the organization rests with the **heads of the divisions**. Coordination of projects or activities that involve several divisions is done by the president's office.

It is important to note here that the divisional structure does *not* preclude functional departments. Indeed, almost all divisional organizations have functional departments as well. For instance, in each product division at General Motors, there is a separate finance department, personnel department, and marketing department. In each geographical division at Walmart, there is a separate finance department, personnel department, and marketing department. Both the residential and the commercial customer divisions of AT&T have separate finance, personnel, and marketing departments. It is simply the case that in divisional organizations, people are separated into product, geographical, or customer groups *before* they are placed in functional departments.[5] If General Motors were not divisionalized, there would be one centralized personnel department for all employees in the corporation (in the tens of thousands). With divisions, GM's personnel officers are still doing only personnel work—but they are doing it for a much smaller subset of people.

Figure 9-2 includes the organizational charts of two divisional organizations, Quaker, Inc., and Federated Department Stores.

In the Quaker organization, employees are first grouped by product divisions: human foods; pet foods; chemicals; Fisher Price toys. Then, within each division, people are organized by function (marketing, personnel, finance). Group vice presidents are responsible for coordinating the activities within their product groups. The president and chief executive officer are responsible for coordinating projects and activities that involve different sets of divisions (e.g., long-range strategic planning).

In the Federated Department Stores organization, employees are first

Figure 9-2 Divisional Organizations.

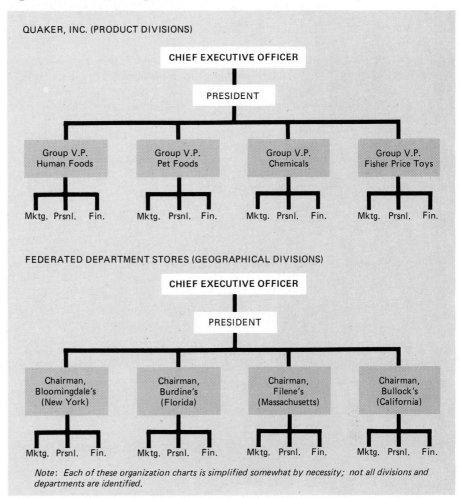

QUAKER, INC. (PRODUCT DIVISIONS)

CHIEF EXECUTIVE OFFICER

PRESIDENT

| Group V.P. Human Foods | Group V.P. Pet Foods | Group V.P. Chemicals | Group V.P. Fisher Price Toys |

Mktg. Prsnl. Fin.   Mktg. Prsnl. Fin.   Mktg. Prsnl. Fin.   Mktg. Prsnl. Fin.

FEDERATED DEPARTMENT STORES (GEOGRAPHICAL DIVISIONS)

CHIEF EXECUTIVE OFFICER

PRESIDENT

| Chairman, Bloomingdale's (New York) | Chairman, Burdine's (Florida) | Chairman, Filene's (Massachusetts) | Chairman, Bullock's (California) |

Mktg. Prsnl. Fin.   Mktg. Prsnl. Fin.   Mktg. Prsnl. Fin.   Mktg. Prsnl. Fin.

Note: Each of these organization charts is simplified somewhat by necessity; not all divisions and departments are identified.

grouped by geographical divisions: New York stores (Bloomingdale's); Florida stores (Burdine's); Massachusetts stores (Filene's); and California stores (Bullock's). Then, within each division, people are organized by function (marketing, personnel, finance). Once again, the chairman of each geographical region is responsible for the activities and projects within that region. Top management is responsible for coordinating all interdivisional activities (e.g., shared transportation and warehousing).

Very few organizations are completely divisionalized by customer. Typically, a division is set up for a client that has a very particular set of needs that could not be handled with standardized procedures. Companies that do a major share of their business with the U.S. government—like General Dynam-

BOX 9-1

Strategy and Structure

In his book *Strategy and Structure,* Alfred Chandler looked at the structural changes of Sears, DuPont, Jersey Standard, and General Motors as they moved from functional structures to divisional structures. The changes in structure of these four organizations are examined in detail below.

Sears: Sears rapidly expanded its mail-order business in the 1920s, but this growth put very little strain on its functional organization structure. During the 1930s, however, Sears entered a whole new line of business: over-the-counter retailing. With this change in the scope of its business, Sears faced too many problems of coordination and supervision for the existing functional organization to handle. General Wood, Sears' chief strategist, became convinced by 1940 of the value of a divisional structure. Because Sears wanted to make sure it could quickly and competently meet the demands of its consumers, Sears divisionalized on the basis of geographical territory. Sears hoped local division managers would be the most responsive to their customers' needs.

DuPont: DuPont's chemical business also expanded in volume after World War I, and, as in the case of Sears, that expansion caused few organizational problems. However, when DuPont started bringing out a larger, more diversified line of chemical products, then the existing functional structure proved inadequate. Top executives were no longer able to give proper attention to the coordination of market demand and product design for all their products or to plan adequately for future expansion. DuPont first experimented with using committees to coordinate all the functions for each product, but found these committees ineffective and cumbersome. Finally, Ireneè DuPont approved a divisional structure using product divisions.

ics (Connecticut) and Harris (Florida)—often set up a ***government systems division.*** Because the U.S. government has very special purchasing and bidding procedures, and because the government is acquiring from these corporations highly sophisticated integrated weapon systems, corporations like General Dynamics and Harris find that government systems divisions are best able to coordinate their government-related activities.

Another type of customer division, which organizations like Coca-Cola and Bendix have added, is an ***international division.*** Doing business overseas or in a foreign country requires a group of specialists who are skilled in handling the political and economic complexities of foreign trade; putting all these people together in the same unit helps to coordinate activities abroad more efficiently. General Electric, for instance, has a Canadian division and a Far East division.

BOX 9-1 *(Continued)*

Jersey Standard: Jersey Standard, a large petroleum products company, experienced remarkable growth after World War I. First, with the coming of the automobile, Jersey Standard was developing many new petroleum products. Second, the company was opening new oil fields in Europe, Latin America, and Asia, and was setting up a worldwide shipping and refining system. Third, the company was expanding its marketing in foreign countries and the United States. This growth and diversification placed too much strain on its functional structure, and in 1933, Jersey Standard, too, decided to implement a product divisional structure.

General Motors: During World War I, General Motors diversified its product lines beyond automotive products. For instance, it became one of the largest manufacturers of refrigerators and bought a majority interest in the Dayton-Wright Airplane Company. General Motors' structure at that time was essentially a functional structure, and it was unable to coordinate such a set of diverse activities. GM, too, then created a divisional structure to manage its businesses. At the same time, GM created interdivisional committees to facilitate coordination and communication across divisions.

Source: Adapted from: Chandler, A. A., Jr. (1962). *Strategy and structure: Chapters in the history of the American industrial enterprise.* Cambridge, MA: MIT Press, pp. 13–16, 299–323.

Advantages of the Divisional Structure

There are three advantages, in particular, of using the divisional structure.[6]

Improves Decision Making

In a divisional structure, it is possible for more high-quality decisions about day-to-day activities to be made, and to be made more quickly. As organizations grow in size (as measured by number of employees, number of products, or number of customers), there are too many decisions to be handled by top management. The divisional structure allows many decisions to be delegated to division managers. These division managers are generally more knowledgeable about the customers, the markets, and the products involved, and therefore have a better grasp of the overall situation than top management would. Moreover, because division managers are closer to the problems, they are often able to take corrective action more quickly.

These improvements in decision making are especially advantageous as organizations expand the scope of their businesses or expand the geographical areas their businesses cover. In his classic study of organizational growth, Alfred Chandler notes that organizations need to divisionalize to reduce the burden of decision making on top manager.[7] Box 9-1 provides descriptions of how Sears, DuPont, Jersey Standard, and General Motors divisionalized. Div-

TABLE 9-2

Advantages and Disadvantages of Divisional Organizations

Advantages

1   Improves decision making
2   Fixes accountability for profits and production
3   Increases coordination of functional departments

Disadvantages

1   Increases difficulty in allocating corporate staff support
2   Loses some economies of scale
3   Fosters little cooperation among divisions

isionalization allowed these companies to expand their businesses without overburdening top management with operational decisions.

Fixes Accountability for Profits and Production

One of the big advantages of the divisional structure is that there are now division heads who are accountable for meeting production quotas and generating specified amounts of profit for the corporation as a whole.[8] Indeed, in many organizations, divisions are called "profit centers."

For instance, at DuPont, the different division chiefs have specific goals in terms of how much product they need to produce and how much profit they are to generate. At Sears, too, the regional division chiefs have specific goals in terms of expected sales volume and profit margins. In both organizations, division heads are evaluated on the overall effectiveness of their units in meeting those goals. By fixing accountability for profits and production at the division head level, organizations make sure that divisions will pull their own weight in meeting overall corporate profit and production goals.

Increases Coordination of Functional Departments

One of the chief advantages of the divisional structure is that it focuses each employee's efforts on one relatively small set of products, customers, or geographical locations. Coordination of functions within each division is made easier because all the employees who are working on the same product (or who are servicing the same customers or geographical locations) are located in the same work unit and report to the same general manager.[9]

For example, imagine that the president of Federated Department Stores had to coordinate purchasing, inventory, hiring, and sales promotions for all Federated stores. The task would be impossible. By using the divisional structure, Federated ensures that the coordination of services within each geographical area will be much smoother. When the president of Burdine's sees that inventory in a particular merchandise area is running high, he or she can get a sales promotion going relatively quickly in the Florida stores, without having to check with, or worry about, the inventories in other geographical areas. Divisions make coordination of functions for each product, customer group, or geographical area much easier.

Disadvantages of the Divisional Structure

While the divisional structure has several strong points, it is not without its drawbacks. Most divisional structures have three distinct disadvantages.[10]

Increases Difficulty in Allocating Corporate Staff Support

While a division contains most of the functions needed to produce its own goods and services, there still remains the problem of allocating those corporate staff functions that *all* the divisions must share.

For instance, most divisions cannot afford to have their own full-time legal or public relations staffs. In most organizations, divisions also have to share advertising staff specialists and personnel support services (e.g., training and counseling). It is often difficult for corporate officers to allocate these staff support services efficiently across the divisions so that each division gets all the support it needs and at the time it requests assistance.

Loses Some Economies of Scale

One of the major costs of a divisional structure is that each division may be duplicating some of the activities of other divisions. For instance, each division of General Motors has its own sales force. These sales people sell only that division's products. Imagine how much money a company like General Motors would save if in every city there was only one GM distributorship! Most cities have a "car row" where there is a Chevy agency, an Olds agency, a Pontiac agency, and a Cadillac agency. Such duplication costs money.

Fosters Little Cooperation among Divisions

Sometimes the autonomy given to divisions to pursue their own goals hinders their achievement of overall corporate goals.

For example, an area in which coordination across divisions is important is compliance with standards set by regulatory agencies like the Environmental Protection Agency (EPA), the Occupational Safety and Health Administration (OSHA), and the Equal Opportunity Commission (EEOC). Noncompliance on the part of any one division can have a substantial negative impact on the organization as a whole, so top management wants to control dealings with these regulatory agencies carefully. However, sometimes the divisions are so independent that it is difficult to get them to comply with the record-keeping demands generated by these agencies. The divisions often view corporate requests for information as "fire drills" made up by headquarters staff, and do not respond in a timely fashion.

Sometimes divisions even get into dysfunctional rivalries with each other. One area in which this often happens is career development. Divisions are typically jealous of their own personnel. They try to develop their human resources internally, and discourage employees from trying for jobs in other divisions. However, the organization as a whole would benefit if it could develop well-rounded, widely trained people to take on top management jobs. When each division pursues personnel policies that are best for itself, an overall corporate goal of developing promotable, top-level management can fall by the wayside.

**Overall
Assessment**

A divisional structure is most appropriate when: (1) the organization is relatively large; (2) it produces a wide range of goods and services; and (3) it is geographically decentralized.

When an organization has these three characteristics, it is best able to capitalize on the advantages that a divisional structure offers. When an organization produces a wide variety of goods and services, it is especially important that the managers who are the most knowledgeable about different sets of operational problems be given responsibility for solving them. Divisional structures accomplish this aim. Moreover, the divisional structure fixes accountability for meeting the production quotas and profit goals for each product, geographical location, or customer group. Finally, when an organization is geographically spread out, it is critical that the coordination of functions for each product or service be made as easy as possible. Divisional structures do this by locating all the people working on the same product or service in the same work unit and having them report to the same general manager.

As we saw above, the major problem with the divisional structure is the lack of coordination among divisions on mutual problems or shared activities. Because of its strong advantages, organizations have tried to fine-tune the divisional structure to compensate for its inherent disadvantages. Several ways have been suggested to improve the lateral relationships among divisions, and in the next section we will examine some of these modifications.

Lateral Relations

Organizations have developed a set of structural devices, called *lateral relations,* to encourage coordination among individuals and groups in different work units. Lateral relations can be used in both functional and divisional organizations. For instance, they have been used to increase coordination across functional departments in a functional structure, and to increase coordination across divisions in a divisional structure.

Five lateral relations, in particular, have been frequently used to achieve effective coordination across work units: (1) dotted-line supervision; (2) liaison roles; (3) temporary task forces; (4) permanent teams; and (5) integrating managers.[12] These structural devices can be incorporated into, or added onto, the regular formal structure.

TABLE   9-3

Lateral Relations

1   Dotted-line supervision
2   Liaison roles
3   Temporary task forces
4   Permanent teams
5   Integrating managers

Dotted-Line Supervision

Dotted-line supervision gives corporate staff officers some indirect supervisory control over their counterparts in the divisions. The corporate staff officers can participate in the hiring (or firing) of divisional staff, can influence their performance evaluations, and can issue them specific guidelines and directives to follow on their jobs.

An example of dotted-line supervision appears in Figure 9-3. The vice president of human resources has a dotted-line (or indirect) supervisory role over the department manager of human resources in each division. The vice president issues guidelines and directives to the divisions' department managers on recruitment practices, affirmative action programs, employee discipline, continuing education, and so forth.

Department managers of human resources in the divisions cannot simply go their own way, bending only to the wishes of their divisional chiefs. They

Figure 9-3   Dotted-line Supervision.

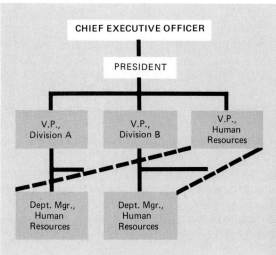

must follow the practices and procedures set for them by headquarters' general management as well. Every year the corporate vice president of human resources will participate in the performance evaluation of the department managers and will make recommendations about their pay raises and promotions. The vice president of human resources is also often given a veto in hiring decisions in his or her area and may initiate the termination of an employee whom he or she feels is technically incompetent or unprofessional.

Liaison Roles

A person in a *liaison role* has the responsibility for coordinating the work of two units. When a considerable amount of contact is needed between two units to complete a project, a liaison position may be formally established to ensure quick and accurate communication.[13] For instance, many organizations use a sales liaison person, whose job it is to coordinate the field sales force with the factory production group.[14]

Another good example of the liaison role is the engineering liaison person in a manufacturing plant. This person is part of the engineering department and reports to the director of engineering. However, this engineer actually works at the manufacturing plant, where his or her job is to expedite communication between design engineers and production/operations supervisors.[15]

Temporary Task Forces

A *temporary task force* is a committee formed to solve a short-run problem involving several different work units. It meets on a regular basis until the problem is solved, and then the task force disbands. Members of the task force still keep their original reporting relationships; they add this temporary work assignment on the task force to their other job duties.[16]

In one manufacturing company, for instance, when a problem arises on the assembly floor, the supervisor calls together the process engineer, a member from the company laboratory, a representative from quality control, and someone from purchasing (if defective parts from a vendor are involved). This group works out the problem. When an acceptable solution is reached, group members return to their normal duties.

Sometimes the establishment of the temporary task force is more formal. At one aerospace firm, weekly design reviews are held. When a significant problem arises, a temporary task force is appointed. The members are given a specific time deadline and some leeway to bypass normal chains of command. The task force then has to report its results formally to management.[17]

Temporary task forces are also formed to launch new products. Representatives from production, engineering, marketing, and sales may meet regularly over a 6-month period to ensure a smooth transition from design to production to initial marketing efforts.

Permanent Teams

A ***permanent team*** is a group of organization members from different work units who meet regularly to address issues or problems of common interest.[18] For instance, in many divisional organizations, there is a permanent team called a ***manpower review committee.*** This committee meets every 6 months to consider which managers should be promoted, which should be terminated, and which should receive training or job rotations. Most divisional organizations also have environmental safety committees, whose job it is to monitor safety hazards and accident rates in the corporation as a whole.

Notice that each of these permanent teams is formed to address a problem or issue that is of interest to all the divisions. Notice, too, that the problems or issues that the committees deal with are recurring ones: manpower planning and environmental safety. For these permanent teams to be most effective, it is important that their members have the knowledge and experience relevant to the problems at hand. For this reason, one often sees senior general managers and human resource managers on manpower review committees, and industrial engineers and first-line supervisors on environmental safety committees.[19]

Integrating Managers

There are some projects in organizations that require constant coordination of several functional activities. When this is the case, organizations will designate certain employees as ***integrating managers.*** Their job is to coordinate all the functional activities on a project on a full-time basis.[20]

The most frequently seen example of an integrating manager is the brand (or product) manager in a consumer goods firm. Quaker, General Foods, General Mills, and Procter and Gamble all use brand managers. General Mills, for instance, assigns a product manager to each of the products in its line, such as Cheerios, Hamburger Helper, and Gold Medal Flour. Product managers are responsible for setting marketing goals, planning market strategy, budgeting funds for promotions and advertising, and coordinating production and shipping of their brand.

Brand managers are regular line employees of the marketing department and report to the vice president of marketing. While the brand managers are responsible and accountable for product success, however, they have no formal authority over employees outside of the marketing department. They must persuade and cajole employees from different units to cooperate. For instance, if the brand manager for Cocoa Puffs wants to bring out Cocoa Puffs in a 6-pack of 1-ounce boxes, he or she has to sell the idea to the production engineers and the sales force.[21]

Obviously, for this system of integrator roles to work, these managers need good interpersonal skills. They need to know when to push their cause aggressively and when to back off. Moreover, they need well-rounded education and experience in the different areas in which they are operating.

Overall Assessment

Lateral relations have proved successful in helping to coordinate activities involving several different work units in organizations. These devices are particularly useful when the amount of integration needed between work units is *relatively limited.* For instance, dotted-line supervision deals solely with the coordination of headquarters and divisional staff groups; liaison roles deal solely with the coordination of two departments; temporary task forces deal solely with problems of a short-run nature.

However, some organizations are so dynamic in their growth, or need so much constant coordination of activities, that these devices simply do not achieve the high level of integration needed. At that point, organizations typically turn to a fourth structural form, the *matrix.*

Matrix Structures

The identifying feature of a matrix structure is that employees report to *two* supervisors rather than to the traditional single supervisor. There is a *dual,* rather than a single, chain of command.[22]

There are two common variants of the matrix structure, one called a ***project management matrix*** and the other called a ***geography-by-product matrix.*** Diagrams of these organization structures appear in Figure 9-4.

Project Management Matrix

Major corporations in such diverse businesses as chemicals (Dow Chemical), petroleum (Shell Oil), electronics (Texas Instruments, General Electric, and TRW), and aeronautics (Lockheed) use the project management matrix structure.

Looking at Lockheed's project management matrix in Figure 9-4, we see there are four critical roles in this type of organization structure.[23]

Functional Managers

Functional managers (e.g., vice president of engineering, vice president of manufacturing) are responsible for the hiring and development of technically competent employees in each functional area. They perform the same activities as department heads in functional and divisional structures.

Project Managers

Project managers (e.g., L-1011 plane project manager, weapons system project manager) are responsible for coordinating the activities of people from different functional areas who are working on the same project. In many ways their job duties are like those of the integrating managers discussed earlier. However, unlike the integrating managers, project managers have some *formal* authority over employees from different functional areas who work on their projects.

Figure 9-4   Matrix Structures.

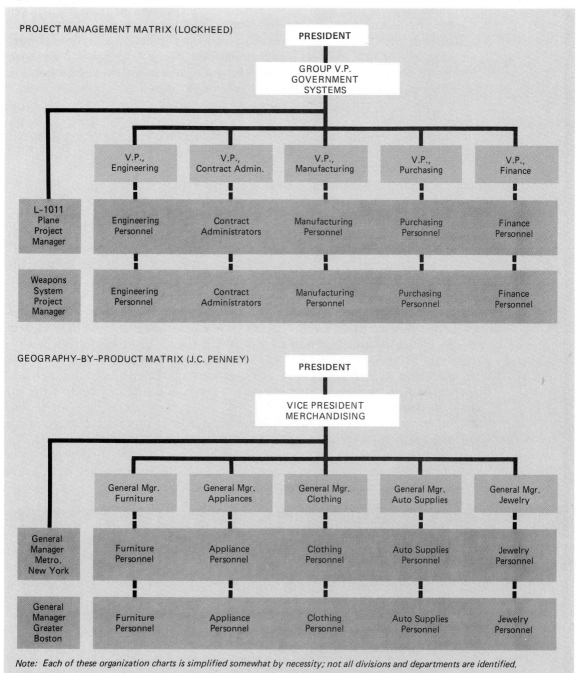

Note: *Each of these organization charts is simplified somewhat by necessity; not all divisions and departments are identified.*

Two-Boss Employees

Each employee who works in the matrix structure reports to two supervisors: a functional manager and a project manager. Typically, an employee is hired by a functional manager to be a member of a functional department, but is "loaned out" (for periods of several months to 2 years) to a project manager to assist on a major project. The functional manager will be mainly responsible for supervising and evaluating the technical aspects of the employee's work. The project manager will be mainly responsible for supervising the employee's day-to-day activities.

Top Managers

The vice president of government systems and the president are responsible for supervising the functional managers and the project managers, and for resolving major disputes among them.

Project management matrix structures were developed in the 1960s. The U.S. government at that time made it a condition for the awarding of research and development contracts that the contracting firms should have a "project management system." The government was afraid projects would get out of hand if each functional manager only had responsibility for one specific part of a project. Instead, the government wanted to make sure that one specific person—a *project manager*—would be responsible for making sure that the entire project got finished on time and within the budget.[24]

On the other hand, many of the government contracts for weapons systems and the like only lasted for one or two years. Organizations did not want to keep on rearranging their formal structures each and every time a government contract was won or lost. The project matrix structure allowed organizations to take on a variety of temporary projects within a stable organization structure but still meet the needs and demands of their major customers.

Finally, it is important to note here that an organization does not need to adopt a matrix structure wholesale. Indeed, particularly for the project management matrix, this structure is adopted *only within certain divisions.* For example, at Harris Corporation (Florida), the matrix structure is only used in the government systems division. This is the division whose major mission is to obtain government contracts and produce information technology systems for the U.S. government.

Geography-by-Product Matrix

Mass market retail chains like J. C. Penney use geography-by-product matrix structures. Employees are grouped, on one hand, by the *type of merchandise* they handle and, on the other hand, by the particular *geographical region* in which they are located.

Looking at Penney's geography-by-product matrix in Figure 9-4, we see that there are four critical roles in this variant of the matrix as well.

Merchandise General Managers

Merchandise general managers (e.g., general manager of furniture, general manager of appliances) are responsible for one category of merchandise items nationwide. They are responsible for choosing items that will be popular in the market and for purchasing those items at the lowest possible prices.

Regional-Level General Managers	***Regional-level general managers*** (e.g., general manager of metropolitan New York, general manager of greater Boston) are responsible for stocking their local stores with items from all the lines of merchandise the national chain carries (e.g., furniture, appliances). Their main duty is to be responsive to the consumer tastes and income levels of their particular communities.
Two-Boss Employees	Managers of the various merchandise departments in each geographical location report to both a merchandise general manager and a regional-level general manager. For instance, the clothing department manager in Fort Lauderdale, Florida, needs to balance the pressures of merchandise general managers to carry items with a high profit margin (like fur-lined gloves) with the local demands of the regional general managers.
Top Managers	The vice president of merchandising and the president are responsible for supervising the merchandise general managers and the regional-level general managers, and for resolving major disputes among them.

Like the project management matrix structures, the geography-by-product matrix tries to balance two conflicting demands. The overall organization needs to carry similar lines of merchandise in all its stores and to buy large quantities of these items at favorable wholesale prices. The regional stores need to identify those merchandise items that will attract buyers to their stores and to stock items that meet local tastes and spending ability.[25]

This type of matrix structure can also be found in the administration of some cities, where functional heads of citywide departments (parks, police, fire, etc.) need to coordinate with the administrators of different neighborhood wards and townships. These two sets of managers are jointly responsible for ensuring the quality of public services to different areas of the city.[26] Recently some international companies have also moved toward this type of matrix structure. Managers of worldwide product lines are now expected to coordinate their activities with the managers of different geographical regions.[27]

Advantages of the Matrix Structure	Let's consider, next, the advantages of the matrix structure that have made it such a popular organizational form in recent years.
Reinforces and Broadens Technical Excellence	By keeping employees grouped by functional activity, the organization ensures that it is hiring and promoting the most technically competent employees. Functional specialists are able to share ideas and suggestions with their colleagues and, at the same time, with professionals in other areas. This broadens their general business perspective and their ability to see a wider range of issues.

For example, when a design engineer and an industrial engineer work together on designing an instrument panel, each of their perspectives on the project broadens. The design engineer becomes more aware of the human factors to be considered in the project; the industrial engineer becomes more

---

TABLE 9-4

Advantages and Disadvantages of Matrix Structures

Advantages

1 Reinforces and broadens technical excellence
2 Facilitates efficient use of resources
3 Balances conflicting objectives of the organization

Disadvantages

1 Increases the number of power conflicts
2 Increases confusion and stress for two-boss employees
3 Impedes decision making

---

aware of the design constraints. In the long run, this makes both types of engineers more effective in their respective jobs.[28]

Facilitates Efficient Use of Resources

Matrix organizations make it easier to share resources among various projects. For instance, at the beginning of a project, employees of the purchasing department are typically very important. Major components for the project have to be purchased, inventoried, inspected, and paid for. In contrast, the busiest time for manufacturing is the second half of the project—after all the components have arrived and the engineering design has been completed. Rather than having several underutilized purchasing agents and manufacturing staff permanently assigned to each project, the organization can shift them from project to project as needed, thereby saving on labor costs.[29]

Balances Conflicting Objectives of the Organization

In project management matrix organizations, the needs of the client to have clear-cut lines of authority and communication on a project have to be balanced with the needs of the organization to economically staff projects with high-quality personnel. In geography-by-product matrix organizations, the needs of the merchandise managers to standardize merchandise and achieve economies of scale across stores have to be balanced with the needs of regional managers to meet the local tastes and preferences of their customers. The matrix organization balances these conflicting objectives so that the way in which the product or service is ultimately delivered is acceptable to all the parties involved.[30]

Disadvantages of the Matrix Structure

Despite its popularity, organizations that have adopted the matrix structure have noted some of its drawbacks. Three disadvantages, in particular, stand out.

Increases the Number of Power Conflicts

One of the disadvantages of the matrix is the constant jockeying for position among managers. There is a tendency for functional managers and project managers to spend too much time in corporate politicking, not only to get their way on projects but also to enhance their own careers. Managers jockey for power in most organizations, but a matrix design, with its overlapping areas of responsibility, almost encourages them to do so.[31]

Increases Confusion and Stress for Two-Boss Employees

Some employees in matrix organizations report that they are often frustrated by working for two supervisors. They complain that when they receive conflicting orders from their two bosses, there is no systematic procedure for resolving the conflict. Moreover, these employees are in a very awkward position: they have to resolve the conflicting demands of people *superior* to them in the organization. This causes them stress and anxiety. No matter which path they pursue, one boss will be displeased.

Another frequent complaint of matrix employees is that they work long hours. Each boss is trying to squeeze as much work out of the employee as possible, and sometimes the only way the employee can cope with those demands is to work excessive hours.[32]

Impedes Decision Making

One of the common complaints heard about matrix organizations is that it takes too many meetings and too many people to make a decision. First, the issue has to be discussed separately among the various functional groups. Next, some sort of compromise has to be achieved in the project group. Then, any conflicts still unsettled need to be decided in additional meetings between the project manager and the various functional managers. All these meetings take time and slow up a final decision.

In one matrix electronics company, the organization required that all business decisions be hammered out in group meetings. However, many of the decisions that had to be made about each product involved detailed matters in which only two or three people were really knowledgeable and interested. Nevertheless, all team members were forced to listen to the deliberations and to participate in the discussions. A large number of people felt their time was being frittered away in needless meetings. Moreover, senior managers complained that decisions got made too slowly and that the groups were hesitant to take new or innovative approaches to problems.[33]

Overall Assessment: Making the Matrix Work

From the discussion above, it is clear that a matrix structure is difficult to sustain. Having *two* chains of command makes the matrix inherently less stable than the functional or the divisional form. However, the matrix structure can be a useful organization form, especially in balancing the different business objectives of the firm.

To make the matrix structure more effective, organizations have adopted three changes in their normal business practices.

Dual Human Resource Management Responsibilities

The human resource practices that a matrix organization uses should support the notion of a dual chain of command. First, both the functional manager and the project manager should participate in the performance appraisal process. Second, both the functional manager and the project manager should participate in making pay raise decisions. Third, promotional decisions should be weighted heavily in favor of workers possessing the ability to work effectively with both functional colleagues and project colleagues.[34]

Selection for Conflict Management Skills

Conflict is inherent in matrix organizations. While some of the conflict can be minimized, most of the conflict is inevitable. Therefore, it is important that organizations hire employees and managers with good conflict management skills.

Clearly the assessment center is the most effective method of identifying employees with these skills. Exercises like the leaderless group discussion, the project planning exercise, and the stock exchange problem give assessors a good idea of how people handle competition and conflict in situations where they also have to cooperate and work with each other (see Chapter 15).

Some corporations, such as TRW, have also used organization development to teach current employees how to manage conflict better. Team building, intergroup conflict resolution exercises, and participative management workshops can all be used to help employees work more effectively with each other under conflict (see Chapter 18).

Changes in Group Decision Making

Probably most critical to the effective implementation of matrix organizations is improved group decision making. One of the consequences of matrix organizations is that people at all different hierarchical levels may be working together on the same project. However, for some issues, people at lower levels of the organization will be the most knowledgeable and possess the most relevant information. For matrix organizations to work, important decisions have to be based on expertise, not on rank.

Moreover, the project manager has to be extremely careful in leading group discussions. As noted in Chapter 7, the project manager has to be especially careful not to let group members bias the data in favor of their preferred alternatives. Even if the decision requires long meetings or several meetings, the project manager cannot let the group make a decision just to be done with it. No organization can operate effectively with poor group decision making, but in a matrix organization such decision making can undermine the very structure itself.[35]

Keys To Effective Management

In these final pages, we examine the circumstances under which organizations should adopt each of the four different types of organization structure discussed in the chapter. We also provide some guidelines for diagnosing when the structure an organization is using is inappropriate and needs to be changed.

1   *Organizations should use functional structures when their firms are small and geographically centralized and when they provide only a few goods or services.*   A functional structure can reduce duplication of activities in a relatively small, geographically centralized corporation. Moreover, the functional structure encourages the hiring and development of technically competent professionals. When the organization is relatively small, some of the disadvantages of functional structures—particularly narrow attitudes on the part of functional departments—are relatively minor.

⇒ 2   *When organizations experience bottlenecks in decision making and difficulties in coordinating interdepartmental activities, they need to recognize that they have outgrown their functional structures.*   As an organization grows and adds more products and services, top managers can become overloaded with interdepartmental problems to resolve. Moreover, it becomes harder for top management to keep an equally attentive eye on all the products and services the organization is providing. At this point, managers are wise to think about switching to a divisional structure.

3   *Organizations should use a divisional structure when the organization is relatively large, is geographically decentralized, and/or when it produces a wide range of goods and services.*   Especially when an organization is large and geographically spread out, the divisional structure is most effective in ensuring that market opportunities for each product are quickly noticed and capitalized upon. The divisional structure is also most effective in ensuring that operations and customer service problems for each product are rapidly diagnosed and corrected. Finally, a divisional structure reduces the need for top managers to coordinate the day-to-day activities of personnel that are physically located quite far away from headquarters.

4   *Organizations should use lateral relations, such as dotted-line supervision and integrating managers, to offset coordination problems in functional and divisional structures.*   Clearly, a major problem facing both functional and divisional organizations is lack of coordination both among departments and among divisions. Corporate staff support services, such as advertising and legal counsel, are hard to allocate. There are duplication expenses and losses of economies of scale. Most seriously, subunits of the organization, in pursuit of their own goals, sometimes work against corporate goals. Lateral relations have proved successful in helping coordinate activities involving several different work units in organizations.

5   *When organizations need constant coordination of activities among functional departments, then lateral relations do not achieve the high level of integration needed. At that point, organizations should seriously consider using the matrix structure.*   Matrix structures force members of different

functional departments to work together closely on projects. Moreover, matrix structures allow members of the organization to broaden their technical training and to view business problems from a variety of perspectives.

6 *To facilitate the use of matrix structures, organizations should modify many traditional management practices.*   Since the matrix organization has a dual chain of command, it is important that both general managers participate in conducting employees' performance appraisals, deciding on pay raises, and evaluating suitability for promotion. Employees need to be selected not only for technical excellence but also for their ability to handle conflict constructively. For matrix organizations to work, important decisions have to be based on expertise, not on rank. Without changes in the supporting management systems, the matrix structure will be quickly undermined.

Review Questions

1   What do we mean by the term *organizational structure?* What goals do organization structures help corporations achieve?

2   What is a functional organization? Give some examples of functional organizations.

3   What are the advantages of a functional structure? What are its disadvantages?

4   What three situational factors seem particularly favorable to the functional structure?

5   What is the key difference between a functional structure and a divisional structure?

6   What are the three most common bases of divisionalization? Give an example of each.

7   What are the advantages of a divisional structure? What are its disadvantages?

8   Why do organizations typically turn to a divisional structure after they expand the volume of their business or diversify their product lines?

9   Name five lateral relations. Give an example of each.

10   Why do organizations incorporate lateral relations into their formal structures?

11   What is the identifying feature of a matrix organization?

12 What are the four critical roles in a project management matrix? In a geography-by-product matrix?

13 What are the chief advantages of a matrix? What are its disadvantages?

14 What changes in traditional management practices need to be made to make the matrix work?

Organization Structure in Practice

Below are pictured the organization charts of two businesses. Figure 1 shows the organization structure of a hospital. Figure 2 shows the organization structure of the Canadian Post Office.

Figure 1 Regional general hospital.

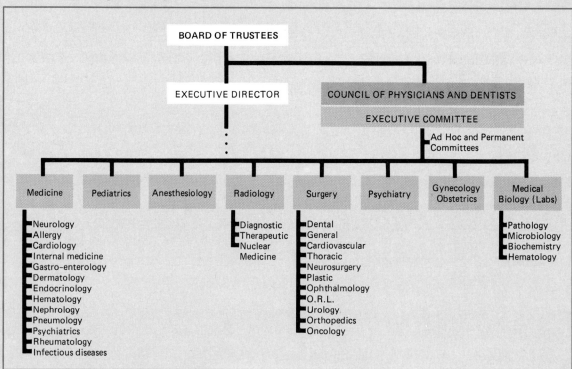

[*Source:* Reprinted from Mintzberg, H. (1979). *The structuring of organizations.* Englewood Cliffs, NJ: Prentice-Hall, p. 109. Used by permission.]

Figure 2 Canadian Post Office.

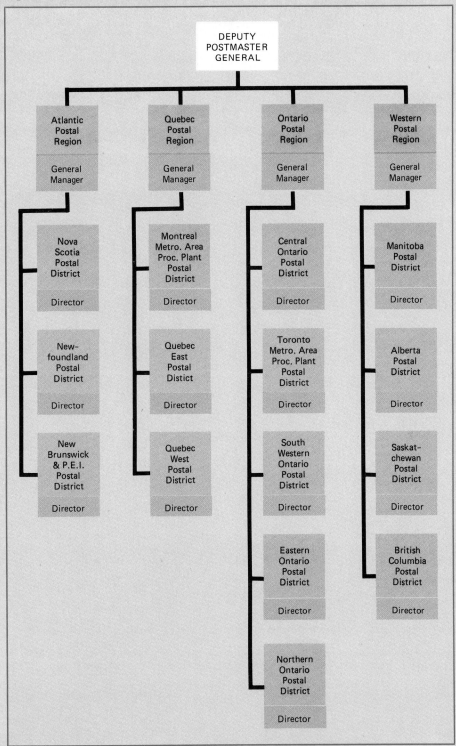

[*Source:* Reprinted from: Mintzberg, H. (1979). *The structuring of organizations.* Englewood Cliffs, NJ: Prentice-Hall, p. 112. Used by permission of the Organization Planning Branch of Post Canada.]

267

Questions for Discussion

1   What type of organization structure does the hospital have? How did you determine this?

2   What type of organization structure does the Canadian Post Office have? How did you determine this?

3   Why do you believe the hospital chose the particular organization structure it did?

4   Why do you believe the Canadian Post Office is structured the way it is?

5   For each structure, give one situation in which a lateral relations structural device could be usefully employed.

Notes

1   Duncan, R. B. (1979). What is the right organization structure? *Organizational Dynamics, 7* (3), 59–80.
   Mintzberg, H. (1979) *The structuring of organizations.* Englewood Cliffs, NJ: Prentice-Hall.

2   Duncan, *op. cit.,* 78.

3   Ibid., 64.

4   Jelinek, M., Litterer, J. A., & Miles, R. E. (1981). Control in organizations. In M. Jelinek, J. A. Litterer, & R. E. Miles (Eds.), *Organizations by design: Theory and practice.* Plano, TX: Business Publications, 417–428.

5   Miles, R. H. (1980). *Macro organizational behavior.* Santa Monica, CA: Goodyear, 1–32.

6   Wallace, M. J., Jr., & Szilagyi, A. D., Jr. (1982). *Managing behavior in organizations.* Glenview, IL: Scott, Foresman, 367.

7   Chandler, A. A., Jr. (1962). *Strategy and structure: Chapters in the history of American industrial enterprise.* Cambridge, MA: MIT Press.

8   Daft, R. L. (1983). *Organization theory and design.* St. Paul, MN: West, 230–233.

9   Mintzberg, *op. cit.,* 380–431.

10   Duncan, *op. cit.,* 66–67.

11   Mintzberg, *op. cit.,* 380–431.
   Duncan, *op. cit.,* 66–67.
   Daft, *loc. cit.*

12   Mintzberg, *op. cit.,* 161–162.

13   Ibid., 162.

14   Landsberger, H. A. (1961). The horizontal dimension in bureaucracy. *Administrative Science Quarterly, 6,* 299–332.

15   Galbraith, J. R. (1977). *Organization design.* Reading, MA: Addison-Wesley, 115.

16   Mintzberg, *op. cit.,* 163–164.

17   Galbraith, *op. cit.,* 116.

18   Mintzberg, *op. cit.,* 164.

19   Galbraith, *op. cit.,* 118–127.

20   Mintzberg, *op. cit.,* 165.

21   Morrison, A. M. (1981, January 12). The General Mills brand of managers. *Fortune,* 99–107.

22   Lawrence, P. R., Kolodny, H. F., & Davis, S. M. (1977). The human side of the matrix. *Organizational Dynamics, 5* (1), 47.

23   Knight, K. Matrix organization: A review (1976). *Journal of Management Studies, 13* (2), 111–118.

24   Kingdon, D. R. (1973). *Matrix organization.* London: Tavistock, 26.

25   Sayles, L. R. (1976). Matrix organization: The structure with a future. *Organizational Dynamics,* (4), 2–17.

26   Mintzberg, *op. cit.,* 171.

27   Stopford, J. J., & Wells, L. T., Jr. (1972). *Managing the multinational enterprise: Organization of the firm and ownership of subsidiaries.* New York: Basic Books.

28   Lawrence, Kolodny, & Davis, *loc. cit.*

29   Knight, *op. cit.,* 119–121.

30   Duncan, *op. cit.,* 71.

31   Knight, *op. cit.,* 119–123.

32   Davis, S. M., & Lawrence, P. R. (1978). Problems of matrix organizations. *Harvard Business Review* (May–June), 131–142.

33   Ibid.

34   Knight, *op. cit.,* 111–130.

35   Galbraith, *op. cit.,* 118–127.

Chapter 10

Designing Effective Organizations

CHAPTER OUTLINE

Classical Theories of Organization Design

Technology and Structure

Environment and Structure

Keys to Effective Management

Review Questions

*C*onsider for a few moments the rise of the Japanese auto industry over the past ten years. Clearly, Japan captured a sizable share of the world auto market, a market in which the United States had been the predominant force in the previous decade. Japan even invaded America's domestic market, manufacturing over 25 percent of the cars sold in the United States. What led Japan to take such a dramatic leap forward?

While the answer to that question has been debated hotly over the past few years, we can conservatively point to two factors that particularly aided Japan in its phenomenal growth. First, Japan has a modern, efficient production *technology.* Japanese companies spend great sums of money on research and development; since World War II, they have invested heavily in designing and purchasing the most technologically advanced equipment in the world.

Second, Japan has done an excellent job in reading its *business environment,* in forecasting how changes in the worldwide economy, political events, and consumer preferences might affect its own industries. The Japanese auto industry, for instance, correctly read the signals that there would be an increased demand for smaller, more fuel-efficient cars.

In the last twenty-five years, there has been increased attention paid to the role these two factors—technology and environment—play in the design of organizations. There is substantial evidence now that if corporations take their technologies and environments into account when deciding on an organization structure, they will be better prepared for technological change and better able to adapt to changes in the business environment.

In this chapter we will be examining the role technology and environment play in the design of effective organizations. First we will explore more closely some of the ideas of early management scholars about organization design. These early theories are often called ***universalistic theories*** because they put forth organization design principles that could be used in all organizations, independent of their technology and environment.

In the second and third sections of the chapters, we will look at how these classical management ideas have been modified over the years by ***contingency theorists.*** These management scholars are called contingency theorists because they argue that how organizations are structured should depend (or be *contingent*) upon a variety of factors, such as technology and environment. In the second section, we will examine the impact technology has on organization design; in the third section, we will examine the impact environment has on organization design. In both these sections, we will look at how our knowledge of contingency theories of organizations can help us plan more effective organization structures.

Classical Theories of Organization Design

Most of the early work on organization design was done by practicing managers. Writing about their own personal experiences in industry and the military, these managers attempted to develop a set of guidelines that would prove useful to other practicing managers. Books defining the general principles of

---

TABLE 10-1

Classical Principles of Organization Design

 1 Division of Work
 2 Unity of Command
 3 Authority and Responsibility
 4 Scalar Chain
 5 Limited Span of Control
 6 Line-Staff Relationships
 7 Use of Rules
 8 Impersonality
 9 Technocracy
10 Written Communication
11 Continuous Employment

effective management, by such writers as Henri Fayol, Lyndall Urwick, and Max Weber, greatly influenced the ways in which managers designed and ran their organizations.[1]

Weber, in particular, advocated a type of organization called a **bureaucracy.** While today the term *bureaucracy* has many negative connotations (e.g., long delays, Catch-22s, red tape), the term originally had positive connotations. It meant an organization run strictly by principles of rationality and efficiency.

Because the principles advocated by Fayol, Urwick, and Weber have had such a lasting impact on the field of management, we will examine them in some more detail below.

Principles of Classical Management

1 *Division of work.* This principle states that each member of the organization should have very clearly defined job duties, and that no two employees' job duties should overlap. Division of work should make each employee most efficient at his or her job.

2 *Unity of command.* This principle of management states that no member of an organization should be responsible to more than one superior. Without unity of command, employees would be hampered by conflicting work orders.

3 *Authority and responsibility.* **Authority** is the right to give orders, while **responsibility** is accountability for getting a job completed. If managers are given responsibility for completing a mission, then they must also be given sufficient authority to exact obedience from their subordinates.

4 *Scalar chain.* All communication from the top of the organization must pass through each successive level of subordinates until it reaches the appropriate lower level. Likewise, all communication from the bottom of the organization must pass through each successive level on its way up the organization.

5 *Limited span of control.* Another principle of management discussed by classical theories involves **span of control,** the number of subordinates who should report to a single supervisor. Generally, it was argued that the ideal span of control is twenty for first-line managers, eight for middle managers, and four for executives. The logic behind these guidelines was as follows: the more routine the work employees are doing, the less supervision they need and the more employees a manager can handle.

6 *Line-staff relationships.* Classical theorists made a careful distinction between **line** personnel and **staff** personnel. Line personnel (e.g., manufacturing and sales) perform the major functions of the organization. Staff

personnel (e.g., corporate law and public relations) provide support, service, and advice to line officials. Classical theorists argued that only line personnel should have formal authority in organizations. Giving staff personnel any formal control over day-to-day operations would violate the "authority equals responsibility" rule.[2]

7 *Use of rules.* Employees can get their work done more efficiently and more quickly if they have routine guidelines they can follow. Moreover, it is easier to coordinate the activities of different individuals or units if there are uniform policies to which everyone adheres.

8 *Impersonality.* Early management theorists recognized that ill will and inefficiency occur in organizations when exceptions to rules are made for the friends and relatives of employees and executives. Therefore, they advocated that organizations use standardized rules for hiring employees and dealing with customers, without regard to the specific individuals involved. While this principle might seem very negative at first glance, its original intent, in contrast, was very positive.

9 *Technocracy.* Technocracy means "rule by the technically competent." Only people who have demonstrated adequate technical training should be hired by organizations. Moreover, technical excellence on the job should be the sole criterion for promoting people in bureaucracies.

10 *Written communication.* All administrative rules, acts, and decisions should be recorded in writing. By putting everything down in writing, organizations ensure that the rules will be followed in a consistent way and that there is a record of past decisions for future reference.

11 *Continuous employment.* Employers should not be able to fire employees for arbitrary or capricious reasons, only for demonstrated incompetence or failure to follow rules. Therefore personnel can expect to be continuously employed as long as they perform satisfactorily.

It will be noted here, of course, that Weber's bureaucracy bears a marked resemblance to traditional functional and divisional organizations. These two structures typically follow the tenets of classical management theory. In contrast, organizations with lateral relations and matrix structures are much less bureaucratic. They are much more decentralized, have fewer distinctions between line and staff, have more informal communication channels, and often violate the "one employee–one boss" rule.

Assessment of Classical Management Principles

In Box 10-1 we present two case examples of bureaucracy. McDonald's is often considered to be an illustration of bureaucracy at its best; the U.S. civil service is often considered to be an illustration of bureaucracy at its worst. These two case examples nicely demonstrate some of the key strengths and weaknesses of classical management principles.

BOX 10-1

Two Bureaucracies: McDonald's and the U.S. Government

McDonald's Corporation: McDonald's Corporation is a tremendously successful bureaucracy. One of the key characteristics that will make or break a fast-food chain is consistency. Customers have to be able to expect the same level of food and service whichever store they enter. McDonald's has achieved remarkable levels of consistency; people can count on getting the same-sized portion, the same-tasting food, and the same restaurant decor no matter what part of the country they are in. How did McDonald's achieve this? McDonald's used a staff of professionals to develop a procedures manual of 385 pages describing the most minute activities. For instance, french fries are kept under the light for only 7 minutes; specially designed scoops determine the precise number of fries to fit in each pouch; a flashing light cues the cook to the exact moment to flip the hamburger.

Routinization is also used in handling personnel. Managers, assistant managers, crew leaders, cooks, and waitresses all have sharply defined responsibilities and very explicit rules to follow. McDonald's even runs a school called Hamburger University in suburban Chicago to train its managerial staff.

The U.S. Civil Service: One of the major criticisms of bureaucracies is that people who "rock the boat," that is, call into question the appropriateness or the effectiveness of the rules, get reprimanded or punished. Such reprimand and punishment discourages other bureaucrats from trying to improve the organization in the future. Robert Vaughan, in a book entitled *The Spoiled System,* gives some examples of this phenomenon in the U.S. civil service.

For instance, Ernest Fitzgerald, an Air Force civilian who exposed a $2.5 billion cost overrun on a C-5A transport plane, was shortly thereafter removed in a Reduction in Force (RIF). Since he was the only person in his job category, he had no right to exercise his seniority in the system in another job. A research scientist for the Agricultural Research Service who questioned the propriety of consultants from private industry using government facilities found himself quickly moved to Alabama from his station in Colorado. One questioning employee at the Department of Agriculture was assigned nothing but the task of organizing departmental beauty contests; another "troublemaker" at the Department of Labor found himself without a phone, secretary, or work assignment.

Source: Adopted from: Lucas, A. (1971, July 4). As American as McDonald's hamburger on the Fourth of July. *New York Times Magazine.*

Boas, M., & Chain, S. (1976). *Big Mac: The unauthorized story of McDonald's.* New York: E. P. Dutton.

Vaughan, R. (1975). *The spoiled system.* Copyright by the Center for the Study of Responsive Law. Charterhouse Books.

1 *Bureaucracies typically insure uniformity and predictability in the quality of their products.*   Certainly this is the biggest boon bureaucracy has brought to McDonald's. McDonald's rule books and training programs help ensure that the quality, portion, and price of food items will be exactly the same no matter which franchise a consumer enters. Since a bad experience in one restaurant will likely turn a consumer off to all McDonald's, this consistency is critical to the growth of McDonald's.[3]

2 *Bureaucracies are generally most effective in those organizations that provide only a limited range of goods and services.*   Bureaucracy does not work efficiently when the organization is offering a wide variety of goods and services, or has to tailor its services to a lot of different types of clients.[4] For instance, McDonald's offers a very limited menu and does not vary the method of food preparation or portion of food for different customers. McDonald's bureaucratic rules could not handle the personal tastes and preferences of millions of customers. In fact, Burger King's "Have It Your Way" advertising campaign draws attention to this drawback of bureaucracy at McDonald's.

3 *Bureaucratic rules can lead to insensitive treatment of subordinates and clients.*   One of the unintended consequences of bureaucracy is that rules meant to protect employees can often be used to punish and harass them.[5] In the U.S. civil service, for instance, rules about employment security and transfers and promotions are meant to protect subordinates from arbitrary, capricious treatment; in the cases we illustrated, they were used to punish junior civil servants.

Bureaucratic rules can also lead to the inhumane treatment of clients or customers.[6] We know of a professor who did not allow makeup exams even for the death of parents. While the rules about makeup exams are made to protect professors from having to write twenty exams, these rules can also be twisted to harass students with legitimate problems.

4 *Bureaucracies do not quickly assimilate the influx of new technology; they are slow to innovate.*[7]   There are two reasons why bureaucracies are slow to adopt new technology. First, there is an information flow problem; news of the technology has to come into the organization and be championed by at least some of its members. In his book on the U.S. civil service, Vaughan describes the way the U.S. Food and Drug Administration (FDA) dealt with the information that new prescription drugs were being marketed without sufficiently rigorous testing. John Nestor, a pediatric cardiologist, was instrumental in blocking the U.S. marketing of thalidomide (a drug that caused hundreds of deformed babies in Europe) through his insistence on using more rigorous drug-testing standards. Instead of rewarding Nestor, the FDA continually changed his job so he would be as far away from the clinical testing area as possible.[8] Well-established bureaucrats often fight a rearguard action to slow down or sabotage the adoption of new technology.

Second, there is a decision-making problem. Administrators have to come to some consensus about how they want to adapt new technologies to their needs. As we saw in Chapter 7, there were substantial decision-making problems in the development of the M-16 rifle. By the time each armed service added what it wanted and all the needs of the contractors were met, the U.S. government had designed a rifle too heavy to carry and impossible to fix in the field—and this was the gun designed to be used in Vietnam.[9] Bureaucracies are often slow to come to decisions and, more importantly, often come to very low quality decisions as well.

5 *Bureaucracies have trouble dealing with unanticipated problems and new issues; they are not flexible and adaptable in changing environments.* A strength of bureaucracies is that they can efficiently handle routine problems in routine environments; a weakness is their inability to handle nonroutine problems in changing environments. When there are unanticipated problems or changes in the environment, bureaucracies are slow to respond.[10]

We have already discussed how difficult it was for the large, bureaucratic U.S. auto companies to deal with technological, economic, and market changes in the 1970s. Even McDonald's, as successful as it has been, has been slow in shifting gears to meet new environmental challenges. It took McDonald's six years to test and market Chicken McNuggets; it has still to successfully launch a product in the growing fast-food salad market. It took the FDA *11 years* to decide how many peanuts needed to be in a jar of peanut butter to be legally marketed as peanut butter![11]

Thus, the classic management principles espoused by Fayol, Urwick, and Weber end up being not so uniformly effective after all. The scalar chain that is supposed to funnel communication upward can, under certain circumstances, choke it altogether. The sharp division of labor that is supposed to increase individual productivity can sometimes demotivate employees and make them callous about the quality of their work. The bureaucratic rules that are made to ensure rational behavior can, under certain circumstances, result in inhumane treatment of employees and clients. The bureaucratic organization, designed to be run by technocrats, can in fact block the adoption of new technology.

Moreover, it is also clear that the principles of bureaucracy are not suited to all types of technologies and environments. When the rate of environmental change is rapid, and the proliferation of new technologies is extensive, the bureaucratic model is much less successful.[12] Contingency theories, theories that modify bureaucratic principles to deal with changes in technology and environments, can clearly be of help to us in designing more effective organizations. We turn to them next.

Technology and Structure

When we hear the word *technology,* we're most likely to think of *machines.* The most common meaning of the word *technology* is the tools and equipment used to transform raw materials into finished products.

However, consider a manufacturing plant as an example of an organization using machine technology. Wouldn't the *knowledge and skills* needed to design and use the machines also be part of the technology? Wouldn't the *mechanisms used for the coordination and control of the production process—* the inventory system, the assembly line, etc.—be part of the technology as well?

For our purposes, we will define the word **technology** as *the transformation process by which mechanical equipment and intellectual skills are used to produce the organization's goods and services.*[13] In the case of an auto manufacturing plant, then, the technology transforms raw materials such as steel and rubber into finished cars. The technology consists of the machinery, the knowledge and skills needed to design and operate the equipment, and the mechanisms used to coordinate and control the production process.

Types and Examples of Technology

Probably the best-known classification of types of technology was devised by Joan Woodward, a British industrial sociologist.[14] She classifies technologies into three types: (1) unit technology; (2) mass production; and (3) continuous process production.

Unit Technology

In **unit technology,** the organization transforms raw materials to meet the particular preferences of the customer. The unit of production is made to order for the customer. A wide variety of techniques are used to produce the unit, and different techniques will be used to produce units for different customers.

The custom home construction industry and the home furnishings industry are examples of unit technology. For instance, in the custom home construction industry, different floor plans and spatial configurations are developed for individual home purchases. In the home furnishings industry, kitchen cabinets, bathroom fixtures, and several types of built-in bookcases and fireplaces are made to order for the customer. Different techniques are used to produce the various units for the different customers.

Mass Production Technology

In **mass production technologies,** standardized operating procedures are used to produce standardized products. The same technology and the same operations can be repeated over and over again.

Many segments of the automobile manufacturing industry and the consumer goods industry (e.g., cosmetics, canned food, paper products) use mass production. The same technology is used repeatedly to produce standardized products. The same control and coordination mechanisms can be used to produce each good; the skills needed to produce each good do not vary; the same tools and equipment can be used repeatedly.

Continuous Process Technology

The manufacture of chemicals, the production of pharmaceuticals, and the refining of oil are all examples of *continuous process technology.* Continuous process production technology often involves the production of liquids or gaseous substances. This technology is called continuous because the chemicals that are made and the oils that are refined flow continuously through pipes from one stage of processing to another, usually without being handled at all by the workers. Automatic controls are used to regulate much of the technology; much of the process is mechanized.[15] Most of the personnel in these firms are professional scientists who design the production process, and highly trained technicians who monitor and maintain the machines and equipment.

Contingency Theories of Technology

How does knowledge of the different types of technology help us better structure and design organizations?

If you think back to the early principles of management and the bureaucratic model, you will remember that classical management theorists advocated "one best way" to design organizations. In contrast, modern contingency theorists claim that the structure of organizations should vary, depending upon factors like the technology of the organization.

Contingency theories of technology have argued the following three propositions:

1   The type of technology in the organization influences the type of organization structure that should be used. If the type of structure fits the type of technology, the organization will be more successful.

2   Different departments and divisions of the organization use different technologies. Therefore, the structure of these subunits should vary, depending upon the type of technology they employ. Not all subunits have to be structured similarly.

3   Different types of coordination and control systems are appropriate for different types of technology.

In short, organizational technology moderates the relationship between organization design and organizational effectiveness (see Figure 10-1). The fit between the type of organization structure and the type of technology influences how effective the organization can be.

Woodward's South Essex Study

Woodward's research on technology contributed a great deal to our understanding of the fit between organization structure and technology. In trying to research the first contingency proposition, Woodward examined 100 South Essex manufacturing firms in great detail. Data were collected on the back-

Figure 10-1   Organizational structure and technology.

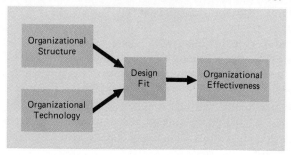

ground and objectives of the firms, the types of manufacturing they did, the forms of organizational structure used, and the methods of control and coordination employed. She also collected data on several criteria of organizational effectiveness: market share, profitability, capital expansion, rate of turnover, and so forth.[16] The results from this research project appear in Table 10-2.

As Woodward's results show, the mass-production technology is the only one of the three types of technology that approaches the bureaucratic model prescribed by classical management. Mass production technology organizations have a wide span of control, rely on written versus oral communication, utilize a high degree of specialization between different types of workers, and rely heavily on formal control and sanction procedures. In contrast, unit and process production firms have much narrower spans of control, use much more verbal communication than written, have much less specialization

TABLE 10-2

A Summary of Woodward's Findings

	Unit	*Mass production*	*Continuous process*
Span of control of first-line supervisors	23	48	15
Amount of written communication	Low	High	Low
Amount of verbal communication	High	Low	High
Specialization between line and staff	Low	High	Low
Use of formal control and sanction procedures	Low	High	Low
Separation of general management from operations supervisors	Low	High	Low
Number of skilled workers	High	Low	High

Source: From Woodward, J. (1965). *Industrial organization: Theory and practice.* London: Oxford University Press, pp. 50–80. Used with permission.

among groups of workers, and use formal control and sanction procedures much less frequently.

Woodward's research also makes clear another key point: those firms that used structures consistent with their technologies were more successful. Let's look at why this might be the case.

Mass production technology lends itself by nature to the bureaucratic type of structure. Since so much of the technology is standardized, there can be well-defined channels of communication and well-defined control and sanction procedures. Because the production operations can be broken down into identifiable subparts, there can be a high degree of specialization among workers. Since the number of skilled workers is low, and the amount of decision-making discretion that those workers have is low, the span of control of first-line supervisors can be high. The bureaucratic structure is efficient for mass production technology. Traditional functional and divisional structures would be successful with this type of technology.[17]

Unit technology, however, does not lend itself by nature to the bureaucratic model. With unit technology particularly, the organization must adapt its technology to meet the specific needs of many different customers or clients. Bureaucratic rules and regulations cannot cover all the situations that will arise. Furthermore, there needs to be close communication and coordination among different job categories. Rigid reporting relationships would inhibit that type of communication.[18]

For continuous production organizations, too, the technology does not lend itself fully to the bureaucratic model. In process production firms, there are large numbers of skilled staff workers. These professionals prefer informal verbal communication to formal written communication and expect to work in a collegial fashion with their supervisors. The span of control in process production firms is therefore much smaller, and there is much less differentiation between superiors and subordinates. Thus, lateral relations and matrix structures are much more appropriate for both unit and continuous process technology firms.

The Aston Studies   A group of industrial sociologists at the University of Aston in Birmingham, England have also conducted a large-scale research program on the relationship between structure and technology.[19] Their research addresses our second technology proposition: that the structures of different subunits of the firm (i.e., departments and divisions) should vary, depending upon the different types of technology they employ.

The Aston group noticed that, particularly in large firms, different departments and divisions used very different technologies. For example, in a hospital setting, immunization clinics used a mass production technology (same flu shots to hundreds of clients), while a psychiatry clinic used a unit technology (different treatments designed for each client).

The Aston group demonstrated that since different departments and divisions use different technologies, their structures should also vary, depending upon the type of technology they employ. Not all subunits have to be structured similarly.[20] For instance, consider again our example of Quaker, Inc., from Chapter 9. The pet foods division uses a mass production technology while the chemicals division uses a continuous process technology. Therefore, the structures of these two divisions should be different. Each division should be structured to fit its technology.

Galbraith's Theory of Organization Design

The work of Jay Galbraith on organization design is relevant to our third, and last, technology proposition: that different types of coordination and control systems are appropriate for different types of technology.

Think back to our initial definition of technology, in which we included the phrase "the mechanisms used for the coordination and control of the production process." If an organization is unable to link the machines and employees of one operation with those of other operations, the organization will be unable to use its technology effectively.

Jay Galbraith developed one of the best-known classifications of coordination and control devices used to link technologies.[21] He identified seven strategies used to coordinate the activities in organizations. These strategies are presented and briefly defined in Table 10-3.

Note that some of these coordination and control devices—(1), (2), and (3)—look very much like those we would expect to see in a bureaucracy. We

---

TABLE 10-3

Galbraith's Classification of Coordination and Control Devices

1 *Rules and programs:* Job incumbents follow prearranged procedures manuals and specified rules
2 *Hierarchy:* Job incumbents refer exceptions to rules and procedures to their supervisors up the hierarchy
3 *Investment in vertical information systems:* The organization uses computers to standardize budgets, inventories, and schedules across units
4 *Goal setting:* Job incumbents have goals to achieve on their jobs but are given some discretion in choosing how to accomplish their jobs
5 *Creation of slack resources:* Job incumbents have some "slack," or "backup," built into their goals (e.g., extra budget money, extra scheduling time) to be used as needed
6 *Creation of self-contained tasks:* Each group of employees responsible for producing a product is given enough resources to accomplish its goals; each group is autonomous in how it carries out its goals
7 *Creation of lateral relations:* The organization uses liaison roles, task forces, and matrix structures to quicken the flow of communication among various groups in the organization

Source: From Galbraith, J. (1974, May). Organization design: An information processing view. *Interfaces, 4,* pp. 28–36. Used by permission.

would expect bureaucracies to use a lot of rules and programs to coordinate the work of various employees and various work groups. We would also expect bureaucracies to have a strict chain of command, with all unusual problems being sent up the hierarchy. We might also expect bureaucracies to want to standardize as much information about budget, inventories, and schedules as possible; bureaucracies are likely to invest in computers to help them standardize their work even further.

On the other hand, note that several of these coordination and control devices—(4), (5), (6), and (7)—are inconsistent with bureaucratic organizations. Classical management theorists would not feel comfortable with either goal setting or self-contained work groups, for these devices leave too much discretion in the hands of the workers. Creation of slack resources violates the bureaucracy's need for total efficiency. Creation of lateral relations is a violation of the classical principles of chain of command and the scalar chain. Let's consider why different types of coordination and control systems are appropriate for different types of technology.

In mass production and continuous process technologies, there are well-established routines that can be applied over and over again. Changes in the raw materials or in the nature of the work to be done occur infrequently. Therefore, bureaucratic control devices like procedures manuals and management information systems are quite efficient; so much of the work is already standardized. The few exceptions to the routine that occur can be passed up the hierarchy to be dealt with; there will not be enough of these exceptions to overload supervisors with decisions to make.[22]

On the other hand, in unit technology (e.g., building a custom home), there is a lot of variability in the work. Raw materials are not standardized, and many products are custom made for consumers. Moreover, employees have to change the way they do their work from job to job. There are very few well-established procedures to follow. Employees need to have a lot of discretion to do their own jobs and to confer freely with coworkers. For this reason, goal setting, creation of self-contained work groups, lateral relations, and creation of slack resources are more critical to unit production. There is simply not enough certainty in the workflow for effective application of rigid bureaucratic control mechanisms.[23]

Overall Impact of Technology on Structure

As we have seen in the section above, technology does indeed influence the design of organizations. The bureaucratic structure is most appropriate for mass production technologies, but not so appropriate for unit or continuous process technologies. Similarly, bureaucratic control devices like rules and procedures are much more appropriate for mass production technologies than for unit or continuous process technologies.

We have also seen substantial support for the contingency approach to organization design. Those organizations that used the organization structures and coordination devices most consistent with their technologies were also the most successful. Moreover, those organizations that let the structures of their subunits vary to meet the demands of their various technologies were also much more effective than those that straitjacketed all subunits into a uniform structure.

However, while technology affects organizational structure, it does not determine it altogether.[24] As we saw in the last chapter, the growth and diversification of the firm certainly influences how it should be designed. And, as we are about to see in the next section, the organization's environment plays as big a role as its technology in determining organizational effectiveness.

Environment and Structure

By the term *environment* we mean those factors *external* to the organization that influence the effectiveness of the firm's day-to-day operations and its long-term growth. Consider IBM as an example of an organization. What are the environmental factors that influence its day-to-day operations and long-term growth?

Certainly changes in *economic conditions* influence IBM's effectiveness. During times of recession, fewer consumers will be buying business machines. *Demographic trends,* as well, can have an impact on the size of IBM's potential market, particularly IBM's sales to schools and universities. *Advances in technology* also influence the success of IBM. To remain competitive, the corporation needs to develop new information-processing technologies and adopt new technologies developed elsewhere. *Changes in market conditions*—for instance, the entry of new competitors into the industry—may mean IBM will have to increase advertising or improve customer service to maintain a competitive edge. The *legal climate,* too, certainly influences IBM's growth; if antitrust laws become more stringent or become more stringently enforced, the rate of IBM's expansion and diversification could be greatly curtailed. Finally, *political conditions,* especially abroad, can influence IBM's success. The stability of foreign governments and their relationships with the United States will influence whether IBM can expand the demand for its products overseas, and whether IBM can manufacture and produce outside the United States.

Thus, we see that environmental factors—the economy, demographic trends, advances in technology, market conditions, the legal climate, and political conditions—all can influence an organization's long-term growth and the effectiveness of its day-to-day operations.

Dimensions of Organization Environments

Environments vary in how *favorable* or *hostile* they are.[25] Favorable environments facilitate the organization's growth; hostile environments impede it. For instance, the most favorable environment for IBM would be one that included a probusiness Congress, good international relations with developing coun-

Figure 10-2   Organizational environment factors.

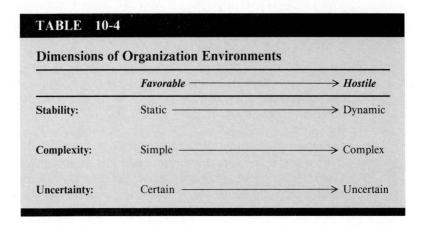

tries, the slow entry of new competitors into the market, and the development of a new technology that would cut costs. In contrast, a hostile environment for IBM would be one that included an antibusiness Congress, the rapid entry of new competitors into its markets, and declining population growth.

Three dimensions of organization environments influence how favorable or hostile the environment will be to the organization (see Table 10-4).[26]

Stability   *Environmental stability* refers to how fast the environment is changing. *Static* environments are those that change very slowly. For instance, the paper goods industry is relatively static. There are very few rapid changes in the economy,

TABLE   10-4

Dimensions of Organization Environments

	Favorable ⟶	*Hostile*
Stability:	Static ⟶	Dynamic
Complexity:	Simple ⟶	Complex
Uncertainty:	Certain ⟶	Uncertain

the technology, or the political climate that influence the production or selling of paper tablets, towels, or tissues.

In contrast, *dynamic* environments are those that change very quickly. The commercial airline industry has a very dynamic environment, in which deregulation policies, price wars, new competitors, and consumer spending patterns on travel all change quickly. In general, dynamic environments are hostile to organizations because they make it difficult for top managers to accurately predict changes in their markets and to adjust their business strategies accordingly.

Complexity

Environmental complexity refers to how many factors in the environment influence an organization. If there are very few factors that influence an organization, then the environment is said to be relatively *simple.* For example, the environment of a clothing store like Brooks Brothers is relatively simple. Brooks's clientele is relatively affluent and not too responsive to economic conditions. Moreover, its clothing styles are conservative and do not change much from year to year.

In contrast, *complex* environments are those in which many factors can influence the organization's operations. Sears operates in a fairly complex environment. Sears sells a wide variety of merchandise, and has to respond to a diversity of different markets. In addition, it operates all over the world in hundreds of stores, and has different types of competitors in each merchandise market in each geographical location. Typically, complex environments are more hostile because they present top management with a larger number of factors to try to predict and control.

Uncertainty

Environmental uncertainty refers to the amount of information managers have about important environmental factors. If managers have fairly complete information about environmental factors that influence major business decisions, then the environment is said to be *certain.* For instance, the environment of canned goods companies is quite certain. The number of companies producing canned tuna fish, for example, is fairly steady, as are consumer preferences for tuna fish. It is relatively easy for Bumble Bee and Starkist to monitor whatever minor changes do occur in the environment.

In contrast, if managers have very little information about environmental factors that influence their business decisions, they are said to be operating in *uncertain* environments. The environments of toy companies like Mattel and Milton Bradley are quite uncertain. It is very difficult to gauge consumer preferences for new toys; some toys take off and others never capture a market. Even if a surefire hit like the Cabbage Patch doll sells a lot, it is very hard to predict how long the toy will sell. There are many more competitors in the market and many more unknown competitors about to enter the field. Uncertain environments are more hostile because they make it more difficult for management to recognize and understand changes in the marketplace, and to cope effectively with them.

Contingency Theories of Organizational Environments

How does the knowledge of different types of organization environments help us to better structure and design organizations?

Contingency theories of environments have argued three propositions, all quite similar to those of contingency theories of technology. These propositions are:

1 The type of environment of the organization influences the type of organization structure which should be used. If the type of structure fits the type of environment, the organization will be more successful.

2 Different departments and divisions of the organization have to respond to different environments. Therefore, the structures of these subunits should vary, depending upon the types of environments they face. Not all subunits have to be structured similarly.

3 Organizations should vary the strategies they use to adapt to their environments, depending upon how hostile their environments are.

In short, organizational environments moderate the relationship between organization design and organizational effectiveness (see Figure 10-3). The fit between the type of organization structure and the type of environment influences how effective the organization can be.

Burns and Stalker: Mechanistic and Organic Structures

Burns and Stalker conducted the classic piece of research on the first proposition: that a fit between organization environment and organization structure leads to increased organizational effectiveness. These researchers looked at twenty industrial organizations in Great Britain. Some of these organizations, like a rayon manufacuring plant, operated in relatively static environments. Other organizations in their study, like an electronics company, operated in very dynamic environments.[27]

In organizations where the environment was static, Burns and Stalker found that organizations using a **mechanistic** structure were most effective. This mechanistic structure is basically what we have called a *bureaucracy*.

Figure 10-3   Organizational structure and environment.

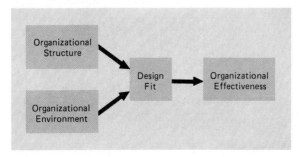

Mechanistic organizations have very formal hierarchies. Power and decision-making are centralized at the top of the organization; orders and communication flow downward. There are many specified rules and procedures for employees to follow; work is highly specialized and routinized. Traditional functional and divisional organizations are mechanistic.

In contrast, Burns and Stalker found that organizations operating most effectively in dynamic environments were *organic* in structure. An organic organization is the antithesis of a bureaucracy. Its structure is flexible; there are fewer rules and less division of labor. Communication is more informal, and employees are freer to communicate upward or laterally to coworkers. Lateral relations and matrix structures are more organic.[28]

We can see why these results, diagrammed in Table 10-5, make sense. If the environment is relatively static, then it is possible for the organization to establish rules and procedures that will cover most situations that could arise. In the rayon plant example, there are few outside disturbances to the production or marketing of rayon. Therefore, the bureaucracy in the rayon plant will run into very few unforeseen difficulties that would make it inefficient. However, if the environment is very dynamic, the organization will be unable to establish rules and procedures to cover all the situations that could arise. Rapid technological advances and rapid changes in the marketplace necessitate quick communication; the formal, top-down bureaucratic chain of command is too slow to deal with a dynamic environment. Thus, companies like the electronics plant need to use more organic structures.

Therefore, as contingency theorists, Burns and Stalker do *not* argue for the universal use of either the mechanistic or the organic structure. Rather, the choice of an organization structure depends on the environment: mechanistic structures for static environments, organic structures for dynamic ones.

TABLE 10-5

Burns and Stalker's Findings

		Organization environment	
		Static	*Dynamic*
Organization Structure	Mechanistic	Effective Organizations	Ineffective Organizations
	Organic	Ineffective Organizations	Effective Organizations

Source: Adapted from Burns, T., & Stalker, G. M. (1961). *The management of innovation.* London: Tavistock, pp. 119–125.

Lawrence and Lorsch's Contingency Theory

A group of management professors at Harvard Business School, led by Paul Lawrence, Jay Lorsch, and John Morse, did the most extensive investigations on our second proposition: that structures of different departments and divisions should vary, depending upon the types of environments they face.[29]

Lawrence and Lorsch looked at the differences among departments within organizations. They observed that different departments of firms were organized in very different ways. Some of the ways these departments differed appear in Figure 10-4.

Lawrence and Lorsch found that for organizations to be effective, different departments had to be structured in different ways. A production group can and should be formally structured because the nature of its work and the nature of its environment are so routine. However, a fundamental research group will not likely succeed if it is formally structured. Research scientists need to be able to have free and easy communication with each other and with their supervisors. They have long-range goals and cannot be evaluated on short-run criteria like "number of ideas generated per day."[30] Lawrence and Lorsch strongly encouraged organizations to let the structures of their subunits vary, depending upon the nature of the work they do and the types of environment they face.

Of course, classical management theorists would be strongly opposed to such a suggestion. They would say: How could we coordinate all these departments if each is going about its own business in its own way?

Lawrence and Lorsch argued that the best way to coordinate, or integrate, subunits is not standardization, but *mutual adjustment*. Top management

Figure 10-4 Lawrence and Lorsch's differences among subunits.

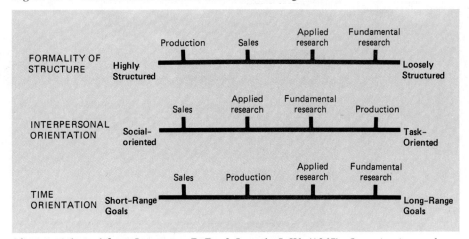

[*Source:* Adapted from Lawrence, P. R., & Lorsch, J. W. (1967). *Organization and environment: Managing differentiation and integration.* Homewood, IL: Irwin, p. 36. Used by permission of Harvard University Graduate School of Business Administration.]

should encourage steady, open communication among different units. Lawrence and Lorsch also argued for the use of lateral relations like task forces and permanent teams that we discussed in the last chapter. Only through mutual adjustment and lateral relations can separate departments do the best jobs they are capable of doing *and* cooperate with other departments to achieve corporate goals.[31]

Coping with Environments

As we have seen in this chapter, all organizations find themselves dependent, in varying degrees, upon their external environments. In fact, if an organization is heavily dependent upon its environment, its very survival can be at stake when the environment changes. For instance, a recent law passed in Florida prohibiting "midnight black" window tinting of automobiles put a large number of window-tinting companies out of business. When the U.S. government banned saccharin, the survival of several types of diet food was seriously called into question. Thus, it is in the organization's best interests to try to control those environmental factors that affect its operations.[32]

Traditionally, organizations have been *reactive* in dealing with their environments. The organization merely took the environment as given and tried to make the most of the situation. However, organizations can also be *proactive* toward their environments. Organizations can try to prevent adverse changes in their environments, or actually try to change the environments themselves.[33]

What does contingency theory have to say about these two approaches to coping with environments? Contingency theorists argue that *the more hostile the organization's environment, the more proactive the organization needs to be in managing its environment.* The more susceptible the organization is to

---

TABLE 10-6

Coping with Organizational Environments

Reactive strategies

1 Creation of special subunits to deal with environmental forces
2 Creation of corporate marketing or public relations departments
3 Creation of boundary-spanning roles

Proactive strategies

1 Acquisition of new businesses and/or sale of existing businesses
2 Diversification
3 Political activity and trade associations

rapid changes in its environment, the more critical it becomes for the organization to be proactive in its coping responses.

Below we discuss three reactive strategies used by organizations in relatively favorable environments, and three proactive strategies used by organizations in relatively hostile environments.

Reactive Strategies

Reactive strategies help organizations fine-tune their structures to make them more responsive to outside environmental forces. The three most common reactive strategies organizations have used to adjust their structures to their environment are: (1) creation of special subunits to deal with environmental forces; (2) creation of corporate marketing or public relations departments; and (3) creation of boundary-spanning roles.

Organizations frequently create special subunits to deal with important environmental forces. A good example of this comes from the consumer goods industry. New products are the lifeblood of this industry, yet the way consumer goods companies were structured inhibited their fast development. Twenty years ago, the responsibility for new products was spread across all product managers. Each manager was responsible for generating one or two products a year. However, the main rewards for product managers were based on short-run profits for existing products. Not surprisingly, the types of new products typically suggested were "flankers"—slight variations on a theme (e.g., introducing Blueberry PopTarts after Cinnamon PopTarts). As a result, some companies failed to innovate and keep up with consumer preferences. Today, most consumer goods companies have established *new products divisions* so that truly new products get generated and supervised from conception through production. The establishment of these divisions makes good structural sense; good basic research would not be done unless a separate unit conducive to that activity was organized.

A second strategy organizations can use to adjust their structures to their environments is the creation of *corporate marketing or public relations departments.* Organizations can use these departments to create friendlier relations with potentially hostile people in the environment.[34] For instance, oil companies like Mobil spend large sums of money advertising the socially beneficial aspects of their business: developing medical technology, building bird feeders for wilderness creatures, and the like. By such advertising, the oil companies hope to counteract consumer opposition to tax incentives for new oil exploration.

A third tactic organizations can use to fit their structures to their environments is the creation of boundary-spanning roles. By the term *boundary-spanning roles,* we mean those people who gather important information about the environment for the organization and/or represent the organization to outside interests. These people bring critical outside information to the attention of top decision-makers and disseminate positive information about the organization to potential clients or suppliers.[35]

For example, universities have started to employ development officers to raise outside funds and obtain grants. There is such a wide variety of funding agencies that might conceivably donate money to the university that individual faculty and departments could not possibly locate all potential sources of financial support. Moreover, proposals to receive funding need a lot of coordination across departments. A proposal for a health services program, for instance, might involve faculty from medicine, psychology, nursing, management, and economics. Without a good deal of centralized coordination, some proposals would never get finished, others would get thrown together piecemeal, and still others would get lost in the funding agency's own bureaucracy. Offices of development now serve as "boundary spanners" for universities. They gather important information about the environment for the rest of the university, and they serve as advocates for the university with funding agencies.

These structural changes are most effective when the organization operates in an essentially stable, certain environment. In this situation, the two or three potential threats to the organization's operations can be readily identified. Reactive strategies take the environment as given and adjust the structure to it.

Proactive Strategies

Proactive strategies help organizations prevent adverse changes in their environments or change the environments themselves. The three most common proactive strategies organizations have used include: (1) acquisition of new businesses and/or sale of existing businesses; (2) diversification; and (3) joining political action groups and trade associations.

One way organizations can be proactive in dealing with their environments is to begin new ventures in what are called *environmental niches.* Environmental niches are very favorable environments—those with little present competition, several barriers to new competition, little or no government regulation, abundant suppliers, and plentiful customers.[36] For example, recently aggressive banks like First Bank of Boston have become heavily committed to financing major mergers, acquisitions, and corporate takeovers. The bank viewed this new venture as one with potentially high profits and little competition or government regulation in the short run.

Conversely, organizations can sell businesses which they feel operate in hostile environments, or move out of hostile environments altogether. Pantry Pride, for instance, recently sold over a third of its supermarkets which were operating with very low profit margins. Industries like Bear Archery have moved to the Sun Belt to find cheaper labor, more nonunion labor, and lower energy costs. Federal Express relocated to Memphis because Memphis Airport has very few closings due to precipitation or fog.

Firms can also *diversify* their businesses (i.e., enter into several different types of business), so that if there is an adverse environmental impact in one area, the survival of the entire business will not be at stake. Builders of new homes, for example, may diversify into home repair, condominium conversion, and apartment construction. If the mortgage rates for new homes sky-rocket, diversified construction companies will have other construction-related activities on which they can still make a profit.

The most proactive strategy organizations can use in dealing with their environments is joining *political action groups* and *trade associations.* Starting particularly with the 1980 elections, political action groups have become a major factor in business-government relations. Political action groups, such as the National Rifle Association, have tried to elect those legislators who favor their business interests and defeat those legislators who are opposed to them. Instead of sitting back and adjusting to whatever results the political elections bring, corporations are actively seeking to elect those legislators who will make their business environments more positive.

Trade associations also help organizations with common interests to change unfavorable elements in their environment. For instance, the major North American auto manufacturers have banded together to lobby Congress for tariffs on Japanese imports. Firms in the coffee industry have engaged in joint advertising of their product to counteract adverse publicity about the side effects of caffeine. Trade associations identify threats to firms in an industry and then use their members' collective funds to combat those adverse environmental influences.[37]

The more dynamic the organization's environment and the more the organization's success depends on effectively coping with its environment, the more the organization should use these proactive strategies. Organizations *can* be successful in highly uncertain environments; we have only to look at the success of many high-technology firms in the past few years. What is especially critical for these companies, however, is that they very carefully monitor and control their environments.

Overall Impact of Environment on Structure

As we have seen in the section above, environment does indeed influence design of organizations. Bureaucratic structures are most appropriate for static, simple, and certain environments but are not so appropriate in dynamic, complex, and uncertain environments. If organizations design their structures around their environments, they are much more likely to be successful. Moreover, if an organization varies the structures of its subunits to meet the particular task and environmental demands each faces, the organization is much more likely to be effective. Finally, the more unstable the environment, the more critical it is for the organization to be proactive in managing external forces.

However, while the environment affects organizational structure, it does not determine it altogether. In the last chapter, we saw how critical the growth and diversification of the firm are to the design of a firm. Even within this chapter, we have seen the importance of the role of technology in organization design. Thus, several factors, environment included, have to be taken into consideration to design the appropriate organization structure.

Keys to Effective Management

Throughout this chapter, we have looked at the impact technology and environment have on the structure of organizations. In these last few pages, we will show how this knowledge about technology and environment can help us choose more appropriate organization structures and design more effective organizations.

1 *Top management should realize that the bureaucratic model is not the ideal formal structure for all organizations.* There is no question that classical principles of management contribute to the rational administration of organizations. However, bureaucracies have trouble dealing with unanticipated problems and new issues, and are slow to innovate and adopt new technology.

2 *Organizations should use traditional functional and divisional structures for mass production technologies.* Mass production technology lends itself by nature to these bureaucratic types of structure. Since so much of the production process can be standardized, a well-defined division of labor, strict communication channels, and centralized decision making can increase the organization's efficiency.

3 *In contrast, organizations should use lateral relations or matrix structures for unit and continuous process technologies.* In both these types of technologies, employees need to have discretion in doing their own jobs and conferring freely with coworkers. Particularly in unit technology, there is a lot of variability in the raw materials and work methods used. Bureaucratic rules and procedures are simply ineffective with these technologies. Lateral relations and matrix structures are more organic and are needed to effectively manage unit and continuous process technologies.

4 *Top management should use traditional functional and divisional structures in stable environments.* Bureaucracies are very good at efficiently handling routine problems in stable environments. If there are very few changes in the environment that could adversely affect the organization, managers of these bureaucratically structured organizations will not be overloaded trying to cope with environmental uncertainty.

5 *In contrast, top management should implement lateral relations and matrix structures in organizations with unstable environments.* When the environment is unstable, the organization needs to constantly monitor changes in its markets and its technology as well as shifts in demographic and economic trends. The organization needs to obtain a lot of information about those external factors and disseminate it rapidly. The strict chains of command and lines of communication of bureaucracies stifle such information sharing and collaboration. Lateral relations and matrix structures are more organic and are needed to effectively cope with a lot of environmental uncertainty.

6   *Organizations should let the structures of their subunits vary, depending upon their technologies and environments.*   The research is convincing that organizations would benefit from not forcing a consistent structure on all departments and divisions, independent of their technology and environment. Consistency of structure across subunits is not as important as the consistency of structures of subunits with their own technologies and environments.

7   *Organizations can implement a variety of structural modifications to increase their effectiveness in dealing with the environment.*   In order to cope with their environments, organizations can create special subunits to deal with environmental problems, enter into political action groups or trade associations with other firms, acquire new businesses in favorable environments, or divest themselves of those in hostile environments. Structures can be changed to better monitor threats from the environment, for example, by the creation of boundary-spanning roles.

8   *Finally, organizations can improve their performance if their formal structures are made consistent with their environments and technologies.*   Over and over again, we have seen that organizations whose structures are congruent with their technologies and environments are more effective. There is not one best way to structure organizations. The underlying principle of organization design has to remain: Fit the structure of the organization to its technology and environment.

Review Questions

1   Identify and explain five classical principles of management.

2   What is the real meaning of the term *bureaucracy?*

3   Discuss the strengths and weaknesses of bureaucracy as a form of organization design.

4   Define the term *technology.*

5   What are the three types of technology defined by Woodward?

6   What type of technology is most suited to a bureaucratic organizational structure? Why?

7   What was the main finding of the Aston research group?

8 According to Galbraith, which types of coordination and control devices are most appropriate for unit and continuous process technologies?

9 Identify six factors that make up an organization's environment.

10 Distinguish among environmental stability, complexity, and uncertainty.

11 What is the difference between a "mechanistic" and an "organic" structure? Which is more appropriate in an unstable environment? Why?

12 Why do the structures of production units and research units have to be different, according to Lawrence and Lorsch?

13 Discuss four strategies organizations can use to cope with environmental uncertainty. Give one example of each.

14 For what type of technology are the functional and divisional structures most appropriate? For what types of technology are lateral relations and the matrix structure most appropriate?

15 For what type of environment are the functional and divisional structures most appropriate? For what types of environment are lateral relations and the matrix structure most appropriate?

Avondale Shipyards, Inc.

Officials of Avondale Shipyards, Inc., a subsidiary of the Ogden Corporation, broke out champagne in 1973 after winning a $309 million, fixed-price contract to build 3 huge liquefied natural gas (LNG) tankers for the El Paso Company. LNG was being promoted as an important new fuel, and Avondale envisioned the El Paso contract as the start of a brisk new business in building ships to haul it.

Since then, however, the champagne has gone flat. The Avondale tankers last year flunked U.S. Coast Guard certification tests to carry the supercold (-250 degrees Fahrenheit) LNG. Algeria shut off El Paso's gas supply. A group of insurance companies led by Lloyd's of London has agreed to pay out $300 million in claims to El Paso on policies covering the ships' completion. The money will go mostly to pay off federally backed bonds sold to finance construction. The Federal Maritime Administration lost $52 million in construction subsidy payments. Now, El Paso is offering the ships for sale at bargain prices—as low as $50 million for all 3—for any use, even for scrap.

Cruelest of all, Avondale's parent company needs three LNG tankers for possible shipment of Indonesian LNG to California, but instead of having Avondale build the ships, Ogden is turning to General Dynamics Corporation's Quincy (MA) shipyard to build them. The Quincy shipyard uses a different tankage system to contain the LNG, and it has sucessfully built nine such ships.

A Nightmare

An Ogden official crisply explains: "The [Avondale] shipyard can be better utilized in other work." Avondale president Albert I. Bossier, Jr., says only that "New York made the decision." But he adds: "I don't have any opposition to it."

Avondale's LNG affair was a seven-year nightmare. Because of the relative newness of LNG as a fuel, there was little experience with

297

the technology for carrying it. Currently, three basic techniques are used for tankage and insulation. Two systems use rectangular tanks combined with elaborate insulation. General Dynamics uses huge aluminum spheres.

In ordering the Avondale ships, El Paso opted for a tankage system developed by Conch LNG, a company jointly owned by Conoco, Inc., USY&T Industries, Inc., and the Royal Dutch/Shell Group. Huge rectangular aluminum tanks were to be insulated with a "secret" formula of polyurethane foam developed by Kaiser Aluminum & Chemical Sales, Inc. Avondale awarded Kaiser a $70 million contract to build and install the tankage system in the 3 ships, including application of the special polyurethane foam insulation.

Lawsuits

Delays and disputes came quickly. The first tanker was completed more than 3 years behind schedule, in the summer of 1979. Then, in July of that year, when the Coast Guard tested the ship with a partial load of LNG, tiny cracks developed in the insulation. As a result, the Coast Guard refused to certify the ships. One reason was that if the cold LNG came into contact with the ship's hull, it would cause the metal to become brittle and then to fracture and crumble.

There followed a year in which experts were called in to solve the problem. Their final analysis was that any corrective measure would cost too much—on the order of $100 million per ship. That doomed the 3 vessels, and the insurance companies finally settled last Sept. 30.

El Paso still must sell the tankers for at least $50 million; otherwise, it is going to have to absorb the difference as a loss. Because it was costing Avondale almost $200,000 a month to keep the ships in its yard, they are now being towed to the Army terminal in Boston for storage until they are sold. Meanwhile, Kaiser has sued Avondale for $40 million, and Avondale has countersued for $169 million in what everyone expects will be a bitter, costly, drawn-out legal battle over who was at fault.

Questions for Discussion

1 What new technological advances influenced Avondale Shipyards?

2 What environmental factors contributed to the business problems at Avondale Shipyards?

3 Using the following three dimensions, characterize Avondale Shipyards' environment.

   a Static-dynamic

   b Simple-complex

   c Uncertain-certain

4 Should Ogden Corporation divest itself of Avondale Shipyards? Why?

Source: Avondale's ill-fated dip into LNG waters. (1980, November 3). *Business Week,* p. 37. Reprinted from the Nov. 3, 1980 issue of *Business Week* by special permission. Copyright 1980 by McGraw-Hill, Inc., New York, NY.

Notes

1   Fayol, H. (1949). *General and industrial management* (C. Storrs, Trans.). London: Pitman.

Urwick, L. (1943). *The elements of administration*. New York: Harper.

3   Weber, M. (1947). *The theory of social and economic organization* (A. M. Henderson and T. Parsons, Trans. & Eds.). Glencoe, IL: Free Press, 328–340.

2   Mooney, J. D. (1947). *The principles of organization*. New York: Harper and Row.

3   Daft, R. L. (1983). *Organization theory and design*. St. Paul, MN: West, 143.

Blau, P. M. (1956). *Bureaucracy in modern society*. New York: Random House, 34.

4   Child, J. (1975). Managerial and organizational factors asociated with company performance—Part II: A contingency analysis. *Journal of Management Studies, 12,* 12–27.

5   March, J. J., & Simon, H. A. (1958). *Organizations*. New York: Wiley, 36–47.

Merton, R. K. (1936). The unanticipated consequences of purposive social action. *American Sociological Review, 1,* 894–904.

Gouldner, A. W. (1954). *Patterns of industrial democracy*. Glencoe, IL: Free Press.

6   Argyris, C. (1960). *Understanding organizational behavior*. London: Tavistock, 7–24.

7   Hall, R. H. (1972). *Organizations: Structure and process*. Englewood Cliffs, NJ: Prentice-Hall.

Thompson, V. (1961). *Modern organizations*. New York: Knopf.

8   Vaughan, R. (1975). *The spoiled system*. Copyright by the Center for the Study of Responsive Law. Charterhouse Books.

9   Fallows, J. (1981). *The national defense*. New York: Vintage.

10   Luthans, F. (1981). *Organizational behavior* (3rd ed.). New York: McGraw-Hill, 513–521.

Drucker, P. (1954). *The practice of management*. New York: Harper & Row, 133–136.

11   Levy, R. (1978, March). Tales from the bureaucratic woods. *Dun's Review,* 95–96.

12 Perrow, C. (1970). *Organizational analysis: A sociological view.* Belmont, CA: Wadsworth, 60.

13 Jelinek, M., Litterer, J. A., & Miles, R. E. (1981). Technology. In M. Jelinek, J. A. Litterer, and R. E. Miles (Eds.), *Organizations by design.* Plano, TX: Business Publications, 162–172.

14 Woodward, J. (1965). *Industrial organization: Theory and practice.* London: Oxford University Press.

15 Thompson, J. D. (1967). *Organizations in action.* New York: McGraw-Hill.

16 Woodward. *loc. cit.*

17 Miles, R. H. (1980). *Macro-organizational behavior.* Santa Monica, CA: Goodyear, 55–59.

18 Zwerman, W. L. (1970). *New perspectives in organization theory.* Westport, CN: Greenwood.
Harvey, E. (1968). Technology and the structure of organizations. *American Sociological Review, 33,* 241–259.

19 Hickson, D. J., Pugh, D. S., & Pheysey, D. C. (1969). Operation technology and organization structure: An empirical reappraisal. *Administrative Science Quarterly, 14,* 378–397.

20 Child, J., & Mansfield, R. (1972). Technology, size, and organization structure. *Sociology, 6,* 369–393.

21 Galbraith, J. (1974). Organization design: An information processing view. *Interfaces, 4* (May), 28–36.

22 Perrow, *op. cit.,* 77–91.

23 Van de Ven, A. H., Delbecq, A. L., & Koenig, R. (1976). Determinants of coordination modes within organizations. *American Sociological Review, 41,* 322–338.
Mahoney, T. A., & Frost, P. J. (1974). The role of technology in models of organization effectiveness. *Organizational Behavior and Human Performance, 11,* 122–138.

24 Daft, *op. cit.,* 180–181.

25 Mintzberg, H. (1979). *The structuring of organizations.* Englewood Cliffs, NJ: Prentice-Hall, 269.

26 Duncan, R. B. (1979). What is the right organization structure? *Organizational Dynamics, 7* (3), 62–63.

27 Burns, T., & Stalker, G. M. (1961). *The management of innovation.* London: Tavistock, 119–125.

28 Burns & Stalker, *loc. cit.*

29 Lawrence, P. R., & Lorsch, J. W. (1967). *Organization and environment: Managing differentiation and integration.* Homewood, IL: Irwin.
Lorsch, J. W., & Morse, J. J. (1974). *Organizations and their members: A contingency approach.* New York: Harper & Row.

30 Lawrence & Lorsch, *op. cit.,* 36.

31 Ibid.

32 Kotter, J. P. (1979). Managing external dependence. *Academy of Management Review, 4,* 87–92.

33 Ibid.

34 Daft, *op. cit.,* 65.

35 Aldrich, H., & Herker, D. (1977). Boundary spanning roles and organization structure. *Academy of Management Review, 2,* 217–239.

36 Daft, *op. cit.,* 66.

37 Kotter, *op. cit.,* 87–92.

Part 5

Improving Employee Performance

Chapter 11   Performance Appraisal

Chapter 12   Reward Systems

Chapter 13   The Design of Work

Chapter 14   Managerial Decision Making

Performance Appraisal

CHAPTER OUTLINE

Functions of Performance Appraisal

What Should Performance Appraisals Measure?

Graphic Rating Scales

Behaviorally Anchored Rating Scales (BARS)

Behavioral Observation Scales (BOS)

Management by Objectives (MBO)

Comparison of Appraisal Techniques

Managing the Appraisal Process

Keys to Effective Management

Review Questions

*A*n essential function for every organization is determining who to reward, who to promote, who requires additional training, and so on. This is done through assessments or appraisals of employee performance. The appraisal process also provides the organization with a mechanism for delivering feedback to its members on how well they have been performing their jobs. If handled effectively, such feedback can help motivate individuals to perform better and can also contribute to employee development by drawing attention to strengths and weaknesses exhibited in previous performance.

The task facing the designers of an organization's performance appraisal system is a formidable one. The appraisal process must generate fair, accurate, and valid information that can serve as a sound basis for organizational decision making regarding salaries, promotions, and so on. At the same time, appraisals must assist and encourage open sharing of information regarding employee strengths and weaknesses, in order to ensure that the process will facilitate employee motivation and development.

In this chapter we examine the performance appraisal process in detail. After looking at the functions, or purposes, of performance appraisal we will discuss the most common methods of employee assessment currently in use. An analysis of some of the problems associated with these techniques will then serve as a basis for exploring some of the newer methods and approaches designed to overcome these problems.

Functions of Performance Appraisal

The fundamental goal of performance appraisal is to generate accurate information regarding the job performance of organization members. The more accurate and valid the information generated, the greater its potential value to the organization.

While all organizations share this basic goal for performance appraisal, there is a great deal of variety in the specific uses that organizations make of the information on performance generated by their appraisals. These uses are summarized in Figure 11-1 and fall into three broad categories: individual evaluation and reward, individual development, and organizational planning and decision making.

Individual Evaluation and Reward

Most organizations use the performance appraisal process to measure and evaluate individuals' performance and to distribute rewards on the basis of these evaluations. Whether an individual is judged to be competent or incompetent, effective or ineffective, promotable or unpromotable is based upon the information generated by performance appraisals. In addition, organizations frequently tie various rewards such as salary increases and promotions to the ratings generated by appraisals.

Figure 11-1 A model of the performance appraisal process.

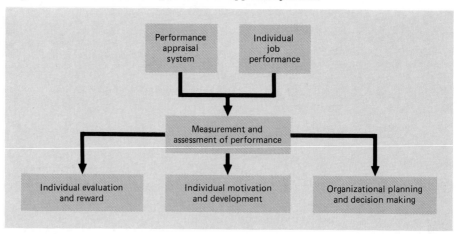

■

**Individual
Motivation and
Development**

In addition to serving as a basis for the administration of organizational rewards and punishments, the information generated by performance appraisals can serve to stimulate the personal development of organization members. Effective appraisals generate information regarding the personal strengths and weaknesses of individual employees. If such information is fed back to individuals in a clear, unambiguous, and nonthreatening manner, the information can serve two valuable purposes. First, if the information indicates that the person is performing effectively, the feedback process itself can be rewarding to the recipient by increasing feelings of self-esteem and personal competence. Second, if the information identifies an area of weakness, this can serve to stimulate training and development in order to overcome the weaknesses identified. Future appraisals then provide a means of monitoring and assessing the improvements arising from attempts to deal with performance problems.

■

**Organizational
Planning
and Decision
Making**

Besides providing the basis for the evaluation, motivation, and development of organization members, effective performance appraisals generate information that can be of significant value to the organization in planning its future human resource needs and policies. The members of an organization can be thought of as the human capital of the organization. The performance appraisal process generates information that permits the organization to assess the state of its human capital and to plan its recruiting, staffing, and development policies in an informed, systematic manner.

Surveys indicate that appraisals are used most frequently by organizations in allocating rewards and in motivating effective performance.[1] They are used much less frequently for organizational planning and decision making. Organizations appear to recognize the value of appraisal information in regard to paying and promoting their members, as well as for facilitating their motivation and personal development. However, organizations are much less likely to make systematic use of the information generated by appraisals in planning their future human resource needs and policies.

What Should Performance Appraisals Measure?

A key issue in performance appraisal is determining what constitute valid criteria or measures of effective performance. Appropriate criteria or measures of effective performance must be identified for each job to which a performance appraisal system is to be applied. Since almost all jobs have many dimensions and aspects, performance appraisals must employ multiple criteria or measures of effectiveness in order to accurately reflect the actual job performance of organization members.[2]

Although it is impossible to identify any universal measures of performance that are applicable to all jobs, it is possible to specify a number of characteristics that a criterion of job performance should possess if it is to be useful for performance appraisal.

1 A good criterion must be capable of being measured *reliably*. The concept of **reliability of measurement** has two components: stability and consistency. **Stability** implies that measures of the criterion taken at different times should yield approximately equal results. **Consistency** implies that measures of the criterion taken by different methods or by different people should be approximately equal to one another.

2 A good criterion should be capable of *differentiating* among individuals according to their performance. If a criterion of performance is such that scores or ratings on the criterion are virtually identical for everyone, the criterion is of no use for distributing pay for performance, recommending candidates for promotion, assessing training and development needs, and so on.

3 A good criterion should be subject to *influence* by the actions of the job incumbent. Since the purpose of performance appraisal systems is to assess the effectiveness of individual organization members, the criteria of effectiveness employed in those systems must be primarily under the discretionary control of the person being assessed.

4 A good criterion should be *acceptable* to those individuals whose performance is being assessed. It is important that the people whose performance is being measured feel that the criteria being employed provide a fair and accurate indication of their performance.[3]

Activities versus Results

A final important issue regarding criteria of effectiveness has to do with whether the criteria adopted for use in performance appraisal focus on the **activities** engaged in by the job incumbent or on the **results** achieved by the incumbent.[4] To take a sales job as an example, an appraisal process employing criteria focused on activities might assess total number of sales calls made, number of "cold" calls, courtesy in dealing with clients, speed with which complaints are handled, and so on. All of these criteria involve assessment of the activities engaged in by the salesperson. Criteria focusing upon results, on the other hand, might include measures of total sales volume, number of new customers added, percentage increase in sales volume, and so on. Measures of results pay no attention to how the results were achieved or what activities on the part of the person are responsible for generating the results.

Measures of activities and measures of results each have advantages and disadvantages as criteria of performance effectiveness.[5] Since organizations are ultimately concerned about the results they achieve, appraisals that focus on results have the advantage of encouraging and rewarding the attainment of the results desired by the organization. However, a disadvantage associated with results-oriented criteria of performance is that they may produce dysfunctional behavior regarding results not measured by the appraisal system. For example, an appraisal system that measures sales volume may result in salespersons selling a great deal, but these sales may have been accompanied by unrealistic claims and promises on the part of the sales staff. If the appraisal system does not include additional measures, such as customer satisfaction or repeat business, as criteria of performance, the organization may not become aware of the dysfunctional behavior until irreparable damage has been done to the organization's reputation. A second disadvantage of results measures as criteria is that they may lead to frustration when failure to achieve results is caused by factors outside the direct control of the person being appraised, for example, by faulty tools and equipment or by lack of support and cooperation from others.[6] Finally, results measures as criteria of performance suffer from the fact that they generate no information regarding a person's activities that can be used in counseling and assisting an individual whose results are inadequate.

This latter weak point of results measures is one of the primary strengths of measures of activities as criteria. When appraisals are based on measures of the activities that a person is or is not engaging in, the information generated can help the organization to design a program of training and development for poor performers. However, a danger associated with appraisals based on activities is that they may serve only to motivate performance of the activities measured, while disregarding the actual results that the activities are designed to encourage. This may result in excessive bureaucratic emphasis on the means and procedures employed rather than on actual accomplishments and results. The successful nonconformist cannot be accommodated within an appraisal system focusing purely on activities.

Effective performance appraisals need to include measures of both results and activities. A well-balanced appraisal process that can both motivate effective performance and assist in the development of individuals' skills and abilities requires both types of criteria of effectiveness.

Graphic Rating Scales

A typical example of a graphic rating scale is contained in Figure 11-2. **Graphic rating scales** consist of a list of general personal characteristics and personality traits, such as quantity of work, quality of work, initiative, cooperativeness, and judgment. The rater judges the employee on each dimension, on a scale whose ratings vary, for example, from *low* to *high* or from *poor* to *excellent*. The scales are referred to as *graphic* because they visually graph performance from one extreme to another. The characteristics being judged are usually extremely broad and general, and the rater is usually given little or no specific

Figure 11-2   Example of a typical graphic rating scale.

	Outstanding	Good	Satisfactory	Fair	Unsatisfactory
Name_____ Dept._____ Date_____					
Quantity of Work: Volume of acceptable work under normal conditions Comments:	☐	☐	☐	☐	☐
Quality of Work: Thoroughness, neatness, and accuracy of work Comments:	☐	☐	☐	☐	☐
Knowledge of Job: Clear understanding of the facts or factors pertinent to the job Comments:	☐	☐	☐	☐	☐
Personal Qualities: Personality, appearance, sociability, leadership, integrity Comments:	☐	☐	☐	☐	☐
Cooperation: Ability and willingness to work with associates, supervisors and subordinates toward common goals Comments:	☐	☐	☐	☐	☐
Dependability: Conscientious, thorough, accurate, reliable with respect to attendance, lunch periods, reliefs, etc. Comments:	☐	☐	☐	☐	☐
Initiative: Earnestness in seeking increased responsibilities; self-starting; unafraid to proceed alone Comments:	☐	☐	☐	☐	☐

[*Source:* Glueck, W. F. (1978). *Personnel: A diagnostic approach.* Dallas: BPI, p. 302. Used by permission.]

guidance regarding what types of work behavior qualify a person for each of the possible ratings along the scales. The rater must use his or her personal judgment in deciding how the employee's work performance can be classified according to one of the available alternative responses on the rating scales.

Whether a graphic rating scale produces accurate ratings of a subordinate's performance depends very much on what specific characteristics or traits are included in the scale. In order for a rating process to produce an accurate appraisal of a person's job performance, the ratings must reflect the most important requirements and demands of the person's job. For example, if a person works alone on a highly standardized job, factors such as cooperation and initiative might be quite irrelevant to how well the person is performing, since cooperation and initiative are not required by the job.

Graphic rating scales can be designed in many different ways, and the sample provided in Figure 11-2 is only a single example. Figure 11-3 illustrates nine different graphic rating formats that could be employed for assessing a single dimension of performance. Although there is no one best way to design a graphic rating scale, in general it is desirable to employ scales in which the meaning and interpretation of each of the response alternatives is clearly identified and defined for the rater.

Problems with Graphic Rating Scales

A common problem with graphic rating scales is that they often fail to reflect the specific nature and demands of the jobs being performed by those whose performance is being evaluated. Unfortunately, it is not uncommon for an organization to use exactly the same graphic rating scale for almost all the employees in the organization. When this is done, any particular employee's evaluation may include ratings on factors quite irrelevant to his or her job and may fail to include ratings on dimensions that are very central to the job. The work performance of people performing many different and varied jobs cannot be accurately evaluated on the basis of a small number of general traits or dimensions. The solution is to ensure that the rating scale used to evaluate a person's job performance is specifically designed to reflect the nature and demands of the job that the person is performing.

A further primary weakness of graphic rating scales lies in the fact that they are not directly tied to the *behavior* of the person being rated. Such scales rate an individual on the basis of the superior's *judgments* regarding various work outcomes, such as quantity and quality of performance, as well as the superior's *judgments* regarding the extent to which the individual possesses certain personal traits, such as initiative and cooperativeness. Thus, graphic rating scales require the rater to draw inferences and to make personal judgments regarding the performance and personal characteristics of the person being rated. Graphic rating scales do not contain ratings or evaluations of the frequency of actual job behaviors that are related to successful performance. Thus, a number of negative consequences arise when graphic rating scales are used to appraise performance.

1   It is extremely difficult for those being rated to determine how they should change their job behavior in order to obtain improved ratings. For example, being told that your personality is unacceptable or that your conscientiousness is inadequate does not provide you with much guidance regarding exactly what you need to start doing differently in order to obtain improved ratings.

Figure 11-3   Examples of alternative graphic rating scale formats for assessing a single dimension of performance.

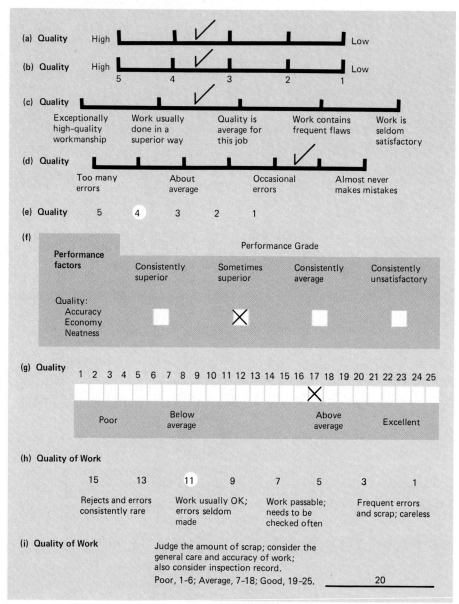

[*Source:* Guion, R. M. (1965). *Personnel testing.* New York: McGraw-Hill, p. 98. Used by permission.]

2 A closely related problem lies in the difficulty of designing a program of training and development for employees whose ratings are low. If the ratings do not identify precisely which behaviors are deficient, then it is impossible to design training activities that could remedy the deficiencies.

3 Since graphic rating scales do not assess specific, concrete behavior, it is difficult to use appraisal systems employing such scales to tie rewards to effective behavior. If appraisals are not based on specific behaviors, then reward systems based on the results of such appraisals are incapable of rewarding specific effective work behavior.

4 Graphic rating scales also suffer from resistance on the part of the superiors doing the ratings. The fact that graphic rating scales require a large amount of inference and judgment on the part of raters has a tendency to make raters uncomfortable. The rating scale forces raters to draw inferences about their subordinates' personalities and characteristics even if they do not feel that they possess adequate information to do so accurately. As a result, raters frequently express displeasure with graphic rating scales and also experience extreme difficulty in discriminating among their subordinates regarding the degree to which they possess such general traits and characteristics.

5 Finally, graphic rating scales frequently generate defensive reactions and arguments when the ratings are fed back to the employee being rated. People are generally quite willing to admit that they have certain shortcomings and that they may have made mistakes or performed less than optimally on certain occasions. However, people also tend to react very negatively and defensively when they feel that they are being stereotyped or classified as an undesirable type of person. Telling workers that their personalities are unsatisfactory or that they lack initiative can often strike at the very heart of their self-concepts and self-esteem and leave them feeling that they have no alternative but to fight back in order to defend themselves.

Common Rating Errors

In addition to the problems already identified regarding graphic rating scales, a variety of factors can introduce bias into the appraisal process.[7] Table 11-1 summarizes a number of the most common errors to which people are prone when making judgments and ratings about others.

Strictness, Leniency, and Central Tendency

Some individuals, when filling out rating scales on their employees, have a tendency to rate everyone quite *strictly* or harshly. A person prone to such a bias would tend to rate good employees as only average and average employees as poor.

Just the opposite problem is involved in a *leniency* bias. Superiors with a leniency bias would tend to rate all their subordinates more positively than the subordinates' performance actually warranted. Such a bias is undesirable since it results in subordinates appearing to be more competent than in fact they are.

TABLE 11-1	
Common Rating Errors	
Strictness	Ratings unduly negative
Leniency	Ratings unduly positive
Central tendency	All ratings near the midpoint
Halo	Similar ratings of one subordinate on all performance dimensions
Recency	Ratings unduly influenced by recent performance of subordinate
Contrast	Ratings influenced by ratings given to previously evaluated subordinates
Attribution	Performance problems unduly attributed to personal characteristics of subordinate rather than to situational factors influencing performance

Some raters are timid about using the extreme endpoints of rating scales. They dislike being too harsh with anyone by giving them an extremely low rating, and they also may feel that no one is really good enough to get the highest possible ratings. This approach results in everyone being rated very close to average, with ratings that tend to be at or close to the center of the rating scale. Individuals whose ratings all converge near the midpoint of the rating scale are said to exhibit a ***central tendency*** bias. The problem created by a central tendency bias is that it makes performance ratings almost useless for identifying either highly effective employees who are candidates for promotion or problem employees who require counseling and training.

Examples of ratings exhibiting strictness, leniency, and central tendency biases are contained in Figure 11-4. The distribution of ratings on the left of the figure would indicate a strictness bias, since the ratings vary only from 1 to 3, with an average of 2. The right-hand distribution indicates a leniency bias, since everyone in this case is rated between 5 and 7, and the average rating is 6. The distribution of ratings in the center of the figure would indicate a central tendency bias, since everyone receives a rating of between 3 and 5, with an average rating of 4. The distribution of ratings in the figure have been stylized to provide clear-cut examples. It is unlikely that any rater would exhibit such dramatic biases in all of his or her ratings.

Halo Effect

Some individuals have a tendency when filling out performance rating scales to rate a subordinate very similarly on all of the dimensions or characteristics being assessed. Thus, the person who is rated high on quantity of performance will also be rated high on quality, high on initiative, high on cooperation, and so on. This is not a problem as long as the person being rated really *is* high on all of the dimensions being assessed (or low on all of them, as the case may be). However, it is frequently the case that an employee may be very high on some dimensions, average on some, and low on still others.[8] A superior who

Figure 11-4 Examples of ratings that would be generated by raters exhibiting strictness, central tendency, and leniency biases.

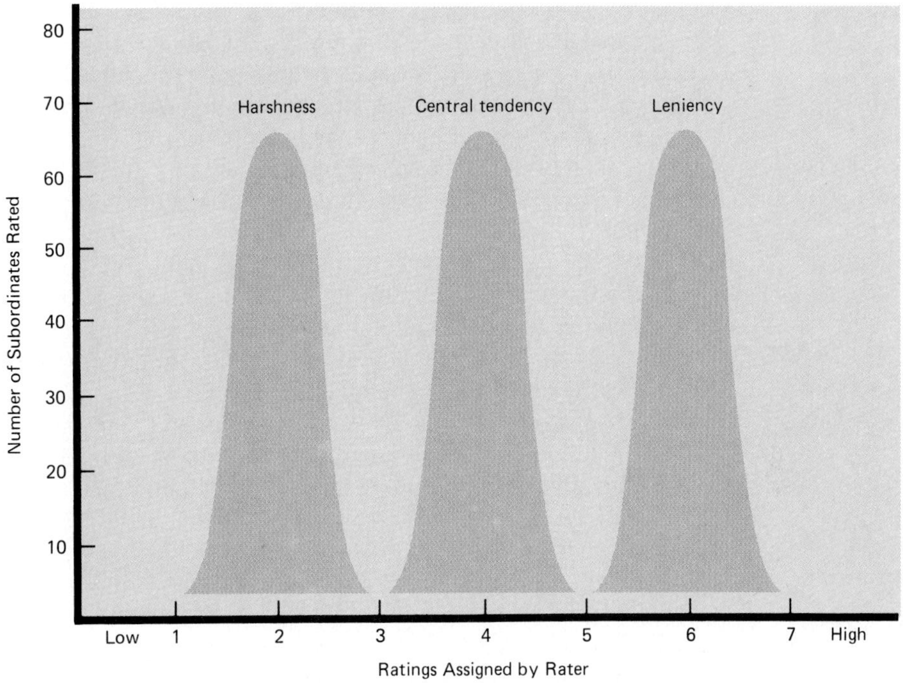

gives such a person the same rating (whether high, medium, or low) on all dimensions is said to exhibit a ***halo effect.*** The term *halo* is used since all of the superior's ratings fall within a narrow range, or within the halo, of one another. The problem created by a halo effect is that it makes it impossible to identify the areas of strength of employees who are generally weak and, conversely, the areas of weakness that need development for employees who are generally strong.[9]

Recency Bias

Ideally, employee ratings should be based upon systematic observations of an employee's performance over the entire rating period (frequently one year). Unfortunately, it is often the case that a rater is strongly influenced by the most *recent* events and observations of the subordinate's performance. Things that happened recently tend to be remembered more clearly and to be most salient in the mind of the superior.[10] Thus, "annual" reviews tend to be inordinately influenced by what the rater has observed of the subordinate over the few weeks or months immediately preceding the performance appraisal. Recency bias can be overcome either by scheduling appraisals more frequently or by encouraging managers to keep frequent written records of the performance of their subordinates to use as references during appraisals.

Contrast Effect

Managers are frequently involved in appraising several subordinates within a fairly short time. When this is the case, the manager's appraisal of each subordinate can be influenced by the evaluation of the preceding subordinate.[11] Thus, a subordinate whose true performance is only average, but who is evaluated immediately after someone whose performance is extremely poor, may receive a fairly positive rating. This can occur as a result of the ***contrast*** created in the appraiser's mind between the very poor performer and the average performer. Exactly the opposite effect could occur if the average performer had the misfortune to be evaluated immediately after a truly outstanding performer.

Attribution Errors

Attributions refer to the assumptions that we make regarding the causes of our own behavior and the behavior of others.[12] As discussed in Chapter 5, attributions fall into two general categories: internal and external. When we assume that the cause of a person's behavior is some characteristic of that person (e.g., his or her personality), we are making an ***internal attribution*** (e.g., "She performed effectively in that situation because she is an intelligent and persistent person"). ***External attributions,*** on the other hand, occur when we conclude that the primary cause of a person's behavior resides not within the person, but somewhere in the external environment (e.g., "She performed effectively in that situation because her boss instructed her in precisely what to do every step of the way").

Research indicates that people have a tendency to make internal attributions regarding the behavior of others even when such attributions are unwarranted or inaccurate.[13] We all have a tendency to assume that the behavior of others is determined primarily by some fairly small number of consistent personality traits or characteristics. In observing and attempting to understand the reasons for another person's behavior we tend to underemphasize the importance of external situational factors and to overemphasize internal personality characteristics as the reasons for the behavior. The implication for performance appraisal is that superiors, in evaluating subordinates, will tend to attribute positive performance to positive personality characteristics and negative performance to negative personality characteristics, and will tend to overlook situational factors that may be influencing behavior.

Reducing Rating Errors

Since rating errors can seriously undermine the value of an organization's performance appraisal system, a good deal of effort has been focused upon the development of methods for reducing or eliminating them.[14] The following steps can help an organization to reduce errors in its appraisal system.

1 Superiors should be encouraged to observe the performance of their subordinates regularly and to keep a record of their observations.[15]

2 Rating scales should be carefully constructed in the following manner:

    a Each dimension on the rating scale should be designed to assess a single important work activity or skill.

    b The dimensions included on the rating scale should all be important and meaningful and should be clearly stated.

    c The words used to define various points along the rating scale ("excellent," "poor," etc.) should be clearly and unambiguously defined for the rater in terms of employee behavior.[16]

3 Raters should not be required to evaluate a large number of subordinates at any one time.

4 Raters should be made conscious of common rating errors such as strictness and leniency, central tendency, halo, and attributional errors, and trained to avoid them.

5 Managers should be provided with training in the effective use of performance appraisal techniques.[17] Errors in performance appraisal cannot be overcome purely by focusing upon the development and design of better rating instruments.[18] Carefully developed training programs have also been found to minimize rating errors in the appraisal process.[19]

Behaviorally Anchored Rating Scales (BARS)

Behaviorally anchored rating scales (BARS) differ from graphic rating scales in two key respects.[20] First, BARS require superiors to evaluate subordinates on a set of dimensions of work *behavior* that have been carefully correlated to the specific job being performed by the person being evaluated. Whereas graphic rating scales evaluate individuals on the basis of their possession of general personality characteristics, BARS evaluate employees in terms of the extent to which they exhibit effective behavior relevant to the specific demands of their jobs. Second, each response alternative along the dimensions of a BARS is labeled, or "anchored," with examples of specific job behavior corresponding to good performance, average performance, poor performance, and so on. These behavioral examples help raters tie their ratings directly to the job behavior of the person being rated. This is in contrast to graphic rating scales, which simply use adjectives such as "good" and "poor" for describing employee characteristics and performance.

    An example of a BARS is contained in Figure 11-5. The example consists of a single dimension of a BARS developed for the job of production control analyst. The dimension of the analyst's job being evaluated by the scale con-

Figure 11-5   A behaviorally anchored rating scale to assess the dimension of ability to communicate and gain cooperation among departments for a production control analyst's job.

Excellent Performance	1	Reports are clear and well organized whether oral or written; speaks and writes clearly and precisely; all departments are continually informed; foresees conflict between departments and handles with initiative.
Very Good Performance	2	Uses language well in conveying ideas; written work is easy to read with few errors; informs and cooperates with other departments; has ability to straighten out misunderstandings after they occur.
Good Performance	3	Conveys the necessary information to other departments, but does not check for misunderstandings; if misunderstandings occur, willingly tries to correct the error.
Fair or Average Performance	4	Is not clear or concise in relaying information; other departments may complain because of lack of communication.
Poor Performance	5	Leaves out essential information when communicating either orally or written; does not know how to handle misunderstandings or conflicts between departments; operating errors occur due to lack of communication.
Very Poor Performance	6	Promotes misunderstanding between departments because of incomplete and unorganized reports (oral and written); often has to depend on others to straighten out misunderstandings.
Unacceptable Performance	7	Does not cooperate with or inform other departments; refuses to improve on reports or handle misunderstandings.

[*Source:* Beatty, R. W., & Schneier, C. E. (1977). *Implementer's manual for personnel administration: An experiential skill-building approach.* Reading, MA: Addison-Wesley, p. 100. Used by permission.]

tained in the figure is the ability to communicate and gain cooperation among departments. As the example makes clear, BARS assist the person doing the evaluation by providing precise examples of the type of expected job behavior associated with each of the ratings along the scale. This reduces the amount of personal judgment and inference required of the rater and helps to tie the appraisal process directly to work behavior.

The process of developing a BARS for a job is fairly complex. First, a group of people familiar with the job are asked to think of as many examples as possible of effective and ineffective performance on the job. This often results in several hundred behavioral examples or incidents of different levels of job performance. These specific incidents of work behavior are then classified into a smaller set of common dimensions of job performance, such as knowledge and skill, judgment, decision making, and problem solving. A second group of people familiar with the job are then presented with the list of job dimensions plus the list of incidents of job behavior. These people are asked to determine which incidents of job behavior they feel are relevant to each of the dimensions of the job. This step is a type of cross-check on the judgments of the first group of people. The only job dimensions and behavioral incidents maintained for actual use in the BARS are those that both groups agreed on as indicating the same levels of performance on the same job dimensions. The final step in the development of the BARS requires judgments to be made regarding which specific incidents of behavior provide the best examples of various levels of job performance varying from very good to very poor along each of the dimensions of the job. A similar process must be followed in developing separate scales for every job in the organization. Considerable time and expense is obviously involved in the design and development of BARS.

Advantages of BARS

A wide variety of potential advantages have been claimed for BARS.

1 Rating errors can be reduced since relevant job dimensions are clearly defined and behavioral anchors clearly indicate the response categories available to the rater.

2 Performance appraisals can become more reliable, valid, meaningful, and complete since the system is developed with the active participation of employees who possess full knowledge of the demands and requirements of the job.

3 Acceptance of and commitment to the appraisal system on the part of both employees and supervisors can be increased as a result of their having been actively and directly involved in the design of the system.

4 The degree of defensiveness and conflict generated by appraisals can be reduced since individuals are evaluated on the basis of their specific job behavior, not their personalities.

5 Employees can be provided with accurate and concrete feedback that can serve to clearly identify specific areas of performance deficiency and needs for training and development activities.[21]

Disadvantages of BARS

While BARS clearly possess these potential advantages, it is equally clear that there are a number of disadvantages associated with them.

1 A primary drawback of BARS is the time, effort, and expense involved in their development, especially since separate BARS are needed for each job (or at least each family of related jobs) in an organization. The investment required for development may thus be justifiable only for jobs having a large number of incumbents.

2   BARS are primarily applicable to jobs whose major components consist of physically observable behavior. Jobs having a high component of mental activity, e.g., that of a research scientist or a creative writer, do not lend themselves as readily to evaluation using behaviorally anchored techniques.

3   Raters sometimes experience difficulty in determining the degree of similarity between the behavior of the employee that they have observed and the particular behavioral examples employed as anchors of the BARS.[22] The examples of job behavior used to anchor the BARS cannot possibly cover every example of employee performance at different levels.

Evaluation of BARS

BARS do provide an effective approach to performance appraisal. BARS clearly outperform graphic rating scales made up on the spur of the moment by a manager in need of an appraisal device for immediate use. While BARS do not always outperform other appraisal techniques that have been carefully designed and tested,[23] BARS are clearly superior to graphic rating scales and must be considered a serious candidate for use in an organization's appraisal system. Recent research has begun to clarify some of the problems in the development and use of BARS,[24] and new results indicate a number of positive spin-offs to the organization from the implementation of BARS in terms of improved attitudes and reduced tension regarding appraisals.[25]

Behavioral Observation Scales (BOS)

Behavioral observation scales (BOS) were developed in an attempt to capitalize on some of the strengths of the BARS approach to performance appraisal while avoiding some of its weaknesses.[26] In the BARS approach, specific examples of work behavior that might be *expected* of the job incumbent are used to "anchor" the various rating points along each dimension of job performance. For each dimension of job performance evaluated by a BOS, on the other hand, a number of specific examples of work behavior are listed, and the appraiser rates the extent to which he or she has actually *observed* the employee engaging in that behavior on a five-point scale varying from "almost never" to "almost always." An example from a BOS evaluating one dimension of job performance is contained in Figure 11-6. An employee's total score on each dimension is determined by adding up his or her ratings on each of the specific examples of job behavior included in that dimension. The process of developing a BOS for a job involves a series of steps very similar to that followed for BARS. Job incumbents, working with expert job analysts, identify the key

Figure 11-6   An example of a BOS performance dimension for evaluating managers.

I. Overcoming Resistance to Change*

   (1) Describes the details of the change to subordinates.
     Almost Never   1   2   3   4   5   Almost Always

   (2) Explains why the change is necessary.
     Almost Never   1   2   3   4   5   Almost Always

   (3) Discusses how the change will affect the employee.
     Almost Never   1   2   3   4   5   Almost Always

   (4) Listens to the employee's concerns.
     Almost Never   1   2   3   4   5   Almost Always

   (5) Asks the employee for help in making the change work.
     Almost Never   1   2   3   4   5   Almost Always

   (6) If necessary, specifies the date for a follow-up meeting to respond to the employee's concerns.
     Almost Never   1   2   3   4   5   Almost Always

                                      Total = _____

Below Adequate	Adequate	Fair	Excellent	Superior*
6–10	11–15	16–20	21–25	26–30

*Scores are set by management.

[*Source:* Latham, G. P., & Wexley, K. N. (1981). *Improving productivity through performance appraisal.* Reading, MA: Addison-Wesley, p. 56. Used by permission.]

dimensions of effective job performance, as well as specific examples of effective and ineffective behavior on each dimension.

Advantages and Disadvantages of BOS

BOS share with BARS the advantages of (1) being relatively reliable and valid as a result of being based upon actual employee behavior; (2) generating high levels of employee acceptance and understanding as a result of employee involvement in their development; and (3) providing employees with useful feedback on their job behavior that can be employed for the design of plans for development and performance improvement. The developers of BOS also argue that since BOS focus attention on actual observed job behavior, rather than on expected behavior, the behavioral items included in a BOS help managers to know what to look for during an appraisal period and also help facilitate the manager's recall of employee behavior during the appraisal process.[27]

Naturally, BOS share many of the disadvantages of BARS as well. BOS are relatively time-consuming and expensive to develop and are difficult to apply to jobs whose primary components may not be physically observable.

No empirical comparisons of BARS and BOS have yet been conducted in industrial settings. Comparisons carried out in university settings have found BOS to be as good as or better than BARS in reducing rating errors and biases.[28] BOS appear to be a promising development on the appraisal scene. Future research should throw light on the specific advantages and disadvantages of BOS compared to other appraisal techniques.[29]

Management by Objectives (MBO)

Management by objectives (MBO) refers to a process in which managers set specific and measurable goals with each individual employee on a regular basis. The employee is then responsible for achieving his or her goals within a certain time. An MBO system can serve as the basis for the design of an organization's performance appraisal system, and is particularly well suited to managerial jobs for which techniques such as BARS and BOS may be inappropriate or inapplicable because behavior is not so readily observable.

MBO is an example of a results-based method of performance appraisal. Under MBO, individuals are evaluated on the basis of what they accomplish, not how they get the job done. There are two important steps involved in the application of MBO to performance appraisal: the first step is goal setting and the second step is performance review.

In the goal-setting phase of MBO each individual meets with his or her immediate supervisor to discuss plans for the coming performance period (usually one year) and to agree on performance goals for the period. As pointed out in our discussion of goal-setting theory in Chapter 3, if goals are to maximize motivation, they must be clear and specific and sufficiently difficult to be challenging, and they must be personally accepted by the individual seeking them. Thus, in the goal-setting phase of MBO the manager's role is to help subordinates to identify specific, realistic, and challenging performance goals for the coming year. Ensuring that goals are specific requires (1) the identification of specific measurement criteria that can be employed in determining whether a goal has been met; and (2) agreement on deadlines and intermediate review dates by which specified levels of progress should have been attained. Ensuring that goals are both challenging and realistic implies a need for the manager to involve the subordinate actively in the goal-setting process. The active participation of the individual performer helps to ensure that goals are set at a sufficiently difficult level to be challenging but not at such a high level that they are completely unrealistic and unattainable. Thus, the outcome of the goal-setting phase of MBO is a set of specific, measurable goals (each with agreed-upon dates for review and accomplishment) that the individual personally identifies with and views as challenging but realistic.

In the second performance review phase of MBO the manager and subordinate meet to discuss the subordinate's progress in attaining his or her goals. The subordinate's performance is appraised and evaluated in terms of the specific goals and objectives agreed to in the initial goal-setting meeting. Appraisal is thus based upon performance and concrete results. It is not based upon what activities the subordinate engaged in to obtain those results, nor is it based on the extent to which the boss feels that the subordinate possesses vague and general personality characteristics such as cooperativeness or initiative. Table 11-2 contains an example of a hypothetical MBO evaluation report for a salesperson. The first column of the report, headed *period objective,* is the outcome

---

TABLE 11-2

An MBO Evaluation Report for a Salesperson

Objectives set	Period objective	Accomplishments	Percent of objective achieved
1 Number of sales calls	100	104	104
2 Number of new customers contacted	20	18	90
3 Number of wholesalers stocking new product 17	30	30	100
4 Sales of product 12	10,000	9,750	97.5
5 Sales of product 17	17,000	18,700	110
6 Customer complaints/service calls	36	24	66%
7 Number of sales correspondence courses successfully completed	4	2	50
8 Number of sales reports in home office within 1 day of end of month	12	10	80

Source: Glueck, W. F. (1978). *Personnel: A diagnostic approach.* Dallas: BPI, p. 307. Used by permission.

---

of the initial goal-setting meeting between the salesperson and his or her manager. At the end of the performance period the *accomplishments* and *percent of objective achieved* columns are filled in and serve as the basis for the salesperson's evaluation in the performance review meeting.

Advantages of MBO

The major advantages claimed for MBO are as follows:

1   By encouraging individuals to set specific, challenging goals, MBO has the potential of increasing employee motivation and performance, in addition to serving as the basis for performance appraisal.

2   Since organizations are ultimately concerned with concrete results, evaluating employees on the basis of the results they have personally accomplished is consistent with the overall needs and objectives of the organization.

3   Employees know precisely what is expected of them and exactly what they must achieve if they are to be evaluated positively.

4   Systematic goal setting throughout the organization facilitates planning and coordination by clarifying exactly what is expected of each person on an ongoing basis.

Disadvantages of MBO

However, a decision to adopt MBO as a performance appraisal technique must take into account not only its advantages, but also the following disadvantages.

1   The heavy emphasis of MBO on results may lead to a lack of attention to how results are being accomplished. Individuals may be accomplishing their goals by cutting corners or by engaging in illegal or unethical behavior. Or, although individuals may know very clearly what they are supposed to accomplish, they may be very unclear regarding how they should go about achieving their goals. Thus, there is a risk that managers may not give

BOX 11-1

Performance Evaluation at Syborn Corporation

Syborn Corporation was like most firms—not very satisfied with its performance evaluation program. It appeared that most raters did not know how to evaluate subordinates effectively and objectively. There seemed to be a preference for rushing through the evaluations in a matter of minutes. Rushing led to more errors and more dissatisfaction with the program.

Syborn decided to provide the managers doing the rating with a training program designed to improve rating skills and the motivation to set objectives. The first part of the training involved managers in interpersonal skill exercises and in learning procedures for setting evaluation reviews and substantiating goals. The firm used lectures, discussions, and videotaping in this part of the program.

The second part of the training presented to the managers involved five general principles to improve their managerial performance. The five principles were presented, discussed, and critiqued. They were:

1   Maintain and enhance self-esteem.

2   Focus on behavior, not personality.

3   Use reinforcement techniques to shape behavior.

4   Listen actively.

5   Maintain communication and set specific follow-up dates.

Since only eight or ten managers participated in each course, there was time for total involvement, thus reinforcing the goals of the program.

Source: "Syborn trains managers to improve performance appraisals" (1981, January). *Management Review,* pp. 32–33.

enough attention to providing their subordinates with advice and assistance regarding how to achieve their goals effectively.

2   MBO makes it difficult to compare the level of performance of different individuals. Since each person is evaluated with regard to his or her personal goals, valid comparisons of individuals require comparisons of both their levels of accomplishment and the difficulty of their goals. Such comparisons can only be based on the judgment of the manager making the comparisons. This shortcoming is particularly salient when personnel decisions regarding promotions, replacements, etc., must be made.

3   MBO programs are difficult to implement effectively. The primary factor distinguishing effective and ineffective MBO programs seems to be the extent to which the implementation of MBO recognizes the need for special skills on the part of managers conducting MBO goal-setting and performance appraisal meetings.[30] The goal-setting process must be participative; the manager must be a skilled listener, taking into account the skills, needs, and aspirations of the individual involved. Similarly, in the appraisal phase of MBO the manager requires skills in listening and coaching, so that the process serves not only to evaluate the past performance of the individual but also to help the subordinate to perform even more effectively in the future. Since managers rarely possess all the skills required for conducting effective goal-setting and appraisal meetings, the implementation of MBO must be accompanied by a program of management training and development designed to assist managers in the acquisition of the necessary skills. An example of such a training program implemented by one organization is described in Box 11-1.

Comparision of Appraisal Techniques

We have now discussed graphic rating scales, behaviorally anchored rating scales (BARS), behavioral observation scales (BOS), and management by objectives (MBO) as performance appraisal techniques. Table 11-3 compares these four approaches to performance appraisal on a number of important dimensions. As the table makes clear, graphic rating scales are clearly the weakest of the alternative techniques available. However, there is still a good deal of variation among the remaining three techniques in terms of their strengths and weaknesses, and no single approach is without its shortcomings. The design and implementation of an appraisal system obviously demands that trade-offs be made. What is essential, given the importance and pervasiveness of the appraisal process in organizations, is that these trade-offs be made in an intelligent and informed fashion.[31]

TABLE   11-3

Evaluation of Performance Appraisal Techniques on a Variety of Key Dimensions

	Graphic rating scales	*BARS*	*BOS*	*MBO*
Accuracy of evaluations	Low	High	High	High
Usefulness for personnel decisions	Moderate	Moderate	Moderate	Moderate
Usefulness for reward allocation	Low	High	High	High
Usefulness for identifying training and development needs	Very low	High	High	Moderate
Costs of development (time and money)	Low	High	High	Moderate
Costs of administration (time and money)	Low	Moderate	Moderate	Moderate
Potential to motivate ratees	Low	Moderate	Moderate	High
Acceptability to ratees	Low	High	High	High
Acceptability to raters	Low	High	High	High
Skills required of raters	Low	Moderate	Moderate	High

Managing the Appraisal Process

Up to this point we have looked at the different uses to which performance appraisals can be put, discussed alternative aspects of work performance that appraisals may focus upon, and reviewed a variety of the methods and techniques employed by organizations in evaluating the performance of their members. We now turn to an examination of the actual implementation of the appraisal process in organizations. We'll discuss who does (or should do) performance appraisals and when and how often appraisals are (or should be) done; finally, we'll take a close look at the actual appraisal interview.[32]

Who Evaluates   In the vast majority of organizations, performance appraisals are conducted by the ***immediate superior*** of the person being evaluated. The immediate superior is often in the best position to observe the employee's performance frequently over the evaluation period. The superior is also well positioned to analyze and interpret the performance of the subordinate in light of the goals and plans of the organization. Finally, depending upon the design of the organization's reward systems (discussed in the next chapter), the superior may be able to link rewards to the evaluations he or she assigns to subordinates. The practice of evaluation by the immediate superior is so common that it is often assumed to be the only feasible way to conduct performance appraisals. There are in fact a variety of options available that are worthy of consideration when appraisal systems are being designed.

A slight variation on appraisals conducted by the immediate superior involves evaluations conducted by a ***group or panel of superiors,*** all from the same hierarchical level, or from the next higher level. All of the managers involved should be in a position to observe the subordinate's performance during the evaluation period. When this is the case, group evaluation can generate more reliable appraisals as a result of the pooling of a variety of opinions.[33] In spite of these potential benefits, such group evaluations are almost never used.

A more radical departure from evaluation by the immediate superior is ***peer evaluation.*** As its name suggests, peer evaluation requires individuals to be evaluated by a group of their work peers from the same hierarchical level in the organization. If peer evaluations are to be successful, those doing the evaluations must have frequent opportunities to observe each other's behavior and effectiveness. In addition, there must be a high level of trust among peers evaluating one another. Finally, the peers must not be in a position of direct competition for the same raises or promotions.[34] Peer evaluations can have a variety of positive outcomes for the organization.[35] In spite of this, the use of peer reviews for appraisal is extremely uncommon because of the rarity of all the conditions for success being met, and because of resistance to their use from organization members.[36]

Subordinates can also be involved in the appraisal process, the argument being that subordinates are often well placed to observe a great deal of their superior's performance. Subordinate evaluations are infrequently used and when they are used tend to be focused upon providing useful developmental feedback to the superior rather than being used as the primary basis for the superior's evaluation.[37]

Self-evaluations similarly tend to be used more for purposes of development than for evaluation itself. Self-evaluation appears to be in slightly wider use than some of the other alternative approaches to evaluation (roughly 5 percent of firms report using self-evaluations). Self-evaluations can be particularly helpful in stimulating an individual to think realistically about his or her areas of personal strength and weakness.[38]

When to Evaluate

Surveys indicate that about two-thirds of employees are evaluated annually, while about one-quarter are evaluated semiannually. Only about 10 percent of employees are evaluated more often than once every 6 months. Unfortunately, there is no straightforward rule that can be applied in determining when and how often individuals should be evaluated. There are, however, certain guidelines that may be followed.

From the standpoint of employee counseling and development, frequent appraisals are desirable. Research indicates that feedback is most effective in influencing and changing behavior when it follows almost immediately after the behavior involved.[39] This implies the desirability of frequent, if not continuous, appraisal meetings between supervisor and subordinate.

From the standpoint of employee evaluation, however, such frequent appraisals may not be so desirable. In order to obtain an accurate picture of an employee's performance, appraisals should be scheduled so that they fit into the natural work cycles of the person's job. Evaluations need to be timed so that they correspond to points at which the positive or negative results of an employee's performance will have had an opportunity to show up.[40] If concrete results cannot be expected to appear for a year, insistence on a semiannual appraisal will be viewed as unfair by the employee. Similarly, if an employee's job is such that results appear quickly but may change rapidly, an annual review may be perceived to be unfair, since it would fail to take adequate account of positive results produced six or eight months previously by the individual.

It is also undesirable for superiors to schedule the evaluations of all their subordinates at the same time. While such a practice may give the appearance of efficiency, it frequently results in fatigue for the superior and a tendency to give inadequate attention to the unique factors relevant to the case of each individual employee. A desirable alternative is to schedule appraisals on the anniversary of the date that each employee joined the organization.

Thus, while there is no single correct approach to the scheduling of performance appraisals, it does appear desirable to (1) schedule frequent feedback meetings to facilitate coaching and development; and (2) schedule formal evaluation reviews at times appropriate to the cycles of the employee's job.

The Appraisal Interview

If the performance appraisal process is to have any potential whatsoever for improving the level of performance of organization members, it is essential that the results of the appraisal process be fed back to the individuals being evaluated. Only in this way can people learn where their strengths and weaknesses lie and subsequently take steps to improve their future performance. However, the fact that some feedback is provided via an appraisal interview does not ensure that the feedback is constructive or that the interview will have a positive motivational influence on the individuals involved.

One major factor that frequently creates difficulties in the appraisal interview is the inherent conflict experienced by the subordinate being evaluated. The subordinate can easily be torn between trying to present him- or herself in the best possible light in order to obtain the highest positive evaluation, on the one hand, and on the other hand wishing to be open and candid about problems and weaknesses in order to obtain assistance and coaching that will facilitate improvement.

A second major source of potential conflict and misunderstanding in appraisal interviews is the tendency for critical comments by the superior to elicit defensive reactions from the subordinate.[41] This is obviously a natural reaction. When we are criticized or our shortcomings are pointed out, our self-concept and self-esteem are threatened and we feel a need to defend ourselves in order to maintain a positive self-image and some degree of self-respect. But the problem is that such automatic defensive reactions interfere with our ability to face our shortcomings realistically and to discuss ways in which we might improve on them in the future.

The likelihood of positive progress arising from appraisal interviews is very much dependent upon the skill of the superior conducting the interview. The superior must be willing to *listen* to the subordinate's side of the story and perhaps to change the evaluation in light of the new information. The superior must also be skillful in communicating negative information to subordinates. The likelihood that negative information will be listened to and acted upon by subordinates depends largely on the extent to which such information is *specific* and *descriptive* of actual performance and the extent to which it is oriented toward *future* performance improvement, rather than toward assigning blame for past problems.[42] The value of appraisal techniques such as BARS, BOS, and MBO can be appreciated in this light, since they are designed to focus appraisals upon specific examples of job behavior or specific performance results. By focusing the discussion upon descriptions of specific problems with a view toward future improvement, a superior can vastly increase the likelihood of constructive dialogue and real performance improvement.[43]

Effective performance appraisal interviews also focus upon a subordinate's areas of strength. In discussing and praising these strengths it is equally desirable that the superior be specific and descriptive of actual events and behaviors that are the source of positive evaluations. Only in this way does the appraisal process help the subordinate to understand exactly which areas of performance are most valued by the organization and, therefore, which areas should continue to receive attention and emphasis.[44]

Keys to Effective Management

The organization depends upon the performance appraisal system for the information required for making critical personnel decisions regarding placement, promotion, development, and termination. The quality of these decisions is directly dependent upon the quality of the information upon which they are based. In light of this, the implications for managerial practice that follow from our discussion of performance appraisal are particularly important.

1 *Managers must recognize and take advantage of the multiple uses to which performance appraisals can be put.* Too often, managers tend to view the performance appraisal system *solely* as a means for judging and evaluating their subordinates. While judgment and evaluation are clearly central components of the performance appraisal process, they are not its only desired outcomes. The appraisal process can and should be a key component in an organization's program of employee development. By reinforcing strengths, identifying weaknesses, and serving as a vehicle for coaching and guidance from the supervisor, performance appraisal can contribute significantly to employee development.

2 *An organization's performance appraisal system should include measures of both activities and results.* Since an organization ultimately succeeds or fails on the basis of the results it achieves, it seems sensible to include measures of results in the evaluation of individual organization members. At the same time, it must be recognized that results are almost always influenced by a number of factors beyond the control of the individual. In light of this, an effective performance appraisal system should also include measures of the activities engaged in by the individual. These activities measures not only serve to supplement results measures but also provide the manager with the information on employee behavior that is essential for feedback, coaching, and development.

3 *Organizations must recognize the severe limitations and shortcomings of graphic rating scales.* Graphic rating scales have serious weaknesses as appraisal methods. They tend not to generate information that can be helpful to the subordinate in improving his or her performance. In addition, they are subject to a wide range of perceptual and judgmental biases that seriously hamper the validity of the appraisals they generate. Such appraisal methods are not to be recommended.

4 *Organizations should seriously consider the implementation of more modern appraisal techniques such as BARS, BOS, and MBO.* The more recently developed appraisal techniques presented in this chapter go a long way in overcoming many of the disadvantages associated with the more traditional appraisal methods. These modern appraisal techniques generate more accurate and valid evaluations and are more likely to provide a sound basis for improved employee motivation, career planning, and personal development.

5 *Managers need to recognize that the effectiveness of performance appraisals depends largely upon their own interpersonal skills in managing the appraisal process effectively.* Frequently, organizations and managers assume that the success of performance appraisals is determined solely by the quality of the design and the nature of the forms and paperwork that are used in the process. This assumption has been the downfall of many *potentially* successful appraisal systems. The value of performance appraisal to organizations and their members is critically determined by the skills and sensitivities of the managers who actually conduct appraisal interviews. Managers must recognize this factor and work hard at devel-

oping and improving the communication skills essential for managing the appraisal process effectively.

Review Questions

1 Discuss some of the alternative uses to which an organization may put its performance appraisal system.

2 How should the uses to be made of performance appraisal information influence the design of an appraisal system?

3 What is meant by the term *criterion?*

4 What are the advantages and disadvantages of using measures of activities versus measures of results as criteria in an appraisal system? Would you recommend using one or the other or both in an appraisal system?

5 Why are graphic rating scales so popular in performance appraisals?

6 Outline several of the common errors that arise in the use of rating scales for appraisals. How might some of these errors be overcome or eliminated?

7 What is a behaviorally anchored rating scale (BARS)? How is a BARS developed and what are its strengths and weaknesses?

8 What is the difference between a BARS and a BOS? What do you see as the primary strengths of the BOS approach to performance appraisal?

9 How can a management by objectives (MBO) program be employed for performance evaluation? In what types of situations would you recommend an MBO-based appraisal system?

10 Who should carry out performance evaluations? Defend and explain your recommendation.

11 How frequently should performance appraisals be conducted? Explain the reasons behind your recommendation.

12 Describe some of the conflicts inherent in an appraisal interview and discuss how these conflicts can be overcome.

13 What types of ethical issues do you feel are raised by the performance appraisal process?

Problems in Performance Evaluation

In a large electric power plant in Saskatoon, Saskatchewan, Canada, they have been having difficulty with their performance evaluation program, by which all operating employees and clerical employees are evaluated semiannually by their supervisors. The form which they have been using appears below. It has been in use for ten years. The form is scored as follows: excellent = 5, above average = 4, average = 3, below average = 2, and poor = 1. The scores for each question are centered in the right-hand column and are totaled for an overall evaluation score.

The procedure used has been as follows: each supervisor rates each employee on July 30 and January 30. The supervisor discusses the rating with the employee. The supervisor sends the rating to the personnel department. Each rating is placed in the employee's personnel file. If promotions come up, the cumulative ratings are considered at that time. The ratings are also supposed to be used as a check when raises are given.

The system was designed by the personnel manager who retired two years ago, Joanna Kyle. Her replacement was Eugene Meyer. Meyer is a graduate in commerce from the University of Alberta at Edmonton. He graduated 15 years ago. Since then, he's had a variety of experiences, mostly in utilities such as the power company. For about five of these years he did personnel work.

Meyer has been reviewing the evaluation system. Employees have a mixture of indifferent and negative feelings about it. An informal survey has shown that about 50 percent of the supervisors fill out the forms, giving about 3 minutes to each form, and send them to personnel without discussing them with the employees. Another 30 percent do a little better. They spend more time completing the forms but communicate about them only briefly and superficially with their employees. Only about 10 percent of the supervisors seriously try to do what was intended.

Meyer found out that the forms were rarely retrieved for promotion or pay raise analysis. Because of this, most supervisors may have felt the evaluation program was a useless ritual.

Where he had been previously employed, Meyer had seen performance evaluation as a much more useful experience, which included giving positive feedback to employees, improving future employee performance, developing employee capabilities, and providing data for promotion and compensation.

Meyer has not had much experience with

Figure 11-7   Performance evaluation form used at the electric power plant.

Performance Evaluation Form of Electric Power Plant

Performance Evaluation

Supervisors: When you are asked to do so by the personnel department, please complete this form on each of your employees. The supervisor who is responsible for 75 percent or more of an employee's work should complete this form on him or her. Please evaluate each facet of the employee's performance separately.

Quantity of work	Excellent	Above average	Average	Below average	Poor	Score
Quality of work	Poor	Below average	Average	Above average	Excellent	
Dependability at work	Excellent	Above average	Average	Below average	Poor	
Initiative at work	Poor	Below average	Average	Above average	Excellent	
Cooperativeness	Excellent	Above average	Average	Below average	Poor	
Getting along with coworkers	Poor	Below average	Average	Above average	Excellent	

Total _____

Supervisor's signature _____

Employee name _____

Employee number _____

design of performance evaluation systems. He feels he should seek advice on the topic.

Questions for Discussion

1   What are the primary strengths and weaknesses of the current evaluation system?

2   What specific changes in the system would you recommend to Meyer?

3   What problems would you anticipate having to overcome in implementing these changes?

Source: Glueck, W. F. (1978). *Cases and excercises in personnel* (rev. ed.). Dallas: BPI, pp. 56–57. Used by permission.

Notes

1   Locher, A. H., & Teel, K. S. (1977, May). Performance appraisal: A survey of current practices. *Personnel Journal.*

2   Dunnette, M. D. (1963). A note on *the* criterion. *Journal of Applied Psychology, 47,* 251–254.

3   Landy, F. J., Barnes-Farrell, J., & Cleveland, J. N. (1980). Perceived fairness and accuracy of performance evaluation: A follow-up. *Journal of Applied Psychology, 65,* 355–356.

4   Porter, L. W., Lawler, E. E., III, & Hackman, J. R. (1975). *Behavior in organizations.* New York: McGraw-Hill.

5   Tosi, H. L., Rizzo, J. R., & Carroll, S. J. (1970). Setting goals in management by objectives. *California Management Review, 12,* 70–78.

6   Peters, L. H., & O'Connor, E. J. (1980). Situational constraints and work outcomes: The influence of a frequently overlooked construct. *Academy of Management Review, 5,* 391–397.
Peters, L. H., O'Connor, E. J., & Rudolf, C. J. (1980). The behavioral and affective consequences of performance-relevant situational variables. *Organizational Behavior and Human Performance, 25,* 79–86.

7   Dipboye, R. L. (1985). Some neglected variables in research on discrimination in appraisals. *Academy of Management Review, 10,* 116–127.
Bazerman, M. H., Beekun, R. I., & Schoorman, F. D. (1982). Performance evaluation in a dynamic context: A laboratory study of the impact of a prior commitment to the ratee. *Journal of Applied Psychology, 67,* 873–876.
Mobley, W. H. (1982). Supervisor and employee race and sex effects on performance appraisals: A field study of adverse impact and generalizability. *Academy of Management Journal, 25,* 598–606.
Pulakos, E. D., & Wexley, K. N. (1983). The relationship among perceptual similarity, sex, and performance ratings in manager-subordinate dyads. *Academy of Management Journal, 26,* 129–139.

8   Cooper, W. H. (1981). Ubiquitous halo. *Psychological Bulletin, 90,* 218–244.
Nathan, B. R., & Lord, R. G. (1983). Cognitive categorization and dimensional schemata: A process approach to the study of halo in performance ratings. *Journal of Applied Psychology, 68,* 102–114.

9   Harvey, R. H. (1982). The future of partial correlation as a means to reduce halo in performance ratings. *Journal of Applied Psychology, 67,* 171–176.

Hulin, C. L. (1982). Some reflections on general performance dimensions and halo rating error. *Journal of Applied Psychology, 67,* 165–170.

Landy, F. J., Vance, R. J., & Barnes-Farrell, J. L. (1982). Statistical control of halo: A response. *Journal of Applied Psychology, 67,* 177–180.

Landy, F. J., Vance, R. J., Barnes-Farrell, J. L., & Steele, J. W. (1980). Statistical control of halo error in performance ratings. *Journal of Applied Psychology, 65,* 501–506.

Murphy, K. R. (1982). Difficulties in the statistical control of halo. *Journal of Applied Psychology, 67,* 161–164.

10   Heneman, R. L., & Wexley, K. N. (1983). The effects of time delay in rating and amount of information observed on performance rating accuracy. *Academy of Management Journal, 26,* 677–686.

11   Ivancevich, J. M. (1983). Contrast effects in performance evaluation and reward practices. *Academy of Management Journal, 26,* 465–476.

Mitchell, T. R., & Liden, R. C. (1982). The effects of the social context on performance evaluations. *Organizational Behavior and Human Performance, 29,* 241–256.

12   Kelley, H. H. (1973). The processes of causal attribution. *American Psychologist, 28,* 107–128.

13   Feldman, J. M. (1981). Beyond attribution theory: Cognitive processes in performance appraisal. *Journal of Applied Psychology, 66,* 127–148.

Knowlton, W. A., Jr., & Mitchell, T. R. (1980). Effects of causal attributions on a supervisor's evaluation of subordinate performance. *Journal of Applied Psychology, 65,* 459–466.

Ross, L. (1977). The intuitive psychologist and his shortcomings: Distortions in the attribution process. In L. Berkowitz (Ed.), *Advances in experimental social psychology* (Vol. 10). New York: Academic Press.

14   Fay, C. H., & Latham, G. P. (1982). The effects of training and rating scales on rating errors. *Personnel Psychology, 35,* 105–116.

Latham, G. P., & Wexley, K. N. (1981). *Improving productivity through performance appraisal.* Reading, MA: Addison-Wesley.

McIntyre, R. M., Smith, D. E., & Hassett, C. E. (1984). Accuracy of performance ratings as affected by rater training and perceived purpose of rating. *Journal of Applied Psychology, 69,* 147–156.

15   Bernardin, H. J., & Walter, C. S. (1977). The effects of rater training and diary keeping on psychometric error in ratings. *Journal of Applied Psychology, 62,* 64–69.

Murphy, K. R., Garcia, M., Kerkar, S., Martin, C., & Balzer, W. K. (1982). Relationship between observational accuracy and accuracy in evaluating performance. *Journal of Applied Psychology, 67,* 320–325.

16   Burnaska, R. G., & Hollman, T. D. (1974). An empirical comparison of the relative effects of rater response bias on three rating scale formats. *Journal of Applied Psychology, 59,* 307–312.

17   Latham, G. P., Wexley, K. N., & Pursell, E. D. (1975). Training managers to minimize rating errors in the observation of behavior. *Journal of Applied Psychology, 60,* 550–555.
    Pulakos, E. D. (1984). A comparison of rater training programs: Error training and accuracy training. *Journal of Applied Psychology, 69,* 581–588.
    Zedeck, S., & Cascio, W. F. (1982). Performance appraisal decisions as a function of rater training and purpose of the appraisal. *Journal of Applied Psychology, 67,* 752–758.

18   Borman, W. C. (1979). Format and training effects on rating accuracy and rater errors. *Journal of Applied Psychology, 64,* 410–421.

19   Bernardin, H. J., & Buckley, M. R. (1979). A consideration of strategies in rater training. Unpublished manuscript.
    Bernardin, H. J., & Pence, E. G. (1980). The effects of rater training: Creating new response sets and decreasing accuracy. *Journal of Applied Psychology, 65,* 60–66.

20   Smith, P. C., & Kendall, L. M. (1963). Retranslation of expectations: An approach to the construction of unambiguous anchors for rating scales. *Journal of Applied Psychology, 47,* 149–155.

21   Hom, P. W., DeNisi, A. S., Kinicki, A. J., & Bannister, B. D. (1982). Effectiveness of performance feedback from behaviorally anchored rating scales. *Journal of Applied Psychology, 67,* 568–576.

22   Borman (1979), *loc. cit.*

23   Jacobs, R., Kafry, D., & Zedeck, S. (1980). Expectations of behaviorally anchored rating scales. *Personnel Psychology, 33,* 595–640.
    Kingstrom, P. O., & Bass, A. R. (1981). A critical analysis of studies comparing behaviorally anchored rating scales (BARS) and other rating formats. *Personnel Psychology, 34,* 263–289.

24   Bernardin, H. J., & Smith, P. C. (1981). A clarification of some issues regarding the development and use of behaviorally anchored rating scales (BARS). *Journal of Applied Psychology, 66,* 458–463.
    Landy, F. J., & Farr, J. L. (1980). A process model of performance ratings. *Psychological Bulletin, 87,* 72–108.

25   Ivancevich, J. M. (1980). A longitudinal study of behavioral expectation scales: Attitudes and performance. *Journal of Applied Psychology, 65,* 139–146.

26   Latham, G. P., & Wexley, K. N. (1977). Behavioral observation scales for performance appraisal purposes. *Personnel Psychology, 30,* 255–268.

Latham, G. P., Fay, C. H., & Saari, L. M. (1979). The development of behavioral observation scales for appraising the performance of foremen. *Personnel Psychology, 32,* 299–311.

27   Latham & Wexley (1981), *loc. cit.*

28   Bernardin, H. J. (1977). Behavioral expectation scales vs. summated ratings: A fairer comparison. *Journal of Applied Psychology, 62,* 422–427.

Bernardin, H. J., Alvares, K. M., & Cranny, C. J. (1976). A recomparison of behavioral expectation scales to summated scales. *Journal of Applied Psychology, 61,* 564–570.

29   Bernardin, H. J., & Kane, J. S. (1980). A second look at behavioral observation scales. *Personnel Psychology, 33,* 809–814.

Latham, G. P., Saari, L. M., & Fay, C. H. (1980). BOS, BES, and baloney: Raising Kane with Bernardin. *Personnel Psychology, 33,* 815–821.

Murphy, K. R., Martin, C., & Garcia, M. (1982). Do behavioral observation scales measure observation? *Journal of Applied Psychology, 67,* 562–567.

Wexley, K. N., & Pulakos, E. D. (1982). Sex effects on performance ratings in manager-subordinate dyads: A field study. *Journal of Applied Psychology, 67,* 433–439.

30   Tosi, H. L., Rizzo, J. R., & Carroll, S. J. (1970). Setting goals in management by objectives. *California Management Review, 12,* 70–78.

Jamieson, B. D. (1973). Behavioral problems with management by objectives. *Academy of Management Journal, 16,* 496–505.

31   Bernardin, H. J., & Beatty, R. W. (1984). *Performance appraisal.* Boston, MA: Kent.

Carroll, S. J., & Schneier, C. E. (1982). *Performance appraisal and review systems.* Glenview, IL: Scott, Foresman.

32   References to the frequency of use of various appraisal techniques are based upon a large national survey conducted by the Bureau of National Affairs entitled "Employee performance: Evaluation and control" (1975, February). *Personnel Policies Forum no. 108.*

33   Cummings, L. L., & Schwab, D. P. (1973). *Performance in organizations.* Glenview, IL: Scott, Foresman.

34   Glueck, W. F. (1982). *Personnel: A diagnostic approach* (3rd ed.). Plano, TX: Business Publications, Inc.

35   Lewin, A., & Zwany, A. (1976). Peer nominations: A model, literature critique, and a paradigm for research. *Personnel Research, 29,* 423–447.

36 Cederblom, D., & Lounsbury, J. W. (1980). An investigation of user acceptance of peer evaluations. *Personnel Psychology, 33,* 567–579.

DeNisi, A. S., Randolph, W. A., & Blencoe, A. G. (1983). Potential problems with peer ratings. *Academy of Management Journal, 26,* 457–464.

Imada, A. S. (1982). Social interaction, observation, and stereotypes as determinants of differentiation in peer ratings. *Organizational Behavior and Human Performance, 29,* 397–415.

Love, K. G. (1981). Comparison of peer assessment methods: Reliability, validity, friendship bias, and user reaction. *Journal of Applied Psychology, 66,* 451–457.

37 Ghorpade, J., & Lackritz, J. R. (1981). Influences behind neutral responses in subordinate ratings of supervisors. *Personnel Psychology, 34,* 511–522.

Wexley, K. N., & Pulakos, E. D. (1983). The effects of perceptual congruence and sex on subordinates' performance appraisals of their managers. *Academy of Management Journal, 26,* 666–676.

38 Levine, E. L. (1980). Introductory remarks for the symposium "Organizational Applications of Self-Appraisal and Self-Assessment: Another Look." *Personnel Psychology, 33,* 259–262.

Levine, E. L., Flory, A., III, & Ash, R. A. (1977). Self-assessment in personnel selection. *Journal of Applied Psychology, 62,* 428–435.

39 Cook, D. (1968). The impact on managers of frequency of feedback. *Academy of Management Journal, 2,* 263–277.

40 Porter, Lawler, & Hackman (1975), *loc. cit.*

41 Kay, E., Meyer, H., & French, J. R. P. (1965). Effects of threat in a performance appraisal interview. *Journal of Applied Psychology, 49,* 311–317.

42 Gibb, J. Defensive communication. (1961). *Journal of Communication, 3,* 141–148.

43 Ashford, S. J., & Cummings, L. L. (1983). Feedback as an individual resource: Personal strategies of creating information. *Organizational Behavior and Human Performance, 32,* 370–398.

Cederblom, D. (1982). The performance appraisal interview: A review, implications, and suggestions. *Academy of Management Review, 7,* 219–227.

Ivancevich, J. M. (1982). Subordinates' reactions to performance appraisal interviews: A test of feedback and goal-setting techniques. *Journal of Applied Psychology, 67,* 581–587.

Larson, J. R., Jr. (1984). The performance feedback process: A preliminary model. *Organizational Behavior and Human Performance, 33,* 42–76.

44   Dipboye, R. L., & dePontbriand, R. (1981). Correlates of employee reactions to performance appraisals and appraisal systems. *Journal of Applied Psychology, 66,* 248–251.

Chapter 12

Reward Systems

CHAPTER OUTLINE

Types and Characteristics of Rewards

Functions of Reward Systems

Pay and Performance

Comparable Worth

Innovative Reward Systems

Keys to Effective Management

Review Questions

*T*he bill for employee wages, salaries, and benefits is typically the largest single cost faced by an organization, often absorbing half or more of the organization's total revenues. Given this fact, it is crucial that the money paid to organization members be administered in a fashion that will encourage the types of performance required for organizational success. The organization must ensure that its reward systems are designed to motivate and maintain effective employee performance throughout the organization. In this chapter we deal with the practical issues involved in designing organizational reward systems in such a way that the organization's monetary investment in its members yields maximum benefits in terms of employee motivation and performance.

The chapter begins by outlining the various types of rewards at the disposal of the organization and the key characteristics of each type of reward. We then go on to examine the different functions and purposes that can be fulfilled by reward systems in organizations. The chapter next focuses in detail on pay and examines alternative methods available for linking pay to performance. Finally, we discuss some of the recent innovations in reward system design and the experiences of organizations that have been experimenting with these innovative approaches.

Types and Characteristics of Rewards

The range of potential rewards that can be employed in organizations is extremely broad. In practice, however, organizations tend to make use of a relatively small number of rewards. Money is the most frequently used reward in organizations and is administered in a variety of forms and on a variety of bases, such as salaries, bonuses, merit increases, and profit-sharing plans. However, money is by no means the only reward that can be used to influence the behavior and performance of organization members. Included in the list of available rewards are promotions, perquisites such as expense accounts, cars, and luxurious offices, benefits such as insurance, pensions, and stock options. special awards and certificates, and so on.[1]

An important point to note is that the individual employee is dependent upon the pay and reward policies of the organization, as well as on the perceptions and judgments of his or her boss, as manifested in performance appraisals, in striving to obtain such organizational rewards. This dependence upon external sources for the administration of rewards, combined with the fact that the majority of extrinsic rewards carry some considerable real cost to the organization, has two important implications for the design of reward systems. First, the organization must attempt to ensure that the costly rewards it is offering are in fact highly valued (and hence experienced as rewarding) by members of the organization. Second, great care must be taken to ensure that the administration of rewards to organization members is linked to effective job performance.

Characteristics of Rewards

Rewards (e.g., pay, promotions, fringe benefits) differ in the extent to which they possess various desirable characteristics from the organization's point of view.[2] An understanding of the characteristics of rewards will put us in a position to analyze systematically the strengths and weaknesses of each type of reward available to the organization.

1 *Importance.*   A reward cannot influence what people do or how they feel if it is not important to them. Given the vast differences that exist among people, it is obviously impossible to find any reward that will be important to everyone in the organization. However, the challenge in designing reward systems is to find rewards that will appeal to as broad a range of employees as possible and also to employ a variety of different rewards in order to ensure that rewards will be available that are important to all the different types of people in the organization.

2 *Flexibility of amount.*   If rewards are to be tailored to the unique characteristics of individual members and are also to be provided contingent upon certain levels of performance, then the rewards themselves must be

flexible. Flexibility of rewards is a necessary prerequisite to the design of individualized reward systems tied to effective job performance.

3 *Frequency.*   The more frequently that a reward can be administered, the greater its potential usefulness as a means of influencing employee performance. Thus, the most desirable rewards are those that can be given frequently without losing their importance.

4 *Visibility.*   Rewards must be highly visible if employees are to perceive a relationship between performance and rewards. Visible rewards have the additional advantage of satisfying employees' needs for recognition and esteem.

5 *Low cost.*   Reward systems obviously cannot be designed without consideration being given to the cost of the rewards involved. Clearly, the lower the cost the more desirable the reward from the organization's viewpoint. High-cost rewards cannot be administered as frequently as low-cost rewards, and by the very nature of the costs involved they detract from organizational efficiency and effectiveness.

Comparison of Rewards

Table 12-1 evaluates some of the most commonly employed organizational rewards in light of these five characteristics of effective rewards. Although the list of rewards contained in Table 12-1 is by no means exhaustive, it does cover the rewards in most frequent and widespread use in organizations.

Pay Raises

The use of pay raises as rewards in organizations is very nearly universal. As Table 12-1 makes clear, pay raises have many desirable characteristics as organizational rewards. They tend to be a highly important reward to most orga-

TABLE   12-1

Characteristics of Commonly Used Rewards

	Average importance	*Flexibility in amount*	*Visibility*	*Frequency*	*Dollar cost*
Pay raises	High	High	Moderate	Moderate	High
Promotions	High	Low	High	Low	High
Benefits	Moderate	Moderate	Moderate	Low	Moderate
Status symbols	Moderate	High	High	Low	Moderate
Special awards and certificates	Low	High	High	Low	Low

nization members, they permit a great deal of flexibility in administration, and they can be provided with almost any desired degree of frequency. Pay raises have the potential to be a highly visible reward as well, although pay secrecy policies in many organizations can inhibit this potential advantage. The sole disadvantage of pay is its high dollar cost to the organization.

Promotions

Promotions are a form of organizational reward whose average level of importance to individuals tends to be quite high. Promotions also have the advantage of being highly visible to all members of the organization. Unfortunately, promotions suffer from a number of disadvantages as well. By their very nature, promotions tend to occur relatively infrequently, given a limited number of levels in the organizational hierarchy. Promotions also have high dollar costs associated with the higher salaries and benefits that generally accompany more senior positions.

Benefits

Organizations commonly have one benefit package for hourly employees, another for salaried personnel, and a third for top-level management. A package usually consists of some combination of benefits, including, for example, a pension plan, life, health, and dental insurance plans, stock option purchase plans, and disability income plans. The main strength of benefits as rewards is that at least some of the benefits included in such packages are usually fairly important to most organization members. Benefit plans have the potential to be moderately flexible and visible, though organizations have only recently begun to recognize the potential for increasing the flexibility and visibility of their benefits packages. The primary weaknesses of benefits as rewards have to do with the low frequency with which benefits tend to be administered and with their costs. Also, employees tend to underestimate their costs and hence their value as rewards.

Status Symbols

Most organizations use various types of status symbols as rewards. A larger office, a personal secretary, a company car, a reserved parking spot, and use of the executive dining room are all visible rewards that can be administered to individuals on a flexible basis. The importance of these rewards to individuals will naturally vary, but many are of at least moderate importance to many people. Status symbols tend to be moderately costly to the organization and can generally only be provided with low frequency.

Special Awards and Certificates

Organizations frequently provide their members with small awards or certificates as a form of recognition for long service or outstanding performance. The primary advantages of such rewards are that they are generally of low cost, that they can be provided with a high degree of flexibility, and that they are highly visible. Unfortunately, such rewards can usually be provided with only low frequency and often are not highly important to their recipients.

Functions of Reward Systems

An organization's reward systems can be designed to accomplish a variety of purposes. There are three broad classes of individual behavior that a reward system may be designed to influence: organizational membership, regularity of attendance, and job performance.

Encouraging Membership

Organizations typically provide individuals with a wide variety of rewards simply on the basis of their membership in the organization. Provision of an adequate level of rewards for organizational membership is important for two reasons. First, it can help the organization to attract and hire new members who are competent and highly motivated. Rewards that are perceived by prospective members to be inadequate or inequitable will make it difficult for the organization to attract the types of people necessary for success. Second, reward systems can help to retain competent organization members. A large body of research discussed in Chapter 4 indicates that people who are dissatisfied with their jobs and dissatisfied with the rewards they are receiving from their jobs are more likely to quit.[3]

While turnover is not inherently harmful to an organization (as when marginal or incompetent employees leave and create opportunities to bring in new blood), it is harmful when the individuals leaving are highly competent and valued organization members.[4] Thus, the organization must ensure that its most valuable members perceive the reward system to be both internally equitable (so that the valuable members feel that they are being fairly treated in light of their contributions) and externally equitable (so that valuable members are not attracted to another organization offering a higher level of rewards for their services).

Rewarding Attendance

Absenteeism and tardiness are clearly costly to an organization. If an individual is absent from work and no one with adequate training and experience is available to step into the person's position, then either the person's work does not get done or it gets done by someone who lacks the necessary skill and expertise to perform the job well. Both situations are undesirable and potentially costly to the organization. On the other hand, if a person is absent and someone with adequate training and experience is immediately available to fill in, this implies that the organization is overstaffed, a situation that is extremely inefficient and costly to the organization in the long run. However you look at it, absenteeism is undesirable and expensive. As discussed in Chapter 4, a great deal of research has shown that levels of satisfaction and absenteeism are inversely related to one another.[5] Reward systems reduce absenteeism to the extent that they create feelings of satisfaction among organization members and provide rewards to members for regular attendance.

Improving Performance

Perhaps the most obvious function of a reward system is to encourage and reward effective performance by organization members. Rewards can facilitate effective performance when people perceive that such performance actually results in obtaining valued rewards within a reasonable period of time.[6] However, successfully linking performance and rewards is extremely difficult to accomplish in practice. Tying rewards to performance requires a good measure of performance, the ability to identify which rewards are important to particular individuals, and the ability to control the amount of these rewards that an individual receives. None of these things are easy to accomplish in most organizational settings.[7]

Table 12-2 indicates the ways in which various types of organizational rewards can fulfill each of the major functions discussed in this section. As the table indicates, pay has the greatest capacity to fulfill all of the various functions that rewards can be designed to accomplish. Promotions may encourage people to stay with the organization and to perform well, but are unlikely to directly influence new membership or regular attendance. Benefits may have an impact upon decisions to join and to stay with the organization, but have little capacity to influence attendance or performance. Status symbols such as cars, large offices, and so on can influence decisions to join and to stay with the organization, but do little in terms of rewarding attendance or improving performance. Finally, while special awards may have some impact upon attendance and perfomance, their ability to encourage membership in the organization is quite limited. The ability of pay to fulfill so many different functions, combined with its strong potential impact upon performance, makes the issue of pay and performance deserving of special attention.

TABLE   12-2

Ability of Alternative Types of Rewards to Fulfill the Different Functions of Reward Systems

| | Functions | | | |
| | Encouraging Membership | | | |
Types of rewards	*Joining*	*Staying*	*Rewarding attendance*	*Improving performance*
Pay	Strong	Strong	Strong	Strong
Promotions	Weak	Strong	Weak	Moderate
Benefits	Strong	Strong	Weak	Weak
Status symbols	Moderate	Moderate	Weak	Weak
Special awards	Weak	Weak	Moderate	Moderate

Pay and Performance

Most organizations claim that they try to link pay and performance for their members. However, a much smaller number of organizations are successful in achieving this objective. In this section we will discuss factors that make this desirable goal so difficult to attain.

Methods of Pay Administration

A tremendous variety of alternative techniques is available for determining how much pay a person performing a particular job should receive. We'll briefly outline the four most common approaches used by organizations in deciding exactly how much pay their members should receive.

Job Evaluation

Methods of pay administration based on job evaluations relate the amount of pay that a person receives to the demands and requirements of the person's job. The more complex the job and the more demands the job puts upon the incumbent, the higher the level of pay provided to the person performing the job. Many organizations employ the services of consulting firms to conduct these job evaluations. Probably the best-known firm conducting such work is Hay Associates, whose consultants evaluate jobs in terms of "Hay points." Points are assigned to a job based upon the number of subordinates supervised, the size of budget responsibility, and the difficulty of decisions made, among other factors. Pay levels are then linked to the number of points assigned to the job. Job evaluation is an extremely widely used method of determining wage and salary levels in organizations, and is used by many companies, including Maremont and American Hospital Supply.

Skill Evaluation

A much newer and less widely used technique of pay administration ties the amount of pay received to what the individual is *capable* of doing rather than to what the person's job *requires* him or her to do. The level of pay that an individual receives is based upon the job-related skills that the person has developed and demonstrated, regardless of the particular skills required by the person's current job. Skill-based pay systems are extremely new and have been implemented primarily in plants recently opened by organizations such as Gaines Foods, Procter & Gamble, and Shell Oil.

Seniority

Some organizations link pay to length of service with the organization, although it is rare that seniority serves as the only or even the primary basis of pay administration. Linking pay to seniority serves to encourage and reward continued membership in the organization, but does nothing to motivate or reinforce productivity and performance.

Performance

Almost all organizations would claim that the amount of pay received by their salaried personnel is related to the level of performance of the individuals involved. While it is true that most organizations attempt to tie individuals' pay to performance, it is much less frequently the case that organizations succeed in accomplishing this worthwhile goal.[8] Some of the difficulties involved in linking rewards to performance have been outlined earlier in this chapter. Many of the problems are related to determining exactly what should be measured in order to obtain an accurate indication of the quality and quantity of an individual's contribution to the effectiveness of the organization. In the next section we'll examine in more detail some of the issues and alternatives involved in relating pay to performance.

The preceding methods of pay administration are not necessarily mutually exclusive. An organization might use one method for nonsalaried personnel at lower levels and a different method for higher-level salaried personnel. In addition, an organization might use several of the methods for determining the salary of organization members. For example, it is extremely common for organizations to use job evaluation as the basis for setting precise wage rates for nonsalaried jobs. At the same time, it is equally common for organizations to use job evaluations for more senior salaried positions, not to set precise salary levels, but rather to define a range within which a person performing the job should be paid. The precise level of pay within the range for a given person is then frequently determined by a combination of performance evaluation and seniority. The higher the level of performance and the longer the person has occupied the position, the more the person's salary would tend toward the high end of the range.

Pay for Performance

As pointed out previously, most organizations make some attempt to relate pay to performance. The precise methods used for linking pay and performance vary widely from one organization to another. Three primary issues can help draw some distinction among the tremendous variety of pay-for-performance schemes that exist.

Whose Performance to Measure

The first issue has to do with whose performance is to be measured. It is possible to design plans to link an individual's pay to his or her own personal performance, to the performance of the work group of which he or she is a member, or to the performance of the total organization.

What Method of Performance Measurement to Use

The second primary issue concerns the method or methods used for measuring performance. In general, performance measurement techniques can be seen as varying on a continuum from the extremely objective to the extremely subjective. Performance criteria such as profit, costs, and sales are quite objective and relatively straightforward to measure. At the other extreme are such highly subjective measures as performance ratings of an individual carried out by his or her boss or work peers.

What Types of Monetary Rewards to Employ

The third major issue has to do with the types of monetary rewards offered by the plan. These generally fall into the two categories of salary increments and cash bonuses. Salary increments have the advantage of being cumulative from year to year, while cash bonuses provide an effective performer with a large lump sum of cash at a single time.

Evaluating Pay-for-Performance Plans

By classifying pay-for-performance plans on the basis of whose performance is measured (individual, group, organization), the type of performance measure used (productivity, cost effectiveness, superior's rating), and type of reward offered (salary, cash bonus), we come up with a total of eighteen different types of pay-for-performance plans. These different alternatives are summarized in Table 12-3 (the table contains only seventeen alternatives since it is not feasible for the effectiveness of a total organization to be rated by a superior and hence this alternative is excluded).

In addition to summarizing the available alternatives, Table 12-3 contains ratings of the effectiveness of each type of plan on a set of four critical dimensions. The ratings vary from 1 to 5; the higher the rating, the stronger the plan is on that dimension, while the lower the rating, the weaker the plan is on that dimension. The four dimensions included in the table are as follows.

1 The first dimension is the extent to which the plan succeeds in creating the perception among members of the organization that pay is in fact tied to their own level of performance. As was previously pointed out, this perception of a direct link between performance and pay is essential if the pay system is to serve to motivate effective performance.

2 The second dimension along which the alternatives are assessed is the extent to which each system produces negative side effects. Although pay-for-performance plans are designed to motivate and encourage effective performance, they sometimes create unintended negative side effects, such as social ostracism, defensive behavior, and a tendency to supply false data about performance. Hence, a low rating on this dimension is desirable.

3 The third dimension is the extent to which the plan encourages cooperative behavior among organization members. The relevance of this dimension in designing a pay-for-performance plan will obviously depend upon the extent to which cooperative behavior among individuals and groups is essential for organizational success.

4 Finally, performance-pay systems can be evaluated with regard to the extent to which they tend to be accepted by organization members. No plan can hope to have an impact upon motivation and performance if it is not accepted by the people to whom it is to be applied.

The ratings reveal a number of patterns regarding the various types of plans. Looking first at the extent to which the plans create the perception that

TABLE   12-3

Ratings of Various Pay Incentive Plans*

		Tie pay to performance	Produce negative side effects	Encourage cooperation	Employee acceptance
Salary reward:					
Individual Plan	Productivity	4	1	1	4
	Cost effectiveness	3	1	1	4
	Superiors' ratings	3	1	1	3
Group	Productivity	3	1	2	4
	Cost effectiveness	3	1	2	4
	Superiors' ratings	2	1	2	3
Organization-wide	Productivity	2	1	3	4
	Cost effectiveness	2	1	2	4
Bonus:					
Individual plan	Productivity	5	3	1	2
	Cost effectiveness	4	2	1	2
	Superiors' ratings	4	2	1	2
Group	Productivity	4	1	3	3
	Cost effectiveness	3	1	3	3
	Superiors' ratings	3	1	3	3
Organization-wide	Productivity	3	1	3	4
	Cost effectiveness	3	1	3	4
	Profit	2	1	3	3

*Ratings range from a low of 1 to a high of 5.

Source: Adapted from Lawler, E. E., III (1977), Reward systems. In J. R. Hackman & J. L. Suttle (Eds.), *Improving life at work.* Glenview, IL: Scott, Foresman. Copyright © 1977. Reprinted by permission.

pay and performance are linked, we notice the following: (1) individual plans rate more highly than group plans, which in turn rate more highly than organization–wide plans; (2) bonus plans rate more highly than salary plans; and (3) plans based on objective measures rate more highly than those employing subjective measures of performance. The perception that pay is tied to performance is most strongly reinforced when an organization member receives a cash bonus based upon objective measures of his or her personal performance.

Turning to the issue of negative side effects, we see that, in general, most of the plans fare quite well in this regard in that they have a low tendency to generate such effects. The notable exceptions are individually based bonus plans. The problem with such plans lies in their potential to create situations in which high performers may be rejected or ostracized by their coworkers, in which people may be encouraged to report false performance data, or in which employees may band together to restrict production in an attempt to force management to lower the performance standards required to obtain the bonus.

With regard to the encouragement of cooperation, the consistent pattern is that group and organization incentive plans tend to encourage cooperation, while individually based plans tend to undermine it. When pay is based upon the performance of the work group or of the total organization, people tend to perceive that they stand to gain personally from improved performance of their coworkers. This perception in turn leads to a greater willingness to be cooperative and helpful. When pay is based on individual performance, on the other hand, such cooperation is not rewarded and hence not facilitated.[9] The Scanlon Plan, described in Box 12-1, is a successful example of a bonus plan based upon measures of work group and organizational performance.

BOX 12-1

The Scanlon Plan

The Scanlon Plan, named for its originator, Joseph Scanlon, involves a combination of group and organization level pay incentives, an employee suggestion system, and a participative approach to assessing and evaluating suggestions that are made. Production committees are set up for each department in the organization. These committees consist of the supervisor or senior manager in the department and representatives of the employees, who may either be elected or appointed by the union. These production committees screen suggestions for productivity improvement from both employees and managers. Experience with this system indicates that the rate of suggestions is double that of normal suggestion plans and that approximately 80 percent of the suggestions made are usable. One organization, the Atwood Vacuum Machine Company, received over 25,000 suggestions from its 2,000 employees during the first 14 years the Scanlon Plan was in operation.

The cost savings generated by suggestions that are accepted are paid to everyone in the department originating the suggestion. This helps encourage suggestions from everyone involved. In addition, under the Scanlon Plan gains resulting from productivity improvements are paid in the form of a monthly bonus to all employees. Everyone receives a share in proportion to his or her wage or salary level.

Overall, the record of the Scanlon Plan is quite positive, as the examples in Table 12-4 make clear. The plan has been implemented in over 100 small- to medium-sized organizations, and by at least one large organization (Midland Ross). The most frequently cited benefits associated with the plan are greater organizational efficiency, increased participation in decision making, a greater willingness on the part of employees to accept change, and an improved climate of union-management relations.[10]

TABLE   12-4

Three Companies Using Scanlon Plans

		Atwood Vacuum Machine Co.		*Parker Pen Co.*	*Pfaudler Co.*
Nature of the organization	Number of employees	2,000		1,000	750
	Number of plants	6		1	1
	Union affiliation	3 (independent)		2 (AFL-CIO)	2 (AFL-CIO)
	Product	Automotive hardware		Writing instruments	Project engineering, glassteel, stainless steel, and food-filling equipment
	Type of production	High volume; competitive		High-volume consumer item	Custom and standard fabricating
Results	Annual bonuses as percent of basic salary	High	20%	20%	17.5%
		Low	5%	5.5%	3%
	Percent of months in which bonus paid		87%	85%	88%
	Highest monthly bonus paid		26%	30%	22%
	Correlation of bonuses paid and division profits		High	High	High

Source: Adapted from Lesieur, F. G., & Puckett, E. S. (1969). The Scanlon Plan has proved itself. *Harvard Business Review, 47,* 109–119. Copyright © 1969 by the President and Fellows of Harvard College; all rights reserved.

Finally, regarding employee acceptance, the ratings indicate that most pay incentive plans can achieve a moderate degree of employee acceptance. The primary exceptions are individually based bonus plans, which generally meet with only a low degree of acceptance because of their tendency to induce competitiveness among individuals and the difficulties involved in administering such plans fairly. These problems are especially severe in the case of managerial jobs because of the difficulty in obtaining accurate and objective measures of managerial performance. There is also a tendency for acceptance of salary plans to be somewhat higher than acceptance of bonus plans, a result that is not surprising since salary increases are cumulative from year to year, while bonuses are not.

Many organizations have been taking steps over the past few years to tighten the links between performance and merit pay. The result is a widening in the ranges of merit increases, with high performers receiving considerable increases and poor performers receiving little or no improvement in their pay. *Business Week* reports that Digital Equipment Corporation's merit increases range from zero to thirty percent, those at Westinghouse vary from zero to

BOX 12-2

Comparable Worth Controversies

"Comparable worth" is becoming an important new rallying cry for several major unions that represent a lot of women or want to represent more.

Labor groups are fighting to get women equal pay for jobs comparable but not necessarily identical to men's in importance, skill, responsibility, and working conditions. The unions are demanding steps to help close the wide gap in wages between historically "women's" and "men's" jobs.

Nurses and city workers in San Jose, California, school secretaries in Anoka, Minnesota, and clerical workers in Allegheny County, Pennsylvania, have engaged in strikes over "pay equity," another name for the concept. About a dozen states and two cities have begun or completed job evaluation studies of their civil service systems, as a result of either legislation or labor negotiations. Other states and localities are considering similar moves.

Organized labor's efforts, concentrated largely in the public sector so far, could have a costly spillover effect on private businesses. Comparable worth "is going to be the compensation issue for the next decade," says Robert Brueckner, administrator of San Jose Hospital, one of four private hospitals struck by 1,500 nurses seeking large pay-equity raises. "I'm sure it will be the issue around which organizing efforts are made and around which strikes occur in existing bargaining units," he says.

Government figures show that a secretary, typically a woman, earns a median of $230 a week, only $11 more than the median wages of a janitor, usually a man. A National Academy of Sciences study issued last fall attributed less than half of the 40 percent difference in men's and women's average earnings to men's greater skills and experience.

nineteen percent, and Xerox's go from zero to thirteen percent. Merit increases are also being given more frequently to outstanding performers and less often to poor performers. High performers at Citicorp may receive merit increases as often as three or four times a year, while at Pullman-Kellogg poor performers may wait up to eighteen months for a merit increase.[11]

Comparable Worth

The issue of *comparable worth* in the determination of wages and salaries has received a great deal of attention recently.[12] The basic issue involved has to do with the notion of "equal pay for work of equal value." Many have charged that jobs and occupations typically filled by women receive lower levels of pay than comparable jobs and occupations filled primarily by men. It has been

BOX 12-2 (*Continued*)

A Supreme Court decision also is fueling union activity over comparable worth. In June 1981, the court held that women could use the controversial theory to bring sex bias suits under federal civil rights law, even if the disputes didn't involve equal jobs. Since the ruling, the American Federation of State, County, and Municipal Employees (AFSCME) has filed suit for sex bias charges against San Jose, Los Angeles, and the states of Connecticut, Hawaii, Washington, and Wisconsin. About 40 percent of its 986,000 members are women. The big public-employees union plans additional legal action, and "I expect others will do so within the next couple of months," predicts Winn Newman, AFSCME's special counsel.

One AFSCME local, representing 2,000 San Jose city workers, staged the biggest, most visible strike so far over comparable worth just weeks after the Supreme Court decision. Employees walked out for 9 days in July 1981, contending city officials had refused to correct pay differences uncovered by a $500,000 city job evaluation study. The study found predominantly women's jobs averaged 15 percent less pay than predominantly men's jobs of comparable value.

The $4.5 million settlement gave all workers a 15.5 percent general wage increase over 2 years. But about 780 of them, including many librarians and accounting clerks, won raises totaling up to 30 percent because they received a "pay equity" bonus.

Source: Big fight looms over gaps in pay for similar "male," "female" jobs. (1982, September 16). *Wall Street Journal,* p. 4.

charged that even when women are performing work that is equally as demanding and equally as difficult as that performed by men, they are paid less and that this constitutes discriminatory treatment.[13]

The comparable worth controversy does not focus on the issue of whether men and women should be paid the same amount for performing *exactly the same job.* There is little if any dispute that they should, and in fact it is illegal not to do so under current laws in both the U.S. and Canada. Instead, the argument is that men and women should be paid equally for performing jobs of "comparable worth" to their organizations. The position of supporters of the comparable worth viewpoint is that even when women are performing work that is equally as valuable to their organizations as that done by men, they tend not to receive pay equal to that of men.

The concept of equal pay for work of equal value is one that has a good deal of common sense appeal. If we believe that people should be paid in relation to their contribution and worth to their organization, then certainly people making equal contributions should receive equal pay regardless of their sex (or any other factor, for that matter). The problems and controversy center around how to go about implementing the concept of comparable worth.[14] In order to ensure that people are receiving equal pay for work of equal value we need some method of determining the value of a person's work to the organization. The most widely accepted method of assessing the nature and demands of a particular job is the job evaluation approach referred to earlier in the chapter.[15] However, the problem is that almost all job evaluation methods themselves involve some degree of subjective judgment regarding the difficulty and demands of the job. It is extremely difficult to accurately measure the worth of a person's job to the organization, and it is practically impossible to do so in a purely objective and detached manner.

Thus, there are two issues involved in the comparable worth controversy. The first has to do with the extent to which we are willing to accept the concept that people should receive equal pay for work of equal value. This is a broad social and political question going beyond the realm of organizations and their managers. It appears that most people and most influential decision makers are willing to accept this basic concept. The second and more difficult issue in the comparable worth controversy has to do with measuring the worth of a job. A concern is that if equal pay for work of equal value were legislated, its main outcome would be the generation of a tremendous amount of work for consultants specializing in job analysis and evaluation. The controversies and disagreements regarding salary levels for different jobs might simply be refocused on the extent to which various groups agreed or disagreed with the methods used by the job analysts in assessing the "worth" of different jobs. The issue of comparable worth is obviously an important one that will command a good deal of attention in the years to come. Some examples of the types of disputes that have arisen over comparable worth are described in Box 12-2.

Innovative Reward Systems

Recently, a number of innovative approaches have been developed to the administration of pay and other rewards for effective performance. Interest in the design of reward systems has been increasing largely as a result of recognition of the fact that pay is such an important determinant of the satisfaction and motivation of organization members. In what follows we will discuss three recent innovations in the design of organizational reward systems.[16] The key strengths and weaknesses associated with each of these innovations are summarized in Table 12-5.

Cafeteria-Style Benefits

Almost every organization rewards its members with some combination of pay and such benefits as life insurance, health insurance, and pension plans. Organizations commonly have one standard benefit package for nonsalaried employees, another for salaried employees, and a third for senior managers. The weakness of such approaches to benefits is that they fail to take into

TABLE   12-5

Overview of Innovative Approaches to Pay

	Major advantages	*Major disadvantages*	*Favorable situational factors*
Cafeteria benefits	Increased pay satisfaction	Cost of administration	Well-educated, heterogeneous work force
Lump-sum salary increases	Increased pay satisfaction; greater visibility of pay increases	Cost of administration	Fair pay rates
Open salary information	Increased pay satisfaction, trust, and motivation; better salary administration	Pressure to pay all the same; complaints about pay rates	Open climate; fair pay rates; pay based on performance

Source: Reprinted, by permission by the publisher, from Lawler, E. E., III (1976). New approaches to pay: Innovations that work. *Personnel, 53*(5), 11–23. Copyright © 1976 AMACOM, a division of American Management Association. All rights reserved.

account differences in the value and importance people place upon the different benefits available. Research consistently indicates that factors such as age, marital status, and number of children influence the extent to which individuals value different types of benefits.[17] For example, young, single people tend to value higher salaries and more vacations, and to be less concerned with things like insurance and pensions. Middle-age people with young families value salaries and bonuses, but tend to be less concerned with vacation time and more concerned with various types of insurance. Older members are concerned less with current salaries and more with pensions and retirement benefits.

A benefits program that ignores these differences among people and treats all organization members identically fails to obtain the maximum payoff from the considerable monetary investment involved in such benefit programs. If benefit plans are to assist the organization by increasing the levels of satisfaction and motivation of their members, the plans must be capable of responding to the significant differences among individuals in the value they place on the benefits available.

An innovative approach to the resolution of this problem is known as a **cafeteria-style benefits program,** under which the organization presents its employees with a whole range of alternative benefits and permits the employees to pick and choose those that they individually value most up to some set maximum value (the employee's total compensation level). At one extreme an individual could take his or her compensation entirely in the form of salary with no other benefits, while at the other extreme an individual could in any given year opt for a reduction in salary and an increase in other benefits, such as insurance or pension contributions. A variant of the cafeteria-style plan requires all employees to accept a minimal level of certain benefits, such as health and life insurance, and then permits free choice in allocation of compensation beyond these minimal levels.

The advantages of cafeteria-style benefit plans are twofold. First, they increase employees' perceptions of the value of their total compensation package. Second, they increase the likelihood that employees will be satisfied with their pay and benefits package. This increased satisfaction is associated with lower levels of turnover and absenteeism and greater ease in attracting new members.

Although cafeteria benefits have significant advantages, they are obviously not without their drawbacks. First, they tend to create bookkeeping difficulties for the organization, which must keep track of exactly who has chosen which benefits and ensure that the benefits are properly administered and dispensed. Fortunately the use of computer systems greatly alleviates such difficulties and brings the problems down to manageable proportions. Second, the uncertainty regarding exactly how many people will choose each benefit can make it difficult for the organization to price certain benefits, such as insurance, for which the cost to the organization is partially dependent upon the number of people choosing the benefit. This difficulty is particularly salient for smaller organizations and may result in some short-term costs to the organization in the early stages of a program, until the numbers of employees choosing various options have stabilized and accurate pricing can be employed. Cafeteria-style benefit programs have been successfully implemented and maintained in both large organizations (e.g., the Systems Division of the TRW Corporation, with 12,000 employees) and small organizations (e.g., the Educational Testing Service, with 3,000 employees). American Can Company found after introducing a cafeteria-style benefits program that 92 percent of its employees felt they had substantially improved their benefits by having the proper mix of items.[18]

Lump-Sum Salary Increases

Almost all organizations review the annual salaries of each of their members once a year to determine the amount by which they will be increased. The amount of increase decided upon is then averaged over the number of pay periods in a year, and each regular paycheck is then incremented accordingly. Thus, it takes an employee an entire year actually to collect the full amount of the annual increase, and the increase is received in small installments. The advantages of this system from the organization's viewpoint are that the organization does not have to part with large amounts of cash at any one time and, further, that the organization does not put itself in a position of having paid for services prior to their being rendered by the employee. At the same time, however, the practice of integrating annual increments into regular paychecks suffers both from the fact that it is an inflexible method of administering pay as a reward and from the fact that even quite large annual salary increases are relatively unnoticeable to the employee when averaged over many pay periods. For example, a 5 percent raise for an employee earning $20,000 amounts to a raise of $1,000 in annual salary. However, split over 50 weeks, this pay raise would only result in the employee's gross pay going up $20 per week; after taxes the employee might only see an additional $14 per week in his or her take-home pay.

An alternative that a number of organizations have begun to experiment with is the administration of annual salary increases in a single lump sum. Under such a system the individual is informed of the amount of his or her annual salary increase and is then given the choice of how and when to receive the increase. The individual may choose to take the full amount immediately, to have the increment integrated into each regular paycheck, or to receive the increment in any combination of lump-sum payments and regular increments that may be convenient. There are a number of advantages to such an approach. First, it is an innovative approach to pay administration and can serve to encourage innovation and experimentation throughout the organization. Second, it makes the organization's pay system much more flexible and permits it to meet the unique needs of individual members rather than treating everyone in an identical fashion. Finally, it serves to make pay increments much more visible as an organizational reward, and hence increases the likelihood that individuals will perceive a link between effective performance and the receipt of rewards. Naturally, the greater visibility afforded by lump-sum increases will only be viewed as desirable by organizations that have in place an equitable pay system that effectively links pay to performance. If an organization's pay system is inequitable or does not tie pay to performance, then the greater visibility afforded by lump-sum increases will be more likely to create than to eliminate problems.

Like all innovative approaches to pay, lump-sum increases are not without their drawbacks. Keeping track of who has chosen which specific mode of receiving salary increases clearly creates bookkeeping and recordkeeping difficulties. Again, computerization has made such problems much more manageable. A more serious problem has to do with the cost to the organization of providing individuals with the full amount of their increase at a single time, prior to the individual actually having earned it. There are two aspects to this problem. First, lump-sum payments are costly to the organization since the full amount of each employee's increase must be paid at one time rather than spread over an entire year. Second, rules must be established and adhered to regarding whether employees are expected to repay some portion of their lump-sum increase if they choose to leave the organization during the year for which the lump-sum increase was granted.

While these potential disadvantages of lump-sum increases must be taken into account, the experience of a Texas company in the oil well service industry indicates that the risks of lump-sum increases are minimal and the benefits considerable. The company introduced a plan in which their field engineers are reviewed once a year to determine merit increases. The amount of the merit increases are based on performance and are paid in cash during the actual performance appraisal interview. The company has experienced increased satisfaction with pay, improved job performance, and reduced turnover among the engineers involved in the program.[19]

Open Salary Information

Secrecy about pay is standard practice in most organizations. The precise amount of money being earned by individual members is treated as confidential information. Pay secrecy is often justified by claiming that members of the organization prefer such a policy and would not like others to know how much they are making. However, an alternative explanation for the prevalence of pay secrecy is that it permits managers to avoid having to explain and justify their pay decisions to their subordinates.

Although pay secrecy does have this advantage of making life easier and less demanding for the manager making pay decisions, it also has a number of disadvantages for the organization. When pay is secret, individuals consistently and significantly overestimate the amount of pay being received by others at the same level in the organization. The more that people overestimate the pay of others, the more dissatisfied they become with their own pay. When pay rates are kept secret, the organization is incapable of correcting such false impressions since the organization's policy is to withhold precisely that information which is necessary to correct the erroneous impressions.

A further disadvantage of pay secrecy is that it reduces the potential of pay to serve as a positive motivating force. When pay is secret it is extremely difficult for the individual to determine whether or not the organization does or does not relate pay to performance. The individual has only his or her own personal experience to go on and is denied access to information regarding how the organization treats all the rest of its members. Further, a policy of pay secrecy is itself a manifestation of a low level of trust between the organization and its members. This low level of trust again impedes the capacity of the pay system to motivate effective performance.

The obvious alternative to pay secrecy is a policy of openness regarding pay. By sharing pay information openly, the organization can contribute to the creation of a climate of greater trust and can help clarify for employees the relationship between pay and performance. A further potential advantage of an open pay system lies in the fact that it may encourage managers to make better and more equitable pay decisions. An organization implementing an open pay policy must, however, take care that managers do not respond by paying all of their subordinates equally in order to avoid having to explain and justify their decisions. Such a practice would obviously undermine any potential benefits to be gained from open pay information.

If an organization is characterized by a long history of pay secrecy and low levels of trust, an abrupt switch to open pay information may be neither feasible nor desirable. A gradual opening of pay information may be more effective in such situations, beginning, for example, with publication of salary ranges and averages for various positions and moving gradually over time to full, open salary information. An organization must also attend to difficulties in measuring performance when implementing open salary information. As jobs become more complex, the criteria for evaluating performance effectiveness frequently become more ambiguous. In such situations, a policy of full salary openness may not be desirable, since individuals may disagree about the quality of performance of different individuals.

Keys to Effective Management

The material covered in this chapter regarding the nature of rewards, the characteristics of organizational reward systems, and innovative approaches to reward system design leads to a variety of implications for management practice concerning the design of effective organizational reward systems.

1 *Managers must carefully determine what types of employee performance they wish to influence prior to making changes in reward systems.*   Reward systems can influence people's desire to join the organization, their willingness to stay with the organization, and the regularity of their attendance, as well as their job performance. Different types of rewards differentially affect these alternative aspects of employee behavior. Changes in reward systems must be carefully thought through to ensure that it is realistic to expect them to result in corresponding improvements in the aspects of employee behavior desired by management.

2 *If reward systems are to encourage effective performance, managers must ensure that rewards are tied to effective performance.*   Organizations invest a tremendous proportion of their resources in the rewards provided to organization members in the form of salaries, benefits, and other job perquisites. If this investment is to achieve the maximum potential payoff in terms of the effective performance of organization members, it is essential that at least some proportion of the rewards be provided contingent upon such performance. It is also essential that the members of the organization be aware of the links that exist between effective performance and obtaining valued rewards.

3 *Managers must take into account differences among their subordinates in designing organizational reward systems.*   It is obvious that people differ in terms of their wants, needs, desires, and values. As a result, different individuals will find different types of rewards differentially satisfying and motivating. This implies the desirability of employing a variety of organizational rewards in a reasonably flexible fashion. Cafeteria-style benefit systems are an example of an approach to rewarding employees that is flexible and capable of accommodating differences among people.

4 *Organizations must ensure that their reward systems treat employees in a fair and equitable fashion.* Individuals who feel that they are being rewarded in an unfair or inequitable fashion are unlikely to be highly motivated to perform effectively and are much more prone to high absenteeism and turnover. As a result, it is essential that managers seek to establish equity in their reward systems and ensure that the reward system is accurately perceived to be fair and equitable by members of the organization.

5 *Managers need to ensure that the organization's reward systems are consistent with the overall management style of the organization.* Problems are almost always created when an organization attempts to make a change in one part of its operations that is inconsistent with the organization's general management style and climate. Organizations can be conceived of as varying along a continuum from being very open, democratic, and participative at one extreme to being very closed, authoritarian, and directive at the other. Innovative approaches to reward system design will be much more likely to be successful in an open and participatively managed organization than in a closed and authoritarian one. Reward systems must be consistent with and reinforced by the organization's predominant style of management.

Review Questions

1 List several of the rewards most commonly employed in organizations. Discuss their relative strengths and weaknesses in terms of the critical reward characteristics presented.

2 Briefly describe three basic functions that reward systems can be designed to fulfill. Which function or functions do you feel organizations should focus their reward systems on? Why?

3 Compare and contrast at least three different methods of determining the amount of pay that an individual should receive. Which methods would you recommend under what circumstances?

4 Discuss the relative merits of individual, group, and organization–wide merit pay plans.

5 What are the key characteristics of the Scanlon Plan? In what types of organizations would you recommend its implementation? Why?

6 Discuss the relative costs and benefits of cafeteria-style benefit plans and lump-sum salary increase plans.

7 What are some of the common problems encountered with skill-based evaluation plans?

8 Under what conditions would you recommend that an organization implement an open salary information system and participative pay decisions?

9 How does the management style of the organization influence the appropriateness of various innovative approaches to reward systems?

10 Why do you think that so many organizations have a policy of pay secrecy? Do you feel that this is a healthy situation?

Recognition Won't Buy Bread

Steve Marks does not particularly like the performance appraisal and merit increase system his company uses but he has to live with it. Not much better or worse than most others, it works on the pool of money available concept. If the total payroll for this fiscal year is one million dollars (and if business is stable and cash available), a fixed percentage is established for promotions and merit increases for the coming period. If this fixed percentage is 5 percent, a pool of money is set aside for salary increases amounting to $50,000. Although usually not official policy, the effect of this pool of money concept is to force each supervisor to increase wages (give raises) in his or her work area to a point that on the average will not exceed 5 percent of current direct payroll. In theory the supervisor is to reward the better producer with a large increase and give the average worker only a nominal increase. The marginal employee should receive no merit increase whatsoever over and above the fixed cost

of living increase allotted to all employees regardless of performance. However, in practice, the situation is often quite different. Faced with the 5 percent rule, a supervisor such as Steve Marks finds that he cannot use his merit pool in a way that will fully reward the most competent performers. In practice, *almost everyone* gets some merit increase, to keep the complaints to a minimum.

Steve Marks describes the inequities of the merit review system as it operates in his organization and tells of other recent experiences.

"Most everyone has to get some kind of increase or you have a near rebellion on your hands. I hate to admit it, but the average performer ends up getting the average (5 percent) merit increase. If the guy is a cut below average he gets 2 to 3 percent. Anything less than that and the man is insulted. So . . . that leaves 7 to 8 percent for the top contributors. As a raise it's not bad, but it's only 2 to 3 percent more than

362

Mr. Average, hardly an incentive for extra output!

"The system really bothered me until I attended a short management seminar which our company sponsored. Seventeen supervisors attended the program, which was conducted by some big name management consultant from New York.

"This consultant made a big issue out of the fact that we place far too much emphasis on money and raises. *He said that money doesn't motivate people!* Then he went on to list his findings on what *did* motivate people. I don't remember the order exactly but it was something like this:

Challenging work

Interesting work

Variety of work

Freedom of action

Responsibility

Sense of accomplishment

Personal growth and development

Recognition

Friendly coworkers

Good working conditions

Salary

"Imagine! *Salary was at the bottom of the list!* At first it was hard to believe, but when I thought about it I could see that all of those other things were pretty important too. Somehow I felt a little less concerned about merit review limitations

for better employees at the conclusion of the seminar.

"The week after the seminar I reviewed the performance of one of my top people. We use an anniversary date (from date of employment) to stagger reviews, and this man had completed his first full year with the company.

"Remembering what I had learned at the management seminar, I stressed the man's contributions and made a special point of recognizing his individual achievements since he had been hired. Then we spoke of ways to enrich his job, to make it more interesting and challenging. We even set objectives for the coming months and yardsticks for measuring goal achievement. I was pretty proud of myself until we got around to the specific amount of his merit increase.

"He was really upset. 'Five percent?' he said. Is that all I'm worth after all those words about what a great job I've done? Save those fancy words for some other guy. . . . Recognition won't buy bread at my store!"

Questions for Discussion

1 Where did Steve Marks go wrong?

2 What are the strengths and weaknesses of the pay-for-performance plan at Steve's company?

3 What changes would you recommend to the plan to increase its capacity to influence performance?

Source: Joyce, R. D. (1972). *Encounters in Organizational Behavior,* with permission of Pergamon Press Ltd., Oxford, England. Used by permission.

Notes

1   Lawler, E. E., III (1971). *Pay and organizational effectiveness.* New York: McGraw-Hill.
   Lawler, E. E., III (1981). *Pay and organization development.* Reading, MA: Addison-Wesley.

2   Lawler, E. E., III (1977). Reward systems. In J. R. Hackman & J. L. Suttle (Eds.), *Improving life at work.* Glenview, IL: Scott, Foresman.

3   Arnold, H. J., & Feldman, D. C. (1982). A multivariate analysis of the determinants of job turnover. *Journal of Applied Psychology, 67,* 350–360.
   Mobley, W. H., Griffeth, R. W., Hand, H. H., & Meglino, B. M. (1979). Review and conceptual analysis of the employee turnover process. *Psychological Bulletin, 86,* 493–522.
   Porter, L. W., & Steers, R. M. (1973). Organizational, work and personal factors in employee turnover and absenteeism. *Psychological Bulletin, 80,* 151–176.

4   Staw, B. M. (1980). The consequences of turnover. *Journal of Occupational Behavior, 1,* 253–273.
   Staw, B. M., & Oldham, G. R. (1978). Reconsidering our dependent variables: A critique and empirical study. *Academy of Management Journal, 21,* 539–559.

5   Breaugh, J. A. (1981). Predicting absenteeism from prior absenteeism and work attitudes. *Journal of Applied Psychology, 66,* 555–560.
   Hammer, T. H., & Landau, J. C. (1981). Methodological issues in the use of absence data. *Journal of Applied Psychology, 66,* 574–581.

6   Vroom, V. H. (1964). *Work and motivation.* New York: Wiley.
   Lawler, E. E., III (1973). *Motivation in work organizations.* Monterey, CA: Brooks/Cole.

7   Lawler, E. E. III (1977), *loc. cit.*

8   Ungson, G. R., & Steers, R. M. (1984). Motivation and politics in executive compensation. *Academy of Management Review, 9,* 313–323.
   Winton, D. G., & Sutherland, C. R. (1982). A performance-based approach to determining executive incentive bonus awards. *Compensation Review,* 11–26.

9   Cotton, J. L., & Cook, M. S. (1982). Meta-analyses and the effects of various reward systems: Some different conclusions from Johnson et al. *Psychological Bulletin, 92,* 176–183.
   Johnson, D. W., Maruyama, G., Johnson, R., Nelson, D., & Skon, L.

(1981). Effects of cooperative, competitive, and individualistic goal structures on achievement: A meta-analysis. *Psychological Bulletin, 89,* 47–62.

Johnson, D. W., Maruyama, G., & Johnson, R. T. (1982). Separating ideology from currently available data: A reply to Cotton and Cook and McGlynn. *Psychological Bulletin, 92,* 186–192.

McGlynn, R. P. (1982). A comment on the meta-analysis of goal structures. *Psychological Bulletin, 92,* 184–195.

10   Driscoll, J. W. (1979, Summer). Working creatively with a union: Lessons from the Scanlon Plan. *Organizational Dynamics,* 61–80.

Glueck, W. F. (1978). *Personnel: A diagnostic approach* (rev. ed.), Dallas, TX: Business Publications, Inc.

Schulz, G., & McKersie, R. (1973). Participation-achievement-reward systems. *Journal of Management Studies, 10,* 141–161.

Scott, K. D., & Cotter, T. (1984, March). The team that works together earns together. *Personnel Journal,* pp. 59ff.

White, J. K. (1979). The Scanlon Plan: Causes and correlates of success. *Academy of Management Journal, 22,* 292–312.

11   The tightening squeeze on white collar pay. (1977, September 12). *Business Week,* 82–94.

12   Cooper, E. A., & Barrett, G. V. (1984). Equal pay and gender: Implications of court cases for personnel practices. *Academy of Management Review, 9,* 84–94.

Livernash, E. R. (1980). *Comparable worth: Issues and alternatives.* Washington, D.C: Equal Employment Advisory Council.

Mahoney, T. A. (1983). Approaches to the definition of comparable worth. *Academy of Management Review, 8,* 14–22.

Treiman, D. J., & Hartmann, H. I. (Eds.), National Research Council, Committee on Occupation Classification and Analysis, Assembly of Behavioral and Social Sciences. (1981). *Women, work and wages.* Washington, D.C.: National Academy of Sciences.

13   Remick, H. (1981). The comparable worth controversy. *Public Personnel Management Journal, 10,* 371–383.

14   Thomsen, D. J. (1980). *Comparable worth analysis.* Pacific Palisades, CA: The Compensation Institute.

15   Treiman, D. J. (1979). National Research Council, Committee on Occupational Classification and Analysis, Assembly of Behavioral and Social Sciences. *Job evaluation: An analytic review.* Washington, D.C: National Academy of Sciences.

16   Lawler, E. E., III (1976). New approaches to pay: Innovations that work. *Personnel, 53* (3), 11–23.

17 Glueck, W. F. (1978). *loc. cit.*

18 Cockrum, R. B. (1982, July). Has the time come for employee cafeteria plans? *Personnel Administrator,* 66–72.

19 Annas, J. W. (1982). The up-front carrot. *Compensation Review,* 45–49.

Chapter 13

The Design of Work

CHAPTER OUTLINE

Historical Development of Work Design

Individual Job Design

Work Design for Groups

Work Design for Groups: An Example

Individual versus Group Work Design

Keys to Effective Management

Review Questions

*T*he topic of work design focuses on the way in which organizations assign tasks and responsibilities to their members. Work design has a critical impact on the motivation, productivity, and satisfaction of organization members. In this chapter we will analyze the reasons some jobs make people unhappy, uncomfortable, and unproductive, while other types of jobs seem to unlock people's creativity, energy, and drive. What is it about assembly line jobs that makes them dull, boring, and alienating, while sales managers working for the same organization may find their jobs interesting, challenging, and fulfilling? An understanding of work design opens up answers to questions such as this. We will examine new ideas and approaches to work design that can increase the productivity and effectiveness of the organization as a whole, while at the same time permitting individual organization members to occupy jobs they find personally meaningful and satisfying.

The chapter begins with a brief historical review of alternative approaches to the design of work. During the first half of this century the prevailing wisdom was that jobs should be made as narrow and specialized as possible in order to maximize productive efficiency. While this point of view has not completely disappeared, more recent thinking about work design has emphasized the payoffs to the organization and its members of providing people with work that is interesting, challenging, and involving. The chapter explores two modern approaches to work design whose goal is to overcome many of the negative effects that accompany highly specialized and routine work. The first approach focuses upon alternative techniques for designing challenging and motivating jobs for individual organization members. The second approach develops new methods of designing work to be performed by groups of employees working as a team.

Historical Development of Work Design

Attempts to outline systematically how work should be designed for maximum efficiency and productivity date back 150 years. As large industrial organizations were coming into existence, the division of labor among various workers became a subject of considerable interest. With the industrial revolution, work was no longer simply carried out by craftsmen working alone or in small groups. For the first time, large factories were created employing large numbers of employees and taking advantage of the new mechanized techniques of production that were being invented. Managers had to think about how to assign job duties and responsibilities to large numbers of people in conjunction with the new machinery and technology.

Scientific Management

The notions of division of labor and task specialization lie at the heart of the **scientific management approach** to the design of work. Scientific management is an approach to work design developed by Frederick W. Taylor in a book entitled *The Principles of Scientific Management,* published in 1911. The ideas expressed in the book have had a tremendous impact upon the design of work, especially in manufacturing organizations, right up to the present day. Taylor argued for an approach to work design that emphasized standardization, specialization, and simplification of work activities in order to maximize productive efficiency. Scientific management emphasizes tearing a job down into its simplest and most basic components and then assigning a person only one of these components to perform over and over again. Scientific management also drew explicit attention to a number of critical managerial functions that must be handled competently if organizations are to be effective.[1]

1 *Task analysis.* This is the heart of the scientific management approach. Managers develop specific guidelines and criteria regarding how to divide the tasks to be performed among individual workers. They also develop rules and procedures for the accomplishment of each particular segment of the work in the most efficient manner.

2 *Selection.* Scientific management places great emphasis upon ensuring a good match between the skills of the worker and the demands of the job. Taylor pointed out the dangers inherent in hiring both underqualified workers who could not perform up to standards and overqualified workers whose skills would not be well utilized in a given position.

3   *Training.*   Training plays a crucial role in the scientific management approach. According to Taylor, training is essential both prior to undertaking work and during work on a job. This emphasis on the role of training is clear from the fact that Taylor referred to supervisors in a scientifically managed organization as "teachers."

4   *Rewards.*   Scientific management recognizes the fact that if high levels of productivity are to be reached and maintained, individuals must be provided with rewards contingent on their performance. Hence the emphasis on monetary bonuses of 30 to 100 percent of ordinary wages when production standards are met.

5   *Goal setting.*   Inherent in the scientific management approach is the setting of specific and challenging goals for each individual to accomplish each workday.

We can see that the success and popularity of scientific management were no accident. First, breaking jobs down into simple, specialized tasks and training workers to perform them with maximum speed increased the overall efficiency of the organization. Second, this emphasis upon standardization and simplification occurred at the same time as significant technological developments in automation and mass production were occurring in the first part of this century. These new production technologies were well suited to the scientific management approach to work design. Third, scientific management had built into it a number of what are usually thought of as much more "modern" approaches to motivation and management whose validity has been demonstrated by much more recent research discussed in Chapter 3. Specifically, it drew attention to (1) the importance of matching individuals and jobs (via selection and training); (2) the value of linking rewards to effective performance; and (3) the influence of specific and challenging, but realistic performance goals on motivation and performance. A final factor relevant to the popularity of scientific management among managers was its emphasis upon placing control and influence in the hands of managers rather than in the hands of workers.

The key problem with scientific management is the tendency for jobs to become highly simplified and routine, and hence monotonous and boring for those performing them. Taylor was correct in drawing attention to the importance of matching the skills of the employee to the demands of the job. However, jobs in scientifically managed organizations tend to be so simplified and routine that all but the dullest and least skilled individuals are overqualified for them. Further, although scientific management correctly notes the importance of contingent rewards, it also assumes that the only contingent reward valued by organization members is money. There is no provision for the use of alternative rewards, such as personal recognition or opportunities for growth and development.

Thus, although scientific management presents many potential advantages

BOX 13-1

Life on The Assembly Line

Workers at the Lordstown, Ohio, assembly plant of General Motors are echoing a rank-and-file demand that has been suppressed by both union and management for the past twenty years: HUMANIZE WORKING CONDITIONS.

Hanging around the parking lot between shifts, I learned immediately that to these young workers, "it's not money."

"It pays good," said one, "but it's driving me crazy."

"I don't want more money," said another, "none of us do."

"I do," said his friend, "so I can quit quicker."

"It's the job," everyone said, but they found it hard to describe the job itself.

"My father worked in auto for thirty-five years," said a clean-cut lad, "and he never talked about the job. What's there to say? A car comes, I weld it. A car comes, I weld it. A car comes, I weld it. One-hundred-and-one times an hour."

I asked a young wife, "What does your husband tell you about his work?"

"He doesn't say what he does. Only if something happened like, 'My hair caught on fire,' or 'Something fell in my face.'"

"There's a lot of variety in the paint shop," said a dapper 22-year old up from West Virginia. "You clip on the color hose, bleed out the old color, and squirt. Clip, bleed, squirt, think; clip, bleed, squirt, yawn; clip, bleed, squirt, scratch your nose. Only now the Gee-Mads* have taken away the time to scratch your nose."

A young man reminisced: 'Before the Go-Mads,* when I had a good job like door handles, I could get a couple of cars ahead and have a whole minute to relax."

I asked about diversions. "What do you do to keep from going crazy?"

"Well, certain jobs like the pit you can light up a cigarette without them seeing."

"I go to the wastepaper basket. I wait a certain number of cars, then find a piece of paper to throw away."

"I have fantasies. You know what I keep imagining? I see a car coming down. It's red. So I know it's gonna have a black seat, black dash, black interiors. But I keep thinking what if somebody up there sends down the wrong color interiors—like orange, and me putting in yellow cushions, bright yellow!"

"There's always water fights, paint fights, or laugh, talk, tell jokes, anything so you don't feel like a machine."

But everyone had the same hope: "You're always waiting for the line to break down."

---

*"Gee-Mads" and "Go-Mads" are nicknames given to the General Motors (GM) engineers who design the jobs on the assembly line.

Source: Reprinted by permission of Barbara Garson c/o International Creative Management. Copyright © 1973, 1974, 1975 by Barbara Garson.

to an organization, it also tends to create high levels of monotony, boredom, and dissatisfaction among organization members. The best example of both the advantages and disadvantages of scientific management is probably the modern automobile assembly line. Although the productive efficiency of the assembly line is legendary, its negative impact upon those working on it is becoming more and more widely recognized. Box 13-1 summarizes the feelings and reactions of individuals working on the General Motors assembly line at Lordstown.

Job Enlargement

Job enlargement emerged in the late 1940s and 1950s in response to the perceived negative consequences of the high levels of specialization, simplification, and routinization generated by the application of the principles of scientific management to the design of work. While scientific management implies the desirability of breaking jobs down into ever smaller and simpler segments, advocates of job enlargement argued that this process could go, and in fact in many cases had gone, too far. Scientific management did contribute to high levels of productive efficiency, but also generated monotony, boredom, dissatisfaction, absenteeism, and turnover among employees. In an attempt to reduce these negative consequences, advocates of job enlargement argued in favor of "putting back together" the highly fractionalized and specialized jobs resulting from scientific management.

The rationale behind job enlargement was that "blue-collar blues" could be overcome if individuals were given jobs that involved a greater variety of operations, had longer cycle times, and required a wider range of skills than scientific management. For example, manufacturing organizations employing the principles of scientific management would generally have one person whose job was to set up jobs to run on a machine, another person to run the machine, and yet another person whose job was to inspect the work produced on the machine. The operator who finished running a job could only sit and wait until an inspector arrived to inspect the work and then wait again for the set-up person to come to set up the next job. There are numerous examples of the application of job enlargement to such situations. Rather than maintaining separate jobs for set-up, operation, and inspection, the organization could combine the three functions into a single "enlarged" job. In some instances this enlargement of tasks and responsibilities was also accompanied by greater latitude for workers in determining some of the methods and procedures employed, and also some freedom (within limits) for workers to set their own work pace. Several such job enlargement experiments resulted in cost savings for the organization (resulting from a reduced need for inspectors and set-up people) as well as considerable increases in both productivity and satisfaction.[2]

While such reported examples of the advantages and positive outcomes of job enlargement are not rare, the approach was not without its critics. For example, some members of the labor movement argued that job enlargement was essentially a management strategy designed to increase productivity and reduce the number of employees required by organizations. Others criticized job enlargement on the basis that it left the essential nature of work unchanged and simply required individuals to perform a wider variety of boring and monotonous jobs. Job enlargement also suffered from the fact that it was not based upon any well-articulated underlying theory that could explain how and why positive results should be expected when jobs were enlarged. Job enlargement was largely an intuitive approach to work design implemented by managers and consultants who could perceive some of the negative effects of over-specialization and who felt that "something had to be done." This lack of a guiding framework made it difficult to develop general principles for the redesign of work in accordance with the job enlargement approach.

Job Enrichment

The difference between job enrichment and job enlargement has to do with the extent to which a job requires workers simply to *do* what others have instructed them to do versus the amount of personal *control* that an individual is given over how the work is to be performed. The job enrichment approach to the design of work has its basis in the "two-factor" theory of motivation and satisfaction developed by Herzberg and his associates.[3] According to Herzberg, characteristics of jobs fall into two separate and distinct categories, labeled **motivators** and **hygiene factors**. Motivators include factors that are inherent to the job, such as achievement, recognition, responsibility, advancement, and personal growth and development. Hygiene factors, on the other hand, are separate from the work itself and refer to things such as company policies, supervision, working conditions, salary, interpersonal relationships, status, and security. Herzberg believes that satisfacton and dissatisfaction with work are not opposite ends of a single continuum, but are separate independent continua. Further, he argues that a person's satisfaction and motivation are solely determined by the extent to which the job contains motivators. Dissatisfaction, on the other hand, is caused by a lack of hygiene factors. Thus, hygiene factors must be present in a job in order to prevent dissatisfaction, but the hygiene factors cannot generate positive motivation and satisfaction. That can only be done by introducing motivators into the job. As indicated in Figure 13-1, if individuals are to be motivated to perform effectively, their jobs must be high on the motivators. Redesigning jobs so that they are high on the motivators is referred to as *job enrichment.*

Most jobs in organizations consist of a very large "doing" component and a very small "controlling" component. Job enlargement can be thought of as improving jobs *horizontally,* since it involves little if any change in the proportions of doing and controlling involved in jobs. When jobs are horizontally enlarged, people are given a greater variety of things to do but are not necessarily given any increased control over how these things are to be done. Job enrichment, on the other hand, changes jobs *vertically* since it increases the controlling component of people's jobs. In job enrichment the authority and control of management are shifted vertically downward in the organization to

Figure 13-1   Predictions of motivation and
satisfaction by Herzberg's two-factor theory.

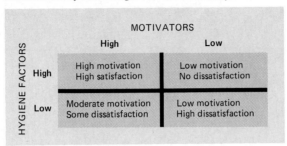

those who actually do the work. This downward vertical shift of control, diagramed in Figure 13-2, is inherent in jobs that are redesigned to contain more of the motivator factors.

While Herzberg's two-factor theory did achieve popularity among practicing managers for some time, his work has been subjected to a good deal of criticism and appears to suffer from a number of serious shortcomings. Trade unionists and industrial engineers in particular question the accuracy and validity of the claims made regarding successful cases of job enrichment. For example, Mitchell Fein, a consulting industrial engineer, reports that a close examination of job enrichment case histories and studies reported between 1964 and 1974 leads to the following conclusions:[4]

1   What actually occurred in the cases was often quite different from what was reported to have occurred.

2   Most of the cases were conducted with handpicked employees, who were usually working in areas or plants isolated from the main operations and thus did not represent a cross-section of the working population. Practically all experiments have been in non-union plants.

Figure 13-2   Changes in the proportion of
"controlling" and "doing" involved in typical jobs
before and after vertical enrichment.

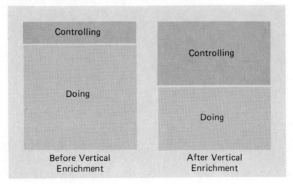

3 Only a handful of job enrichment cases have been reported in the past ten years, despite the claims of gains obtained for employees and management through job changes.

4 In all instances the experiments were initiated by management, never by workers or unions.

Perhaps the most serious criticisms of Herzberg's approach to job enrichment have focused upon the validity of the two-factor theory itself. The theory argues that only motivators can increase motivation and satisfaction, while hygiene factors can only reduce dissatisfaction. Evidence in favor of two-factor theory is reported in a number of studies carried out by Herzberg and his associates.[5] However, the vast majority of other independent researchers who have attempted to replicate Herzberg's findings have consistently failed to obtain results similar to Herzberg's.[6] Researchers other than Herzberg consistently find that both motivators and hygiene factors can lead to both satisfaction and dissatisfaction. Characteristics of jobs do not appear to fall into such a neat two-way classification as Herzberg's theory suggests, and satisfaction and dissatisfaction do not appear to be two separate and independent continua.

Overall then we can say that Herzberg's theory of job enrichment played an extremely valuable role in drawing attention to the nature of the work itself as a key determinant of employees' motivation and satisfaction. On the other hand, the details of Herzberg's approach, especially the distinction between motivators and hygiene factors, do not appear to provide a sound basis for dealing with work design problems in organizations.

Individual Job Design

Recently, researchers interested in the design of work and in the impact of work design on motivation, satisfaction, and performance have been focusing increasing attention upon the specific aspects or characteristics of jobs that appear to have a significant impact upon how people respond to their work. The job characteristics model put forward by Hackman and Oldham[7] is probably the most well articulated theory available regarding the impact of the design of work upon the thoughts, feelings, and actions of job incumbents. For this reason we will examine the job characteristics model closely.

Critical Psychological States

The Hackman-Oldham *job characteristics model* is primarily concerned with the conditions under which jobs generate high levels of motivation and satisfaction. Three key conditions must all be met if workers are to be motivated and satisfied. First, individuals must experience their work as *personally meaningful.* People must view their work and its outcomes as something that they personally care about and feel is important. In other words, the work must be something that "makes a difference" to people. Second, for motivation and satisfaction to be high people must experience a sense of *personal responsibility* for the work and its outcomes. People will only experience positive feelings following good performance and negative feelings following poor performance if they feel personally responsible for the good or poor performance themselves. The third key condition for the existence of high levels of motivation and satisfaction is *knowledge of the results* of the work. Regardless of how meaningful a job is to people or how personally responsible people feel for the performance of their jobs, if they are unable to determine whether they have performed effectively or ineffectively, it is impossible for them to experience the positive feelings of accomplishment that are essential ingredients of high work motivation.

These three key conditions for the existence of high levels of motivation and satisfaction are referred to as ***critical psychological states.*** They are given this label since the three key conditions for high motivation and satisfaction are all internal to the people doing the work (hence "psychological"), and because the presence of all three conditions is argued to be necessary for the existence of high levels of motivation and satisfaction (hence "critical"). In order to be able to design jobs that will create high levels of motivation and satisfaction among employees, we must know what types of jobs are likely to cause people to experience these three psychological states.

Core Job Characteristics

The links that exist between job characteristics and the critical psychological states are outlined in Figure 13-3. According to the job characteristics model there are a total of five core characteristics of work that influence the critical psychological states. Three job characteristics influence the experienced meaningfulness of the work, while one characteristic each has a direct impact upon experienced responsibility and knowledge of results.

Experienced Meaningfulness

The three core job characteristics that influence the extent to which an individual experiences work as personally meaningful are defined as follows.

Skill variety: The degree to which carrying out a job involves a variety of activities, requiring the use of a number of the person's different skills and talents.

Task identity: The degree to which a job requires completion of a "whole" and identifiable piece of work, that is, doing a job from beginning to end with a visible outcome.

Task significance: The degree to which the job has a substantial impact on the lives of other people, whether those people are in the immediate organization or in the world at large.

Figure 13-3 Job characteristics that foster the three psychological states.

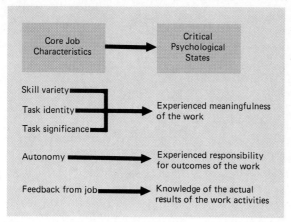

[*Source:* Hackman, J. R., & Oldham, G. R. (1980). *Work redesign,* Reading, MA: Addison-Wesley, p. 77. Used by permission.]

As an example, a person operating a small ceramic pottery business would have a job high on skill variety (requiring all the skills of making pottery plus business skills of marketing products, keeping accounts, etc.), high on task identity (starting with lumps of clay and ending with attractive finished products), and high on task significance (feeling that the products brought pleasure to many people by their beauty and usefulness). At the other extreme, a person working as a typist in a typing pool would probably have a job low on skill variety (doing nothing but typing all day), low on task identity (simply typing what was required, seldom doing major pieces of work from beginning to end), and low on task significance (not feeling that the job made much of a difference to others).

Experienced Responsibility

The job characteristic that has a direct impact upon the extent to which a person experiences personal responsibility for outcomes of the work is autonomy.

Autonomy: The degree to which the job provides substantial freedom, independence, and discretion to the individual in scheduling the work and in determining the procedures to be used in carrying it out.

If an individual is to feel personally responsible for performing effectively or ineffectively, it is essential that the job provide him or her with some degree of freedom, independence, and discretion in determining precisely how and when the work is to be performed. Such a situation creates the conditions under which people can attribute success or failure on the job to themselves rather than to someone or something else. Our pottery businessperson discussed above would have almost total autonomy in determining what to do and how to do it, while the typist in the typing pool would have almost no autonomy regarding what work was to be done, when, and how.

Knowledge of Results

The extent to which an individual possesses knowledge of the actual results of the work activities is determined by the amount of direct feedback that the job provides the incumbent. The relevant job characteristic is defined as follows:

Job feedback: The degree to which carrying out the work activities required by the job provides the individual with direct and clear information about the effectiveness of his or her performance.

The emphasis here is upon feedback that the individual receives directly as a result of performing the job. Although superiors and coworkers provide other sources of feedback regarding performance, our interest is focused exclusively upon the extent to which the individual is able to obtain feedback directly as a result of performing the work. The person running their own pottery business would get almost instant feedback regarding the quality of the pottery produced. The typist could potentially receive feedback from the job if typists also checked their own work and corrected errors. If checking and corrections were done by other workers, feedback from the job would be very low.

Differences among People

The more that a job possesses the five core characteristics, the greater the ***motivating potential*** the job is said to have. However, the job characteristics model does not suggest that jobs high in motivating potential will always generate high levels of motivation and satisfaction for all people. In fact, three separate factors influence, or "moderate," the effect of work design on internal work motivation. The three factors included in the complete model conained in Figure 13-4 are employee knowledge and skill, the growth need strength of employees, and the extent to which employees are satisfied with work "context" factors, such as pay and working conditions.

Knowledge and Skill

Workers with a high degree of job-relevant knowledge and skill, when placed on a job with high motivating potential, are likely to perform well and, as a result, will be both motivated and satisfied. On the other hand, workers lacking knowledge and skill required for the job will be unable to perform well regardless of the high levels of motivation generated by the work itself. The result will be poor performance and eventually a drastic reduction in the capacity of the job to generate motivation and satisfaction.

Growth Need Strength

Growth needs refers to individuals' needs for such things as personal accomplishment, learning, and personal growth and development. Individuals with strong needs for growth are likely to respond much more positively to jobs high in motivating potential than are individuals with weak growth needs.

Figure 13-4 The complete job characteristics model.

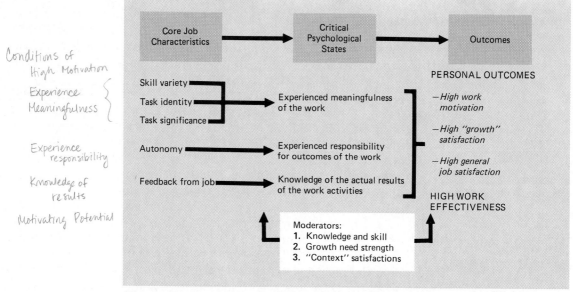

Conditions of
  High Motivation

Experience
  Meaningfulness }

Experience
  responsibility

Knowledge of
  results

Motivating Potential

[*Source:* Hackman, J. R., & Oldham, G. R. (1980). *Work redesign.* Reading, MA: Addison-Wesley, p. 90. Used by permission.]

Context Satisfactions

Obviously, the nature of the work itself is not the only factor that influences a person's motivation and satisfaction. A variety of other important work *context* factors such as pay, supervision, coworkers, and working conditions also influence motivation and satisfaction. If an individual is extremely dissatisfied with these context factors, then the potential of an enriched job to result in high levels of motivation and satisfaction is greatly diminished. A reasonable degree of satisfaction with work context factors is a necessary prerequisite if the work itself is to generate high levels of motivation and satisfaction.

Outcomes of Enriched Work

Job characteristics theory specifies a variety of outcomes that are influenced by work design. These outcomes are summarized in Figure 13-4 and fall into two categories: personal outcomes and work effectiveness.

Personal Outcomes

Personal outcomes refers to those outcomes experienced personally by the individual performing an enriched job. There are three such outcomes influenced by the nature of the work itself. *Internal work motivation* is motivation that is self-generated by the job incumbent and is completely independent of external factors such as pay, supervision, and coworkers. When internal work motivation is high, good performance on the job generates positive feelings and serves as an occasion for self-reward. In contrast, poor performance leads to negative feelings and a denial of personal internal rewards. Besides generating high levels of internal work motivation, enriched jobs also provide individuals with greater opportunities for personal growth and development. As a result, ***growth satisfaction*** should be higher for individuals performing enriched work. Finally, ***general satisfaction*** with work should be higher on enriched jobs as a result of a spillover effect from satisfaction with the work itself.

Work Effectiveness

Work effectiveness is a summary term employed to capture both the quality and quantity aspects of work performance. Work effectiveness is predicted to be higher for enriched jobs than for more simplified and routine jobs. Since jobs high in motivating potential generate high levels of motivation among individuals to perform *well,* the quality of performance on enriched jobs should be particularly high.

Job Design in Practice

The principles of effective job design outlined by the job characteristics model can be used in either of two ways. Organizations may make use of these principles in designing new jobs created as a result of expansion or reorganization. Alternatively, the principles of effective job design can be used to *redesign* existing jobs that may currently be creating low levels of motivation and satisfaction among employees. Since the redesign of existing jobs is both more common and more complicated than the design of new jobs from scratch, we will focus our attention on the implementation of job redesign in organizations.

Diagnosing Problems

The job characteristics approach emphasizes the need for careful and systematic diagnosis of the nature of the jobs in an organization as the first step in any job redesign project. This diagnosis involves assessing both the *need* for job redesign in the organization and the *feasibility* of successful implementation of changes in the design of jobs in the organization. There is a need for job redesign only when a real problem or opportunity exists in the organization, when the problem has to do with low levels of motivation and satisfaction, when the work itself appears to be the source of the problem as indicated by low motivating potential, and when the most problematic characteristics of the job can be identified. Even when a need for job redesign has been identified, job redesign may not be feasible unless employees are ready for change, that is, unless they possess adequate knowledge and skills, have strong needs for growth, and are reasonably satisfied with context factors such as pay and supervision. In addition, the feasibility of successful job redesign is dependent upon the organization's overall receptivity to change and its willingness to live with some short-term disruption while changes are being implemented. A questionnaire entitled the Job Diagnostic Survey has been developed to be used in assessing both the need for and the feasibility of job redesign in organizations.[8]

TABLE 13-1

Implementing Principles Useful in Job Redesign

Combining tasks	Putting together existing, fractionalized tasks to form new and larger modules of work.
Forming natural work units	Arranging the items of work handled by employees into logical or inherently meaningful groups. Possible bases for forming natural work units include geography, type of business, organization unit, and customer group.
Establishing client relationships	Putting the employee in direct contact with the recipients or "clients" of the work and giving him or her continuing responsibility for managing relationships with them.
Vertically loading the job	Giving workers increased control over the work by pushing down responsibility and authority that formerly were reserved for higher levels of management.
Opening feedback channels	Creating conditions for employees to learn directly from doing the job itself how they are performing and whether their performance is improving or deteriorating over time.

Implementing Solutions

Even if job redesign *is* the appropriate strategy to pursue, we still require some guidelines regarding how to go about implementing changes in job design. There are really two sets of issues here: the first is *what* specific changes should be made to jobs; and the second is *how* the change process should be handled.

A set of five *implementing principles* defined in Table 13-1, can assist in determining what changes are most appropriate for a given job. Each implementing principle influences a different set of the core job characteristics. Figure 13-5 summarizes the relationships between the implementing principles and the core job characteristics. In making actual changes to jobs, managers should choose those implementing principles that influence the core job characteristics that are most problematic (i.e., lowest) in the jobs being redesigned.

If job redesign is to be successful, it is also essential that the process of implementing changes be managed competently. A number of key factors differentiate successful job redesign projects from those that fail.[9] First, prior to the implementation of any changes, management must ensure that a careful diagnosis of the changes needed in the target jobs is conducted. Further, specific changes being contemplated in jobs must be openly discussed with all affected employees and must be based explicitly on the diagnosis. In addition, the people responsible for managing the job redesign project must prepare contingency plans ahead of time to deal with both the problems and the oppor-

Figure 13-5   Links between the implementing principles and the core job characteristics.

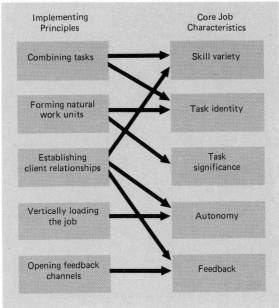

[*Source:* Hackman, J. R., & Oldham, G. R. (1980). *Work redesign.* Reading, MA: Addison-Wesley, p. 135. Used by permission.]

tunities that emerge from job redesign activities. Finally, success requires those responsible for the job redesign project to be prepared to evaluate the project continuously and to confront difficult problems quickly and openly.

Although job redesign is not a panacea for all organizational problems, when job redesign projects are competently managed in accordance with these key ingredients, job redesign can improve levels of motivation, satisfaction, and work effectiveness and has the long-run potential to help organizations rehumanize rather than dehumanize the people who work in them.

Work Design for Groups

The job characteristics model of individual job design discussed in the previous section assumes that each member of the organization is assigned responsibility for the effective performance of a single job. However, assigning individuals to jobs is not the only possible approach to designing work for organization members. An alternative is to establish *groups* of employees who are jointly responsible for carrying out a broad set of duties and responsibilities assigned to the group as a whole. When such teams are also given the authority to determine for themselves how they will carry out their responsibilities, they are referred to as *self-managing,* or *autonomous, work groups.*

Hackman and Oldham have extended their earlier work on job design to develop a model of effective work design for such self-managing groups.[10] According to the model summarized in Figure 13-6 there are two key ingredients of work group effectiveness. First, all members of the group must be prepared to invest a high level of effort in the work of the group. Second, the members of the group must possess among themselves the knowledge and skill necessary for effective performance of the work the group is responsible for. Each component of work group effectiveness is directly influenced by a number of work design factors under the control of management. We will briefly discuss the work design factors influencing the components of work group effectiveness in order to see how organizations should go about designing work for groups in order to maximize group performance.

Figure 13-6 How group work design factors influence work group effectiveness.

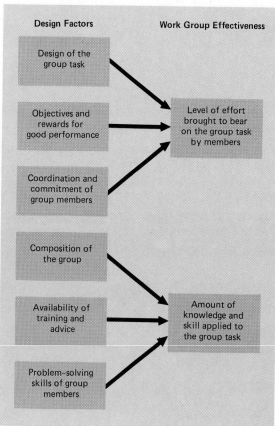

Key Ingredients

Design Factors Influencing Effort of Group Members

In designing work for groups, three factors can be manipulated by management that will have an impact on the level of effort group members bring to bear on their work. The first factor is the way in which the *group task* is designed. Just as individual jobs must be challenging and involving if they are to encourage high levels of individual effort, so when work is designed for groups the group task must be sufficiently complex and challenging to capture the interest and involvement of all group members. The task for which the group is responsible must possess characteristics similar to those outlined previously for enriched individual jobs. Thus, the group's task must require the use of a variety of skills for successful performance and must permit group members to perform a whole and identifiable piece of work from start to finish. The task should provide group members with substantial latitude to decide among themselves how they will carry out the work, and should provide group members with useful feedback regarding the adequacy of their performance on an ongoing basis. Finally, the group task should be something that group members feel makes a difference or has some impact on other people.

The second factor influencing the effort that group members put into their work is the way the organization sets *objectives* and provides *rewards* for effective performance. If group members are to work together effectively as a team, then the organization must ensure that objectives are set and rewards provided on the basis of the performance of the *group* as a whole. Only in this way can the organization send a consistent message to group members that their efforts should be directed toward contributing to the performance of the group as a whole. For example, if a group of employees is promised a bonus based upon achieving an objective of producing fifty units per week of some product, group members will be motivated not only to achieve a high level of personal productivity but also to assist their fellow group members, since everyone in the group must work effectively to achieve the group objective and obtain the bonus.

Finally, a high level of effort from group members requires management to take steps to encourage *commitment* to the group. This can be facilitated by setting aside time for regular group meetings in which members of the group discuss how they have been working together and generate new ideas regarding how they might coordinate their work even more effectively in the future. Such team-building meetings can also contribute to the development of a sense of team spirit and commitment.

Design Factors Influencing Group Knowledge and Skill

If a group is to effectively perform its work, it is obvious that group members must possess among themselves all of the knowledge and skill required by the group task. Management has three design factors at its disposal to influence the amount of knowledge and skill available in the group.

The first and most obvious design factor is *group composition.* Members should be chosen for the group on the basis of the task-relevant knowledge, skill, and experience that they possess. However, in designing work for groups it is not essential that every group member possess all of the knowledge and skills necessary for performance of the group task. Instead, members should be chosen in such a way that their knowledge and skills are complementary. When each group member brings a unique set of skills to the group, the result is a team that possesses a total set of skills greater than that possessed by any one of its members alone.

The second design factor at the organization's disposal is the provision of *training and advice* to group members. The task the group is responsible for will almost always be sufficiently broad and complex that no individual member will possess all of the knowledge and skills required by the task. Thus, there will always be room for the improvement and broadening of the knowledge and skills of group members relevant to task performance. To achieve this broadening, organizations may offer formal training for group members or make experts or consultants available to provide advice and direction to group members when problems arise.

Finally, the knowledge and skill brought to bear on the group task is also influenced by the *problem-solving skills* of the group members. Members of the group must know how to share their knowledge and experience effectively with one another. When problems arise the group must work together cooperatively to arrive at solutions rather than simply argue with one another about who has the best idea regarding what should be done. Management can influence the problem-solving skills of group members by providing advice and direction to group members regarding how they should go about resolving problems and disagreements when they arise.

Work Design for Groups: An Example[11]

In 1968 General Foods made a decision to open a new dry dog food plant in Topeka, Kansas. The plant started production in January 1971. From its initial conception a decision was made that this plant would attempt to incorporate in its design and functioning the latest behavioral science knowledge regarding work design in order to maximize both the plant's productive efficiency and the quality of life and personal satisfaction of the plant's employees. This commitment was made and followed through on by the General Foods managers in charge of the design and operation of the new plant, working in conjunction with a behavioral science consultant (Richard Walton of the Harvard Graduate School of Business Administration).

Work Design

Work in the new plant was organized around self-managing work groups, each of which was given responsibility for a major segment of the work to be accomplished. The total work force of seventy operators was divided into three *pro-*

cessing teams and three *packaging* teams (one processing team and one packaging team work each of the plant's three shifts). Each team consisted of between seven and seventeen operators and a team leader. The goal was to make the teams large enough that they could be given responsibility for a whole task requiring many different skills, but at the same time to keep the size small enough to permit face-to-face meetings for decision making and coordination.

Both job specialties and separate staff departments were avoided. Individuals were not assigned to a particular job; rather, each team reached a consensus via discussion regarding who should be assigned to perform particular tasks for a given period of time. In addition, there were no separate departments responsible for maintenance, quality control, custodial services, industrial engineering, or personnel. All of these functions were carried out by the operating teams themselves. Each team member was responsible for maintaining the equipment he operated and housekeeping his own work area. Each team was responsible for conducting its own quality testing and ensuring that quality standards were met. Team members themselves screened new job applicants and made selection decisions by consensus.

Status Differentials

The goal of the work design at Topeka was to make all of the operators' jobs equally challenging and meaningful. In order to accomplish this, the dullest and most routine jobs were eliminated from the plant either by automation (wherever possible) or by contracting work out (e.g., grounds maintenance). In addition, the set of tasks assigned to each work group always included a variety of challenging responsibilities, such as planning, problem solving, and managing relationships with other work groups. In order to reinforce the perceptions of equality among all of the operators jobs, steps were taken to minimize or eliminate status differentials within the plant. All operators were placed in a single job classification, whereas in another General Foods plant manufacturing similar products there were over twelve separate job classifications for operators. Status differences were further minimized by a lack of status symbols. For example, a single parking lot was used by everyone at the plant, a common entrance was used by everyone, and common decor was used throughout offices and the production areas.

The minimization of status differentials was designed to facilitate the group work design in two ways. First, by creating and reinforcing only a single job classification it was possible to increase flexibility and the capacity to shift individuals from job to job within groups and also from group to group when necessary. Second, the lack of status differences helped facilitate communication and trust among operators and between operators and management. High levels of communication and trust greatly facilitate the creation of cohesive and committed work groups.

Authority and Decision Making

In line with the concept of responsible autonomy for self-managing groups, decision-making authority in the Topeka plant was shifted to the lowest possible level in the organization. Teams were given broad scope for making decisions regarding matters affecting them. Steps were taken to facilitate decision making at the team level by ensuring that operators were provided with the economic information and decision rules necessary to permit them to make sound production decisions.

Reward System

A skills-based reward system was implemented in the plant from the outset. (See Chapter 12 on reward systems for further discussion of such plans.) An operator's pay was based upon the number of jobs or skills that had been mastered. Operators began at the starting rate, moved up to the single-job rate after one job had been mastered, went to the team rate when all of the jobs in the team had been learned, and finally achieved plant rate when a person was capable of performing any job in the plant. Further pay advances beyond plant rate could be obtained for learning various specialty skills, such as electrical maintenance. Decisions on levels of skill that had been attained were made by team leaders, with input from other team members as an important factor influencing the decision.

The skills-based reward system is well suited to the system of autonomous work teams, since it permits pay progression without the existence of a complex job hierarchy. The system also provides an incentive for individuals to learn new skills and helps reinforce the importance of personal development, both of which contribute to increased work force flexibility.

Results

Overall, the innovative approach to work design for groups implemented at Topeka qualifies as highly successful, both in terms of job satisfaction and quality of work life and in terms of productive efficiency.

Several studies have been conducted assessing the attitudes and motivation of the work force at the Topeka plant. One study reported high levels of work participation, freedom to communicate, expressions of warmth, minimization of status distinctions, human dignity, commitment, and individual self-esteem.[12] Another study, carried out by researchers from the University of Michigan, concluded that positive work attitudes were prevalent among operators at the plant.[13] Indeed, these researchers reported that the levels of satisfaction and involvement in all parts of the plant were the highest they had ever observed in any plant they had studied.

On the economic side there is clear evidence for the productive efficiency of the plant. General Foods' corporate analysts attribute savings in the neighborhood of $1 million annually to the innovative use of self-managing groups at Topeka. This million-dollar annual saving can be appreciated in light of the fact that the plant has a total work force of approximately 100 and involved a capital investment in the $10 to $15 million range.

Further evidence of the effectiveness of the group work design is contained in the fact that the plant started up and ran for 3 years and 8 months (1.3 million employee hours) without a single lost-time accident. During the first 3 years of operation absenteeism ranged from 0.8 to 1.4 percent, while turnover was approximately 10 percent per year. These results were sufficiently impressive to General Foods' management that a corporate policy was developed favoring similar approaches to work design in other plants where conditions were suitable. While any new approach to designing work generates some difficulties in implementation, the picture that emerges of the Topeka plant is of an innovative and highly effective organization.[14]

Individual versus Group Work Design

In the first part of the chapter we discussed work design focused upon the individual job, while in the latter part of the chapter our attention has been turned to designing work for groups. The question we need to answer now is "Which approach is better?" or perhaps more accurately, "When is individual job design appropriate and under what alternative conditions are group designs for work called for?"

First, we need to be reminded that neither approach should be implemented until a careful diagnosis of the organization has clearly indicated the existence of a *need* for changes in work design. Once a need has been established, the next step is to determine whether new work designs are *feasible* in the organization. Under different conditions, either or both approaches may simply not be feasible for the organization. A difficult decision arises only when both individual and group designs are feasible. Under such circumstances it appears best to choose the group design *only* when it is *substantially* more attractive than the best possible individual design.[15] The reason lies in the greater complexity involved in implementing and managing work groups. First, work groups are inherently more complex to manage than individuals working on separate jobs. Once a group is created, many interpersonal relationships are established and many issues arise regarding how the group should manage itself to be effective and efficient. Second, creating self-managing groups frequently involves a fairly dramatic change from traditional patterns of organization. The more dramatic the changes are, the more difficult they are to manage. Finally, implementing work groups frequently requires changes well beyond the design of the work groups themselves, for example, when reward systems must be redesigned to be based upon group rather than individual performance.

In general, then, it appears that work design based upon self-managing groups is a more difficult and more complex process than individual job enrichment. That is not to say that work design for groups is never desirable or appropriate. There clearly are instances in which group-based work design is *the* appropriate route to pursue in improving the design of work. However, unless the conditions calling for a group-based approach are clear and compelling, the probability of success and ease of implementation suggest the choice of individually based job enrichment.

Keys to Effective Management

Our discussion of alternative approaches to work design leads to a number of implications for managerial practice.

1 *Managers must recognize that the way in which work is designed for employees is not fixed, but can be altered and manipulated.* It is often assumed that the way in which jobs are designed or tasks are assigned to people is the way that things have to be in an organization. Frequently, managers simply haven't thought about alternative ways in which responsibilities and activities could be assigned to individuals. Managers need to recognize that within certain bounds set by technology and physical facilities, there always exist a variety of ways in which jobs can be designed for organization members.

2 *Managers must take into account differences among people in their desire for more enriched work.* Not everyone wants a more challenging and enriched job. As a result, redesigned work is not for everyone and will not have universal positive benefits if implemented with employees who do not desire it. Prior to undertaking a work redesign project, managers must assess their employees carefully to determine the extent to which they are likely to respond positively to more enriched work.

3 *Managers must undertake careful diagnosis of their situation prior to implementing group-based work designs.* The implementation of autonomous self-managing work groups represents a major change for most organizations. Such a change inevitably generates complex managerial problems. In order to ensure that coping with these complex problems is indeed worthwhile, managers need to diagnose their situations carefully prior to implementing group-based work designs. Such diagnosis involves an assessment of both the need for new designs for work and the feasibility of group-based work design in any particular situation.

4 *Managers must devote significant attention to the design factors at their disposal when group-based work designs are implemented.* When autonomous self-managing work groups are established, management must ensure that the work assigned to the group is sufficiently complex and challenging to be motivational for group members. The setting of objectives and provision of rewards by the organization must be based upon the performance of the group as a whole. In addition, care must be taken in composing the groups, in order to ensure that group members possess the knowledge and skill necessary to perform their work effectively. Group composition is doubly important since it is also essential that group members be capable of working effectively and harmoniously with one another.

5   *Managers require a theoretical model or framework to assist in the diagnosis, planning, and implementation of work redesign.*   The likelihood of achieving successful results from work redesign is directly dependent on the extent to which the redesign activities are carefully planned on the basis of a systematic diagnosis of the target jobs and employees involved. A theoretical model provides the manager with a framework that can guide the diagnosis, planning, and implementation of changes in a systematic fashion.

Review Questions

1   Why is the design of work an important issue for a manager to be concerned about?

2   What is scientific management and why has it been so influential?

3   According to the Hackman and Oldham job characteristics model, what are the essential ingredients of high motivation and satisfaction?

4   Describe the relationship between the core job characteristics and the three psychological states in the job characteristics model.

5   What characteristics of individuals influence the extent to which changes in the core job dimensions will result in changes in the psychological states and the personal and work outcomes? Discuss.

6   What diagnostic steps must be taken prior to implementing job redesign?

7   Describe some of the specific implementing principles that can be employed to increase the motivating potential of a job.

8   Describe several of the design factors for self-managing work groups and discuss how they influence work-group effectiveness.

9   How should managers go about deciding whether individual or group work redesign is most appropriate for their organizations?

10 Discuss the advantages and disadvantages of trying to influence employee motivation, satisfaction, and performance via extrinsic methods (e.g., pay and other rewards) as opposed to intrinsic methods (e.g., the design of jobs).

11 Is the nature of job design in an organization strictly a management prerogative, or do you feel that the employees themselves should have some say in how their jobs are designed? Defend your position.

Job Enrichment in Data Processing

The job of keypunch operator in a large insurance company involved transferring information from written documents onto computer cards. The keypunch department consisted of ninety-eight operators, seven assignment clerks, and one supervisor. Work came in to the keypunch department from other client groups in the organization. Jobs were of variable size and differed in terms of whether a delivery date was specified. Jobs were received by the assignment clerks who reviewed them for obvious errors, omissions, and legibility problems. After this initial inspection the assignment clerks broke the job up into batches that could each be performed in about one hour. Each one-hour batch was then assigned to an operator who was under these constant instructions: "Punch only what you see. Don't correct errors, no matter how obvious they look."

Once a job had been punched it was then verified, a process that essentially involved doing the job a second time, to ensure that no errors had been made the first time. Completed cards were then returned to the supervisor, who checked for errors and assigned corrections to any available operator.

The keypunch department was a clear problem area for the organization. A variety of factors indicated the existence of serious motivation problems. The supervisor was constantly dealing with crises and employee grievances. Operators appeared apathetic and at times openly hostile to their jobs. The output of the department (as compared to work standards) was inadequate and error rates were high. Due dates and schedules were frequently missed. Employee absenteeism was high.

A diagnosis of the keypunch operators' job in light of the five core job characteristics indicated clearly that the motivating potential of the job was extremely low. Skill variety was nonexistent; operators sat at their machines and keypunched and did nothing else. Task identity was equally low. Operators were given work in one-hour batches, not in units that had any identifiable beginning or end. Task significance was low. Since operators were insulated from the client groups by the assignment clerks and supervisor, they had no idea what impact, if any, their work had upon anyone or anything. Autonomy was near zero. Operators were to punch what they saw on the page in front of them. They had no freedom to influence what they did, how they did it, or when it was to be done. Finally, feedback from the job was nonexistent. Errors were detected by the supervisor and corrections were done by someone other than the original operator. No means existed for an operator to assess how well she was performing (all the operators were female).

Questions for Discussion

1   Based upon the diagnosis, would you recommend changes in work design in this situation? Why or why not?

2   Develop a plan for individual job enrichment and also a plan for a group-based work design in this situation.

3   Would you recommend individual job enrichment or the formation of self-managing work groups in this case? Why?

Source: Adapted from Hackman, J. R., Oldham, G R., Janson, R., & Purdy, K. (1975, Summer). A new strategy for job enrichment. *California Management Review,* 57–71.

Notes

1   Porter, L. W., Lawler, E. E., III, & Hackman, J. R. (1975). *Behavior in organizations.* New York: McGraw-Hill.

2   Walker, C. R. (1950). The problem of the repetitive job. *Harvard Business Review, 28,* 54–58.

3   Herzberg, F. (1966). *Work and the nature of man.* Cleveland: World.
Herzberg, F. (1968, January-February). One more time: How do you motivate employees? *Harvard Business Review,* 53–62.
Herzberg, F. (1974, September-October). The wise old Turk. *Harvard Business Review,* 70–80.
Herzberg, F. (1976). *The managerial choice.* Homewood, IL: Dow Jones-Irwin.
Herzberg, F., Mausner, B., Peterson, R. D., & Capwell, D. F. (1957). *Job attitudes: Review of research and opinion.* Pittsburgh: Psychological Service of Pittsburgh.
Herzberg, F., Mausner, B., & Snyderman, B. (1959). *The motivation to work.* New York: Wiley.
Hinton, B. L. (1968). An empirical investigation of the Herzberg methodology and two-factor theory. *Organizational Behavior and Human Performance, 3,* 286–309.

4   Fein, M. (1974). Job enrichment: A reevaluation. *Sloan Management Review, 15,* 69–88.

5   Herzberg (1966) *loc. cit.*
Herzberg, et al. (1957, 1959), *loc. cit.*
Whitsett, D. A., & Winslow, E. K. (1967). An analysis of studies critical of the motivator-hygiene theory. *Personnel Psychology, 20,* 391–415.

6   Dunnette, M. D., Campbell, J. P., & Hakel, M. D. (1967). Factors contributing to job satisfaction and dissatisfaction in six occupational groups. *Organizational Behavior and Human Performance, 2,* 143–174.
Hinton, B. L. (1968). An empirical investigation of the Herzberg methodology and two-factor theory. *Organizational Behavior and Human Performance, 3,* 286–309.
House, R. J., & Wigdor, L. (1967). Herzberg's dual factor theory of job satisfaction and motivation: A review of the evidence and a criticism. *Personnel Psychology, 20,* 369–389.
King, N. A. (1970). A clarification and evaluation of the two-factor theory of job satisfaction. *Psychological Bulletin, 74,* 18–31.

7   The discussion in this section is based upon:
Hackman, J. R., & Oldham, G. R. (1976). Motivation through the

design of work: Test of a theory. *Organizational Behavior and Human Performance, 16,* 250–279.

Hackman, J. R., & Oldham, G. R. (1980). *Work redesign.* Reading, MA: Addison-Wesley.

Hackman, J. R., Oldham, G. R., Janson, R., & Purdy, K. (1975, Summer). A new strategy for job enrichment. *California Management Review,* 57–71.

8   Hackman, J. R., & Oldham, G. R. (1975). Development of the Job Diagnostic Survey. *Journal of Applied Psychology, 60,* 159–170.

9   Hackman, J. R. (1975, September-October). Is job enrichment just a fad? *Harvard Business Review,* 129–139.

10   The discussion in this section is adapted from the model of work design for groups presented by Hackman & Oldham (1980), *loc. cit.*

11   Walton, R. E. (1972, November-December). How to counter alienation in the plant. *Harvard Business Review, 50,* 70–81.

Walton, R. E. (1975). From Hawthorne to Topeka and Kalmar. In E. L. Cass & F. G. Zimmer (Eds.), *Man and work in society.* New York: Van Nostrand Reinhold.

Walton, R. E. (1977). Work innovations at Topeka: After six years. *Journal of Applied Behavioral Science, 13,* 433–448.

12   Schrank, R. (1974). On ending worker alienation: The Gaines pet food plant. In R. Fairfield (Ed.), *Humanizing the workplace.* Buffalo, NY: Prometheus, 119–140.

13   Lawler, E. E., III, Jenkins, G. D., Jr., & Herline, G. E. (1974, July 12). Initial data feedback to General Foods—Topeka Pet Food plants—Selected survey items. Ann Arbor, MI: Institute for Social Research.

14   Walton (1977), *loc. cit.*

15   Hackman & Oldham (1980), *loc. cit.*

Chapter 14

Managerial Decision Making

CHAPTER OUTLINE

Classical Decision Theory

Behavioral Theory of Decision Making

Group Decision Making

Keys to Effective Management

Review Questions

*R*egardless of their level in the organization, managers are constantly called upon to make decisions regarding a wide variety of issues, from the first-line supervisor making a decision about how to discipline a problem employee, to the chief executive officer making strategic organizational decisions regarding new policies, products, or procedures.[1] In all these situations the manager must somehow sort out what alternatives are available, try to assess the likely consequences of the various alternatives, and then make a decision regarding which course of action will be pursued. In this chapter we will take a close look at the process of decision making in organizations. Our goal will be to understand exactly what's involved in organizational decision making and what can be done to improve the quality of decisions that managers make.

The first part of the chapter focuses on decision making by individual managers. We begin by discussing the classical model of decision making, which emphasizes a highly rational and comprehensive approach to decision making. We'll analyze and critique this classical model and then discuss more recent thinking regarding behavioral decision theory, which offers a more realistic and workable approach to the decision-making process. The chapter then goes on to issues related to decision making by groups. We'll examine the relative advantages and disadvantages of groups for making high-quality decisions that are both creative and acceptable to organization members.

Classical Decision Theory

Classical decision theory assumes that decision making is (or should be) a rational process whereby decision makers seek out and choose the course of action that is most likely to maximize the attainment of their goals and objectives. According to classical theory, the decision-making process can be broken down into a series of sequential steps. These steps are summarized in Figure 14-1.

Steps in the Decision-Making Process

Perceive a Problem or Opportunity

The decision-making process can get started in either of two ways. First, a decision maker may perceive the existence of a problem, something that is not going well and that requires action. For example, a manager may notice that absenteeism and turnover among the employees in his or her department have been steadily increasing to the point that adequate staff are not always available to complete work assignments on schedule and productivity is declining. A second possible trigger to the decision-making process is the perception of a unique opportunity that may have presented itself and that should be taken advantage of. For example, a manager may discover that a competing organization is planning to close its office in a particular city, opening up opportunities for the manager's organization to expand its own operations in that location. Notice that it is the *perception* of problems and opportunities, not their actual *existence,* that gets the decision-making process started. Problems and opportunities may exist all around us, but if they are not perceived and noticed, they do not initiate the decision-making process.

Set Goals and Objectives

Once a problem or opportunity has been identified, the decision maker must clearly identify the goals and objectives that a good decision should achieve. For example, if an individual is experiencing a lack of satisfaction and fulfillment with his or her current job, the individual's goals for the decision-making process might be to identify, obtain, and accept a new job that is most likely to maximize his or her future satisfaction, development, and feelings of accomplishment. The manager concerned about declining productivity and increased turnover in his or her particular department might set goals of identifying and implementing changes in the work system that are most likely to result in increased productivity and reduced employee turnover.

Generate Alternatives

Once goals and objectives have been set, the decision maker then generates alternative courses of action that might result in goal attainment. This is the stage in the decision-making process that requires the greatest component of

Figure 14-1 Model of the decision-making process.

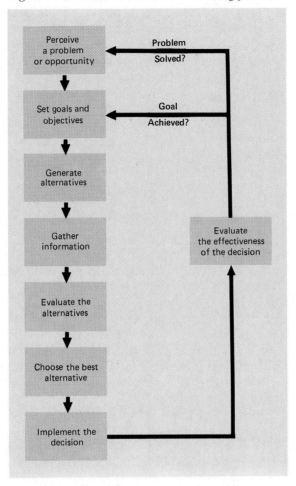

creativity and imagination. Ideally, the decision maker should seek to generate as many alternatives as possible and should try to ensure that the set of alternatives is relatively diverse (i.e., the alternatives should not all be highly similar to one another). In this way the decision maker increases the likelihood that some very good potential alternatives will not be excluded from further consideration in the decision-making process. For example, the manager concerned about high rates of absenteeism and turnover should consider changing the pay and reward systems, changing the design of work for employees, changing the leadership styles of supervisors, changing the methods of work assignments and scheduling, and so on. Restricting the consideration of alternatives to changes in the pay system, for example, might result in many potentially effective courses of action not being considered in the decision-making process.

Gather Information

The alternatives that have been generated must be systematically evaluated. However, before evaluation can proceed, information must be collected regarding each of the alternatives and their likely consequences. More specifically, the decision maker must seek to learn as much as possible regarding the likelihood that each alternative will result in the achievement of the goals and objectives being sought. For example, the individual who is dissatisfied with his or her current job must gather a great deal of information regarding other jobs that might be available. Information is required on what specific opportunities are available in other organizations, how those organizations treat their employees, what the person's long-term prospects might be in each organization, and so on.

Evaluate the Alternatives

Once all available information has been collected regarding all of the alternatives under consideration, the decision maker must use that information to evaluate the alternatives in a systematic fashion. This requires the decision maker to employ some technique that permits all of the information collected regarding each of the alternatives under consideration to be used to analyze and compare the relative advantages of each alternative. The outcome of this evaluation process should then be a rank ordering of the alternatives from best to worst according to their likelihood of leading to the attainment of the goals and objectives of the decision maker. For example, the manager dealing with the problem of increased absenteeism and turnover must systematically evaluate all of the consequences anticipated to follow each course of action under consideration. If changes in the pay system were made, what improvements would be expected in absenteeism and turnover at what increased payroll costs? If changes in job design were implemented, how disruptive would they be and how much improvement could be expected?

Choose the Best Alternative

This step should be quite straightforward if the evaluation of alternatives has been conducted comprehensively and systematically. The decision maker simply chooses the alternative that the evaluation process has indicated to be most desirable. Problems may arise at this stage, however, if the evaluation process leads to the conclusion that two or more alternatives appear equally likely to be "best." For example, a graduating MBA student majoring in marketing may have thought she always wanted to work for Procter and Gamble (P&G). At the conclusion of the interviewing process she simultaneously receives offers from P&G and IBM. No matter how much information she gathers or how much careful evaluation of alternatives she does, it may remain almost impossible to tell which of the two offers would be best for her.

Implement the Decision

Although, strictly speaking, the decision-making process has ended once a decision has been reached regarding the best alternative, it is also true that the decision-making process is no more than a mental exercise if the chosen course of action is not implemented. Further, issues of implementation (e.g., the ease and feasibility of putting a solution into practice) are frequently important factors in the choice of an alternative in the previous stages. After a great deal of thought and analysis, the manager concerned about high absenteeism and turnover may have decided that job redesign was the best solution to his problem. While his decision may be a good one, he still has much work ahead of him if that decision is to be effectively implemented, as our discussion in Chapter 13 made clear.

Evaluate Decision Effectiveness

The decision-making cycle should not end until the decision maker evaluates the extent to which the chosen alternative has succeeded in solving the initial problem and achieving the goals identified at the outset of the process. If such evaluation indicates success, then the decision-making cycle is concluded. However, if the chosen alternative has not solved the problem or achieved stated objectives, then the decision maker must recycle through the decision-making process to generate a new alternative. If, after implementing job enrichment, absenteeism and turnover decline to acceptable levels, the manager can feel satisfied that a decision has resulted in his problem being effectively solved. If, however, absenteeism and turnover remain at high levels, the manager must go back to the alternative-generating phase and attempt to arrive at a new course of action.

Figure 14-2 provides an example of these steps in the decision-making process. The figure helps draw attention to the fact that there are three major phases in this process. The first phase in decision making consists of framing the problem or opportunity, in other words determining exactly what the decision maker is faced with and what objectives are to be accomplished. The next phase in the process requires the active generation of ideas, alternatives, and information. The final phase in the process requires the systematic analysis of the information and alternatives generated in the earlier steps. In this latter phase, the complex set of information generated must be distilled down to a single choice regarding which course of action will be pursued and actually implemented.

Assumptions of Classical Theory

Classical theory of decision making not only assumes that decision making follows the above series of steps; it also makes certain strong assumptions regarding what happens at various stages in the decision-making process. We'll outline several of the most critical assumptions.

1   *Goals are given.*   Classical theory assumes that the goals to be achieved in any decision situation are either predetermined or else so obvious as to be straightforward. Classical theory does not address itself to situations in which goals are unclear, in which disagreement exists regarding goals, or in which several goals are in conflict with one another.

2   *All alternatives are considered.*   According to classical theory, decision makers must generate and evaluate *all* possible courses of action. Decision

Figure 14-2   An example of steps in the decision-making process in which five alternatives are considered and evaluated.

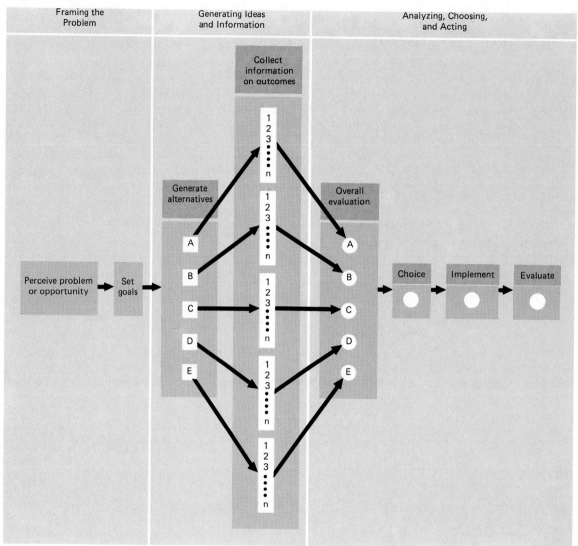

making is thus an exhaustive (and probably exhausting) process in which no potential solution to a problem is excluded from consideration.

3   *All outcomes are taken into account.*   Classical theory assumes that decision makers are aware of and take into account *every* possible outcome associated with each alternative under consideration.

4   *Perfect information is freely available.*   It is assumed that decision makers either possess or can obtain (at no cost) perfect information regarding (1) the value of every outcome that may be obtained; and (2) the likelihood that each alternative course of action will result in obtaining each of the outcomes.

5   *Decision makers are rational maximizers.*   Classical theory views decision makers as totally rational. This total rationality results in the decision maker always choosing the optimal course of action, that is, the alternative that maximizes the attainment of desirable outcomes that meet the goals of the decision maker.

Assessment of Classical Theory

Classical theory has enjoyed a good deal of popularity partly because it is intuitively appealing. It appears to provide a good description of how people at least *should* go about making decisions (even if they aren't always quite so systematic as the theory implies they ought to be). In addition, it provides specific guidance to decision makers regarding how to improve the quality of decision making. The classical theory position that decision making should proceed systematically through the series of steps that are outlined in Figures 14-1 and 14-2 is sound. Better decisions result when decision makers carefully analyze problems, evaluate multiple alternatives, and make systematic choices on the basis of their analyses.[2] The problem with classical theory lies in the assumptions it makes regarding how decision makers can or should deal with each of the steps in the decision-making process. The assumptions of classical theory are overstated, inaccurate, and generally impossible to implement in practice. We'll look at the shortcomings of each of classical theory's assumptions in turn.

1   *Goals are given.*   In almost all real decision-making situations goals are *not* given. Indeed, a central problem in most decision-making situations is determining precisely which goal or goals are most important to attempt to attain. For example, does the graduating MBA with two job offers in hand choose the job with the highest salary (monetary goal), the best career advancement prospects (development goal), or the most interesting initial work assignments (challenge and interest goal)? Similarly, does an organization making decisions regarding changes in its organizational strategy choose a strategy that it hopes will maximize profit, total sales, market share, long-term growth and stability, or does it choose a strategy that will minimize costs, reduce overhead, and decrease turnover? The decision maker must almost always determine which of a multitude of goals (many of which may be conflicting) are most important to pursue. Goals are rarely, if ever, given.

2   *All alternatives are considered.*   For all but the most trivial decisions it is foolish to suggest that all alternatives can even be identified, much less con-

sidered. How realistic is it to suggest that a graduating MBA should consider and evaluate *all* possible potential employers and jobs before choosing to accept an offer? The ambiguity and complexity of organizational decisions make this assumption even more untenable for organizational decisions. The manager seeking to reduce absenteeism and turnover has a massive number of potential solutions available to choose from, including any number of changes to the pay system, new approaches to job design, and changes in supervisory styles. Since the number of potential courses of action is so large, adherence to this assumption of classical decision theory would make it almost impossible for such a manager ever to arrive at a decision, since he or she might never finish generating and evaluating all of the alternatives available.

3   *All outcomes are taken into account.*   Just as it is impossible to generate all possible alternatives, it is impossible to anticipate and predict all possible outcomes of each alternative. The MBA student choosing between two job offers cannot know for sure exactly what it will be like working for either organization. Will all of the hoped-for opportunities in each company actually materialize? Will the new MBA get along well with his or her new boss? How will his or her coworkers feel about a new person coming into the department? The future is inherently uncertain and unpredictable, and no decision maker can ever be sure that all possible outcomes of a decision have been taken into account.

4   *Perfect information is freely available.*   Information is not free, and only rarely is it even feasible to obtain perfect information regarding the ramifications of a course of action. Generating and evaluating alternatives takes time, energy, and resources. Thus, the process of obtaining information for use in decision making frequently has high costs associated with it. As a result, almost all decisions are based upon information that is to some extent inadequate and incomplete.

5   *Decision makers are rational maximizers.*   The classical model assumes that decision makers have a tremendous mental capacity both for remembering and storing huge quantities of information and for processing that information in order to assess which available alternative is the optimal one. A great deal of psychological research indicates that people are simply incapable of the kinds of mental arithmetic implied by classical theory.[3] The conclusion is not simply that people *don't* make decisions in the manner suggested by classical theory; more to the point, they *can't.*

Given these limits on his or her capacity to analyze and process information, and given the constraints imposed by time, the complexity of the problem, and the costs of information, how should a manager approach a decision situation in order to make the best possible decision? The behavioral theory of decision making discussed in the next section deals with this question.

Behavioral Theory of Decision Making

Given the difficulties and shortcomings of classical decision theory, we clearly need an approach to decision making that is (1) more likely to provide an accurate description of how individuals *actually* make decisions; and (2) more likely to provide realistic guidance to decision makers regarding how they *should* approach decision situations. Behavioral decision theory provides such an alternative approach. The central ideas of behavioral decision theory have been developed by Herbert Simon, James March, and their colleagues.[4]

Bounded Rationality

A major problem with the classical view of rational decision making is that it assumes that decision makers have mental capacities for analysis and evaluation that vastly exceed those actually possessed by people. In addition, recent research into the underlying nature of problem complexity and techniques of searching for solutions to complex problems indicates that neither larger computers nor smarter people are likely to be able to implement the classical theory approach to decision making in the face of the enormous complexity of most real-world problem situations.[5]

In response to this recognition of the inherent complexity of most real-world problems and the impossibility of actually implementing the classical theory approach to rational decision making, Simon has developed the notion of **bounded rationality**.[6] According to the principle of bounded rationality, "the capacity of the human mind for formulating and solving complex problems is very small compared with the size of the problems whose solution is required for objectively rational behavior in the real world—or even for a reasonable approximation to such objective rationality."[7] Thus, bounded rationality implies the following:

1   Decisions will always be based upon an incomplete and to some degree inadequate comprehension of the true nature of the problem situation being faced.

2   Decision makers will never succeed in generating all possible alternative solutions for consideration.

3   Alternatives are always evaluated incompletely since it is impossible to foresee and predict accurately all of the outcomes associated with each alternative.

4   The ultimate decision regarding which alternative to choose must be based upon some criterion other than maximization or optimization, since it is impossible ever to determine which alternative is *the* optimal one.

If everyone in every organization were perfectly rational, every individual and every organization would always be making the best possible decisions, and as a result problems of organizing and managing organizations effectively would be nonexistent. These problems continue to exist precisely because individuals have limited abilities to agree on goals and to analyze situations in the rational manner assumed by classical decision theory.[8]

Satisficing

If people are not perfectly rational and if they are not capable of making decisions on the basis of all of the detailed and exhaustive analyses assumed by classical theory, how then can they go about determining which alternative to choose when faced with a decision? Simon has suggested that the key to understanding how people actually go about simplifying complicated decision situations lies in the notion of *satisficing.* While the assumptions of classical theory suggest that a decision maker must continue to generate and evaluate alternatives until the best alternative has been identified, the principle of satisficing suggests that a decision maker continues to generate and evaluate alternatives until one alternative that is *good enough* to be acceptable is identified.

The advantages of satisficing as a basis for decision making are obvious. First, it is manageable to implement since it does not require a decision maker to generate a potentially infinite list of alternatives. Second, it more realistically acknowledges the bounded rationality of human beings. Finally, satisficing appears to provide a valid description of how people actually do go about making decisions. Given the time, effort, and expense that must go into the process of generating and evaluating alternatives, satisficing keeps the decision-making process within manageable bounds and cuts off the process when an acceptable solution has been identified.

Stress and Decision Making

The process of choosing among alternatives whose outcomes can never be perfectly anticipated generates a degree of psychological stress and conflict.[9] The level of stress experienced can vary from the relatively minor (as in choosing which of several pairs of shoes to buy) to the totally debilitating (as in deciding which career to pursue or which job to accept). A moderate level of stress appears to be essential to create the motivation for the decision maker to engage in a systematic process of analysis and choice among alternatives. If only a low level of stress is generated by the decision problem (as in choosing a pair of shoes), then it is unlikely that the decision maker will invest the time, energy, and effort required in a rational decision-making procedure. If, on the other hand, a decision situation generates an extremely high level of stress (as in choosing between alternative career paths), the high stress level itself may impede the decision maker's ability to engage systematically and objectively in careful analysis and choice. Hence, effective decision making only occurs when stress levels are sufficiently high to motivate the decision maker to engage in the process, but not so high as to be debilitating for the decision maker.

Procedural Rationality

Given the reality of bounded rationality and satisficing, and the impossibility of making optimal decisions in the sense implied by classical decision theory, what should decision makers do to ensure that they are making the best possible decisions within the constraints inherent in all real decision situations? In order to deal with this question, Simon has introduced the concept of ***procedural rationality,*** which says that since it is impossible for decision makers ever to ensure that they have made the optimal rational decision, they should instead turn their attention to the design of methods, or *procedures,* for decision making that will be most likely to generate the best possible decisions within the constraints of human judgment and insight.[10] Such rational procedures need to be designed in such a way that they capitalize on the strengths of human beings as problem solvers and decision makers. These strengths appear to lie not in any capacity to generate, process, and analyze huge amounts of information, but in the ability to employ insight and experience in identifying a small number of promising alternatives for further exploration and analysis.[11]

Successive limited comparisons is an example of a method of decision making that incorporates the principle of procedural rationality.[12] This method of decision making does not require total agreement on objectives, exhaustive analysis of all possible alternatives and outcomes, or determination of the optimal alternative. Instead, the approach views decision making as a process of successively comparing alternative courses of action until decision makers arrive at an alternative they can agree upon.

Instead of proposing an exhaustive analysis of many possible courses of action, the method of successive limited comparisons (as its name suggests) involves a drastically limited analytical process that ignores many alternatives and many important outcomes. It requires decision makers to consider only alternatives that are very *similar* to the current state of affairs, to focus analysis only upon *differences* between the current state and the alternative under consideration, and to *ignore* all outcomes of any alternative that are outside their own sphere of interest and concern. In this way the complexity of the decision-making process is brought within the feasible physical and mental bounds of decision makers.

By considering only alternatives very similar to the current course of action, decision makers limit themselves to a manageable set of alternatives and are faced only with prospects whose outcomes may be reasonably predicted with some accuracy. By focusing attention only upon differences between alternatives, decision makers don't waste time and energy analyzing outcomes that will not help them distinguish between the alternatives. Finally, by focusing only upon outcomes within their own sphere of interest and concern, they avoid the paralysis generated by attempts to analyze and predict every possible outcome of a given course of action.

In general, the concept of procedural rationality implies that organizations need to design rational procedures for coping with problems and deciding upon solutions. These procedures must be designed to focus managers' attention upon key aspects of problems and must permit managers to bring to bear their insight, creativity, and experience in generating a manageable number of solutions.[13]

A key issue to be addressed in the design of organizational decision-making systems is whether individual managers should make decisions acting alone or in concert with groups of involved organization members. There is no single straightforward answer to this question. The factors that must be taken into account in determining whether groups should be used for decision making are discussed in the next section.

Group Decision Making

There are both strengths and weaknesses associated with using groups to make decisions. We will examine the relative advantages and disadvantages of group decision making in terms of the *quality* of the decisions arrived at, the *creativity* of those decisions, and the degree of *acceptance* of decisions among those who must implement them.

Quality of Decisions

potential higher quality

The **quality** of a decision refers to the extent to which the decision is ultimately successful in meeting the goals and objectives of the decision makers. There are two reasons why groups generally make decisions of higher quality than those made by individuals working alone.

First, groups can bring a *greater sum total of knowledge and information* to bear on a problem. A single individual who makes a decision is constrained to rely on his or her own limited personal knowledge. When several people make a decision jointly, more information can be brought to bear on the issue. Other individuals might be able to fill in "missing pieces of the puzzle."[14] In fact, some studies have shown that groups are five to six times as likely to correctly solve judgment problems as individuals working alone.[15] For example, a manager may be trying to decide how to allocate funds for pay raises among entry-level subordinates. If the manager were to sit down alone to make the pay raise decisions, he or she would have only formal performance evaluations and some random anecdotal evidence about the performance of these employees. By meeting with the employees' immediate supervisors to discuss worker evaluations, the manager could elicit much richer data about the employees' individual performances.

Second, groups provide *a greater number of approaches to a problem.* Sometimes individuals can get into ruts in how they approach problems. If we're from marketing, we tend to focus primarily on the advertising and selling aspects of business decisions. If we're from finance, we focus mostly on the accounting and cash flow aspects of business decisions. If we're from operations, we focus mainly on the logistics of producing and distributing products when we make business decisions. When a decision has to be made that affects many parts of the organization, it is often useful to employ a group so that "blind spots" in the decision can be identified early and better solutions devised.[16] Groups can point out errors or false assumptions that any one individual member might be unaware of.

For example, a consumer goods company may be trying to decide whether to introduce a new product into the market. From a marketing standpoint, it may be "all systems go"; from the financial standpoint, it may seem a little risky; from an operations standpoint, it may seem impossible. Someone from marketing may be unaware of a potential labor strike at a major plant; someone from operations may not be aware of corporate cash flow problems that affect the expansion into new areas; someone from finance may not realize the very positive results of market research and market pretests. By bringing these points of view together, not only is more information brought to bear on the decision but also more different types of information. Each person's assumptions can be tested by others.

Group Composition

variety

However, groups are no guarantee of high-quality decisions. The composition of the group strongly influences the relative advantage of groups over individuals in the quality of the decisions they arrive at.[17]

The source of the group's advantage over individuals in making decisions is based upon its ***heterogeneity.*** As we discussed earlier, having people with different perspectives interacting with each other can lead to both the generation of more innovative suggestions and the elimination of poor proposals. Groups make better judgments than individuals when the group members have varied skills and experiences.[18] Just adding more people to a group without increasing its diversity is unlikely to add to the quality of group decisions. The group must also be composed of individuals with skills and experiences *relevant* to the problem at hand. Experience can facilitate a group's decision making only if members have the right kind of experience.[19]

expertise

For example, a study was carried out that compared the abilities of four groups of engineers to successfully solve design problems. One group was composed of only engineers who had experienced previous success with similar problems. The second group was composed of engineers who had had both successful and unsuccessful experiences on similar design problems. The third group consisted of engineers who had had only unsuccessful experiences, and the fourth group was composed of engineers with no prior relevant experience at all. The results revealed that the "successful" engineers correctly solved 80 percent of the problems, the "mixed success" engineers correctly solved 50 percent of the problems, the "no experience" group correctly solved 43 percent of the problems, and the "unsuccessful" engineers solved only 25 percent of the problems.[20]

Another group composition factor that will determine the quality of the decision a group will make is whether the individuals with the most competence in an area have the most influence on the decision. If people with the most information have the least influence, then the decision suffers; if people with the most information have the most influence, then the decision quality is enhanced.[21]

leader
competence

Needless to say, the competence of the group's leader strongly influences the quality of a group decision. When the leader plays a dominant role in influencing a decision on which he or she has little expertise, the decision quality suffers.[22] Low-status members are often unwilling to criticize the suggestions of high-status members, even if the lower-status members have more expertise. Moreover, people tend to overestimate the expertise of group leaders and tend to underestimate the competence of lower-status members.[23] Groups make decisions of better quality when the people with the highest status have the most expertise on the topic under discussion.

The quality of group decisions generally exceeds that of the average individual member. However, the quality of group decisions rarely exceeds that of the *most* competent group member. The reason is that groups use the diversity of their members' points of view to eliminate clearly faulty reasoning so that groups will generally do better than their average individual members would have done alone. However, it is frequently the case that the most proficient group members do not have the highest status or cannot argue their views most persuasively. Thus, there is some "process loss," which leaves the group with a better decision than the average group members would have made—but not always the best possible decision given the data available.[24]

Creativity of Decisions *Dis.*

Do groups come up with more creative, imaginative ideas than individuals? Unfortunately, the general answer to this question seems to be no. The reasons have to do with the tendency for groups to get into a rut in terms of how they think about a problem, as well as the fear of criticism that may inhibit group members from expressing their ideas.

One of the most well-known techniques for stimulating creativity in groups is known as **brainstorming**.[25] The purpose of brainstorming is to enhance creativity through group discussion. Certain procedural rules are enforced to permit all group members to express their ideas and to reduce critical evaluations that might inhibit creativity. Three rules in particular are central to the technique.

1 Freewheeling discussion is encouraged. No idea is to be considered too far-out.

2 Using or building upon others' ideas is supported. No idea is any one member's property. All ideas belong to the group.

3 Criticism is completely forbidden. Ideas are to be generated, not evaluated.

The enthusiastic advocacy of brainstorming by its developers argued persuasively for the creative potential of this technique. Even today, many organizations still use brainstorming or a similar procedure in making group decisions. However, the popularity of the technique has resulted in a good deal of systematic evaluation of its impact on creativity. Most of that research has failed to support the claim that brainstorming can increase the creativity of a group making decisions.

A series of studies have disclosed that a set number of individuals working alone can consistently generate more ideas than the same people can working together in brainstorming groups. When individuals work alone and subsequently pool their ideas, they produce on average nearly twice as many ideas as brainstorming groups do working together. The total set of ideas generated by the individuals working alone are also more original and qualitatively superior to those of the brainstorming groups.[26] The research has consistently found that not only do groups not increase creativity; they also frequently inhibit it.[27]

Why do groups get in the way of creativity? First of all, groups can fall into a rut and pursue a single train of thought for long periods of time. Instead of trying to generate different types of ideas, brainstorming groups often tend to go off on tangents or on variations of one idea.[28]

Second, despite rules against criticism in brainstorming, some individuals still feel that judgments are being made about them, even if they are not expressed.[29] This further inhibits the expression of unconventional or unusual ideas.

Third, the interpersonal dynamics of the group can negatively influence whether the group comes to a creative solution. In some groups, the desire to be a good group member and to be accepted can silence disagreement. Majority opinions can get accepted regardless of whether their objective quality is logically and scientifically sound. Reaching consensus is confused with finding the best solution. In other groups, individuals try to "win" their case through sheer stubbornness and high participation. Caught up in a competitive spirit, some members become more committed to winning the argument than to finding the best solution.[30]

Creativity in generating new ideas is inhibited, in part, by fear of criticism. However, it is precisely this "critical" ability of groups that makes them so effective in evaluating ideas and alternative solutions. The collective judgment of the group, with its wider range of views, seems superior to that of the individual decision maker.[31] While individuals are better than groups in *generating* new ideas, groups are better than individuals in *evaluating* them. Groups can contribute to creative solutions by being used only for evaluative purposes.

Acceptance of Decisions

Does participation in group decision making increase the level of understanding and acceptance of group decisions among individual members? Does participation in group decision making increase members' commitment to executing group decisions? The answer to these questions is generally *yes.*

When a decision is made by an individual, he or she still has to communicate that decision to others and persuade them of its merits. Often the failure to communicate the reasoning behind a decision can create new problems that are just as difficult to resolve as the initial problem was. When other group members work together in solving a problem or making a decision, the chances for communication failure are greatly reduced. People who have participated understand the solution because they saw it develop and contributed to it. Moreover, they will be aware of several alternatives that were considered and the reasons why they were discarded.[32]

Participation has similarly positive effects on individual members' acceptance of and commitment to group goals. While one person may be formally authorized to make a policy decision, he or she will likely be dependent upon the support of others to carry out the decision. A manager can decide to increase minority hiring, but unless subordinates who actually do the recruitment and screening share the same goal, it will be difficult to accomplish. When a group makes a decision, a greater number of people accept it and feel responsible for making the policy work.[33] An example of the impact of participation on the acceptance of decisions is summarized in Box 14-1.

A Caveat about Participation

As beneficial as group participation can be, it is often used indiscriminately. Vroom and Yetton's model of managerial decision making, discussed in Chapter 5, points out that group participation is more effective in some circumstances than in others. The Vroom and Yetton model gives us some guidelines to follow.[34]

1   Participation is more appropriate when a manager does not possess enough information to solve a problem alone. In these circumstances, the leader needs the expertise of subordinates to reach a high-quality decision.

2   Participation is more appropriate when the nature and the dimensions of the problem are unclear. Then, the group's help is needed to define the problem and to separate symptoms of the problem from the true problem.

3   Participation is more appropriate when subordinates share the leader's goals in solving a problem. If subordinates sense that the "best" solution might work against their own personal interest, the probability of reaching a good group decision is substantially lowered.

4   Participation is more appropriate when acceptance of the decision by subordinates is critical to effective implementation. Participation is necessary when a course of action is likely to fail because it is resisted or opposed by those who have to execute it.

5   Participation is more appropriate when there are no pressing time constraints. Since group decision making takes much more time, participation is most appropriate when there is not a deadline close at hand.

BOX 14-1

Participation Improves Productivity

The interesting field experiment conducted on participation at the Harwood Manufacturing Corporation illustrates that participation increases acceptance of organizational policies and increases commitment to executing them. Harwood produced pajamas in its plants. However, style changes and engineering improvements frequently necessitated changing work routines and work procedures. Employees resisted these changes strongly, experienced high absenteeism and turnover, and took a long time to reach their former production levels after job changes took place. Researchers introduced changes into the Harwood Corporation in three different ways to three different groups.

1 In the control groups, change was introduced in the "traditional" way. Supervisors told production employees that the changes were necessary because of competitive conditions and that a new piece rate had been set.

2 In the representative condition, representatives of the workers met with management to help with the redesign of the job, the setting of the piece rate, and the training of the production employees in the new methods. These representatives were then partially responsible for enlisting the aid of all the other operators in making the changes.

3 In the participative condition, all employees met in small groups with management and participated directly in the redesign of the job, the setting of the pay rate based on productivity, and the design of operator training.

The results showed that the participative group "relearned" their jobs much more quickly and experienced much lower turnover. Participation facilitated the acceptance of the new procedures as a group goal. Moreover, the participative groups developed norms around this new group goal and exerted pressures on individuals to comply. In the participative groups, workers accepted the new pay rate based on production as reasonable and exerted effort to meet their former levels of productivity as quickly as possible. In the control group, in contrast, the workers purposely restricted production to "prove" that the new pay rates were arbitrary and unreasonable and that the old rate should be reinstated.

Source: Coch, L., & French, J. R. P., Jr. (1948). Overcoming resistance to change. *Human Relations, 1,* 512–532.

6 Participation is more appropriate when the decision or problem is important and relevant to subordinates. Employees often find extended consultation on matters of little relevance to them to be a waste of their time rather than a favor.

7   Participation is more appropriate when subordinates have strong desires to exercise their own judgment. Individuals differ in how much they care about influencing what goes on around them and how much they care about exerting direct influence themselves. Employees with low needs for independence are just as satisfied being given orders without having to participate in decision making.

In short, participation does bring many benefits to groups and organizations.[35] Used more discriminately, it can bring even more benefits to organizations at less cost.

Groupthink: Group Decision Making Gone Awry

Some special problems can occur in decision-making groups when the group becomes very highly cohesive and demands high levels of conformity from its members. Groups characterized by high levels of cohesiveness and conformity sometimes exhibit a very dysfunctional approach to decision making that has been labeled *groupthink*.[36] Groupthink occurs when maintaining the pleasant atmosphere of the group becomes more important to members than coming up with good decisions. As a result, decision making suffers tremendously.

The symptoms of groupthink are as follows.

1   *The illusion of invulnerability.*   Groups suffering from groupthink share an illusion of invulnerability. They overestimate their ability to succeed against high odds and extraordinary risks.

2   *Collective rationalization.*   Victims of groupthink are much less likely to perceive any blind spots in their plans. When faced with feedback that suggests the plans are failing, victims of groupthink put a lot of energy into thinking of rationalizations for the failure and ways to discount the warnings.

3   *Belief in the inherent morality of the group.*   Groups that demand too much conformity develop a sense of self-righteousness, a conviction that what they are doing is not only logically but also ethically correct. This belief dulls members' sensitivity to the ethical and moral consequences of their actions.

4   *Stereotypes of out-groups.*   Victims of groupthink hold biased, or stereotyped, views of competing groups. They assume the competition is too inept or too impotent to counter their offensives.

5   *Direct pressure on dissenters.*   Groups that demand a lot of conformity place a great deal of pressure on people who call into question the rightness or morality of the group's position. Group members are reinforced only when they acknowledge the rightness of the group and are punished for disagreeing with the group's position.

6 *Mindguards.* Just as bodyguards provide physical protection, mindguards provide intellectual protection to group members. Members of a group suffering from groupthink will often actively discourage group members from talking with people who may hold views in conflict with those of the group. Mindguards may also choose not to present certain reports or information to the group because they are sure that the group would disagree with the information anyway.

7 *Self-censorship.* These groups also pressure members to keep silent regarding their misgivings about the group's decisions and to minimize the importance of their self-doubts.

8 *Illusion of unanimity.* Largely as a result of self-censorship and the pressures to affirm the rightness of the group's decisions, the victims of groupthink share an illusion of group unanimity. They mistake silence for conversion to the group's position, and lukewarm assent for genuine agreement.

Groups that are highly cohesive and demand a high level of conformity from their members are less likely to accurately examine the risks of their proposed courses of action. They are also less likely to pay careful attention to negative data. When faced with failure, they are less likely to reconsider alternatives. Convinced by the rightness of their position, they fail to work out ahead of time any contingency plans for operations going wrong. All of these factors taken together contribute to the increased likelihood of decision-making fiascos.

Examples of groupthink can be observed in a variety of foreign policy decision-making fiascos by the U.S. government over the past forty years. For instance, the Kennedy cabinet backed a plan for Cuban exiles to invade Cuba against Fidel Castro, even when news of the "surprise" invasion of the Bay of Pigs was leaked in the *New York Times*. Later, the Johnson administration misread the strategic problems of winning the war in Vietnam and rationalized away continuous "setbacks" (as opposed to "defeats"). Further examples might be the lack of preparedness of U.S. forces for the Japanese attack on Pearl Harbor, and President Truman's strategic errors in the Korean War.

Groupthink can be avoided if the group leader is aware of the phenomenon and works to prevent its occurrence. Groupthink sometimes occurs because members of the group wish to show that they are in agreement with the leader's point of view. This can be prevented if the leader is careful to avoid expressing his or her personal opinions until all of the other group members have made their own views known. Groupthink can also be avoided if someone is appointed at each group meeting to play the role of devil's advocate. This person is then expected to be constructively critical of any ideas that may be brought up.

Alternative Group Techniques

Two techniques developed fairly recently for group problem solving try to take advantage simultaneously of the creativity of individual members and the critical ability of groups. These two methods are called the ***Delphi Technique*** and the ***Nominal Group Technique.***

Delphi Technique

Developed by researchers at the Rand Corporation, the Delphi method aims at providing members with each others' ideas while avoiding the inhibitions characteristic of face-to-face interaction. Indeed, in Delphi groups, there is no face-to-face contact at all. There are five steps to the Delphi technique.

Step 1 Each individual member independently and anonymously writes down comments, suggestions, and solutions to the problem confronting the group.

Step 2 All the comments are sent to a central location, where they are compiled and reproduced.

Step 3 Each member is sent the written comments of all other members.

Step 4 Each member provides feedback on the others' comments, writes down new ideas stimulated by their comments, and forwards these to the central location.

Step 5 Steps 3 and 4 are repeated as often as necessary until consensus is reached.[37]

Nominal Group Technique

The nominal group technique has also gained some currency in industry. The term *nominal* refers to the fact that individuals are not allowed to communicate verbally; the collection of people is a group "nominally," or "in name only." The process of decision making in nominal groups also has five steps.

Step 1 The group meets face-to-face, but each member is given the problem in writing and is asked to silently and independently write down ideas on how to solve the problem.

Step 2 Each member in turn verbally presents *one* idea to the group. There is no discussion until all ideas are exhausted.

Step 3 The group discusses ideas, both to clarify and elaborate on them and to provide evaluation.

Step 4 Each individual independently and anonymously ranks the ideas.

Step 5 The group decision is determined to be the idea with the highest aggregate ranking.[38]

The research on the effectiveness of these two techniques is encouraging.[39] To be sure, the procedures are time-consuming, and there is some artificiality in not being able to communicate more openly with other group members (especially in the Delphi technique). However, both techniques allow for fuller expression of creative ideas by individuals and for fuller critical assessment of ideas by groups. While many managers today still advocate brainstorming and may be less aware of Delphi and Nominal Group techniques, these latter two techniques offer much greater promise for effective group decision making.

Managers do not need to take a position on whether they advocate decision making by groups.[40] Instead, they need to become sensitive to when and under what circumstances it is appropriate to use groups for decision making. Managers must also develop the skills necessary to make effective use of groups and to avoid pitfalls such as groupthink that can occur when groups are brought together. Knowledge regarding when to use groups for decision making, combined with the skill to use decision-making groups effectively, is a key ingredient of managerial success.

Keys to Effective Management

In light of our discussion of the nature of decision making and the various theories that attempt to explain and describe the process, what conclusions can we draw regarding managerial decision making in organizations? A number of implications emerge fairly clearly and forcefully from our analysis.

1 *Managers must recognize and accept that the model of decision making put forward by classical theory is impossible to implement in practice.*   Classical theory, with its assumptions of rationality and comprehensive analysis, appears at first glance to offer a good model of how managers should go about making decisions. However, the assumptions of classical theory do not at all reflect the way in which managers actually go about making important decisions. In addition, classical theory does *not* provide an "ideal" model of how managers *should* attempt to make decisions. The complexity of most important managerial problems and the limited analytical capacities of all decision makers make the classical model not only inefficient but also impossible to implement in real decision situations.

2 *Managers must focus their attention on the development of effective decision-making procedures.*   A common thread in most recent research on decision making is the impact of the decision-making *procedures* employed on the ultimate quality and effectiveness of decisions that are made. Managers must design decision-making procedures that will assist them in (1) systematically developing a manageable set of realistic alternatives; (2) analyzing the alternatives generated in as comprehensive a fashion as is feasible within the constraints of time, information, and attention; and (3) planning for the implementation of the course of action that is ultimately decided upon.

3 *Managers need to control group membership carefully to increase the quality of group decisions.*   To take advantage of two key potential assets of groups—a greater sum total of knowledge and a greater number of approaches to a problem—managers have to be especially careful in composing decision-making groups. Group members should have competencies relevant to the problem at hand, and the group as a whole should represent diverse points of view.

4   *Managers can use groups effectively to increase acceptance of decisions.*
Frequently managers view their main task—if not their only task—as coming up with a high-quality decision or solution. However, coming up with a high-quality decision is only half the battle. The other half is getting a decision accepted as reasonable by other group members. Often, the failure to communicate the reasoning behind the decision can create problems of a magnitude equal to that of the initial problem that was to be solved. Managers need to spend more energy than they typically do on gaining commitment and acceptance of group decisions and doing so before the decision is finalized. Subordinates who participated in decision making will understand the solution because they saw it develop. Moreover, they will be aware of alternatives that were considered and why they were discarded. Especially when the manager needs subordinate cooperation to effectively execute a decision, this early participation is critical.

5   *Managers can put more energy into skillfully handling group discussions.*
Many interpersonal problems can emerge as groups try to reach decisions. At each stage in the group decision-making process, the group leader can manage group discussions in such a way that more contributions and insights of members are brought to bear on a problem without much "process loss." In problem diagnosis, managers need to focus the group's attention on problem diagnosis itself and discourage premature consideration of solutions. In solution generation, managers need to encourage members who are shy or inhibited to contribute their ideas. In solution evaluation, managers need to encourage group members to systematically evaluate the costs and benefits of different solutions, using quantitative data where possible. In solution choice, managers need to ensure that everybody participates and that no "false consensus" develops.

Review Questions

1   Discuss the role and importance of decision making in organizations.

2   Outline the basic assumptions of classical decision theory and describe steps that classical theory assumes occur in the decision-making process.

3   How accurate a description of actual managerial decision making does classical theory provide? Be specific.

4 Should managers attempt to make decisions according to the procedures outlined by classical theory? If so, why? If not, why not?

5 Discuss the implications of bounded rationality and satisficing for managerial decision making.

6 What do we mean by the term *procedural rationality?* What's the relevance of procedural rationality to managerial decision making? Provide an example of a procedurally rational approach to decision making.

7 What advice would you give a manager who wanted to improve his or her ability to make good decisions?

8 Do groups make better decisions than individuals acting alone? Why or why not?

9 Describe brainstorming. Evaluate its effectiveness as a method of generating creative ideas.

10 What is groupthink, why does it occur, and how can it be prevented?

11 Describe the Delphi technique and the Nominal Group technique. Evaluate their effectiveness as methods of generating creative solutions to problems.

12 Under what circumstances is group participation most effective?

The Structure of a Business Decision

The Nakamura Lacquer Company of Kyoto, Japan, was one of the many hundred small handicraft shops making lacquerware for the daily table use of the Japanese people when the American GIs of the occupation army began to buy lacquerware as souvenirs. Young Mr. Nakamura, who in 1948 had just taken over the old family business, saw therein an opportunity, but soon found that traditional handicraft methods were both too slow and too expensive to supply this new demand. He developed ways of introducing simple methods of machine-coating, machine-polishing, and machine-inspecting into what had been purely a handicraft, carried out with the simplest tools. And while the American GI and his souvenir-hunting disappeared with the American occupation in 1952, Nakamura built a substantial business, employing several thousand men, and produced 500,000 sets of lacquer tableware each year for the Japanese mass-consumer market. The Nakamura "Chrysanthe-mum" brand had become Japan's best known and best-selling brand—good quality, middle-class, and dependable. Ouside of Japan, however, Nakamura did practically no business, except for selling occasionally to American tourists through his established Japanese outlets, such as the big department stores.

This was the situation when, early in 1960—with U.S. interest in things Japanese beginning to grow—Mr. Nakamura received in rapid sequence two visitors from the United States, both very highly recommended and equipped with the very highest and best credentials.

"Mr. Nakamura," the first one said, "I am Phil Rose of the National China Company—VP marketing. As you probably know, we are the largest manufacturer of good-quality dinnerware in the United States with our "Rose & Crown" brand, which accounts for almost 30 percent of total sales. We think that we can successfully introduce lacquer dinnerware to a small but discriminating public in the United States. We have investigated the Japanese industry and found that you are by far the best and most modern producer. We are willing to give you a firm order for 3 years for annual purchases of 400,000 sets of your lacquer dinnerware at 5 percent more, delivered in Japan, than your Japanese jobbers pay you, provided the merchandise is made for us with our trademark, "Rose & Crown," and provided that you undertake not to sell to anyone else in the United States lacquerware either with your brand or with any other brand during that period."

Mr. Nakamura had scarcely recovered from this shock when the next visitor appeared. "I am Walter Semmelbach," he said, "Semmelbach, Semmelbach and Whittacker, Chicago—largest supplier of hotel and restaurant supplies in the States, and buyers of dinnerware and similar goods for a number of department stores. We think we can successfully introduce good-quality Japanese lacquer dinnerware to our market. In fact, all our customers are willing to try it out. We think there is a market for at least 600,000 sets a year. Within five years it should be a couple of million. We have investigated your industry and feel you are the only man in Japan who can exploit this opportunity. Now we know your government does not allow you to invest any money abroad; we don't ask you for a penny. We are willing to pay the full costs of introduction. We are willing to budget $1.5 million for the next 2 years for introduction and promotion. You don't owe us that money. All we ask of you is (1) that we get the exclusive representation for your "Chrysanthemum" brand for 5 years at standard commission rates; and (2) that the first 20 percent on all the sales we make during that time—which we figure is roughly YOUR profit margin—be used to pay off the money we actually spend for promotion and introduction as certified by a firm of independent accountants we want you to name."

Questions for Discussion

1   How should Mr. Nakamura go about deciding which offer (if any) to accept?

2   What types of information will he require in order to make a good decision?

3   Which steps in the decision-making process do you feel will be most problematic or difficult?

Source: Drucker, P. F. (1977). *Management cases.* New York: Harper & Row, pp. 133–135. Used by permission.

Notes

1   Mintzberg, H. (1973). *The nature of managerial work.* New York: Harper & Row.

Mintzberg, H. (1975, July-August). The manager's job: Folklore and fact. *Harvard Business Review, 49–61.*

Stewart, R. (1967). *Managers and their jobs.* London: Macmillan.

2   Janis, I. L., & Mann, L. (1977). *Decision making.* New York: The Free Press.

3   MacCrimmon, K. R., & Taylor, R. N. (1976). Decision making and problem solving. In M. D. Dunnette (Ed.), *Handbook of industrial and organizational psychology.* Chicago: Rand McNally.

Miller, G. A. (1956). The magical number seven, plus or minus two. *Psychological Review, 63,* 81–97.

Simon, H. A. (1957). *Models of man.* New York: John Wiley & Sons.

Simon, H. A. (1976). *Administrative behavior* (3rd ed.) New York: The Free Press.

4   Cyert, R., & March, J. G. (1963). *A behavioral theory of the firm.* Englewood Cliffs, NJ: Prentice-Hall.

March, J. G., & Simon, H. A. (1958). *Organizations.* New York: Wiley.

Simon, H. A. (1957). *Models of man.* New York: John Wiley & Sons.

Simon, H. A. (1960). *The new science of management decision.* New York: Harper & Row.

Simon, H. A. (1976a). *Administrative behavior* (3rd ed.). New York: The Free Press.

Simon, H. A. (1976b). From substantive to procedural rationality. In S. J. Latsis, (Ed.), *Method and appraisal in economics.* Cambridge, England: Cambridge University Press.

Simon, H. A. (1978). Rationality as process and as product of thought. *American Economic Review, 68,* 1–16.

5   Simon (1978), *ibid.*

6   Simon (1957), *loc. cit.*

7   Ibid., p. 198.

8   Klein, N. M. (1983). Utility and decision strategies: A second look at the rational decision maker. *Organizational Behavior and Human Performance, 31,* 1–25.

9   Janis, I. L., & Mann, L. (1977), *loc. cit.*

10   Simon (1976b, 1978), *loc. cit.*

11 Simon (1978), *loc. cit.*

12 Lindblom, C. E. (1959). The science of muddling through. *Public Administration Review, 19,* 79–99.

13 Beach, L. R. (1983). Muddling through: A response to Yates and Goldstein. *Organizational Behavior and Human Performance, 31,* 47–53.
Beach, L. R., Campbell, F. L., & Townes, D. B. (1979). Subjective expected utility and the prediction of birth planning decisions. *Organizational Behavior and Human Performance, 24,* 18–28.
Yates, J. F., & Goldstein, W. M. (1983). Personal decision aiding: Some observations about the Beach birth-planning procedure. *Organizational Behavior and Human Performance, 31,* 26–46.

14 Maier, N. R. F. (1967). Assets and liabilities in group problem solving: The need for an integrative function. *Psychological Review, 74,* 239–249.

15 Shaw, M. E. (1981). *Group dynamics* (3rd ed.). New York: McGraw-Hill.

16 Maier (1967), *loc. cit.*
Shaw (1981), *loc. cit.*

17 Yetton, P., & Bottger, P. (1983). The relationships among group size, member ability, social decision schemes, and performance. *Organizational Behavior and Human Performance, 32,* 145–159.

18 Shaw (1981), *loc. cit.*

19 Reitz, H. J. (1981). *Behavior in organizations* (2nd ed.). Homewood, IL: Irwin.

20 Allen, T. J., & Marquis, D. G. (1964). Positive and negative biasing-sets: The effects of prior experience on research performance. *IEEE Transactions on Engineering Management,* EM-11, 158–161.

21 Maier, N. R. F. (1970). *Problem solving and creativity in individuals and groups.* Belmont, CA: Brooks Cole.
Miner, F. C., Jr. (1984). Group versus individual decision making: An investigation of performance measures, decision strategies, and process losses/gains. *Organizational Behavior and Human Performance, 33,* 112–124.
Yetton, P., and Bottger, P. (1982). Individual versus group problem solving: An empirical test of a best-member strategy. *Organizational Behavior and Human Performance, 29,* 307–321.

22 Hoffman, L. R., & Maier, N. R. F. (1961). Quality and acceptance of problem solutions by members of homogeneous and heterogeneous groups. *Journal of Abnormal and Social Psychology, 62,* 401–407.

23 Harvey, O. J. (1953). An experimental approach to the study of status relations in informal groups. *American Sociological Review, 18,* 357–367.

Sherif, M., White, B. J., & Harvey, O. J. (1955). Status in experimentally produced groups. *American Journal of Sociology, 60,* 370–379.

24 Shaw (1981), *loc. cit.*

25 Osborn, A. F. (1957). *Applied imagination.* New York: Scribner.

26 Taylor, D. W., Berry, P. C., & Block, C. H. (1958). Does group participation when using brainstorming facilitate or inhibit creative thinking? *Administrative Science Quarterly, 3,* 23–47.

27 Bouchard, T. J. (1971). Whatever happened to brainstorming? *Journal of Creative Behavior, 5,* 182–189.

Van de Ven, A. H., & Delbecq, A. (1974). The effectiveness of nominal, Delphi, and interaction group decision-making processes. *Academy of Management Journal, 17,* 605–632.

28 Dunnette, M. D., Campbell, J. P., & Jaastad, K. (1963). The effect of group participation on brainstorming effectiveness for two industrial samples. *Journal of Applied Psychology, 47,* 30–37.

29 Collaras, P. A., & Anderson, L. R. (1969). Effect of perceived expertise upon creativity of members in brainstorming groups. *Journal of Applied Psychology, 53,* 159–163.

30 Maier, N. R. F. (1973). *Psychology in industrial organizations.* Boston: Houghton Mifflin.

31 Harrison, E. F. (1975). *The managerial decision-making process.* Boston: Houghton Mifflin.

Vroom, V. H., & Grant, L., & Cotton, T. (1969). The consequences of social interaction in group problem solving. *Organizational Behavior and Human Performance, 4,* 75–95.

32 Maier (1967), *loc. cit.*

33 Maier (1967), *loc. cit.;* Shaw (1981), *loc. cit.*

34 Vroom, V. H., & Yetton, P. W. (1973). *Leadership and decision making.* Pittsburgh: University of Pittsburgh Press.

35 Guzzo, R. A., & Waters, J. A. (1982). The expression of affect and the performance of decision-making groups. *Journal of Applied Psychology, 67,* 67–74.

Jackson, S. E. (1983). Participation in decision making as a strategy for reducing job-related strain. *Journal of Applied Psychology, 68,* 3–19.

Tjosvold, D., & Field, R. H. G. (1983). Effects of social context on consensus and majority vote decision making. *Academy of Management Journal, 26,* 500–506.

36 Janis, I. L. (1982). *Victims of groupthink* (rev. ed.). Boston: Houghton Mifflin.

37 Payne, J. W. (1982). Contingent decision behavior. *Psychological Bulletin, 92,* 382–402.

38 Dalkey, N. (1969). *The Delphi method: An experimental study of group opinion.* Santa Monica, CA: Rand Corporation.

39 Delbecq, A. L., Van de Ven, A. H., & Gustafson, D. H. (1975). *Group techniques for program planning.* Glenview, IL: Scott, Foresman.

40 Jewell, L. N., & Reitz, H. J. (1981). *Group effectiveness in organizations.* Glenview, IL: Scott, Foresman.

Part 6

Improving Organizational Effectiveness

Chapter 15   Organizational Entry

Chapter 16   Managing Job Stress

Chapter 17   Innovative Approaches to Organizing

Chapter 18   Organization Development

Chapter 19   Careers in Organizations

Organizational Entry

CHAPTER OUTLINE

Job Choice: The Individual's Perspective

Selection: The Organization's Perspective

Job Interviews

Tests

Assessment Centers

Keys to Effective Management

Review Questions

*O*ne question looms above all others for students as they enter their last year of school: Where am I going to get a job? Students anxiously await their entry into "the real world"—but are equally anxious about the process of getting hired. Will I get a job using what I learned in school? Will I get a job I like? Will I get a job *at all?*

As the annual recruiting season approaches, the selection process weighs heavy on the minds of organizations as well. Organizations, too, are anxious about the success of their recruiting and selection efforts. Will they be able to hire enough people to fill their vacancies? Will they be able to hire the best individuals available? After all the time and money spent on recruitment, will the people they hire actually succeed on the job?

Thus we see that the selection process, in reality, is a *two-way* street. Individuals are trying to obtain jobs that fulfill their personal needs and aspirations; organizations are trying to obtain employees with the right skills, training, and motivation. Individuals are trying to decide on which jobs to take just as organizations are trying to decide on which individuals to hire.[1]

In this chapter we will be looking at the entry of individuals into organizations. The chapter has five sections. In the first section, we will examine how *individuals* decide on what jobs they will pursue and what jobs they will accept. In the second section, we will focus on how *organizations* decide which employees to hire. In the following three sections, we will look more closely at the three most popular devices organizations use to select employees: interviews, tests, and assessment centers. Throughout the chapter, we will explore why the joining-up process can fail, and what both individuals and organizations can do to make the entry process more successful.

Job Choice: The Individual's Perspective

Most people think of their job hunting as beginning when they actually start sending out résumés and going for job interviews. However, the process of deciding which jobs to pursue actually begins much earlier. The immediate decision about which job to accept comes after years of thinking about what they like to do, what tasks they are particularly good at performing, and what type of life they want to lead. Let's look first at the factors that heavily shape individuals' early thinking about careers, and then look more closely at the way they actually make job choice decisions (see Figure 15-1).

Developing a Career Identity

Between ages 11 and 16, individuals start to engage in concrete career planning. Adolescents think about what their interests are, where their talents lie, and what their personal values are. Then, they try to find careers and occupations that fit those interests, talents, and values.[2] There is, in fact, a *career success cycle.* Individuals try to major in subjects and find jobs in areas where they have been successful in past endeavors; success reinforces a particular career

Figure 15-1   Job choice: The individual's perspective.

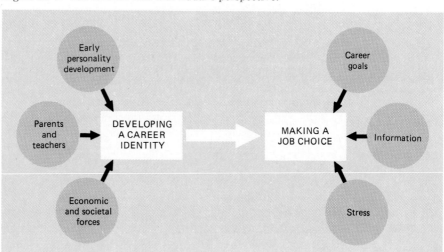

choice. Individuals avoid taking courses and searching out jobs in which their past efforts have been unsuccessful; failure extinguishes their desire to pursue a particular career.[3]

In their search for suitable vocations, teenagers are strongly influenced by three factors: (1) their early personality development; (2) their parents and teachers; and (3) economic and societal forces.

Early Personality Development

Probably the most well-known research on the link between personality development and career selection was done by John Holland.[4] Holland has identified six personality types and shown to which occupations each personality type will be most attracted (see Table 15-1).

Holland categorizes individuals into six kinds of personal orientation: realistic; investigative; artistic; social; enterprising; or conventional. The group of people within each personal orientation share similar needs and values. For

---

TABLE   15-1

Holland's Model of Vocational Choice

Personal orientation		*Occupational environment*
1 **Realistic:** Involves aggressive behavior, physical activities requiring skill, strength, and coordination	⟶	Forestry, farming, architecture
2 **Investigative:** Involves cognitive processes (thinking, organizing, understanding) rather than affective activities (feeling, acting, emotional)	⟶	Biology, mathematics, oceanography
3 **Social:** Involves interpersonal rather than intellectual or physical activities	⟶	Clinical psychology, foreign service, social work
4 **Conventional:** Involves structured, rule-regulated activities and subordination of personal needs to an organization or person of power and status	⟶	Accounting, finance, bookkeeping
5 **Enterprising:** Involves verbal activities to influence others, to attain power and status	⟶	Management, law, publications
6 **Artistic:** Involves self-expression, artistic creation, expression of emotions, and individual activities	⟶	Art, music, drama

Source: Reprinted from Holland, J. L. (1973). *Making vocational choices: A theory of careers.* Englewood Cliffs, NJ: Prentice-Hall, 112–117.

instance, "conventional" personalities have a high need for structure and rules to follow. In contrast, "enterprising" personalities have a high need for power and status. Holland's research suggests that people in each personality type do indeed gravitate to a small subset of jobs. "Conventional" personalities, with their high need for structure and rules to follow, gravitate toward accounting and finance. "Enterprising" personalities, with their high need for power and status, gravitate to management and law.

Why do different personality types gravitate to different jobs? First, people want jobs whose duties are consistent with their likes and dislikes. Artistic personalities will want to avoid jobs like mathematician or biologist because they allow so little self-expression or expression of emotion; on the other hand, investigative personalities will be attracted to math and science jobs for just that reason. Second, people will gravitate to jobs where their coworkers share similar attitudes and values. Conventional personalities will feel much more comfortable working with others who also have a high need for structure, for instance, than with artistic personalities who typically dislike structure.[5]

Parents and Teachers

Parents and teachers influence the career aspiration levels of children. Some adults push children to excel in school and compete for high-level professional and managerial jobs. In contrast, others may not encourage children to set their sights very high: "Why go to college when there's a good job in the factory right here in town?"

Second, parents and teachers also influence how much value and importance children put on achievement and financial success. Some parents and teachers stress to children that the rewards of high-paying jobs are worth the effort to obtain them. Getting A's is worth foregoing baseball practice; studying for college boards is worth foregoing television. On the other hand, some adults convey to children that short-run pleasures are much more important than long-run plans and goals: "No job is worth going to school eight years for."

Third, parents and teachers influence how much information children receive about different career opportunities. Some parents and teachers give adolescents a great deal of information about a wide variety of career options. Other teenagers, however, receive very little, if any, information about careers from their parents and teachers; their career options are more limited as a result.

Economic and Societal Forces

Economic and societal forces also influence the types of careers to which young adults aspire.[6] For instance, during times of recession, students are more likely to gravitate toward what they see as "you can always get a job doing. . ." occupations, such as accounting, computer programming, and nursing. A strong economy and a strong labor market encourage students to take more risks and allow them to consider getting Ph.D.'s or starting their own small businesses.

Societal forces, too, can influence vocational choice. During the anti-Vietnam war era of the 1960s, antibusiness fervor turned more people away from business into law, which was seen as a more noble way of influencing society.[7]

The Watergate scandals of the 1970s, which saw lawyer after lawyer sent to jail for criminal activity, reversed the trend. Management schools became as popular, if not more popular, than law schools.

These economic and societal forces do not override basic personality needs and orientations, but modify the ways in which individuals seek to fulfill themselves. Economic and social forces can influence whether an individual becomes a CPA or an accounting professor, a corporate lawyer or a government official, an actor or a high school dramatics coach. People's basic desires remain the same, but how they seek to satisfy them will be influenced by immediate situational factors.

Making a Job Choice

Starting around age 17, and continuing until a person graduates college or graduate school, individuals begin to make much more realistic, focused decisions about which career to settle on and which job to accept. They become much more sensitive to what it means to work in a particular job ("medicine means long hours") or a particular organization ("IBM means 'I've been moved'").

Individuals' decisions about which jobs to take are influenced by their career goals, the amount of information they have about different job options, and the amount of stress they are under when they make their decisions.

Career Goals

Probably the most informative study done on the role of career goals in job choice decision making was conducted at Carnegie-Mellon University.[8] MBA students were asked to rank fifteen career goals in order of importance to them. Then they were asked to rate the actual jobs they were considering, based on (1) the extent to which the jobs would help them achieve their career goals, and (2) how likely they were to obtain each of these fifteen career goals on each of the jobs. When it came time to make their actual job choices, 76 percent of the MBA students picked the job which they had rated as most instrumental in meeting their career goals. From among the several offers of employment extended to individuals, people are most likely to select the offer that they expect to provide the greatest rewards.

Information

If people were completely rational decision makers, however, their job choice decision process would look something like the following. First, individuals would clearly identify their career goals and objectives. Second, they would generate several job alternatives to consider. Third, they would gather complete information about each of these alternatives. Fourth, they would evaluate all the alternatives against all their goals, and choose the highest ranking alternative.

Does this sound like the way you made your decision about which college to attend? Does it sound like the way you have made past job decisions? If you answered "no" to both these questions, you are like most other people. A series of studies conducted at Yale University demonstrate quite convincingly that most people cannot and do not make important decisions in a perfectly rational manner.[9] Why is this the case?

First of all, people have trouble identifying exactly what their career and job goals are. Moreover, some career goals can be in conflict. Should a person choose a job with the highest salary (monetary goal), the best career advancement prospects (development goal), or the most interesting current work assignment (challenging work goal)? One job will not maximize all goals; working toward one goal can mean working away from another.

Second, people do not have perfect information about potential jobs. Organizations frequently do not give new recruits realistic information about the jobs being offered.[10] It is particularly difficult for individuals to get accurate information about the intrinsic aspects of jobs, such as opportunities for growth and development at work.[11]

Third, most individuals simply do not have the mental capacity for remembering, storing, and processing all the information required to make *the* best decision. They are not capable of evaluating many job offers against many criteria and calculating what the highest ranking solution is.[12] Thus, while individuals may want to maximize their career goals, they often do not have enough information or the information-processing capacities to do so.

Stress

Making a job decision is a stressful situation, and stress lowers people's ability to make objective job choices (see Chapter 16). Job choice decisions are major steps in people's lives and have important consequences for them. However, individuals often have to make these decisions with very imperfect information and under time pressure. Sometimes the stress causes people to accept the first offer that comes along just to get the decision over with, rather than engaging in a fuller search. Other people will put off deciding until the last minute, so they will not have to think about the potential negative consequences of their decisions.[13]

In addition, it appears that most people make up their minds about what jobs they will take subconsciously before they are consciously aware of having made their decision. An intensive study of MBA job decision making found that people often make a decision deep down inside weeks before they admit to themselves and others that they have done so.[14] Between the time they subconsciously make the decision and the time they openly accept an offer, they engage in all sorts of tactics to bolster their chosen course of action. For instance, they exaggerate the favorable consequences of their preferred job choice and minimize its unfavorable consequences. They also avoid hearing counterarguments or any information that would make them want to reconsider their "choice."[15]

Improving Job Choice Decision Making

Thus, we see that an individual's decision about which career to follow involves both "rational" and "emotional" decision making. A person's actual job choice is influenced not only by realistic perceptions of his or her abilities and goals, but also by the anxiety and confusion experienced while making the decision. Let's look at some ways job choice decision making can be improved.

Seeking Out Job-Related Information	First, job applicants can spend much more time and energy seeking out job-related information. Many times people will spend more time researching which car or stereo to buy than assessing which company to work for! Job candidates should seek out information from diverse sources (written materials, faculty, practitioners, friends). Moreover, at least at the beginning stages of the job search, individuals should seek out information on a wide range of alternatives, not limiting themselves by faulty stereotypes (e.g., I could never live in a big city; I could never live in the Midwest).[16]
Seeking Out Negative Data	Second, job candidates need to seek out negative data as well as positive data about their job alternatives. Job seekers often suffer from ***defensive avoidance***—they avoid or ignore hearing negative information about potential jobs because such information is anxiety-arousing.[17] However, ignoring the risks of a decision does not make the decision less risky; it only puts off the day of reckoning. Job candidates should systematically evaluate the pros *and* cons of each alternative on all their relevant criteria (pay, geographical location, etc.). When it comes to job searches, no news about some aspect of a job does not mean good news.
Seeking the Help of Counselors	Third, job seekers can often benefit from the help of a respected individual—be it a career counselor, a friend, or a mentor—who will *confront* rather than allay the job seeker's anxieties during decision making. A variety of career self-assessment materials (such as Richard Bolles's *What Color is Your Parachute?*) can help people obtain a better handle on their own strengths, weaknesses, and career preferences. However, while certainly self-assessment is a good place to start in career development, exclusive reliance on self-insight and introspection can lead to bad decision making. People want to see themselves in a positive light and sometimes don't want to grapple with the really important issues (e.g., How much do I care about working for a high-status organization? Am I competitive enough for this job?) An objective outsider can confront a job seeker with issues that should be addressed, with rationalizations or false hopes, and with what the real consequences of each job choice might be. While such confrontation will be less comforting than the traditional counsel of "I'm sure you can do it," it more often results in better long-run decisions.[18]
Improving University-Employer Links	Organizations can assist individuals, too, in their job choice decision making. One way in which organizations can improve the accuracy of information with which applicants can make job choice decisions is through improved university-employer links. Employers can provide college career counselors with more accurate information about what the job markets in various occupations and geographical areas are like. Companies can also provide students access to practitioners through campus visits, class projects, and guest speakers. Such activities can give students useful information about what skills they should be trying to acquire to obtain the types of jobs they want.

Employers, too, stand to gain from better university-organization links.

Universities can provide companies with useful feedback on the effectiveness of their interviewing and recruitment efforts. Through summer or part-time internship programs, firms can get a first-hand look at those students whom they might be interested in hiring on a permanent basis. Such mutual exchanges can lead to both more efficient job searches on the part of students and more effective selection decisions on the part of companies.[19]

Giving Realistic Job Previews

Another way organizations could help improve the decision making of job applicants is through realistic job previews. The joining-up process frequently fails because firms do not give recruits realistic information about job openings. For instance, a major study of recruiting at Harvard Business School revealed that recruiters gave "glowing" rather than "balanced" descriptions of the jobs being offered to students.[20]

The negative consequences of unrealistic job previews are threefold. First, individuals who receive unrealistic job previews are much more anxious about their performance in their first few months on the job, and this anxiety hurts their performance. Second, giving unrealistic job previews sometimes leads recruits to accept jobs they find unchallenging or unsuited to their talents.[21] Third, there is consistent evidence that unrealistic job previews result in higher turnover among disgruntled new hires.[22]

Giving realistic job previews does not mean that employers need to instigate feelings of discontent by relaying to new recruits every negative aspect of every personality of every work group. What giving realistic job previews does imply, however, is giving a more balanced description of the jobs being offered. More honest disclosure on the part of organizations can substantially improve the decision making of individuals, and do so *without* impairing the organization's ability to recruit.[23]

Selection: The Organization's Perspective

The organization's selection and hiring of new employees is also a two-stage process (see Figure 15-2). In the first stage, organizations assess job applicants' skills and abilities. Organizations first have to identify those applicants who

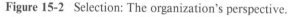

Figure 15-2   Selection: The organization's perspective.

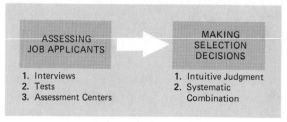

can successfully perform the jobs offered, and can perform them the best. In the second stage, organizations make the actual selection decisions about which of the qualified applicants they should hire.

Assessing Job Applicants

Organizations use a variety of measurement devices to assess whether job applicants have the skills and abilities needed to successfully perform the jobs offered. Probably the most frequently used selection device is the *job interview.* Even for summer jobs, job applicants are asked questions by potential supervisors about their qualifications, their reasons for wanting a job, and the days or hours they could work.

Organizations also use a variety of *tests* to select potential employees. For instance, "Big Eight" accounting firms use CPA exam grades to decide which accountants to hire; manufacturing firms use typing tests to decide which applicants to hire as secretaries. Recently, organizations have also developed a new selection device, called an *assessment center.* Assessment centers are designed specifically to assess managerial skills, such as communication and analytical decision making.

We will look at all these selection devices—job interviews, tests, and assessment centers—in much more detail shortly. Before looking at these devices, however, we need to first briefly discuss what the criteria of good selection devices are. What qualities must these devices possess if they are to help us make sound personnel selection decisions?

Criteria for Selection Devices

A brief summary of the major criteria for evaluating selection devices appears in Table 15-2.[24]

1 *Job-relatedness.*   First, managers want to make sure their selection devices measure the skills and abilities that are actually used on the jobs being offered. If managers are trying to fill sales positions, for instance, they want to make sure that applicants have good oral presentation skills. Only if selection devices are job-related will they accurately predict on-the-job performance.

TABLE 15-2

Criteria of Effective Selection Devices

1. Job-relatedness	**4.** Inoffensiveness
2. Reliability	**5.** Differentiation among applicants
3. Validity	**6.** Legality

2 *Reliability.* Reliability refers to the extent to which a selection device yields stable and consistent results. In an interview, for instance, do different interviewers agree on the quality of a candidate's answers? If a person took the CPA exam today, and then again tomorrow, would he or she obtain similar results? Stability and consistency of results are desirable, since they indicate that the selection device is in fact yielding a true measure of the applicant's abilities.

3 *Validity.* Validity refers to the extent to which a selection device really measures what it purports to measure. A CPA exam is valid if it really measures accounting knowledge, and not just test-taking smartness. An interview is invalid if all it measures is how much applicants can appease an interviewer, and not real social skills.

4 *Inoffensiveness.* The organization has a thin line to walk during selection. On one hand, it wants to get the information it needs from job applicants to make good decisions, even if the information might reflect negatively on the applicants. On the other hand, the organization does not want to turn off job applicants in the process, so that even if they receive job offers they will reject them. For example, a major U.S. corporation used to ask job applicants during their interviews such questions as: "What would your worst enemy tell me about you?" and "If you could be an insect, which one would you want to be, and why?"

5 *Differentiation among applicants.* It is important to keep in mind that the point of using selection devices is to identify differences among applicants that will predict different levels of on-the-job performance. If a selection device does not differentiate among job applicants, it cannot be useful in identifying the most promising candidates.

Consider two interview questions, "How many years' experience have you had of directly supervising others?" and "Do you enjoy working with people?" The first question differentiates among job applicants and can be used to predict performance. The second question doesn't differentiate among candidates and will be of little use in making selection decisions.

6 *Legality.* In recent years a wide variety of federal legislation, executive orders, guidelines, and court decisions have had a tremendous impact upon how organizations can assess job applicants. For instance, it is illegal to ask for information about religious affiliation, to ask for a recommendation or reference from a clergyman, or to inquire about willingness to work on a particular religious holiday. It is also illegal to ask for information about pregnancy or plans for marriage.[25] In assessing job applicants, organizations must be careful to use selection devices that do not discriminate against applicants on the basis of their age, religion, gender, race, or national origin.

As we discuss job interviews, tests, and assessment centers in the pages to come, keep these criteria in mind. They will help us to evaluate just how effective these selection devices can be.

**Making
Selection
Decisions**

The second step in the organization's selection process is deciding which candidate to hire, based on the information the organization has collected via interviews, tests, and assessment centers. The vast majority of selection decisions are made by *intuitive judgment.* That means that one individual reviews all the information on an applicant and then makes a hiring decision based upon his or her best judgment and overall impression of the applicant. After all those efforts to measure job candidates, most organizations do not scientifically combine the information to make accurate predictions. Why is this the case?

First of all, many organizations are unaware that there is any alternative to using intuitive judgment to make selection decisions. Second, some people are of the opinion that it is dehumanizing to reduce a job applicant to a series of numbers and then to make an important decision based solely on those numbers. Finally, some personnel decision makers hold strong beliefs that their intuitive judgment is excellent and could never be surpassed by a system lacking their personal brand of sensitivity and insight into the nature of people.

While the widespread use of intuitive judgment in making hiring decisions is understandable, it is also unfortunate. The evidence is now overwhelming that another method of combination, called *systematic combination,* is superior to intuitive judgment as a method of making rational and valid selection decisions. In systematic combination, all of the information on an applicant is coded in numerical terms. This information is then simply added up, with the more important pieces of information being given greater weight than less important pieces of information. The hiring decision is then based purely upon the final score assigned to the applicant as a result of this systematic combination of numerical scores.

The research evidence strongly demonstrates the superiority of systematic combination over intuitive judgment.[26] Fifty-one different studies have compared intuitive judgment to systematic combination as methods of making decisions. In 33 of the 51 studies (about 65 percent), systematic combination of numerical data yielded better predictions than did intuitive judgment. All of the remaining eighteen studies were judged to be a tie. There was not a single example of intuitive judgment outperforming systematic combination.[27]

Thus, organizational decision making, like individual decision making, has both its rational and its nonrational elements. Some decisions are made by careful analysis of the data, and others are made by gut reaction.

Job Interviews

No method of selecting employees into organizations holds more fascination for job applicants than the *job interview.* Graduating students speculate endlessly about what companies are *really* looking for. How should they dress?

How assertive should they be? What are "good" answers to questions like "Where do you want to be in five years?" and "What are your greatest weaknesses?"

The selection interview has been the object of a good deal of study and much controversy. It is unquestionably the most widely used selection device. It is considered by managers and practitioners alike to be an excellent means of assessing job applicants, and it is almost always treated as the final hurdle in the selection process.

However, its popularity with managers and practitioners as a selection device is equalled by its lack of popularity—indeed, its downright bad reputation—among scholars and researchers. Research on the job interview suggests that it is generally the most unreliable, invalid, and ineffective selection device around.[28]

The Negative Side

Why are job interviews so unreliable and invalid? Two large-scale research projects examined this question, and their results throw a great deal of light on the problems with the selection interview. Their results, along with others summarized below, lead to a rather unflattering picture of the typical selection interview.[29]

1 Interviewers have their own personal stereotypes of what constitutes a "good" employee and about how a potential "good" employee should appear in an interview situation.

2 Interviewers tend to make an accept-or-reject decision very early in the interview (often in the first five to ten minutes) and then spend the remainder of the interview seeking out information that confirms this initial impression.

3 Negative information supplied by an applicant tends to have a much greater impact upon an interviewer's judgment than does positive information.

4 An interviewer's judgment regarding an applicant is not determined solely by the applicant's characteristics, but is also influenced by the relative strength or weakness of immediately preceding interviewees. When an average applicant is interviewed immediately following one or more below-average applicants, the average applicant tends to be rated well above average. The same process works in reverse if an average applicant has the misfortune to follow immediately after an outstanding applicant.

5 Interviewers have great difficulty in reliably and validly assessing personality traits of job applicants. The social skills that interviewers feel confident they are assessing are often, in reality, good performances by well practiced interviewees.[30]

BOX 15-1

Job Interviews: The Hidden Hurdle

Corporations like to say that competence overwhelmingly decides who gets managerial jobs. But executive recruiters say subjective chemistry—deciding whether the candidate is "our kind of person"—often is far more important than the executives doing the hiring realize. Some examples:

■   One California engineering executive lost a job because he spoke with enthusiasm about coaching his son's Little League baseball team. In most cases, Little League might seem safe enough. But in this case, the executive recruiter said it "made the company president feel the executive's work wasn't really his top priority."

■   A 5-foot 5-inch candidate for a $60,000-a-year midwestern manufacturing vice presidency encountered clear sailing until a rainstorm ruined his chances. The short executive lent his tall prospective employer his raincoat. The employer later explained that until he put on the raincoat, he never fully realized how short the applicant was—or how uncomfortable he was with short people. The boss was so uncomfortable he couldn't hire the man, even though the two would have worked 700 miles apart.

■   Artichokes were the Waterloo of one company president seeking the $300,000-a-year presidency of another consumer goods company. Though the executive was generally well polished, he revealed at dinner with the chairman a pitiable incompetence at handling the unfamiliar first course. At one point, he even tried carving the leaves with a knife and fork. The executive recruiter reports that the candidate was rejected; "the chairman said he just didn't want a guy who didn't know how to eat properly."

Of course, chemistry probably won't get an obvious bungler a good job, and where one candidate is clearly superior, it may play no role at all. But in the common situation where three or four candidates all could handle the job, executives often lean to people who share their personal values, manner of dressing, and even personal habits.

Moreover, recruiters say executives often don't recognize the chemistry that influences their hiring decisions, especially when they're avoiding a strong executive who might prove threatening. Says one recruiter: "They often want an aggressive, dynamic person but one who is slightly less aggressive and dynamic than they are."

Source: Reprinted from Job interviews: The hidden hurdle. (1979, September 19). *Wall Street Journal,* p. 1. Used with permission of Dow Jones.

6 An interviewee's appearance (e.g., the types of clothes worn) and nonverbal behavior (e.g., whether the applicant "looks" interested) can greatly influence the evaluation made by the interviewer. For instance, interviewers might infer from an unstylishly dressed job applicant that he or she was unsophisticated, or from a blank facial expression that the job applicant was unenthusiastic.[31]

7 Interviews are potentially discriminatory in legal terms.[32] As we have noted above, many factors in the interview that get weighed heavily in decision making, like physical appearance, are not job-related. Moreover, interviewers often ask questions that violate applicants' legal rights to privacy, such as "What church do you belong to?" or "Are you planning on getting pregnant?"

Thus, the interview, which plays such an important role in selection decisions, is in reality a very unreliable and invalid selection device.[33] The utter frustration that this creates, even for applicants for high-level jobs, is made clear in Box 15-1. As these examples of interviews gone awry illustrate, random events can present hidden hurdles to getting hired.[34]

The Positive Side

Despite its many weaknesses, the job interview does possess several characteristics that make it an attractive selection device for organizations. Now let's look more closely at the positive side of job interviews, and discover what attributes make them so popular with companies that are hiring.[35]

1 The interview gives the organization an opportunity to provide information to the applicant about the job duties of the specific position being offered and about the organization in general.

2 If an applicant is particularly outstanding, the organization can try to use the interview to sell itself to the applicant.

3 The interview may be used as a public relations device by the organization to help project a positive image of the firm to all potential job applicants.

4 The interview provides the organization with an opportunity to obtain missing or incomplete data from interviewees, information that may be required to make selection decisions.

5 The interview permits interviewers to make assessments of their ability to get along with job applicants. This may be valuable if an interviewer will be the interviewee's immediate superior if the applicant is hired.

6 Finally, the interview may be the only appropriate or acceptable form of assessment available for many senior management and professional positions (e.g., doctors, lawyers, and professors). The most desirable potential candidates may be unwilling to subject themselves to any other form of selection.

Improving the Interview

Despite the interview's problems, interviews are solidly entrenched in current hiring procedures. Interviews seem to be here to stay. Therefore, in this last section on interviews, let's focus on ways to minimize or overcome some of the problems and pitfalls with which the interview is fraught. A summary of these suggestions appears in Table 15-3.

1 *Use a structured interview format.*   The interview can be made much more systematic and objective if a specific structure for the interview is laid out and adhered to by all interviewers. Such a structure may take the form of a list of topics to be covered, the order in which the topics should be covered, and/or a list of specific questions to be asked.[36]

2 *Provide a complete job description to interviewers.*   All interviewers should be provided with a clear description of what the job requires of a person, and what personal characteristics are likely to be indicative of success. Interviewers should also know *in advance* which interview answers should be considered favorable and which answers should be considered unfavorable.[37]

3 *Use trained interviewers.*   Effective interviewing requires specific skills in asking questions, probing for details, and listening carefully. First, interviewers need to give job applicants enough time to answer their questions. Second, interviewers need to avoid giving "stress interviews," in which job

---

TABLE   15-3

Suggestions for Improving the Interview

1. Use a structured interview format.

2. Provide a complete job description to interviewers.

3. Use trained interviewers.
    - Give applicants a chance to talk.
    - Avoid stress interviews.
    - Avoid questions that are discriminatory.

4. Use multiple interviewers.

5. Avoid quotas.

6. Keep structured written records.

7. Use the interview as only one aspect of an overall selection system.

applicants are embarrassed or intimidated on purpose. Third, interviewers have to be given explicit instructions about which questions discriminate on the basis of sex, age, or race, and which do not. Questions like "Do you plan on having children?" are not simply bad taste; they are bad business and illegal as well.[38]

4 *Use multiple interviewers.*   If interviewers have different perceptions of what a "good" job candidate looks like, then it makes sense to use multiple interviewers. With multiple interviewers, no one interviewer's bias will weigh too heavily in selection decision.

5 *Avoid quotas.*   The evidence is clear that when interviewers are told they must find a certain number of suitable candidates, they do. However, they do so by lowering their standards and recommending candidates of lower quality. Organizations would be well advised not to set quotas for interviewers.[39]

6 *Keep structured written records.*   Human memory is very limited and very fallible. Keeping structured written records insures that the information generated in each interview will be accurately maintained.[40]

7 *Use the interview as only one aspect of an overall selection system.*   Even with these improvements, the interview can never be a highly reliable or highly valid assessment measure. For that reason, the interview should never be the *sole* basis on which candidates are selected. Used in conjunction with other selection devices, the interview can provide additional insights into candidates' strengths and weaknesses. Used alone, the interview can be a hurdle that trips up as many good candidates as bad.

Tests

A second category of selection devices that organizations use to assess job applicants are paper-and-pencil tests that measure individual abilities and interests. In order to perform effectively on a job, an individual must have both the ability and the motivation to do so. Therefore, organizations have developed different types of tests to measure these different aspects of a person's performance potential.

Ability Tests

Organizations have been particularly interested in measuring five different types of individual abilities:[41]

Intellectual ability: the ability to comprehend readily and accurately what is said; the ability to do speedy and accurate math calculations; the ability to discover a rule or principle and apply it to the solution of a problem (needed for a scientist's job).

Spatial ability: the ability to understand and to use machines and equipment (needed for an architect's job).

Mechanical ability: the ability to understand and to use machines and equipment (needed for skilled mechanical trades jobs).

Clerical ability: the ability to quickly and accurately perform systematic clerical operations (needed for a secretary's job).

Motor ability: the ability to perform tasks requiring manual dexterity and eye-hand-foot coordination (needed for many skilled craft jobs).

Some examples of items from these different types of ability tests appear in Figure 15-3.

In general, research results indicate that ability tests are indeed helpful in predicting who will subsequently be successful on the job.[42] If we think back to the criteria of effective selection devices, it is easy to understand why. These tests are job-related, and they measure skills and abilities actually used on the job in question. Because they have been developed over a long period of time

Figure 15-3 Examples of ability test questions.

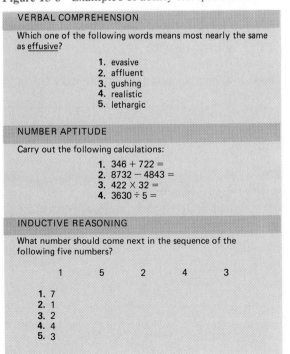

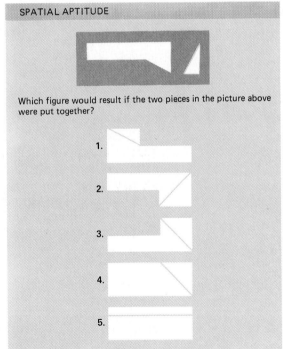

[*Source:* Reprinted with permission from Dunnette, M. D. (1966). *Personnel selection and placement.* Belmont, CA: Wadsworth, pp. 47–48.]

and with a lot of care, they are generally reliable and valid. They do indeed differentiate among applicants; differences among applicants do predict different levels of on-the-job performance.

One final point needs to be made about ability tests. Legal questions have been raised about intellectual ability tests; they may discriminate unfairly against minority job applicants. Therefore, organizations must be especially careful to demonstrate the validity of these tests for their own work force.

Personality Tests

If one were to ask a group of managers the most common reason for employee failure on the job, they would undoubtedly say that "personality" was the main problem; the employee was "difficult to get along with," "touchy," "neurotic," and so on. For this reason, organizations have used personality tests to isolate individuals with personality pathologies that would get in the way of performing successfully on the job.[43] There are two broad categories of personality tests: projective and objective.

Projective Personality Tests

Projective personality tests are those in which the subject is asked to project his or her own interpretation onto an ambiguous stimulus. Probably the most well-known of these personality tests is the Rorschach test. Each person is shown ten inkblots, of different colors and shapes, and is asked to explain what he or she sees in each blot. Another well-known projective test is the Thematic Apperception Test (TAT). The TAT consists of a series of twenty pictures; the person tested must interpret each picture by telling a story about it in terms of what he or she believes is happening and what will be the outcome. The meaning each person attaches to these inkblots and pictures depends upon his or her own personality and background. The way people respond reveals clues to their values, attitudes, and motivations.[44]

Objective Personality Tests

Objective personality tests are paper-and-pencil tests that ask subjects to check off items that best describe themselves. Probably the most well-known are the Minnesota Multiphasic Personality Inventory (MMPI), the Edwards Personal Preference Schedule (EPPS), the California Psychological Inventory (CPI), and the Bernreuter Personality Inventory (BPI). These tests yield a series of scores for the applicant on a number of personality dimensions, such as neurotic tendency, self-sufficiency, introversion-extraversion, dominance, self-confidence, decisiveness, and sociability.[45]

Usefulness of Personality Tests

Personality tests have been widely and strongly criticized. One recurrent criticism of personality tests has been that they are not reliable and valid measures of personality because they are so easy to fake; job applicants are motivated to give socially acceptable answers. For instance, consider these word association questions:[46]

Night   (dark, sleep, moon, morbid)

Umbrella (rain, prepared, cumbersome, appeasement)

Autumn   (fall, leaves, season, sad)

One doesn't have to be Freud to see that choosing morbid, appeasement, and sad reflects depression.

Another criticism of personality tests has been that they are unethical and an invasion of privacy. These personality tests give top-level managers access to the very personal, private thoughts and feelings of their future employees. In the wrong hands, the results can be used to manipulate individuals or to ruin their careers.[47]

Personality tests were originally developed by psychiatrists and clinical psychologists to diagnose emotional disorders, and the evidence is reasonably positive that their results are useful in planning and carrying out therapy.[48] However, the evidence on their adaptation from counseling settings to corporate settings is much more negative. On many of these tests, the interpretation is highly subjective, and no quantitative scores are developed. For this reason, they have had only very limited success in predicting actual on-the-job performance.[49]

Assessment Centers

The final selection device we will discuss is the *assessment center.* In the assessment center, job candidates go through a series of individual and group exercises in which they have to solve the same types of problems and make the same types of decisions they will face on the jobs being offered. They are used almost exclusively to select candidates for management jobs and to evaluate employees for promotion to supervisory positions. Assessment centers are used by over 2,000 corporations today, including IBM, AT&T, General Electric, J.C. Penney, and Sears.[50]

Structure of Assessment Centers

The evaluation of candidates in assessment centers generally lasts one to three days. During this period, a group of ten to twenty managerial candidates, referred to as *assessees,* engage in a wide variety of structured exercises. They are assessed for such attributes as oral and written communication skills, decision-making skills, energy level, originality, analytical ability, and reactions to stress. Unlike other selection devices, assessment centers also measure individual job candidates as they interact with other people. Therefore, assessment centers can also measure candidates' initiative and leadership capacities, planning and organizing skills, and human relations competence.

Generally, there are three to four assessors who observe the job candidates' performance in these exercises. These assessors can be professional psychologists, or senior-level managers who have received at least a few days' training (and sometimes several weeks' training) in assessment techniques. Assessors are required to take copious notes on their observations and to write up their impressions and evaluations systematically. Each assessee also evaluates each and every other assessee's performance (peer evaluations).[51]

Content of Assessment Centers

Generally, each organization using an assessment center will design tests and exercises directly related to its own job situations. However, most assessment centers contain some combination of the following evaluation methods.[52]

1 *Personal history forms.*   Each candidate fills in some form of biographical information blank that records work experiences, educational history, special accomplishments, and so on.

2 *In-depth structured interviews.*   Each candidate is interviewed by two or more assessors about his or her current interests and career plans. Some organizations also use these interviews to do extensive personality assessment.

3 *In-basket exercises.*   Typically, the job candidates are given an accumulation of memos, reports, notes of incoming telephone calls, letters, and other materials supposedly collected in the in-basket of the jobs that they are about to take over. The candidates are then given a limited amount of time to work through the contents of the in-basket, making decisions, responding to requests, setting agendas for meetings, and so forth. Each candidate's responses are subsequently evaluated by assessors on a set of criteria (e.g., ability to set priorities, organizational skills) and given a numerical score.

4 *Leaderless group discussions.*   Candidates work together as a group on some simulated managerial problem that requires a group meeting. Assessees are evaluated on such dimensions as willingness to listen to others, openness to alternative points of view, ability to communicate effectively, and initiative in taking the leadership role.

  In one variant of the leaderless group discussion, six job candidates play the roles of managers meeting to discuss who among their subordinates is the best candidate for a promotion to a first-line management position. Each participant has one subordinate whom he or she feels is the best candidate, and each is instructed to "do the best he/she can" for the employee from his or her department. The group has to decide how to rank order their subordinates in terms of promotability.

5 *Interpersonal role-play exercises.*   Candidates work in pairs on simulated role-play situations designed to assess candidates' abilities to listen carefully, to communicate effectively, to handle disagreement and conflict constructively, and to handle problem employees and customers tactfully. A commonly used role-play situation is a simulated appraisal interview in which the boss has been provided with incomplete information about his or her subordinate's performance. The exercise permits an assessment of the boss's ability to draw out information from the subordinate, to listen effectively, to overcome barriers to communication set up by differences in

rank, and to use the appraisal interview as an opportunity for constructive coaching and development.

6 *Case analyses.* Candidates are provided with a written case study of an organization and asked either to write up an analysis of the case or to prepare themselves for a group discussion of the case. Candidates are scored on logical and analytic thinking, organization of ideas, and written or oral communication skills. Cases can also be scored for specific knowledge of different business areas (e.g., marketing, finance, accounting, personnel).

7 *Oral presentations.* Candidates are required to make a speech on some business topic relevant to the organization. The presentation may be either immediately observed and evaluated by assessors, or it may be videotaped for subsequent, and more detailed, evaluation of poise and persuasiveness.

8 *Management games.* Management games usually require small subgroups of assessees to compete against other subgroups on some task. For instance, in "Stock Exchange," groups of job candidates play investment banking teams managing investment portfolios. Each group has a ticker tape running continuously during its meeting and is under pressure to come to quick, high-quality decisions. These games permit observations of behavior under stress.

Success of Assessment Centers

Overall, assessment centers have been very successful in predicting who will become successful managers. In the most comprehensive study of assessment centers conducted, researchers at AT&T evaluated 422 male employees in assessment centers—and then kept the results secret from AT&T's top management for eight years! Of the total number of employees who did reach middle management, 78 percent were correctly identified as promotable by the assessment staff. Moreover, of the employees who did *not* reach middle management in 8 years, 95 percent were correctly identified as *lacking* managerial potential.[53] In all but one of twenty-three subsequent studies comparing company assessment centers to other selection devices, the assessment center outperformed other assessment techniques.[54] The research evidence on the success of assessment centers is compelling.

If we think back to the criteria for good selection devices, it is easy to see why the assessment center has fared so well. Validity is increased because the exercises used are designed to bring out the specific skills and aptitudes needed for managerial positions. Validity is also increased because applicants' behavior is observed in situations that mirror closely the real job setting. Reliability is increased because exercises are standardized so assessors can evaluate the candidates under relatively constant conditions and can make relevant comparative judgments. Reliability is also increased because assessments are based upon the composite judgments of several assessors, most of whom do not know the job applicants. Consequently, there is much less chance that personal biases, mistaken impressions, and unfounded inferences will enter the selection process.[55]

Potential Problems and Solutions

While assessment centers have generally been well received, two problems have surfaced repeatedly.[56]

1   Assessment centers are very expensive in terms of both money and time. It costs a lot of money to design exercises, to hire psychologists, and to rent or buy appropriate assessment facilities. The labor costs of releasing job candidates and assessors from work can be quite high as well. It can cost as much as $2,000 per candidate to run an assessment center.

2   Those who do exceedingly well in assessment centers may suffer delusions of being a crown prince or princess. They may expect rapid advancement on the basis of potential only. Management may exacerbate this problem by treating these individuals so well that their future success becomes a self-fulfilling prophecy. In contrast, candidates who do poorly at an assessment center may feel that they have been given the kiss of death as far as their future with the company is concerned.

As organizations have gained in experience in using assessment centers, they have become more sophisticated in dealing with these issues. Two recent innovations in assessment centers have addressed these problems.[57]

1   Costs can be cut by requiring candidates to do many of the exercises before coming to the center. For example, candidates may complete a personal history form and go through an in-basket exercise before coming to the center. Companies can use commercially available exercises instead of exercises developed specifically for them. Assessment centers can be run on company property, instead of in expensive outside facilities. Moreover, assessment centers can be conducted on Saturday and Sunday to avoid disrupting work.

2   Feedback procedures and follow-up training can be used to blunt the effects of the "Crown Prince" and "Kiss of Death" syndrome. Professional psychologists can give successful candidates positive but realistic feedback on their future prospects in the corporation. For those not chosen, accurate feedback and remedial training can help offset a natural letdown. For instance, at Four-Phase System, Inc., a California computer systems company, the second half of the assessment center is used for immediate remedial training in areas where the assessment center turned up an employee weakness.

While no selection device is without flaws, the assessment center is clearly the best selection device for choosing managerial employees. When one considers how long the selection interview has been used and how far away it is from being a valid predictor of success, the short, successful history of the assessment center is even more impressive.

Keys to Effective Management

Obtaining a good fit between the needs of the individual and the needs of the organization is equally important to both parties. If such a fit can be achieved, employees are more likely to exhibit greater productivity, experience higher job satisfaction, and demonstrate greater loyalty to the organization. Below we look at some ways to systematically improve the organizational entry process.

1 *Organizations can improve their selection programs by making their selection devices more job-related, reliable, and valid.* Selection devices have to tap the actual skills used on the specific jobs that are being filled. Only if selection devices are job-related will organizations be able to accurately predict on-the-job performance. Organizations should also make their selection devices more reliable and valid. Selection devices provide stable measures of individual abilities and interests, and should really measure what they purport to measure. More extensive selection device development and more extensive evaluation of past hiring decisions can help organizations increase both the reliability and the validity of their selection measures.

2 *Organizations should avoid overreliance on the typical unstructured job interview.* Interviewers do not agree on what constitutes a "good" employee; they evaluate the same information about job applicants in very different ways; the job applicant's physical appearance and nonverbal behavior can greatly influence the evaluation made by the interviewer. Therefore, these interviews tend to be poor selection devices.

However, sometimes the interview is needed to sell the organization to job candidates and to obtain missing data from job applicants. Interviews can be improved by using a structured interview format, training interviewers in communication skills, using multiple interviewers, and keeping structured written records.

3 *Ability tests are excellent predictors of performance and should be used more frequently by organizations.* Ability tests have been very useful in making selection decisions. They are job-related, and they measure skills and abilities critical to effective job performance. Because most ability tests have been developed over a long period of time and with a lot of care, they are also generally reliable and valid.

4   *Personality tests, on the other hand, may be effective in counseling situations, but are not generally effective as selection devices.*   Answers on personality tests may be faked by job applicants. These tests are also considered an invasion of privacy by many job applicants. For these reasons, personality tests should be used very sparingly, if at all, by organizations.

5   *Organizations should use assessment centers more frequently to select job candidates for managerial positions.*   The validity of assessment centers is high because they use exercises designed to bring out the decision-making, analytical, and communication skills of managers. Moreover, managers are observed in interaction with other people and in situations which mirror closely the real job setting. The reliability of assessment centers is high because exercises are standardized and because assessments are based upon the composite judgments of several assessors. The research evidence on the success of assessment centers in choosing managers is convincing.

6   *Organizations should use systematic combination rather than intuitive judgment to combine the various pieces of information they collect on job candidates.*   The evidence is compelling that the systematic combination approach to making hiring decisions is superior to intuitive judgment. Systematic combination can take into account many more pieces of information in making a decision than any individual decision maker could, and can do so without distorting, changing, or omitting any relevant data. Unfortunately, intuitive judgment is too often contaminated by personal bias and faulty first impressions.

7   *Organizations can help applicants make better job choice decisions through improved university-employer links and realistic job previews.*   While ultimately individuals are responsible for their own career decisions, organizations can help job applicants obtain more accurate information through campus visits, in-company class projects, guest speakers, and internships. Realistic job previews can also improve the decision making of job applicants without impairing the organization's ability to recruit.

Review Questions

1   What factors influence which careers people pursue?

2   In Holland's model, why do people with different types of personality gravitate to different types of jobs?

3   Why is it the case that most people cannot make important decisions in a perfectly rational manner?

4   What can individuals do to make better job choice decisions?

5 What is the difference between the intuitive judgment and systematic combination methods of evaluating job candidates? Which is preferable, and why?

6 What are realistic job previews? Why are they important?

7 Name five criteria of good selection devices. Briefly explain why each criterion is important.

8 What is the difference between reliability and validity?

9 Why is the job interview generally considered such an ineffective selection device?

10 What are the advantages of interviews? How can interviews be improved to make them more reliable and valid?

11 Which type of test—ability or personality—is a better predictor of job performance? Why?

12 What are the three major objections to the use of personality tests in selecting job candidates?

13 What is the difference between *projective* and *objective* personality tests?

14 What is an assessment center? Briefly identify five data-collection exercises that generally occur in an assessment center.

15 What are some potential problems in assessment centers, and how might these problems be addressed?

Gigantic Aircraft Company

Gigantic Aircraft Company is a large firm with a plant near Santa Barbara, California. The personnel manager has called in Boyce Piersol, a management consultant specializing in personnel, for advice on selection policies. Bill Fabris invited Piersol to come in the first thing in the morning. When Piersol arrived, Fabris said:

Boyce, I'm glad you're here. I've been having a lot of trouble in selection recently. My long suit has always been collective bargaining. I'm a lawyer by training, and I think I need help. Briefly, let me outline how we handle selection here now:

***Blue-collar employees**—Screening interview to separate out the misfits; then a test battery—mostly abilities tests—and then interview the best of the lot. For crucial jobs, either securitywise, or if the job involves expensive equipment, get two letters of reference from prior employers.*

***White-collar employees**—Clerical, and so forth—same as blue-collar procedures except references always are checked out.*

***Managerial employees**—Multiple interviews, intelligence tests, personality tests, and references.*

I've also been making a list of what's happened in selection in the last six months since I've been in this job.

1. Our best managerial candidate was lost because she refused to take the personality test we use, the Minnesota Multiphasic Personality Inventory. She said it was an invasion of her privacy.

2. For employees who handle expensive supplies, we use a polygraph test, too. We've had

a few refuse to take it. Our thefts are high. We wonder if it's any good! My boss feels the polygraph is essential.

3. One man we hired is doing a good job. We accidently found out he has a prison record. His supervisor wants to know how we missed that and wants to let him go. We have no policy on this, but I feel he's proved himself in three months on the job.

4. We're having a lot of trouble on the reference letters. When we ask people to rate the applicants on the basis of all factors, including references, we find the supervisors read different things into these letters.

5. Our turnover has been high. My boss thinks it's because we aren't matching the best people to the right jobs. I need your help.

Questions for Discussion

1 What are the biggest strengths of Gigantic's selection system?

2 What are the biggest weaknesses of Gigantic's selection system?

3 Imagine you are Boyce Piersol. Based on what you know now, what specific recommendations would you make to the personnel manager? Why?

Source: Glueck, W. F. (1974). *Cases and exercises in personnel.* Dallas, TX: Business Publications, Inc. Used by permission.

Notes

1   Kotter, J. P. (1973). The psychological contract: Managing the joining-up process. *California Management Review, 15,* 91–99.

2   Clausen, J. A. (Ed.). (1968). *Socialization and society.* Boston: Little, Brown.

3   Hall, D. T. (1976). *Careers in organizations.* Pacific Palisades, CA: Goodyear.

4   Holland, J. L. (1973). *Making vocational choices: A theory of careers.* Englewood Cliffs, N.J.: Prentice-Hall.
Feldman, D. C. & Arnold, H. J. (1985). Personality types and career patterns: Some empirical evidence on Holland's model. *Canadian Journal of Administrative Sciences, 2,* 192–210.

5   Glaser, B. G. (1968). *Organizational careers: A sourcebook for theory.* Chicago: Aldine.
Roe, A. (1957). Early determinants of vocational choice: *Journal of Counselling Psychology, 4,* 212–217.

6   Hall, *loc. cit.*

7   Reich, C. (1970). *The greening of America.* New York: Random House.

8   Vroom, V. H. (1966). Occupational choice: A study of pre- and post-decision processes. *Organizational Behavior and Human Performance, 1,* 212–225.

9   Janis, I. L., & Mann, L. (1977). *Decision making: A psychological analysis of conflict, choice, and commitment.* New York: Free Press.

10   Ward, L. B. & Athos, A. G. (1972). *Student expectations of corporate life.* Boston: Division of Research, Graduate School of Business Administration, Harvard University.

11   Wanous, J. P. (1981). *Organizational entry.* Reading, MA: Addison-Wesley.

12   Simon, H. A. (1957). *Models of man.* New York: John Wiley.

13   Janis, I., & Wheeler, D. (1978, May). Thinking clearly about career choices. *Psychology Today,* 66–68, 70, 75–76, 121–122.

14   Soelberg, P. O. (1966). Unprogrammed decision making. *Proceedings of the Academy of Management,* 26th Annual Meeting, San Francisco.

15   Janis & Mann, *loc. cit.*

16 Feldman, D. C. (1980). A socialization process that helps new recruits succeed. *Personnel, 57,* 11–23.

17 Janis and Mann, *op. cit.*

18 Janis and Wheeler, *op. cit.*

19 Hall, *op. cit.,* 152.

20 Ward and Athos, *op. cit.*

21 Feldman, D. C. (1976a). A contingency theory of socialization. *Administrative Science Quarterly, 21,* 433–452.

22 Weitz, J. (1956). Job expectancy and survival. *Journal of Applied Psychology, 40,* 245–247.

23 Wanous, *op. cit.*

24 Dunnette, M. D. (1966). *Personnel selection and placement.* Belmont, Calif.: Wadsworth.

25 Connolly, W. B. (1975). *A practical guide to equal employment opportunity: Laws, principles, and practices,* Vols. 1 and 2. New York: Law Journal Press.

26 Sawyer, J. (1966). Measurement and prediction, clinical and statistical. *Psychological Bulletin, 66,* 178–200.
  Dawes, R. M. (1979). The robust beauty of improper linear models in decision making. *American Psychologist, 34,* 571–582.

27 Meehl, P. E. (1965). Seer over sign: The first good example. *Journal of Experimental Research in Personality, 1,* 27–32.

28 Valenzi, E. R., and Andrews, I. R. (1973). Individual differences in the decision process of employment interviewers. *Journal of Applied Psychology, 58,* 49–53.
  Wright, O. R., Jr. (1969). Summary of research on the selection interview since 1964. *Personnel Psychology, 22,* 391–413.

29 Webster, E. C. (1964). *Decision making in the employment interview.* Montreal: Industrial Relations Center, McGill University.
  Carlson, R. C., Thayer, P. W., Mayfield, E. C., and Peterson, D. A. (1971). Improvements in the selection interview. *Personnel Journal, 50,* 268–274.

30 Mayfield, E. C. (1964). The selection interview: A re-evaluation of published research. *Personnel Psychology, 17,* 239–260.

31 Schmitt, N. (1976). Social and situational determinants of interview decisions: Implications for the employment interview. *Personnel Psychology, 29,* 79–102.

32 Arvey, R. D. (1979). Unfair discrimination in the employment interview: Legal and psychological aspects. *Psychological Bulletin, 86,* 736–765.

33 Carlson, R. C. (1971). The effect of interview information in altering valid impressions. *Journal of Applied Psychology, 55,* 66–72.

34 *Wall Street Journal* (1979, September 19), 1.

35 Miner, J. B., & Miner, M. G. (1977). *Personnel and industrial relations: A managerial approach* (rev. ed.). New York: Macmillan.

36 Mayfield, E. C., Brown, S. H., & Hamstra, B. W. (1980). Selection interviewing in the life insurance industry: An update of research and practice. *Personnel Psychology, 33,* 725–740.

37 Osburn, H. G., Timmreck, C., & Digby, D. (1981). Effect of dimensional relevance on accuracy of simulated hiring decisions by employment interviewers. *Journal of Applied Psychology, 66,* 159–165.

38 Rothstein, M., & Jackson, D. N. (1980). Decision making in the employment interview: An experimental approach. *Journal of Applied Psychology, 65,* 271–283.

39 Carlson, Thayer, Mayfield, & Peterson, *loc. cit.*

40 Webster, *loc. cit.*

41 Dunnette, *loc. cit.*

42 Ghiselli, E. E. (1973). The validity of aptitude tests in personnel selection. *Personnel Psychology, 26,* 461–478.

43 Beach, D. S. (1980). *Personnel* (4th ed.). New York: Macmillan, 244.

44 Beach, *loc. cit.*

45 Barrett, R. S. (1963). Guide to using psychological tests. *Harvard Business Review, 41*(5), 138–146.

46 Whyte, W. H., Jr. (1956). *The organization man.* New York: Simon and Schuster, 199–200.

47 Guion, R. M., & Gottier, R. F. (1965). Validity of personality measures in personnel selection. *Personnel Psychology, 18*(2), 135–164.

48 Whyte, *loc. cit.*

49 Gellerman, S. W. (1958). The ethics of personality testing. *Personnel, 35*(3), 30–35.

50 Finkle, R. B. (1976). Managerial assessment centers. In M.D. Dunnette (Ed.), *Handbook of industrial and organizational psychology.* Chicago: Rand McNally, 861–888.

51   Byham, W. C. (1970, July-August). Assessment centers for spotting future managers. *Harvard Business Review,* 150–167.

52   Howard, A. (1974). An assessment of assessment centers. *Academy of Management Journal, 17,* 115–117.

53   Bray, D. W., Campbell, R. J., & Grant, D. L. (1974). *Formative years in business.* New York: Wiley.

54   Byham, *op. cit.,* 150–167.

55   Byham, *op. cit.,* 150–167.

56   Howard, *op. cit.,* 130–134.

57   Byham, *op. cit.,* 150–167.

Chapter 16

Managing Job Stress

CHAPTER OUTLINE

The Nature of Job Stress

Sources of Job Stress

Consequences of Job Stress

Individual Differences and Stress

Coping with Job Stress

Keys to Effective Management

Review Questions

A recent survey conducted by the Gallup Organization for the *Wall Street Journal* found that over one-third of the executives sampled considered job stress to be a substantial personal concern. About 40 percent of the executives sampled say they frequently lie awake at night or wake up thinking about work problems, while another 33 percent report they often feel incapable of relaxing at home because of stress.[1] In the 1960s, America came to terms with the "blue-collar blues"; in the 1970s, it discovered "white-collar woes." In the 1980s, America is learning that workers at all levels of the organization are feeling tension and pressure in their jobs—and that this job stress takes a heavy toll.

In this chapter, we'll explore the nature of job stress from the perspective of both the individual and the organization. In the first section of the chapter, we will define job stress and discuss how it operates in our daily work lives. Then we'll look at the major sources of stress and the reasons why we experience certain aspects of our work environments as stressful. In the third section, we'll discover what the consequences of stress are—for our psychological well-being, for our physical health, and for the effectiveness of the organizations of which we are members. Fourth, we'll look at individual characteristics that make some people more prone to stress, and others less so. Finally, we'll examine coping with job stress, and what organizations can do to help their employees cope with the inevitable stress they will face at work.

The Nature of Job Stress

The nature of job stress has been studied by scholars in a wide range of academic disciplines. Physicians, psychiatrists, and researchers in management have all studied its causes and its symptoms, and have defined the term in a variety of different ways. For our purposes, we will define *stress* as the reactions of individuals to new or threatening factors in their work environments.

The Dual Nature of Stress

An important characteristic of job stress that our definition highlights is that it can be either positive or negative. Some new work situations can bring us positive challenges and excitement, while others are very threatening and anxiety-arousing.[2]

For example, a new downturn in the economy can create negative stress for sales personnel, because they will be much more anxious about making sales commissions and sales quotas. When managers are given major projects to complete under severe time pressure, they also experience negative stress. They feel very tense and nervous about being able to get their work done on time.

On the other hand, promotions to new jobs present employees with positive stress. While employees may feel anxious about their new work assignments, they also anticipate them eagerly and look forward to the additional challenges, rewards, and excitement.[3] In these cases, the new and uncertain job situations create positive stress (also called *eustress*).

Inevitability of Stress

Our definition of job stress also suggests that job stress is inevitable for most individuals. Most people have both living situations and job situations that constantly produce stress. Simply the logistics of living can create stress: the car breaking down on the way to an appointment; reaching the post office five seconds after it closed; going out of the way to pick up merchandise that is not ready when promised. At work, people either miss important phone calls or can't reach those whom they need; they can't figure out exactly what's expected of them; they have too much work to do and too little time to do it in. It is impossible to imagine what a life or a job with no stress would be like—and it is not certain that such a life would be terribly attractive. In fact, in the Gallup Poll just cited, fewer than 10 percent of those surveyed thought they would be happier in less stressful jobs. Almost 60 percent of the managers in this survey felt exhilarated by job stress.[4]

Personal Reactions to Stress

Our definition of job stress also highlights the fact that individuals can have a variety of reactions to job stress. They can react *emotionally* by feeling frustrated or anxious, happy or excited, bored or depressed. The way they view the world *perceptually* can also change under stress; they may experience mental blocks, be hypersensitive to criticism, or have trouble concentrating. People can respond to stress *behaviorally;* they may eat more, drink more, lose their appetites, or stop going out socially.

People's bodies also respond to stress *physiologically.* In fact, the physiological response to stress follows a fairly consistent pattern known as the ***General Adaptation Syndrome.***[5] In the first stage, ***alarm,*** the body prepares for stress by releasing hormones from the endocrine glands. Hearts beat faster, breathing quickens, blood-sugar levels rise, muscles tense up, pupils dilate, and digestion slows. During the second stage, ***resistance,*** the body tries to repair the shock caused by the stress and to return the body to its normal state. However, if the stress continues long enough, the body's capacity for adaptation becomes exhausted. In this third stage, ***exhaustion,*** the body's resistance level progressively weakens. The body is then more susceptible to diseases like ulcers and heart attacks.

What is even more frightening to note is that the effects of stress are cumulative. Like exposure to x-rays or toxic chemicals, stress builds up inside the body. Once the health level has reached the danger point, continued chronic stress can precipitate a major health breakdown. It is indeed a fact of life for twentieth-century Americans that stress can kill.[6]

Importance for Organizational Effectiveness

The impact stress has on organizational performance is no less dramatic. Many executives feel they could make better decisions and perform more effectively if they worked under less stress. Stress has also been linked to absenteeism, turnover, and industrial accidents.[7] In a new development, many workers are suing companies for compensation payments for emotional and physical illnesses traced to their jobs—and winning. Consider some examples:[8]

1   A Burroughs Corporation secretary became hysterical when her boss constantly criticized her for going to the bathroom too often. She said he also asked prying questions about her new husband's family. The state workers' disability compensation bureau awarded her $7,000.

2   A Maine state trooper became severely depressed because he was on call 24 hours a day. He claimed his sex life deteriorated because he never knew when the phone would ring. He settled out of court for $5,000.

3   In California there are now 3,000 to 4,000 claims per year for psychiatric injury resulting from work-related experiences. About half of these result in workers' compensation awards. A Ventura law firm solicits cases with ads that ask "Does your job make you sick?"

Just as stress accumulates in our bodies, stress accumulates in organizations. At high levels, it destroys organizational climate, lowers organizational performance, and weakens organizational effectiveness. We turn next to examine what causes the most stress in organizations today.

Sources of Job Stress

Individuals will experience stress when they face new or threatening factors in their work environments. While individuals will vary, of course, in what they experience as stressful, there are some aspects of work that systematically create job stress for employees.

A summary list of these major sources of stress appears in Table 16-1. One major source of job stress is *the job itself.* The way the job is designed, the amount of time pressure an individual faces, and the amount of expectations others have of a person at work can all lead to job stress. *Interpersonal relationships* are a second source of job stress. How much contact an individual has with coworkers and bosses, how much time he or she deals with clients or consumers, and how pleasant those interactions are all influence how much stress an individual experiences at work. Third, *problems in personal lives* can spill over into the work environment, adding further tension to an already stressful work situation.

Job Characteristics

A major source of job stress is a person's *role* in the organization. A **role** is simply the set of expectations that other people in the organization have of an individual in his or her job. Supervisors, coworkers, clients, customers, suppliers, and inspectors—all of these people expect an individual to behave in

---

TABLE   16-1

Sources of Job Stress

Job Characteristics

Role ambiguity
Role conflict
Role overload
Role underload

Interpersonal Relationships

Amount of contact with others
Dealing with people in other departments
Organizational climate

Personal Factors

Career concerns
Geographical mobility
Rate of life change

certain predictable ways. Often, the expectations others have of an employee are unclear, in conflict, or too high for the employee to meet within the time allotted, and he or she experiences stress.

Role Ambiguity

In order for people to perform their jobs well in organizations, they need to know their job objectives, what they are expected to do and not do, and what the scope and responsibilities of their jobs are. When there is a lot of uncertainty surrounding job definitions or job expectations, people experience *role ambiguity.*[9]

With the recent increase in mergers and acquisitions among major corporations, for instance, more and more employees are experiencing job stress as a result of role ambiguity. When two corporations merge, employees are often unsure who is to perform which job duties. Employees wonder if they are duplicating other people's work, and are uncertain about whom they should be reporting their problems to. All this role ambiguity is anxiety-arousing to employees, and they consequently experience job stress.

Role Conflict

Often employees discover that different groups of people in an organization have widely varying expectations of them, and that they cannot meet all these expectations. This inconsistency of expectations associated with a role is called *role conflict.*[10] There are two general types of role conflict in organizations.

The first type is *intersender role conflict:* two different groups have expectations of an individual that are incompatible or inconsistent.[11] For example, admissions clerks in hospitals are expected by public relations officers to be pleasant, sympathetic, and helpful to incoming patients and their families, but are also expected by the comptroller's office to get detailed insurance and financial information. It is difficult for admissions clerks to achieve both goals simultaneously.

The second type is *intrasender role conflict:* one group has incompatible or inconsistent expectations of another.[12] The plight of air traffic controllers is a good illustration of such role conflict. Air traffic controllers are under order from the Federal Aviation Administration to properly space all aircraft traffic. Nevertheless, control tower supervisors encourage air traffic controllers to ignore some of these regulations because aircraft traffic would get too heavy if all rules were followed to the letter. However, if a near-miss or an error occurs, the controllers are disciplined by these same supervisors for not following the regulations. Air traffic controllers are receiving inconsistent messages from their bosses (ignore regulations; follow regulations) and experience tremendous stress as a result. In one year alone at Chicago's O'Hare Airport, seven controllers experienced such acute hypertension that they had to be carried out of the control tower on a stretcher.[13]

Role Overload

Role overload is a situation in which employees feel they are being asked to do more than time or ability permits. Working under time pressure is especially stressful. People are anxious when they have a lot to do before some deadline; as time runs out, a feeling of impending disaster increases.[14]

Two particularly interesting studies have been conducted on the impact of role overload on job stress. One study was done with tax accountants approaching the April 15 tax deadline;[15] the other was done wth medical students before an impending examination.[16] In both studies, physiological symptoms of stress increased dramatically prior to the time deadline, and decreased sharply after the deadline had passed. The general adaptation syndrome does activate itself as the threat of time deadlines draws near, and the body returns to equilibrium after the threat is over.

Role Underload

Most frequently, employees experience stress from having to respond to the role expectations of too many people. For some jobs and some workers, though, stress comes from role underload. *Role underload* is the condition in which employees have too little work to do or too little variety in their work. Salespeople in a store with no customers, standing around all day with nothing to do, could be said to experience role underload. Assembly line workers also generally experience role underload; rarely do they perform more than one or two tasks day after day after day.

Ironically, role underload can lead to many of the same problems as role overload: low self-esteem; increased frequency of nervous symptoms and complaints; increased health problems. One of the most disturbing outcomes of role underload is passivity. Workers with role underload report they feel both physically and psychologically weary; even when they are not at work, they do not show much interest in social activity or physical exercise.[17]

Interpersonal Relationships

A second major source of stress in organizations is poor interpersonal relationships with others, be they supervisors, subordinates, coworkers, or clients. When interpersonal relationships at work are unpleasant, employees develop a generalized anxiety, a diffuse feeling of dread about upcoming meetings and interactions. Three aspects of interpersonal relationships at work, in particular, have a negative impact on job stress: (1) amount of contact with others; (2) amount of contact with people in other departments; and (3) organizational climate.[18]

Amount of Contact with Others

Jobs vary in terms of how much interpersonal contact is built into them. Some jobs, like security guard or research scientist, involve relatively little interaction with others. In contrast, jobs like administrative assistant or waitress require constant human interaction. While most of these interactions proceed smoothly, over time people become burned out and feel a need for privacy. Too much prolonged contact with other people can cause stress.[19]

This stress is exacerbated when the people we come into contact with are in distress themselves. For this reason, employees in the "helping professions"—health care, social service, education, and law—report the highest levels of stress. The clients' stress rubs off on people who are acting in the helping capacity. It is ironic that doctors have the highest rate of alcoholism of any of the professions and that psychiatrists have the highest rate of suicide.[20]

Amount of Contact with People in Other Departments

Having contacts with people outside one's own department creates a special sort of stress. People in other departments do not always have an adequate understanding of jobs outside their own areas. As a result, they are more likely to make requests that cannot be honored or set deadlines that cannot be met.[21]

In hospitals, for example, employees in service departments like x-ray and pharmacy report high amounts of stress. The x-ray technicians and pharmacists report that doctors and nurses from the medical and surgical units make unreasonable demands on them and set very unrealistic deadlines for their services. Two x-ray technicians on call all night, for instance, cannot respond to all calls for service quickly when one always has to be on duty in the emergency room.

Organizational Climate

Finally, the overall psychological climate of the organization can create stress. When day-to-day life in an organization is marked by unfriendly, distant, or hostile exchanges, employees are continually tense. They have little trust in each other and do not express their true concerns and desires. They are unsupportive of each other and spend little time helping each other with problems.[22]

In Box 16-1, we have a description of a person working in such a hostile organization. The manager in this excerpt, Larry Ross, sees the organization as a minefield, waiting to go off at the first misstep.[23] The stress such organizations create for their employees is severe; the damage such stress creates, incalculable.

Personal Factors

Frequently, employees' personal lives have a marked effect on their lives at work. If things are going well personally, they are more likely to be upbeat and optimistic. They have more energy and patience for dealing with problems at work. On the other hand, if employees are having some personal problems, they might be more tense or distracted when they go to work. Little problems at work make them angry and irritable. Their nerves may already be a little frayed; it takes less to get them upset.

Three factors, in particular, influence how much stress people bring from their personal lives to the work setting: (1) their career concerns; (2) their geographical mobility; and (3) the rate of change in their personal lives.

Career Concerns

One major career concern that can cause stress is lack of job security. With the exception of some unionized employees, very few workers in America have job security—and in recessions, even those employees enjoy few guarantees. Even top-level managers can lose their jobs on short notice. When the economy worsens or the profits of the firm go flat, people become especially worried about how they could support themselves if they lost their jobs.

A second career concern that can cause employees stress is status incongruity, i.e., having jobs with less status (power, prestige) than they think they deserve. People are likely to feel stress if they are in a job that they consider beneath them. Status incongruity makes an individual feel defensive at work:

BOX 16-1

Larry Ross: One Man's View of Organizational Life

Most corporations I've been in, they were on the New York Stock Exchange with thousands and thousands of stockholders. The last one—whereas, I was the president and chief executive, I was always subject to the board of directors, who had pressure from the stockholders. I owned a portion of the business, but I wasn't in control. I don't know of any situation in the corporate world where an executive is completely free and sure of his job from moment to moment.

The danger starts as soon as you become a district manager. You have men working for you and you have a boss above. You're caught in a squeeze. The squeeze progresses from station to station. I'll tell you what a squeeze is. You have guys working for you that are shooting for your job. The guy you're working for is scared stiff you're gonna shove him out of his job. Everybody goes around and says, "The test of the true executive is that you have men working for you that can replace you, so you can move up." That's a lot of baloney. The manager is afraid of the bright young guy coming up.

Fear is always prevalent in the corporate structure. Even if you're a top man, even if you're hard, even if you do your job—by the slight flick of a finger, your boss can fire you. There's always the insecurity. You bungle a job. You're fearful of losing a big customer. You're fearful so many things will appear on your record, stand against you. You're always fearful of the big mistake. You've got to be careful when you go to corporation parties. Your wife, your children have to behave properly. You've got to fit in the mold. You've got to be on guard.

As he struggles in this jungle, every position he's in, he's terribly lonely. He can't confide and talk with the guy working under him. He can't confide and talk to the man he's working for. To give vent to his feelings, his fears and his insecurities, he'd expose himself. This goes all the way up the line until he gets to be president. The president *really* doesn't have anybody to talk to, because the vice presidents are waiting for him to die or make a mistake and get knocked off so they can get his job.

He can't talk to the board of directors, because to them he has to appear as a tower of strength, knowledge, and wisdom, and have the ability to walk on water. The board of directors, they're cold, they're hard. They don't have any direct-line responsibilities. They're interested in profits. They're interested in progress. They're interested in keeping a good face in the community—if it's profitable. You have the tremendous infighting of man against man for survival and clawing to the top.

Source: Reprinted from Terkel, S. (1974). *Working.* New York: Pantheon, pp. 405–407. Used with permission.

What am I doing wrong? What could I do to get ahead? Such career concerns also create self-induced pressure to perform at super-high standards, and make individuals overly sensitive to criticism and resentful of the success of others.[24]

Geographical Mobility

Geographical moves create stress because they disrupt the routines of daily life. Everything in employees' lives is in flux. Simple activities like shopping or driving to work take more effort. Workers have fewer friends to turn to for social support. When geographical moves are undertaken as part of a job transfer, the moves can be even more stressful. The transferred employees are likely to feel out of control at work, too, and experience their new work environments as unpredictable.[25]

Moving also creates problems for the spouses and children of employees. They, too, are uprooted from schools, jobs, and friends. They are often lonely, and need help in getting settled and adjusted. For employees who have just moved, it is not uncommon for the stress at work and the stress at home to start feeding off each other in a negative cycle.[26] The more changes that occur in a person's social relationships, financial affairs, or family life, the greater the person's stress will be. The faster those changes occur, the more that stress is exacerbated.

A scale developed by T. H. Holmes and R. H. Rahe and their colleagues at the University of Washington provides a quantitative measure of how quickly people's lives have changed over a twelve-month period. This scale appears in Table 16-2. Each of the forty-three different events listed in Table 16-2 is rated for the amount of stress it typically creates; the more points assigned, the more stressful the life event. By totaling the number of points associated with all the changes that occurred over the past year, people can obtain a good measure of how much stress they have had to contend with.[27]

Holmes and Rahe found they could predict stress-related diseases from scores on this rating scale. If a person experiences changes that add up to more than 200 scale points in a single year, he or she has a 50-50 chance of incurring a serious health problem the following year. If someone experiences changes which add up to more than 300 points in a given year, that person has a 75 percent chance of serious health problems in the upcoming year. The general adaptation syndrome that we discussed earlier in the chapter explains these results. If the body's defenses for resisting illness are exhausted from constant adjustment to new stresses, the person is more vulnerable to diseases such as heart attacks and ulcers.[28]

Holmes and Rahe's scale points out another phenomenon: as far as stress goes, there *can* be too much of a good thing. Several of the life events in the rating scale are positive (e.g., marriage, outstanding personal achievement, and vacations). However, even these positive events require some adjustment. Marriage, for instance, requires many compromises and changes in daily routines. Even if the stress is associated with a positive event, it still takes its toll.

TABLE 16-2

Scale of Stressful Life Events

Life event	Scale value
Death of spouse	100
Divorce	73
Marital separation	65
Jail term	63
Death of close family member	63
Major personal injury or illness	53
Marriage	50
Fired from work	47
Marital reconciliation	45
Retirement	45
Major change in health of family member	44
Pregnancy	40
Sex difficulties	39
Gain of a new family member	39
Business readjustment	39
Change in financial state	38
Death of a close friend	37
Change to a different line of work	36
Change in number of arguments with spouse	35
Mortgage over $10,000	31
Foreclosure of mortgage or loan	30
Change in responsibilities at work	29
Son or daughter leaving home	29
Trouble with in-laws	29
Outstanding personal achievement	28
Wife begins or stops work	26
Begin or end school	26
Change in living conditions	25
Revision of personal habits	24
Trouble with boss	23
Change in work hours or conditions	20
Change in residence	20
Change in schools	20
Change in recreation	19
Change in church activities	19
Change in social activities	18
Mortgage or loan less than $10,000	17
Change in sleeping habits	16
Change in number of family get-togethers	15
Change in eating habits	15
Vacation	13
Christmas	12
Minor violations of the law	11

Source: Ruch, L. O., & Holmes, T. H. (1971, June). Scaling of life change: Comparison of direct and indirect methods. *Journal of Psychosomatic Research, 11,* 213.

Consequences of Job Stress

While Holmes and Rahe are concerned mainly with the physiological consequences of stress, there is a wide array of attitudes and behaviors that are affected by stress as well. In this next section, we will explore the impact job stress has on all these variables (cf. Table 16-3).

Physical Health

Job stress has a substantially negative impact on physical health. First, job stress increases the frequency of *minor physical ailments*. People who are experiencing stress are more likely to have headaches, stomach aches, back aches, and chest pains.[29]

Second, job stress has a major impact on *contributory factors to major illnesses*. People under stress are more likely to have a quickened heart beat and

TABLE 16-3
Consequences of Job Stress
Physical Health
Physical ailments Contributory factors to major illnesses Major physical illnesses Longevity
Psychological Well-Being

Anxiety
Frustration:
    Passivity
    Aggression
    Depression
    Suicide

Performance
Absenteeism and turnover Sabotage Productivity
Decision Making
Procrastination Less search for new information Difficulty in concentrating

greater difficulty breathing. Blood pressure rises with stress, as do cholesterol levels. All of these factors make the body more susceptible to major illnesses like heart disease.[30]

Indeed, the research quite strongly suggests that people who undergo prolonged periods of stress are more likely to suffer more *major physical illnesses*. In particular, stress is a major contributor to ulcers, arthritis, drug and alcohol abuse, and heart disease. Some researchers suggest that managers with high levels of stress may be twice as prone to heart disease, five times as prone to a second heart attack, and twice as prone to fatal heart attacks as low-stress managers.[31]

Finally, and not surprisingly in light of the evidence presented above, job stress influences *longevity*. There is strong evidence that job stress shortens one's life.[32] Job stress not only makes bodies more susceptible to major illnesses, but also contributes directly to life-threatening diseases.

Even the courts have been making worker compensation awards on the basis of stress-induced disabilities. Courts have ruled that in stress cases, "the central consideration isn't the actual work environment, but how the employee reacts to it." Employers can be held liable if the illness has been "aggravated, accelerated, precipitated, or triggered" by the conditions of the job.[33]

Psychological Well-Being

Stress has a marked impact on mental as well as physical health. Probably the most noticeable impact job stress has on people psychologically is that it increases their anxiety. *Anxiety* is a vague sense of apprehension and foreboding. People may not know exactly how to put their finger on what's bothering them, but they feel vulnerable to people and events in their work environments. They worry more about how they will deal with potential threats that may not even materialize.

Stress also increases *frustration.* When people are blocked from behaving the way they would like to behave or from getting what they want, they are said to be frustrated.[34] When people get passed over for a promotion, for instance, they feel frustrated. They can't do the job they want, and they can't obtain the status and rewards they desire. There are several ways in which individuals respond to frustration.

One response to frustration is *passivity.* If a person constantly fails at a job despite increased efforts, or keeps on getting the bad breaks, he or she is likely to give up or become disinterested. When you read in the newspapers about unemployment among those "actively seeking employment," for instance, these figures exclude those workers who have not looked for a job in six months. These workers are so frustrated by constant rejection that they have withdrawn from the work force and have stopped looking for work altogether.

Another response to frustration is *aggression.* Aggressive employees strike out at those around them. If employees feel aggressive toward their supervisors and coworkers, they may snipe at them in meetings. They may become irritable, losing their temper over relatively unimportant matters. They may become more negative, finding fault with everyone and everything.

A third response to frustration is **depression.** When people are frustrated at work, they often become sad. They may become pessimistic and lose their self-confidence and self-esteem. Individuals may start to avoid social contacts and feel more lonely. For instance, sometimes people will become depressed if they do not win some special award or recognition they had hoped for. They blame themselves for their failure and feel helpless to control events around them.

Most people have suffered from *acute* depression occasionally. Individuals may be really depressed after getting poor performance evaluations, or getting job rejection letters, or breaking up a marriage. Generally, after a short while, they are like their "old selves" again, with confidence renewed. However, if the depression does not self-correct and becomes *chronic,* more serious problems can ensue.[35]

A fourth response to frustration, although much rarer, is **suicide.** For a variety of reasons, an individual may feel unable to cope with all the negative aspects of his or her life and decide to end it. Unfortunately, the occurrence of suicide has increased over the past decade, particularly among executives. In February, 1975, the chairman and president of United Brands rode the elevator to his office on the forty-fourth floor of the Pan Am Building, raised a venetian blind, swung his briefcase against the glass window, and jumped to his death. Subsequent investigations revealed that the executive was plagued by poor business decisions and suggestions that an insurrection was brewing among his aides. In August, 1981, the president of Continental Airlines, who had been fighting—and losing—a takeover battle against Texas International, lay down on a couch in his office and put a bullet through his brain. At the time of the takeover bid, the executive was also despondent over the loss of his wife to cancer.[36]

Performance

Stress may also have a negative impact on individual performance. Stress can lead to increased turnover and absenteeism, for instance. Turnover and absenteeism allow workers to withdraw from unpleasant environments. In addition, stress has been frequently associated with industrial sabotage. Workers sometimes create mechanical failures on the assembly line to give themselves a break from the monotony and strain of their work. A report from the Department of Health, Education, and Welfare noted, in fact, that "breaking a machine in order to get some rest may be a sane thing to do."[37]

Job stress also has an impact on individual productivity. As will be seen in Figure 16-1, as individuals start feeling more stress at work, their performance will *increase.* They are energized to take advantage of new opportunities or to deal with potential problems. In fact, they will work more intensely or more rapidly than when they are experiencing little or no stress. People will push themselves to their performance limits under moderate amounts of stress.

Figure 16-1   Job stress and performance.

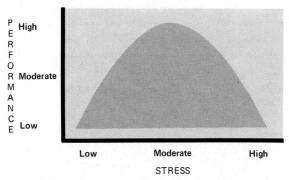

[*Source:* Adapted from McGrath, J. E. (1976). Stress and behavior in organizations. In M. D. Dunnette (Ed.), *Handbook of industrial and organizational psychology.* Chicago: Rand McNally, p. 1363. Used by permission of John Wiley and Sons.]

However, if the stress becomes too high or persists a long time, performance begins to *decrease*. People burn out; they can only work at a fever pitch for so long. Moreover, the longer the stress lasts, the more their physical and emotional energy gets drained.[38]

Consider, for instance, the difference between studying for a midterm and studying during finals' week. When studying for a midterm, students get energized for a short period of time. They will study hard and try to reread a lot of class material. When they get into the exam, the stress often energizes them to write especially quickly and to cram in as much as they can. During finals' week, however, students are already tired from a whole semester's work. Sometimes for five consecutive days they have to try to get "psyched" for an exam. They get behind in their sleep, start eating more junk food, and become more lethargic. Students find they cannot perform as well on the last exam as on the first. While they may want to sustain their high levels of effort, they are often simply too drained to do so by the end of the week.

Thus, we see that the relationship between stress and performance is *curvilinear*. People perform best under *moderate* amounts of stress.

Individual Decision Making

Stress also impedes effective decision making. When people are feeling stress, they are more likely to procrastinate and to avoid having to make decisions. They have more trouble concentrating and often forget important pieces of information. They are less likely to seek out new information that could help them make better decisions. As a result, the quality of the decisions they make suffers.

For example, when individuals are trying to decide which job offers to accept, they frequently feel stress. While there are several good opportunities that lie ahead, there is also much uncertainty about what these jobs are really like. The costs of a wrong decision can be high. Moreover, often these decisions have to be made within a few days' time. As a result of this stress, many people delay making the decision until the last moment; they keep on trying to put it out of their minds. They have trouble concentrating on the information they already have, and feel too distracted to search out additional data on their options. As a result, individuals often make bad job decisions when they are operating under high stress.[39]

Individual Differences and Stress

Not everybody experiences stress in the same way, and not everybody responds to stress in the same way. There are strong differences in the ways individuals experience and respond to stress. As Figure 16-2 suggests, these individual differences moderate the relationship between the causes and consequences of stress. They influence whether people experience their jobs as stressful, and how negatively people react to the stress they do feel.

Self-Esteem

Individuals who have positive images of themselves and their abilities are less likely to experience work as stressful. Moreover, people with high self-esteem have more confidence in themselves that they can deal successfully with stress.

Two research findings are particularly interesting here. First, studies suggest that the critical difference between those who survived being prisoners of war and those who did not survive was self-esteem. Those who had high levels of self-esteem were better able to cope with the strain and deprivation of being held captive.[40] Secondly, physicians doing research on coronary heart disease risk factors have discovered that the higher a person's self-esteem, the less likely he or she is to be heart attack–prone.[41]

Tolerance for Ambiguity

People also differ in their tolerance for ambiguity. Some people are comfortable with the fact that not everything in their work situation is black and white. For instance, they are not upset when they know generally what they are supposed to do but don't receive very detailed, precise, step-by-step instructions. Other people have a low tolerance for ambiguity. They are uncomfortable with unstructured situations. They want to know *exactly* what they are supposed to do and *exactly* how they will be evaluated.

People with high tolerance for ambiguity are less likely to suffer from job stress. They are less likely to see role ambiguity and role conflict as stressful, for example. When faced with unclear or inconsistent demands, they are less likely to feel tense. Moreover, people with high tolerance for ambiguity are much more likely to cope effectively with stress.[42]

Figure 16-2   Individual differences and stress.

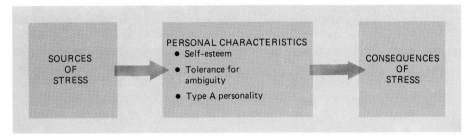

Type A Personality

Probably the most talked about personal characteristic in the job stress litera-ture today is the ***Type A personality.*** This personality type was first identified by two cardiologists, Meyer Friedman and Ray Rosenman, who were con-ducting research on the impact job stress has on heart disease.[43]

Table 16-4 gives a comprehensive list of the characteristics of the Type A personality. Type A personalities are aggressive. They are willing to oppose others to get what they want. When placed in circumstances where there are a

---

TABLE   16-4

Type A Personality

Test yourself. How many of these Type A personality characteristics do you possess?

1. Move, walk, and eat rapidly
2. Have a habit of hurrying the ends of your sentences
3. Hurry the speech of others; say very quickly, over and over again, "Uh huh, uh huh" or "Yes, yes, yes" to get others to speed up their rate of talking
4. Try to do two or more things simultaneously (e.g., read the mail while you are on the phone)
5. Try to bring conversations around to work-related topics that particularly intrigue you
6. Feel guilty when you relax or do absolutely nothing for several hours to several days
7. Tend not to notice noninstrumental aspects of a situation (e.g., not noticing a new carpet, a new hairdo, etc.)
8. Feel acquisitive of money and personal possessions
9. Overschedule yourself; don't make allowances for unforeseen contingencies
10. Feel challenged and threatened by the success of others
11. Have nervous tics like clenching your fists or banging your hand upon the table
12. Keep on trying to do things faster and faster
13. Evaluate your own performance and the activities of others in terms of "numbers"

Source: Adapted from Friedman, M., & Rosenman, R. H. (1974). *Type A behavior and your heart.* New York: Knopf, pp. 83–85. Reprinted by permission of the publisher.

lot of obstacles, they will keep on plugging away rather than give up. Type A people are ambitious and hard-driving. They have very high standards for themselves. They will take on increasing amounts of work, even when they are overloaded; they will work at incredible speed rather than miss (often self-imposed) deadlines. Type A personalities are also competitive; they have to win all the time, even in leisure activities and casual conversations.

In contrast, ***Type B personalities*** feel less pressure. They keep a steadier pace, rather than working against the clock. The Type B personality is more likely to try to extend the deadline or to accept a lower standard of work from themselves in the short-run. Type B people are likely to "let things roll off their backs" rather than fight every issue.

The clearest finding of the medical research on Type A personalities is that they are much more prone to coronary disease. In one study of 3,000 men, for instance, 77 percent of those who suffered heart attacks were clearly identified as Type A personalities in earlier test scores. Particularly startling was the fact that in the 39- to 49-year age group, Type A men experienced 6½ times the incidence of heart disease that Type Bs did. In short, Type A people are much more likely to put themselves in highly stressful situations and to push themselves the hardest in those situations. Unfortunately, they are also more likely to suffer the consequences of such high stress.[44]

As physicians, Friedman and Rosenman are interested not only in diagnosing problems, but also in alleviating them. Psychologists and managers, too, are concerned with helping workers both avoid needless stress and cope with what stress they do experience more effectively. In the next and final section, we examine more closely a variety of strategies for dealing with job-related stress.

Coping with Job Stress

As we have pointed out before, it is not true that employees do not want any stress at work. Indeed, there is substantial evidence that employees are energized and motivated by moderate amounts of stress. However, most people want to reduce their stress to the point where they feel they have some control over what is going on around them.

In this section, we will be looking at a variety of ways in which individuals cope, or deal, with stress at work. A summary list of these coping strategies appears in Table 16-5. The first set of these coping strategies are ***work-focused***. Employees can decrease stress by directly changing their own work habits or the work environments they are in. The second set of these coping strategies are ***emotion-focused***. These strategies do not directly change the work environment per se, but rather help employees adjust to the stress more easily.[45]

TABLE   16-5

Coping with Job Stress

Work-Focused Coping Strategies

Role clarification
Time management
Delegation
Search for more information and direct task help
Cooperative work strategies
Departure from the job

Emotion-Focused Coping Strategies

Reduced perfectionism
Increased social support
Increased tolerance of ambiguity
Relaxation techniques
Health maintenance

Work-Focused Coping Strategies

Role Clarification

Probably the most direct way in which individuals can cope with stress is by trying to clarify or change the role expectations of others. If employees feel their job assignments are unclear, they can ask their supervisors for clarification of what is expected. If they feel that they are getting conflicting signals from their managers (for instance, "I don't care how you get this done, just get it done" but "Don't step on any toes") they can confront their managers about the lose-lose situations they find themselves in. One overlooked coping strategy in this area is changing the constraints put upon a job assignment. If a job is due in two days and there is no way it can be accomplished even by working twelve-hour days, it is rational to ask for more time or help when the assignment is initially given.

Time Management

Another way of coping with stress is to manage time more effectively. People can learn to get better organized so that they can do their work more efficiently and fritter away less time needlessly. For example, managers often waste time by answering all calls and letters as they come in. Instead, they could put off unimportant activities until slack periods and try to do their most important work in the morning when they are feeling fresh.[46]

Delegation

A third way of coping with job stress is to delegate some responsibilities to others.[47] Managers can let subordinates gather some of the data they need, or represent them at some meetings. Secretaries can take care of many of the bureaucratic details managers don't need to attend to personally. Delegation can directly decrease work demands put upon the manager—and often the tasks the manager delegates to subordinates are seen as challenging by those who receive them.

Search for More Information and Direct Task Help

Some employees may think it is a sign of weakness to ask for more information or some initial assistance when given an unfamiliar task. It is not uncommon, for instance, to see new employees work three times longer on a job than necessary rather than admit they are not sure what they are doing. It is much more efficient, effective, and anxiety-reducing to get some help before getting lost.

Cooperative Work Strategies

Sometimes an effective way of dealing with too much work is to cooperate with other people in the same situation. For instance, in preparing major reports, dividing the work and sharing information can help employees complete their projects faster and with much less effort. People worry, of course, that they will be taken advantage of; they will work hard, but others will not. However, more often than not, people will realize it is in their own best interest to share the load and will cooperate enthusiastically.

Departure from the Job

Finally, it is important to note that sometimes the stress on a job is too great, and that not much can be done to relieve it. The organization may be greatly understaffed, and the person greatly overworked. An employee might be in a job for which he or she is simply not well trained. Whatever the reason, it is not a sign of weakness to leave a job before one gets physically sick or emotionally depressed.

Emotion-Focused Coping Strategies

Reduced Perfectionism

One of the biggest sources of stress in people's lives is the attempt to live up to the impossible standards they set for themselves. People expect themselves to perform consistently at high levels, even when they are trying to get too much done in too little time. They expect themselves to be efficient "machines" at work even when they are ill or preoccupied with personal problems. Sometimes a good way of dealing with stress is to accept less than one's very best every once in a while. Not that people should become lazy or lackadaisical, but rather they should realize that not every performance can be stellar, and the world will not stop turning if they are not perfect every time.

Employees also have fantasies about what the perfect job or perfect manager would be like. They imagine there are saintly, compassionate, competent supervisors out in the world—and they feel ill-used because they don't have them. However, their managers have the same stresses they have, probably more, and expecting ideal behavior from them inevitably leads to disappointment. There is no perfect boss and there is no perfect job. Learning to live with a little less is not compromising standards; it is dealing with the job more realistically.

Increased Social Support

A very effective way of coping with job stress is to seek out social support from others. When people feel stressed, it helps to have friends and colleagues who are supportive. Friends can provide an outlet for blowing off steam; they can support lagging self-confidence or self-esteem; they can be confided in about personal and work-related problems.[48]

Increased Tolerance of Ambiguity

Throughout school, most people receive clear homework assignments, objective tests, and frequent feedback. The work world is not like that. Most of the problems managers work on are ill-defined; little feedback is received; the criteria for success are much fuzzier. Certainly, it makes sense to try to reduce role ambiguity wherever possible. However, employees can never obtain the role clarity they had as students, and they might be better off becoming more tolerant of ambiguity.

Relaxation Techniques

Relaxation techniques are another type of emotion-focused coping device. When individuals can't change the stressful work situation, they can sometimes cope with it more effectively if they are calmer. Some researchers have found that people experience a "relaxation response" if: (1) they are in a quiet environment; (2) they close their eyes; (3) they get into a comfortable position; and (4) they keep on repeating a simple sound to block out work-related thoughts.[49] While the research in this area is still relatively new and sketchy, there is some evidence that such a "relaxation response" can decrease muscle tension, heart rate, blood pressure, and rate of breathing.[50]

Health Maintenance

Researchers in the area of job stress have advocated increased health maintenance for those in high-stress jobs. Proper diet, proper exercise, and enough sleep can keep the body in better shape for dealing with stress. When employees are tired and run down, they are much more likely to let their jobs get on their nerves. They eat too much junk food, drink coffee to keep them going, and consider walking to the vending machine as sufficient exercise. People are much more likely to get physically sick or emotionally depressed if they are out of shape, over tired, or poorly nourished.

Organizational Programs to Manage Stress

Before concluding this chapter, we also want to look briefly at some programs organizations are using to help their employees better deal with sress. While a wide variety of stress programs have been experimented with, three types of programs have become the most widespread.

Probably the most frequently used organizational stress management program is ***health maintenance.*** The Sun Valley Health Institute in Idaho, for instance, runs four-day programs that not only monitor employees' current health, but also emphasize to participants what changes are needed in their diets and exercise routines.[51] Many companies, such as Xerox, Kimberly-Clark, Weyerhaeuser, Pepsi-Cola, and Rockwell International, have invested large sums of money in gym facilities staffed with full-time physical education and health care personnel.[52]

Another type of stress management program that organizations are experimenting with is *supervisor training.* For instance, organizations like American Express have systematically trained managers to be more effective in delegating authority and including subordinates in decisions that affect their work assignments and workloads. Other organizations, such as First Union National Bank of North Carolina, have used leadership training to teach managers better counseling skills.[53] Central to many of these supervisory training programs is an emphasis on preventing job stress. Managers are trained to give better performance appraisals, to listen to employees' problems more effectively, and to communicate job assignments and instructions more clearly.

Third, some organizations have also sponsored *individual stress reduction workshops* for their employees. These programs have run the gamut from biofeedback, sensitivity groups, and transcendental meditation to career counseling, time management, and interpersonal skills workshops. Kaiser-Permanente, a health maintenance organization in California, runs a four-day stress management program for its staff. In lectures and seminars, participants are given a basic understanding of the causes of stress and its consequences for their well-being. Then, participants are given materials to help them identify the major sources of stress in their own lives, and some strategies for dealing with that stress more effectively.[54]

The future of such stress management programs, ironically, is itself uncertain. In recent years, a thriving industry has sprouted to teach corporations and their employees—at rates as high as $2,700 per person—how to deal with stress. Unfortunately, some charlatans have been drawn to the area, casting doubt upon the many good stress programs also available.[55] One company active in stress management, Drilco (a Texas tool manufacturer), has discontinued its program because it found that much of the stress of its employees was personal, and better handled outside the company. IBM, a company otherwise noted for its generous employee policies, has no psychological counseling program for employees, labeling such programs "deadly paternalism."[56]

In the final analysis, then, the management of stress lies by necessity with the individual. Even if organizations continue to remain active in stress management programs, ultimately it is the individual who has to be responsible for his or her own well-being.

Keys to Effective Management

Since stress is inevitable for most people in most jobs today, the main problem facing managers is how to diagnose, prevent, and reduce *needless* stress. Let's look at the implications of what we know about job stress for the effective management of human resources in organizations.

1 *Managers can alleviate some of the stress in the workplace by clarifying role expectations.* Workers experience stress from not knowing what the scope and responsibilities of their jobs are. They also experience stress from getting conflicting demands from other people in the organization and having too much work to do in too little time. Managers can help subordinates reduce stress by giving straightforward instructions and timely, constructive performance reviews, and by including subordinates in decisions that affect their work assignments and workloads.

2 *Managers need to be aware that when employees are under too much stress, their productivity and decision-making ability decline.* Employees under too much stress make poorer decisions, frequently procrastinate, have trouble concentrating, and forget important pieces of information. Individual productivity also suffers as a result of stress; people burn out at high levels of stress, and they lose their energy and capacity to do their best work. Moreover, organizations with high levels of stress experience higher levels of turnover, absenteeism, and industrial sabotage.

3 *Even though some of the stress people experience at work is due to their own personalities or their personal lives, managers can still help these employees with effective counseling.* Simply by becoming better listeners, managers can help subordinates to blow off some steam and discover alternative ways of behaving. They can encourage more teamwork and cooperation in their work units. Managers can help subordinates set more realistic goals and standards for performance. Finally, managers can become more aware of how their own management style creates stress and tension for subordinates. Indeed, in commenting on why some top managers seem less prone to stress, Herbert Benson, a noted Boston psychiatrist, wryly observes: "Those guys don't have stress, they create it."[57] Managers can help subordinates the most by becoming more a part of the solution and less a part of the problem.

4 *Organizations can implement programs and policies that can help individuals deal with their stress more effectively.* Organizations can institute health maintenance programs, supervisor training programs, and stress reduction workshops. Liberal time-off and vacation policies can also help workers—even in such jobs as air traffic controller and stockbroker—remain more effective in their jobs for longer periods of time.

5 *Managers can develop more effective strategies for coping with their own stress at work.* For example, supervisors can improve their time management skills, delegate some tasks to others, and seek out more information and assistance when needed. They can lower some of their self-imposed standards of perfection and become more comfortable dealing with ambi-

guity. Finally, managers can cope more effectively with stress by using some relaxation devices and getting enough sleep, exercise, and proper nutrition.

Review Questions

1   What is job stress?

2   Can stress be positive? What are some factors in your life that are stressful in a positive sense?

3   What is the General Adaptation Syndrome? What happens in each of the three stages?

4   Define each of these role terms: *role ambiguity; role conflict; role overload.* Do you ever experience any of these as students?

5   Why do people in the "helping professions" report the highest levels of stress?

6   What personal factors can create stress for people? What factors in your personal life right now create the most stress?

7   What is the Social Readjustment Rating Scale? What does a score on Holmes and Rahe's scale predict?

8   What are the consequences of job stress for people's physical health? For their mental health?

9   Why do people make poorer decisions when they are under stress?

10   What is the relationship between level of stress and individual productivity?

11   Name three personality traits that make people more susceptible to stress.

12   What is a Type A personality? How do Type B personalities differ?

13   What is the difference between work-focused coping strategies and emotion-focused coping strategies? Give some examples of each.

14   What are the most frequently used organizational programs to manage stress?

The Company Man

He worked himself to death, finally and precisely, at 3:00 a.m. Sunday morning.

The obituary didn't say that, of course. It said that he died of a coronary thrombosis—I think that was it—but everyone among his friends and acquaintances knew it instantly. He was a perfect Type A, a workaholic, a classic, they said to each other and shook their heads—and thought for five or ten minutes about the way they lived.

This man who worked himself to death finally and precisely at 3:00 a.m. Sunday morning—on his day off—was 51 years old and a vice-president. He was, however, one of six vice-presidents, and one of three who might conceivably—if the president died or retired soon enough—have moved to the top spot. Phil knew that.

He worked six days a week, five of them until eight or nine at night, during a time when his own company had begun the four-day week for everyone but the executives. He worked like the Important People. He had no "extracurricular interests," unless, of course, you think about a monthly golf game that way. To Phil, it was work. He always ate egg salad sandwiches at his desk. He was, of course, overweight, by 20 or 25 pounds. He thought it was okay, though, because he didn't smoke.

On Saturdays, Phil wore a sports jacket to the office instead of a suit, because it was the weekend.

He had a lot of people working for him, maybe sixty, and most of them liked him most of the time. Three of them will be seriously considered for his job. The obituary didn't mention that.

But it did list his "survivors" quite accurately. He is survived by his wife, Helen, 48 years old, a good woman of no particular marketable skills, who worked in an office before marrying and mothering. She had, according to her daughter, given up trying to compete with his work years ago, when the children were small. A company friend said, "I know how much you will miss him." And she answered, "I already have."

"Missing him all these years," she must have given up part of herself which had cared too much for the man. She would be "well taken care of."

His "dearly beloved" eldest of the "dearly beloved" children is a hard-working executive in a manufacturing firm down South. In the day and a half before the funeral, he went around the neighborhood researching his father, asking the neighbors what he was like. They were embarrassed.

His second child is a girl, who is 24 and newly married. She lives near her mother and they are close, but whenever she was alone with her father, in a car driving somewhere, they had nothing to say to each other.

The youngest is 20, a boy, a high school graduate who has spent the last couple of years, like a lot of his friends, doing enough odd jobs to stay in grass and food. He was the one who tried to grab at his father, and tried to mean enough to him to keep the man at home. He was his father's favorite. Over the last two years, Phil stayed up nights worrying about the boy.

The boy once said, "My father and I only board here."

At the funeral, the 60-year old company president told the 48-year old widow that the 51-year old deceased had meant much to the company and would be missed and would be hard to replace. The widow didn't look him in the eye. She was afraid he would read her bitterness and, after all, she would need him to straighten out the finances—the stock options and all that.

Phil was overweight and nervous and worked too hard. If he wasn't at the office, he was worried about it. Phil was a Type A, a heart attack natural. You could have picked him out in a minute from a lineup.

So, when he finally worked himself to death, at precisely 3:00 a.m. Sunday morning, no one was really surprised.

By 5:00 p.m. the afternoon of the funeral, the company president had begun, discreetly of course, and with care and taste, to make inquiries about his replacement. One of three men. He asked around: "Who's been working the hardest?"

Questions for Discussion

1 What characteristics of the Type A personality did Phil have?

2 What impact did job stress have on his professional life? His personal life?

3 What characteristics of the work environment created the job stress?

4 What might Phil have done to alleviate the stress?

Source: Goodman, E. (1980). *Close to home.* New York: Fawcett Crest, pp. 14–16. Copyright 1976, The Boston Globe Newspaper Company/Washington Post Writers Group. Reprinted with permission.

Notes

1 *Wall Street Journal* (1982, September 29), 35.

2 Brief, A. P., Schuler, R. S., & Van Sell, M. (1981). *Managing job stress.* Boston: Little, Brown, 50–53.

3 Feldman, D. C., & Brett, J. M. (1983). Coping with new jobs: A comparative study of new hires and job changers. *Academy of Management Journal, 26* (2), 258–272.

4 *Wall Street Journal, loc. cit.*

5 Selye, H. (1956). *The stress of life* (rev. ed.). New York: McGraw-Hill.

6 Albrecht, K. (1979). *Stress and the manager.* Englewood Cliffs, NJ: Prentice-Hall, 35.

7 Brief et al., *op. cit.*, 33–63.

8 Rice, B. (1981, June). Can companies kill? *Psychology Today,* 78, 80–85.

9 French, J. R. P., Jr., & Caplan, R. D. (1973). Organizational stress and individual strain. In A. J. Marrow (Ed.), *The failure of success.* New York: AMACOM, 30–66.

10 Kahn, R. L., Wolfe, D. M., Quinn, R. P., Snoek, J. D., & Rosenthal, R. A. (1964). *Organizational stress: Studies in role conflict and ambiguity.* New York: Wiley.

11 Rizzo, J. R., House, R. J., & Lirtzman, S. I. (1970). Role conflict and ambiguity in complex organizations. *Administrative Science Quarterly, 15,* 150–163.

12 Ivancevich, J. M., & Matteson, M. T. (1980). *Stress and work.* Glenview, IL: Scott, Foresman, 118–120.

13 Martindale, D. (1977, February). Sweaty palms in the control towers. *Psychology Today,* 71–73.

14 Albrecht, *op. cit.*, 88.

15 Friedman, M., Rosenman, R. H., & Carroll, V. (1958). Changes in serum cholesterol and blood clotting time in men subjected to cyclic variation of occupational stress. *Circulation, 17,* 852–861.

16 Dreyfuss, F., & Czaczkes, J. W. (1959). Blood cholesterol and uric acid of healthy medical students under stress of examination. *Archives of Internal Medicine, 103,* 708.

17 Katz, D., & Kahn, R. (1978). *The social psychology of organizations* (2nd ed.). New York: John Wiley.

18 French & Caplan, *op. cit.*, 30–66.

19 Albrecht, *op. cit.*, 93.

20 Albrecht, *op. cit.*, 96.

21 French & Caplan, *op. cit.*, 30–66.

22 Albrecht, *op. cit.*, 86.

23 Terkel, S. (1974). *Working.* New York: Random House, 405–407.

24 Cooper, C. L., & Marshall, J. (1977). *Understanding executive stress.* New York: Petrocelli, 16–53.

25 Lazarus, R. H. (1977). Cognitive and coping processes on emotions. In A. Monat and R. S. Lazarus (Eds.), *Stress and coping.* New York: Columbia University Press.
  Pinder, C. C. (1978). Multiple predictors of post-transfer satisfaction: The role of urban factors. *Personnel Psychology, 30,* 543–556.

26 Brett, J. M. (1981). The effect of job transfer on employees and their families. In C. L. Cooper and R. Payne (Eds.), *Current concerns in occupational stress.* Chichester, England: John Wiley.
Feldman, D. C., & Brett, J. M. (1985). Trading places: The management of employee job changes. *Personnel, 62,* 61–65.

27 Holmes, T. H., & Rahe, R. H. (1967). Social readjustment rating scale. *Journal of Psychosomatic Research, 11,* 43–218.

28 Ruch, L. O., & Holmes, T. H. (1971, June). Scaling of life changes: Comparison of direct and indirect methods, *Journal of Psychosomatic Research, 11,* 213.

29 Burke, R. J. (1969, Winter). Occupational and life strains, satisfaction, and mental health. *Journal of Business Administration, 1,* 35–41.

30 Cooper, C., & Payne, R. (1978). *Stress at work.* London: Wiley.

31 Rosenman, R., & Friedman, M. (1971). The central nervous system and coronary heart disease. *Hospital Practice, 6,* 87–97.

32 Palmore, E. (1969). Predicting longevity: A follow-up controlling for age. *The Gerontologist, 9,* 247–250.

33 Rice, *op. cit.*

34 Organ, D. W., & Hamner, W. C. (1982). *Organizational behavior: An applied psychological approach* (2nd ed.). Plano, TX: Business Publications, 263.

35   Organ & Hamner, *loc. cit.*

36   *Wall Street Journal, loc. cit.*

37   Department of Health, Education, and Welfare (1973). *Work in America.* Cambridge, MA: MIT Press, 88.

38   McGrath, J. E. (1976). Stress and behavior in organizations. In M. D. Dunnette (Ed.), *Handbook of industrial and organizational psychology.* Chicago: Rand McNally, 1351–1396.

39   Janis, I. L., & Mann, L. (1977). *Decision making: A psychological analysis of conflict, choice, and commitment.* New York: The Free Press.

40   Bettleheim, B. (1958). Individual and mass behavior in extreme situations. In E. E. Maccoby (Ed.), *Readings in social psychology.* New York: Holt, Rinehart, and Winston.

41   Kasl, S., & Gobb, S. (1970, January–February). Blood pressure changes in men undergoing job loss: A preliminary report. *Psychosomatic Medicine,* 19–38.

42   Lyons, T. (1971). Role clarity, need for clarity, satisfaction, tension, and withdrawal. *Organizational Behavior and Human Performance, 6,* 99–110.

43   Friedman, M., & Rosenman, R. H. (1974). *Type A behavior and your heart.* New York: Knopf, 67–88.

44   *Ibid.*

45   Folkman, S., & Lazarus, R. S. (1980). An analysis of coping in a middle-aged community sample. *Journal of Health and Social Behavior, 21,* 219–239.

46   Lakein, A. (1973). *How to get control of your time and your life.* New York: Wyden.

47   Much of the following discussion is taken from Feldman, D. C., & Brett, J. M. (1983). Coping with new jobs: A comparative study of new hires and job changers. *Academy of Management Journal, 26* (2), 258–272.

48   *Ibid.*

49   Benson, H. (1975). *The relaxation response.* New York: Morrow.

50   Kuna, D. (1975, June). Meditation and work. *Vocational Guidance Quarterly,* 342–346.
Lazarus, R. H. (1977). Cognitive and coping processes on emotion. In A. Monat & R. S. Lazarus (Eds.), *Stress and coping.* New York: Columbia University Press.

51   *Wall Street Journal* (1982, September 30), 33.

52 Ivancevich, J. M., & Matteson, M. T. (1980, Autumn). Optimizing human resources: A case for preventive health and stress management. *Organizational Dynamics,* 5–23.

53 *Wall Street Journal* (1982, September 30), *loc. cit.*

54 Goldberg, P. (1978). *Executive health.* New York: McGraw-Hill, 240.

55 *Wall Street Journal* (1982, September 30), *loc. cit.*

56 Rice, *loc. cit.*

57 *Wall Street Journal* (1982, September 28), 37.

Chapter 17

Innovative Approaches to Organizing

CHAPTER OUTLINE

Factors Generating the Need for Innovation

Quality of Work Life

Japanese Management

Excellent Companies Research

Keys to Effective Management

Review Questions

*B*ooks on management and organizational behavior usually attract a fairly narrow audience of researchers, students, and managers. Recently, however, a dramatic shift has been occurring in the level of interest and enthusiasm shown for books on these topics among a much larger segment of the population. Books such as *Theory Z* on Japanese management and *In Search of Excellence* dealing with excellent U.S. companies have captured the attention of hundreds of thousands of people and have spent many months at or near the top of the best-seller lists. *In Search of Excellence,* in fact, has sold nearly three million copies, making it one of the most popular books ever published on any topic.

The wide-ranging success and popularity of books such as these signals a tremendous surge of interest in the topics of management and organization. This in turn raises two important and interesting questions. First, why suddenly have so many people become interested in how organizations can be managed more effectively and successfully? What factors may account for such wide-ranging interest in topics that were previously of concern to only a relatively small segment of the population? The second important question has to do with the content of these newly popular books. What are the authors of these books saying and what can we learn from them about organizations and organizational behavior?

This chapter presents answers to these questions. In the first part of the chapter we look at some important changes that have been occurring in society. These changes have resulted in serious concerns among many people regarding how our organizations are managed and have generated strong forces in favor of new and innovative approaches to management. In the subsequent sections of the chapter we examine three of the most influential and widely debated innovative approaches to designing and managing organizations to have emerged in recent years. The three approaches are the Quality of Work Life (QWL) movement, the Japanese approach to management, and the "excellent companies" research arising from the work of Peters and Waterman.

Factors Generating the Need for Innovation

Up until very recently the preeminent position of North American business in the world marketplace was not only unquestioned but also widely assumed to be unassailable. However, a number of recent events have led to serious concerns being raised about how North American organizations are managed. This concern and questioning have also generated a strong interest in new and innovative approaches to the management and organization of North American business. While many factors are doubtless responsible for the current state of concern and the accompanying desire for innovative solutions, four key factors, summarized in Figure 17-1, can be identified as significant contributors to this situation. These four factors are the lagging rates of growth in productivity among North American businesses, the increasing presence of foreign competitors in world markets, the tremendous rate of technological change brought about by the revolution in microelectronics, and significant changes in the labor market in North America in terms of education, values, and expectations.

Lagging Productivity Growth

Productivity is defined as the value of goods or services produced by a firm per unit of cost incurred by the firm in the production process. Thus, a firm's productivity can be increased in either of two ways. First, productivity goes up if the organization is able to increase the value of goods or services produced without incurring a corresponding increase in costs. Second, productivity is increased if the firm is able to reduce the costs associated with producing the same level or amount of goods and services. Productivity can be increased by improving technology, plant, and equipment, by improving work and production methods, and by improving the effectiveness of the management and organizational systems of the firm.

Increasing productivity is a key management function and productivity

Figure 17-1   Factors contributing to concerns regarding
North American approaches to management.

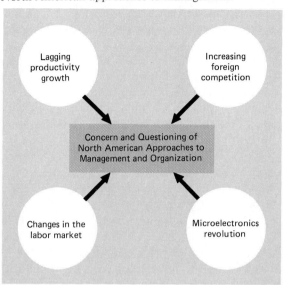

growth is an important indicator of the health and viability of an organization. Although productivity levels in the United States and Canada have continued to rise, they have not been going up as quickly as was the case in the past, nor have North American productivity improvements been keeping pace with those of the Japanese. The fact that improvements in productivity among North American firms are declining and lagging behind those achieved in other countries is a serious source of concern and an indicator of the need to explore new and innovative approaches to improving our levels of productivity and efficiency.[1]

Increasing Foreign Competition

Only a few years ago the North American automobile market was dominated by the U.S. auto manufacturers. In 1967 only 9 percent of all cars sold in the United States were foreign-made. That situation has changed radically today, with imported cars alone accounting for approximately 27 percent of U.S. sales in the 1980s. Similar changes have occurred in other industries as well. U.S. manufacturers of consumer electronics such as television sets and stereo equipment have all but given up in the face of superior Japanese products. Japanese motorcycle manufacturers have been so successful that there now remains only a single company in North America making motorcycles (Harley-Davidson). That company has been so badly hurt by Japanese competition that in 1983 it had to request (and was granted) tariff protection by the U.S. government in order not to go out of business. The increasing foreign threat to the viability of North American business has not only come from the Japanese, however.

Textile manufacturers in countries such as South Korea and Taiwan, where labor costs are low, have been making dramatic inroads in clothing markets in North America and elsewhere.

What these developments imply is that if North American businesses are to remain competitive, and indeed are to survive, methods must be found of equaling or surpassing the levels of productivity and quality being achieved by the Japanese and other foreign competitors. While part of the solution to meeting the challenge of foreign competition will no doubt lie in the implementation of new and improved production technologies, innovative approaches to organizing and managing North American businesses will be essential as well.

The Revolution in Microelectronics

The computer chip has had and will continue to have a dramatic impact on the management and functioning of organizations. Every facet of organizational life will be influenced by the new microelectronics, from the shop floor to the executive suite. At the shop-floor level, computer-aided design (CAD), computer-aided manufacturing (CAM), and computer-aided testing (CAT) are rapidly becoming the norm rather than the exception in new manufacturing facilities. In the automobile industry and many other sectors, tedious and repetitive tasks previously associated with assembly line manufacturing are increasingly being taken over by robots.

The new technology is having an equally pervasive impact on white-collar workers. Word processing equipment and electronic mail systems are fundamentally altering the nature of secretarial and clerical work, as well as changing the patterns of communication among organization members. And the proliferation of microcomputers is adding a new dimension to the work performed by many managers.

The implementation of microelectronics will require organizational and managerial innovations, as well, to permit optimal utilization of the new technology. The new technologies offer opportunities not only to increase productivity and efficiency, but also to improve the quality of work life for members of the organization.[2]

A Changing Work Force

The kinds of people working in today's organizations have changed from those of a generation or even a decade ago. Many more women than ever before are participating in the full-time work force, and women are becoming increasingly (and justifiably) evident in senior managerial and professional positions previously occupied almost exclusively by men.[3] In 1950, women represented 30 percent of the total civilian labor force; by 1980, 42 percent. The work force is also aging, as people live longer and continue to work until later in life and as the population bulge of the "baby boom" (those born between 1946 and 1964) moves through the career cycle. Other conflicting forces are at work influencing the goals and expectations individuals bring to their jobs. On the one hand, the self-actualization and personal growth orientation fostered during the 1960s and 70s created increasing demands for interesting, involving, and personally meaningful work. On the other hand, the combination of new technologies and economic recession that led to high unemployment levels in the 1980s has tempered many of these demands and expectations.

These and other factors influencing the nature and composition of the work force pose new challenges for managers and demand innovative organizational responses from modern organizations. In the remainder of the chapter we will discuss three sets of such innovative ideas regarding organization and management: quality of work life, Japanese management, and the excellent companies research.

Quality of Work Life (QWL)

Quality of work life (QWL) has been defined as "the quality of the relationship between employees and the total working environment, with human dimensions added to the usual technical and economic dimensions."[4] Some of the characteristics of a high quality of work life are summarized in Table 17-1. As the definition of QWL and its characteristics in Table 17-1 make clear, the goal of QWL is the creation of organizational conditions that foster individual

TABLE   17-1

Characteristics of a High Quality of Work Life

Security
Equitable pay and rewards
Justice in the workplace
Relief from bureaucratic and supervisory coercion
Meaningful and interesting work
Variety of activities and assignments
Challenge
Control over self, work, workplace
Own area of decision making (or responsibility)
Learning and growth opportunities
Feedback, knowledge of results
Work authority—authority to accomplish that for which one is held responsible
Recognition for contributions—financial, social and psychological rewards, status, advancement
Social support—reliability of others when needed; mutual expectation of sympathy and understanding when needed
Futures that are viable (no dead-end jobs)
Ability to relate one's work and accomplishments to life outside the workplace
Options or choices to suit the individual's preferences, interests, and expectations

Source: Adapted from Davis, L. E. (1983). Learnings from the design of new organizations. In H. F. Kolodny & H. van Beinum (Eds.), *The quality of working life and the 1980's.* New York: Praeger, pp. 80–81. Used by permission.

learning and development, that provide individuals with substantial influence and control over what they do and how they are to do it, and that provide individuals with interesting and meaningful work that serves as a source of personal satisfaction and a means to valued personal rewards.[5]

Advocates of QWL do not believe that the provision of a high quality of work life for members of the organization must be achieved at the expense of the productivity and effectiveness of the organization. In fact, the argument made in favor of enhancing the quality of work life is quite the contrary. QWL advocates believe that the factors leading to a poor quality of work life for the employees of an organization are precisely the same factors that account for the declining productivity and effectiveness of many modern organizations.[6]

Advocates of QWL argue that organizations setting out to provide a high quality of work life for their members will, at the same time, be designing organizations more likely to be effective and to succeed in the modern era of rapid change, unpredictable events, and increasing foreign competition. But how are organizations to accomplish this? How are they to go about establishing a higher quality of work life for their members, and in the process, more effective and adaptive systems of management?

First, management must seek to establish a good fit between the technical and the social aspects of the organization.[7] It is no longer acceptable for new technological systems to be designed and implemented without consideration for the impact of the new technology upon the people in the organization and the nature of their work. If optimal benefit is to be achieved from technological advances, the implementation of new technology must take into account the nature and the needs of the people who will be operating the technological systems. Organizational effectiveness requires that the organization's technical and social systems be planned and designed in concert with one another.

Organizations must also be designed to permit maximum *adaptability* to changing conditions and to maximize the *motivation* of members to perform effectively. The route to both adaptability and motivation advocated by QWL is the use of *autonomous, or self-managing work groups* as the primary basis for performing the work of the organization.[8] As discussed in Chapter 13, the use of such autonomous work groups can facilitate motivation since the members of the group experience a high degree of freedom and personal responsibility, and also must perform a variety of challenging tasks in order to complete the overall primary task for which they are responsible. Adaptability is increased since the groups are self-managing and contain individuals with many different skills.

Finally, the QWL approach emphasizes that organizational effectiveness is dependent upon a high degree of *commitment* on the part of everyone in the organization to the attainment of organizational goals. Achieving this commitment requires a managerial approach stressing open lines of communication and a high level of participation in the decision-making process by all members of the organization.

The implementation of QWL requires management to adopt a new role and new attitudes toward employees. A high quality of work life cannot be established in a climate of mistrust and adversarial relationships. High quality of work life demands that management view employees as cooperating members of a single team. The manager must become less a directive supervisor and more a coach or helper available to provide assistance and support when these are required.[9]

Examples of QWL Programs

QWL programs come in a wide variety of shapes and sizes and may result in organizational changes as varied as new work systems, flexible working hours, and new compensation plans. Examples of some of the types of changes that have resulted from QWL programs are summarized in Table 17-2. In what follows we will briefly describe several QWL programs and the changes resulting from them in order to provide a picture of what QWL is all about in practice.

Buick Division of General Motors[10]

One of the earliest and most dramatic QWL projects at General Motors occurred in the Buick division of the company. Buick, which had specialized in large and luxurious automobiles with poor gas mileage, was particularly hard-hit by the energy crisis of the 1970s. In addition, the division was characterized by very poor labor relations (with strikes and strike threats occurring

---

TABLE 17-2

Examples of Different Types of Innovations Implemented as Part of QWL Programs

1   Work teams, where the isolation of the worker doing one task repeatedly is replaced by groups of workers responsible for a variety of tasks
2   Quality circles, a Japanese technique, in which workers meet to solve job problems, especially those related to improving the quality of their products
3   Worker participation in the design of jobs and in decisions about their day-to-day work lives
4   More flexible work scheduling and job assignments so that, for example, two married individuals can both work and still "manage" a household and children
5   More flexible compensation plans, so that workers can get more of the benefits they desire and can participate in cost savings and company profits
6   Less supervision, under which production teams help select and train new team members, forecast material and manpower requirements, and evaluate their own performance
7   More attention to the design and maintenance of the physical plant and workplace, as well as to health and safety hazards
8   In-house training programs, free tuition for higher education, or a firm policy of promoting from within
9   Increased provision for job security
10   New forms of union-management cooperation and increased involvement of unions in bargaining for quality of working life programs

Source: (1979, September 16). *Chicago Tribune,* p. 14.

about every six months) and a poor record of product quality. By 1975 sales were down dramatically and the number of UAW members employed by the division had shrunk to 18,000 from 26,000 in the 1950s.

At this point both Buick management and UAW leaders recognized that some form of dramatic change was essential if the division was to survive and further job losses be avoided. Management and union leaders held a series of meetings that resulted in agreement on a QWL program designed with the goals of improving the quality of work life for employees and increasing the quality of the division's products. The various components of this QWL program are summarized in Figure 17-2. Worker participation programs were established to solicit employees' ideas on ways to improve production methods and product quality. Autonomous work groups were set up in a number of the division's locations and given responsibility for both assembling and inspecting entire components. Workers were given training to permit them to perform a number of the different jobs required within their group. In addition, both workers and managers were trained in listening skills, settling conflicts in groups, and goal setting.

The results have been dramatic. Sales climbed to a record 854,011 cars, up 77 percent from the 1975 low point. Quality improvements were such that by 1981 the number of defective engines had fallen from two per 1000 to one in 10,000. In addition to these improvements in the company's performance there has been strong evidence of an improvement in the quality of work life for employees. Buick has not had a strike since 1974 and absenteeism has fallen in the QWL plants to 2 percent (compared to the GM average of 5 percent).

Figure 17-2 Components of QWL improvements at Buick.

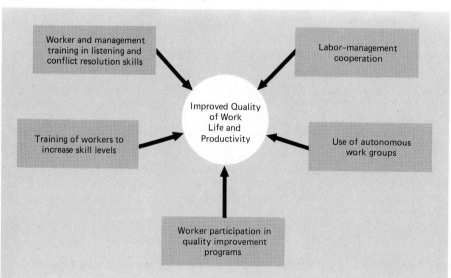

Comments by the workers reinforce this picture of an improved quality of work life at Buick. One union officer stated "I believe there is total trust beween the company and the union." Another worker, who was eligible for retirement, chose to stay on in order to participate in the QWL program. He stated that after thirty-two years "of never having any say in how my job is done the program is fantastic."

Volvo

Volvo has a long history of commitment and innovation in the implementation of QWL programs.[11] Volvo's most famous QWL project is the final assembly plant at Kalmar, completed in 1974. This plant represented the first radical departure from traditional automobile assembly techniques, with the aim of improving the quality of work life for assembly workers. The workers at Kalmar are organized into autonomous teams, each of which is responsible for the assembly of a particular identifiable portion of the car (e.g., electrical system, instrumentation, interior, doors, engine compartment). The members of each team decide how the work will be divided among themselves on each shift.

Considerable effort was taken to provide a pleasant work environment in the plant. All work stations are located along an outside wall next to large picture windows and are decorated in light colors. Special attention was also paid to noise levels in the plant in order to keep noise at or below the level at which normal conversation can be carried on.

Volvo management has indicated a high level of satisfaction with the results achieved at Kalmar. So much so in fact that nine Volvo plants finished since that time have incorporated some of the ideas first attempted at Kalmar. Overall, Volvo continues to innovate in its application of QWL activities in its existing operations. The programs are supported by various series of lectures and discussions about products and a number of courses in interpersonal relations, working in groups effectively, and problem solving.

Future Prospects for QWL

Given the number and variety of successful examples of QWL programs that have been reported, the future prospects for QWL should be bright. A recent international conference entitled "QWL and the 80s" attracted over 1,700 participants from all over the world. Participants represented a broad cross-section of academics, managers, union members, and government workers. Of particular interest is the fact that the primary issues of concern to participants tended to be less "Should we undertake QWL projects" than "How do we go about implementing QWL."[12]

At the same time, however, there are several issues that must be raised regarding the current state of our knowledge of the effectiveness of QWL. In addition, several factors can be identified that will likely influence the future acceptance and implementation of QWL programs in a larger number of organizations.

1   There does not yet exist a sufficient body of scientifically sound research regarding the impact and effectiveness of QWL projects. While the number of case studies of QWL projects is growing, these do not constitute an adequate scientific basis for assessing the overall impact of QWL. We require more complete theoretical explanations of how and why QWL projects achieve the results claimed for them and a more substantial body of sound research data to substantiate such theories.

2   Because QWL is based upon new ideas and new approaches to managing organizations, some of the people associated with QWL have in the past tended to advocate the desirability of QWL programs with an almost messianic zeal. While enthusiasm for QWL may be well-founded, there is a danger in the overly enthusiastic endorsement of any single approach to the improvement of organizational effectiveness. In order to prevent QWL from becoming a passing fad, those associated with QWL must adopt a balanced view of the strengths as well as the weaknesses of the approach, and describe more fully when and under what circumstances QWL programs should be implemented.[13]

3   The very term *quality of work life* tends to draw immediate attention to the fact that a primary goal of QWL is the creation of an improved quality of life at work for organization members. The inherent danger is that the impression may be created in the minds of managers considering QWL programs that such programs have as their sole aim improving the levels of job satisfaction of employees, with little or no regard for the productivity and effectiveness of the organization. As our previous discussion has made clear, this is not the case. QWL seeks to improve organizational productivity and effectiveness via organizational changes that also result in a higher quality of work life for organization members. This issue must be kept clearly in mind and communicated unequivocally to practicing managers considering undertaking QWL programs.

Japanese Management

There has been a tremendous surge of interest among North American managers in the Japanese approach to management.[14] This interest has been sparked by the dramatic successes of the Japanese in the international marketplace, and by the relative decline in the competitive position of once-dominant North American industries. The Japanese gross national product (GNP) has increased thirteen-fold over the past thirty years and continues to exhibit steady growth at twice the rate of the U.S. economy. These spectacular gains have been achieved by a country with about half the population of the United States and a landmass approximately equal to that of the state of Montana or the province of Alberta. The country has very few natural resources and is highly dependent on imports of such crucial products as food, coal, iron, and oil. In addition, these gains have been achieved within a society in which the cost of doing business is high: wages are relatively high, real estate is extremely expensive, pollution controls are stringent, and dependence on imported materials is extremely high.

North American managers have been both concerned by the decline in their competitive position and intrigued by what may lie at the root of the tremendous surge in the success of Japanese organizations. Given the many constraints and problems faced by the Japanese, there has been a natural tendency to focus on the Japanese approach to management as a potential key factor explaining the rise in Japanese productivity and competitiveness. If the success of the Japanese cannot be explained in terms of such factors as cheap labor and abundant raw materials, perhaps the key lies in their approach to organizing and managing.[15] If North American businesses are to reestablish their competitive position, it may well be essential for them to study and learn from the Japanese approach to managing.

The Nature of Japanese Management

The Japanese approach to management has a variety of unique characteristics. Among these are factors summarized in Figure 17-3, such as lifetime employment, relatively slow evaluation and promotion of new managers, the use of nonspecialized career paths, a consensus approach to decision making, and strong emphasis on quality and production efficiency. We shall look briefly at

Figure 17-3   Major components of the Japanese approach to management.

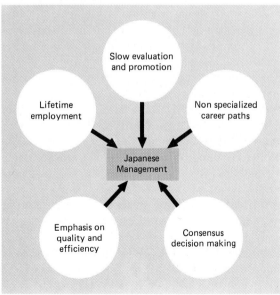

each of these components of the Japanese approach to management and assess their applicability and potential value to the North American business environment.

Lifetime Employment

The concept of lifetime employment has received a good deal of attention in the popular press recently. The concept is an intriguing one and is argued by some proponents to lead to a work force characterized by a high degree of loyalty, very low uncertainty regarding staffing, and a willingness on the part of management to invest significantly in training in order to develop "experts" who will be with the organization for a long period of time.[16] While the concept of lifetime employment undoubtedly may yield a number of these benefits, it is essential for managers to realize that the lifetime employment concept does *not* apply to the vast majority of workers in Japan. In fact, only about one-third of the organizations in Japan practice lifetime employment, and these are the large, high-profile firms about which we hear a great deal. In addition, and perhaps of even greater relevance, is the fact that the concept of lifetime employment in Japan applies only to men. Women are not granted lifetime employment by Japanese organizations and are treated as temporary workers subject to layoff in times of economic downturn. Further, even lifetime employees are expected to retire at approximately age 55, at which time the worker receives an amount equal to approximately 5 or 6 times his annual salary. Japanese organizations do not, as a matter of course, provide anything equivalent to the pensions provided by most large North American organizations.

Slow Evaluation and Promotion of Managers

Japanese organizations also take a dramatically different approach to their treatment of new managerial talent within their organizations. In the United States or Canada, a young, bright, highly educated management trainee expects to move rapidly through a variety of different jobs and to be promoted quite frequently during the early years of his or her career. There tends to be frequent use of formal evaluations, and frequent promotions are taken as a sign of high potential and effective performance. In Japan, salaries and ranks within the organization are much more strongly determined by age. Salary differences among managers occur only in the later career stages. New managers hired into the organization at the same time tend to move through the organization as a group, and it is not expected that younger workers will be in management positions senior to those occupied by older managers. Formalized individual evaluations of the type so commonly used in North America are not employed. The emphasis is not upon distinguishing yourself from others on the basis of your performance, but rather on demonstrating the ability to get along with others and work effectively with them.[17] This approach obviously differs quite dramatically from both the practices and the expectations of managers in North American firms. It is unlikely that a change from current North American evaluation and promotion practices to those in use in Japan could be achieved quickly or easily.

Nonspecialized Career Paths

In addition to this deemphasis upon formal evaluation and rapid promotion, the career paths of managers in Japanese organizations tend to be quite nonspecialized. Managers are viewed as "company employees," not as "area specialists." While managers in their early career years are not promoted rapidly, they are moved from one area or department to another with some frequency.[18] This nonspecialized approach to developing the careers of managers has a variety of long-run payoffs to the Japanese organization. By the time they reach midcareer, Japanese managers have developed a commitment to the overall organization rather than to any specialized function within it. Their experience in a variety of departments tends to encourage recognition of the validity of the viewpoints and problems faced by members of other departments. This results from the fact that each manager will either have had previous experience in that department or will recognize that he will at some point in the future be a member of that department himself. This approach can go a long way in facilitating coordination across functional areas and in reducing the sources of the conflict and competition between different functional departments that is so common within North American organizations. In addition, from the viewpoint of the individual manager, the nonspecialized career path can lead to greater vitality, learning, personal growth, and satisfaction as a result of the variety of experiences and viewpoints to which each manager is exposed.

Consensus Decision Making

The nonspecialized approach to career planning contributes to the effectiveness of another key characteristic of the Japanese approach to management: consensus decision making. While many organizations in North America are characterized by an assumption that it is the boss's job to make decisions and *tell* his or her subordinates what is to be done, the prevailing attitude and practice in Japanese organizations is that decisions are to arise out of a long process of mutual exploration and discussion among all those involved in and influenced by the decision.[19] This consensus approach to decision making has a variety of important advantages and payoffs. Multiple inputs and viewpoints help to ensure that decisions are made in the best interest of the organization as a whole rather than simply in the self-interest of any particular manager or department. In addition, the consensus approach helps to generate high degrees of understanding, acceptance, and commitment to implementing decisions once they have been arrived at. While a top-down, autocratic approach to decision making may result in decisions being made quickly, it often results in many problems at the implementation stage. Japanese organizations take a relatively long time to arrive at a decision, but they are able to implement decisions extremely quickly and smoothly.

Quality Emphasis

A further defining characteristic of the Japanese approach to management is its strong emphasis upon quality and efficiency of production systems.[20] One manifestation of this emphasis on quality is the existence of "quality circles" in Japanese organizations. Quality circles consist of groups of employees and managers who meet regularly to engage in joint problem solving in order to reduce defects and improve quality of products.[21] Quality circles have high prestige both within Japanese organizations and within the broader society. An annual prize is awarded to the organization achieving the most significant improvements in quality, and receipt of this award is accorded national recognition and extremely high prestige throughout the country. However, quality circles are only one manifestation of the Japanese concern for quality. A commitment to quality tends to pervade Japanese organizations from the top down. Japanese organizations now measure their defects in parts per million (as opposed to parts per hundred or parts per thousand as in North America) and have as their goal the achievement of zero defects. The concern for quality and the direct involvement of line workers in the quest for zero defects results in a relatively sophisticated work force with both a concern for quality and sophisticated skills in the detection of defects and the improvement of production processes. Japanese workers are expected not only to run their machines, but also to maintain them, to correct minor problems, to help fellow workers experiencing difficulties, to keep the workplace clean, and to constantly engage in the search for ways to improve methods and eliminate problems.

Sophisticated Production and Control Systems

Combined with this strong emphasis on quality is a high degree of sophistication in production planning and inventory control. Japanese organizations are able to reduce costs tremendously by keeping extremely low inventories of supplies, work in progress, and finished products. Japanese manufacturing organizations tend to be characterized by iron discipline in production planning, vendor relations, industrial engineering, and manufacturing and process engineering.[22] This sophistication and discipline in managing the production process results in high degrees of efficiency within manufacturing firms. As an example of the magnitude of efficiency improvement that can be achieved, the changeover process of presses in hood and fender stamping in the auto industry requires an average of six hours for General Motors in the United States, four hours for Volvo in Sweden, and *twelve minutes* for Toyota in Japan. Because of their high degrees of efficiency and discipline, Japanese manufacturing organizations tend to be characterized by a "no crisis" atmosphere; managers spend their time training, planning, and identifying techniques for further improvement in quality and efficiency, rather than running around dealing with day-to-day crises.

Japanese Techniques Applicable in North America

What then can managers and organizations in the United States and Canada learn from Japan? What can we import and make use of on the one hand, and what aspects of Japanese management are likely only to work within the unique environment of Japan and Japanese society?[23]

Lifetime employment is probably not a candidate for wholesale importation into North American business. Japanese organizations do not practice lifetime employment as a general principle applicable to all employees, and its workability is dependent upon its differential application to males and females, and also upon the unique characteristics of the Japanese retirement and pension systems. In addition, it is unlikely that the Japanese practices of slow promotion and lack of evaluation in the early career could be quickly adopted and implemented in North America. Neither new managers nor those currently in the firm are likely to tolerate such a dramatic shift in their expectations and practices.

On the other hand, organizations in the United States and Canada can probably make relatively immediate use of the nonspecialized career path approach, the consensus decision-making approach, and the strong emphasis on quality and efficient production management. Nonspecialized career paths need not necessarily violate the expectations of new management trainees in North American organizations. In addition, they have the potential to facilitate the development of strong generalist managers and to break down some of the barriers and sources of conflict between functional departments that characterize many organizations in North America.

Consensus decision making, while running contrary to the natural instincts of some North American managers, also has significant potential for benefit. The skills and techniques necessary to implement the consensus decision approach can be developed via training and practice. While it would be a mistake for an organization to attempt to implement consensus decision making as the "rule" throughout the organization, a greater use of the consensus approach in situations in which it is appropriate is likely to yield significant long-run benefits to the organization.

A strong emphasis upon quality improvement and efficient production management is likely to pay significant dividends to North American organizations.[24] Sophisticated techniques for production management are now available and should be used to their fullest to increase the efficiency of manufacturing processes. In addition, the emphasis upon quality offers a method for organizations to involve not only their management but their line workers in improving the products and the competitiveness of their organizations. A concern for quality can be shared by all members of the organization and has a strong potential to provide a vehicle for the development of more cooperative relationships between management and workers. Box 17-1 describes how Sanyo achieved dramatic quality improvements after taking over a plant manufacturing television sets in Arkansas.

While it is certainly desirable for North American management to look to the Japanese in order to learn from their strategies and techniques of management, there are also some inherent dangers in the recent rise in interest in Japanese management techniques.[25] While there is doubtless a great deal to be learned from the Japanese, certain of their approaches will prove inapplicable and inappropriate in the North American context, as they are based on the unique characteristics of Japan and Japanese society. As a result, managers in North America should not adopt the goal of imitating or emulating the Japa-

BOX 17-1

Sanyo's Emphasis on Quality[26]

The Sanyo plant in Forest City, Arkansas, provides an example of Japanese management dealing with an American union (the International Union of Electrical Workers). The atmosphere, while noisy and busy, is very casual.

Yet the Japanese management is highly visible at Sanyo, most notably vice president of administration "Michi" Sohma. Sohma recalls that in 1975, when Sanyo took over the company (which was producing television sets for Sears), quality was so bad that bankruptcy loomed. Only 500 workers remained; but by 1977, only a year later, the product and sales were so improved that the work force ballooned to 1,500. Sears, needless to say, was delighted: "As long as we do our best to please the Customer God, we never can fail," Sohma explains.

How did Sanyo do it? One obvious answer is Sohma himself, who was uniquely qualified to help the Japanese managers and engineers and the American workers understand and work with each other. Step one, Sohma recalls, was opening his door to the union leaders and talking to them as friends. "We could have dismissed everybody and started from scratch without a union," he says, "But we didn't. Why should we be afraid of unionism? I told them, I cannot do everything you ask, but I will openly tell them whatever we decide and why."

With the union's cooperation tentatively won, the next step was to bring in Japanese technicians to work side by side with the Americans on the assembly line. "Not teaching, but just working together," says Sohma. "I warned all the Japanese here [twenty-six supervisors] not to be bossy and not to try to tell people what to do. Anyhow, their English wasn't good enough."

For the Arkansas workers, this proved to be a frustrating but rewarding period. "My initial impression was that they were overly concerned with what we would call minor-type details—like putting the labels on perfectly straight," says Charles Green, now the director of the microwave division. "At first it annoyed us tremendously—but it shows their dedication to quality compared to what we used to look at." But as the television set reject rate dropped from 10 percent to below 2 percent, the Americans started getting the message.

"Morale, which had been so low, began soaring," says Sohma. "People saw the product moving and more orders coming in. So they started feeling like they were okay, that they could make good television sets and weren't such bad guys after all."

No one at Sanyo denies there were and still are problems, however. "We learned their ways, but through hard knocks," admits Green. "Instead of going home at 5 or 6 o'clock, I found myself going home at 8 or 9—and the Japanese kept working until midnight if there was something that wasn't going right." He was also surprised by Sanyo's willingness to put more people on the line when there were problems: "That's cost. But cost is not as big a factor to Japanese as getting good quality."

nese approach to management. Instead, it is essential to look to the Japanese, to study their management techniques carefully, and to assess thoughtfully what can be applied here and what cannot.

Excellent Companies Research[27]

During the late 1970s the large and highly respected U.S. management consulting firm of McKinsey and Company undertook a study to find out how the most successful and best-run U.S. companies are managed. During the 1970s the United States had begun to lose its place as the world leader in business productivity and efficiency. No longer could it be taken for granted that the "American way" was the best, most productive, and most efficient approach to management and business success. There was a natural tendency among Americans to look for external factors accounting for the decline in the position of U.S. businesses. Factors such as energy shortages and the new-found competitiveness of the Japanese were often used to explain the problems being faced by U.S. organizations.

The McKinsey researchers were skeptical of these types of explanations, which tended to place the blame for poor performance on factors outside the control of management and the organizations themselves. If factors such as higher energy costs and Japanese competition were the sources of the problem, why were not *all* U.S. corporations suffering from declining productivity and effectiveness? Even though U.S. businesses in general were performing less well in the 1970s than they had historically, it was still the case that there were many U.S. companies that continued to be world leaders in their fields and that were characterized by high productivity, effectiveness, and profitability. The McKinsey researchers felt that there might well be a great deal to learn about effective management by studying the best-run and most effective companies in the United States. Their work culminated in a book entitled *In Search of Excellence: Lessons from America's Best-Run Companies* by Thomas J. Peters and Robert H. Waterman. In what follows we will describe what these researchers did, the common problems they identified with U.S. management, and the key factors they feel characterize the management of the most effective and successful businesses in the United States.

The Nature of the Research

The McKinsey researchers began by polling a wide variety of businesspeople, consultants, business school professors, and members of the business press for their nominations of companies felt to be innovative and excellent. The outcome of this process was a list of sixty-two companies generally agreed to be well run and highly effective. The companies chosen are listed in Table 17-3, which also classifies the companies into six major industry groupings. Next, the researchers evaluated the companies selected in terms of a variety of eco-

TABLE 17-3

U.S. Companies Surveyed in the McKinsey & Co. Excellent Companies Research

High technology	Consumer goods	General industrial	Service	Project management	Resource based
Allen-Bradley	Atari (Warner	Caterpillar Tractor	Delta Airlines	Bechtel	Dow Chemical
Amdahl	Communications)	Dana Corporation	Disney Productions	Boeing	Du Pont
Data General	Avon	Minnesota Mining &	K mart	Fluor	Standard Oil
Digital Equipment	Bristol-Myers	Manufacturing	Merriott		(Indiana)/
Emerson Electric	Chesebrough-		McDonald's		Amoco
Hewlett-Packard	Pond's		Wal-Mart		
Hughes Aircraft	Eastman Kodak				
Intel	Frito-Lay				
International	(PepsiCo)				
Business Machines	Johnson &				
National	Johnson				
Semiconductor	Levi Strauss				
Raychem	Mars				
Schlumberger	Maytag				
Texas Instruments	Merck				
Wang Labs	Procter & Gamble				
	Revlon				
	Tupperware (Dart				
	& Kraft)				

nomic measures of long-term superior performance. Selected industry experts were also asked to rate the companies in terms of their long-term record of innovativeness. Only those companies agreed upon as continuously generating new products and services and responding rapidly to changes in their markets and external factors were retained. This screening process resulted in nineteen of the original sixty-two companies being dropped from the study. The remaining forty-three companies served as the basis for the detailed research.

The research process led to two sets of findings. The first set has to do with what factors may be accounting for the declining competitiveness and productivity of some U.S. companies. The second set concerns the factors that appear to characterize the management and philosophy of the excellent companies. We will examine each set of findings in turn.

Problems with American Management
The Business Schools

The five specific factors summarized in Figure 17-4 were identified as contributing to the declining performance of U.S. companies.

The curriculum in most leading business schools places strong emphasis on rational analysis and quantitative techniques. Courses in financial management and decision analysis teach students models and techniques that are designed to lead to the "right" answer. They reinforce the belief that all business decisions are, or should be, amenable to quantification and that if the

Figure 17-4   Problems contributing to lack of innovation and poor performance in U.S. companies.

student can "get the numbers right," he or she will definitely be on the road to success. Such courses have enjoyed high prestige in business schools, and as a result the brightest students have been attracted to these subjects. However, this type of training does not leave students with an appreciation of the role of factors such as loyalty, commitment to quality, and concern for the customer, which appear to be so essential to business success. Because of this, business schools have been coming under increasing attack as contributors to the problems currently experienced by American companies.

Narrow Managerial Perspectives

American managers often spend their entire careers prior to taking on senior management positions in a single specialized functional area such as marketing or finance. One outcome of this type of career path can be a relatively narrow perspective and a lack of a broad appreciation for the needs of the organization as a whole. Tied in with this can be a failure to understand the capabilities and skills that are required at key points in the organization and that make the difference between success and failure.

Lack of Personal Identification with the Company

Because American managers often follow a specialized career path and frequently move from company to company several times in their careers, they tend to identify more with their area of specialty (e.g., finance, marketing, manufacturing) than they do with their company and what it does. As a result, managers often lack commitment and a sense of values and concern for their organization. This is in marked contrast to the Japanese, whose personal identity is strongly intertwined with the company they work for and who evidence a strong concern, even a love, for the products they produce.

Lack of Concern for People

U.S. business places great emphasis upon technological innovation and investment policy as key determinants of success. People are often viewed as a "set of hands" that must somehow be integrated into the technological solutions generated by the rational analysts. People, with their needs, loyalties, values, and ideas, are seen as a sort of necessary evil that often get in the way of "clean" solutions to technical problems. The Japanese on the other hand view people as the key resource contributing to the success of the organization. Loyalty, commitment, personal identification with the company's success, and the human relationship between the employee and his supervisor are the basic elements of productivity to the Japanese.

Overreliance on Planning and Analysis

Managers have tended to pay too little attention to their products and their people, and instead have been relying too much on planning and analysis. Because planning is interesting and intellectually challenging, and because it lacks the pressure of day-to-day operations, senior managers have increasingly turned their attention to strategic planning and long-term policy issues. Managers have become more concerned with their plans than with their products or their people. Planning has become almost an end in itself, and the value of plans is assessed in terms of the sophistication of the techniques employed in the planning process, rather than in terms of the utility of the plans for the success of the organization.

Overall, then, many U.S. organizations have adopted a narrow analytical approach that is not conducive to experimentation and innovation. The critical role of the human element in shaping organizational success, as well as the crucial role of values, loyalty, commitment, and enthusiasm in effective management, have been ignored. There has been an obsession with avoiding errors, rather than a commitment to experimentation and creativity. Organizations have tended to become abstract, heartless, overly complex, and inflexible. However, this approach did not characterize the management style and philosophy of the excellent companies surveyed by the McKinsey researchers. These successful organizations made effective use of the rational techniques of planning and analysis, but were managed in a style that also emphasized and took advantage of the key human elements crucial to innovation and effectiveness. We now turn to a discussion of the distinguishing characterstics of these excellent companies.

Characteristics of Excellent Companies

The search for factors accounting for the success of the excellent companies did not unearth any previously unknown "secret weapons" that the companies had been hiding from their competitors. Neither did success appear to lie in their use of or reliance upon the rational techniques of planning and analysis.

To be sure, the excellent companies did use these techniques and use them well. But they also appeared to recognize clearly the limitations and appropriate uses of such techniques.

Instead, the success of these companies appeared to lie in their ability to handle the basic skills and techniques of management well. They were characterized by an emphasis on taking action quickly, by a strong commitment to serving their customers, by the ability to innovate practically, and above all by a recognition of the key role of people in generating the success of the company and the need for the active commitment of everyone in the organization to its success. These characteristics are outlined in Figure 17-5 and are described more fully below in terms of the eight attributes that appeared to distinguish the excellent, innovative companies from the rest.

1 *A bias for action.*   While the excellent companies recognized the need for rational analysis and planning, they also recognized its limitations. They were particularly adept at avoiding the "paralysis of analysis" that so often occurs in large companies. One manifestation of this bias for action was a strong emphasis upon experimentation. People were encouraged to try out new ideas and approaches and were not punished if their initial solutions

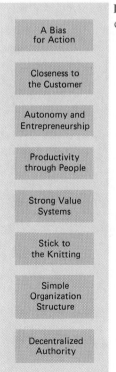

Figure 17-5   Characteristics of the management styles of the excellent companies studied by the McKinsey & Co. researchers.

to problems were imperfect. This emphasis on taking action in response to problems contributed to a high degree of vitality and innovation, even as organizations became large.

2 *Closeness to the customer.*   The excellent companies recognized clearly that they are dependent on their customers for their continued success. This concern for the customer manifested itself in two ways. First, there was a tremendous stress placed by everyone in the companies on quality, service, and the reliability of their products and services. Second, concern for the customer was manifested in a willingness to listen to customers, to find out what they want and what ideas customers may have for product improvement. In fact, many of the excellent companies claimed they get their best ideas for new products from their customers.

3 *Autonomy and entrepreneurship.*   Innovative companies worked hard to encourage leadership and innovation throughout the organization. New ideas and new products were not the sole responsibility of a single specialized "research and development" department. People in all parts of the organization were encouraged to be creative, to experiment, and to take practical risks. Mistakes were viewed as a natural occurrence in an innovative environment. In order to minimize the cost of mistakes, the excellent companies avoided investing all their resources in a single "home run" product or project, and instead encouraged multiple individuals and teams to take on a variety of innovative projects.

4 *Productivity through people.*   The excellent companies viewed every one of their members from the bottom up as a valued resource and an important contributor to the company's success. Rank and file members were seen as the key source of ideas for improvements in quality and productivity.

5 *Strong value systems.*   Managers of innovative companies tended not to isolate themselves in analytic ivory towers. They stayed close to the key activities in the organization and close to the people, many by practicing what has become known as "management by walking around" (MBWA for short). In addition, top managers of the excellent companies tended to see their role as that of managing the values of their organization by setting and reinforcing its basic philosophy.

6 *Stick to the knitting.*   Excellent companies did not seek to become conglomerates managing a portfolio of businesses in order to spread their risk and exposure. Instead, they stayed close to what they knew and could do well. Robert W. Johnson, former Johnson and Johnson chairman, stated: "Never acquire a business you don't know how to run."

7 *Simple organization structure.*   While almost all the companies studied in the excellent companies research had sales well in excess of a billion dollars annually (and many much more than that), their organizational structures were invariably simple. In addition, there was a strong tendency to avoid large corporate staff groups.

8 *Decentralized authority.*   The management of excellent companies was decentralized in the sense that authority and responsibility tended to be pushed down in the organization to the people actually doing the work. There was a high degree of autonomy and a great deal of emphasis on individual initiative.

BOX 17-2

Who's Excellent Now

The turmoil and product-development problems plaguing Hewlett-Packard (HP)—the third largest computer maker after International Business Machines Corp. and Digital Equipment Corp.—hardly make it look like one of America's most innovative, best-run companies. Although its earnings are still strong, HP has stumbled badly in the critical microcomputer and superminicomputer markets.

To regain its stride, HP is being forced to abandon attributes of excellence for which it was praised. Its technology-driven, engineering-oriented culture, in which decentralization and innovation were a religion and entrepreneurs were the gods, is giving way to a marketing culture and growing centralization. The continuing exodus of disenchanted managers—twelve have left in just the last six months—tells the story. "The time spent in coordinating meetings has increased by an order of magnitude in the last four years," sighs André Schwager, a former HP general manager who left in September. "It's clear that the culture is beginning to change."

Hewlett-Packard is not the only "excellent company" that is not looking so excellent these days. According to studies by *Business Week,* management consultants McKinsey & Co., and Standard & Poor's Compustat Services, Inc., at least fourteen of the forty-three "excellent" companies highlighted by Peters and coauthor Robert H. Waterman, Jr., in their book just two years ago have lost their luster.

One major lesson from all this is that the excellent companies of today will not necessarily be the excellent companies of tomorrow. But the more important lesson is that good management requires much more than following any one set of rules. *In Search of Excellence* was a response to an era when management put too much emphasis on number-crunching. But companies can also get into trouble by overemphasizing Peters and Waterman's principles. Says Waterman: "The book has been so popular that people have taken it as a formula for success rather than what it was intended to be. We were writing about the art, not the science of management."

Source: Who's excellent now? (1984, November 5). *Business Week.* Used by permission.

Implications of the Excellent Companies Research

The findings of Peters and Waterman in their research on the sources of excellence are rich in ideas and approaches with which the practicing manager might experiment. There seems little doubt that an organization that values its customers and employees, listens to them, and generates high levels of commitment, enthusiasm, and loyalty is going to be better off than one that does not.

At the same time, however, it is important to keep in mind that the excellent companies research consists of an in-depth case study of a set of high-performing organizations. It does not contain the characteristics of a carefully controlled scientific investigation that can in any sense offer *proof* that the factors identified are in fact the key to the success of the excellent companies. The authors studied only excellent companies; they did not include in their study a group of similar but less successful organizations. As a result, we do not know the extent to which less successful organizations also practice the management techniques argued to account for the success of the excellent companies.[28] In addition, questions have been raised regarding just how "excellent" some of the companies studied really were, and whether they will continue to perform well.[29] Box 17-2 describes the problems that some of the excellent companies described by Peters and Waterman have encountered.

Rather than scientific facts, the excellent companies research offers a rich set of speculative ideas regarding the sources of excellence and effectiveness. Doubtless many of their ideas are correct, but a clear picture of the precise causes of effectiveness and excellence must await further analysis and carefully controlled scientific investigation.

Keys to Effective Management

Our discussion of factors generating the need for organizational innovation and of a variety of the important new approaches to management and organization leads to a number of implications for the practicing manager.

1 *Managers must be sensitive to critical changes occurring in the environments of their organizations and be prepared to respond innovatively.* New technologies, increased foreign competition, and changing expectations of the work force all constitute new challenges to the organizations of today and tomorrow. Organizations and their managers cannot hope to be successful if they insist on attempting to apply yesterday's solutions to today's problems. Managers must be sensitive to the changes that are occurring and be willing to respond innovatively to the challenges represented by such changes.

2 *Managers must take care to avoid "fads" and must learn to pick and choose carefully and sensibly from new ideas and approaches to management as they appear.* Innovative management is not the corporate equivalent to "keeping up with the Joneses." An organization that is constantly trying to implement every one of the latest ideas to appear in the business press is probably more desperate than it is innovative. While managers must be open and willing to consider innovative ideas and approaches, they must also adopt a hardheaded and critical approach in determining whether any particular set of innovative ideas are in fact appropriate to their own situations.

3 *Managers should make use of consensus decision making and nonspecialized career paths to enhance decision making and flexibility.* Japanese organizations' emphasis on consensus decision making and nonspecialized career paths appears to have high potential for successful implementation in North America. Consensus decision making can result in better decisions that are more readily implemented. Nonspecialized career paths can create a more flexible work force that is knowledgeable and informed regarding the problems and issues faced by everyone in the organization.

4 *Management styles emphasizing the active involvement, loyalty, and commitment of organization members characterize many of the most effective and innovative organizations in the world.* It does not appear that organizations must choose between having a happy and satisfied work force on the one hand and being productive and efficient on the other. Rather than being mutually exclusive, these goals are highly compatible. Many of the most effective and innovative companies place great stress on the value of their employees and the importance of providing a high quality of work life for their members.

5 *Managers should give their people the freedom to innovate and be prepared to tolerate mistakes when they occur.* Managers need to create a climate that fosters and encourages innovation and risk-taking among their people. Individuals will only be willing to take risks with new ideas if they feel confident that they won't be punished if any particular idea is unsuccessful. When mistakes are not tolerated, innovation and risk-taking rapidly disappear.

Review Questions

1 Discuss some of the key factors generating the need for innovation on the part of organizations in North America.

2 What are some of the implications of the revolution in microelectronics for today's managers?

3 Discuss some important changes in the nature of the work force over the past twenty years and describe some of the challenges these changes have created for management.

4 What is meant by the term *quality of work life* (QWL)?

5 Are productive efficiency and a satisfied work force mutually consistent? Discuss.

6 Describe an example of a QWL program and discuss what you believe to be the key factors leading to its success.

7 What limitations if any do you see regarding the application and implementation of QWL programs?

8 Discuss some of the key characteristics of the Japanese approach to management.

9 Which components of the Japanese approach to management do you feel are applicable in North America and which components are not? Defend your position.

10 What problems with American management were identified by the excellent companies researchers? Do you agree with their characterization of the problems?

11 Discuss some of the characteristics identified by the McKinsey researchers as contributing to the success of the excellent companies they studied. Do you feel that all of these factors must be present if an organization is to be innovative and successful?

12 What are some of the limitations of the McKinsey & Co. research on excellent companies? What conclusions do you feel practicing managers should draw from this research?

Nissan: Robotics Comes to Tennessee

Costing $660 million, Nissan's small truck factory in Smyrna, Tennessee, is the single largest investment made by a Japanese company in the United States. Reputed to be the most technically advanced automotive facility in the world, this incredible complex houses seventy-two acres of workspace under one roof. The sheer size and the somewhat spooky presence of 220 robots is impressive—but the most striking thing is the work force. The 2,000 employees at this factory were selected from a pool of 40,000 applicants, after an intensive screening and training process.

Moreover, Nissan sent about 425 of these Tennesseans to Japan for orientation and training before production began in June 1983—not just managers and supervisors, but hourly workers as well. "I think they all got a frontal lobotomy while they were over there," comments one labor economist who can't quite believe that American workers could so quickly embrace the Japanese way of work life that prevails at the Smyrna plant.

For starters, most workers and managers wear uniforms (called "company dress") and join in morning exercises at 7:30 a.m.—although both practices are voluntary. After the physical warm-up, morning meetings are held. "We sit down for ten or fifteen minutes to discuss ideas and personal problems," explains Larry Swoopes, a paint-plant worker who was recently promoted to group leader. "It brings everybody closer together. It's a big family effort, putting our best foot forward to get the job done."

Many of the top Americans in the plant, like Joseph Kieltyka, manager of the trim and chassis plant, are former employees of the Ford Motor Company. "I have about ten times more to say as plant manager here as I did at Ford," Kieltyka says. "Here, I only have to talk to two people to get to the top man. At Ford, I had to talk to fifteen or twenty people and I never did get to the top man." At Nissan, he adds, he spends about four hours a day walking around the plant talking to workers and making sure they're happy and doing a good job. At Ford, he recalls, "I rode around in a golf cart and I wore a tie instead of a company uniform."

For the moment, Nissan workers insist that all the surprises have been pleasant ones. "What you have here is a lot of people who are dedicated because we want to see the plant make it," says Swoopes. "As the plant goes up, we go up with it." The fact that workers are taught a variety of skills—and get paid more for each new skill—is another big plus, in his opinion. (Hourly wage rates start at $8.90 and can go up to $12.54, and there's an additional $1.35 per hour bonus paid twice a year.) As for labor unions, Swoopes declares: "I don't see it happening here and I hope I never see it. I don't believe the union can offer us anything that we don't already have here."

Questions for Discussion

1 Which aspects of the Japanese management approach have been implemented at the Tennessee plant? Which have not?

2 Do you feel that Nissan has made a good decision in terms of which aspects of Japanese management to implement in the United States?

3 How would you describe the quality of work life in the new plant?

Source: Adapted from "How the Japanese Run U.S. Subsidiaries" (1983, October). *Dun's Business Month.* Used by permission of *Dun's Business Month,* © 1983, Dun and Bradstreet Publications Corporation.

Notes

1   Maital, S., & Meltz, N. (Eds.). (1980). *Lagging productivity growth: Causes and remedies.* Cambridge, MA: Ballinger.

2   Mumford, E., & Hensall, D. (1979). *A participative approach to computer systems design.* London: Associated Business Press.
Mumford, E., & Sackman, H. (Eds.). (1975). *Human choice and computers.* Amsterdam: North Holland.
Walton, R. E. (1983). Social choice in the development of advanced information technology. In H. F. Kolodny & H. Van Beinum (Eds.), *The quality of working life and the 1980s.* New York: Praeger.

3   Warr, P., & Parry, G. (1982). Paid employment and women's psychological well-being. *Psychological Bulletin, 91,* 498–516.

4   Davis, L. E. (1983). Learnings from the design of new organizations. In Kolodny & van Beinum, *loc. cit.*

5   Davis, L. E., & Cherns, A. B. (1975). *The quality of working life.* New York: Free Press.

6   Trist, E. L. (1981). The evolution of sociotechnical systems. In A. Van de Ven & R. Joyce (eds.), *Organization design and performance.* New York: Wiley.

7   Emery, F. E., & Trist, E. L. (1965). The causal texture of organizational environments. *Human Relations, 18,* 21–32.
Emery, F. E., & Trist, E. L. (1969). Socio-technical systems. In F. E. Emery (Ed.), *Systems thinking.* Harmondsworth, England: Penguin.

8   Davis, L. E. & Cherns, A. (1975), *loc. cit.*
Walton, R. E. (1972, November–December). How to counter alienation in the plant. *Harvard Business Review, 50,* 70–81.

9   Cherns, A. (1977, Spring). Can behavioral science help design organizations? *Organizational Dynamics,* 44–64.

10   (1981, July 5). *New York Times, 3.*

11   Gyllenhammar, P. (1977, July–August). How Volvo adapts work to people. *Harvard Business Review,* 102–113.

12   Kolodny & van Beinum (1983), *loc. cit.*

13   Yorks, L., & Whitsett, D. A. (1985). Hawthorne, Topeka, and the issue of science versus advocacy in organizational behavior. *Academy of Management Review, 10,* 21–30.

14 Keys, J. B., & Miller, T. R. (1984). The Japanese management theory jungle. *Academy of Management Review, 9,* 342–353.

Levine, S. B., & Kawada, H. (1980). *Human resources in Japanese industrial development.* Princeton: Princeton University Press.

Ouchi, W. G. (1981). *Theory Z: How American business can meet the Japanese challenge.* Reading, MA: Addison-Wesley.

Pascale, R. T., & Athos, A. G. (1981). *The art of Japanese management: Applications for American executives.* New York: Simon & Schuster.

15 Vogel, E. (1979). *Japan as number one: Lessons for America.* Cambridge, MA: Harvard University Press.

16 Ouchi, W. G. (1981), *loc. cit.*

17 Pascale, R. T., & Athos, A. G. (1981), *loc. cit.*

18 Hatvany, N., & Pucik, V. (1981, Spring). Japanese management practices and productivity. *Organizational Dynamics,* 5–21.

19 Ouchi, W. G. (1981), *loc. cit.*
Pascale, R. T., & Athos, A. G. (1981), *loc. cit.*

20 Hayes, R. H. (1981, July–August). Why Japanese factories work. *Harvard Business Review,* 57–66.

21 Munchus, G., III. (1983). Employer-employee based quality circles in Japan: Human resource policy implications for American firms. *Academy of Management Review, 8,* 255–261.

Werther, W. B., Jr. (1982). Quality circles: Key executive issues. *Journal of Contemporary Business, 11*(2), 17–26.

22 Quality: The U.S. drives to catch up. (1982, Nov. 1). *Business Week,* 66–77.

23 Rehder, R. R. (1981). What American and Japanese managers are learning from each other. *Business Horizons, 24,* 63–70.

24 Schonberger, R. J. (1982). The transfer of Japanese manufacturing management approaches to U.S. industry. *Academy of Management Review, 7,* 479–487.

25 Peterson, R. B., & Sullivan, J. (1982). Applying Japanese management in the United States. *Journal of Contemporary Business, 11*(2), 5–15.

Sugimoto, Y., & Mouer, R. (1982). *Do the Japanese fit their stereotype?* Tokyo: Tooyoo Keizai.

Sullivan, J. J. (1983). A critique of theory Z. *Academy of Management Review, 8,* 132–142.

26 From "How the Japanese run U.S. subsidiaries" (1983, October). *Dun's Business Month.* Used by permission.

27 Peters, T. J. & Waterman, R. H., Jr. (1982). *In search of excellence: Lessons from America's best-run companies.* New York: Harper & Row, 132–142.

28 Carroll, D. T. (1983, November–December). A disappointing search for excellence. *Harvard Business Review,* 78–88.

29 Who's excellent now? (1984, November 5). *Business Week.*

Chapter 18

Organization Development

CHAPTER OUTLINE

The Nature of Organization Development

The Organization Development Process

Phases in Organization Development

Organization Development Interventions

Keys to Effective Management

Review Questions

*I*t is increasingly common to hear and read about the rapid pace of change in the world around us. Books such as *Future Shock* and *The Third Wave* by Alvin Toffler have documented many of the phenomenal changes we are experiencing and have made predictions as to how these changes will influence the way we live and work. "Think tanks" such as the Hudson Institute have been established for the purpose of predicting the course and direction of fundamental changes in society in the future. The rapid pace of change in the modern world has important implications for organizations and their managers. Managers can no longer expect to be successful if they are unaware of the need for adaptation and unable to bring about changes in their organizations and their methods of management.

In this chapter we will focus upon techniques that have been developed to facilitate the process of change in organizations. The term *organizational development* (OD) refers to a broad range of behavioral science–based strategies used to diagnose the need for change in organizations and to implement changes when necessary. We will first look at the nature of OD as a comprehensive approach to organizational change, then examine in some detail the steps or phases in the OD process and discuss some specific techniques (often called *interventions*) that are employed in OD to help bring about change in organizations. The chapter concludes with a look at some of the factors that appear essential to making the OD process work effectively for organizations and their managers.

The Nature of Organization Development

Organization development (OD) is a general strategy or approach to organizational change that can be employed to analyze and diagnose the sources of organizational problems and to develop and implement action plans for their solution.[1] OD is a collaborative process in that members of the organization who will be affected by change are actively involved in diagnosing the problems and in designing new ways of operating in their organization.

Examples of Organizational Problems Calling for Change

Organizations of all types and sizes experience problems from time to time that require internal change. Changes may be required in the attitudes and values of organization members, the patterns of behavior employed by organization members in dealing with one another, the structure and strategy of the organization, or any combination of these factors.[2] The following examples indicate some of the types of problems that arise in organizations that OD can help deal with.

Interpersonal Conflict

Two managers within the same department dislike one another personally. Their working relationship is characterized by frequent arguments and a great deal of political infighting. Each manager feels that the other is responsible for their poor relationship and the ongoing conflict that exists. Their inability to work together creates serious problems for the head of the department when the successful completion of work assignments demands cooperation between them. The department head wonders how she can get the two managers to resolve their differences.

Team Building

A project team has been formed with responsibility for the development of a new project that the organization views as the key to its future competitiveness and success. The team is made up of high-powered talent drawn from several departments within the organization. Each of the members has very strong ideas regarding what the team should be doing and how the work should be organized. The outcome is that in their first few weeks of working together, little progress has been made in agreeing upon the activities and priorities of the group. Disagreements and conflicts are commonplace. Rather than a cooperating "team," the organization has a group of strong-willed, intelligent individuals, each going in his or her own direction. Little progress is being made on the project, which is critical to the success of the organization. How can the manager in charge overcome these problems and turn this group into an effective work team?

Intergroup Conflict

Members of the marketing department of a large organization view their job as maximizing the sales of the organization's products and increasing market share against competitors. Members of the manufacturing department of the same organization see their primary goal as reducing production costs while maintaining an adequate standard of product quality. Marketing is often willing to make special commitments to customers regarding product changes and delivery dates if this will lead to increased orders and sales. At the same time, manufacturing is always highly resistant to such demands, since they result in increased costs associated with special work and overtime payments, all of which impede their ability to meet their cost-reduction targets. The result is that the relationship between the two departments is characterized by frequent conflict, mistrust, and poor communication. How can this unhealthy relationship between marketing and manufacturing be turned around?

Rapid Growth

In recognition of the increasing threat to the organization of new products and technology, an organization decides to increase the budget of the research and development (R&D) department by 200 percent. With this budget increase, the staff of the R&D department jumps from 50 people to almost 200 in the space of 9 months. While almost all the new staff members are competent, talented individuals, the output of the expanded department does not seem much greater than was the case prior to the huge increase in size and budget. Senior management wonders whether the decision to invest so heavily in R&D was a good one. Many of the new staff members complain of being underutilized and begin to question whether they want to stay with the organization. Why is this investment not paying off?

Economic Recession

A prolonged recession has cut deeply into an organization's markets and sales. Management recognizes that drastic changes will be needed but is unsure precisely what changes are required. Morale in the organization is low as members wonder whether they will be fired or laid off. How should management proceed?

New Competition

An organization has been extremely stable and successful for many years in light of its near monopoly position in the markets within which it has been operating. The organization has always been reputed for offering the highest-quality products and excellent service to customers. Recently, however, overseas competitors have moved into the company's markets with products that are more technologically sophisticated and lower-priced than those the company has been offering for years. Senior management, unaccustomed to competitive pressures, is perplexed regarding how to respond to this severe threat to their position.

| Changing Aspirations and Goals of Managers | The cornerstone of a large organization's approach to the development of future senior managers has been to move high-potential young executives frequently among the company's various locations around the world. In the past, these moves were viewed as highly desirable by younger managers, since they meant significant salary increases, new responsibilities, and an opportunity eventually to enter the senior management ranks. Recently, an increasing proportion of very talented young managers have been refusing moves planned for them by the company, citing family and personal reasons as the basis for their refusals. Many have indicated they would leave the company if forced to move. The organization is perplexed at this change in attitudes and unsure how to respond. |

Distinguishing Features of Organization Development

Organization development consists of a series of steps aimed first at diagnosing the sources of organizational problems such as the foregoing, and then at generating solutions to the problems in a collaborative fashion. Three distinguishing features of the OD approach to solving organizational problems are particularly important.

Application of Behavioral Science Knowledge and Technology

OD represents a planned attempt to bring to bear what we know about organizations and organizational behavior in order to facilitate organizational change. We know that organizations and their members are not always logical and rational. If attempts to bring about organizational change are to be successful, they must recognize that people's attitudes, emotions, and perceptions play a large part in influencing their behavior, and specifically their willingness to undertake changes whose outcomes may appear uncertain, risky, or threatening. OD addresses this fact by actively involving the members of the organization in the change process. People are less likely to fear, and are more likely to accept, changes that they have had an active voice in designing and implementing.

Use of a Knowledgeable and Skilled Change Agent

While OD actively involves members of the organization in the change process, OD activities are managed under the direction of a change agent (or consultant) who is knowledgeable in the behavioral sciences and skilled in working with individuals and groups.[3] The change agent may be a professional consultant engaged by the organization specifically to provide advice and direction to the OD process, or may alternatively be a member of the organization who possesses the necessary knowledge and skills and whose job is the facilitation of OD work in the organization on a continuing basis.

Collaboration and Active Participation of Organization Members

Members of the organization itself are actively involved as collaborators in all phases of the OD process for two reasons. First, organization members are themselves the richest source of knowledge about the organization and its problems, and this intimate knowledge places them in an often unique position to contribute creatively to the design of solutions to organizational problems.

Second, no "solution," regardless of its elegance and potential effectiveness on paper, is a "real" solution to an organizational problem until it has been implemented. The likelihood of actual implementation is far higher when organization members themselves have been actively involved in diagnosing problems and generating solutions to those problems. Participation and collaboration result in organization members feeling that proposed changes are their *own* ideas, greatly facilitating the effective implementation of real change in the organization.

The Organization Development Process

Any change process influencing people can be thought of as involving a series of three steps that the individuals affected must move through. These three steps, labeled ***unfreezing***, ***movement,*** and ***refreezing***, are diagramed in Figure 18-1.[4]

Unfreezing

In any organizational situation, a variety of forces tend to be operating against change and in favor of maintenance of the status quo. People become comfortable in situations that are predictable and understandable. Change may involve the loss of comfort and predictability in the world, and hence be resisted. In this sense, people can be thought of as "locked in" or "frozen" in their current situations and patterns of behavior. As a result, in order to prepare people for change and make them more willing to accept changes that may be required, an "unfreezing" process is a necessary prerequisite to the implementation of movement or change. The unfreezing may take the form of increasing levels of awareness regarding previously hidden problems, or of drawing attention to the existence of alternative styles of behavior, organization, and management.[5]

Movement

Once people have been prepared for change via a process of unfreezing, actual changes can be designed and implemented in organizations. Change necessarily involves *movement* to new patterns of behavior and organization from

Figure 18-1   Three-step procedure of change.

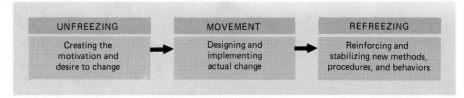

those that have existed in the past. We have a natural tendency to identify change almost exclusively with this movement stage, since it is here that change is actually occurring. However, the advantage of thinking about change as a three-step procedure is that it helps draw attention to the fact that fundamental change can occur only if movement is preceded by an unfreezing process, and followed by a refreezing stage.

Refreezing

After changes have been implemented and movement has occurred, there is a universal tendency for people and organizations to regress, or slip back into old habits and patterns of behavior. In order to avoid this, it is necessary to ensure that new modes of behavior and organization are constantly reinforced and supported. This process of reinforcing and supporting changes following their implementation can be thought of as a "refreezing" of newly acquired methods of operating and managing. Without refreezing, change is likely to be temporary and to have minimal lasting impact on the organization and its members.[6]

OD is a process designed to move organizations and their members through these steps in the change process. In order to achieve this in practice, OD proceeds through a series of steps or phases of activity as a change agent guides the organization toward fundamental change. We now turn to a detailed examination of these phases in the OD process.

Phases in Organization Development

Although every OD project is designed to respond to the unique problems and issues that exist in an organization, it is possible to outline a series of steps, or phases, that characterize the OD process in general.[7] These phases in the process are summarized in Figure 18-2. While in practice the different phases often overlap, each phase has some unique characteristics and activities associated with it.[8] In what follows we will briefly discuss the key issues associated with each of the phases. The discussion of the phases is accompanied by a series of boxes describing what occurred in an actual OD project.[9]

Problem Recognition

Before the OD process can get off the ground, someone or some group of people in the organization must recognize that a problem or problems exist that require change. In other words, people in the organization must feel some need to change. Without this, the OD process cannot get started.

Once a problem has been recognized and members of the organization feel a need to take action to deal with the problem, the organization may contact an OD consultant in order to explore the possibility of using the OD approach to deal with the problems being experienced. An OD consultant is someone

Figure 18-2   Phases in the OD process.

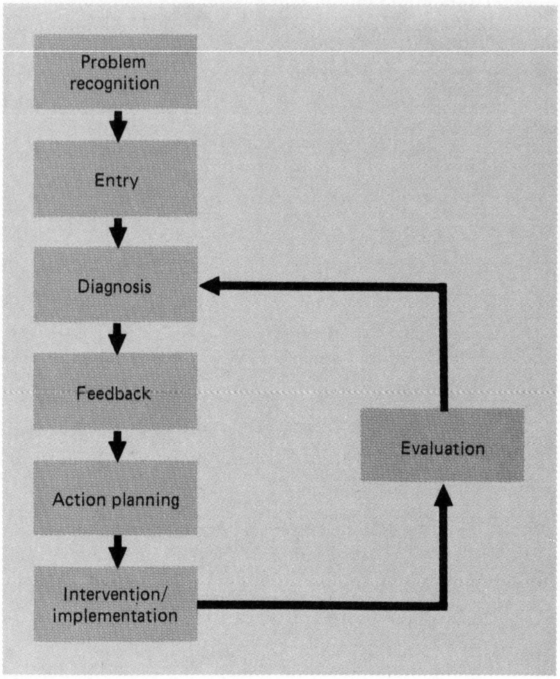

knowledgeable about organizational behavior and OD who is experienced in helping organizations use the OD process to solve problems and implement changes. It is at this stage that the entry phase of OD begins.

Entry

The term *entry* refers to the entry of the OD consultant into the client organization. There are three components to the entry process: contact, exploration, and contracting.[10]

Contact

Contact refers to the initial meetings between the organization and an OD consultant. In the case of an external consultant (an OD specialist who is not a member of the client organization), contact will almost always be initiated by the organization. A member or members of the client organization may know an OD consultant personally or by reputation, and contact him or her for the purpose of discussing the possibility of undertaking OD work in the organization. In the case of an internal consultant (an OD specialist who is employed by the organization on a continuing basis), contact may be initiated either by the organization or by the consultant.

Exploration

Once contact has been made between consultant and client, a process of mutual **exploration** follows. This exploration takes the form of a meeting or meetings between the consultant and the client. At this stage, the client is generally represented by the senior manager in charge of the organizational unit considering undertaking OD. The exploration process is designed to give the client organization and the consultant an opportunity to assess one another to permit both parties to determine the desirability of establishing a working relationship for OD.

During the exploration process the organization seeks to assess whether the consultant is suitably qualified to work with the organization as an OD change agent. The client is thus interested in exploring the consultant's previous OD experience, the extent to which the consultant possesses suitable skills to serve as an effective change agent, and also the depth of the consultant's knowledge regarding OD, organizational behavior, and the nature of the client organization itself.

The consultant, on the other hand, is interested in learning as much as possible about the organization, the problems that the organization is experiencing, and the *readiness* of the members of the organization to undertake fundamental change. The likelihood of success when undertaking OD is dependent upon (1) the readiness of the client to acknowledge openly the existence of problems in the organization; (2) a willingness on the part of the client to take some personal responsibility for the existence of problems; and (3) the willingness of the client to commit time, energy, and resources to the OD process. The consultant must explore all of these factors in deciding whether to undertake OD work with the client.

Contracting

The importance of a clear and explicit **contract** between client and consultant at the outset of OD cannot be overemphasized.[11] The client and the consultant need to know what each expects from the other and from the OD process. In order to operate effectively, the consultant requires cooperation and commitment from the organization in terms of things such as access to information and people and willingness to attend meetings. The client needs to know the consultant's plans, how much time the process will take, what results can be expected when, and what the consultant's services will cost the organization. Getting these sorts of issues out in the open and reaching clear and explicit agreements on them paves the way for a productive and fruitful OD process. Box 18-1 describes the problem recognition and entry phases of an OD project in a major pharmaceutical firm.

Diagnosis

The planning and implementation of organizational change in OD is based upon a systematic diagnosis of the organization and the work-related problems that its members are experiencing. In addition, since OD is also a collaborative process, the diagnosis phase of OD actively involves the members of the orga-

BOX 18-1

Problem Recognition and Entry: Getting OD Started at Galen Pharmaceuticals

Galen Pharmaceuticals, because of increasing levels of absenteeism and turnover among employees, had decided to conduct a job satisfaction survey throughout the company. All 3,000 employees, including management, were surveyed by an outside opinion research firm. The results of the survey showed clearly that there was considerable dissatisfaction throughout the company, especially among the rank and file. The major problem concerned managerial style and the general approach adopted by various levels of supervision, particularly in the management of people. The survey indicated that most managers were perceived as autocratic, rather rigid in their approach and style, and unilateral (top-down) in the decision-making process. Another serious problem was the perception by employees that the company lacked a sense of purpose, or that there was a lack of clarity regarding the organization's mission. Galen's president, John Edwards, concluded that change was in order and that the company could use expert help in bringing it about.

Bob Williams, an experienced OD consultant, was invited to explore the possibility of consulting with Galen. Williams met with the top management committee for about three hours. He was shown the survey results and asked what he might do as a change agent. Williams stated that he would want to conduct a more in-depth diagnosis of the organization to discover the underlying causes of Galen's problems. He also agreed to outline a process, or flow of events, that he would recommend the organization follow, and explained some of the types of changes that might ultimately be recommended.

Williams' perception of the president (Edwards) was that Edwards definitely wanted to take corrective action in response to the survey. Edwards also impressed Williams with the scope of his understanding of what was needed and with his commitment to starting a change effort. Williams emphasized that he believed organizational change was a management responsibility and that the managers of the company were the real change agents. He would provide direction in terms of *how* to determine what needed changing and *how* to implement the changes, not necessarily *what* to change.

Approximately one month following the entry meeting Williams was contacted again and told that Galen had selected him to consult with them. Immediately following this, a meeting was arranged with Edwards. The consultant wanted Edwards to understand and agree to what he intended to do in the OD process. Williams and Edwards agreed to a rough timetable and an outline of the initial steps in the change process. They also agreed to an informal consulting contract covering an initial period of six months.

nization in the process of generating data and information about the organization and its problems. The role of the consultant in the diagnosis phase is to determine, with the client, the types of information that will be most helpful in assessing the current state of the organization and the existing barriers to its effective functioning.

A variety of data collection techniques are available to the consultant for use in the diagnosis phase. The most commonly used techniques are summarized in Table 18-1 and discussed below.

TABLE 18-1

A Comparison of Different Methods of Data Collection

Method	*Major advantages*	*Major potential problems*
Interviews	1. Richness of data 2. Empathy—potentially high 3. Flexibility—possibility of revision as interview proceeds 4. Increased validity based on positive rapport	1. Efficiency—large expenditure of time and money 2. Validity—responses and analysis subject to interviewer bias 3. Ease of analysis—difficulty of coding and quantifying
Questionnaires	1. Efficiency—coverage of large samples at relatively low cost 2. Validity—quantifiable responses, not subject to bias of analyst 3. Ease of analysis and presentation—large volume of data can be analyzed and presented	1. Empathy—little, and thus reduced depth of data 2. Richness of data—low; difficulty of interpretation 3. Flexibility—possible neglect of important issues 4. Validity—various response biases such as leniency; hence reduced validity 5. Ease of presentation—numerical data uninspiring
Observation	1. Validity—data on actual behavior rather than reports of behavior 2. Validity—real time, not retrospective 3. Flexibility—ease in shifting focus *any or all org*	1. Ease of analysis—difficulty of coding and quantifying 2. Efficiency—large expenditure of time and money 3. Validity—limited sample and potential observer bias 4. Empathy—potential for creating feelings of being manipulated, unless unobtrusive
Supplementary data	1. Validity—high credibility and no response bias 2. Ease of analysis—good for financial data 3. Efficiency—not costly to obtain and usually not costly to analyze	1. Flexibility—analyzable data limited 2. Validity—data largely self-report 3. Ease of analysis—coding and interpretation problems except for financial data 4. Empathy—no relationship developed with people 5. Richness of data—generally low

Source: Adapted from Nadler, D. A. (1977). *Feedback and organization development: Using data-based methods.* © 1977, Reading, MA: Addison-Wesley. Table 7.1. Reprinted with permission.

Interviews

Interviews are probably the most widely used method of collecting data in OD, partly because they are an extremely flexible tool for gathering information about an organization and its problems. During interviews with the consultant, organization members are free to mention any sources of problems or difficulties that they may be experiencing. In addition, when particular issues are mentioned, the consultant is free to ask additional probing questions in order to understand more clearly the nature of a particular problem and what may be causing it. Interviews also give the consultant an opportunity to develop rapport and understanding with members of the organization.

Interviews are not without their drawbacks however. Collecting diagnostic information by interviews is time-consuming and expensive. Since interviews are so time-consuming, it is also generally necessary to select only a small sample of members of the organization to be interviewed. This introduces the risk that the consultant may not obtain a valid picture of the entire organization and its problems. The information collected in interviews is also subject to potential bias by the interviewer, who may unconsciously ask certain types of questions and not others. The final problem associated with interviews is the difficulty of generating clear and accurate summaries from a large number of interviews. This is a problem that questionnaires, the other extremely common method of gathering data, are well suited to avoid.

Questionnaires

The diagnostic phase of OD frequently involves the administration of a questionnaire especially designed to focus on the major problem areas being experienced in the organization. A sample segment of an OD questionnaire is contained in Figure 18-3. Questionnaires have the advantage of providing a large amount of standardized information in a short period of time. The perceptions and opinions of everyone (or almost everyone) in the organization can be obtained in response to a standard set of questions that people answer in terms of numerical response scales. The fact that the data generated from questionnaires is standardized and numerical greatly facilitates its analysis and the determination of general trends in the results.

While the ease and efficiency of questionnaires are strong positive points, there are also some problems associated with their use. Questionnaires lack the flexibility of interviews. With a questionnaire, you have no way of determining whether you have asked the correct questions. The questionnaire may ignore some important problems in the organization that might have come to light during an interview. In addition, administering a questionnaire does little or nothing to develop rapport and understanding between the OD consultant and members of the organization. Questionnaire administration does not usually involve a face-to-face, one-on-one meeting and can be experienced as relatively cold and impersonal.

Observation

The consultant can often learn a great deal about the client organization simply by being sensitive to his or her observations of the organization and its members. By witnessing relationships, the tone of interaction among members, and

Figure 18-3   Sample OD data collection questionnaire.

This part of the questionnaire asks you to describe aspects of your job environment and management practices in the engineering division as you see them. Please indicate the degree to which you agree or disagree with each statement. Write a number in the blank beside each statement, based on the following scale.

HOW MUCH DO YOU AGREE WITH THE STATEMENT?

1	2	3	4	5	6	7
Disagree Strongly	Disagree	Disagree Slightly	Neutral	Agree Slightly	Agree	Agree Strongly

_____   Deadlines for projects are realistic (they take into account the demands that are being placed on my time).

_____   People in the engineering division are more interested in building up their own group or department than in building better products.

_____   In this organization people are encouraged to perform at a high level of engineering quality.

_____   Management practices are such that I feel motivated to assume personal responsibility for doing high quality work.

_____   I feel personally responsible for making sure that all of the work I do is of the highest possible quality.

_____   The attitude in the engineering division seems to be to do a job "good enough to get into production" rather than to do a job in "the best possible way."

_____   The meetings I attend are often poorly organized and conducted.

_____   I feel I am involved in the process of setting the goals and deadlines that apply to my work.

_____   There is a lot of "empire building" going on within the engineering division.

_____   Deadlines are taken seriously in this organization.

_____   When goals and deadlines are established my input is seriously considered.

_____   I am held accountable for performing at a high level of excellence.

_____   I feel personally responsible for meeting deadlines that I am given.

the general climate of the organization, the consultant can gain considerable insight into the nature of the organization and the types of problems it is experiencing. The consultant can focus attention on any or all parts of the organization and in the process obtain a great deal of useful information.

Observation is also unfortunately very time-consuming and difficult to do in a systematic fashion. While the consultant may gain certain insights from his or her observations, it is difficult to ensure that these observations are representative of what occurs in the organization in general. Further, it is extremely difficult to adequately record and summarize the results of observations for systematic feedback to members of the organization. Finally, it is difficult to know to what extent the behavior observed by the consultant was influenced by the very fact that the consultant was present observing the members of the organization. Would the organization members have acted differently if the consultant had not been present? These problems are formidable, and as a result observation tends to serve as a supplementary, rather than a primary, source of diagnostic information for OD.

Supplementary Data

Supplementary data refers to other sources of information existing within the organization that were not collected explicitly for purposes of the diagnostic phase of OD. Examples of supplementary data sometimes used in OD are measures of absenteeism, turnover, financial performance, output rates, quality or reject rates, and so on. Supplementary data may provide a cheap source of independent information regarding the operation and effectiveness of the organization. On the other hand, the use of supplementary data is limited to what exists in the organization. In addition, the consultant has no control over and often no way to assess the accuracy of supplementary data since they have been collected and maintained by others.

The diagnosis phase of the OD project at Galen Pharmaceuticals is described in Box 18-2.

Feedback

Once data collection for diagnosis has been completed, the OD process then moves into the feedback phase. ***Feedback*** consists of the consultant reporting back to the client organization a summary of the data collected during diagnosis. The goals of the feedback phase are twofold. The first goal is to ensure that the members of the client organization receive and accept as valid an accurate picture of the current state of the organization and its problems. The second goal is to use the feedback process to create enthusiasm among the members of the client organization for undertaking changes designed to solve the problems identified.[12]

Feedback usually occurs in a group meeting attended by the consultant and a small group of key managers from the client organization. The consultant's role in the feedback meeting is to present the data collected during diagnosis and then to assist the members of the client organization in their discussion and interpretation of the data. The consultant does *not* tell the members of the organization what action should be taken based on the data presented. The consultant's job is to provide the client with an objective description of the data collected and then to help the members present deal with the data in a constructive manner.

Action Planning

There is often a natural flow during the same meeting from the feedback to the ***action planning*** phase of OD. Once problems have been identified and consensus achieved on the need to resolve them, the next step is to develop plans for dealing with these problems. Since OD is a collaborative process between the

BOX 18-2

The Diagnosis Phase of OD: Learning about Problems at Galen

The initial step taken at Galen by consultant Bob Williams was to establish an advisory committee for the OD project. The committee was composed of president John Edwards plus a vertical cross-section of company members: a member of the top management team (the vice president of marketing), a representative from the next level of management from the finance department, a first-line supervisor, a nonsupervisory administrator, two production employees, and the director of human resources. The committee met once a month for the following purposes: (1) to monitor the change effort; (2) to advise Edwards and Williams about the effectiveness of the OD project; (3) to keep Williams informed and on track regarding the consequences of the various activities within the overall change effort; and (4) to suggest additional plans and activities.

The next step was to conduct individual interviews with each member of the top management team, including the president. The questions asked in the interviews were as follows:

1   What are your reactions to the results of the job satisfaction survey completed earlier this year?

2   What are the major managerial strengths of the company?

3   What are the major managerial weaknesses of the company?

4   What are your hopes for this OD project?

5   What are your fears regarding the OD project?

The purpose of these interviews was to determine more thoroughly the views of these top managers regarding the need for organizational change, to determine their individual motivation and commitment to change, and to establish rapport between them and Williams.

Ground rules were established with each manager at the outset of his or her interview. First, information collected would become public among the top management team at a later feedback session but would go no further. Second, no person would be identified as the source of any specific statement. Third, the information would be used to clarify the top management team's view of the current state of the company and would serve as the basis for planning action steps for the OD project

consultant and the client, the consultant's role during action planning is to help the client generate and explore the consequences of various alternatives. The consultant's role is *not* to tell the client what actions should or should not be undertaken, since such an approach would make the solutions the consultant's rather than the client's, and would not generate the sense of ownership and the commitment to implementing changes that are essential to the success of the OD process.

There are three ways in which the consultant can be particularly helpful to the client during the action planning phase. First, he or she can suggest alternative approaches or solutions to the problems, based upon his or her personal experience and knowledge. While members of the client organization are the ones most knowledgeable about their own organization, they may be unaware of innovative approaches to managing and organizing and may have difficulty envisioning alternative ways of doing things in their own organization.

Second, the consultant can assist members of the client organization in thinking through the implications of alternative courses of action. It is often extremely difficult to anticipate and plan for all the unexpected problems that may arise when important changes are undertaken in an organization. The consultant can use his or her knowledge and experience with the OD process to help the client anticipate such problems and develop plans for addressing them when they arise.

Third, the consultant can enhance motivation to implement action plans. If organization members are to be motivated to implement action plans, it is essential that they be clearly informed of the plans, that specific measurable goals be set for the implementation of plans, that people clearly understand

---

BOX 18-3

The Feedback and Action Planning Phases of OD: Identifying Problems and Planning Changes

Approximately one week following the completion of data collection, consultant Bob Williams arranged a meeting with the Galen top management group. The agenda for this half-day session was the feedback report to the management of the consultant's summary of his interviews. Williams began the feedback meeting by giving the managers his summary of the interviews, organized simply and straightforwardly according to the five interview questions. The second phase of the feedback meeting was the reorganization and categorization of the interview data. During the meeting the managers indicated whether their interview data had been categorized appropriately, and some changes were made accordingly.

The group then began the process of action planning. The action planning process consisted of defining desired changes for the organization and developing strategies for implementing those changes. Specifically, the following steps were planned. A one-day meeting was to be held with the top management team in which the president and his six department heads would define their desired state for the organization. A two-day meeting would then be held in which the top forty key managers of the company, including the president and his six executives, would define the desired state for the organization. The previous work by the top team would provide an overall picture and lead for the next level of management to become more specific regarding the desired state for their respective organizational units.

what their personal responsibilities are and *when* they are to be accomplished, that the time allotted for accomplishing change objectives is realistic, and that people are recognized and rewarded for their accomplishments in implementing planned changes. If these implementation steps are not taken, there is a high risk that the motivation and commitment necessary to achieve real change in the organization will not be sustained. Box 18-3 describes what occurred during the feedback and action planning phases of the OD process at Galen Pharmaceuticals.

Intervention/ Implementation

This phase of the OD process involves actually undertaking the changes decided upon during action planning. It is at this point that change actually occurs in the organization.

Intervention activities can take a wide variety of forms. Some of the alternative types of interventions commonly employed in OD are summarized in Table 18-2. As the table indicates, intervention activities can be classified into two major types. First are *individual interventions.* When diagnosis and feedback lead to the conclusion that organizational problems are arising from shortcomings in the ability and/or motivation of organization members, then some type of individual-based intervention activity is called for. *Process interventions,* on the other hand, are designed to improve the interaction processes that go on between individuals, among the members of work teams, and between different groups in the organization. Process interventions are called for when organizational problems appear to be rooted in the interaction processes between and among people in the organization. Each of these different categories of interventions will be examined in more detail in the next section, after we have discussed the final evaluation phase of OD.

Evaluation

The final phase in the OD process is the evaluation of the impact of the changes undertaken on the functioning and effectiveness of the organization. Following intervention and implementation of changes in the organization, additional

TABLE   18-2

Alternative Types of Interventions

Individual	*Process*
Counseling and coaching	Interpersonal peacemaking
Training and development	Group development/team building
Recruitment and selection	Intergroup meetings

data are collected on how the organization is functioning. The goal is to assess the extent to which problems identified in the initial diagnosis have been solved or at least improved upon.

While in one sense evaluation can be thought of as the final phase in the OD process, the evaluation phase can also be seen, as Figure 18-2 indicates, as a kind of recycling of the OD process back to the diagnosis phase. During evaluation, the organization is interested in diagnosing the extent to which problems previously identified have been solved, as well as in determining whether any new problems may have arisen. In order for this evaluation data to be of any value to the organization it must then be fed back to members of the organization and be used as a basis for further action planning and intervention activities. Thus OD, when it is truly effective, is an ongoing process of identifying problems, developing and implementing solutions to those problems, and evaluating the effectiveness of the changes made. The more that this ongoing process becomes institutionalized as part of the organization's "normal" activities, the brighter the outlook for the ongoing health and effectiveness of the organization, since new problems and issues that need to be addressed and that may require change are constantly arising in organizations. Box 18-4 describes how the implementation and evaluation phases were handled at Galen Pharmaceuticals.

Organization Development Interventions

Some of the alternative types of OD interventions were mentioned in the previous section and summarized in Table 18-2. In this section we will examine these different types of intervention activities in greater detail.

Individual Interventions

Sometimes the diagnosis and feedback phases of OD lead to the conclusion that organizational problems have their roots in certain shortcomings or inadequacies of individual organization members. In this type of situation intervention activities need to be designed that will enable organization members to develop the abilities or skills they currently lack. Such activities can take a variety of forms.

Counseling and Coaching

Certain individuals may require support and direction if they are to adjust to organizational changes effectively. Some individuals may be unaware of ways in which their own job performance is dysfunctional to the organization. In addition, such individuals may not be conscious of alternative ways of approaching and carrying out their work. Counseling and coaching by the consultant may stimulate self-awareness and lead to the development of new behavior patterns on the job for these individuals.

BOX 18-4

Implementation and Evaluation: Making Changes and Following Up

The outcome of the one-day top management meeting and the two-day meeting of forty key managers had been agreement on the state that management wished to achieve for the organization within two years. The objectives included not only reduced absenteeism and turnover, but specific goals regarding net profit, return on investment, number of new products developed, and market share.

Following the initial off-site meetings, consultant Bob Williams began working with each of the six primary units of the company. Williams helped them plan action steps for implementing the transition phase for their particular functions. These action steps took many different forms, including supervisory and management skills training in some departments, team-building sessions, and intergroup problem-solving meetings between the marketing and manufacturing groups. Williams also continued to meet with the advisory committee, in order to keep all members of the organization informed about the change effort and to monitor progress and rectify problems that arose during the transition.

In order to plan for the evaluation of the OD project at Galen, Williams recommended to president Edwards that essentially the same survey that had been administered approximately a year before he began his consultation should be administered two years later. The overall schedule can be summarized as follows:

Year 1	Survey conducted
Year 2	Change effort (OD) begins
Year 3	Survey conducted again
Year 4	Organization reaches desired state

By the fourth year Williams might recommend that the survey be administered for yet a third time. Other comparative data should also be collected to determine if the company is performing better in the areas of performance targeted for improvement.

Training and Development	Individuals may simply lack the skills necessary to perform their work more effectively. It is often the case that, as part of the OD process, individuals will be provided with training in interpersonal and problem-solving skills. The development of such skills can often lead to improved communication and a more positive and cooperative attitude among members of the organization.
Recruitment and Selection	As the OD process takes hold in an organization, some fundamental changes may occur in organization structure, management practices, and so on over time. These changes may be such that the organization needs to be recruiting

and hiring different types of people from those who have tended to be hired in the past. This implies a need for coordination between the management of the OD process and the management of the organization's procedures for recruiting and selection.

Process Interventions

Process interventions are designed to improve the interaction *process* (or working relationships) between individual organization members, among members of work groups or teams, or between groups or departments in the organization. We will briefly examine a number of the most common process interventions employed in OD.

Interpersonal Peacemaking

Interpersonal peacemaking refers to actions that an OD consultant can undertake with the goal of resolving a serious conflict between two organization members. There are two phases to the process. In the first phase the consultant meets with the parties to the conflict individually in order to assess their readiness and willingness to work on resolving the conflict. If, as a result of these meetings, the consultant concludes that there is potential for progress, then the process moves to the second phase. This consists of a meeting between the two individuals in conflict. The consultant is in attendance and serves as a sort of chairman of the meeting by setting the agenda, controlling the interaction, and so on. A summary of the key activities of the consultant in an interpersonal peacemaking meeting is contained in Table 18-3. The consultant's goal is to help the parties begin discussing how and why they have come into conflict and what can be done to resolve their differences in order to establish a positive working relationship.

Group Development/ Team Building

A problem commonly identified in the diagnosis phase of OD is the failure of work groups to achieve their full potential due to lack of coordination, poor leadership, conflict among individual members, and so on. When these sorts of problems regarding the process going on within work groups are identified,

---

TABLE   18-3

Key Consultant Activities during an Interpersonal Peacemaking Meeting

Refereeing the interaction process
Initiating the agenda for the meeting
Restating the issue and the participants' views
Eliciting reactions and offering observations
Diagnosing the conflict
Prescribing discussion methods
Diagnosing conditions causing poor dialogue

the OD consultant can help resolve them by conducting what are known as *group development*, or *team building*, activities with the members of the group involved.

There are two phases to the group development process. The first phase is a data collection process during which the consultant employs some combination of interviews and questionnaires to find out from members of the group the problems and frustrations each of them is experiencing within the group. A sample questionnaire that can be employed in this phase of the process is contained in Figure 18-4. The second phase is a meeting of all members of the group, usually held off-site (away from regular job duties and responsibilities) for a period of two to three days. At this meeting the consultant first presents the results of the data collection process in summary form to the group members, highlighting the major problems or issues identified by the group members individually. For the remainder of the meeting the consultant serves as a chairperson and general resource person to the group as the members begin to grapple with the problems identified and develop plans for dealing with them. The group development process can result in increased self-awareness among individual group members regarding their own role in the group and insight regarding ways in which they need to change their own behavior in order to facilitate coordination and cooperation within the group.

Intergroup Meetings

When the diagnosis phase of OD brings to light serious, dysfunctional conflict between groups in the organization, *intergroup meetings* may be recommended by the consultant as an intervention strategy for attempting to resolve the conflict. The first step in the intergroup intervention process involves a series of meetings between the consultant and members of each of the two groups in conflict. During these meetings the consultant's goals are to gather information regarding sources or causes of the conflict and to assess whether there exists a real desire and commitment on the part of members of the groups to resolve the conflict. If the groups share little common ground and are not motivated to resolve their differences, the likelihood of progress in an intergroup meeting is slim.

If from these meetings the consultant reaches a positive conclusion regarding the likelihood of progress, an intergroup meeting is scheduled, usually at an off-site location. Such a meeting consists of the following steps.

Step 1   The consultant meets with everyone present to go over the agenda for the meeting and to set up ground rules or norms regarding how individuals will need to behave at the meeting if progress is to be made.

Step 2   The two groups are sent off by themselves to develop the following lists:
a   How we see ourselves
b   How we see the other group
c   How we think the other group sees us

A sample of the types of perceptions that can emerge from this process is contained in Table 18-4.

Figure 18-4   Sample OD team-building questionnaire.

Directions:

This form is designed to help you think about your behavior in your work group. First, read over the scales and on each one circle the number on the scale that describes you when you are at your best. Label this mark "B". Do the same for the point that describes you when you are your worst. Mark this circle "W".

After marking all the scales, pick out the 3 or 4 along which you would most like to change. On these scales draw an arrow above the line to indicate the desirable direction for changing your behavior.

1. Ability to listen to others in an understanding way.

1	2	3	4	5	6	7
Low			Moderate			High

2. Ability to influence others in the group.

1	2	3	4	5	6	7
Low			Moderate			High

3. Willingness to trust others to do what they have said they will do.

1	2	3	4	5	6	7
Low			Moderate			High

4. Willingness to discuss my feelings about how the group is working.

1	2	3	4	5	6	7
Very Unwilling			Neither Willing or Unwilling			Very Willing

5. Willingness to be influenced by others.

1	2	3	4	5	6	7
Very Unwilling			Neither Willing or Unwilling			Very Willing

6. Tendency to run the group.

1	2	3	4	5	6	7
Low			Moderate			High

7. Sensitivity to the feelings of others.

1	2	3	4	5	6	7
Not Sensitive			Somewhat Sensitive			Very Sensitive

8. Reaction to conflict and antagonism in the group.

1	2	3	4	5	6	7
Low Tolerance			Moderate Tolerance			High Tolerance

9. Reaction to opinions opposed to mine.

1	2	3	4	5	6	7
Low Tolerance			Moderate Tolerance			High Tolerance

TABLE 18-4

Sample Intergroup Perceptions Emerging During an Intergroup Meeting

Engineering	*Manufacturing*
We see ourselves:	
Stable	Competent
Cooperative	Error prone
Creative	Hard working
We see them:	
Unstable	Error prone
Not creative	No sense of urgency
Industrious	Unified as a group
They see us:	
In ivory towers	Constantly changing
Error prone	Error prone
Intrusive	Inflexible

Source: Hackman, J. R. & Suttle, J. L. (1977). *Improving life at work: Behavioral science approaches to organizational change.* Santa Monica, CA: Goodyear, p. 285. Reprinted by permission.

Step 3   The two groups come back together and post up their three lists in the room. At this stage, no discussion of the material on the lists is permitted; only questions of clarification are allowed.

Step 4   The members of the two groups again go off separately and are asked to:
a   discuss what they have learned from seeing the other group's list
b   develop a set of priority issues that need to be addressed if the working relationship between the groups is to be improved

Step 5   The groups come back together and each presents its list of priority issues. The whole group discusses these issues and agrees on a single set of priorities.

Step 6   The priority items are discussed and action plans are developed to address the key problem areas identified.

When members of both groups are motivated to improve their working relationship, the intergroup meeting intervention has been shown to have a high degree of effectiveness.[13] It achieves this by initiating a process of communication, listening, and cooperative behavior between groups that had previously not been present.

The key issue in planning OD interventions is to ensure that the intervention activities are appropriate to the problems that have been diagnosed. Many interventions are available that can be very effective in helping organizations overcome serious impediments to their effectiveness. When the diagnosis of problems has been conducted carefully and interventions are completely implemented, the OD process has significant potential to increase organizational effectiveness.

Keys to Effective Management

Our discussion of the nature of OD and the process of implementing it in organizations brings to light a variety of key issues managers must be conscious of if the OD process is to be successful.

1 *Managers must adopt a systematic approach to planning the OD process.* To implement successful change, managers must begin by unfreezing old attitudes and behaviors, replacing these with new, more effective ways of behaving, and providing the necessary support to refreeze the new ways of doing things. Planning and implementing change is a complex process that requires the coordination of many elements in the organization.

2 *The OD process must be managed in a collaborative and participative manner.* OD, by its very nature, places strong emphasis on the need to generate problem solutions that are *acceptable* to members of the organization. The key to achieving acceptance is the active participation of organization members in a collaborative process.

3 *Managers must ensure that planned changes are based on a careful diagnosis of organizational problems.* Before deciding on solutions, managers must be sure that they have a clear understanding of the problems they are faced with in their organization. This requires an in-depth diagnosis of the organization using multiple methods of collecting information about the organization and its problems. This diagnosis then provides the basis for sound planning of intervention strategies that are highly likely to lead to organizational improvement.

4 *Top management support for OD must be established and maintained.* If senior managers are skeptical of OD and its potential to help the organization, it is unlikely that the process can be successful. OD takes time, requires resources, and demands the enthusiastic commitment of those involved in the process. As a result, the material and moral support of top management are key ingredients to success.

5 *Management must set realistic goals and expectations for OD.*   It is important that initial OD work in an organization not be overly ambitious. If the organization tries to take on too much, the process may get out of hand or may become bogged down. A more focused and smaller-scale starting point is more likely to lead to success. In addition, management must recognize that OD is not a process that "turns around" organizations overnight. Fundamental organizational change is a time-consuming process and one whose most important results may not be measurable for a period of two years or more after the outset of the change process.

Review Questions

1 What is organization development (OD)?

2 What kinds of organizational problems do you feel are best suited to the OD approach to change?

3 What factors distinguish OD from other approaches to bringing about change in organizations?

4 What is meant by the terms *unfreezing, movement,* and *refreezing,* and what is their relevance to organizational change?

5 Briefly outline the phases in the OD process. Which phase do you feel is most critical to the success of OD?

6 Discuss the different issues that must be dealt with during the contact, exploration, and contracting stages of the entry process.

7 Discuss the strengths and weaknesses of some of the alternative data collection techniques that can be used in the diagnosis phase of OD.

8 What is the appropriate role of the consultant during the action planning process? What things should the consultant be attempting to do during this phase?

9 How do you feel that the evaluation phase should fit into the overall OD process?

10 Describe two major categories of OD interventions and provide examples of each.

11 Describe some different types of individual interventions and discuss when each is appropriate.'

12 What is interpersonal peacemaking? When is it appropriate and how is it carried out?

13 Describe how you would organize and conduct a group development meeting with a management team.

Resolving Intergroup Conflict

A manufacturing plant and regional sales district were locked in an intergroup conflict that not only resulted in stormy interchanges but also caused problems in customer relations. The plant perceived sales as concerned only about volume and pleasing the customer, not about the plant's costs. The district sales manager and his salespeople saw the plant as unresponsive to customers, conservative, and overly concerned about costs and long manufacturing runs.

One particular phone conversation on a Friday afternoon was often cited as an example of the conflict. The district sales manager was calling to find out why the sales service department had been turned down by the plant on a special request to send products to a large and important customer. The plant manager explained that three days was too short a time for turning around a large order and that it would disrupt operations in the plant, other customer orders,

and the whole month's production schedule. Besides, the plant manager told the district manager, "You guys are just not willing to tell the customer that he can't have what he wants. It's your job to manage the customer, not respond to every wish." At this, the district manager lost his temper and accused the plant manager of caring only about his "gross margin" (plant profit). The shouting match that ensued resulted in the plant manager hanging up.

As part of a larger OD program that was aimed at improving cooperation and coordination between functional groups, a corporate OD consultant met with the plant manager and district sales manager to determine their interest in working to improve relations and coordination. They both agreed to an intergroup meeting as a means of improving cooperation. The plant manager and his staff and the district manager and his salespeople came together at a motel for two days to work on the problems in their relationship. The manager of the sales service organization, which often found itself in the middle of this conflict because of its responsibility to represent sales to manufacturing, was also present as a neutral observer.

Questions for Discussion

1 What issues should the OD consultant have discussed with the plant manager and the district sales manager prior to the intergroup meeting?

2 How would you plan the agenda of the intergroup meeting? Outline the steps you would employ?

3 If you were the consultant, what would you plan to do during the meeting? What role would you play? What would you do and not do? Why?

Source: Adapted from Beer, M. (1980). *Organization change and development: A systems view,* p. 153. Glenview, IL: Scott, Foresman. © 1980. Used by permission of the author.

Notes

1   Beer, M. (1980). *Organization change and development: A systems view.* Santa Monica, CA: Goodyear.

2   Winn, A. (1968, September). The laboratory approach to organizational development: A tentative model of planned change (paper read at the Annual Conference of the British Psychological Society, Oxford). Cited in R. T. Golembiewski (1969, July–August). Organizational development in public agencies: Perspectives on theory and practice, *Public Administration Review.*

3   Beer (1980), *loc. cit.*

4   Lewin, K. (1958). "Group decision and social change." In Maccoby, E. E., Newcomb, T. M., & Hartley, E. L. (Eds.), *Readings in social psychology.* New York: Holt, Rinehart, & Winston.

5   Blake, R. R., Mouton, J. S., Barnes, L. B., & Greiner, L. E. (1964). Breakthrough in organizational development. *Harvard Business Review, 42,* 133–155.
  Bowers, D. G. (1973). OD techniques and their results in 23 organizations: The Michigan ICC study. *Journal of Applied Behavioral Science, 9,* 21–43.

6   Lewin (1958), *loc. cit.*

7   French, W. L. (1969). Organizational development: Objectives, assumptions, and strategies. *California Management Review, 12,* 23–34.

8   Burke, W. W. (1982). *Organization development: Principles and practice.* Boston, MA: Little, Brown, and Company.
  Kolb, D., & Froham, A. (1970). An organizational development approach to consulting. *Sloan Management Review, 12*(1), 51–65.

9   The descriptions are adapted from a case presented by Burke (1982), *loc. cit.,* 306–313.

10   Burke (1982), *ibid.*

11   Weisbord, M. R. (1973). The organizational development contract. *OD Practitioner, 5*(2), 1–4.

12   Beer, M. (1980), *loc. cit.*

13   Alderfer, C. P. (1976). Boundary relations and organizational diagnosis. In L. Meltzer & F. Wickert (Eds.), *Humanizing organizational behavior.* Springfield, IL: Charles C Thomas.
  Beer, M. (1976). The technology of organizational development. In M. D. Dunnette (Ed.), *Handbook of industrial and organizational psychology.* Chicago, IL: Rand McNally.

Chapter 19

Careers in Organizations

CHAPTER OUTLINE

The Nature of Careers

Early Career Issues

Transfers and Promotions

Middle- and Later-Career Issues

Career Development

Keys to Effective Management

Review Questions

*M*ost people today will change the type of work they do, the organizations in which they work, and the cities in which they live, several times during their work lives. For this reason, we need to examine not only the first professions and jobs individuals choose, but also the series of occupations and jobs they will hold over a forty-year period. These sequences of jobs and occupations are called *careers* and are the subject of this chapter.

The chapter is divided into five sections. In the first section, we will look closely at the changing nature of careers in organizations, and why careers are so different today than they were a quarter century ago. In this section we will also look at how changes in individuals' personal lives influence their aspirations and satisfactions at different points in their careers.

The next three sections of the chapter focus on the career issues people face at different stages of their lives. In the second section of the chapter, we will look at experiences of college graduates as they enter the work force. We examine here the typical problems individuals face when they first join organizations, and how organizations "socialize" these new recruits into the workplace. In the third section of the chapter, we will look at how managers in their

20s and 30s establish themselves early in their careers. We look here at how organizations transfer and promote their employees, and how employees adjust to these job changes. In the fourth section, we will look at the careers of middle-age and older managers, and the special challenges and frustrations these employees face.

The fifth and final section of the chapter focuses on the management and development of careers in organizations. At this point, we will examine programs and policies that organizations can use to better develop their employees, as well as strategies that individuals can use to better manage their own careers.

The Nature of Careers

In *The Organization Man,* the classic critique of corporate life in America, William H. Whyte attacked the lack of control that executives and managers were exerting over their own careers. In the organizations Whyte described in 1957, career success was largely determined by willingness to conform to organizational values and expectations, both at work and at home. Corporations valued individuals who were willing to get along by going along:

They are all, as they say, in the same boat. But where is the boat going? No one seems to have the faintest idea; nor for that matter, do they see much point in even raising the question. Once people liked to think, at least, that they were in control of their destinies, but few of the younger organization men cherish such notions. Most see themselves as objects more acted upon than acting—and their future, therefore, determined as much by the system as by themselves.[1]

People's ideas about careers and career success have changed substantially since that time in at least eight ways.

1   The term *career* has in a sense been democratized. No longer does it pertain to only individuals in high-status or rapid-advancement occupations. *Career* now refers to the sequence of jobs people hold during their work histories, regardless of occupation or organizational level.[2] Executives have careers, but so do executive secretaries.

2   While a large majority of workers are still striving to move up the organization hierarchy, there are increasing numbers of employees who are turning down more responsible jobs to remain in positions they currently hold and enjoy. There are now more frequent career moves in a horizontal, and sometimes downward, direction.

3   Today there is evidence that more and more individuals are experiencing "multicareers," career paths that include two or three different fields and

two or three different organizations. Very few people will work in one area or in one organization their whole lives.[3]

4 Colleges, graduate schools, the government, and the media have all made individual employees more sensitive to the benefits that can be reaped from actively planning and managing their own careers. No longer is it assumed that the organization has unilateral control over the individual's career. Individuals are a lot less willing to sit back and see how things turn out.

5 Managers today are not implicitly guaranteed lifetime work security. Today, if managers begin to lose their drive or talent, they are no longer shunted off to a less critical assignment. They are simply fired. Starting particularly with the recession of 1973, white-collar workers are laid off in poor economic times. This change in organizational values has fueled a "me-first" careerism among managers.

6 At the time Whyte wrote his book, there were so few women executives that the phrase "organization man" was likely to offend very few managers. Today, more and more women are going to business school (often more than 25 percent of the entering class are women), and more and more women are succeeding to top management positions.

7 Today career success is *personally* defined. No longer is it assumed that career success should be measured by high salary and high occupational status alone. For some the traditional goals of money, advancement, and prestige remain the same, but for others these goals are no longer attractive. Many people now define career success as having a job that allows them time to pursue relationships and leisure activities outside the job.[4]

8 Finally, people no longer assume that their career aspirations will remain stable over a forty-year period. What is challenging to a 25-year old may not prove motivating to a 45-year old. People's personal needs change as they grow older, marry, have children; what they find satisfying in their 20s they may find deadening in their 40s.

Career and Life Stages

To understand the different attitudes managers have about their jobs at different points in their lives, we have to understand both the career challenges they face *and* the personal problems they confront. In Tables 19-1 and 19-2, we outline some of the major changes that occur in people's personal lives and careers as they grow older. In the next few pages, we'll briefly consider some of the highlights of these stages. Before proceeding, however, it is important to note that not all individuals experience all these feelings at the different stages in their lives and careers. What we will be discussing next are the *typical* concerns people in different age groups experience.

The adolescent years are ones in which an individual tries to develop a self-identity. A teenager strives to become an independent person, someone

TABLE 19-1

Career Stages of Managers

Age group	Career stage	Career concerns
15–22	Exploration	Finding the right career Getting the appropriate education
22–30	Early career: Trial	Getting the first job Adjusting to daily work routine and supervisors
30–38	Early career: Establishment	Choosing specialty and deciding on level of commitment Transfers and promotions Broadening perspective of occupation and organization
38–45	Middle career: Growth	Establishing professional or organizational identity Choosing between alternative career paths (e.g., technical vs. managerial)
45–55	Middle career: Maintenance	Being an independent contributor to the organization Taking on more areas of responsibility
55–62	Later career: Plateau	Training and developing subordinates Shaping the future direction of the organization Dealing with threats to position from younger, more aggressive employees
62–70	Later career: Decline	Planning for retirement Developing one's replacement Dealing with a reduced work load and less power

Source: Based upon the works of: Schein, E. H. (1978). *Career dynamics: Matching individual and organizational needs.* Reading, MA: Addison-Wesley, 40–46; Dalton, G. W., Thompson, P. H., & Price, R. L. (1977). The four stages of professional careers: A new look at performance by professionals. *Organizational Dynamics, 6,* 19–42; Van Maanen, J., & Schein, E. H. (1977). Career development. In Hackman, J. R. & Suttle, J. L. (Eds.), *Improving life at work.* Santa Monica, CA: Goodyear, 54–57.

who can stand apart from his or her parents and still succeed. Choosing a career and deciding on what type of education to pursue are integral to this defining of self-identity.

If adolescent years are marked by the striving to become independent, early adult years are marked by the establishing of intimacy. People in their 20s try to develop close friendships and often make a commitment to a spouse.

TABLE   19-2

Life Stages and Concerns of Managers

Age group	Life stage	Life concerns
15–22	Adolescence	Developing a self-identity Reconciling others' views of self with self-perceptions
22–30	Entering the adult world	Developing close friendships Making a commitment to a spouse Becoming involved seriously with work
30–38	Young adulthood	Introspection and questioning about commitments made to career and family Struggle between desire for order and stability and desire for freedom from all restraints
38–45	Mid-life transition	Questioning of all values Feeling that there is only one last chance for major success Frustration with adolescence of children
45–55	Middle adulthood	Settling down; more realistic views of family, friends, and work Increased attachment to spouse; decreased attachment to children leaving the household
55–62	Late adulthood	A softening of feelings; a tendency to avoid emotion-laden issues A preoccupation with everyday joys and frustrations Concern with establishing and guiding the next generation
62–70	Maturity	Increased awareness of death Developing a sense of satisfaction with one's life choices

Source: Based upon the works of: Levinson, D. J. (1977). The mid-life transition: A period in adult psychosocial development. *Psychiatry, 40,* 99–112; Erikson, E. H. (1963). *Childhood and society* (2nd ed.). New York: Norton; Valliant, G. E. (1977). *Adaptation to life.* Boston: Little, Brown.

At this point most people also become seriously involved with work and begin to establish their careers. As people enter their 30s, they try to broaden their knowledge of the occupations and organizations they have chosen; they also try to achieve some balance between their commitments to work and their commitments to families and friends.

In their late 30s and early 40s, many people realize that this may be the last chance to make a major change in their professional or personal lives. This may be the last chance to go back to school, or switch fields, or move geographically. On the personal front, it may mark a turning point in a marriage or other significant relationships.

The mid-40s to mid-50s are typically a very happy and productive time. Many people settle down at work and become major contributors to organizational success. As children leave home, adults have more time and energy to invest in their spouses and friends.

As people reach their middle and later 50s, it is generally clear how far they can go professionally; the top of their professional career is in sight. Just as their children are beginning to produce grandchildren, many of these older adults find satisfaction in training and developing the next generation of subordinates in the organization or becoming mentors.

After age 60, most individuals begin to plan for retirement. They disengage themselves from work and spend more energy rekindling old leisure pursuits or developing new ones. While the deaths of friends and spouses increase their awareness of death, many older adults develop a sense of satisfaction with their choices in life and a sense of pride in their accomplishments.

In the next three sections of the chapter, we will explore the careers of managers at different stages in their lives. As we do so, keep in mind how changes in professional lives and personal lives constantly reinforce each other. The need for intimacy and commitment in the 20s fuels the need to demonstrate competence at work; the need to make major career changes in the 40s fuels the reexamination of family commitments and other life choices; the "empty nest" syndrome of children leaving home and starting their own families turns older workers' attention to developing the next generation of leaders in the firm.

Early Career Issues

The change from student to employee is a dramatic transition for most students—and for many it can be quite a shock. Let's consider for a moment, then, the "entry shock" most students experience as they start their first jobs.

Entry Shock

There are seven major ways in which the environment of a student and that of a full-time employee differ.[5] The adjustment required by these differences is what causes new entrants into the work force to feel such discomfort in the "real world."

1   *Supervisors.*   Students, at any point in time, will have four or five supervisors (teachers). These teachers usually change every four months and are

often selected by the students themselves. In contrast, an employee usually has one manager, sometimes for years, with little (perhaps no) influence over the choice of that superior. New workers mistakenly treat their supervisors as they treated their professors, with unfortunate results.

2 *Feedback.* Students learn to expect brief, quantitative performance evaluations (grades) on numerous specific occasions throughout the year. An employee, on the other hand, may never get any concrete feedback from superiors outside of pay raises or promotions. It is not unusual for new workers to feel that they are working in a vacuum and to become angry that they are not receiving more feedback. Many young managers detest being treated as "average" and resent being considered nothing special or unique.

3 *Time horizons.* Students learn to think in terms of time cycles of one or two hours (a class), a week (after which a sequence of classes repeats itself), or four months (a semester, when classes and professors change). Time horizons in the working world are much more likely to be either very short (as short as a few hours in some production/operating jobs) or very long (as long as several years in some planning jobs). These changes in time cycles can leave new employees feeling disoriented.

4 *Magnitude of decisions.* Business students often get used to making a number of major decisions (hypothetically) every day. At least at first, the new employee will rarely make any major decisions in his or her job. This often leads to feelings of being underused or ignored.

5 *Speed of change.* Because students are encouraged to think about planning and implementing innovative programs, they often develop highly unrealistic expectations concerning the ease and quickness of making changes in the real world. Organizations often move slowly, and changes are often based on political, rather than on technical or business, considerations. Very little change can be effected by one person alone, especially a newcomer.

6 *Promotions.* A student with a master's degree and no full-time work experience has lived in an environment where promotions occur once every twelve months—eighteen promotions in eighteen years. It is not surprising that students are frustrated that they are not moving up the corporate hierarchy as quickly. Moreover, students are frustrated that movement through an organization can depend on nothing more than luck or having the right connections.

7 *The nature of problems.* Professors typically assign problems that can be solved in a short period of time, using some specific method or theory that is currently being taught. Such a process is efficient by many educational standards. However, new workers often find it incredibly frustrating when the problems they are given aren't neat and easily solvable.

The overall result of this entry shock is that many new recruits' self-confidence is shaken. Recent graduates become anxious about their ability to succeed and feel uncertain about the correctness of their job choices. Others question whether they are willing to make the sort of commitments needed to succeed on the organization's terms.

The issue becomes, then, how to start the initial work period off on the right foot. In the next section, we'll examine how organizations can help recruits adjust to their new work environments more effectively.

Organizational Socialization

The process by which recruits are transformed from total outsiders into participating and effective members of companies is called ***organizational socialization.***[6] Organizational socialization involves not only adjusting to new work tasks, but also adjusting to new work groups and new organizational practices. Newcomers actually undergo a "multiple socialization process" in which they simultaneously develop new work skills, new friends, new values, and new behavior patterns.[7]

Becoming accepted by coworkers and superiors can be as difficult as learning the job itself. In a study of organizational socialization at hospitals, one accounting clerk commented that she "felt like an orphan, hoping someone would take me in," while another clerk reported that she spent over $50 per month in long-distance phone calls to get support from old friends about her present problems with coworkers. A radiology technologist experiencing a good deal of difficulty in his working relationships with coworkers commented: "I've been here two months, and even now I don't feel accepted. . . . I worry about my relationships with other workers all the time. . . . This worry drives out concern for patients, for work, for everything."[8]

Learning the organization's special practices can be trying as well. In the hospital study cited above, a very important part of the accounting clerk's job is dealing with patients and lawyers who are trying to unravel payment problems or billing errors. It takes a while to learn the shortcuts to solving problems, to find the people in the informal network who can cut through the red tape, and so forth. The clerks who never learn the informal system never really succeed at the job. On the other hand, one billing clerk responsible for clients whose last names began with the letters O through Z learned the ropes so quickly she became known affectionately as "The Wizard of Oz."[9]

Stages of Organizational Socialization

The socialization process does not occur in one or two days, but is achieved over a period of weeks and months. Usually, organizational socialization takes place in three stages (see Figure 19-1).[10]

Stage 1 **"Getting in."**   For many new hires, the process of socialization starts before the person actually enters the organization. Hoping to get a job with a particular type of organization, students will try to acquire the types of skills and

Figure 19-1 Stages of organizational socialization.

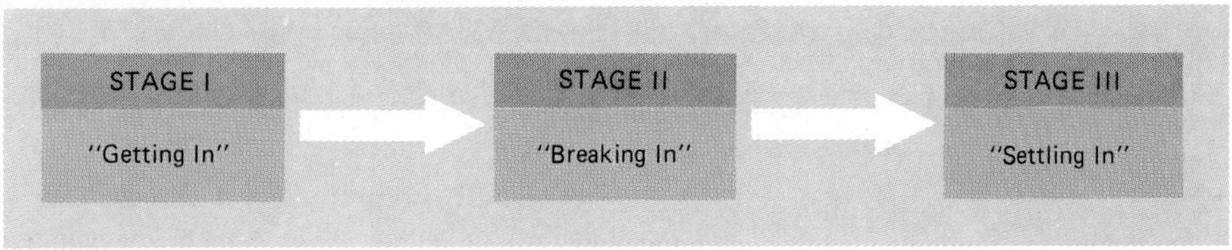

[*Source:* Adapted from Feldman, D. C. (1980). A socialization process that helps new recruits succeed. *Personnel, 57,* 11–23.]

abilities that will gain them acceptance into the organization. Moreover, students' values and attitudes may change in anticipation of their new status in life.[11] Business students, for instance, may start dressing more conservatively or acting more businesslike even before they actually enter the corporate world.

Stage 2 **"Breaking in."** In this second stage, individuals see what the organization is really like and attempt to become participating members of it.[12] Organizations may provide recruits with some training or orientation, and some initial feedback on their technical performance.

Stage 3 **"Settling in."** In this third stage, newcomers actually begin to settle down and to truly adjust to the organization. They are over their initial anxieties about being fired or feeling isolated; they now feel really comfortable with their coworkers and their own performance on the job. The organization starts making longer-range career plans for these individuals.

In many ways, the adjustment process that students go through as they enter college and graduate school parallels the socialization process that newcomers experience when they enter work organizations. To see some of the changes that occur in students as they get socialized to business school, consider the three diary entries from a Harvard Business School MBA student in Box 19-1. The first excerpt expresses the student's feelings about getting into the business school; the second excerpt shows the student as he tries to break into the school setting; the third excerpt shows the student as he settles into a daily routine.[13]

Managing Organizational Socialization

Although the initial entry period is a crucial one to the development of an individual's career, many organizations leave the socialization process to chance. However, because it is so important to get newcomers' careers off to a positive start, it is imperative that organizations take more initiative in creating conditions for successful socialization right from the start. There are several strategies organizations can use to design more effective organizational socialization programs, which we will discuss below.[14] These are summarized in Table 19-3.

BOX 19-1

The Socialization of an MBA Student: The Gospel According to the Harvard Business School

Stage 1: "Getting in"   "You remember the people who started out with you in grade school; who haven't, some of them, made it through high school; who haven't, most of them, made it through college. How the faces got fewer and fewer, until you are dead sure somebody has to be a real genius to get into the Harvard Business School.

And the more you think about it, the more you become convinced that it really is going to be like the pictures in the catalogue. With everybody running around in suits and ties, probably saying 'sir' to each other. That these are going to be unbelievably smart, unbelievably aggressive people, and that a regular, willing guy like yourself is going to be in very hot water."

Stage 2: "Breaking in"   "Over to Aldrich 108, at 9:30, to meet your 94 new friends who, from now til next June, will be known collectively as Section B. These are the people you will be together with, four and a half hours a day, five days a week, always in this same room. Too many new names to remember, even with the name tags everybody is wearing.

Then, in the third and final class, we meet Duncan McKay. Looking at nobody in particular, he says that he doesn't want us to love him. That he doesn't care if we hate him. That if we are lucky, *some* of us are going to be leaders and that we shouldn't bother to come to his class without a coat and tie.

That said, he takes his foot off the table, announces tomorrow's case, and piles into the classroom door so that its wings scream in their hinges for some time after he has left. The class is too stunned to even breathe."

Stage 3: "Settling in"   "The name of the game is to make a point. Both, the kind that proves something and the kind that can be added up to give a grade. . . .

The trouble is that with 94 players and the time per game limited to ninety minutes, it's difficult to score. To overcome these difficulties we are developing a number of special techniques. Like the 'preventive attack' in which you start the class by laying out the case, showing what according to you is the problem and what should be done, which gives you some five to ten uninterrupted minutes.

There are also a number of 'defensive' techniques. Of these, the most effective is the 'questioning of premises.' While the guy who is laying out the case is building the second and third levels of his argument, you demolish the foundations. . . .

As a kind of last resort, you can always fall back on sheer 'trifling.' You may not score, but at least you show you are there."

Source: Adapted from Cohen, P. (1973). *The gospel according to Harvard Business School.* New York: Doubleday, pp. 1–21. Used by permission.

TABLE   19-3

Managing Organizational Socialization

1   Provide a challenging first job
2   Provide relevant training
3   Provide timely and reliable feedback
4   Design a relaxed orientation program
5   Place recruits in work groups with high morale and with supportive supervisors
6   Do not demand overconformity to the organization's norms

Source: Feldman, D. C. (1976, Autumn). A practical program for employee socialization. *Organizational Dynamics,* 64–80.

Provide a Challenging First Job

When newcomers are given challenging job assignments, they are motivated to perform well; they become more involved in the organization as a whole, and they increase their capacity to work long, hard hours. On the other hand, when newcomers are given unimportant or trivial first assignments, they become bored, frustrated, and impatient. For this reason, organizations need to provide newcomers with first jobs that allow them to use the skills for which they were hired and to develop new skills reasonably soon.

Provide Relevant Training

It is generally a good idea to have a relatively short, structured training program, in which recruits are taught the basic skills and methods to perform their jobs properly. (If the training period is too long, recruits may feel they are simply back at school.) Then newcomers can start their jobs and receive on-the-job training; they can get coaching and feedback from trainers and supervisors on what they are doing properly and what they need to change. Any systematic deficiencies can be helped through additional structured training aimed at specific deficiencies. Organizations should avoid just letting newcomers "sink or swim" on their own.

Provide Timely and Reliable Feedback

Newcomers' assessments of themselves and their future in the organization are heavily influenced by their first probationary performance evaluation reviews. These probationary reviews not only provide feedback on performance to date, but also signal to employees the organization's initial "letting-in" response to their "breaking-in" efforts. When a full year goes by before the first feedback is given, high performers are kept waiting needlessly for affirmation. As a nurse in the hospital socialization study remarked, "Even a well-trained pigeon should be positively reinforced more than once every 365 days."[15] Newcomers should receive comprehensive feedback on their performance within the first few months on the job, and less extensive positive or negative feedback as their performance warrants.

Design a Relaxed Orientation Program

Orientation programs are too often geared toward selling the company or creating organizational loyalty. Indeed, some of these programs provide such a slick, packaged indoctrination that they are considered overkill by newcomers.

Instead, the orientation should be geared to giving new employees the *specific* information they want and need immediately (e.g., information about payroll, training programs, their work assignments, and the products or divisions in which they will be working). Because recruits can only absorb so much information at one time, items of interest that do not have to be immediately relayed can be communicated at a later date.

Moreover, the tone of the orientation program should be a relaxing one, rather than an anxiety-building one. A particularly successful orientation program was developed at Texas Instruments. It stressed making four points clear to the recruits:

1 Your opportunity to succeed is very good.

2 Disregard "hall talk," "hazing," and rumors.

3 Take the initiative in communication.

4 Get to know your supervisor.

The employees who went through this orientation program initiated a lot more communication with their supervisors, reached preestablished levels of competence a month earlier than expected, and experienced much less anxiety.[16]

Place Recruits in Work Groups with High Morale, and with Supportive Supervisors

There is virtually no aspect of the socialization process that a supervisor, if so inclined, cannot help go more smoothly. Therefore, it is particularly important to put the more supportive, helpful supervisors in charge of new recruits. They can provide the best coaching about how to make an effective transition into the world of work from the world of school.

Which work group a new recruit is placed in can also affect the ease of socialization. If new employees are placed in work groups in which there is high morale, they will develop much more positive attitudes about the organization as a whole, and are much more likely to make friends with the people in their work group. However, putting new recruits into groups with low morale can really hinder effective socialization. When recruits are placed in groups with low morale, they are much more likely to develop negative, cynical attitudes about the organization.

Do Not Demand Overconformity to the Organization's Norms

Forcing new recruits into an iron mold is not an effective socialization strategy. Two of the greatest assets new recruits bring with them to their jobs are a fresh perspective on the way the organization does business and a strong desire to improve the way the organization functions. By forcing new recruits to strictly conform, organizations dampen this enthusiasm.[17] After all, sometimes new ideas and good suggestions come from those employees who are marching to a slightly different drummer. By being somewhat flexible, organizations can be as—perhaps more—effective in socializing new recruits.

Transfers and Promotions

So far we have discussed the first jobs that college graduates and MBAs face. However, very few young managers stay in the same organization—never mind the same job assignment—for very long. The late 20s and 30s are a time when most young managers make several job changes and some organizational changes as they try to become established in their careers.

Two types of job changes are particularly common in this career stage. The first type of job change a young manager might receive is a ***promotion.*** Here, an employee would move up the organization's hierarchy and take on increasing responsibilities. The second type of job change a young manager might receive is a ***lateral transfer.*** In a transfer, an employee does not move up the hierarchy, but takes over another assignment at the same level of the organization. In the next few pages we will look at transfers and promotions in more detail and examine how organizations can manage the job change process more effectively.

Benefits of Transfers and Promotions

Job transfers and promotions can be beneficial to both organizations and employees.[18]

The Organization's Perspective

From the organization's point of view, moving employees from job to job can broaden employees' skills. Managers who change jobs can learn about a variety of different problems in a variety of different departments. Consequently, when these mobile managers mature and are ready for top management positions, they will have a broader business perspective with which to make decisions.

Transfers and promotions also help solve staffing and manpower planning problems. If an organization expands its business operations or merges with another organization, transfers and promotions provide needed staff for new positions or provide a gentle alternative to layoffs. Transfers and promotions help fill vacancies left by resignations and retirements, too.[19]

The Individual's Perspective

Individuals also have much to gain from transfers and promotions. As we saw in Table 19-1, the 20s and 30s are a time when most managers want to develop a broader view of the occupation and the organization in which they work. Transfers and promotions facilitate this career growth. They can open up opportunities for young managers to branch out from their first jobs and to develop whole new sets of skills and competencies.

Second, as managers reach their early 30s, they get tired of being viewed as subordinates; they want to start exerting authority as well as receiving orders. Transfers and promotions typically open up jobs with increased authority and supervisory responsibilities. These management jobs will be the first for many.

Third, transfers and promotions at this age can mean substantial pay raises and a new standard of living. As these managers marry and have children, the possibility of making more money is particularly alluring.[20]

Special Problems of Transferred and Promoted Employees

At first glance, it might seem that there would be very few adjustment problems for transferred and promoted employees. After all, they have already demonstrated their competence in the organization, and they can anticipate even greater challenges and responsibilities ahead. However, a recent study comparing the adjustment of job changers to new hires suggests that getting "resocialized" into new positions is not as easy as it might appear. Let's look at the special problems of transferred and promoted employees more closely below.[21]

1   *Increased demands for high performance.*   Newly hired employees are often given some time to get their performance up to par. Very few people expect new hires to be highly competent from day one. However, transferred and promoted employees are expected to take charge immediately and to perform at the same high level they were performing at before the job change. This can be very stressful for job changers, especially for those working in new functional areas or with completely different product lines.

2   *Less training for new jobs.*   Most new hires are given some formal training for their new jobs; they are also often encouraged to seek out help when they need it. In contrast, most organizations view job changers as needing less training for their new positions. Having been promoted or transferred because of their performance to date, these managers are expected to pick things up easily as they go along. However, many times the new jobs are very different from the old jobs; it is particularly difficult to perform effectively under these circumstances.

3   *Incomplete mastery of previous jobs.*   Many times employees are promoted or transferred so quickly that they are moving on to jobs with increased responsibility before they have mastered their old jobs. In a study examining the career paths of production/operations managers, one participant had been promoted from plant manager to director of national operations to vice president of international operations within eighteen months. These changes meant the manager went from being responsible for producing nine products in one region to producing twenty-nine products worldwide. At first, such quick promotions leave managers feeling exhilarated. Later, though, these managers feel frightened and out of control as they realize they are responsible for products or services about which they know virtually nothing.[22]

4 *Need to unlearn old behaviors and attitudes.*   As people move from job to job within a company, they have to be sensitive to the local organizational culture and unlearn some of the behaviors and attitudes of the old job. For instance, in the study of transferred and promoted employees cited above, managers talked about how hard it was to adjust from working in a field operation to working at corporate headquarters. In field operations, people were not as sensitive to status differences. Managers and employees at all levels of the organization socialized extensively with each other outside of work. At corporate headquarters, in contrast, it was only acceptable to initiate social contacts with people at one's own level in the organization; socializing with subordinates was seen as very inappropriate. To people used to drinking or playing football with their subordinates, this shift to headquarters meant a lot of painful unlearning.[23]

5 *Less social support for changers.*   Because most new hires are coming right out of school, their coworkers expect them to feel somewhat disoriented. Coworkers anticipate that these new employees will have some self-doubts, and some may readily offer social support to them. While job changers, too, may feel uncertain or alone in their new positions, their coworkers are less likely to be attuned to the anxiety or tension they are feeling.

6 *Special problems of geographical moves.*   Many transfers and promotions involve a major geographical relocation. There are houses to sell, community ties to sever, new jobs to find for working spouses, and new schools to find for children. Most employees still believe that refusal to move may hurt their careers, and some undertake their moves with reluctance.[24]

However, the true picture of what happens to transferred families is not as gloomy as it is sometimes portrayed in the media. For instance, recent research suggests that frequent moves can strengthen a marriage. Most spouses of transferred employees have positive attitudes about the prospect of moving again, and only 12 percent report they would be unwilling to relocate another time. Also, moving is not as hard on young children who go through it as was once thought. They develop a greater tolerance for new or uncertain situations and become more independent and adaptable than their less mobile peers. The one piece of bad news: moving is very difficult on teenage children, and they may experience more adjustment problems than their younger siblings.[25]

Managing the Transfer and Promotion Process

The costs of transferring and promoting employees can be quite high. Employees who change jobs are often out of work two weeks during the move and may have several more weeks before and after the move in which they are not working at peak efficiency. Just the direct dollar costs of moving an employee are quite high. It is not unusual for the transportation of employee families and their belongings, as well as subsidies for the sale and purchase of homes, to exceed $25,000.[26] For this reason, it is particularly important for organizations to manage the transfer and promotion process judiciously. Below we look at three strategies organizations can use to manage the transfer and promotion process more effectively.[27]

1   *Better manpower planning.*   Many transfers and promotions are needed solely for staffing purposes; some employees retire or resign, and a whole shifting of other employees occurs as a result. If organizations made more accurate estimates of manpower needs and did more systematic human resource planning, many of these job changes could be eliminated.

For instance, some organizations require managers to indicate yearly, for each position they supervise, three backup employees who could conceivably move into each slot if needed. Managers also have to indicate what type of training or experience these backup employees would need to be able to take over a job. This procedure forces executives to do more systematic human resources planning and can eliminate the need for some of the transfers that take place merely to fill vacancies.

2   *Better timing and spacing of job changes.*   As we discussed earlier, it takes awhile to master a new job and to get up to speed on the new assignment. When employees are asked to change jobs before they have mastered the old ones, they start off their next assignments with only shaky technical background, not to mention shaky self-confidence. In general, it is a good strategy not to move employees until they have been on an assignment at least one year.

The second aspect of the timing issue involves giving employees advance warning of job changes. One study of transferred and promoted employees suggests that more than half of these managers received less than two weeks' notice of the job change.[28] It is difficult enough to make a job transition, but the task is made so much more burdensome without at least a month to get prepared for the new assignment—especially when the job change involves a geographical move.

3   *Better training and orientation of job changers.*   While job changers may not need the type of training and orientation new employees need, it is not true that they can do without any. The same training that is given to a new employee on a position can be modified and given to a transferred or promoted employee in a shortened form. The same courtesies given to new employees—introductions, social invitations, tours of the company or the city—should be extended to job changers as well. Such an approach to the training and orientation of job changers will help them get back into the swing of things much more quickly and much more easily.

Middle- and Later-Career Issues

The problems of middle- and later-career employees—plateaued performance, obsolescence, and forced retirement—seem very distant and vague to new, young college graduates. However, to the older managers who have these anxieties, the problems are very immediate and concrete. In this section, we'll be examining both the professional and the personal challenges of managers in the later stages of their careers.

Professional Concerns of Mid- and Late-Career Managers

There are five major professional problems which surface and become salient after age 40. These problems are outlined in Table 19-4 and are discussed in more detail below.

Slower Promotions

The speed at which employees get promoted slows down after the first few job changes. Early in their careers, employees pass fairly easily from one echelon to the next (e.g., from junior financial analyst to senior analyst to manager). However, as employees get older and reach middle management, the frequency of promotions decreases sharply. It may take five to ten years to make director or vice president from manager—and many employees don't even make it this far.[29]

Different Criteria for Transfers and Promotions

As employees become older and advance in the organization, they realize that the criteria for which they were selected into the organization are no longer the criteria on which future promotions will be based. While initial selection decisions may be based on specific technical competence, promotions to upper management are more likely to be based on political acumen, social compatibility with superiors, or just being in the right place at the right time when an unexpected opening occurs.[30]

TABLE 19-4

Middle- and Late-Career Issues

Professional Concerns

1 Slower promotions
2 Different criteria for transfers and promotions
3 Different types of work demands
4 Threatening work environments
5 Frustration by changes in organizations and careers

Personal Concerns

1 Awareness of advancing age and death
2 Awareness of physical aging
3 Awareness of personal limitations
4 Marked changes in family relationships
5 Increases in hostile, defensive feelings

**Different Types
of Work
Demands**

When employees are young, they work on mainly technical, small-scope projects. However, as employees mature and gain experience, they take on greater responsibilities. They are expected to be able to work independently, to be able to manage and train others, and to exert some authority and power.

If older employees are unwilling to grow and to accept new responsibilities—no matter how competent they are at lower-level jobs—they will become less and less valued by the organization. Organizations would rather hire new employees with potential for career growth than tie up positions with employees who have no potential at all.[31]

**Threatening Work
Environments**

While the work environments which new employees face are uncertain, most recruits are optimistic about the chances for success. For middle- and late-career stage employees, there are several reasons for pessimism.[32]

These employees feel a growing sense of obsolescence. Young subordinates have more recent technical knowledge and need to be relied on heavily for technical advice. Moreover, older managers face a harder time obtaining jobs outside the organization. Organizations are more likely to promote top managers from within their own corporation than to recruit externally. Thus, older employees are caught between bright, young subordinates who are competing with them for promotions, and a tight external job market for managers who don't make it in their own organizations.

**Frustration
by Changes
in Organizations
and Careers**

Organizations change, just as people do. The atmosphere of an organization, which may have been so attractive at the time young college graduates signed on, can change dramatically over the course of twenty years. Small, informal organizations can grow into large, formal organizations; people-oriented top management can change in favor of technically oriented bureaucrats. Mid-career managers may be frustrated by seeing the corporate world around them changing in ways they find undesirable.[33]

Some mid-career managers are frustrated by the demands or limitations of the careers they have chosen. For some, the combination of inadequate career development guidance, insufficient training, and plain bad luck have left them at levels of responsibility well below their potential. Others have seen the demands for their services deteriorate, forcing them to consider new careers late in life.

**Personal
Concerns of
Mid- and Late-
Career
Managers**

At different stages in their lives, people have different needs and goals and feel vulnerable in different ways. The middle and later years of a career present a particularly stressful set of personal circumstances for workers. Let's consider next the systematic personal problems of older employees that produce such stress and frustration.[34] A brief summary of these problems also appears in Table 19-4.

Awareness of Advancing Age and Death	After age 40, many people report the sudden feeling that life is half over, that they now have as much or more time behind them as ahead of them. After age 65, people become much more acutely aware of death. Most people at this age have buried their parents, and many have buried their spouses and/or close friends.
Awareness of Physical Aging	After age 40, many people become more aware of signs of their physical aging. Despite exercise, there is a decrease in muscle tone. Weight redistributes itself in sometimes unflattering ways, and skin becomes more wrinkled and less firm. Particularly after age 65, heart attacks and strokes are more likely to occur. Hearing and vision often become impaired.
Awareness of Personal Limitations	By the time people reach their 40s they have a fairly good idea of how far they can advance in their jobs. If people know they will be unable to attain some of their important goals, they are forced to confront their unrealistic expectations and personal failings. They are no longer rising stars but merely middle managers who aren't going to make it all the way. For people over 65, there is a feeling of being yesterday's news.
Marked Changes in Family Relationships	The decisions about marriage and children which seemed so right in the 20s often seem wrong-headed in the 40s. People's values and interests change as they mature, and many people find their spouses do not fulfill their emotional needs anymore. The cute toddlers have turned into teenagers ready to rebel against parental authority; no longer can parents control the actions of their children. For people over 65, the loss of a spouse is the major source of pain. The person with whom one has shared most of one's life is now gone, and with that comes increased loneliness. Children have established their own lives, often far away, and visits with children and grandchildren may occur only once or twice a year.
Increases in Hostile, Defensive Feelings	Middle-age managers often have significant anger toward younger employees, who have greater professional opportunities and make more money than the older managers did when they were young. There is anger, too, that younger employees have more flexibility in their lives and do not operate under the accumulated constraints of work and home responsibilities. Just as their children are rebelling against their authority, their subordinates are competing with them and questioning their judgment.

The Mid-Life Crisis

This overlap of personal and professional problems at age 40 can lead to a cycle of anxiety and depression, often labeled a ***mid-life crisis.*** There is a gnawing feeling that life isn't turning out the way it was dreamed and that this is the last chance to take some corrective action. Four traps lay in store for those who experience this mid-life crisis:[35]

The "Frying Pan into the Fire" Syndrome	If an individual's mid-life crisis is precipitated by some specific negative event (such as a divorce or being laid off), the individual is likely to be confused, restless, and prone to make precipitous decisions that will relieve this anxiety. He or she is likely to remarry or jump into another job situation too quickly.
The "My Whole World Flew Apart at Once" Syndrome	Some people, when they reach middle age, feel compelled to throw their whole lives up for grabs. They feel the urge to change spouses, homes, jobs, and personal appearance all at the same time.
The "Expression of Individuality" Syndrome	Impatience and frustration with the politics and bureaucracy of organizations may impel individuals to seek a total professional independence that they are not ready to handle. Mid-life managers sometimes decide to pick up and move to the country, or start their own business, or try to become an independent consultant. However, many miss the social contacts with those left behind; others miscalculate how much money they will earn in their new businesses or how precarious their financial futures have become.
The "Overchoice" Syndrome	Some people undergoing a mid-life crisis become overwhelmed by the variety of choices and options available to them. Having been constrained by one career path and one family for years, these individuals flit from one relationship to another and from one job to another, without making any new commitments.

Of course, not all individuals will undergo a mid-life crisis, and not all 40-year olds will fall into one of the four traps we've just enumerated. However, for most middle managers age 40 is a time of reassessment and rethinking of career and personal life decisions.

Career Development

One of the lessons organizations have learned about career management is that they cannot help employees with career problems in their 40s and 50s unless they have a systematic career management program for employees of all ages. Organizations cannot ignore the career development issues facing their employees in the first twenty years of their careers and then expect to solve their mid-career problems with some quick solution. The same lesson has been learned by managers themselves. Career development is an activity they have to work on throughout their careers; they cannot let it slide for twenty years and then try to find some quick solutions in their 40s. In this next and final section, we'll examine what organizations can better do to manage their employees' careers, and what managers can better do to develop their own potential.

■

Career Management: The Organization's Perspective

Particularly over the past twenty years, organizations like Sears, General Electric, Exxon, and IBM have implemented a wide variety of programs to help employees further develop their potential and avoid obsolescence. Let's look more closely at some of the more frequently used and successful of these programs.[36]

Career Counseling

Three types of career counseling are done to help employees in planning and implementing their career goals. First, supervisors are trained to discuss career issues with their employees in performance review sessions. Second, personnel staff are prepared to conduct one-on-one counseling sessions with interested employees. Third, some organizations run workshops on career development. Participants receive workbooks and engage in exercises to help them identify career goals and plan future job moves.

Charting Career Paths

Instead of letting job changes be random, organizations are beginning to plan job sequences for employees. Managers can be moved in a logical way; people can utilize their present skills and can develop new ones as well. Some organizations are using management development committees to review middle managers' strengths and weaknesses and to develop five-year career paths for each middle manager. High-potential employees are slated for a series of moves through various departments to prepare them for upper-management positions.

Career Information Systems

Many organizations are disseminating more complete and accurate information about career opportunities in their firms. All jobs are posted, and individuals can nominate themselves for these openings. Information about typical career paths into popular jobs in the organization is also provided.

Human Resource Planning

Some organizations have developed computerized skills inventories of their employees. When job openings occur, management has access to a list of all employees who have the appropriate skills for the positions. Also, many organizations are requiring managers to document what training each of their subordinates would need to be promoted and their plans for providing that training.

Periodic Skill Assessment

Several organizations are beginning to use assessment centers to help in career development of middle- and later-career managers. Managers are assessed for their readiness for promotion. Those lacking specific skills can be given remedial training; those who are unlikely to be able to advance are given realistic feedback about their future in the organization.

Training

There are certain career moves that especially require additional training; without this training, employees are much less likely to be able to succeed on their new jobs. The move from hourly employment to management and the move from technical specialist to general management, for instance, both require more intensive training. More organizations are beginning to run their own training programs to facilitate these career moves. Others have started to reimburse employees to obtain relevant training from university-based degree programs.

Special Help for Disadvantaged Groups

Organizations are aware today that some groups have historically been denied career opportunities and may need an extra boost to obtain and succeed in higher-level jobs. Many organizations have special career management seminars for minorities, women, and those entering the work force for the first time in middle age. Some organizations are allowing two-career couples more flexibility in planning job moves, as well as providing assistance to the spouse in finding a job. Other organizations have experimented with flexible working hours, providing assistance for day care and even allowing two spouses in the same field to share one job. For older employees, organizations have experimented with sabbaticals (to retool or change career interests), early retirement bonuses, and extensive preretirement counseling.

Several organizations that are particularly serious about career development have combined the different practices discussed above into systematic, comprehensive career development programs. Descriptions of some of the more innovative of these programs at AT&T, 3M, Lawrence Livermore Laboratory, and Syntex appear in Box 19-2.[37]

Key Ingredients of Successful Programs

Three key ingredients contribute to the success of these organizations in designing and implementing career management programs.[38]

First, career management activities are most successful when they are coordinated with other activities in human resource management, such as selection, training, manpower planning, and performance appraisal. Career management succeeds best when it is not relegated to the periphery, but becomes integrated with other key personnel functions.

Second, career management is most likely to succeed when immediate line supervisors are actively involved. While personnel departments may provide the structure to career development programs, their actual content should be largely the responsibility of line management. The line supervisors are frequently in the best position to assess employee competence, provide relevant training, and engage in career counseling.

Third, career management is most likely to succeed when there is equal access to its benefits. While companies may focus extra attention later on high-potential employees, in the successful programs we have discussed each employee has the opportunity to volunteer to be assessed, to receive training, and to obtain counseling.

Next let's look at career development from the individual's perspective.

BOX 19-2

Career Development Programs in Action

AT&T   Three career development programs are in use in the telephone system. The first program is a one-day assessment program for noncollege, nonmanagement people. This "early identification program" consists of an eight-hour skills assessment, followed by extensive feedback and career counseling by a trained professional. The second program, geared for high-potential female college graduates, combines assessment centers with career planning. Career plans, training needs, and interim assignments are reviewed every six months. The third program focuses on training supervisors in job restructuring, joint goal setting, and appraisal skills.

3M   Minnesota Mining and Manufacturing (3M) currently has a two-day management assessment program that helps employees identify career goals, training needs, and placement opportunities. Each program consists of about fifteen participants, chosen from young, nonmanagement employees who have volunteered or been nominated by management. 3M also has a career information center, a staff of career counselors, and a regular series of career development workshops.

Lawrence Livermore Laboratory   Lawrence Livermore Laboratory provides a regular series of career development workshops open to all employees. These workshops involve the assessment of individual interests and abilities. After the workshop, a personalized career strategy is developed for each employee. In addition, individual career counseling, career-interest testing, and access to a career information center are provided to interested employees. A key feature of the laboratory's program is the utilization of technical and scientific professionals—who also hold graduate degrees in counseling psychology—as career counsellors.

Syntex   Syntex runs assessment centers to provide management candidates with feedback on their present job skills and future promotability. The company also gives seminars to employees about different job and career opportunities. These seminars provide information about different functional areas and descriptions of the experiences, education, and skills necessary for each area. In addition, Syntex has developed its own career-planning workbook for use by all employees, and provides both individual counseling and group workshops to assist employees in career planning.

Source: Miller, D. (1978). Career planning and management in organizations. In M. Jelinek (Ed.), *Career management for the individual and the organization.* Chicago: St. Clair Press, pp. 353–360. Permission granted by John Wiley and Sons.

Career Development: The Individual's Perspective

We noted that with the onset of layoffs during the recession of 1973, managers began to develop a "me-first" careerism. They started to realize that organizations would not take care of them in a paternalistic way and that they had to fend for themselves. In the wake of this change, a variety of books and articles were written offering career advice to those aspiring to get ahead in the world. Among the most frequently proffered suggestions are the following.[39]

Obtain a Challenging Job

When job choices are being made, career growth should weigh more heavily than shorter-term considerations such as small pay differences. Learning the job as quickly as possible, being a strong performer, and training a replacement makes it easier to move on to more broadening work assignments.

Actively Manage your Own Career

Individuals should be prepared to practice self-nomination, to make it known to superiors that they want a particular job and are prepared to work to qualify for it.

Seek out a Sponsor

Employees should try to become protégés of mobile senior executives who could help speed their rise in the organization.

Seek to Broaden the Scope of the Job

Employees should avoid being trapped by formal, narrow job descriptions and should seek out additional responsibilities of interest and jobs with higher responsibility.

Develop Additional Skills

Individuals should nominate themselves for training programs or job assignments where they could broaden their business knowledge or learn new skills.

*   *   *

No doubt all of these suggestions can help individuals at different points in their careers make better career management decisions. However, success in the business world can never be achieved simply by following this set of strategies.

A much more useful and enduring way to develop career plans would be to periodically engage in the following four-step process.[40]

Step 1   **Situational analysis and self-management.**

Ask yourself:

Which facets of my current situation are satisfying or at least tolerable? Which facets impel me to change my career, my life style, or both?

What are my real or potential skills and abilities? What actively have I done or might I do that really interests me?

What are my essential emotional and financial needs?

Step 2   **Examination of alternatives.**

Ask yourself:

What reasonable alternatives do I see in the near- and long-term future?

In regard to my own skills, interests, and financial situation, which alternatives can I cancel out?

What are my priorities? How would I rank the remaining alternatives?

Step 3   **Goal setting.**

Ask yourself:

What goals do I want to achieve during the rest of my life and career?

Of these goals, which do I need to start work on now?

How long can I postpone work on the other goals? What degrees of flexibility have I left myself?

Step 4   **Career planning.**

Ask yourself:

In order to reach the immediate goals I have set for myself, what do I need to do now?

In looking ahead, what additional activities will be necessary to enable me to reach my long-term goals?

What kind of help can I get to assist me in realizing this career plan? Who can provide the help I need?

*   *   *

In short, career development cannot succeed if it is reduced to a series of short-run strategies to get over immediate hurdles. It can only succeed if it begins with an examination of oneself rather than the manipulation of others.

Keys to Effective Management

As the programs at AT&T, 3M, Lawrence Livermore Laboratory, and Syntex suggest, it is possible for both individuals and organizations to better manage careers in organizations today. Let's look now at some of the more important keys to effective career management.

1   *Both individuals and organizations need to plan for more mobility in careers today.*   More and more individuals are hoping for "multicareers," career paths that include two or three different fields and two or three different organizations. Moreover, organizations are transferring, promoting, and moving employees geographically much more frequently than in the past. Individuals can no longer count on paternalistic treatment from organizations, and organizations can no longer count on enduring loyalty from employees. Therefore, both individuals and organizations need to do more goal setting and examination of alternative courses of action to meet their own career management objectives.

2 *The transition from school to work is a critical time in individuals' careers, and needs to be managed more carefully by both individuals and organizations.* Most students experience quite an entry shock when they start to work; they are surprised by the routine nature of the work, the lack of feedback, and the slowness of decision making. Organizations are frustrated, too, by the overambition, the unrealistic expectations, and the political immaturity of their new hires. In order to better socialize new recruits into organizations, firms should try to provide challenging first job assignments, relevant training, timely and reliable feedback, and relaxed orientation programs. Individuals should strive for excellent performance from the start, initiate conversations with their supervisors to obtain feedback, seek to broaden their own skills and abilities, and search out opportunities to increase the scope of their jobs.

3 *Transfers and promotions can be beneficial to both organizations and employees, but much of their positive impact is lost if these job changes are improperly timed.* Transfers and promotions can broaden the business perspective of employees as well as help solve staffing problems. However, if organizations move employees too frequently and without enough advance warning, problems develop that counteract the positive results of transfers and promotions. Employees may not have mastered their current jobs and may not be ready to meet new challenges; they may not have the time to get prepared or trained for the next assignment; they may become overloaded with the stresses of uprooting themselves and their families at frequent intervals. Organizations should give employees several weeks' notice of a job change and not move employees more than once a year.

4 *Organizations can implement a variety of programs to help managers deal with the particular stresses and frustrations of middle age.* Over the past twenty years, organizations have implemented a wide variety of programs to help employees further develop their potential and avoid obsolescence in middle age. Elements of these programs include: career counseling; career pathing; career information systems; skills inventories of employees; periodic skill assessment; additional training; and special help for disadvantaged groups. However, for these programs to be successful, career management has to be coordinated with other human resource activities such as personnel selection, human resource planning, and performance appraisal. Moreover, immediate line supervisors as well as personnel staff

should be actively involved in the assessment, training, and counseling of middle-age employees.

5   *Finally, individuals should rely less heavily on the "get ahead quick" advice of popular writers about careers and rely more heavily on long-run, systematic career planning.* Career self-development cannot succeed if it is reduced to a series of short-run strategies to get over short-run hurdles. It can only succeed if it involves continual self-appraisal, goal setting, examination of alternatives, and concrete career planning.

Review Questions

1   How have people's ideas about careers and career success changed over the past twenty-five years?

2   Why is the first job such a shock to new college graduates?

3   What do we mean by the term *organizational socialization?* What are the three stages of organizational socialization?

4   Identify six strategies organizations can use to better manage the organizational socialization process.

5   Why is a relaxed orientation program preferable to a slick, formal orientation program?

6   What are the benefits to organizations of job transfers and promotions? What are the benefits to individuals?

7   Name five special problems of transferred and promoted employees.

8   Discuss the following statement: "Geographical moves have consistent negative effects on employees' families."

9   What is the optimal spacing of job changes? How much advance notice should job changers receive of their new assignments?

10   Discuss the five major professional problems that surface and become salient after age 40.

11   Discuss the five major personal problems that surface and become salient after age 40.

12   What is meant by the term *mid-life crisis?*

13   What four traps lay in store for those who experience this mid-life crisis?

14   Identify six strategies organizations can use to help employees develop their potential and avoid obsolescence.

15   What is the four-stage process individuals should use to develop their own careers?

Gordon Company

Scene 1

The top financial managers of the Gordon Company are attending the monthly staff meeting. The latter part of the discussion is about recruiting problems. Harry Brown, chief financial officer of Gordon, listens as the financial managers tell about the problems they are having with the personnel department in attempting to fill position vacancies. Many ideas are brought up, but two apparent facts emerge that upset Brown:

1 In the financial organization, 15 percent of the exempt (professional and managerial) positions are vacant. Some of them have been vacant for more than three months.

2 The turnover of exempt employees in his organization has reached 25 percent.

This is the first time in the monthly meetings that this situation has surfaced, and Brown does not know why it has not come up before or the reason for the high turnover rate.

Scene 2

Tom Jones is a manager who reports directly to Brown. As he returns to his office after the meeting, he realizes that now is the time for him to propose some plans that he has been developing with Bill White, one of his subordinates. Both Jones and White have been well aware of the low morale among the management employees in their division and have been working on possible solutions. In their judgment, most exempt employees feel that there is little opportunity for professional or career development in the company and that the top managers are not interested.

Together with several other younger managers who have been concerned about the situation, they have developed a plan that would establish a management development program. The primary purpose of the program would be to attract and to keep highly motivated employees in the company. Some of the features of the proposed program are: (1) regular, periodic discussions between managers and subordinates about performance and career plans; (2) an organized method of filling vacancies from within, through promotion or rotation of qualified employees; and (3) planned rotations of stalemated employees.

Jones and White have discussed how quickly they should move on their plan and how far the plan should go. Bill White believes that, given the company's conservative psychological environment, a slow evolutionary approach consisting of several phases would be the most acceptable to the more conservative managers who hold the key second-level positions in the organization. Tom Jones, on the other hand, favors the introduction of a complete and far-reaching program that would really take care of the problem, even if a few of the more conservative managers might be put on the defensive.

Scene 3

White receives a phone call from Dick Gray, the manager of management and organization development in the industrial relations department. Gray, who has been working on this problem in other areas of the company, requests a meeting with Jones and White to review the status of each other's plans. At the meeting, the three find that their plans are very similar and that they have all included the same considerations about the conservative management environment of the company. However, Gray has faced opposition to similar programs in the past in other parts of the organization and therefore advises a cautious approach. Jones, on the other hand, reiterates his feeling that a complete program is necessary to satisfy the desires of the employees.

Scene 4

Everyone agrees that the success of the plan depends on Bob Johnson, the number two man in the organization and the one considered to be the leader of the conservative faction. Jones considers himself the spokesman for the group of newer managers in the company, who have taken a very progressive approach toward the company's problems. He is apprehensive about Johnson's reaction to these progressive tactics and decides that a face-to-face confrontation would be the best approach.

During the meeting, Tom Jones and Dick Gray review the situation about the vacancies, turnover, and low morale. Bob Johnson tends to discount the seriousness of the problems, feeling that the turnover has been, for the most part, among people who were not good contributors

anyway and that their loss does not harm the company. Regarding the Jones-White plan, which includes annual career counseling sessions, an organized method of promotions from within, and a method of rotating assignments to rejuvenate stagnating managers, Johnson expresses a very negative reaction. He feels that the organization isn't ready for such a program and that the objectives of the plan have, in fact, already been accomplished in an informal manner.

Jones is now convinced that the plan can be instituted only if Harry Brown convinces Johnson of the need. He calls Brown and tells him over the phone about the plan that has been developed and requests a meeting to gain management support.

Scene 5

Brown calls Johnson and asks him what the plan is all about. Johnson gives a very sketchy outline, minimizing the need for the plan and its value to the company. On the day of the meeting, Brown knows that he is faced with the struggle between an older, more conservative faction that has grown up with the company and a newer, more progressive group of younger people who are needed to ensure the company's continued growth.

During the meeting, Dick Gray gives a great deal of support to the plan, indicating that if the Jones-White plan is not adopted in the financial organization, a similar plan could well be implemented companywide within a year. Johnson reiterates his feelings about the people who have left and his concern about the high level of expectations that the plan would create and, in his opinion, would not fulfill. Brown adjourns the meeting, saying that he will get in touch with all parties in a few days about the decision.

Questions for Discussion

1   What are the career development problems the Gordon Company faces?

2 What are the key elements of the career development program developed by Jones and White?

3 What are Johnson's objections to the Jones-White plan? Do you believe they are valid, or not? Why?

4 If you were Harry Brown, what would you do? Briefly justify your decision.

Source: Case originally written by R. T. Nealon, Jr., under the supervision of E. F. Huse. Reprinted from: Huse, E. F., & Cummings, T. C. (1985). *Organization development and change* (3rd ed.). St. Paul: West Publishing, 527–529. Reprinted by permission. All rights reserved.

Notes

1   Whyte, W. H., Jr. (1957). *The organization man.* Garden City, New York: Doubleday Anchor Books, 437.

2   Hall, D. T. (1976). *Careers in organizations.* Pacific Palisades, CA: Goodyear, 1–4.

3   Hall, *op. cit.,* 4–9.

4   Beach, D. S. (1980). *Personnel* (4th ed.). New York: Macmillan, 320.

5   Kotter, J. P. (1975). The first year out. Unpublished note, Harvard Business School.

6   Feldman, D. C. (1976a). A contingency theory of socialization. *Administrative Science Quarterly, 21,* 433–452.

7   Feldman, D. C. (1981). The multiple socialization of organization members. *Academy of Management Review, 6,* 309–318.

8   Feldman, D. C. (1976b, Autumn). A practical program for employee socialization. *Organizational Dynamics,* 64–80.

9   Feldman, *ibid.*

10   Feldman, *ibid.*

11   Van Maanen, J. (1976). Breaking in: Socialization to work. In R. Dubin (ed.), *Handbook of work, organization, and society.* Chicago: Rand McNally.

12   Schein, E. H. (1964). How to break in the college graduate. *Harvard Business Review, 42,* 68–76.

13   Cohen, P. (1973). *The gospel according to Harvard Business School.* New York: Doubleday, 1–21.

14   Much of the discussion that follows is based upon Feldman, D. C., (1980). A socialization process that helps new recruits succeed. *Personnel, 57,* 11–23.

15   Feldman (1976b), *loc. cit.*

16   Gomersall, E. R., and Myers, M. S. (1966). Breakthrough in on-the-job training. *Harvard Business Review, 44,* 62–72.

17   Schein, E. H. (1968). Organizational socialization and the profession of management. *Industrial Management Review, 9,* 1–16.

18   Feldman, D. C., & Brett, J. M. (1985). Trading places: Managing employee job changes. *Personnel, 62,* 61–65.

19   Pinder, C. C., and Das, H. (1979). Hidden costs and benefits of employee transfers. *Human Resource Planning, 2,* 135–145.

20   Feldman & Brett (1985), *loc. cit.*

21   The discussion in the following section is based upon Feldman, D. C., & Brett, J. M. (1983). Coping with new jobs: A comparative study of new hires and job changers. *Academy of Management Journal, 26,* 258–272.

22   Feldman & Brett (1985), *loc. cit.*

23   Feldman & Brett (1985), *loc. cit.*

24   Singular, S. (1983, June). Moving on. *Psychology Today, 40–47.*

25   Brett, J. B. (1981). The effect of job transfer on employees and their families. In C. L. Cooper and R. Payne (Eds.), *Current concerns in occupational stress.* Chichester, England: John Wiley and Sons.

26   Pinder & Das, *loc. cit.*

27   The discussion in the following section is based upon Feldman & Brett (1985), *loc. cit..*

28   Feldman & Brett (1983), *loc. cit.*

29   Levinson, H. (1969). On being a middle-aged manager. *Harvard Business Review, 47,* 51–60.

30   Feldman & Brett (1983), *loc. cit.*

31   Rosenbaum, J. E. (1979). Tournament mobility: Career patterns in a corporation. *Administrative Science Quarterly, 24,* 220–241.

32   Orth, C. D., III. (1974). How to survive the mid-career crisis. *Business Horizons, 17,* 12–18.

33   Dalton, G. W., Thompson, P. H., & Price, R. L. (1977). The four stages of professional careers: A new look at performance by professionals. *Organizational Dynamics, 6,* 19–42.

34   Much of this discussion is based upon Levinson, Harry. (1969). On being a middle-aged manager. *Harvard Business Review, 47,* 51–60; and Hall, D. T. (1976). *Careers in organizations.* Pacific Palisades, CA: Goodyear, 80–84.

35   Orth, *loc. cit.*

36   Morgan, M. A., Hall, D. T., and Martier, A. (1979). Career development activities in industry. *Personnel, 66,* 16.

37   Miller, D. B. (1978). Career planning and management in organizations. In M. Jelinek (Ed.), *Career management for the individual and the organization.* Chicago: St. Clair, 353–360.

38   Hall, *loc. cit.*

39   Much of the discussion which follows is based upon Webber, R. A. (1976). Career problems of young managers. *California Management Review, 18,* 11–33, and Hall, D. T. (1976). *Careers in organizations.* Pacific Palisades, CA: Goodyear, 185–187.

40   Orth, *loc. cit.*

Bibliography

Adams, J. S. (1965). Injustice in social exchange. In L. Berkowitz (Ed.), *Advances in experimental social psychology* (Vol. 2). New York: Academic Press.

Adorno, T., et al. (1950). *The authoritarian personality.* New York: Harper & Brothers.

Albrecht, K. (1979). *Stress and the manager.* Englewood Cliffs, NJ: Prentice-Hall.

Alderfer, C. P. (1972). *Existence, relatedness, and growth: Human needs in organizational settings.* New York: Free Press.

Alderfer, C. P. (1976). Boundary relations and organizational diagnosis. In L. Meltzer & F. Wickert (Eds.), *Humanizing organizational behavior.* Springfield, IL: Charles C. Thomas.

Alderfer, C. P. (1977). Group and intergroup relations. In J. R. Hackman & J. L. Suttle, *Improving life at work.* Santa Monica, CA: Goodyear, 227–296.

Aldrich, H. & Herker, D. (1977). Boundary spanning roles and organization structure. *Academy of Management Review, 2,* 217–239.

Allen, T. J., & Marquis, D. G. (1964). Positive and negative biasing sets: The effects of prior experience on research performance. *IEEE Transactions on Engineering Management,* EM-11, 158–161.

Alvarez, R. (1968). Informal reactions to deviance in simulated work organizations: A laboratory experiment. *American Sociological Review, 33,* 895–912.

Anderson, C. R. (1977). Locus of control, coping behaviors, and performance in a stress setting: A longitudinal study. *Journal of Applied Psychology, 62,* 446–451.

Andrew, J. (1983, May 6). Terminal tedium. *Wall Street Journal,* 1, 15.

Annas, J. W. (1982) The up-front carrot. *Compensation Review,* 45–49.

Argyris, C. (1960) *Understanding organizational behavior.* London: Tavistock.

Arnold, H. J. (1981). A test of the multiplicative hypothesis of expectancy-valence theories of work motivation. *Academy of Management Journal, 24,* 128–141.

Arnold, H. J., & Feldman, D. C. (1982). A multivariate analysis of the determinants of job turnover. *Journal of Applied Psychology, 67,* 350–360.

Aronson, E. (1976). *The social animal* (2nd ed.). San Francisco: W. H. Freeman.

Arvey, R. D. (1979). Unfair discrimination in the employment interview: Legal and psychological aspects. *Psychological Bulletin, 86,* 736–765.

Ashford, S. J., & Cummings, L. L. (1983). Feedback as an individual resource: Personal strategies of creating information. *Organizational Behavior and Human Performance, 32,* 370–398.

Ashour, A. S. (1982). A framework of a cognitive-behavioral theory of leader influence and effectiveness. *Organizational Behavior and Human Performance, 30,* 407–430.

Athanassiades, J. (1973). The distortion of upward communication in hierarchical organizations. *Academy of Management Journal, 16,* 207–226.

Atkinson, J. W., & Raynor, J. O. (1974). *Motivation and achievement.* Wash., DC: Winston.

Back, K. W. (1951). Influence through social communication. *Journal of Abnormal and Social Psychology, 46,* 190–207.

Bales, R. F., & Slater, P. E. (1955). Role differentiation in small groups. In T. Parsons, R. F. Bales, et al., *Family, socialization, and interaction process.* Glencoe, IL: Free Press.

Barnowe, J. T., Mangione, T. W., & Quinn, R. P. (1972). The relative importance of job facets as indicated by an empirically derived model of job satisfaction. Unpublished report, University of Michigan, Survey Research Center, Ann Arbor.

Barrett, R. S. (1963). Guide to using psychological tests. *Harvard Business Review, 41,* 138–146.

Bartley, S. H. (1980). *Introduction to perception.* New York: Harper & Row.

Bass, B. M. (1982). *Stogdill's handbook of leadership.* New York: Free Press.

Beach, D. S. (1980). *Personnel* (4th ed.). New York: Macmillan.

Beach, L. R. (1983). Muddling through: A response to Yates and Goldstein. *Organizational Behavior and Human Performance. 31,* 47–53.

Beach, L. R., Campbell, F. L., & Townes, D. B. (1979). Subjective expected utility and the prediction of birth planning decisions. *Organizational Behavior and Human Performance, 24,* 18–28.

Beer, M. (1976). The technology of organization development. In M.D. Dunnette (Ed.), *Handbook of Industrial and Organizational Psychology.* Chicago: Rand McNally.

Beer, M. (1980). *Organization change and development: A systems view.* Santa Monica, CA: Goodyear.

Benson, H. (1975). *The relaxation response.* New York: W. Morrow.

Bernardin, H. J., & Beatty, R. W. (1984). *Performance appraisal.* Boston: Kent.

Bernardin, H. J., & Kane, J. S. (1980). A second look at behavioral observation scales. *Personnel Psychology, 33,* 809–814.

Bernardin, H. J., & Smith, P. C. (1981). A clarification of some issues regarding the development and use of behaviorally anchored rating scales (BARS). *Journal of Applied Psychology, 66,* 458–463.

Bettelheim, B. (1958). Individual and mass behavior in extreme situations. In E. E. Maccoby (Ed.), *Readings in social psychology.* New York: Holt, Rinehart, and Winston.

Birnbaum, M. H. (1983). Perceived equity of salary policies. *Journal of Applied Psychology, 68,* 49–59.

Bittel, L. R. (1985). *What every supervisor should know* (5th ed.). New York: McGraw-Hill.

Blake, R. R., & Mouton, J. S. (1961). Comprehension of own and of outgroup positions under intergroup competition. *Journal of Conflict Resolution, 5,* 304–310.

Blake, R. R., & Mouton, J. S. (1961). Loyalty of representatives to ingroup positions during intergroup competition. *Sociometry, 24,* 177–183.

Blake, R. R., & Mouton, J.S. (1962). The intergroup dynamics of win-lose conflict and problem-solving collaboration in union-management relations. In M. Sherif (Ed.), *Intergroup relations and leadership.* New York: Wiley. (1964).

Blake, R. R. & Mouton, J.S. (1964). *The managerial grid.* Houston: Gulf.

Blake, R. R., Mouton, J. S., Barnes, L. B., & Greiner, L. E. (1964). Breakthrough in organizational development. *Harvard Business Review, 42,* 133–155.

Blake R. R., Shepard, H. A., & Mouton, J. S. (1964). *Managing intergroup conflict in industry.* Houston: Gulf.

Blau, P. M. (1956). *Bureaucracy in modern society.* New York: Random House.

Boas, M., & Chain, S. (1976). *Big Mac: The unauthorized story of McDonald's.* New York: Dutton.

Bouchard, T. J. (1971). Whatever happened to brainstorming? *Journal of Creative Behavior, 5,* 182–189.

Bowers, D. G. (1973). OD techniques and their results in 23 organizations: The Michigan ICC study. *Journal of Applied Behavioral Science, 9,* 21–43.

Bray, D. W., Campbell, R. J., & Grant, D. L. (1974). *Formative years in business.* New York: Wiley.

Breaugh, J. A. (1981). Predicting absenteeism from prior absenteeism and work attitudes. *Journal of Applied Psychology, 66,* 555–560.

Brett. J. M. (1980). The effect of job transfer on employees and their families. In C. L. Cooper & R. Payne (Eds.), *Current concerns in occupational stress.* Chichester, England: Wiley, 99–136.

Brett, J. M. (1980, Spring). Why employees want unions. *Organizational Dynamics, 8,* 47–59.

Brief, A. P., Schuyler, R. S., & Van Sell, M. A. (1981). *Managing job stress.* Boston: Little, Brown.

Bruner, J. S., & Tagiuri, R. (1954). The perception of people. In G. Lindzey (Ed.), *Handbook of social psychology.* Reading, MA: Addison-Wesley. *2,* 601–633.

Burke, R. J. (1969, Winter). Occupational and life strains, satisfaction, and mental health. *Journal of Business Administration, 1,* 35–41.

Burke, W. W. (1972). Managing conficts between groups. In J. D. Adams (Ed.), *Theory and method in organization development: An evolutionary process.* Arlington, VA: NTL Institute, 1972, 255–268.

Burke, W. W. (1982). *Organization development: Principles and practice.* Boston: Little Brown.

Burnaska, R.G., & Hollman, T. D. (1974). An empirical comparison of the relative effects of rater response bias on three rating scale formats. *Journal of Applied Psychology, 59,* 307–312.

Burns, T., & Stalker, G. M. (1961). *The management of innovation.* London: Tavistock.

Business Week/Harris Poll: Middle managers still think positively (1983, April 25). *Business Week,* 64.

Byham, W. C. (1970, July–August). Assessment centers for spotting future managers. *Harvard Business Review,* 150–167.

Byrne, D., & Kelley, K. (1981). *An introduction to personality* (3rd ed.). Englewood Cliffs, NJ: Prentice-Hall.

Cameron, K. S., & Whetten, D. A. (Eds.) (1983). *Organizational effectiveness: A comparison of multiple models.* New York: Academic Press.

Campbell, J. P., Dunnette, M. D., Lawler, E. E., III, & Weick, K. E. (1970). *Managerial behavior, performance and effectiveness.* New York: McGraw-Hill.

Carlson, R. E. (1971). The effect of interview information in altering valid impressions. *Journal of Applied Psychology, 55,* 66–72.

Carlson, R. E., Thayer, P. W., Mayfield, E. C., & Peterson, D. A. (1971). Improvements in the selection interview. *Personnel Journal, 50,* 268–274.

Carroll, D. T. (1983, November–December). A disappointing search for excellence. *Harvard Business Review,* 78–88.

Carroll, S. J., Jr., & Schneier, C. E. (1982). *Performance appraisal and review systems.* Glenview, IL: Scott, Foresman.

Carroll, S. J., Jr., & Tosi, H. L., Jr. (1973). *Management by objectives.* New York: Macmillian.

Cederblom, D. (1982). The performance appraisal interview: A review, implications, and suggestions. *Academy of Management Review, 7,* 219–227.

Cederblom, D., & Lounsbury, J. W. (1980). An investigation of user acceptance of peer evaluations. *Personnel Psychology, 33,* 567–579.

Chacko, T. I., & McElroy, J. C. (1983). The cognitive component in Locke's theory of goal setting: Suggestive evidence for a causal attribution interpretation. *Academy of Management Journal, 26,* 104–118.

Chadwick-Jones, J. K. (1969). *Automation and behavior.* New York: Wiley.

Chandler, A. A., Jr. (1962). *Strategy and structure: Chapters in the history of the American industrial enterprise.,* Cambridge, MA: MIT Press.

Chapple, E., & Sayles, L. R. (1961). *The measure of management.* New York: Macmillan.

Chemers, M. M., & Skrzypek, G. J. (1972). An experimental test of the contingency model of leadership effectiveness. *Journal of Personality and Social Psychology, 24,* 172–177.

Cherns, A. (1977, Spring). Can behavioral science help design organizations? *Organizational Dynamics,* 44–64.

Child, J. (1975). Managerial and organizational factors associated with company performance–Part II: A contingency analysis. *Journal of Management Studies, 12,* 17–27.

Choran, I. (1969). The managers of a small company. Unpublished MBA thesis. McGill University, Montreal.

Clausen, J. A. (Ed.) (1968). *Socialization and society.* Boston: Little, Brown.

Coch, L. & French, J. R. P., Jr. (1948). Overcoming resistance to change. *Human Relations, 1,* 512–532.

Cockrum, R. B. (1982, July). Has the time come for employee cafeteria plans? *Personnel Administrator,* 66–72.

Cohen, P. (1973). *The gospel according to the Harvard Business School.* New York: Doubleday.

Collaras, P. A., & Anderson, L. R. (1969). Effect of perceived expertise upon creativity of members in brainstorming groups. *Journal of Applied Psychology, 53,* 159–163.

Connolly, W. B. (1975). *A practical guide to Equal Employment Opportunity: Laws, principles and practices* (Vols. 1 & 2) New York: Law Journal Press.

Cook, D. (1968). The impact on managers of frequency of feedback. *Academy of Management Journal, 11,* 263–277.

Cooper, C. L., & Marshall, J. (1977). *Understanding executive stress.* New York: Petrocelli Press.

Cooper, C. L., & Payne, R. (1978). *Stress at work.* London: Wiley.

Cooper, W. H. (1981). Ubiquitous halo. *Psychological Bulletin, 90,* 218–244.

Copley News Service (1975, November). *Reader's Digest,* 82.

Cosier, R. A., & Dalton, D. R. (1983). Equity theory and time: A reformulation. *Academy of Management Review, 8,* 311–319.

Costa, P. T., Jr., McCrae, R. R., & Holland, J. L.

(1984). Personality and vocational interests in an adult sample. *Journal of Applied Psychology, 69,* 390–400.

Crozier, M. (1964). *The bureaucratic phenomenon.* Chicago: University of Chicago Press.

Cummings, L. L., & Schwab, D. P. (1973). *Performance in organizations.* Glenview, IL: Scott, Foresman.

Cyert, R., & March, J. G. (1963). *A behavioral theory of the firm.* Englewood Cliffs, NJ: Prentice-Hall.

Daft, R. L. (1983). *Organization theory and design.* St. Paul, MN: West.

Dalkey, N. (1969). *The Delphi method: An experimental study of group opinion.* Santa Monica, CA: Rand Corporation.

Dalton, G. W., Thompson, P. H., & Price, R. L. (1977). The four stages of professional careers: A new look at performance by professionals. *Organizational Dynamics, 6,* 19–42.

Dalton, M. (1959). *Men who manage.* New York: Wiley.

Dansereau, F., Jr., Graen, G. B., & Haga, W. J. (1975). A vertical dyad linkage approach to leadership within formal organizations: A longitudinal investigation of the role-making process. *Organizational Behavior and Human Performance, 13,* 46–78.

Davis, K. (1953). Management communication and the grapevine. *Harvard Business Review, 31,* 43–49.

Davis, K. (1968). Success of chain-of-command oral communication in a manufacturing group. *Academy of Management Journal, 11,* 379–387.

Davis, K. (1978). *Human relations at work* (5th ed.). New York: McGraw-Hill.

Davis, L. E. (1983). Learnings for the design of new organizations. In Kolodny, H.F. & van Beinum, H. (Eds.). *The quality of working life and the 1980's.* New York: Praeger.

Davis, L. E., & Cherns, A. B. (1975). *The quality of working life.* New York: Free Press.

Davis, S. M., & Lawrence, P. R. (1978, May–June). Problems of matrix organizations. *Harvard Business Review,* 131–142.

Davis, T. R. (1984). The influence of the physical environment in offices. *Academy of Management Review, 9,* 271–283.

Dawes, R. M. (1979). The robust beauty of improper linear models in decision making. *American Psychologist, 34,* 571–582.

Delbecq, A. L. Van de Ven, A. H., & Gustafson, D. H. (1975). *Group techniques for program planning.* Glenview, IL: Scott, Foresman.

DeNisi, A. S., Randolph, W. A., & Blencoe, A. G. (1983). Potential problems with peer ratings. *Academy of Management Journal, 26,* 457–464.

Dentler, R. A., & Erikson, K. T. (1959). The function of deviance in groups. *Social Problems, 7,* 98–107.

Department of Health, Education, and Welfare. (1973). *Work in America.* Cambridge, MA: MIT Press.

Deutsch, M. (1949). An experimental study of the effects of cooperation and competition upon group process. *Human Relations, 2,* 199–232.

Deutsch, M. (1949). A theory of cooperation and competition. *Human Relations, 2,* 129–152.

Dion, K. L. (1973). Cohesiveness as a determinant of ingroup-outgroup bias. *Journal of Personality and Social Psychology, 28,* 163–171.

Dipboye, R. L. (1985). Some neglected variables in research on discrimination in appraisals. *Academy of Management Review, 10,* 116–127.

Dipboye, R. L., & dePontbriand, R. (1981). Correlates of employee reactions to performance appraisals and appraisal systems. *Journal of Applied Psychology, 66,* 248–251.

Dossett, D. L., & Hulvershorn, P. (1983). Increasing technical training efficiency: Peer training via computer-assisted instruction. *Journal of Applied Psychology, 68,* 552–558.

Dorwick, P. W., & Hood, M. (1981). Comparison of self-modeling and small cash incentives in a sheltered workshop. *Journal of Applied Psychology, 66,* 394–397.

Dreher, G. F., & Mai-Dalton, R. R. (1983). A note on the internal consistency of the Manifest Needs Questionnaire. *Journal of Applied Psychology, 68,* 194–196.

Dreyfuss, F., & Czaczkes, J. W. (1959). Blood cholesterol and uric acid of healthy medical students under stress of examination. *Archives of Internal Medicine, 103,* 708.

Driscoll, J. W. (1979, Summer). Working creatively with a union: Lessons from the Scanlon Plan. *Organizational Dynamics,* 61–80.

Drory, A., & Gluskinos, U. M. (1980). Machiavellianism and leadership. *Journal of Applied Psychology, 65,* 81–86.

Drucker, P. (1954). *The practice of management.* New York: Harper & Row.

Duchon, D., & Jago, A. G. (1981). Equity and the performance of major league baseball players: An extension of Lord and Hohenfeld. *Journal of Applied Psychology, 66,* 728–732.

Duncan, R. B. (1979). What is the right organization structure? *Organizational Dynamics, 7,* 59–80.

Dunham, R. B., and Smith, F. J. (1979). *Organizational surveys.* Glenview, IL: Scott, Foresman.

Dunnette, M. D. (1963). A note on *the* criterion. *Journal of Applied Psychology, 47,* 251–254.

Dunnette, M. D. (1966). *Personnel selection and placement.* Belmont, CA: Wadsworth.

Dunnette, M. D. (1976). Aptitudes, abilities, and skills. In M. D. Dunnette (Ed.), *Handbook of industrial and organizational psychology.* New York: Wiley.

Dunnette, M. D., Campbell, J. P., & Hakel, M. D. (1967). Factors contributing to job satisfaction and dissatisfaction in six occupational groups. *Organizational Behavior and Human Performance, 2,* 143–174.

Dunnette, M. D., Campbell, J. P., & Jaastad, K. (1963). The effect of group participation on brainstorming effectiveness for two industrial samples. *Journal of Applied Psychology, 47,* 30–37.

Eden, D., & Ravid, G. (1982). Pygmalion versus self-expectancy: Effects of instructor- and self-expectancy on trainee performance. *Organizational Behavior and Human Performance, 30,* 351–364.

Eden, D., & Shani, A. B. (1982). Pygmalion goes to boot camp: Expectancy, leadership and trainee performance. *Journal of Applied Psychology, 67,* 194–199.

Elizur, D. (1984). Facets of work values: A structural analysis of work outcomes. *Journal of Applied Psychology, 69,* 379–389.

Emery, F. E., & Trist, E. L. (1965). The causal texture of organizational environments. *Human Relations, 18,* 21–32.

Emery, F. E., & Trist, E. L. (1969). Sociotechnical systems. In F. E. Emery (Ed.), *Systems thinking.* Harmondsworth, England: Penguin.

England, G. W. (1971). *Development and use of weighted application blanks.* Minneapolis: University of Minnesota Industrial Relations Center.

Erez, M., & Kanfer, F. H. (1983). The role of goal acceptance in goal setting and task performance. *Academy of Management Review, 8,* 454–463.

Erez, M., & Zidon, I. (1984). Effect of goal acceptance on the relationship of goal difficulty to task performance. *Journal of Applied Psychology, 69,* 69–78.

Erikson, E. H. (1963). *Childhood and society* (2nd ed.). New York: Norton.

Erikson, K. T. (1966). *Wayward puritans.* New York: Wiley.

Etzioni, A. (1964). *Modern organizations.* Englewood Cliffs, NJ: Prentice-Hall.

Evans, M. G. (1970). The effects of supervisory behavior on the path-goal relationship. *Organizational Behavior and Human Performance, 5,* 277–298.

Evans, M. G. (1974). Extensions of a path-goal theory of motivation. *Journal of Applied Psychology, 59,* 172–178.

Fallows, J. (1981). *The national defense.* New York: Vintage Books.

Farris, G. F., & Lim, F. G., Jr. (1969). Effects of performance on leadership, cohesiveness, satisfaction, and subsequent performance. *Journal of Applied Psychology, 53,* 490–497.

Fay, C. H., & Latham, G. P. (1982). The effects of training and rating scales on rating errors. *Personnel Psychology, 35,* 105–116.

Fayol, H. (translated by C. Storrs). (1949). *General and industrial management.* London: Pitman.

Fein, M. (1974). Job enrichment: A reevaluation. *Sloan Management Review, 15,* 69–88.

Feldman, D. C. (1976). A contingency theory of socialization. *Administrative Science Quarterly, 21,* 433–452.

Feldman, D. C. (1976). A practical program for employee socialization. *Organizational Dynamics, 5,* 64–80.

Feldman, D. C. (1980). A socialization process that helps new recruits succeed. *Personnel, 57,* 11–23.

Feldman, D. C. (1981). The multiple socialization of organization members. *Academy of Management Review, 6,* 309–318.

Feldman, D. C. (1984). The development and enforcement of group norms. *Academy of Management Journal, 9,* 47–53.

Feldman, D. C. (1985). A taxonomy of intergroup conflict resolution strategies. In L. Goodstein (Ed.), *Developing human resources.* La Jolla, CA: University Associates, 169–176.

Feldman, D. C. & Arnold, H. J. (1985). Personality types and career patterns: Some empirical evidence on Holland's model. *Canadian Journal of Administrative Sciences, 2,* 192–210.

Feldman, D. C., & Brett, J. M. (1983). Coping with new jobs: A comparative study of new hires and job changers. *Academy of Management Journal, 26,* 258–272.

Feldman, D. C. & Brett, J. M. (1985). Trading places: Managing employee job changes. *Personnel, 62,* 61–65.

Feldman, J. M. (1981). Beyond attribution theory: Cognitive processes in performance appraisal. *Journal of Applied Psychology, 66,* 127–148.

Festinger, L., Schachter, S., & Back, K. (1950). *Social pressures in informal groups.* Stanford, CA: Stanford University Press.

Fiedler, F. E. (1962). Employee grievances and turnover. *Personnel Psychology, 15,* 43–56.

Fiedler, F. E. (1964). A contingency model of leadership effectiveness. In L. Berkowitz (Ed.), *Advances in experimental social psychology.* New York: Academic Press.

Fiedler, F. E. (1967). *A theory of leadership effectiveness.* New York: McGraw-Hill.

Fiedler, F.E. (1967). Validation and extension of the contingency model of leadership effectiveness: A review of empirical findings. *Psychological Bulletin, 76,* 128–148.

Fiedler, F. E. (1972). Personality, motivational systems, and the behavior of high and low LPC persons. *Human Relations, 25,* 391–412.

Field, R. H. G. (1982). A test of the Vroom-Yetton normative model of leadership. *Journal of Applied Psychology, 67,* 523–532.

Filley, A. C. (1977). Conflict resolution: The ethic of the good loser. In R. C. Huseman, C. M. Logue, & D. L. Freshly (Eds.), *Readings in interpersonal and organizational psychology.* Boston: Holbrook Press 234–252.

Finkle, R. B. (1976). Managerial assessment centers. In M.D. Dunnette (Ed.), *Handbook of industrial and organizational psychology.* Chicago: Rand McNally, 861–888.

Fleishman, E. A. (1962). The description and prediction of perceptual-motor skill learning. In R. Glaser (Ed.), *Training in research and education.* Pittsburgh: University of Pittsburgh Press.

Fleishman, E. A., & Harris, E. F. (1962). Patterns of leadership behavior related to employee grievances and turnover. *Personnel Psychology, 15,* 43-56.

Fleishman, E. A., Harris, E. F., & Burtt, H. E. (1955). *Leadership and supervision in industry.* Columbus: Ohio State University, Bureau of Educational Research.

Flowers, V. S., et al. (1975). *Managerial values for working.* New York: American Management Association.

Folkman, S., & Lazarus, R. S. (1980). An analysis of coping in a middle-aged community sample. *Journal of Health and Social Behavior, 21,* 219–239.

Ford, J. D. (1981). Departmental context and formal structure as constraints on leader behavior. *Academy of Management Journal, 24,* 274–288.

Ford, J. D., & Schellenberg, D. A. (1982). Conceptual issues in the assessment of organizational performance. *Academy of Management Review, 7,* 49–58.

French, J. R. P., Jr., & Caplan, R. D. (1972). Organizational stress and individual strain. In A. J. Marrow (Ed.), *The failure of success.* New York: AMACOM, 30–66.

French, J. R. P., & Raven, B. (1959). The bases of social power. In D. Cartwright (Ed.), *Studies in social power.* Ann Arbor, MI: Institute for Social Research.

French, W. L. (1969). Organization development: Objectives, assumptions, and strategies. *California Management Review, 12,* 23–34.

Friedman, M., & Roseman, R. H. (1974). *Type A behavior and your heart.* New York: Knopf.

Friedman, M., Roseman, R. H., & Carroll, V. (1958). Changes in serum cholesterol and blood clotting time in men subjected to cyclic variation of occupational stress. *Circulation, 17,* 852–861.

Fusilier, M. R., Ganster, D. C., & Middlemist, R. D. (1984). A within-person test of the form of the expectancy theory model in a choice context. *Organizational Behavior and Human Performance, 34,* 323–342.

Gaertner, G. H., & Ramnarayan, S. (1983). Organizational effectiveness. An alternative perspective. *Academy of Management Review, 8,* 97–107.

Galbraith, J. R. (1974). Organization design: An information processing view. *Interfaces, 4,* 28–36.

Galbraith, J. R. (1977). *Organization design.* Reading, MA: Addison-Wesley.

Gannon, M. J., & Noon, J. P. (1971). Management's critical deficiency. *Business Horizons, 14,* 49–56.

Garland, H. (1982). Goal levels and task performance: A compelling replication of some compelling results. *Journal of Applied Psychology, 67,* 245–248.

Garland, H. (1983). Influence of ability, assigned goals, and normative information on personal goals and performance: A challenge to the goal attainability assumption. *Journal of Applied Psychology, 68,* 20–30.

Garland, H. (1984). Relation of effort-performance expectancy to performance in goal-setting experiments. *Journal of Applied Psychology, 69,* 79–84.

Gellerman, S. W. (1958). The ethics of personality testing. *Personnel, 35,* 30–35.

Getman, J. G., Goldberg, S. B., & Herman, J. B. (1976). *Union representation elections: Law and reality.* Russell Sage Foundation.

Ghiselli, E. E. (1973). The validity of aptitude tests in personnel selection. *Personnel Psychology, 26,* 461–478.

Ghorpade, J., & Lackritz, J. R. (1981). Influences behind neutral responses in subordinate ratings of supervisors. *Personnel Psychology, 34,* 511–522.

Gibb, J. (1961). Defensive communication. *Journal of Communication, 3,* 141–148.

Gilbreth, F. B., & Gilbreth, L. M. (1919). *Fatigue study.* New York: Macmillian.

Glaser, B. G. (1968). *Organizational choices: A source book for theory.* Chicago: Aldine.

Glass, A. (1975, May 31). Paperwork bogs down paperwork probe. *The Miami News,* 1.

Glueck, W. F. (1978). *Personnel: A diagnostic approach* (rev. ed.). Dallas, TX: Business Publications.

Glueck, W. F. (1982). *Personnel: A diagnostic approach* (3rd ed.). Plano, TX: Business Publications.

Goffman, E. (1955). On face-work: An analysis of ritual elements in social interaction. *Psychiatry, 18,* 213–231.

Goldberg, P. (1978). *Executive health.* New York: McGraw-Hill.

Golembiewski, R. T. (1962). *The small group.* Chicago: University of Chicago Press.

Gomersall, E. R., & Myers, M. S. (1966). Breakthrough in on-the-job training. *Harvard Business Review, 44,* 62–72.

Goodman, P. S. (1974). An examination of referents used in the evaluation of pay. *Organizational Behavior and Human Performance, 12,* 170–195.

Goodman, P. S., & Friedman, A. (1971). An examination of Adams' theory of inequity. *Administrative Science Quarterly, 16,* 271–288.

Goodman, P. S., & Pennings, J. M. (1977). *New perspectives on organizational effectiveness.* San Francisco: Jossey-Bass.

Gough, H. G. (1984). A managerial potential scale for the California Psychological Inventory. *Journal of Applied Psychology, 69,* 233–240.

Gouldner, A. W. (1954). *Patterns of industrial democracy.* Glencoe, IL: Free Press.

Graen, G. B., Alvares, K. M., Orris, J. B., & Martella, J. A. (1970). Contingency model of leadership effectiveness: Antecedent and evidential results. *Psychological Bulletin, 74,* 285–296.

Graen, G. B., Liden, R. C., & Hoel, W. (1982). Role of leadership in the employee withdrawal process. *Journal of Applied Psychology, 67,* 868–872.

Green, S. G., Blank, W., & Liden, R. C. (1983). Market and organizational influences on bank employees' work attitudes and behaviors. *Journal of Applied Psychology, 68,* 298–306.

Green, S. G., & Mitchell, T. R. (1979). Attributional processes of leaders in leader-member interactions. *Organizational Behavior and Human Performance, 23,* 429–458.

Greenberg, J. S., & Ornstein, S. (1983). High status job title as compensation for underpayment: A test of equity theory. *Journal of Applied Psychology, 68,* 285–297.

Greene, C. N. (1979). *A longitudinal investigation of modification to a situational model of leadership effectiveness.* Paper presented at the National Meeting of the Academy of Management, Atlanta.

Guilford, J. P. (1959). Three faces of intellect. *American Psychologist, 14,* 469–479.

Guilford, J. P. (1967). *The nature of human intelligence.* New York: McGraw-Hill.

Guion, R. M., and Gottier, R. F. (1965). Validity of personality measures in personnel selection. *Personnel Psychology, 18,* 135–164.

Guzzo, R. A., & Waters, J. A. (1982). The expression of affect and performance of decision-making groups. *Journal of Applied Psychology, 67,* 67–74.

Gyllenhammar, P. (1977, July–August). How Volvo adapts work to people. *Harvard Business Review,* 102–113.

Hackman, J. R. (1975, September–October). Is job enrichment just a fad? *Harvard Business Review,* pp. 129–139.

Hackman, J. R. (1976). Group influences on individuals. In M. Dunnette (Ed.). *Handbook of industrial and organizational psychology.* Chicago: Rand McNally.

Hackman, J. R., & Oldham, G. R. (1975). Development of the Job Diagnostic Survey. *Journal of Applied Psychology, 60,* 159–170.

Hackman, J. R., & Oldham, G. R. (1976). Motivation through the design of work: Test of a theory. *Organizational Behavior and Human Performance, 16,* 250–279.

Hackman, J. R., & Oldham, G. R. (1980). *Work redesign.* Reading, MA: Addison-Wesley.

Hackman, J. R., Oldham, G. R., Janson, R., & Purdy, K. (1975, Summer). A new strategy for job enrichment. *California Management Review,* 57–71.

Haire, M. (1955). Role perception in labor-management relations: An experimental approach. *Industrial and Labour Relations Review, 8,* 204–216.

Haire, M., & Grunes, W. F. (1950). Perceptual defenses: Processes protecting an organized perception of another personality. *Human Relations, 3,* 403–412.

Hall, E. T. (1959). *The silent language.* New York: Doubleday.

Hall, D. T. (1976). *Careers in organizations.* Pacific Palisades, CA: Goodyear.

Hall, R. H. (1972). *Organizations: Structure and process.* Englewood Cliffs, NJ: Prentice-Hall.

Hall, T. (1984, October 23). Demanding PepsiCo is attempting to make work nicer for managers. *Wall Street Journal,* 31.

Hammer, T. H., & Landau, J. C. (1981). Methodological issues in the use of absence data. *Journal of Applied Psychology, 66,* 574–581.

Hammond, L. K., & Goldman. M. (1961). Competition and noncompetition and its relationship to individual and group productivity. *Sociometry, 24,* 46–60.

Hamner, W. C., & Hamner, E. P. (1976, Spring). Behavior modification on the bottom line. *Organizational Dynamics,* 12–24.

Hamner, W. C., & Smith, F. J. (1978). Work attitudes as predictors of unionization activity. *Journal of Applied Psychology, 63,* 415–421.

Haney, W. V. (1973). *Communication and organizational behavior.* Homewood, IL: Irwin.

Harrel, A. M., & Stahl, M. J. (1981). A behavioral decision theory approach for measuring McClelland's trichotomy of needs. *Journal of Applied Psychology, 66,* 242–247.

Harrison, E. F. (1975). *The managerial decision-making process.* Boston: Houghton Mifflin.

Harvey, E. (1968). Technology and the structure of organizations. *American Sociological Review, 33,* 241–259.

Harvey, O. J. (1953). An experimental approach to the study of status relations in informal groups. *American Sociological Review, 18,* 357–367.

Harvey, R. H. (1982). The future of partial correlation as a means to reduce halo in performance ratings. *Journal of Applied Psychology, 67,* 171–176.

Hatvany, N., & Pucik, V. (1981, Spring). Japanese management practices and productivity. *Organizational Dynamics,* 5–21.

Hayes, R. H. (1981, July–August). Why Japanese factories work. *Harvard Business Review,* 57–66.

Haynes, R. S., Pine, R. C., & Fitch, H. G. (1982). Reducing accident rates with organizational behavior modification. *Academy of Management Journal, 25,* 407–416.

Henchy, T., & Glass, D. C. (1968). Evaluation apprehension and the social facilitation of dominant and subordinate responses. *Journal of Personality and Social Psychology, 10,* 466–454.

Heneman, R. L., & Wexley, K. N. (1983). The effects of time delay in rating and amount of information observed on performance rating accuracy. *Academy of Management Journal, 26,* 677–686.

Herman, J. B. (1973). Are situational contingencies limiting job attitude-job performance relationships? *Organizational Behavior and Human Performance, 10,* 208–224.

Herzberg, F. (1966). *Work and the nature of man.* Cleveland: World.

Herzberg, F. (1968, January–February). One more time: How do you motivate employees? *Harvard Business Review,* 53–62.

Herzberg, F. (1974, September–October). The wise old Turk. *Harvard Business Review,* 70–80.

Herzberg, F. (1976). *The managerial choice.* Homewood, IL: Dow Jones-Irwin.

Herzberg, F., Mausner, B., Peterson, R. D., & Capwell, D. F. (1957). *Job attitudes: Review of research and opinion.* Pittsburgh: Psychological Service of Pittsburgh.

Herzberg, F., Mausner, B., & Snyderman, B. (1959). *The motivation to work.* New York: Wiley.

Hickson, D. J., Pugh, D. S., & Pheysey, D. C. (1969). Operation technology and organization structure: An empirical reappraisal. *Administrative Science Quarterly, 14,* 378–397.

Hill, W. (1973). Leadership style: Rigid or flexible? *Organizational Behavior and Human Performance, 9,* 35–47.

Hinton, B. L. (1968). An empirical investigation of the Herzberg methodology and two-factor theory. *Organizational Behavior and Human Performance, 3,* 286–309.

Hodgetts, R. M., & Altman, S. (1979). *Organizational behavior.* Philadelphia: W. B. Saunders.

Hoffman, L. R., & Maier, N. R. F. (1961). Quality and acceptance of problem solutions by members of homogeneous and heterogeneous groups. *Journal of Abnormal and Social Psychology, 62,* 401–407.

Holland, J. L. (1973). *Making vocational choices: A theory of careers.* Englewood Cliffs, NJ: Prentice-Hall.

Hollander, E. P. (1958). Conformity, status, and idiosyncrasy credit. *Psychological Review, 65,* 117–127.

Holmes, T. H., & Rahe, R. H. (1967). The social readjustment rating scale. *Journal of Psychosomatic Research, 11,* 213–218.

Hom, P. W., DeNisi, A. S., Kinicki, A. J. & Bannister, B. D. (1982). Effectiveness of performance feedback from behaviorally anchored rating scales. *Journal of Applied Psychology, 67,* 165–170.

House, R. J. (1971). A path goal theory of leader effectiveness. *Administrative Science Quarterly, 16,* 321–339.

House, R. J. & Baetz, M. (1979). Leadership: Some generalizations and new research directions. In B. H. Staw (Ed.), *Research in organizational behavior,* Greenwich, CT: JAI Press.

House, R. J., & Dessler, G. (1974). The path goal theory of leadership: Some post hoc and a priori tests. In J. G. Hunt & L. L. Larson (Eds.), *Contingency approaches to leadership.* Carbondale, IL: Southern Illinois University Press.

House, R. J., & Mitchell, T. R. (1974, Autumn). Path-goal theory of leadership. *Journal of Contemporary Business, 3,* 81–98.

House, R. J., & Wigdor, L. (1967). Herzberg's dual factor theory of job satisfaction and motivation: A review of the evidence and a criticism. *Personnel Psychology, 20,* 369–389.

How to earn well-pay (1978, June 12). *Business Week,* 143–146.

How the Japanese run U.S. subsidiaries. (1983, October). *Dun's Business Month.*

Howard, A. (1974). An assessment of assessment centers. *Academy of Management Journal, 17,* 115–134.

Hulin, C. L. (1982). Some reflections on general performance dimensions and halo rating error. *Journal of Applied Psychology, 67,* 165–170.

Hunter, J. E., & Hunter, R. F. (1984). Validity and utility of alternative predictors of job performance. *Psychological Bulletin, 96,* 72–98.

Ilgen, D. R., Mitchell, T. R., & Frederickson, J. W. (1981). Poor performers: Supervisors' and subordinates' responses. *Organizational Behavior and Human Performance, 27,* 386–410.

Ilgen, D. R., Nebeker, D. M., & Pritchard, R. D. (1981). Expectancy theory measures: An empirical comparison in an experimental situation. *Organizational Behavior and Human Performance, 28,* 189–223.

Imada, A. S. (1982). Social interaction, observation, and stereotypes as determinants of differentiation in peer ratings. *Organizational Behavior and Human Performance, 29,* 397–415.

Ivancevich, J. M. (1980). A longitudinal study of behavioral expectation scales: Attitudes and performance. *Journal of Applied Psychology, 65,* 139–146.

Ivancevich, J. M. (1982). Subordinates' reactions to performance appraisal interviews: A test of feedback and goal-setting techniques. *Journal of Applied Psychology, 67,* 581–587.

Ivancevich, J. M. (1983). Contrast effects in performance evaluation and reward practices. *Academy of Management Journal, 26,* 465–476.

Ivancevich, J. M. and Matteson, M. T. (1980). Optimizing human resources: A case for preventive health and stress management. *Organizational Dynamics, 9,* 5–23.

Ivancevich, J. M., & Matteson, M. T. (1980). *Stress and work.* Glenview, IL: Scott, Foresman.

Ivancevich, J. M., & McMahon, J. T. (1982). The effects of goal setting, external feedback, and self-generated feedback on outcome variables: A field experiment. *Academy of Management Journal, 25,* 359–372.

Ivancevich, J. M., & Smith, S. V. (1981). Goal-setting interview skills training: Simulated and on-the-job analysis. *Journal of Applied Psychology, 66,* 697–705.

Jackson, D. N., & Paumonen, S. V. (1980). Personality structure and assessment. *Annual Review of Psychology, 31,* 503–551.

Jackson, J. (1966). A conceptual and measurement model for norms and roles. *Pacific Sociological Review, 9,* 35–45.

Jackson, S. E. (1983). Participation in decision making as a strategy for reducing job-related strain. *Journal of Applied Psychology, 68,* 3–19.

Jackson, S. E., & Zedeck, S. (1982). Explaining performance variablity: Contributions of goal setting, task characteristics, and evaluative contexts. *Journal of Applied Psychology, 67,* 759–768.

Jacobs, R., Kafry, D., & Zedeck, S. (1980). Expectations of behaviorally anchored rating scales. *Personnel Psychology, 33,* 595–640.

Jago, A. G., & Vroom, V. H. (1978). Predicting leader behavior from a measure of behavioral intent. *Academy of Management Journal, 21,* 715–721.

Jago, A. G., & Vroom, V. H. (1980). An evaluation of two alternatives to the Vroom-Yetton normative model. *Academy of Management Journal, 23,* 347–355.

Jamieson, B. D. (1973). Behavioral problems with management by objectives. *Academy of Management Journal, 16,* 496–505.

Janis, I. L. (1982). *Victims of groupthink* (rev. ed.). Boston: Houghton-Mifflin.

Janis, I. L., & Mann, L. (1977). *Decision making: A psychological analysis of conflict, choice, and commitment.* New York: Free Press.

Janis, I. L. & Wheeler, D. (May 1978). Thinking clearly about career choices. *Psychology Today,* 66–68, 70, 75–76, 121–122.

Janz, T. (1982). Manipulating subjective expectancy through feedback: A laboratory study of the expectancy-performance relationship. *Journal of Applied Psychology, 67,* 480–485.

Jelinek, M., Litterer, J. A., & Miles, R. E. (1981). Control in organizations. In M. Jelinek, J. A. Litterer, & R. E. Miles (Eds.), *Organization by design: Theory and practice.* Plano, TX: Business Publications. 417–428.

Jelinek, M., Litterer, J. A., & Miles, R. E. (1981). Technology. In M. Jelinek, J. A. Litterer, & R. E. Miles, (Eds.), *Organization by design: Theory and practice.* Plano, TX: Business Publications, 169–172.

Jewell, L. N., & Reitz, H. J. (1981). *Group effectiveness in organizations.* Glenview, IL: Scott, Foresman.

Johnson, D. W., Maruyama, G., & Johnson, R. T. (1982). Separating ideology from currently available data: A reply to Cotton and Cook and McGlynn. *Psychological Bulletin, 92,* 186–192.

Johnson, D. W., Maruyama, G., Johnson, R., Nelson, D., & Skon, L. (1981). Effects of cooperative, competitive, and individualistic goal structures on achievement: A meta-analysis. *Psychological Bulletin, 89,* 47–62.

Kahn, R. L., Wolfe, D. M., Quinn, R .P., Snoek, J. D., & Rosenthal, R. A. (1964). *Organizational stress: Studies in role conflict and ambiguity.* New York: Wiley.

Kasl, S. and Gobb, S. (1970, January–February). Blood pressure changes in men undergoing job loss: A preliminary report. *Psychosomatic Medicine,* 19–38.

Katterberg, R., Smith, F. J., & Hoy, S. (1977). Language, time, and person effects on attitude scale translations. *Journal of Applied Psychology, 62,* 385–391.

Katz, D. & Kahn, R. (1978). *The social psychology of organizations* (2nd ed.). New York: Wiley.

Kay, E., Meyer, H., & French, J. R. P. (1965). Effects of threat in a performance appraisal interview. *Journal of Applied Psychology, 49,* 311–317.

Kelley, H. H. (1973). The processes of causal attribution. *American Psychologist, 28,* 107–128.

Kelley, M. (1982). Participant based theories of organizational effectiveness. Paper presented at the 42nd Annual Meeting of the Academy of Management, New York.

Kenny, D. A., & Zaccaro, S. J. (1983). An estimate of variance due to traits in leadership. *Journal of Applied Psychology, 68,* 678–685.

Kerr, S., & Schriesheim, C. A. (1974). Consideration, initiating structure, and organizational criteria—An update of Korman's 1966 review. *Personnel Psychology, 27,* 555–568.

Keys, J. B., & Miller, T. R. (1984). The Japanese management theory jungle. *Academy of Management Review, 1,* 342–353.

Kidder, T. (1981). *The soul of a new machine.* New York: Avon.

Kim, J. S. (1984). Effect of behavior plus outcome goal setting and feedback on employee satisfaction and performance. *Academy of Management Journal, 27,* 139–149.

King, N. A. (1970). A clarification and evaluation of the two-factor theory of job satisfaction. *Psychological Bulletin, 74,* 18–31.

Kingdon, D. R. (1973). *Matrix organization.* London: Tavistock.

Kingstrom, P. O., & Bass, A. R. (1981). A critical analysis of studies comparing behaviorally anchored rating scales (BARS) and other rating formats. *Personnel Psychology, 34,* 263–289.

Klein, N. M. (1983). Utility and decision strategies: A second look at the rational decision maker. *Organizational Behavior and Human Performance, 31,* 1–25.

Knight, K. (1976). Matrix organization: A review. *Journal of Management Studies, 13,*(2) 111–118.

Knowlton, W. A., Jr., & Mitchell, T. R. (1980). Effects of causal attributions on a supervisor's evaluation of subordinate performance. *Journal of Applied Psychology, 65,* 459–466.

Kolb, D., & Frohman, A. (1970). An organization development approach to consulting. *Sloan Management Review, 12*(1), 51–65.

Kolodny, H. F. & van Beinum, H. (1983). *The quality of working life and the 1980s.* New York: Praeger.

Komaki, J., Barwick, K. D., & Scott, L. R. (1978). A behavioral approach to occupational safety: Pinpointing and reinforcing safe performance in a food manufacturing plant. *Journal of Applied Psychology, 63,* 434–445.

Komaki, J., Heinzmann, A. T., & Lawson, L. (1980). Effect of training and feedback: Component analysis of a behavioral safety program. *Journal of Applied Psychology, 65,* 261–270.

Kotter, J. P. (1973). The psychological contract: Managing the joining-up process. *California Management Review, 15,* 91–99.

Kotter, J. P. (1975). The first year out. Unpublished note, Harvard Business School. Boston, MA: Harvard Business School Division of Research, 1975.

Kotter, J. P. (1979). Managing external dependence. *Academy of Management Review, 4,* 87–92.

Kuna, D. (1975, June). Meditation and work. *Vocational Guidance Quarterly,* 342–346.

Kurke, L. B., & Aldrich, H. E. (1983). Mintzberg was right!: A replication and extension of the nature of managerial work. *Management Science, 29,* 975–984.

Lakein, A. (1973). *How to get control of your time and your life.* New York: Wyden.

Landsberger, H. A. (1961). The horizontal dimension in bureaucracy. *Administrative Science Quarterly, 6,* 299–232.

Landy, F. J., Barnes-Farrell, J., & Cleveland, J. N. (1980). Perceived fairness and accuracy of performance evaluation: A follow-up. *Journal of Applied Psychology, 65,* 355–356.

Landy, F. J., & Farr, J. L. (1980). A process model of performance ratings. *Psychological Bulletin, 87,* 72–108.

Landy, F. J., Vance, R. J., & Barnes-Farrell, J. L. (1982). Statistical control of halo: A response. *Journal of Applied Psychology, 67,* 177–180.

Landy, F. J., Vance, R. J., Barnes-Farrell, J. L., & Steel, J. W. (1980). Statistical control of halo error in performance ratings. *Journal of Applied Psychology, 65,* 501–506.

Larson, J. R., Jr. (1984). The performance feedback process: A preliminary model. *Organizational Behavior and Human Performance, 33,* 42–76.

Latham, G. P., Fay, C. H., & Saari, L. M. (1979). The development of behavioral observation scales for appraising the performance of foremen. *Personnel Psychology, 32,* 299–311.

Latham, G. P., & Saari, L. M. (1979). Importance of supportive relationships in goal setting. *Journal of Applied Psychology, 64,* 151–156.

Latham, G. P., Saari, L. M., & Fay, C. H. (1980). BOS, BES, and baloney: Raising Kane with Bernardin. *Personnel Psychology, 33,* 815–821.

Latham, G. P., & Steele, T. P. (1983). The motivational effects of participation versus goal setting on performance. *Academy of Management Journal, 26,* 406–417.

Latham, G. P., & Wexley, K. N. (1977). Behavioral observation scales for performance appraisal purposes. *Personnel Psychology, 30,* 255–268.

Latham, G. P., & Wexley, K. N. (1981). *Improving productivity through performance appraisal.* Reading, MA: Addison-Wesley.

Latham, G. P., Wexley, K. N. & Pursell, E. D. (1975). Training managers to minimize rating errors in the observation of behavior. *Journal of Applied Psychology, 60,* 550–555.

Latham, G. P., & Yukl, G. A. (1975). A review of the research on the application of goal setting in organizations. *Academy of Management Journal, 18,* 824–845.

Lawler, E. E., III. (1971). *Pay and organizational effectiveness: A psychological view.* New York: McGraw-Hill.

Lawler, E. E., III. (1973). *Motivation in work organizations.* Monterey, CA: Brooks/Cole.

Lawler, E. E., III. (1976). New approaches to pay: Innovations that work. *Personnel, 53*(3), 11–23.

Lawler, E. E., III. (1977). Reward systems. In J. R. Hackman & J. L. Suttle (Eds.), *Improving life at work.* Glenview, IL: Scott, Foresman.

Lawler, E. E., III. (1981). *Pay and organization development.* Reading, MA: Addison-Wesley.

Lawler, E. E., III, Jenkins, G. D., Jr., & Herline, G. E. (1974, July 12). Initial data feedback to General Foods—Topeka Pet Food Plants—Selected survey items. Ann Arbor, MI: Institute for Social Research.

Lawler, E. E., III, & Porter, L. W. (1967). The effects of performance on job satisfaction. *Industrial Relations, 7,* 20–28.

Lawler, E. E., III, Porter, L. W., & Tannenbaum, A. (1968). Managers' attitudes toward interaction episodes. *Journal of Applied Psychology, 52,* 432–439.

Lawrence, P. R., Kolodny, H. F., and Davis, S. M. (1977). The human side of the matrix: *Organizational Dynamics, 5,* 40–53.

Lawrence, P. R., & Lorsch, J. W. (1967). New management job: The integrator. *Harvard Business Review, 45,* 142–151.

Lawrence, P. R., & Lorsch, J. W. (1969). *Organization and environment: Managing differentiation and integration.* Homewood, IL: Irwin.

Lazarus, R. H. (1977). Cognitive and coping processes on emotions. In A. Monat and R. S. Lazarus (Eds.), *Stress and coping.* New York: Columbia University Press.

Leavitt, H. J. (1951) Some effects of certain communication patterns on group performance. *Journal of Abnormal and Social Psychology, 46,* 38–50.

León, F. R. (1981). The role of positive and negative outcomes in the causation of motivational forces. *Journal of Applied Psychology, 66,* 45–53.

Levine, E. L. (1980). Introductory remarks for the symposium "Organizational Applications of Self-Appraisal and Self-Assessment: Another Look." *Personnel Psychology, 33,* 259–262.

Levine, E. L., Flory, A., III, & Ash, R. A. (1977). Self-assessment in personnel selection. *Journal of Applied Psychology, 62,* 428–435.

LeVine, R. A., & Campbell, D. T. (1972). *Ethnocentrism: Theories of conflict, ethnic attitudes, and group behavior.* New York: Wiley.

Levine, S. B., & Kawada, H. (1980). *Human resources in Japanese industrial development.* Princeton: Princeton University Press.

Levinson, D. J. (1977). The mid-life transition: A period in adult psychosocial development. *Psychiatry, 40,* 99–112.

Levinson, H. (1969). On being a middle-aged manager. *Harvard Business Review, 47,* 51–60.

Levy, R. (1978, March). Tales from the bureaucratic woods. *Dun's Review,* 95–96.

Lewin, A., & Zwany, A. (1976). Peer nominations: A model, literature critique, and a paradigm for research. *Personnel Psychology, 29,* 423–447.

Lewin, K. (1958). Group decision and social change. In E. E. Maccoby, T. M. Newcomb, & E. L. Hartley (Eds.), *Readings in social psychology.* New York: Holt, Rinehart, & Winston.

Lewis, P. V. (1980). *Organizational communication: The essence of effective management* (2nd ed.). Columbus, OH: Grid.

Liden, R. C., & Graen, G. B. (1983). Generalizability of the vertical dyad linkage model of leadership. *Academy of Management Journal, 23,* 451–465.

Likert, R. (1961). *New patterns of management.* New York: McGraw-Hill.

Lindblom, C. E. (1959). The science of muddling through. *Public Administration Review, 19,* 79–99.

Litwin, G. H., & Stringer, R. A., Jr. (1968). *Motivation and organizational climate.* Boston: Division of Research, Graduate School of Business Administration, Harvard University.

Livernash, E. R. (1980). *Comparable worth: Issues and alternatives.* Washington, D.C.: Equal Employment Advisory Council.

Locher, A. H., & Teel, K. S. (1977, May). Performance appraisal: A survey of current practices. *Personnel Journal.*

Locke, E. A. (1968). Toward a theory of task performance and incentives. *Organizational Behavior and Human Performance, 3,* 157–189.

Locke, E. A. (1976). The nature and causes of job satisfaction. In M. D. Dunnette (Ed.), *Handbook of industrial and organizational psychology.* Chicago: Rand McNally. 1297–1349.

Locke, E. A. (1978). The ubiquity of the technique of goal setting in theories of and approaches to employee motivation. *Academy of Management Review, 3,* 594–601.

Locke, E. A. (1982). Relation of goal level to performance with a short work period and multiple goal levels. *Journal of Applied Psychology, 67,* 512–514.

Locke, E. A., Frederick, E., Bobko, P., & Buckner, E. (1984). Effect of previously assigned goals on self-set goals and performance. *Journal of Applied Psychology, 69,* 694–699.

Locke, E. A., Frederick, E., Bobko, P., & Lee, C. (1984). Effect of self-efficacy, goals, and task strategies on task performance. *Journal of Applied Psychology, 69,* 241–251.

Locke, E. A., Shaw, K. N., Saari, L. M., & Latham, G. P. (1981). Goal setting and task performance: 1969–1980. *Psychological Bulletin, 90,* 125–152.

London, M. (1985). *Developing managers.* San Francisco: Jossey-Bass.

Longworth, R. C., & Neikirk, B. (1977, September 16–19). The changing American worker. *Chicago Tribune.*

Lorsch, J. W., & Morse, J. J. (1974). *Organizations and their members: A contingency approach.* New York: Harper & Row.

Lott A. J., & Lott, B. E. (1965). Group cohesiveness as interpersonal attraction: A review of relationships with antecedent and consequent variables. *Psychological Bulletin, 64,* 259–309.

Lucas, A. (1971, July 4). As American as McDonald's hamburgers on the Fourth of July. *New York Times Magazine.*

Luthans, F. (1985). *Organizational behavior* (4th ed.). New York: McGraw-Hill.

Luthans, F., & Kreitner, R. (1974, July–August). The management of behavioral contingencies. *Personnel,* 7–16.

Luthans, F., & Kreitner, R. (1975). *Organizational behavior modification.* Glenview, IL: Scott, Foresman.

Luthans, F., Paul, R., & Baker, D. (1981). An experimental analysis of the impact of a contingent reinforcement intervention on salespersons' performance behaviors. *Journal of Applied Psychology, 66,* 314–323.

Luthans, F., & Schweizer, J. (1979, September). How behavior modification techniques can improve total organizational performance. *Management Review,* 43–50.

Lyons, T (1971). Role clarity, need for clarity, satisfaction, tension and withdrawal. *Organizational Behavior and Human Performance, 6,* 99–110.

MacCrimmon, K. R., & Taylor, R. N. (1976). Decision making and problem solving. In M. D. Dunnette (Ed.), *Handbook of industrial and organizational psychology.* Chicago: Rand McNally.

Maddi, S. R. (1980). *Personality theories. A comparative analysis* (4th ed.). Homewood, IL: Dorsey.

Mahoney, T. A. (1983). Approaches to the definition of comparable worth. *Academy of Management Review, 8,* 14–22.

Mahoney, T. A., & Frost, P. J. (1974). The role of technology in models of organization effectiveness. *Organizational Behavior and Human Performance, 11,* 122–138.

Maier, N. R. F. (1967). Assets and liabilities in group problem solving: The need for an integrative function. *Psychological Review, 74,* 239–249.

Maier, N. R. F. (1970). *Problem solving and creativity in individuals and groups.* Belmont, CA: Brooks/Cole.

Maier, N. R. F. (1973). *Psychology in industrial organizations* (4th ed.). Boston: Houghton-Mifflin.

Maital, S., & Meltz, N. (Eds). (1980). *Lagging productivity growth: Causes and remedies.* Cambridge, MA: Ballinger.

Mann, F. C., & Hoffman, L. R. (1960). *Automation and the worker.* New York: Holt.

March, J. G., & Simon, H. A. (1958). *Organizations.* New York: Wiley.

Martindale, D. (1977, February). Sweaty palms in the control towers. *Psychology Today,* 71–73.

Maslow, A. H. (1954). *Motivation and personality.* New York: Harper.

Matsui, T., Okada, A., & Mizuguchi, R. (1981). Expectancy theory prediction of the goal theory postulate, "The harder the goals, the higher the performance." *Journal of Applied Psychology, 66,* 54–58.

Mayfield, E. C. (1964). The selection interview: A re-evalaution of published research. *Personnel Psychology, 17,* 239–260.

Mayfield, E. C., Brown, S. H., & Hamstra, B. W. (1980). Selection interviewing in the life insurance industry: An update of research and practice. *Personnel Psychology, 33,* 725–740.

McCall, M. W., Jr., Morrison, A. M., & Hannan, R. L. (1979). *Studies of managerial work: Results and methods* (Tech. Rep. No. 9), Center for Creative Leadership. .

McCaul, K. D., & Kopp, J. T. (1982). Effects of goal setting and commitment on increasing metal recycling. *Journal of Applied Psychology, 67,* 377–379.

McClelland, D. C., & Boyatzis, R. E. (1967). Leadership motive pattern and long-term success in management. *Journal of Applied Psychology, 67,* 737–743.

McGehee, W., & Tullar, W. L. (1978). A note on evaluating behavior modification and behavior modeling as industrial training techniques. *Personnel Psychology, 31,* 477–484.

McGlynn, R. P. (1982). A comment on the meta-analysis of goal structures. *Psychological Bulletin, 92,* 184–192.

McGrath, J. E. (1976). Stress and behavior in organizations. In M. D. Dunnette (Ed.), *Handbook of industrial and organizational psychology.* Chicago: Rand McNally, 1351–1396.

McIntyre, R. M., Smith, D. E., & Hassett, C. E. (1984). Accuracy of performance ratings as affected by rater training and perceived purpose of rating. *Journal of Applied Psychology, 69,* 147–156.

Meehl, P. E. (1965). Seer over sign: The first good example. *Journal of Experimental Research in Personality, 1,* 27–32.

Merton, R. K. (1936). The unanticipated consequences of purposive social action, *American Sociological Review, 1,* 898–904.

Merton, R. K. (1940). Bureaucratic structure and personality. *Social Forces, 18,* 560–568.

Meyer, H. E. (1975, June). How the boss stays in touch with the troops. *Fortune, 91,* 152–155.

Miles, R. H. (1980). *Macro organizational behavior.* Santa Monica, CA: Goodyear.

Miller, D. B. (1978). Career planning and management in organizations. In M. Jelinek (Ed.), *Career management for the individual and the organization.* Chicago: St. Clair, 353–360.

Miller, D., Kets de Vries, M. F. R., & Toulouse, J.-M. (1982). Top executive locus of control and its relationship to strategy-making, structure, and environment. *Academy of Management Journal, 25,* 237–253.

Miller, G. A. (1956). The magical number seven, plus or minus two. *Psychological Review, 63,* 81–97.

Miller, L. K., & Hamblin, R. L. (1963). Interdependence, differential rewarding, and productivity. *American Sociological Review, 28,* 768–777.

Mills, J., & Aronson, E. (1965). Opinion change as a function of communicator's attractiveness and desire to influence. *Journal of Personality and Social Psychology, 1,* 173–177.

Miner, F. C., Jr. (1984). Group versus individual decision making: An investigation of performance measures, decision strategies, and process losses/gains. *Organizational Behavior and Human Performance, 33,* 112–124.

Miner, J. (1980). *Theories of organizational behavior.* Hinsdale, IL: Dryden.

Miner, J. B., & Miner, M. G. (1977). *Personnel and industrial relations: A managerial approach* (rev. ed.). New York: Macmillan.

Mintzberg, H. (1973). *The nature of managerial work.* New York: Harper & Row.

Mintzberg, H. (1975, July–August). The manager's job: Folklore and fact. *Harvard Business Review,* 49–61.

Mintzberg, H. (1979). *The structuring of organizations.* Englewood Cliffs, NJ: Prentice-Hall.

Mitchell, T. R. (1982). Motivation: New directions for theory, research, and practice. *Academy of Management Review, 7,* 80–88.

Mitchell, T. R., & Kalb, L. S. (1982). Effects of job experience on supervisor attributions for a subordinate's poor performance. *Journal of Applied Psychology, 67,* 181–188.

Mitchell, T. R., Larson, J. R., Jr., & Green, S. G. (1977). Leader behavior, situational moderators, and group performance: An attributional analysis. *Organizational Behavior and Human Performance, 18,* 254–268.

Mitchell, T. R., Smyser, C. M., & Weed, S. E. (1975). Locus of control: Supervision and work satisfaction. *Academy of Management Journal, 18,* 623–631.

Mitchell, T. R., & Wood, R. E. (1980). Supervisors' responses to subordinate poor performance: A test of an attributional model. *Organizational Behavior and Human Performance, 25,* 123–138.

Mobley, W. H. (1982). Supervisor and employee race and sex effects on performance appraisals: A field study of adverse impact and generalizability. *Academy of Management Journal, 25,* 598–606.

Mobley, W. H., Griffeth, R. W., Hand, H. H., & Meglino, B. M. (1979). Review and conceptual analysis of the employee turnover process. *Psychological Bulletin, 86,* 493–522.

Mooney, J. D. (1947). *The principles of organization.* New York: Harper & Row.

Morgan, C. T., & King, R. A. (1966). *Introduction to psychology* (3rd ed.). New York: McGraw-Hill.

Morgan, M. A., Hall, D. T., & Martier, A. (1979). Career development activities in industry. *Personnel, 66.*

Morrison, A. M. (1981, January 12). The General Mills brand of managers. *Fortune,* 99–107.

Mowday, R. (1983). Equity theory predictions of behavior in organizations. In R. M. Steers & L. W. Porter (Eds.), *Motivation and work behavior* (3rd ed.). New York: McGraw-Hill.

Mowen, J. C., Middlemist, R. D., & Luther, D. (1981). Joint effects of assigned goal level and incentive structure on task performance: A laboratory study. *Journal of Applied Psychology, 66,* 598–603.

Mumford, E., & Hensall, D. (1979). *A participative approach to computer systems design.* London: Associated Business Press.

Mumford, E., & Sackman, H. (Eds.). (1975). *Human choice and computers.* Amsterdam: North Holland.

Munchus, G., III. (1983). Employer-employee based quality circles in Japan: Human resource policy implications for American firms. *Academy of Management Review, 8,* 255–261.

Murphy, K. R. (1982). Difficulties in the statistical control of halo. *Journal of Applied Psychology, 67,* 161–164.

Murphy, K. R., Garcia, M., Kerkar, S., Martin, C., & Balzer, W. K. (1982). Relationship between observational accuracy and accuracy in evaluating performance. *Journal of Applied Psychology, 67,* 320–325.

Murphy K. R., Martin, C., & Garcia, M. (1982). Do behavioral observation scales measure observation? *Journal of Applied Psychology, 67,* 562–567.

Murray, H. A. (1938). *Explorations in personality.* New York: Oxford University Press.

Myers, M. S. (1967). How attitude surveys can help you manage. *Training and Development Journal, 21,* 34–41.

Nathan, B. R., & Lord, R. G. (1983). Cognitive categorization and dimensional schemata: A process approach to the study of halo in performance ratings. *Journal of Applied Psychology, 68,* 102–114.

Naylor, J., Pritchard, R., & Ilgen, D. (1980). *A theory of behavior in organizations.* New York: Academic Press, 159–223.

Nord, W. R. (Ed.) (1976). *Concepts and controversy in organizational behavior.* Santa Monica, CA: Goodyear.

O'Day, R. (1974). Intimidation rituals: Reactions to reform. *Journal of Applied Behavioral Science, 10,* 373–386.

Oldham, G. R., & Brass, D. J. (1979). Employee reactions to an open-plan office: A naturally occurring quasi-experiment. *Administrative Science Quarterly, 24,* 267–284.

O'Reilly, C. A., & Pondy, L. R. (1979). Organizational communication. In S. Kerr (Ed.), *Organizatonal behavior.* Columbus, OH: Grid, 119–150.

Organ, D. W., & Hamner, W. C. (1982). *Organizational behavior: An applied psychological approach* (2nd ed.). Plano, TX: Business Publications.

Orth, C. D., III. (1974). How to survive the mid-career crisis. *Business Horizons, 17,* 12–18.

Osborn, A. F. (1957). *Applied imagination.* New York: Scribner.

Osburn, H. G., Timmreck, C., & Digby, D. (1981). Effect of dimensional relevance on accuracy of simulated hiring decisions by employment interviewers. *Journal of Applied Psychology, 66,* 159–165.

Ouchi, W. G, (1981). *Theory Z: How American business can meet the Japanese challenge.* Reading, MA: Addison-Wesley.

Palmore, E. (1969). Predicting longevity: A follow-up controlling for age. *The Gerontologist, 9,* 247–250.

Parsons, T. (1956). Suggestions for a sociological approach to the theory of organizations I and II. *Administrative Science Quarterly, 1,* 63–85, 225–239.

Pascale, R. T., & Athos, A. G. (1981). *The art of Japanese management: Applications for American executives.* New York: Simon & Schuster.

Payne, J. W. (1982). Contingent decision behavior. *Psychological Bulletin, 92,* 382–402.

Pecotich, A., & Churchill, G. A., Jr. (1981). An examination of the anticipated satisfaction importance valence controversy. *Organizational Behavior and Human Performance, 27,* 213–226.

Perrow, C. (1970). *Organizational analysis: A sociological view.* Belmont, CA: Wadsworth.

Peters, L. H., & O'Connor, E. J. (1980). Situational constraints and work outcomes: The influence of a frequently overlooked construct. *Academy of Management Review, 5,* 391–397.

Peters, L. H., O'Connor, E. J., & Rudolf, C. J. (1980). The behavioral and affective consequences of performance-relevant situational variables. *Organizational Behavior and Human Performance, 25,* 79–86.

Peters, T. J., & Waterman, R. H., Jr. (1982). *In search of excellence: Lessons from America's best-run companies.* New York: Harper & Row.

Peterson, R. B., & Sullivan, J. (1982). Applying Japanese management in the United States. *Journal of Contemporary Business, 11*(2), 5–15.

Pfeffer, J. (1977). Power and resource allocation in organizations. In B. Staw & G. Salancik (Eds.),

New directions in organizational behavior. Chicago: St. Clair.

Pinder, C. C. (1978). Multiple predictors of post-transfer satisfaction: The role of urban factors. *Personnel Psychology, 30,* 543–566.

Pinder, C. C. (1984). *Work motivation.* Glenview, IL: Scott, Foresman.

Pinder, C. C., & Das, H. (1979). Hidden costs and benefits of employee transfers. *Human Resource Planning, 2,* 135–145.

Podsakoff, P. M. (1982). Determinants of a supervisor's use of rewards and punishment: A literature review and suggestions for future research. *Organizational Behavior and Human Performance, 29,* 58–83.

Podsakoff, P. M., Todor, W. D., Grover, R. A., & Huber, V. L. Situational moderators of leader reward and punishment behaviors: Fact or fiction? *Organizational Behavior and Human Performance, 34,* 21–63.

Podsakoff, P. M., Todor, W. D., & Skov, R. (1982). Effects of leader contingent and noncontingent reward and punishment behaviors on subordinate performance and satisfaction. *Academy of Management Journal, 25,* 810–821.

Porter, L. W. (1961). A study of perceived need satisfaction in bottom and middle management jobs. *Journal of Applied Psychology, 45,* 1–10.

Porter, L. W., Lawler, E. E., III, & Hackman, J. R. (1975). *Behavior in organizations.* New York: McGraw-Hill.

Porter, L. W., & Steers, R. M. (1973). Organizational, work and personal factors in employee turnover and absenteeism. *Psychological Bulletin, 80,* 151–176.

Pringle, C. D., & Longenecker, J. G. (1982). The ethics of MBO. *Academy of Management Review, 7,* 305–312.

Pritchard, R. D., Hollenback, J., & DeLeo, P. J. (1980). The effects of continuous and partial schedules of reinforcement on effort, performance, and satisfaction. *Organizational Behavior and Human Performance, 25,* 336–353.

Pruitt, D. G. (1971). Indirect communication and the search for agreement in negotiations. *Journal of Applied Social Psychology, 1,* 205–239.

Pulakos, E. D. (1984). A comparison of rater training programs: Error training and accuracy training. *Journal of Applied Psychology, 69,* 581–588.

Pulakos, E. D., & Wexley, K. N. (1983). The relationship among perceptual similarity, sex, and performance ratings in manager-subordinate dyads. *Academy of Management Journal, 26,* 129–139.

Quality: The U.S. drives to catch up. (1982, November 1). *Business Week,* 66–77.

Rabbie, J. M. (1963). Differential preferences for companionship under threat. *Journal of Abnormal and Social Psychology, 67,* 643–648.

Reber, R. A., & Wallin, J. A. (1984). The effects of training, goal setting, and knowledge of results on safe behavior: A component analysis. *Academy of Management Journal, 27,* 544–560.

Rehder, R. R. (1981). What American and Japanese managers are learning from each other. *Business Horizons, 24,* 63–70.

Reich, C. (1970). *The greening of America.* New York: Random House.

Reitz, H. J. (1981). *Behavior in organizations.* Homewood, IL: Irwin.

Remick, H. (1981). The comparable worth controversy. *Public Personnel Management Journal, 10,* 371–383.

Renwick, P. A., Lawler, E. E., III, & the *Psychology Today* staff. (1978). What you really want from your job. *Psychology Today, 11,* 53–64, 118.

Rice, B. (1981, June). Can companies kill? *Psychology Today, 78,* 80–85.

Rice, R. W. (1981). Leader LPC and follower satisfaction: A review. *Organizational Behavior and Human Performance, 28,* 1–25.

Rizzo, J. R., House, R. J. & Lirtzman, S. I. (1971). Role conflict and ambiguity in complex organizations. *Administrative Science Quarterly, 15,* 150–163.

Robbins, S. P. (1978). Conflict management and conflict resolution are not synonymous terms. *California Management Review, 21,* 67–75.

Roberts, K. H., & Savage, F. (1973). Twenty questions: Utilizing job satisfaction measures. *California Management Review, 15,* 21–28.

Roe, A. (1957). Early determinants of vocational choice. *Journal of Counselling Psychology, 4,* 212–217.

Roethlisberger, F. J., & Dickson, W. J. (1939). *Management and the worker.* Cambridge, MA: Harvard University Press.

Rogers, C., & Farson, R. E. Active listening. In C. Anderson & M. J. Gannon, (Eds.), *Readings in management.* Boston: Little, Brown, 284–303.

Rosenbaum, J. E. (1979). Tournament mobility: Career patterns in a corporation. *Administrative Science Quarterly, 24,* 220–241.

Rosenberg, M. J. (1960). A structural theory of attitudes. *Public Opinion Quarterly,* 319–340.

Rosenman, R., & Friedman, M. (1971). The central nervous system and coronary heart disease. *Hospital Practice, 6,* 87–97.

Ross, L. (1977). The intuitive psychologist and his shortcomings: Distortions in the attribution process. In L. Berkowitz (Ed.), *Advances in experimental social psychology* (Vol. 10). New York: Academic Press.

Rothstein, M., & Jackson, D. N. (1980). Decision making in the employment interview: An experimental approach. *Journal of Applied Psychology, 65,* 271–283.

Rotter, J. B. (1966). Generalized expectancies for internal versus external control of reinforcement. *Psychological Monographs, 80* (609).

Ruch, L. O., & Holmes, T. H. (1971). Scaling of life change: Comparison of direct and indirect methods. *Journal of Psychosomatic Research, 11,* 213.

Rue, L. W., & Byars, L. (1980). Communication in organizations. In L. L. Cummings & R. B. Dunham (Eds.), *Introduction to organizational behavior: Text and readings.* Homewood, IL: Irwin, 556–572.

Saari, L. M., & Latham, G. P. (1982). Employee reactions to continuous and variable ratio reinforcement schedules involving a monetary incentive. *Journal of Applied Psychology, 67,* 506–508.

Salancik, G. R. (1984). A single value function for evaluating organizations with multiple constituencies. *Academy of Management Review, 9,* 617–625.

Salancik, G. R., & Pfeffer, J. (1974). The bases and uses of power in organizational decision making. *Administrative Science Quarterly, 19,* 453–473.

Sampson, E. E., & Brandon, A. C. (1964). The effects of role and opinion deviation on small group behaviour. *Sociometry, 27,* 261–281.

Sarbin, T. R., & Allen, V. L. (1968). Increasing participation in a natural group setting: A preliminary report. *The Psychological Record, 18,* 1–7.

Sawyer, J. (1966). Measurement and prediction, clinical and statistical. *Psychological Bulletin, 66,* 178–200.

Sayles, L. R. (1976). Matrix organization: The structure with a future. *Organizational Dynamics, 5*(2), 2–17.

Sayles, L. R., & Strauss, G. (1981). *Managing human resources* (2nd ed.). Englewood Cliffs, NJ: Prentice-Hall.

Scandura, T. A., & Graen, G. B. (1984). Moderating effects of initial leader-member exchange status on the effects of a leadership intervention. *Journal of Applied Psychology, 69,* 428–436.

Schachter, S., Ellerston, N., McBride, D., & Gregory, D. (1951). An experimental study of cohesiveness and productivity. *Human Relations, 4,* 229–238.

Schein, E. H. (1964). How to break in the college graduate. *Harvard Business Review, 42,* 68–76.

Schein, E. H. (1968). Organizational socialization and the profession of management. *Industrial Management Review, 9,* 1–16.

Schein, E. H. (1970). *Organizational psychology* (2nd ed.). Englewood Cliffs, NJ: Prentice-Hall.

Schein, E. H. (1978). *Career dynamics: Matching individual and organizational needs.* Reading, MA: Addison-Wesley.

Schmitt, N. (1976). Social and situational determinants of interview decisions: Implications for the employment interview. *Personnel Psychology, 29,* 79–102.

Schmitt, N., & Son, L. (1981). An evaluation of valence models of motivation to pursue various post high school alternatives. *Organizational Behavior and Human Performance, 27,* 135–150.

Schneider, B. (1978). Person-situation interaction: A review of some ability-situation interaction research. *Personnel Psychology, 31,* 281–295.

Schneider, B., Reichers, A. E., & Mitchell, T. M. (1982). A note on some relationships between the aptitude requirements and reward attributes

of tasks. *Academy of Management Journal, 25,* 567–574.

Schonberger, R. J. (1982). The transfer of Japanese manufacturing management approaches to U.S. industry. *Academy of Management Review, 7,* 479–487.

Schrank, R. (1974). On ending worker alienation: The Gaines pet food plant. In R. Fairfield (Ed.), *Humanizing the workplace.* Buffalo, NY: Prometheus Books, 119–140.

Schrank, R. (1978). *Ten thousand working days.* Cambridge, MA: MIT Press.

Schriesheim, C. A. (1978). Job satisfaction, attitudes toward unions, and voting in a union representation election. *Journal of Applied Psychology, 63,* 548–552.

Schriesheim, J. F. (1980). The social context of leader-subordinate relations: An investigation of the effects of group cohesiveness. *Journal of Applied Pscyhology, 65,* 183–194.

Schulz, G., & McKersie, R. (1973). Participation-achievement-reward systems. *Journal of Management Studies, 10,* 141–161.

Scott, K. D., & Cotter, T. (1984, March). The team that works together earns together. *Personnel Journal,* 59ff.

Scott, W. E., Jr. (1966). Activation theory and task design. *Organizational Behavior and Human Performance, 1,* 3–30.

Scott, W. E., Jr., & Erskine, J. A. (1980). The effects of variation in task design and monetary reinforcers on safe behavior. *Organizational Behavior and Human Performance, 25,* 311–335.

Seashore, S. (1954). *Group cohesiveness in the individual work group.* Ann Arbor: Institute for Social Research, University of Michigan.

Secord, P. F., & Backman, C. W. (1964). *Social psychology.* New York: McGraw-Hill.

Secord, P. F., Backman, C. W., & Slavitt, D. R. (1977). Impression formation and interaction. In B. M. Staw (Ed.). *Psychological foundations of organizational behavior.* Santa Monica, CA: Goodyear 147–157.

Selye, H. (1956). *The stress of life* (rev. ed.). New York: McGraw-Hill.

Shapiro, B. S. (1977, September–October). Can marketing and manufacturing coexist? *Harvard Business Review,* 104–114.

Shaw, M. E. (1981). *Group dynamics* (3rd ed.). New York: McGraw-Hill.

Sherif, M., & Sherif, C. W. (1953). *Groups in harmony and tension.* New York: Harper.

Sherif, M., White, B. J., & Harvey, O. J. (1955). Status in experimentally produced groups. *American Journal of Sociology, 60,* 370–379.

Simon, H. A. (1952). Comments on the theory of organization. *American Political Science Review, 46,* 1130–1139.

Simon, H. A. (1957). *Models of man.* New York: Wiley.

Simon, H. A. (1960). *The new science of management decision.* New York: Harper & Row.

Simon, H. A. (1976). *Administrative behavior* (3rd ed.). New York: The Free Press.

Simon, H. A. (1976). From substantive to procedural rationality. In S. J. Latsis (Ed.), *Method and appraisal in economics.* Cambridge, England: Cambridge University Press.

Simon, H. A. (1978). Rationality as process and as product of thought. *American Economic Review, 68,* 1–16.

Sims, H. P., Jr., & Manz, C. C. (1984). Observing leader verbal behavior: Toward reciprocal determinism in leadership theory. *Journal of Applied Psychology, 69,* 222–232.

Singh, R. (1983). Leadership style and reward allocation: Does least preferred coworker scale measure task and relation orientation? *Organizational Behavior and Human Performance, 32,* 178–197.

Singular, S. (1983, June). Moving on. *Psychology Today,* 40–47.

Sirota, D. (1959). Some effects of promotional frustration on employees' understanding of, and attitudes toward, management. *Sociometry, 22,* 273–278.

Skinner, B. F. (1953). *Science and human behavior.* New York: Macmillan.

Smith, F. J. (1977). Work attitudes as predictors of attendance on a specific day. *Journal of Applied Psychology, 62,* 16–19.

Smith, F. J., & Porter L. W. (1977). What do executives really think about their organizations? *Organizational Dynamics, 6,* 68–80.

Smith, J. E., Carson, K. P., & Alexander, R. A. (1984). Leadership: It can make a difference. *Academy of Management Journal, 27,* 765–776.

Smith, P. C., & Kendall, L. M. (1963). Retranslation of expectations: An approach to the construction of unambiguous anchors for rating scales. *Journal of Applied Psychology, 47,* 149–155.

Smith, P. C., Kendall, L. M., & Hulin, C. L. (1969). *The measurement of satisfaction in work and retirement.* Chicago: Rand McNally.

Snyder, C. A., & Luthans, F. (1982, August). Using O. B. Mod to increase hospital productivity. *Personnel Administrator,* 67–73.

Soelberg, P. (1966). Unprogrammed decision making. In *Papers and proceedings.* Academy of Management 26th Annual Meetings, San Francisco.

Spector, P. E. (1982). Behavior in organizations as a function of employees' locus of control. *Psychological Bulletin, 91,* 482–497.

Spray, S. L. (1976). *Organizational effectiveness: Theory, research and application.* Kent, OH: Kent State University Press.

Stahl, M. J., & Harrell, A. M. (1981). Modeling effort decisions with behavioral decision theory: Toward an individual differences model of expectancy theory. *Organizational Behavior and Human Performance, 27,* 303–325.

Stahl, M. J., & Harrell, A. M. (1982). Evolution and validation of a behavioral decision theory measurement approach to achievement, power, and affiliation. *Journal of Applied Psychology, 67,* 744–751.

Staw, B. M. (1980). The consequences of turnover. *Journal of Occupational Behavior, 1,* 253–273.

Staw, B. M., & Oldham, G. R. (1978). Reconsidering our dependent variables: A critique and empirical study. *Academy of Management Journal, 21,* 539–559.

Steele,, F. (1973). *Physical settings and organization development.* Reading, MA: Addison-Wesley.

Steers, R. M. (1977). *Organizational effectiveness: A behavioral view.* Santa Monica, CA: Goodyear.

Steers, R. M., & Braunstein, D. N. (1976). A behaviorally based measure of manifest needs in work settings. *Journal of Vocational Behavior, 9,* 251–266.

Steiner, I. D. (1966). Models for inferring relationships between group size and potential group productivity. *Behavioral Science, 11,* 273–283.

Stewart, R. (1967). *Managers and their jobs.* London: Macmillan.

Stewart, R. (1982). A model for understanding management jobs and behavior. *Academy of Management Review, 7,* 7–13.

Stogdill, R. M. (1948). Personal factors associated with leadership: A survey of the literature. *Journal of Psychology, 25,* 35–71.

Stogdill, R. M. (1974). *Handbook of leadership: A survey of theory and research.* New York: Free Press.

Stopford, J. M., & Wells, L. T., Jr. (1972). *Managing the multinational enterprise: Organization of the firm and ownership of subsidiaries.* New York: Basic Books.

Strauss, G. (1964). Work flow frictions, interfunctional rivalry, and professionalism: A case study of purchasing agents. *Human Organization, 23,* 137–149.

Strauss, G., & Sayles, L. R. (1980). *Behavioral strategies for managers.* Englewood Cliffs, NJ: Prentice-Hall.

Strube, M. J., & Garcia, J. E. (1981). A meta-analytic investigation of Fiedler's contingency model of leadership effectiveness. *Psychological Bulletin, 90,* 307–321.

Sugimoto, Y., & Mouer, R. (1982). *Do the Japanese fit their stereotype?* Tokyo: Tooyoo Keizai.

Sullivan, J. J. (1983). A critique of theory Z. *Academy of Management Review, 8,* 132–142.

Sutton, H., & Porter, L. W. (1968). A study of the grapevine in a governmental organization. *Personnel Psychology, 21,* 223–230.

Tagiuri, R. (1965). Value orientations and relationships of managers and scientists. *Administrative Science Quarterly, 10,* 39–51.

Taylor, D. W., Berry, P. C., & Block, C. H. (1958). Does group participation when using brainstorming facilitate or inhibit creative thinking? *Administrative Science Quarterly, 3,* 23–47.

Taylor, F. W. (1911). *The principles of scientific management.* New York: Harper.

Terborg, J. R. (1981). Interactional psychology and research on human behavior in organizations. *Academy of Management Review, 6,* 569–576.

Terborg, J. R., Richardson, P., & Pritchard, R. D. (1980). Person-situation effects in the prediction of performance: An investigation of ability, self-esteem, and reward contingencies. *Journal of Applied Psychology, 65,* 574–583.

Terkel, S. (1974) *Working.* New York: Pantheon Books.

Thomas, K. W. (1977). Toward multidimensional values in teaching: The example of conflict behaviors. *Academy of Management Review, 2,* 484–490.

Thomsen, D. J. (1980). *Comparable worth analysis.* Pacific Palisades, CA: The Compensation Institute.

Thompson, J. D. (1967). *Organizations in action.* New York: McGraw-Hill.

Thompson, V. (1961). *Modern organizations.* New York: Knopf.

Thurstone, L. C. (1938). Primary mental abilities. *Psychometric Monographs, 4.*

The tightening squeeze on white collar pay. *Business Week* (September 12, 1977), 82–94.

Tjosvold, D. (1984). Effects of leader warmth and directiveness on subordinate performance on a subsequent task. *Journal of Applied Psychology, 69,* 422–427.

Tjosvold, D., & Field, R. H. G. (1983). Effects of social context on consensus and majority vote decision making. *Academy of Management Journal, 26,* 500–506.

Tosi, H. L., Jr., Rizzo, J. R., & Carroll, S. J., Jr. (1970). Setting goals in management by objectives. *California Management Review, 12*(4), 70–78.

Treiman, D. J., & Hartmann, H. I. (Eds.) (1981). *Women, work and wages.* Washington, D.C.: National Academy of Sciences, National Research Council, Committee on Occupation Classification and Analysis, Assembly of Behavioral and Social Sciences.

Treiman, D. J. (1979). *Job evaluation: An analytic review.* Washington, D.C: National Academy of Sciences, National Research Council, Committee on Occupational Classification and Analysis, Assembly of Behavioral and Social Sciences.

Triandis, H. C. (1971). *Attitudes and attitude changes.* New York: Wiley.

Trist, E. L. (1981). The evolution of sociotechnical systems. In A. Van de Ven & R. Joyce (Eds.), *Organization design and performance.* New York: Wiley.

Ungson, G. R., & Steers, R. M. (1984). Motivation and politics in executive compensation. *Academy of Management Review, 9,* 313–323.

Urwick, L. (1944). *The elements of administration.* New York: Harper and Row.

Valenzi, E. R., & Andrews, I. R. (1973). Individual differences in the decision process of employment interviewers. *Journal of Applied Psychology, 58,* 49–53.

Valliant, G. E. (1977). *Adaptation to life.* Boston: Little, Brown.

Van de Ven, A. H., & Delbecq, A. (1974). The effectiveness of nominal, Delphi, and interaction group decision-making processes. *Academy of Management Journal, 17,* 605–632.

Van de Ven, A. H., Delbecq, A. L. & Koenig, R. (1976). Determinants of coordination modes within organizations. *American Sociological Review, 41,* 322–338.

Van Maanen, J. (1976). Breaking in: Socialization to work. In R. Dubin (Ed.), *Handbook of work, organization, and society.* Chicago: Rand McNally.

Van Maanen, J., & Schein, E. H. (1977). Career development. In J. R. Hackman & J. L. Suttle (Eds.), *Improving life at work,* Santa Monica, CA: Goodyear.

Vaughan, R. (1975). *The spoiled system.* Center for the Study of Responsive Law.

Vecchio, R. P. (1977). An empirical examination of the validity of Fiedler's model of leadership effectiveness. *Organizational Behavior and Human Performance, 19,* 180–206.

Vecchio, R. P. (1982). A further test of leadership effects due to between-group variation and within-group variation. *Journal of Applied Psychology, 67,* 200–208.

Vecchio, R. P. (1982). Predicting worker performance in inequitable settings. *Academy of Management Review, 7,* 103–110.

Vecchio, R. P. (1984). Models of psychological inequity. *Organizational Behavior and Human Performance, 34,* 266–282.

Vecchio, R. P., & Gobdel, B. C. (1984). The vertical dyad linkage model of leadership: Problems and prospects. *Organizational Behavior and Human Performance, 34,* 5–20.

Vogel, A. (1967, May–June). Why don't employees speak up? *Personnel Administration, 30,* 20–22.

Vogel, E. (1979). *Japan as number one: Lessons for America.* Cambridge, MA: Harvard University Press.

Vroom, V. H. (1964). *Work and motivation.* New York: Wiley.

Vroom, V. H. (1966). Occupational choice: A study of pre-and post-decision processes. *Organizational Behavior and Human Performance, 1,* 212–225.

Vroom, V. H., Grant, L., & Cotton, T. (1969). The consequences of social interaction in group problem solving. *Organizational Behavior and Human Performance, 4,* 75–95.

Vroom, V. H., Grant, L., & Cotton, T. (1969). The consequences of social interaction in group problem solving. *Organizational Behavior and Human Performance, 4,* 75–95.

Vroom, V. H. & Jago, A. G. (1978). On the validity of the Vroom-Yetton model. *Journal of Applied Psychology, 63,* 151–162.

Vroom, V. H., & Mann, F. C. (1960). Leader authoritarianism and employee attitudes. *Personnel Psychology, 13,* 125–140.

Vroom, V. H., & Yetton, P. W. (1973). *Leadership and decision-making.* Pittsburgh, PA: University of Pittsburgh Press.

Wahba, M. A., & Bridwell, L. G. (1976). Maslow reconsidered: A review of research on the need hierarchy theory. *Organizational Behavior and Human Performance, 15,* 212–240.

Walker, C. R. (1950). The problem of the repetitive job. *Harvard Business Review, 28,* 54–58.

Walker, C. R., & Guest, R. H. (1952). *The man on the assembly line.* Cambridge, MA: Harvard University Press.

Walker, J., & Marriott, R. (1951). A study of some attitudes to factory work. *Occupational Psychology, 25,* 181–191.

Wallace, M. J., & Szilagyi, A. D., Jr. (1982). *Managing behavior in organizations.* Glenview, IL: Scott, Foresman.

Walton, R. E. (1972, November–December). How to counter alienation in the plant. *Harvard Business Review, 50,* 70–81.

Walton, R. E. (1975). From Hawthorne to Topeka and Kalmar. In E. L. Cass & F. G. Zimmer (Eds.), *Man and work in society.* New York: Van Nostrand Reinhold.

Walton, R. E. (1977). Work innovations at Topeka: After six years. *Journal of Applied Behavioral Science, 13,* 422–433.

Walton, R. E. (1982). Social choice in the development of advanced information technology. In H. F. Kolodny & H. Van Beinum (Eds.), *The quality of working life and the 1980's.* New York: Praeger.

Walton, R. E., & McKersie, R. B. (1965). *A behavioral theory of labor negotiations: An analysis of a social interaction system.* New York: McGraw-Hill.

Wanous, J. P. (1981). *Organizational entry.* Reading, MA: Addison-Wesley.

Ward, L. B. & Athos, A. G. (1972). *Student expectations of corporate life.* Boston: Division of Research, Graduate School of Business Administration, Harvard University.

Warr, P., & Parry, G. (1982). Paid employment and women's psychological well-being. *Psychological Bulletin, 91,* 498–516.

Watson, K. M. (1982). An analysis of communication patterns: A method for discriminating leader and subordinate roles. *Academy of Management Journal, 25,* 107–120.

Weaver, C. N. (1980). Job satisfaction in the United States in the 1970's. *Journal of Applied Psychology, 65,* 364–367.

Webber, R. A. (1976). Career problems of young managers. *California Management Review, 18,* 11–33.

Weber, M. (1947). *The theory of social and economic organization* (A. M. Henderson & T. Parsons, Trans. & Eds.). Glencoe, IL: Free Press.

Webster, E. C. (1964). *Decision making in the employment interview.* Montreal: Industrial Relations Center, McGill University.

Weisbord, M. R. (1973). The organization development contract. *OD Practitioner, 5*(2), 1–4.

Weiss, D. J., Dawis, R. V., England, G. W., & Lofquist, L. H. (1967). *Manual for the Minnesota Satisfaction Questionnaire* (Minnesota Studies in vocational rehabilitation No. 22). Minneapolis: University of Minnesota Industrial Relations Center.

Weissenberg, D., & Kavanaugh, M. H. (1972). The independence of initiating structure and

consideration: A review of the evidence. *Personnel Psychology, 25,* 119–130.

Weitz, J. (1956). Job expectancy and survival. *Journal of Applied Psychology, 40,* 245–247.

Werther, W. B., Jr. (1982). Quality circles: Key executive issues. *Journal of Contemporary Business, 11*(2), 17–26.

Wexley, K. N., & Pulakos, E. D. (1982). Sex effects on performance ratings in manager-subordinate dyads: A field study. *Journal of Applied Psychology, 67,* 433–439.

Wexley, K. N., & Pulakos, E. D. (1983). The effects of perceptual congruence and sex on subordinates, performance appraisals of their managers. *Academy of Management Journal, 26,* 666–676.

Wexley, K. N., & Yukl, G. A. (1977). *Organizational behavior and personnel psychology.* Homewood, IL: Irwin.

White, J. K. (1979). The Scanlon plan: Causes and correlates of success. *Academy of Management Journal, 22,* 292–312.

Whitsett, D. A., & Winslow, E. K. (1967). An analysis of studies critical of the motivator-hygiene theory. *Personnel Psychology, 20,* 391–415.

Who's excellent now? (1984, November 5). *Business Week.*

Whyte, W. F. (1955). *Money and motivation.* New York: Harper.

Whyte, W. H., Jr. (1957). *The organization man.* Garden City, NY: Doubleday Anchor Books.

Wiggins, J. A., Dill, F., & Schwartz, R. D. (1965). On status-liability. *Sociometry, 28,* 197–209.

Winn, A. (1968, September). *The laboratory approach to organizational development: A tentative model of planned change.* Paper read at the Annual Conference of the British Psychological Society, Oxford, and cited in R. T. Golembiewski, Organizational development in public agencies: Perspectives on theory and practice, *Public Administration Review.*

Winton, D. G., & Sutherland, C. R. (1982). A performance-based approach to determining executive incentive bonus awards. *Compensation Review, 1,* 1–26.

Woodward, J. (1965). *Industrial organization: Theory and practice.* London: Oxford University Press.

Wright, O. R., Jr. (1969). Summary of research on the selection interview since 1964. *Personnel Psychology, 22,* 391–413.

Yates, J. F., & Goldstein, W. M. (1983). Personal decision aiding: Some observations about the Beach birth-planning procedure. *Organizational Behavior and Human Performance, 31,* 26–46.

Yetton, P., & Bottger, P. (1982). Individual versus group problem solving: An empirical test of a best-member strategy. *Organizational Behavior and Human Performance, 29,* 307–321.

Yetton, P., & Bottger, P. (1983). The relationships among group size, member ability, social decision schemes, and performance. *Organizational Behavior and Human Performance, 32,* 145–159.

Yorks, L., & Whitsett, D. A. (1985). Hawthorne, Topeka, and the issue of science versus advocacy in organizational behavior. *Academy of Management Review, 10,* 21–30.

Yukl, G. A. (1971). Toward a behavioral theory of leadership. *Organizational Behavior and Human Performance, 6,* 414–440.

Yukl, G. A. (1981). *Leadership in organizations.* Englewood Cliffs, NJ: Prentice-Hall.

Zahn, G. L., & Wolf, G. (1981). Leadership and the art of cycle maintenance: A simulation model of superior-subordinate interaction. *Organizational Behavior and Human Performance, 28,* 26–49.

Zajonc, R. B. (1965). Social facilitation. *Science, 149,* 269–273.

Zammuto, R. F. (1982). *Assessing organizational effectiveness.* Albany, NY: State University of New York Press.

Zammutto, R. F. (1984). A comparison of multiple models of organizational effectiveness. *Academy of Management Review, 9,* 606–616.

Zedeck, S., & Cascio, W. F. (1982). Performance appraisal decisions as a function of rater training and purpose of the appraisal. *Journal of Applied Psychology, 67,* 752–758.

Zimbardo, P. G., Ebbesen, E. B., & Maslach, C. (1977). *Influencing attitudes and changing behavior* (2nd ed.). Reading MA: Addison-Wesley.

Zwerman, W. L. (1970), *New perspectives in organization theory.* Westport, CT: Greenwood.

Indexes

Name Index

Adams, J. S., 80
Adorno, T., 49
Albrecht, K., 483, 484
Alderfer, C. P., 47, 79, 236, 237
Aldrich, H. E., 19, 301
Alexander, R. A., 148
Allen, T. J., 421
Allen, V. L., 206
Altman, S., 178
Alvarez, R. A., 150, 208, 337
Anderson, C. R., 49
Anderson, L. R., 422
Andrews, I. R., 455
Andrews, J., 89
Annas, J. W., 366
Argyris, C., 299
Arnold, H. J., 80, 114, 364, 454
Aronson, E., 178–179, 206
Arvey, R. D., 455
Ash, R. A., 338
Ashford, S. J., 338
Ashour, A. S., 148
Athanassiades, J., 177
Athos, A. G., 366, 454, 455
Atkinson, J. W., 79

Back, K., 206
Backman, C. W., 48, 178
Baetz, M., 50, 148, 150
Baker, D., 83
Bales, R. F., 207
Balzer, W. K., 335
Bannister, B. D., 336

Barnes-Farrell, J., 334, 335
Barnowe, J. T., 113, 114
Barrett, G. V., 365
Barrett, R. S., 456
Bartley, S. H., 48
Barwick, K. D., 83
Bass, A. R., 336
Bass, B. M., 148
Bazerman, M. H., 334
Beach, D. S., 456, 575
Beach, L. R., 421
Beatty, R. W., 337
Beekun, R. I., 334
Benson, H., 485
Bernardin, H. J., 335–337
Berry, P. C., 422
Bettleheim, B., 485
Birnbaum, M. H., 80
Bittel, L., 168, 178
Blake, R. R., 237, 238
Blank, W., 50
Blau, P. M., 299
Blencoe, A. G., 338
Block, C. H., 422
Boas, M., 275
Bobko, P., 48, 81, 82
Borman, W. C., 336
Bottger, P., 421
Bouchard, T. J., 422
Boyatzis, R. E., 148
Brandon, A. C., 208
Brass, D. J., 49
Braunstein, D., 79
Bray, D. W., 457

Breaugh, J. A., 114, 364
Brett, J. M., 114, 116, 207, 483–485, 575, 576
Bridwell, L. G., 79
Brief, A. P., 483
Brown, S. H., 456
Bruner, J. S., 178
Buckley, M. R., 336
Buckner, E., 82
Burke, R. J., 484
Burke, W. W., 238
Burnaska, R. G., 336
Burns, T., 287, 288, 300, 301
Burtt, H. E., 113
Byars, L., 179
Byham, W. C., 457
Byrne, D., 49

Cage, J. H., 151
Calder, B. J., 152
Cameron, K. S., 18
Campbell, D. T., 237
Campbell, F. L., 421
Campbell, J. P., 393, 422
Campbell, M. P., 47
Campbell, R. J., 457
Caplan, R. D., 483, 484
Carlson, R. C., 455, 456
Carroll, D. T., 517
Carroll, S. J., Jr., 82, 334, 337
Carroll, V., 483
Carson, K. P., 148
Cascio, W. F., 336

Cederblom, D., 338
Chacko, T. I., 81
Chadwick-Jones, J. K., 114
Chain, S., 275
Chandler, A. A., Jr., 248–249, 269
Chapple, E., 238
Chemers, M. M., 150
Cherns, A. B., 515
Cherrington, D. J., 114
Child, J., 299–300
Choran, I., 19
Clausen, J. A., 454
Cleveland, J. N., 334
Coch, L., 113
Cockrum, R. B., 366
Cohen, P., 554, 575
Collaras, P. A., 422
Connolly, W. B., 455
Cook, D., 338
Cook, M. S., 364
Cooper, C. L., 484
Cooper, E. A., 365
Cooper, W. H., 334
Cosier, R. A., 81
Costa, P. T., Jr., 80
Cotter, T., 365
Cotton, J. L., 364
Cotton, T., 422
Craig, J. R., 151
Cranny, C. J., 337
Crozier, M., 237
Cummings, L. L., 337–338
Cyert, R., 420
Czaczkes, J. W., 483

Daft, R. L., 269, 299–301
Dalkey, N., 423
Dalton, D. R., 81
Dalton, G. W., 548, 576
Dalton, M., 206, 236
Dansereau, F., Jr., 149
Das, H., 576
Davis, K., 177
Davis, L. E., 515
Davis, S. M., 270
Davis, T. R., 49
Dawes, R. M., 455
Dawis, R. V., 115
Delbecq, A. L., 300, 422, 423
DeLeo, P. J., 83
Denisi, A. S., 151, 336, 338
Dentler, R. A., 207, 208
DePontbriand, 339

Dessler, G., 150
Deutsch, M., 236
Dickson, W. J., 207
Digby, D., 456
Dill, F., 208
Dion, K. L., 206
Dipboye, R. L., 334, 339
Dossett, D. L., 48
Dowrich, P. W., 82
Dreher, G. F., 47
Dreyfuss, F., 483
Driscoll, J. W., 365
Drory, A., 148
Drucker, P., 299
Duchon, D., 81
Duncan, R. B., 238, 269, 270, 300
Dunham, R. B., 115, 116
Dunnette, M. D., 47, 48, 334, 393, 422, 443, 455, 456

Ebbesen, E. B., 178, 179
Eden, D., 79, 81, 148
Elizur, D., 47
Ellertson, N., 206
Emery, F. E., 515
England, G. W., 115
Erez, M., 82
Erikson, E. H., 549
Erikson, K. T., 207, 208
Erskine, J. A., 83
Etzioni, A., 18
Evans, M. G., 130, 150

Fallows, J., 191, 207, 299
Farr, J. L., 336
Farris, G. F., 151
Farson, R. E., 178
Fay, C. H., 335, 337
Fayol, H., 299
Fein, M., 393
Feldman, D. C., 114, 207, 237, 335, 454, 455, 483–485, 553, 555, 575, 576
Festinger, L., 206
Fiedler, F. E., 127, 149, 150
Field, R. H. G., 151, 422
Filley, A. C., 237
Finkle, R. B., 456
Fitch, H. G., 83
Fleishman, E. A., 48, 113, 149
Flory, A., III, 338
Flowers, V. S., 47

Folkman, S., 485
Ford, J. D., 18, 152
Frederick, E., 48, 81, 82
Frederickson, J. W., 152
French, J. R. P., Jr., 113, 148, 338, 483, 484
Friedman, A., 80
Friedman, M., 473, 483–485
Frost, P. J., 300
Fusilier, M. R., 80

Gaertner, G. H., 18
Galbraith, J. R., 238, 269, 270, 282, 283, 300
Gannon, M. J., 114
Ganster, D. C., 80
Garcia, J. E., 150
Garcia, M., 335, 337
Garland, H., 47, 79, 82
Gellerman, S. W., 456
Getman, J. G., 114
Ghiselli, E. E., 48–49, 456
Ghorpade, J., 338
Gibb, J., 338
Gibbs, J., 178
Gilbreth, F. B., 113
Gilbreth, L. M., 113
Glaser, B. G., 454
Glass, A., 177
Glass, D. C., 207
Glueck, W. F., 337, 365, 366
Gluskinos, U. M., 148
Gobb, S., 485
Gobdel, B. C., 149
Goffman, E., 207
Goldberg, P., 486
Goldberg, S. B., 114
Goldman, M., 236
Goldstein, W. M., 421
Golembiewski, R. T., 206
Gomersall, E. R., 575
Goodman, P. S., 18, 80, 113
Gottier, R. F., 456
Gough, H. G., 49
Gouldner, A. W., 299
Graen, G. B., 148–150
Grant, D. L., 457
Grant, L., 422
Green, S. G., 50, 152
Greenberg, J. S., 80
Greene, C. N., 152
Gregory, D., 206
Griffeth, R. W., 364

Grover, R. A., 151
Grunes, W. F., 178
Guest, R. H., 113
Guilford, J. P., 48
Guion, R. M., 456
Gustafson, G. H., 423
Guzzo, R. A., 422
Gyllenhammar, P., 515

Hackman, J. R., 18, 206, 208, 334, 393, 394
Haga, W. J., 149
Haire, M., 178
Hakel, M. D., 393
Hall, D. T., 454, 455, 575–577
Hall, E. T., 177
Hall, R. H., 299
Hall, T., 106, 116
Hamblin, R. L., 236
Hammer, T. H., 364
Hammond, L. K., 236
Hamner, E. P., 83
Hamner, W. C., 83, 114, 484, 485
Hamstra, B. W., 456
Hand, H. H., 364
Haney, W. V., 177
Hannan, R. L., 19
Harrell, A. M., 47, 79, 80
Harris, E. F., 113, 149
Harrison, E. F., 422
Hartmann, H. I., 365
Harvey, E., 300
Harvey, O. J., 421, 422
Harvey, R. H., 334
Hassett, C. E., 335
Hatvany, N., 516
Hayes, R. H., 516
Haynes, R. S., 83
Heilman, M. E., 151
Heinzmann, A. T., 83
Henchy, T., 207
Heneman, R. L., 335
Hensall, D., 515
Herker, D., 301
Herline, G. E., 394
Herman, J. B., 114
Herschlag, J. K., 151
Herzberg, F., 393
Hickson, D. J., 300
Hill, W., 149
Hinton, B. L., 393
Hodgetts, R. M., 178
Hoel, W., 148

Hoffman, L. R., 113, 421
Holland, J. L., 47, 429, 430, 454
Hollander, E. P., 208
Hollenback, J., 83
Hollman, T. D., 336
Holmes, T. H., 466, 467, 484
Hom, P. W., 336
Hood, M., 82
Hornstein, H. A., 151
House, R. J., 39, 50, 130, 148, 150, 393, 483
Howard, A., 457
Hoy, S., 115
Huber, V. L., 151
Hulin, C. L., 115, 335
Hulvershorn, P., 48
Hunter, J. E., 48
Hunter, R. F., 48

Ilgen, D. R., 79, 80, 152
Imada, A. S., 338
Ivancevich, J. M., 81, 82, 335, 336, 338, 483, 486

Jaastad, K., 422
Jackson, D. N., 49, 456
Jackson, J., 207
Jackson, S. E., 81, 422
Jacobs, R., 336
Jago, A. G., 81, 151
Jamieson, B. D., 337
Janis, I. L., 420, 422, 454, 455
Janz, T., 79
Jelinek, M., 269, 300
Jenkins, G. D., 394
Jewell, L. N., 236, 423
Johnson, D. W., 364, 365
Johnson, R. T., 364, 365

Kafry, D., 336
Kahn, R. L., 484
Kalb, L. S., 152
Kane, J. S., 337
Kanfer, F. H., 82
Kasl, S., 485
Katterberg, R., 115
Katz, D., 484
Kavanaugh, M. H., 148
Kawada, H., 516
Kay, E., 338
Kelley, H. H., 335

Kelley, K., 49
Kelley, M., 18
Kendall, L. M., 115, 336
Kenny, D. A., 148
Kerkar, S., 335
Kerr, S., 149
Kets de Vries, M. F. R., 49
Keys, J. B., 516
Kidder, J. T., 184, 206
Kim, J. S., 47, 81
King, N. A., 393
King, R. A., 179
Kingdon, D. R., 270
Kingstrom, P. O., 336
Kinicki, A. J., 336
Klein, N. M., 420
Knight, K., 270
Knowlton, W. A., Jr., 152, 335
Koenig, R., 300
Kolodny, H. F., 270, 515
Komaki, J., 83
Kopp, J. T., 81
Kotter, J. P., 301, 454, 575
Kreitner, R., 83
Kuna, D., 485
Kurke, L. B., 19

Lackritz, J. R., 338
Lakein, A., 485
Landau, J. C., 364
Landsberger, H. A., 269
Landy, F. J., 334–336
Larson, J. R., Jr., 152, 338
Latham, G. P., 48, 81–83, 335–337
Lawler, E. E., III, 18, 28, 47, 50, 79, 91, 93, 113, 114, 177, 334, 365, 393, 394
Lawrence, P. R., 236–238, 270, 289, 290, 301
Lawson, L., 83
Lazarus, R. H., 484, 485
Lazarus, R. S., 485
Lee, C., 48, 81
León, F. R., 80
Levine, E. L., 338
LeVine, R. A., 237
Levine, S. B., 516
Levinson, D. J., 549
Levinson, H., 576
Levy, R., 299
Lewin, A., 337
Lewis, P. V., 178
Liden, R. C., 50, 148, 149, 335

Likert, R., 177
Lim, F. G., Jr., 151
Lindblom, C. E., 421
Lirtzman, S. I., 483
Litterer, J. A., 269, 300
Litwin, G. H., 79
Livernash, E. R., 365
Locher, A. H., 334
Locke, E. A., 48, 81, 82, 113, 114
Lofquist, L. H., 115
London, M., 19
Longenecker, J. G., 82
Longworth, R. C., 115
Lord, R. G., 334
Lorsch, J. W., 236–238, 289, 290, 301
Lott, A. J., 206
Lott, B. E., 206
Lounsbury, J. W., 338
Love, K. G., 338
Lowen, A., 151
Lucas, A., 275
Luthans, F., 83, 177, 178, 299
Luther, D., 80, 82
Lyons, T., 485

McBride, D., 206
McCall, M. W., Jr., 19
McCaul, K. D., 81
McClelland, D. S., 148
McCrae, R. R., 47
MacCrimmon, K. R., 420
McElroy, J. C., 81
McGehee, W., 83
McGlynn, R. P., 365
McGrath, J. E., 471, 485
McIntyre, R. M., 335
McKersie, R. B., 238, 365
McMahon, J. T., 81
Maddi, S. R., 49
Mahoney, T. A., 300, 365
Mai-Dalton, R. R., 47
Maier, N. R. F., 49, 421, 422
Maital, S., 515
Mangione, T. W., 113, 114
Mann, F. C., 113, 114
Mann, L., 420, 454, 455, 485
Mansfield, R., 300
Manz, C. C., 152
March, J. G., 18, 420
March, J. J., 299
Marquis, D. G., 421
Marriott, R., 113, 114
Marshall, J., 484

Martella, J. A., 150
Martier, A., 576
Martin, C., 335, 337
Martindale, D., 483
Maruyama, G., 364, 365
Maslach, C., 178, 179
Maslow, A. H., 47, 52, 53, 79
Matsui, T., 80
Matteson, M. T., 483, 486
Mayfield, E. C., 455, 456
Meehl, P. E., 455
Meglino, B. M., 364
Meltz, N., 515
Merton, R. K., 236, 299
Meyer, H. E., 158, 177, 338
Middlemist, R. D., 80, 82
Miles, R. E., 269, 300
Miles, R. H., 269, 300
Miller, D. B., 49, 567, 576
Miller, G. A., 420
Miller, L. K., 236
Miller, T. R., 516
Mills, J., 178
Miner, F. C., Jr., 421
Miner, J. B., 79, 456
Miner, M. G., 456
Mintzberg, H., 18, 19, 50, 177, 269, 270, 300, 420
Mitchell, T. M., 48
Mitchell, T. R., 49, 79, 150–152, 335
Mizuguchi, R., 80
Mobley, W. H., 334, 364
Mooney, J. D., 299
Morgan, C. T., 179
Morgan, M. A., 576
Morrison, A. M., 19, 270
Morse, J. J., 289, 290, 301
Mouer, R., 516
Mouton, J. S., 237, 238
Mowan, J. C., 80, 82
Mowday, R., 81
Mumford, E., 515
Munchus, G., III, 516
Murphy, K. R., 335, 337
Murray, H. A., 47, 79
Myers, M. S., 115, 575

Nathan, B. R., 334
Naylor, J. G., 48
Nebeker, D. M., 80
Neikirk, B., 115
Nelson, D., 364

Noon, J. P., 114
Nord, W. R., 48

O'Connor, J. B., 334
O'Day, R., 197, 207
Okada, A., 80
Oldham, G. R., 49, 364, 393, 394
O'Reilly, C. A., 179
Organ, D. W., 484, 485
Ornstein, S., 80
Orris, J. B., 150
Orth, C. D., III, 576, 577
Osborn, A. F., 422
Osburn, H. G., 456
Ouchi, W. G., 516

Palmore, E., 484
Parry, G., 515
Parsons, T., 18
Pascale, R. T., 516
Paul, R., 83
Paumonen, S. V., 49
Payne, J. W., 423
Payne, R., 484
Pecotich, A., 80
Pence, E. G., 336
Pennings, J. M., 18
Perrow, C., 300
Peters, L. H., 334
Peters, T. J., 517
Peterson, D. A., 455, 456
Peterson, R. B., 516
Pfeffer, J., 237
Pheysey, D. C., 300
Pinder, C. C., 47, 80, 484, 576
Pine, R. C., 83
Podsakoff, P. M., 150, 151
Pondy, L. R., 179
Porter, L. W., 18, 81, 93, 102, 114–116, 177, 334, 364, 393
Price, R. L., 548, 576
Pringle, C. D., 82
Pritchard, R. D., 49, 79, 80, 83
Pruitt, D. C., 237
Pucik, V., 516
Pugh, D. S., 300
Pulakos, C. D., 334, 336–338
Pursell, E. D., 336

Quinn, R. P., 113, 114, 483

Rabbie, J. M., 207
Rahe, R. H., 466, 467, 484
Ramnarayan, S., 18
Randolph, W. A., 338
Raven, B., 148
Ravid, G., 79, 81
Raynor, J. O., 79
Reber, R. A., 82
Rehder, R. R., 516
Reich, C., 454
Reichers, A. E., 48
Reitz, H. J., 113, 114, 152, 236, 421, 423
Remick, H., 365
Renwick, P. A., 114
Rice, B., 483, 484, 486
Rice, R. W., 150
Richardson, P., 49
Rizzo, J. R., 82, 334, 337, 483
Robbins, S. P., 236
Roberts, K. H., 115
Roe, A., 454
Roethlisberger, F. J., 207
Rogers, C., 178
Rosenbaum, J. E., 576
Rosenberg, M. J., 47
Rosenman, R. H., 473, 483–485
Rosenthal, R. A., 483
Ross, L., 335
Rothstein, M., 456
Rotter, J. B., 49
Ruch, L. O., 466, 467, 484
Rudolf, C. J., 334
Rue, L. W., 179
Runyon, K. E., 151

Saari, L. M., 81–83, 337
Sackman, H., 515
Salancik, G. R., 18, 237
Sampson, E. E., 208
Sarbin, T. R., 206
Savage, F., 115
Sawyer, J., 455
Sayles, L. R., 164, 178, 179, 238, 270
Scandura, T. A., 149
Schachter, S., 206
Schein, E. H., 18, 548, 575
Schellenberg, D. A., 18
Schmitt, N., 80, 455
Schneider, B., 48, 49
Schneier, C. E., 337
Schonberger, R. J., 516
Schoorman, F. D., 334

Schrank, R., 186, 206, 394
Schriesheim, C. A., 114, 149, 151
Schriesheim, J. F., 149
Schuler, R. S., 483
Schulz, G., 365
Schwab, D. P., 337
Schwartz, R. D., 208
Scott, K. D., 365
Scott, L. R., 83
Scott, W. E., Jr., 83, 113, 114
Seashore, S., 206
Secord, P. F., 48, 178
Selye, H., 483
Shani, A. B., 148
Shapiro, B. S., 216, 236
Shaw, K. N., 81
Shaw, M. E., 206, 207, 421, 422
Shepard, H. A., 238
Sherif, C. W., 236, 237
Sherif, M., 236, 237, 422
Simon, H. A., 18, 299, 420, 421, 454
Sims, H. P., Jr., 152
Singh, R., 150
Singular, S., 576
Sirota, D., 113
Skinner, B. F., 68, 82
Skon, L., 364
Skov, R., 151
Skrzypek, G. J., 150
Slater, P. E., 207
Slavitt, D. R., 178
Smith, D. E., 335
Smith, F. J., 114–116
Smith, J. E., 148
Smith, P. C., 115, 336
Smith, S. V., 82
Smyser, C. M., 49, 151
Snoek, J. D., 483
Snyder, C. A., 84
Soelberg, P. O., 454
Son, L., 80
Spector, P. E., 49
Spray, S. L., 18
Stahl, M. J., 47, 79, 80
Stalker, G. M., 287, 288, 300, 301
Staw, B. M., 364
Steele, F., 49
Steele, T. P., 81
Steers, R. M., 18, 79, 81, 364
Steiner, I. D., 188, 206, 207
Stewart, R., 19, 420
Stogdill, R. M., 148, 149
Stopford, J. M., 270
Strauss, G., 164, 178, 179, 236

Stringer, R. A., Jr., 79
Strube, M. J., 150
Sugimoto, Y., 516
Sullivan, J. J., 516
Sutherland, C. R., 364
Sutton, H., 177
Szilagyi, A. D., 207, 269

Tagiuri, R., 47, 178
Taylor, D. W., 422
Taylor, F. W., 47, 81
Taylor, R. N., 420
Teel, K. S., 334
Tennenbaum, A., 177
Terborg, J. R., 49
Terkel, S., 87, 113, 465, 484
Thayer, P. W., 455, 456
Thomas, K. W., 237
Thompson, J. D., 300
Thompson, P. H., 548, 576
Thompson, V., 299
Thomsen, D. J., 365
Thurstone, L. C., 48
Timmreck, C., 456
Tjosvold, D., 149, 422
Todor, W. D., 151
Tosi, H. L., Jr., 82, 334, 337
Toulouse, J.-M., 49
Townes, D. B., 421
Treiman, D. J., 365
Triandis, H. C., 178
Trist, E. L., 515
Tullar, W. L., 83

Ungson, G. R., 364
Urwick, L., 299

Valenzi, E. R., 455
Valiant, G. E., 549
Van Beinum, H., 515
Vance, R. J., 335
Van de Ven, A. H., 300, 422, 423
Van Maanen, J., 548, 575
Van Sell, M., 483
Vaughan, R., 275, 299
Vecchio, R. P., 80, 81, 149, 150
Vogel, A., 177
Vogel, E., 516
Von Glinow, M. A., 151
Vroom, V. H., 47, 79, 113, 114, 133, 149, 151, 364, 422, 454

Wahba, M. A., 79
Walker, C. R., 113, 393
Walker, J., 113, 114
Wallace, M. J., 207, 269
Wallin, J. A., 82
Walter, C. S., 335
Walton, R. E., 238, 394, 515
Wanous, J. P., 454, 455
Ward, L. B., 454, 455
Warr, P., 515
Waterman, R. H., Jr., 517
Waters, J. A., 422
Watson, K. M., 152
Weaver, C. N., 115
Webber, R. A., 577
Weber, M., 272–277, 299
Webster, E. C., 455, 456
Weed, S. E., 49, 151
Weick, K. E., 47

Weiss, D. J., 115
Weissenberg, D., 148
Weitz, J., 455
Wells, L. T., Jr., 270
Werther, W. B., Jr., 516
Wexley, K. N., 177, 236, 237,
  334–338
Wheeler, D., 454
Whetten, D. A., 18
White, B. J., 422
White, J. K., 365
Whitsett, D. A., 393, 515
Whyte, W. F., 206
Whyte, W. H., Jr., 456, 575
Wigdor, L., 393
Wiggins, J. A., 208
Winslow, E. K., 393
Winton, D. G., 364
Wolf, G., 152

Wolfe, D. M., 483
Wood, R. E., 152
Woodward, J., 278–281, 300
Wright, O. R., Jr., 455

Yates, J. F., 421
Yetton, P. W., 133, 149, 151, 421,
  422
Yorks, L., 515
Yukl, G. A., 81, 148, 149, 177, 236,
  237

Zahn, G.L., 152
Zajonc, R. B., 207
Zammuto, R. F., 18
Zedeck, S., 81
Zidon, I., 82
Zimbardo, P. G., 178, 179
Zwerman, W. L., 300

Subject Index

Ability, 25, 30–34, 131
Absenteeism:
  relationship to satisfaction, 94,
    103–104
  relationship to stress, 470–471
Achievement-oriented leadership, 131
Acquisition of new businesses, 290,
  292–293
Action planning in OD, 530–533
Active listening, 164
Affirmative Action, 435–436
Aggression, 469–470
Anxiety, 469
Appraisal interviews, 328–329
Appraisals (*see* Performance appraisal)
Aptitudes:
  mental, 32
  nature of, 31–32
  physical, 33
Assessment centers, 445–450
  content of, 446–447
  defined, 445
  improving, 447–450
  problems of, 447–448
  research at AT&T on, 447–448
  structure of, 445–446
  success of, 447–448
Attitude(s), 104
  and behavior, 26
  changing, 165–169
  nature of, 26
  similarity of, 181, 183–184
Attitude surveys, 99–107
  administration of, 105–107
  design of, 99–103

Attitude surveys (*Cont.*):
  examples of, 99–102
  measurement issues in, 102–103
  uses of, 103–105
Attribution errors, 316
Authoritarianism, 38
Authority, 272–273
Autonomous work groups, 382–384
Autonomy, 376–377

Background noise, 156
  in communication, 156
Bargaining, 227–228
Behavior, individual, 23
Behavioral observation scales (BOS),
  320–321
Behavioral theories of leadership,
  124–127
Behavioral theory of decision making,
  403–406
Behaviorally anchored rating scales
  (BARS), 317–320
Beliefs:
  accuracy of, 27
  and behavior, 27
  nature of, 26
Belongingness needs, 53
Benefits:
  cafeteria-style, 354–356
  characteristics of, 343
Bernreuter Personality Inventory, 444
Blue-collar workers, satisfaction of, 98
Bolstering, 166–168, 471–472, 479
Boundary-spanning roles, 291–292

Bounded rationality, 403–404
Brainstorming, 408–409
Brand managers, 91–92
Bureaucracy, 272–277, 280–283,
  294–295
  assessment of, 274–277, 294–295
  defined, 273
  impact on decision making, 276–277
  standardized rules in, 274–277

California Psychological Inventory, 444
Career(s), 545–571
  changing nature of, 546–547
  choice of, 428–434
  defined, 525
  early-career issues, 428–434,
    550–560
  impact on stress, 464–466
  late-career issues, 560–564
  middle-career issues, 560–564
  self-management of, 568–571
  stages, 547–550
Career aspirations, 429–431
Career counselling, 433, 565
Career development programs,
  251–252, 564–567
Career goals, 431
Career identity, 428–432
  development of, 428–431
  factors influencing, 428–432
Career information systems, 431–434,
  565
Career mobility, 557–560, 569–570
Career paths, 565, 569–570

Career success cycle, 428–431, 547
Central tendency errors, 314
Classical decision theory, 396–402
  assessment of, 401–404
  assumptions of, 399–401
  steps in, 396–399
Coalition formation, 221
Coercive power, 121
Cognitive dissonance, 167
Cohesiveness, 182–187, 200–201,
  219–220
  consequences of, 184–185
  defined, 182
  improving, 200
  influence on productivity, 185–187
  influence on satisfaction, 184
  relationship to intergroup conflict,
    185
  sources of, 183
Communication, 154–179
  ambiguity of, 159–161, 172
  amount of, 104, 156
  attention to, 155–159
  channels of, 104, 156–158, 241
  comprehension of, 159–164
  credibility of, 165–168
  defensive, 166–168, 172
  defined, 154
  directionality of, 156–157
  importance of, 154
  improving systems of, 104
  informal, 158
  networks in, 157–158
  nonverbal, 161
  novelty of, 159
  oral, 170–172, 280–281
  redundancy in, 171–172
  relationship to cohesiveness, 185
  relationship to intergroup conflict,
    218–223
  repetition of, 169–172
  retention of, 169–172
  tacit, 227–228
  timing, 171–172
  written, 170–171, 274, 280–281
Comparable worth, 352–354
Competition:
  in relationship to conflict, 217, 231
  in relationship to motivation, 217
Compromise, 227–228
Conflict avoidance, 223–226, 231
Conflict confrontation, 224–225, 231
Conflict containment, 224–225, 231
Conflict defusion, 224–225, 231

Conflict resolution strategies, 225–230
Conflict smoothing, 226
Conformity, 195–200
  during socialization, 556–557
Consideration, 125
Context satisfactions, 378
Contracting as a conflict resolution
  strategy, 221
Contrast effect, 316, 438
Control systems, Galbraith's typology
  of, 282–283
Cooperation:
  relationship to cohesiveness,
    181–186
  relationship to intergroup conflict,
    231
  relationship to job satisfaction,
    87–90
  relationship to job stress, 475–476
Cooptation, 221
Coordination, 5
Coordination of work:
  impact of groups on, 190, 200
  impact of intergroup conflict on,
    212–215, 231
  impact of organizational structure on,
    241–242, 245, 250–251, 282–283
Core job characteristics, 375–377
Counselling, 479
Criteria, 307–309
Critical psychological states, 375–377

Decentralization of organizational
  structure, 245–250
Decision acceptance, 134
Decision making, 221–222, 432–434
  behavioral theory of, 403–406
  in bureaucracies, 276–277
  classical theory of, 396–402
  group, 406–415
  impact of stress on, 432, 471–472,
    479
  impact of structure on, 244–245,
    249–250, 261–262
Decision quality, 134
Decision styles, 133
Defensive avoidance, 167, 433
Delegation, relationship to stress,
  475–476
Delphi technique, 414
Depression, 470
Design, organization (*see* Organization
  design)

Deviance, 195–201
  amount of, 196–200
  defined, 195–196
  functions of, 196
  rejection of deviants, 196–201
  relationship to group effectiveness,
    199–201
Diagnosis in OD, 525–530
  data collection, 528–530
  interviews, 528
  observation, 528–530
  questionnaires, 528
  supplementary data, 530
Diffusion of responsibility, 190–191, 200
Directive leadership, 130
Diversification, 290, 292–293
Division of labor, 272–273, 280–281
Divisional organization, 245–252, 263
  advantages of, 249–252
  bases of divisionalization, 245–248
  defined, 245–246
  disadvantages of, 250–252
  examples of, 246–249
  overall assessment of, 252
Divisions:
  customer, 246–248
  geographical, 246–247
  international, 248
  product, 245–247, 291
Dominance, 40
Dotted-line supervision, 253–254
  defined, 253
  examples of, 253–254
Dual-career couples, 547
Dual-ladder careers, 565–566

Economies of scale, 244, 251
Edwards Personal Preference Schedule,
  444
Effort, impact of groups on, 189
Entry process in OD, 524–525
  contact, 524
  contracting, 525
  exploration, 525
Entry shock, 550, 570
Environment:
  dependence on, 6–7
  organization, 6
  types of, 6
Environment (organization), 271, 277,
  284–295
  Burns and Stalker model of,
    287–288

Environment (organization) (*Cont.*):
  complexity of, 285–286
  contingency theories of, 272, 287–293
  coping with, 290–293
  defined, 284
  dimensions of, 284–286
  elements of, 284–286
  favorability of, 284–286, 294–295
  fit with structure, 287–295
  impact on structure, 287–295
  Lawrence and Lorsch model of, 289–290
  stability of, 285–286, 294–295
  subunit, 289–290, 294–295
  uncertainty of, 285–286
Environmental niches, 292
Equal Employment Opportunity, 436, 440
Equity theory, 61–64
ERG theory, 55–56
Esteem needs, 53
Ethnocentrism, 218–220
Eustress, 459
Evaluation of OD, 533–534
Excellent companies research, 503–510
  characteristics of excellence, 506–509
  implications of, 510
  nature of, 503–505
  problems identified, 505–506
Exception principle, 171
Expectancies, 58
Expectancy theory, 57–61
Experienced meaningfulness, 375–376
Experienced responsibility, 376–377
Expert power, 121
Extinction, 69
Extroversion, 40

Feedback:
  of attitude surveys, 106–107
  in communication, 163–164
  to new employees, 551, 555
  during socialization, 551, 555
Feedback in OD, 530
Fiedler's contingency theory, 127–130
Filtering, 156–157
  of communication, 156–157
Forewarning, 170, 172–173
Fringe benefits, satisfaction with, 86
Frustration, 469

Functional organizations, 242–245, 263
  advantages of, 243–244
  defined, 242
  disadvantages of, 244–245
  examples of, 242–243
  managers in, 242–245
  overall assessment of, 245

Gatekeepers, 157
General Adaptation Syndrome, 460
  defined, 460
  stages of, 460
Geographical mobility, 466–467, 559–560
Goal setting:
  relationship to career planning, 568–569
  relationship to organization design, 282–283
  (*See also* Goals)
Goals:
  characteristics of, 66–67
  and motivation, 29–30
  of organizations, 5
Grapevine, 157
Group-based work design, 381–387
Group decision making, 191, 195, 406–415
  in matrix organizations, 259–262
  (*See also* Group decisions)
Group decisions, 406–412
  acceptance of, 412–413
  creativity of, 408–409
  quality of, 406–407
Group performance, 187–191
  assets of groups, 188–189
  liabilities of groups, 189–191
  Steiner model of, 188–190
Group size, 187–191
Groups, 180–208
  autonomous, 382
  command, 182
  defined, 181
  goal acceptance, 67
  goal difficulty, 66–67
  goal setting, 64–68
  goal specificity, 66
  goals of, 182–187, 196–200
  graphic rating scales, 309–317
  informal, 182
  joining, 182
  perspective on OB, 7–8
  satisfaction with, 90

Groups (*Cont.*):
  self-contained, 282–283
  self-managing, 382
  social, 481–482
  task, 182
  work, 90, 181–182
Groupthink, 412–413
Growth need strength, 377–378

Halo effect, 314–315
Health, 468–470
  emotional, 469–470
  maintenance of, 477–479
  physical, 468–469
  relationship to stress, 468–470, 477–479
Holland's model of vocational choice, 429–430
Holmes and Rahe Stress Scale, 466–468
Hygiene factors, 372

Idiosyncrasy credits, 198–200
Implementing principles, 380–381
In Search of Excellence (*see* Excellent companies research)
In-basket exercises, 446
Individual perspective, 7
Inequity, 63–64
Information overload, 156
Initiating structure, 125
Innoculation effect, 170, 172–173
Innovation, 276–277, 294–295
  need for, 488–491
Inputs, 6, 62
Integrating managers, 230, 255–256
  defined, 255
  examples of, 255
Integrative problem solving, 218–223
Interdependence, 7
Intergroup conflict, 209–238, 520
  amount of, 211, 232
  causes of, 212–217
  consequences of, 222–223
  contemporary view of, 210–211
  defined, 209
  diagnosing, 212–217
  dynamics of, 217–223
  managing, 223–230
  resolving, 223–230
  traditional view of, 210
Intergroup interventions, 537–540

Interpersonal conflict, 519
Interpersonal peacemaking, 536
Interventions in OD:
  nature of, 533
  types of: individual, 534–536
    process, 536–540
Interviews, 437–442, 449–450
  legal environment of, 440–442
  multiple, 442
  strengths of, 440–441
  stress, 428–432
  structured, 441
  suggestions for improving, 441–442
  weaknesses of, 438–440
Introversion, 40

Japanese management, 85, 161,
    497–503
  applicable techniques, 500–503
  nature of, 497–500
Jargon, 160–161
Job choice, 428–434
  counselling, 433
  decision making, 431–434
  factors influencing, 428–431
  impact of selection process on,
    432–434
  improving effectiveness of, 432–434
  information, 433
  role of stress in, 471–472
Job Descriptive Index, 99–100
Job design, 88, 187, 374–381
  control over work methods, 88, 187
  control over work pace, 88, 187
  feasibility of, 387–388
  job characteristics model of,
    374–381
  in practice, 379–381
  skill variety, 88, 187
Job enlargement, 371–372
Job enrichment, 372–374
  diagnosing feasibility of, 379
  diagnosing need for, 379
  implementation of, 380
  outcomes of, 378–379
Job evaluations, pay and, 346
Job feedback, 377
Job performance:
  relationship to cohesiveness,
    185–187
  relationship to satisfaction, 92–95,
    188–189
  relationship to stress, 470–471, 479

Job satisfaction, 85–116
  consequences of, 92–95
  defined, 86
  discrepancy model of, 91–92
  impact of groups on, 87–90,
    188–189
  sources of, 85–91
  surveys, 99–107
  trends in, 95–98
Job security, 274, 546–547

Knowledge of results, 377

Lateral relations, 252–256, 263–264,
    274, 277, 280–283, 294–295
  defined, 252
  overall assessment of, 256
  purposes of, 252
  relationship to intergroup conflict, 230
  types of, 252–256
Leaderless group discussions, 446
Leadership:
  attribution theory of, 140–142
  behavioral theories of, 124–127
  constraints on, 138–139
  defined, 120
  employee-centeredness, 88
  Fiedler's contingency theory of,
    127–130
  influence on behavior, 42
  during intergroup conflict, 218–220
  mutual influence, 138
  nature of, 120–122
  participative, 90
  path-goal theory of, 130–133
  satisfaction with, 88–90
  trait theories of, 122–124
  Vroom and Yetton model of,
    133–137
Learned needs theory, 56–57
Least Preferred Coworker Scale, 128
Legitimate power, 121
Leniency errors, 313–314
Levels of analysis of OB, 7
Liaison roles, 254
  defined, 254
  examples of, 254
Lifetime employment, 498
Line positions, 212–213, 273–274
Locus of control, 40, 131
Longevity, 469
Lump-sum salary increases, 356–358

Macro perspective on OB, 9
Management by objectives (MBO),
    67–68, 322–325
Management games, 447
Management information systems:
  relationship to intergroup conflict,
    221–222
  relationship to organization design,
    482–483
Managerial work, 13–15
Managers:
  jobs of, 13–15
  nature of, 13
Manpower planning, 560, 565
Manpower review committees, 255
Maslow's need hierarchy theory, 52–55
Matrix structures, 256–264
  advantages of, 259–260
  defined, 256
  disadvantages of, 260–261
  examples of, 256–259
  geography-by-product, 257–258
  improving effectiveness of, 262
  overall assessment of, 261–262
  project management, 256–258
  types of, 256–259
Mediators, 228–229, 231
Mental health, 464–469
Merchandise general manager, 258–259
Micro perspective on OB, 7
Mid-life crisis, 548–549, 563–564,
    570–571
  defined, 563
  symptoms of, 564
  traps of, 564
Middle managers, satisfaction of, 97–98
Minnesota Multiphasic Personality
    Inventory, 444
Minnesota Satisfaction Questionnaire,
    99, 101
Moderators of impact of job design,
    377–378
Motivating potential score, 377
Motivation:
  competition as a strategy of, 217
  defined, 51
  as determinant of behavior, 25
  equity theory of, 61–64
  expectancy theory of, 57–61
  goal theory of, 64–68
  impact of groups on, 189–191, 200
  nature of, 26–30
  need theories of, 52–57
  reinforcement theory of, 68–74

Motivators, 372
Mutual influence, 138

Need for achievement, 57
Need for affiliation, 57
Need for power, 57
Need hierarchy theory, 52–55
Need theories of motivation, 52–57
Needs, 29
Negative reinforcement, 69
Nominal group technique, 414–415
Norms, 192–196, 200–201
  behavior, 192
  changing, 200–201
  defined, 192
  development of, 194–195
  diagnosing, 200–201
  enforcement of, 193–194
  performance, 192–193
  relationship to group dynamics,
    192–195
  relationship to group effectiveness,
    192–195, 199–200
  types of, 192–193

OB Mod, 71–74
Obsolescence, 561–564
Ohio State studies, 125–127
Open salary information, 358–359
Organization design, 9, 271–301
  classical theories of, 272–277
  contingency theories of, 277–301
  principles of, 273–274
  to resolve conflict, 230
  universalistic theories of, 271–277
Organization development (OD),
    518–540
  distinguishing features of, 521–522
  interventions, 534–540
  nature of, 519–522
  phases in, 523–534
  process of, 522–523
Organization size, relationship to
    structure, 245
Organization structure, 9, 42,
    239–270, 294–295
  defined, 241
  divisional, 245–251, 263, 274, 277,
    280–281, 294–295
  functional, 242–245, 263, 274, 277,
    280–281, 294–295

Organization structure (*Cont.*):
  lateral relations, 251–256, 263–264,
    274, 277, 280–281, 294–295
  matrix, 256–264, 274, 277,
    280–281, 294–295
  mechanistic, 287–288
  organic, 287–288
  purposes of, 241–242
  relationship to strategy, 248–250
  types of, 241–242
Organizational behavior:
  defined, 4
  nature of, 3
Organizational behavior modification,
    71–74
Organizational climate, impact on
    stress, 464–465
Organizational effectiveness;
  assessment of, 10–11
  components of, 10
  determinants of, 12
  nature of, 9–10
  perspectives on, 11
  standards of, 11–12
  time frame, 11
Organizational systems, influence on
    behavior, 25
Organizations:
  defined, 4–5
  nature of, 4–5
  systems view of, 5–7
Orientation, 555–556, 560
Outcomes, 58–59, 62
Outputs, 6

Participation (*see* Participative decision
    making)
Participative decision making, 406–412
  (*See also* Group decision making)
Participative leadership, 131
Passivity, 469–470
Path-goal theory, 130–133
Pay, satisfaction with, 86
Pay administration, methods of,
    346–347
Pay equity, 352–354
Pay for performance, 346–352
  characteristics of, 342–343
  evaluation of, 348–352
  methods of, 347–348
Peer evaluation, 327

Perceptions:
  defined, 162
  determinants of, 34–37
  impact on communication, 162–163
  nature of, 25
  relationship to conflict, 218–223
Performance, 24
  relationship to satisfaction, 92–95,
    188–189
  relationship to stress, 470–471, 479
Performance appraisal, 305–339
  criteria of, 307–309
  functions of, 306–307
  timing of, 327–328
Permanent teams, 252–255
  defined, 255
  examples of, 255
Personality:
  determinants of, 40–41
  impact on job choice, 428–430, 438
  impact on stress, 469–470
  influence on behavior, 25, 41
  nature of, 37–38
  tests, 444–445
  traits, 38–41
Physical facilities, 41–42
Physical health, 466–468
Physiological needs, 52
Piece-rate incentives, 185–187
Plateaud performance, 561–564
Political activity, 290, 292–293
Porter Need Satisfaction Questionnaire,
    101–102
Positive reinforcement, 69
Power:
  relationship to conflict, 220–223
  relationship to organization structure,
    261
  sources of, 120–122
Pressure tactics, 222
Procedural rationality, 405–406
Product managers, 254
Productivity, 185, 187–191
Project managers, 256–261
Projection, 163
Promotions, 343, 551, 557–562, 570
  benefits of, 557–558
  criteria for, 561–562
  defined, 557
  managing process of, 559–560
  orientation for, 558, 560
  problems of, 558, 560
  satisfaction with, 88
  social support for, 559

Promotions (*Cont.*):
  stress reactions to, 464–470,
    558–559
  timing of, 558, 560
  training for, 558–560
Psychological well-being, 469–470
Psychology:
  individual, 7
  social, 8
Punishment, 69

Quality of work life (QWL), 491–496
  characteristics of, 491–492
  contributors to, 492–493
  examples of programs, 493–495
  future prospects of, 495–496
Queuing of communication, 171

Rate of life change, 464–467
Ratebusting, 192–200
Rating errors, 313–317
Realistic job previews, 97, 434, 450
Recency bias, 315
Recruitment, 427–434, 440–441
Referent power, 121
Refreezing process in OD, 523
Regional general managers, 259
Reinforcement:
  negative, 69
  positive, 69
  schedules of, 70–71
Reinforcement theory, 68–74
Relaxation techniques, 477
Reliability, 308
  of satisfaction surveys, 102
  of selection devices, 435–436
Resource allocation:
  relationship to conflict, 215–217
  relationship to organization structure,
    251
Resource interdependence, 215–217
Responsibility, 272–273
Reward power, 120–121
Reward systems:
  conflicts in, 215–217, 231
  functions of, 344–345
  influence on behavior, 42
  innovations in, 354–359
  nature of, 42
Rewards:
  for attendance, 344
  characteristics of, 341–343

Rewards (*Cont.*):
  comparison of, 342–343
  cost of, 342
  extrinsic, 93–94
  flexibility of, 341–342
  frequency of, 342
  importance of, 341
  intrinsic, 93–94
  for membership, 344
  for performance, 345
  types of, 341
  visibility of, 342
Role(s), 194, 461–463
  defined, 194, 461
  relationship to norms, 194
Role ambiguity, 461–462
Role clarification, 475, 479
Role conflict, 461–462
  intersender, 462
  intrasender, 462
Role overload, 462–463
Role-play exercises, 446–447
Role underload, 463
Rorschach Test, 444–445

Safety needs, 52
Salary:
  information, 358–359
  lump-sum increases, 356–358
  (*See also* Pay)
Satisfaction surveys (*see* Attitude
  surveys)
Satisficing, 404
Scalar chain, 272–273
Schedules of reinforcement, 70–71
Scientific management, 368–371
Selection, 427–457
  legal environment of, 440–442
  stages of process, 434–435
Selection decisions, 437, 449–450
  by intuitive judgment, 437, 450
  by systematic combination, 437, 450
Selection devices, 434–450
  criteria of, 435–436
  types of, 437–450
Self-actualization, 53
Self-esteem, 472–473
Self-evaluation, 327
Self-managing work groups, 382–384
Semantics, 159–160
Situational favorability, 128–129
Skill-based evaluation, pay and, 346
Skill variety, 375
Smoothing, 227

Social facilitation, 189
Social needs, 53
Social psychology, 8
Socialization (organizational), 552–557
  agents of, 556
  anticipatory, 552–553
  characteristics of, 552
  defined, 552
  designing programs of, 553–557
  individual coping strategies for,
    568–569
  models of, 552–553
  multiple processes of, 552
  stages of, 552–554
Sociology, 9
Span of control, 272–273, 280–281
Specialization, 5
Staff positions, 212–213, 273–274
Status symbols, 343
Stereotyping, 35–36
  in communication, 162–163
  defined, 162
  in selection decisions, 438
Stress, 458–480
  causes of, 461–467
  consequences of, 468–472
  coping with, 474–477, 479–480
  and decision making, 404
  defined, 459
  dual nature of, 459–460
  impact on decision making, 432,
    471–472, 479
  impact on job choice, 432
  impact on organizational
    effectiveness, 460
  individual differences in, 472–474
  inevitability of, 459
  legal environment of, 460
  management programs, 477–480
  in matrix organizations, 261
  prevalence of, 458–459
  reactions to, 89
Strictness errors, 313
Structure, organizational (*see*
  Organization Structure)
Successive limited comparisons, 405
Suicide, 463, 470
Superordinate goals, 227
Supervision (*see* Leadership)
Supportive leadership, 131
Synergy, 180–181
Systems:
  nature of, 6
  view of organizations, 5–7

Task ambiguity, 213–215
Task forces, 254–255
  defined, 254–255
  examples of, 230, 254–255
Task identity, 375
Task interdependence, 212–213
  defined, 212
  reciprocal, 213
  sequential, 212–213
Task significance, 375
Team building, 184, 519–520,
  536–537
Technocracy, 274
Technology, 271, 276–277, 278–284,
  294–295
  Aston studies of, 281–282
  contingency theories of, 272,
    279–283
  continuous process, 279–283,
    294–295
  defined, 278
  fit with structure, 278–284, 294–295
  Galbraith's theory of, 282–283
  impact on structure, 283–284,
    294–295
  mass production, 278, 280–283,
    294–295
  subunit, 281–282, 294–295
  types of, 278–279
  unit, 278, 280–283, 294–295
  Woodward's theory of, 279–281
Tests, 442–445, 449–450
  ability, 442–444, 449–450
  examples of, 443–444
  personality, 444–445, 449–450
  types of, 442–444
  usefulness of, 444–445

Thematic Apperception Test, 444–445
Time management, 475
Tolerance for ambiguity, 472–473, 477
  defined, 472
  relationship to stress, 472–473, 477
Topeka, Kansas, plant design, 384–387
Training, 33–34, 555, 558, 566
Trait theories of leadership, 122–124
Transfers, 557–560, 570
  benefits of, 557–558
  defined, 557
  geographical, 559
  impact on families, 559
  lateral, 557
  managing process of, 559–560
  orientation for, 560
  problems of, 558–559
  social support for, 559
  stress reactions to, 464–470,
    558–559
  timing of, 558, 560
  training for, 558, 560
Transformation processes, 6
Turnover:
  relationship to satisfaction, 94,
    103–104
  relationship to stress, 470–471, 476
Two-factor theory, 372–373
Type A personality, 473–474
  defined, 473
  relationship to stress, 473–474
  test for, 473

Unfreezing process in OD, 522
Unions, 104–105
  contract negotiations, 227–229
  desire for, 95

Unions (*Cont.*):
  grievances, 95
  mediators, 227–229
  organizing, 95
  strikes, 95
Unity of command, 272–273

Valence, 58–59
Validity:
  of satisfaction surveys, 102
  of selection devices, 435–436
Values, 28–29, 183
Vocational choice, 428–431
  Holland's model of, 429–430
Vroom and Yetton model, 133–137

Withdrawal behavior:
  relationship to satisfaction, 94
  relationship to stress, 470–471
Work design:
  group-based, 381–387
  historical development of, 368–374
  individual-based, 374–381
  nature of, 367–368
  satisfaction with, 88–89
  as a source of stress, 461–463
Work group:
  impact on new employees, 556
  satisfaction with, 90
Work groups (*see* Groups)
Working conditions, satisfaction with,
  90–91

Young workers, satisfaction of, 96–97